MARKETING AND DISTRIBUTION RESEARCH

By

LYNDON O. BROWN, Ph.D.

Vice-President and Director of Media, Merchandising, and Research,
Dancer-Fitzgerald-Sample, Inc.
Lecturer in Marketing Research, Columbia University

THIRD EDITION

THE RONALD PRESS COMPANY • NEW YORK

Library of Congress Catalog Card Number: 55-7720

PREFACE

This new edition is a comprehensive treatment of the science of marketing and distribution research—its methods, uses, scientific foundations, and relation to business operations. It embodies the practices of outstanding marketing and distribution researchers and brings together the discoveries and experiences of the research departments of a number of leading American corporations with whom the author and his associates collaborate from day to day.

This book is deliberately broad in scope, embracing all phases of marketing and distribution research that have proved of value. To be fully equipped to understand the field and play a part in its most useful application, the student, executive, or practitioner must be aware of the multiplicity of ways in which marketing research operates. One of the limiting factors in the effective use of marketing and distribution research is the tendency of some individuals to identify it with a restricted activity such as the consumer survey. Marketing research is valuable as a management tool largely because it can be applied in many ways to the solution of basic marketing problems. Sometimes the most useful contribution can be made through a controlled price experiment, sometimes by an analysis of distribution costs, at other times through one of the many other kinds of research.

The exposition of the basic principle that marketing and distribution research is one phase of applied science rather than some new or unique discovery is generally recognized as a major contribution of the original edition of this work. The present revision holds to that position and examines the entire field from this perspective. To be sure, some techniques are still rather limited, and the occasional necessity to employ temporary stop-gap methods causes certain individuals to doubt at times that marketing research can truly be called a science. But we do not deny the existence of a science of weather forecasting because weather forecasters err. The failure of practitioners to be scientific is simply evidence of the fact that human beings do not as yet know all about the science of marketing. This fact in itself makes the entire area an exciting one because we are constantly exploring and seeking to discover additional, more scientific methodology.

In both organization and content this edition differs in certain ways from the previous one. The material is now so organized that it can be adapted readily to the various needs of instructors offering courses in different institutions. Where the course provides ample time, the entire book can be covered as the basic text. In shorter courses, the instructors may limit their text assignments to Parts I and II, using Part III as outside reading as desired.

Throughout the book the material has been carefully brought up to date. The chapters on sampling are entirely new and incorporate developments that have brought the sampling problem well under control in marketing research. This edition also contains new chapters on motivational research and on operations research. Lists of selected readings at the ends of chapters guide the reader to material in other publications, including books of problems available to the instructor for use as supplementary teaching aids.

The reader can use this book with the confidence that it embodies the methods and standards of outstanding marketing and distribution researchers. The chapters on sampling, for example, have been reviewed by Lester Frankel, Technical Director of Alfred Politz, Inc., and Willard R. Simmons, of W. R. Simmons and Associates, Inc. These two organizations are recognized as the leaders in sampling methods in the field of marketing and distribution research. Dr. Wallace Wulfeck, Chairman of the Advertising Research Foundation Committee on Motivational Research, has read and criticized the chapter on this new and difficult subject. Other parts of the book have been subjected to the criticisms of other practitioners.

The names of all the business associates and university colleagues who have helped are too numerous to list. Faculty members in many universities who use the book as a text have been most helpful in their suggestions for this revision. Richard Lessler, William Weilbacher, and Lloyd Miller have made contributions. Mrs. John Hastings has been of great assistance in production, and Marie Mason in editing. My chief indebtedness is to my wife, Blanche B. Brown, who has taken an active part in the preparation of this book.

LYNDON O. BROWN

New York City
February, 1955

CONTENTS

PART I

Principles of Marketing and Distribution Research

PART II

Marketing and Distribution Research Practice

CONTENTS

PART III

Specialized Fields and Techniques of Marketing and Distribution Research

ILLUSTRATIONS

ILLUSTRATIONS

Part I

PRINCIPLES OF MARKETING AND DISTRIBUTION RESEARCH

1

SCOPE AND IMPORTANCE OF MARKETING
AND DISTRIBUTION RESEARCH

You drive into a filling station in Yourtown, U. S. A. While attendants fill your gasoline tank and service the car, you stroll into the station, pick up a soft drink, and purchase a pack of cigarettes. This is a commonplace type of experience for most Americans. However, few of them realize that back of this simple kind of buying transaction lies a vast complex of industry, and that marketing research is now an essential part of it.

The process may seem casual, but it was not by accident that you drove into that particular station, agreed to the attendant's suggestion that he "check your oil," bought the cigarettes you did, or enjoyed that brand of soft drink. The chances are that the selection of that particular location for the station itself was based on a considerable amount of marketing research in the community, competitive situations, neighborhood characteristics, and traffic-flow counts. The gasoline you purchased may have been priced on the basis of careful marketing studies to determine optimum prices. Even the words spoken to you by the attendant may have been developed as a result of research which tested the effect of various personal sales approaches.

While waiting for your car to be serviced, you were subjected to a variety of silent influences in the form of station layout, merchandise display, and a barrage of advertising signs. Again, these matters were not left to the opinion of company personnel or the dealer. The important ones were based on marketing research studies of the effectiveness of various forms of store layout, merchandise display, and advertising. The selection and training of the dealer and his employees, the supplementary services performed free or for a charge, and the quantities of stocks maintained are only a few of the other items in connection with which marketing research very likely played a major role in that filling station.

After you leave the filling station, you drive to a chain supermarket. Here you make only a few simple purchases—perhaps a package of breakfast cereal, a few bars of soap, and a can of dog food. Again, casual as this process may seem, a whole host of sales influences operating on you were probably based on marketing research. A few examples of research by the retailer himself are the location and layout of the store, the items handled, pricing, and the design of selling displays. Undoubtedly, the cereal you selected had been tested time and again on other consumers by its manufacturer to insure that the product would have maximum consumer acceptance and the package design was also carefully developed through marketing research. Back of your simple purchase of a few bars of soap lies a tremendous advertising campaign. The television commercial which you thought made no particular impression on you was probably designed and executed on the basis of extensive research to determine the relative effectiveness of various types of advertising appeals, even of individual words and devices. You perhaps had not planned to buy dog food that day, certainly not that particular brand. But you picked it up because of a special promotion designed by its manufacturer on the basis of marketing research.

On the way home, you are held up at a railroad crossing while a passenger train passes through Yourtown. You may not realize that the design of the coaches, the types of services offered, even the schedule of the train itself, were probably determined to a large extent by marketing research studies of the desires and needs of the public.

As you read a magazine at home in your easy chair, you may be completely unaware that marketing research, through studies of thousands of readers similar to you, has provided the foundation for the editorial material as well as the advertisements you read. When another member of your family glances at an advertisement for a motion picture and urges that the family go to see it, probably none of you realizes that the title of the picture, the scenario, the selection of leading actors, as well as the methods by which it is publicized, were all influenced by marketing research.

Your home is a veritable display of the evidences of applications of marketing research. You live among the end products of the American economy, brought to you by the process of marketing. There is no item in your home today that is not subject to marketing research.

The products which you, as a consumer, purchase are but the end products of an intricate industrial economy. Back of these consumer goods lies a complex industrial organization to market the raw materials, processed goods, machinery, and other industrial products needed to manufacture consumer goods. Every time a product moves from one producer to another, directly or through some form of dealer, the marketing process takes place and creates an opportunity for marketing research to guide management.

Definition of Marketing and Distribution Research

The all-pervasive importance of marketing and distribution research in present-day industry is suggested by its definition: *Marketing and distribution research is the use of scientific method in the solution of marketing or distribution problems for the purpose of increasing sales, decreasing marketing and distribution costs, and maximizing profits.* Three essential elements in this definition are: (1) application of scientific method, (2) solution of problems, and (3) marketing and distribution.

Application of scientific method means that marketing research is limited to those activities which employ truly scientific methods according to currently accepted standards. Casual observation of a situation, reading of general literature, or going through the motions of "making a study" does not constitute scientific method, helpful as these activities may be. Only to the extent that procedures such as those discussed in this book are employed can the operation be considered scientific.

Solution of problems implies a restriction of marketing and distribution research to those instances in which a specific problem or group of problems is identified as the subject for the research. There is no marketing policy or operating decision which cannot be reduced to a problem. However, it would be folly to attempt to apply scientific research methods, which are costly and take time, to provide a basis for every decision that must be made. It is a prime function of management to make thousands of decisions on the basis of judgment and experience. When a particularly significant problem arises, these management decisions should be based on marketing research. Thus, the prime application of marketing research is at the policy-making level.

It should be noted at the outset that marketing problems are not solved in terms of absolute or final certainty. What research does is to reduce the probability of error in marketing policy and operations. In a complex economic and business activity such as marketing, one is confronted with the necessity of choice among several alternative courses of action. "Problem solving" means the reduction of uncertainty to a point where it is possible to choose among various alternatives with confidence in the outcome. This condition does not depreciate the value or necessity of research in the least. In fact, even in the physical sciences problems are not solved with absolute certainty, but rather in terms of probability.

Marketing and distribution embrace the entire process of getting goods and services from the factory or institution to the final consumer

	Market Characteristics	Market Potentials	Competitive Position	Distribution Research	Sales Research	Advertising Research	Product Research	Market Trends
Administration								
General Policy Decisions	X	X	X	X	X	X	X	X
Budget Control	−	X	X	X	X	X	X	X
Price Policies	X	−	X	X	−	−	X	X
Employee Relations	X	−	X	−	−	−	−	X
Government Relations	X	−	X	−	−	−	−	X
Finance								
Capital Requirements	−	X	−	−	X	X	X	X
Development Policy	−	X	X	−	X	X	X	X
Financial Control	−	X	−	X	X	X	−	X
Credit Policy	−	−	−	X	−	−	−	X
Stockholder Relations	X	X	X	−	−	X	X	X
Production								
Capacity Requirements	−	X	X	−	−	−	X	X
Plant Location	−	X	X	X	X	−	−	−
Manpower Requirements	−	X	X	−	−	−	X	X
Purchasing	−	X	−	−	−	−	X	X
Inventories	−	−	X	X	X	−	X	X
Transportation	−	X	−	X	X	−	−	−
Product Changes	X	X	−	−	X	−	X	X
Packaging Requirements	X	−	−	X	−	−	X	X
Sales								
Sales Forecasts	−	X	X	−	X	−	−	X
Market Areas	−	X	−	X	X	−	−	−
Sales Potentials	−	X	X	−	−	−	−	X
Method of Distribution	−	−	X	X	X	−	−	X
Selection of Distributors	−	−	−	X	X	−	−	X
Sales Force Needed	−	X	−	X	X	−	−	−
Sales Training	−	−	−	X	X	−	−	−
Sales Organization	−	X	X	X	X	−	−	−
Sales Compensation	−	−	−	X	X	−	−	−
Organization of Force	−	−	−	X	X	−	−	−
Advertising								
Size of Appropriation	−	X	X	−	−	X	X	X
Territorial Allocation	−	X	X	−	−	X	−	X
Selection of Media	X	X	X	X	−	X	−	X
Advertising Copy	X	−	−	−	−	X	X	−
Promotions	X	−	X	X	−	X	−	−

See caption for Figure 1 on opposite page.

6

for ultimate consumption. By definition, marketing and distribution research is applicable to all phases of this process. The magnitude of marketing in a modern economy is quickly demonstrated by the fact that approximately 60 per cent of the ultimate consumer cost of the products of American industry are marketing and distribution costs.

Marketing and distribution processes per se are limited to activities involved in getting products or services from the producer into the hands of buyers or consumers. However, the scope of marketing and distribution research embraces all economic and business activities that affect or are affected by marketing. For example, the product or service itself is a primary concern of marketing research just as much as are the means of getting it marketed. In some situations the product is the most important single problem calling for marketing research.

The reader will note that the terms "marketing" and "distribution" are generally used jointly and synonymously in this book. This is in accordance with current practice. In certain sections of the country and among certain groups of marketing practitioners, the term "distribution" is commonly employed to describe the entire process of getting goods and services from producer to consumer. In other instances it is restricted to the more limited area of wholesale and retail distribution. However, the American Marketing Association recommends that the terms "marketing" and "distribution" be used synonymously.

Importance of Marketing and Distribution Research

Marketing Research as a Management Tool. Business is rapidly coming to recognize that the greatest opportunity for increasing profits lies in increasing the efficiency of distribution and, in turn, decreasing the costs of distribution. The generalized estimate that marketing and distribution costs represent approximately 60 per cent of the final cost of commodities to the ultimate consumer has been substantiated by studies of the A. C. Nielsen Company. Nielsen's clients in the food and drug industries sell their products for an aggregate consumer price of about 15 billion dollars. Only about $7 billions represent the cost of production, taxes, and profit; the remaining $8 billions represent the cost of distribution incurred by the manufacturer and the trade combined.

Figure 1. Marketing Research as a Management Tool. This check chart shows the wide variety of applications of marketing and distribution research to many different areas of the modern business enterprise. The left hand column lists areas in which vital problems arise. The column headings show the chief types of marketing and distribution research. The crosses indicate situations in which marketing and distribution research has been applied effectively in the solution of problems.

There is ample evidence that the reduction of distribution costs offers the greatest opportunity for securing competitive advantages. Other cost factors, such as labor, raw materials, factory production facilities, and taxes, are becoming progressively more standardized within industries. For example, manufacturers have much less opportunity today to gain a competitive advantage in labor costs; in fact, management is rapidly losing most of its control over these costs.

Those who are in any way responsible for the operation or control of business activities have a direct interest in the rapidly increasing application of scientific method in the field of marketing. Manufacturers, service enterprises, wholesalers, retailers, and business consultants are compelled to devote more and more of their time to marketing problems. Top management is most directly interested, for it knows that the continued existence of a business requires that haphazard methods of selling and distribution be replaced by more efficient policies and operations based on scientific measurement of consumers, dealers, and markets. The executive must reduce the cost burdens involved in selling his products and services, and must see to it that every possible waste is eliminated. The sales manager is forced to develop more efficient means to increase his sales volume economically. Individual salesmen are using the results of marketing analyses to make their daily work more effective. Advertising managers and agency practitioners apply results of marketing studies in their specialized functions. Even the general public has a direct interest, for lower costs of marketing reduce prices and efficient marketing makes goods more widely available to the ultimate consumer.

Many examples of the importance attached to marketing research as a tool of management by present-day business may be cited. The attitude of the General Electric Company has been expressed as follows:

The management of the General Electric Company is sold on the use of market research, not only as a sales tool, but also as an operating tool. And with good reason. For just as physical research and engineering lower the cost of making things, market research lowers the cost of putting those things into the hands of the people. Together they result in not only less costly, but better and more useful products for more people.

And just as General Electric pioneered in industrial research, it also pioneered in industrial market research. . . . General Electric started market research as long ago as 1921. . . . Today, each of the six operating departments of the Company has organized market research units, and one or more of our affiliated companies. In addition, there is a general company market research organization that reports directly to the President's staff.[1]

[1] Robert S. Peare, Vice President, General Electric Company, in an address before the Market Research Council of New York, December 13, 1946.

The following statements by business leaders reflect the status of marketing research in a wide variety of different types of business.[2]

In this fast moving age of electronics, the atomic bomb, record births, an economy moving at break-neck speed, and other developments, I would as soon attempt to steer a ship without charts as to direct an enterprise without the benefit of market research.

> Gale F. Johnston, President
> Mercantile Trust Company

Market research is indispensable to the operation of a sound sales program. Facts, not hunches, must be behind all important decisions.

> O. Parker McComas, President
> Philip Morris & Co. Ltd., Inc.

Here at National Bank of Detroit we are constantly engaged in research to find the most efficient methods of serving customers, the most expeditious manner of handling transactions and the most desirable locations for facilities from the standpoint of the convenience of present and prospective customers. . . .

> Charles T. Fisher, Jr., President
> National Bank of Detroit

Market research is as important to the over-all planning of a consumer goods business as accounting is to the financial aspect of any company.

> Philip Liebmann, President
> Liebmann Breweries, Inc.

Air transportation is one of the most competitive enterprises in the field of public service and is, therefore, particularly sensitive to customer opinion. In American Airlines we rely on market research to (a) provide service when and where it is needed, (b) improve the quality of the service and (c) locate new markets in which to exert promotional effort.

> C. R. Speers, Assistant Vice President
> General Sales Manager, American Airlines

Market research, the most accurate technique for finding out what consumers want and at what price, is important under any conditions for the manufacturer, wholesaler, and retailer. The economic era which we are entering will be characterized by distribution as the chief problem rather than production. Market research must supply the answers for distributing the huge additional quantities of goods and services that we are now capable of producing.

> John C. Williams, President
> L. Bamberger & Company

The stakes we are playing with today are so large and the return is so small, that business executives cannot afford to gamble on hunches, they must have reliable

---

[2] See *What Marketing Research Can Do for Business Executives*, prepared by the Research Committee of the Sales Executives Club of New York, May, 1952.

and quick information to enable them to make decisions with their eyes open—to take the calculated risk. Market research is perhaps their most vital tool in this regard.

Don G. Mitchell, President
Sylvania Electric Products, Inc.

Effect on Business Success. Marketing and distribution research activities increase business success in several specific ways:

1. *They delineate the significant marketing problems.* In the constant pressure of day-to-day operations, the business executive frequently has a mistaken impression of the factors which really handicap marketing activities. The isolation of the basic causes of marketing inefficiency is often the most important single contribution marketing research makes to management.

2. *They keep a business in touch with its markets.* Marketing researches interpret markets to the business organization, so that business policies may be aimed in the right direction and based on facts rather than hunch, guesswork, opinion, or casual impressions. They overcome the danger that the modern, complex, and highly organized business enterprise will lose the feel of the demands of the markets.

3. *They reduce waste in marketing methods.* The effectiveness of different methods employed by the business is measured in order to eliminate those which are inefficient. More effective and less expensive methods of marketing and advertising may be found.

4. *They develop new sources of profit* through the discovery of new markets, new products, and new uses for established products.

5. *They are insurance* against unanticipated changes in the market which have the power to make a product or an industry obsolete. They show the business where it is going.

6. *They are used for sales promotion.* Many business firms are now using the results of their research work as direct means of increasing sales in sales meetings, publicity and advertising.

7. *They reduce costs of production and other administrative expense.* While marketing and distribution research is designed primarily to make distribution more efficient and to cut its costs, there are many ways in which its results lower costs of manufacturing. Examples of such results are simplification of the product line or production in larger volume.

8. *They indicate the direction which technical research should take.* By providing concrete data on customer preference relating to composition, design, or other attributes of the product or service, marketing research guides the research laboratories in their activities.

9. *They infuse enthusiasm into the business organization.* With the knowledge that a company bases its marketing activities on scientific knowledge of the market, employees have a confidence which kindles their enthusiasm. The executives know that they are operating intelligently and are following the proper course. Every salesman, for example, knows that his product is right, that there is a market for the product, that he is being backed up by sound advertising, and that the selling methods he employs have been proved.

10. *They foster good will,* both in the consumer market and in the industrial market. As the activities become more firmly rooted in scientific methodology and professional viewpoint, a cooperative spirit is introduced between producer and consumer, between producers of complementary products, between producer, wholesaler, and other factors. Thus marketing research results in improved marketing methods for entire industries.

Growth and Present Status

The Rise of Marketing and Distribution Research. Engineering research based on the physical sciences was adopted in the production phases of business many years before the introduction of marketing research. There are few firms which do not, to a marked degree, apply the principles of engineering research. Marketing research, on the other hand, is generally regarded as being little more than a quarter of a century old.

Several factors account for the earlier development and widespread use of research in the field of production. One of the most important is that production research deals with physical elements which can be handled with standard laboratory procedures. The tools and technique for physical research had been developed in the scientific laboratories and a well-trained body of engineers was readily available. Furthermore, the direct financial gain resulting from the application of research to production is readily seen. Lowered costs which follow changes in the product or production methods may be accurately measured and credited to the production research laboratory. Another important reason for its rapid growth has been the constant demand for greater production in a rapidly expanding country. During the early part of the twentieth century this expansion focused the attention of business executives upon the problems of production, largely to the exclusion of problems of marketing.

After the first World War the excess production capacity and the shrinkage of world markets created pressures which shifted much of the attention of executives from production to marketing. At the same time, with the development of large-scale production, the gap between producer and consumer widened. The introduction of complex and highly specialized forms of business organization also contributed to the need for some definite procedure to keep firms in touch with requirements of the market.

Present Use by Industry. The volume of marketing and distribution research has increased steadily since the late 1920's. Today there are few firms which do not employ research to some extent. Extensive marketing research departments are now found in hundreds of business firms. Large and small organizations alike use independent research organizations to solve critical marketing and distribution problems, for these facilities may be employed as effectively by smaller firms as by the largest corporations. In the past some companies were willing to pay dearly for engineering studies of their factories and products, but were reluctant to appropriate large sums for distribution research. However, at the present time there is a growing appreciation of the need for continuous marketing research. Furthermore, recognition of the fact that marketing and distribution research is a basic tool of top management, rather than a supplementary device to be employed only as an administrative aid at the lower levels of business organization, has placed it in a vital position in American industry.

Marketing and distribution research has recently been undergoing a period of rapid expansion. The development of techniques of demonstrated accuracy, the growth of trained personnel, the building of facilities, and the expanding demand of business for this new management tool have all contributed. It is clear that its importance and use are growing at a pace which taxes its limited personnel and facilities to the utmost.

A survey made by the American Marketing Association reported that approximately 38 per cent of 4,786 business firms engaged in marketing research of some kind.[3] Eleven per cent of the companies questioned had organized research departments, while 27 per cent conducted marketing research as a line executive function, relying on outside sources for actual work. The survey also showed that the extent to which marketing research was used varied considerably according to volume of sales and type of industry. Only 23 per cent of the firms doing an annual sales volume of under $500,000 engaged in marketing research, whereas 73 per cent of those doing over $5,000,000 per year did so. The greater use by larger companies is further indicated by the fact that 45 per cent of them maintain organized research departments. Consumer-goods companies were

[3] W. W. Heusner, C. M. Dooley, G. A. Hughes, and Percival White, "Marketing Research in American Industry: I," *Journal of Marketing*, April, 1947, pp. 338–54.

larger users of marketing research than were those producing industrial goods, as only 35 per cent of the latter type engaged in marketing
and distribution research.

In 1952, the American Management Association made a survey of
180 of their member companies regarding their marketing research
practices. Admittedly this study was biased in the direction of larger
and more progressive corporations. They found that 93 per cent of
the firms covered in the study engage in marketing research.[4] The
results by type of company were as follows:

Manufacturers of both consumer and industrial goods 97%
Manufacturers of consumer goods only 94
Manufacturers of industrial goods only 93
Retailing, service, etc. 86

Another indication of the continued spreading of marketing
research through American business is the recent development of the
cooperative research program of the Super Market Institute. This
institute serves over 650 firms operating over 7,000 large retail food
stores with a combined sales volume of approximately six billion
dollars per year. The research program provides for cooperation
among members and with manufacturers or other organizations. The
program provides for marketing research projects which employ
statistics furnished by members of the Super Market Institute from
their acounting records as well as special experiments conducted in
their retail stores.

The total volume of marketing research has increased steadily
during recent years, but there is every indication that its greatest
period of expansion lies ahead. That this field has not yet begun to
find its full stature is indicated by estimates that about one cent out
of every sales dollar is spent for research of all types, and that approximately one tenth of a cent is spent for marketing research. In this
connection, the National Industrial Conference Board says:

Distribution is far behind production in the race for greater efficiency and
lower costs. . . . Scientific market research offers industry an objective approach to the problems of distribution that has helped many companies to
improve their products, broaden their markets, and cut distribution costs. . . .
All companies, whether they realize it or not, engage to some extent in market
research. . . .[5]

Marketing and distribution research is a peculiarly American
institution. It developed first in this country as a result of the

[4] American Management Association, *Company Practices in Marketing Research*,
Research Report No. 22, 1953, p. 17.
[5] National Industrial Conference Board, *Organization for Market Research*, Studies
in Business Policy No. 12, 1945, p. 1.

intense pressures created by our economic growth. In its early days, some limited applications were made in England, but the science was scarcely known throughout the rest of the world. However, in recent years there has been a growing interest in the subject, particularly in England, the Scandinavian countries, and Germany. Today the movement is rapidly spreading to other parts of the world. One important result is broader contribution to the improvement of procedures, through varied experiences and the cross-fertilization of many scientific minds.

Vocational Opportunities. With the recent expansion in marketing research, the field offers growing and unusual vocational opportunities to well-trained individuals who choose this calling. While many of the present practitioners have learned solely through experience, a growing number are preparing themselves on a more professional basis.

The various job opportunities in marketing research are described in detail in a vocational guidance manual. Such a variety of tasks is involved that an individual may readily find a specialized aspect of the work which fits his particular talents. While the greatest number of marketing researchers are in the larger industrial cities, people now engage in this vocation in all types of cities and all sections of the country.

Marketing research offers vocational opportunities for both men and women. In fact, it offers relatively unusual opportunities for women interested in either full-time or part-time careers. A further indication of the expanding opportunities in marketing research is found in the annual directory of independent marketing research agencies. The 1954 edition lists over 250 firms.[6]

Economic and Social Aspects

A profound shift in the basic economics of the United States has come about as a result of the development of marketing and distribution research. Traditionally, the economic process has begun with the producer. Until recent years the manufacturer, farmer, or service entrepreneur marketed a product which he thought he could produce most efficiently and at the greatest profit. On the basis of his personal experience and skills, he set up an organization and established price and marketing policies. The product was then promoted by aggressive sales methods and by advertising directed to the consumer.

---

[6] Ernest S. Bradford, *Bradford's Survey and Directory of Marketing Research Agencies in the United States and Abroad*, 6th ed. (New York: Privately printed, 1954).

Today, modern industry begins at the opposite end. It studies the market to determine the products needed, the characteristics of demand, and the prices the market will pay. With a myriad of marketing data, it literally produces to the market. Thus, management thinking now begins with the demand side of the economic equation. Production to a carefully measured demand provides a much sounder and more efficient economic structure.

To an amazing extent, the daily lives of people living in America, the things they eat, wear, and enjoy, as well as the methods by which they obtain them, are influenced by marketing and distribution research. The size, shape, texture, color, packaging, price, and distribution of disposable tissues in which the public blows its nose have been largely determined by a vast amount of marketing research. More important, from the social point of view, marketing research is the means by which the ultimate consumer literally becomes king of the market place, with his desires, prejudices, and every whim translated to the producer and distributor by research.

The ultimate aim of marketing research is to reduce the cost of distribution, and, consequently, the price which the consumers pay for the things they need. In a free competitive economy, the ultimate effect is bound to be a significant increase in the consumer's standard of living. The present relatively high distribution costs, already referred to, indicate the great extent to which the growing application of marketing research by industry can be a major factor in improving the general standard of living.

One of the most significant economic aspects of marketing and distribution research is its dynamic contribution to the expansion of the American economy. Business grows to the extent that it is nurtured by consumption of its goods and services. Marketing research stimulates business by discovering new products and services that are desired by consumers. The expansion of industry into fields such as baking mixes, frozen foods, and air conditioning has been accompanied by extensive research which has demonstrated the readiness of the market to accept innovations on a broad scale.

The influence of marketing and distribution research in this respect operates in two ways. First, it discovers new market opportunities and gives management the necessary confidence to make investments in production facilities and aggressive marketing campaigns in order to capitalize on the opportunities. Secondly, research directly increases consumer demand by helping the producer design products and services so that they bring greater satisfaction to consumers and by increasing the efficiency with which those products and services are marketed.

Marketing and distribution research has broad social implications. In addition to its general contribution to an increased standard of living it makes the life of the consumer much more pleasant and rewarding. In the process of helping industry design goods and services in accordance with the needs and desires of the buyer, it simultaneously increases the degree of customer satisfaction in the use of those goods and services. Every product irritation or annoyance that is eliminated through research helps the user. Research on distribution methods makes more and better products available to buyers in surroundings which make shopping a pleasant experience rather than a disagreeable chore.

Evidences that consumers understand and appreciate their own gains from marketing and distribution research are common. For example, industrial buyers and other executives will give freely of their time to cooperate in providing information for a well-designed marketing research. Consumers will make lengthy and sometimes arduous tests of experimental products with no compensation other than their recognition that they are contributing to the ultimate satisfaction of other consumers. Contrary to the impression held by some, people like to be interviewed if properly approached and will work hard at cooperating with a marketing investigator.

The present free enterprise economic system is based fundamentally upon the principle of individual initiative and the profit motive. There is no need to go into the limitations of this system. However, it should be pointed out that a fundamental weakness of the self interest theory, which has dominated the economic structure since Adam Smith, is not so much in the viciousness of businessmen as in their errors. Business mistakes beget sharp business practices and many of the present wasteful methods. If one takes individual cases of business failure, he will find that in most of them false judgment of market possibilities played an important part. Accurate measurement of markets, reducing errors caused by ignorance, removes one of the chief weaknesses of the individual-initiative, free enterprise system.

Production in anticipation of demand is another fundamental characteristic of the present economic structure. Custom work has been relegated to an insignificant role, as practically all products are first made and later sold. This scheme leads to huge forward commitments, both in the field of consumer goods and in that of industrial products. Manufacturers must be prepared to forecast demand accurately. Failure to evaluate markets properly must of necessity lead to economic waste.

Large-scale production methods require large-scale and adequate markets. In the desire for increased volume, there is a constant tendency to overestimate the capacity of markets to absorb a product. The result is that even in relatively "normal" business conditions, industries suffer from excess plant capacity. During periods of so-called prosperity, plant capacity rises sharply, so that in depression the excessive capacity, in itself, becomes a great economic burden.

In periods of business depression a plethora of theories concerning the business cycle is advanced. While almost everyone seeks for the touchstone which will explain by one theory the fundamental cause of these swings, there are many factors which contribute.

The overproduction theory is not in very good repute at present, perhaps because of the orthodox economists' logical refutation of the possibility of long-range economic overproduction. A historical examination of depressions, however, points to overextended plant capacity and overproduction as a major cause. The depression of 1873, for example, was preceded by immense expansion of industry, particularly in railroads. In 1920 the country was faced with plant capacity overextended by war needs. In 1929 we had plant capacity predicated on an abnormal expansion of the domestic market, development of foreign trade, installment selling, and an effort to retain the expansion of war times.

The depression of 1929 has been analyzed by many as primarily a monetary and credit depression. Yet the bulk of those credits were originally for purposes of plant expansion; the speculation was based on Pollyanna concepts of the future volume of industry. Had production been curtailed as soon as markets began to shrink (this shrinkage began in most cases a year before the financial crash), the huge superstructure would never have attained the heights to which it climbed. It is interesting to note that the wildest speculation came after sales volume in many lines was actually curtailed.

Marketing and distribution research also contributes to both economic stability and growth by producing facts which allay unnecessary fears of businessmen. Lack of confidence caused by ignorance of the true market situation can cause business to retrench production and reduce demand-creation effort. By doing so, management itself compounds its difficulties by further reducing market demand. In the extremely complex free enterprise system, each retrenchment tends to multiply itself by stimulating further retrenchment in additional areas.

A classic example of this contribution of marketing and distribution research occurred after the end of World War II. On the basis of historical experience, it was assumed that the war would be followed by a severe business depression. In spite of the forecasts of many economists, the anticipated depression did not occur. Readjustment was made rather painlessly and spread out over a long period of time so that the economy remained healthy. Many improvements in management methods, in financial institutions, and in communications undoubtedly contributed to this situation. However, marketing research was unquestionably a major factor. All during the war, for the first time in our history, business firms were engaged in marketing researches designed to develop new products which could take up the slack in production when peace returned. These activities continued at an increasing pace after hostilities ceased. Marketing and distribution research also contributed by directing the attention of business management to the true levels of purchasing power which had been created during the war. A notable example was the contribution of Arno Johnson, who, with others, demonstrated the new levels of purchasing power and helped arouse management to the need for aggressive selling to capitalize on new opportunities.[7] Thus, marketing research not only created much needed confidence but also discovered new sales opportunities in critical times.

The Role of Marketing Research in the Theory and Practice of Marketing

Limitation of Scientific Principles in Marketing. In marketing, as in all fields of human activity, basic laws or general principles are constantly sought. Just as the engineer employs fundamental scientific principles in his daily work, the marketing man seeks to use basic generalizations in meeting the problem of his business. In marketing, however, the solid foundations of physical phenomena which give permanence and universality to the principles of the older sciences are lacking.

Markets are in a state of constant flux. Nearly 4,000,000 babies are born in the United States every year. Over 37,500,000 new people enter the marketing picture every ten years. Markets are composed of human beings whose habits, attitudes, and desires are subject to constant change. Furthermore, one of the prime purposes of many marketing activities is to keep the public constantly dissatisfied with its habitual method of living and to develop new desires.

In view of these conditions, broad scientific principles have only limited application in the field of marketing. Their application must be made in the light of exceptions and unusual circumstances which are nearly always present. Most marketing problems are peculiar to particular conditions of time and space. Marketing management can

---

[7] Arno H. Johnson, *Marketing in a Defense Economy* (New York: J. Walter Thompson Co., 1951); and "Peace Can Bring Opportunity to Advertising to Improve U. S. Living," *Advertising Age*, May 11, 1953, p. 1 *et seq.*

therefore be scientific for the most part only in so far as it employs scientific methods to solve specific problems, rather than by attempting to solve them on the basis of established laws or principles.

Potential Development of Marketing Principles. By means of marketing and distribution research, however, it is possible to develop principles and generalizations based upon facts, rather than upon casual observation or individual experiences. Although the application of general principles of marketing is now restricted, progress in the field will in a sense be measured largely by the extent to which workable basic principles can be developed. These principles may be based on hunch, guesswork, isolated cases, or the experience of individuals and groups of individuals. Such principles must of necessity be unsound. On the other hand, many of the basic generalizations or principles of marketing which are now being developed are based on the cumulative results of different marketing researches. Principles which grow out of facts have a true scientific foundation and therefore are much more valuable.

Increased Size and Complexity of Modern Business. The continuing growth of large-scale production, with the widening of the physical distance between the manufacturer and the consumer, has been the chief single factor which has brought about the large increase in interest in marketing in recent years. A century ago the typical business unit was the one-man shop. Under these conditions there was no need for much attention to marketing because the producer was constantly in touch with the consumer. Even during the early growth in the size of business units, there was no great gulf between producer and consumer.

With the development of specialized marketing agencies, however, a tendency for manufacturers to be out of touch with their markets appeared. Consumers bought from retailers, who in turn bought from wholesalers, who often dealt with the manufacturer through other intermediaries. Each of these units tended to erect a sort of dam which blocked the backward flow of the consumer's needs and desires to the manufacturer.

With the current tendency toward integration, the manufacturer is nominally brought more directly in contact with the consumer, but size and specialization within the business unit may separate the consumer from the directing heads of the business even more than the intervention of middlemen. Within the firm itself, the engineering, production, finance, sales, and advertising departments are often set off rigidly from one another. The result is that unless some definite effort to keep in touch with the market through research is pursued, the firm is likely to find policies dangerously out of tune with the market.

The principle that the consumer is the ultimate objective of all business enterprise, that business must be directed fundamentally toward the most efficient satisfaction of the needs and desires of consumers, has long been recognized in a theoretical way by economists and businessmen. Just as the economist has generally glossed over the subject of the economics of consumption, the businessman has permitted himself to become embroiled in immediate problems of production, finance, and the details of operation.

The interests of society, industrial groups, and the individual business enterprise demand more effective and less costly methods of marketing. Both the general public and businessmen have come to realize that a large share of the gains accomplished through efficient production has been lost through expensive and wasteful marketing methods. Today there are few businessmen who do not constantly seek an opportunity to replace guesswork with factual knowledge of the market. Thus marketing and distribution research have become the foundation of modern marketing practice in the United States.

SELECTED READINGS

Cowan, Donald R. G. (ed.) *Annual Marketing Research Conference*, Michigan Business Papers, No. 27. Ann Arbor: University of Michigan, Bureau of Business Research.

Hobart, Donald M. *Dynamic Marketing*. Philadelphia: The Curtis Publishing Co., 1954.

Lockley, Lawrence C. "Notes on the History of Marketing Research," *Journal of Marketing*, April, 1950, pp. 733–36.

Luck, David J., and Wales, Hugh G. *Marketing Research*. New York: Prentice-Hall, Inc., 1952, pp. 53–72.

Mulvihill, Donald F. "Market Research for the Small Business," *University of Alabama Business News*, XXII, 4 (December 15, 1951).

Rewoldt, Stewart H. *Economic Effects of Marketing Research*, Michigan Business Studies, Vol. XI, No. 4. Ann Arbor: University of Michigan, 1953.

Smith, Charles W. "Increasing Distribution Efficiency by Better Organized Research," *Journal of Marketing*, January, 1953, pp. 233–45.

Westfall, Ralph. "Marketing Research—Milestone or Millstone?—A Reply," *Journal of Marketing*, October, 1953, pp. 174–77.

CASE

Applebaum, William, and Spears, Richard F. "Marketing Research Studies in a Grocery Chain," *Journal of Marketing*, July 1952, pp. 52–56.

GENERAL BIBLIOGRAPHY

Blankenship, Albert B. (ed.) *How to Conduct Consumer and Opinion Research*. New York: Harper & Bros., 1946.

Blankertz, Donald F., Ferber, Robert, and Wales, Hugh G. *Cases and Problems in Marketing Research*. New York: The Ronald Press Co., 1954.

BRADFORD, ERNEST S. *Marketing Research.* New York: McGraw-Hill Book Co., Inc., 1951.

HOBART, DONALD M. *Marketing Research Practice.* New York: The Ronald Press Co., 1950.

HOBART, DONALD M., and WOOD, J. P. *Selling Forces.* New York: The Ronald Press Co.. 1953.

LORIE, JAMES H., and ROBERTS, HARRY V. *Basic Methods of Marketing Research.* New York: McGraw-Hill Book Co., Inc., 1951.

LUCK, DAVID J., and WALES, HUGH G. *Marketing Research.* New York: Prentice-Hall, Inc., 1952.

Printers' Ink. Articles on Research and Market Analysis. New York: *Printers' Ink,* Readers' Service Department, 1952.

REVZAN, DAVID A. *A Comprehensive Classified Marketing Bibliography,* Parts I, II, and III. Berkeley, California: University of California Press, 1951.

A Short Annotated Bibliography of Marketing and Advertising Research. New York: Advertising Research Foundation, 1953.

THOMPSON, RALPH B. *A Selected and Annotated Bibliography of Literature on Marketing Research.* Austin, Texas: University of Texas, College of Business Administration, 1950.

WALES, HUGH G., and FERBER, ROBERT. *Marketing Research—Selected Literature.* Dubuque, Iowa: William G. Brown Co., 1952.

WHEELER, FERDINAND C. (ed.) *The Technique of Marketing Research.* New York: McGraw-Hill Book Co., Inc., 1937.

2

ORGANIZATION OF MARKETING AND
DISTRIBUTION RESEARCH

In order to meet the growing demands of American industry for marketing and distribution research, an extensive and clearly defined organization of this field has emerged. This general structure has grown in response to specific needs as they have developed. However, as a result of its rapid expansion, serious problems of organization have arisen between and within various units engaging in research. As a result, considerable attention is now being devoted to matters of staff, procedures, activities, and relations between different firms. Furthermore, a considerable expansion in facilities is required to keep pace with demands, so that there is a growing need for more competent organizations and personnel.

Firms Engaged in Marketing and Distribution Research

Twelve major types of organizations are involved in the use and conduct of marketing research. They are:

1. Manufacturers of consumer goods
2. Manufacturers of industrial products
3. Wholesalers
4. Retailers
5. Service organizations
6. Advertising agencies
7. Channels of communication
8. Trade associations
9. Cooperative associations
10. Government and public agencies
11. Independent consultants
12. Syndicated research services

Manufacturers of Consumers' Goods. National manufacturers of products designed for the ultimate consumer, in such form that they can be used by him without further commercial processing, are the most important single class of users of marketing and distribution research. As a result of the complexity of their marketing problems, almost all producers of packaged food products, soaps, household appliances, and similar products make extensive use of this management tool.

Some manufacturers maintain rather elaborate marketing research departments with annual budgets running well over $1,000,000. Regardless of the size of the internal department, they rely heavily on outside organizations such as their advertising agencies, independent consultants, and syndicated services for much of their research.

Manufacturers of Industrial Products. For many years manufacturers of goods used in producing other goods hesitated to use marketing and distribution research extensively. This hesitancy arose chiefly because of the large share of sales made direct, without any middlemen, and because of large unit sales, the relatively small number of customers, and the close personal contact between buyer and seller. In recent years, however, manufacturers of industrial goods have employed marketing research in ever-increasing volume as opportunities to eliminate marketing wastes and to increase sales volume have been discovered through research. Today these manufacturers constitute the largest single numerical group of users.

Wholesalers. During the period when channels of distribution were shifting so rapidly that the wholesaler was fighting for his existence, there was little inclination to employ the modern tool of marketing research in this field. As the emphasis shifted to more efficient performance of the wholesaling function, however, leading wholesale firms in various lines came to rely more and more on marketing research techniques. The field offers fertile opportunities, particularly in internal analysis, in defining territories, in controlling dealer operations, and in increasing the efficiency of warehousing and transporting goods.

Retailers. The pioneering work in the use of marketing research by retail establishments has largely been done by the chainstore systems, possibly because of their decentralized operations and because they have found through experience that marketing research can play a vital role in the solution of such crucial problems as store location. The department stores have not developed the use of marketing research as extensively as many expected they would, in view of their obvious opportunities to do so. This may be explained in part by the emphasis placed on extremely complex systems of internal accounting controls and on personal merchandising skills.

Various types of retailing organizations are becoming increasingly aware of the broader implications of marketing research, and are employing it more and more extensively, particularly in connection with defining retail trading areas, store location, variations of merchandise handled, selling policies, and advertising.

Service Organizations. Marketing research techniques are not limited in their application to the marketing of physical products. Those firms which purvey services find that its principles are fully applicable to their marketing problems. Banks, insurance companies, hotels, restaurants, airlines, and utilities are examples of active users. For example, the Life Insurance Sales Research Bureau has analyzed regional statistics to develop market potentials for many years. Studies of consumer types, surveys of agents, estimates of uncovered insurable risks, opinion polls on management policies and on distribution methods are other forms of marketing research applied in the insurance field. The American Telephone and Telegraph Company was one of the pioneers in marketing research, notably in their forecasts of future demand for service in various localities.

Advertising Agencies. Advertising agencies were largely responsible for pioneering the acceptance of marketing and distribution research. Today the larger advertising agencies maintain extensive research departments both for their own needs and as an additional service to their clients. It is universally recognized that an advertising agency must work on the basis of facts in order to plan effectively and execute advertising campaigns under today's complex and highly competitive conditions. As their services expanded beyond the purchase of space and preparation of copy, agencies have historically become more actively concerned with the planning of complete marketing campaigns. As a result, they have come to do a great deal of marketing research for their clients in areas other than advertising.

The advertising agency employs specialists who are especially well qualified to conduct those phases of research—such as testing advertisements, media, and merchandising research—which are closely associated with advertising. It also has broad experience with different products and types of marketing problems. Furthermore, because of its close and continuous relations with clients, it knows the latter's marketing problems intimately.

The disadvantages of advertising agency research are possible bias and the speed with which agency work is usually conducted. Whether bias is actually present in any given case depends on the research policy of the organization and its relationship with the client. If the agency has an ethical management and the full confidence of the client, bias will not be present in research it conducts. The general tempo of an advertising agency is very fast. Its management sometimes expects that the work of the research division should be conducted at the same speed as that of other functions. This point of view can lead to unfortunate results because of the need for time in good research.

The practice of charging a fee to clients for research conducted in their interest has done a great deal to improve the quality of agency research work. Increased emphasis on advertising research per se has also contributed. The attraction of superior personnel has placed a number of the larger advertising agencies in a position to do outstanding marketing research.

Channels of Communication. Magazines, newspapers, radio, television, and other channels of communication are extensive users of marketing research. They employ its techniques in two general ways: (1) for editorial research designed to study the reading or listening audience in order to provide a foundation for editorial and management policy; and (2) for promotional research to provide information for advertisers using the medium. Their promotional use of research has been a great stimulus in arousing others to the importance of this field.

The most common forms of promotional research by media are studies which break down the market reached, show the extent of audience and duplication, check reader interest, and analyze circulations. Data from these surveys are often valuable guides in marketing policy. Publications also often prepare rather extensive analyses of the markets for individual products.

The specialized knowledge of the market which each medium covers is one of its chief advantages. The trade contacts which publications have established should not be overlooked as valuable sources of information for any specific study.

There is wide variation in the quality of research done by advertising media. A good deal of superficial and biased research is done by some of them. On the other hand, some of the highest quality research has been conducted by media for promotional purposes because it is there for all to see and must measure up to critical inspection by many technicians. The chief governing elements are the quality of the research personnel and the standards set by management.

Trade Associations. Extensive marketing research is conducted by trade associations in manufacturing, wholesaling, and retailing, as well as by associations of companies engaged in finance, insurance, real estate, construction, and transportation. An increasing number are sponsoring market studies for the mutual benefit of members. Examples include such varied fields as those served by the National Electrical Manufacturers Association, the National Furniture Association, and the National Institute of Diaper Services.

The trade asociation often provides facilities for carrying on a continuous research service for its members, particularly in the matter of pooling marketing data. Outside research organizations are frequently employed by the associations to make the larger, more basic studies of markets for the products of the industry and of the more significant problems common to various individual firms within the industry. Trade associations have an unusual opportunity to serve their members by engaging in marketing researches beyond the means of individual firms. Furthermore, costs of special studies can be shared by cooperating companies.

The extent of marketing research by trade associations is indicated by a survey made by the U. S. Department of Commerce. This study showed that of the 2,000 national and regional trade associations, 31 per cent carried on some form of marketing research activities. An analysis of the current research of 75 associations showed that their activities embraced product research, consumer research, market analysis, and research relating to marketing functions, policies, and costs. The Department of Commerce, in commenting on the results of its survey, stated that "more and more emphasis is being placed on marketing research." [1]

Examples of special studies sponsored by trade associations are the following:

1. Gray Iron Founders Society—a study of the principal markets for products of the industry and the extent of market areas served by the industry.
2. International Association of Ice Cream Manufacturers—an annual survey of production and distribution.
3. National Association of Independent Tire Dealers—a study to determine the kinds of merchandise and services sold by independent tire dealers.
4. Cotton Textile Institute—studies designed to discover new outlets for cotton products.
5. Wholesale Dry Goods Institute—a study of distribution practices, plans, and preferences of dry-goods retailers, wholesalers, and manufacturers.
6. National Shoe Manufacturers Association—consumer research.

[1] See Theodore K. Pasma, *Trade Association Opportunities in Marketing Research*, U. S. Department of Commerce, Industrial Series No. 78, 1948.

Cooperative Associations. Both producer cooperative organizations and consumer cooperatives now employ marketing research extensively. The producer cooperative is in the same position as the national manufacturer. The California Fruit Growers Association, the Walnut Growers, and several others were quick to sense the importance of scientific marketing and distribution studies. The consumer cooperatives, such as farmers' purchasing associations and cooperative stores, have learned that they are essentially in the same position as the regular wholesaler and retailer; therefore, these groups are making extensive use of marketing research.

Governmental and Other Public Agencies. The United States Government is the outstanding statistical organization in this country. In recent years more and more of its branches have borrowed the techniques of marketing research in making surveys to guide their operations, as well as in making marketing studies for the use of business firms. State and local governments also employ the techniques of marketing research as a basis for determining public policy. Welfare agencies, educational institutions, and philanthropic groups are making increasing use of marketing research techniques. Opinion studies and consumer surveys are among the most common forms used by this latter class.

Governmental agencies are indispensable sources of general statistical data which may be used in marketing research. The individual firm could not hope to duplicate their fact-gathering facilities. They have legal authority and funds to gather vast quantities of basic data. Their chief weakness is that the information is often very general and hence applicable to only a limited number of problems.

Universities and foundations conduct many marketing research studies. Their chief advantage is that they are usually conducted without bias by men of real scientific caliber. However, they are often too generalized to be adapted readily to the specific needs of the individual firm.

From the point of view of the researcher, the broad studies made by governmental agencies, universities, and foundations are regarded chiefly as sources for secondary data. Many of their studies have also contributed greatly to the improvement of research methods.

Independent Consultants. There are numerous organizations which specialize in conducting marketing research on a fee basis for manufacturers, distributors, service organizations, and other users. These specialists render chiefly two basic services: (1) they advise in the planning, interpretation, and application of marketing research, and (2) they provide the physical facilities for conducting various parts of the work, such as the field investigations and the tabulation and analysis.

The chief advantages of these organizations are the caliber of their principals, the experience which they have obtained through making different studies for many clients, adequate mechanical facilities, and an unbiased, outside point of view. The better ones are headed by persons who have broad experience in the field of marketing and distribution research and can render valuable advice in planning and interpretation. While the fees which they charge sometimes appear large, the actual cost is usually lower than the expense involved in maintaining an extensive staff in the average individual company.

The disadvantages of organizations specializing in marketing research are their lack of intimate knowledge of the internal problems of a business and the superficial character of the work which is done by some of the poorer ones. The lack of a detailed knowledge of the internal problems of the business is not necessarily a real handicap, however, since management can provide this ingredient.

It is very difficult to estimate in advance the exact cost of a marketing research, particularly one which involves extensive field work. Unfortunately, many clients, in an effort to reduce costs, demand that a flat fee be set before giving the work to the consulting firm. In such cases the firm must include a rather large cushion to take care of unanticipated expenses and to make up for unexpected losses which may be incurred. If the prospective client shops around in an effort to obtain the lowest possible price, it is inevitable that he will eventually find a firm which will accept the work at a low fee and will then cut corners in order to make expenses. The result is that the user of the research gets superficial work, sometimes to the point of actually getting erroneous and misleading results.

This pressure to obtain low costs and the tendency to shop around are characteristics of a new field which has not yet attained full professional status. As marketing research matures, in the sense in which the legal and accounting professions have matured, however, the users of research tend to rely more upon well-equipped independent marketing research counselors.

Under no circumstances should the user of research allow himself to be the potential victim of a situation in which his outside source is working under the handicap of an inadequate budget or too great a time pressure. The research director who sets the standards of cheap and speedy research is failing in his primary obligation—to obtain for his management the best scientific solution to its most significant marketing problems. Good research in any field takes both money and time.

The best marketing research usually results from a combination of a competent research director within the organization using the research and a competent outside organization. The importance of the skill of the research director in making the most effective use of outside facilities is emphasized in the following statement:

> It should be reiterated that outside organizations can perform, and have performed, an important service for industry in the field of marketing research. The value of this service to any one company depends on the discrimination with which the research organization, agency or private consultant is selected, and the skill with which the findings are interpreted and utilized in the company. By far the best use of outside organizations involves integration of their work with that of the company's own permanent organization.[2]

Syndicated Services. Syndicated services gather standardized marketing facts on a continuous basis for their clients. They provide a vast fund of vital marketing information for management as well as basic raw data for the research department. In the sense of research which is planned and executed in order to solve the specific problems of an individual firm, the information supplied by these services is limited, as they are primarily fact-gathering agencies. The better organizations, however, make every effort to interpret the facts which they present for their clients.

An important form of syndicated service is the *store audit*. This type of service reports the flow of competitive products through a sample of retail channels of trade. National audits are available for food and drug items from the A. C. Nielsen Company. They show purchases by retailers, sales to consumers, inventories, prices, and related information by individual brands, package sizes, etc. Local store auditing services for individual markets are also maintained by several organizations.

A second important form of syndicated service is the *consumer panel*, which reports consumer purchases by brands. This service is based on diaries which are kept by a sample of families scattered throughout the country. The housewife records purchases of a number of products, showing the amount purchased, brands, source of purchase, and other related information. In return for prizes and premiums, the housewife fills out the diary and mails it to a central office where the data are analyzed. The Market Research Corporation of America maintains a national consumer panel. A number of local panels are maintained by advertising media.

Both the store audit and the consumer panel provide important marketing information. Since they both report competitive sales by

---

[2] American Management Association, *A Company Guide to Marketing Research*, Report No. 5, pp. 29–30.

individual brands and the facts presented do not always agree, there is considerable controversy as to the relative merits of each method. The store audit has the following advantages: It is based on physical auditing of records by trained observers and it obtains merchandising information which cannot be furnished by the consumer panel. The consumer panel has these advantages: It obtains buying information regardless of the retail source, and it provides analysis data on consumers, such as economic class, which are unavailable through store audits. In spite of the current controversy, it is clear that the two services are complementary and that the company which uses both types of information is most fully served.

A number of syndicated services operate in the advertising field. One of the oldest of these reports the percentage of magazine and newspaper readers who see and read various advertisements. Prominent in the broadcasting field are services which measure the size of audiences. Other syndicated services used in advertising studies report advertising expenditures and advertising circulations.

The Research Department

Some companies do not maintain separate marketing research departments, either because they do not engage in research extensively or because they rely upon outside agencies for their research. However, any company which uses marketing research, regardless of its extent or source, is the hub of those activities. Furthermore, the transfer of the research findings into management policies and operations occurs within the company. Therefore, even if no formal department exists, every firm should have at least one major executive who is more or less expert in marketing research and is made responsible for the general direction of its planning, supervision, and interpretation.

Organization of the Department. A company may be of sufficient size to warrant the full-time employment of a considerable research staff. The following factors should be taken into account in determining the size of the department:

1. The number of actual marketing research functions it performs.
2. The amount of routine work assigned to the department.
3. The amount of statistical accounting done by the department; i.e., customer sales analysis, area or geographic distributions of sales, sales by item, sales cost distribution, etc.
4. The use of company service departments such as stenographic and computation pools and tabulating departments.

5. The promotional uses made of marketing research findings and other promotional activities assigned the department.

6. The degree of centralization of marketing research activities prevailing in the organization.

The American Management Association survey shows that the average marketing research department consists of six persons. Except in a few large organizations, a big department is uneconomical. Too often firms get the "research fever," set up a big department, and then discontinue it in a wave of economy. It is much better to employ one good man who understands the field thoroughly and rely on outside sources. To be really effective, marketing research must be a continuous activity which is welded into the regular activities of the organization.

The following examples show the number and type of employees in typical marketing research departments: [3]

A. *Manufacturer of Food*
    Director of Market Research
    2 Analysts
    3 Statisticians
    Librarian
    2 Tabulators
    Chartist
    Secretary
    Typist
    Comptometer Operator

B. *Manufacturer of Plastic Materials*
    Director of Market Research
    2 Analysts
    Statistician
    Librarian

C. *Manufacturer of Soap*
    Research Director
    Assistant Director
    Assistant to Director
    11 Analysts
    Interviewer
    Field Investigator
    Librarian
    5 Machine Operators
    5 Secretaries and Stenographers
    3 Clerical Personnel

[3] *Ibid.*

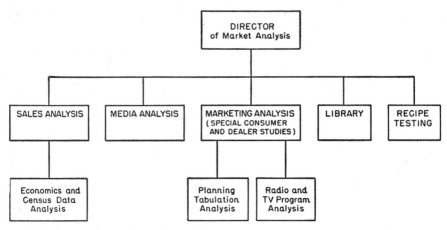

FIGURE 2. Organization of a Marketing Research Department. This chart shows the functional organization of the Marketing Analysis Department of General Mills, Inc. Personnel of the department has been eliminated from the chart in order to clarify the organization of functions. Note that the organization has been adapted to the special needs and requirements of the corporation. For example, a specialized unit, ranking with Sales Analysis, Marketing Analysis, etc., is maintained for recipe testing because of the nature of the business.

It must be remembered that the qualifications of research personnel are always more important than the organization. The guiding factors in building an organization are the research requirements of the company and the personal skills and characteristics of the Director of Research.

An important consideration in organizing the department is to have a definite operating budget. Good research takes time and costs money. Its dollars-and-cents return is often unmeasurable. If one is forced to work from hand to mouth, he will eventually find that his work is curtailed by someone who sees an easy chance to save money. It is better to have a small but definite budget than to work in constant fear that too much is being spent and to be forced to justify costs from day to day. Above all, the support and evaluation of a research organization must be considered over a relatively long term and not, as in the case of production, sales, and profits, over the short-term period of the annual budget and the president's report.

Position and Qualifications of the Person in Charge. The all-important factor in organizing market research is to place a person with proper qualifications in charge of it. He must have an unusual combination of practical and theoretical talents. On the practical side, he must have a sound management understanding of business, and at the same time be a good liaison man and a salesman who can talk the language of other departments and keep them enthusiastic about the work. He must have the imagination to present the work of his department vividly and pictorially. On the theoretical side, he must know methods—not so much the mechanics as the philosophy and use of them. He must be constantly researching research itself, looking for new and better procedures. He must, of course, be thoroughly familiar with the business in which his firm is engaged. In the meat-packing industry, for example, there are countless well-established policies and practices with which one must reckon. This industry, for example, has special problems of pricing, so the analyst must be familiar with the executive thinking on this subject peculiar to the field.

The person who is responsible for marketing research should be either a key executive in the organization or in direct and constant contact with those actively directing the affairs of the company. Much otherwise good marketing research is barren of productive results because the person in charge does not rank high enough in the personnel of the company. Marketing research is one of the most fundamental of management activities, and its operation should be kept close to the directing heads of the company.

It has frequently been reiterated that a program of marketing research has a much better chance to produce good results if the individual in charge of the function is of high calibre, has definite standing in the organization, and enjoys strong executive sponsorship. Obviously, *a carefully selected, adequately compensated executive is in a more favorable position to gain the respect of other department heads than one of uncertain rank who has only the half-hearted backing of management.*[4]

Place of the Marketing Research Department. The marketing research department should ideally be separate from others and responsible directly to the head of the business or to a general executive whose authority is not limited to a few departments. Sometimes it is made part of the industrial engineering department or planning division. While the research department should work constantly in harmony with this division, its work will be done better if it operates separately. Some firms maintain extensive statistical departments, but where a large volume of routine statistical work is carried on it is better not to bury creative marketing research in it. Since most firms have separate sales and advertising departments, it is best not to set up the marketing research work in either. Placing it in one of these departments may embroil it in interdepartmental politics; harmonious relation with all other departments is essential.

[4] *Ibid.*

That management is coming to recognize the importance of giving more independence to the marketing research department and having its head report to general management is shown by the following:

TABLE 1

EXECUTIVE TO WHOM MARKETING RESEARCH HEAD REPORTS [5]

Head of the company (president, boards of directors, partner)	33.6%
Vice presidential level.	32.3
More than one of above.	11.7
Selling department managers (sales, advertising, etc.)	15.5
Financial department managers (treasurer, secretary, computing department)	2.1
Committee and others.	1.7
No answer	3.1
Total	100.0%

Functions of the Research Department. The discussion in the next chapter of the various types of marketing and distribution research reveals a wide variety of possible departmental activities. Many of them require highly technical procedures and extensive research resources. In planning the research program for any given organization, it is essential that it be concentrated in those research areas which will be most productive.

Surveys of the research activities of various companies are frequently made in order to determine those which are most commonly pursued. These studies of departmental activity show that quantitative market analysis, sales analysis, product research, and competitive position are ranked high in importance. As a guide to establishing company policy there is value in reviewing these surveys. However, the overriding consideration in defining the functions of the department is critical examination and selection of areas to be researched in the light of the special requirements of the business. Thus, the value of the department may be enhanced by concentrating its activities on those types of research offering the optimum investment of time and expenditures.

SELECTED READINGS

AMERICAN MANAGEMENT ASSOCIATION. *A Company Guide to Marketing Research*, Research Report, No. 5, 1944, and *Company Practices in Marketing Research*, Research Report No. 22, 1953.

LUCK, DAVID J., and WALES, HUGH G. *Marketing Research*. New York: Prentice-Hall, Inc., 1952, pp. 25–52.

[5] Heusner *et al.*, "Marketing Research in American Industry: I," *Journal of Marketing*, April, 1947, p. 348. A more recent survey by the American Management Association did not obtain information on this subject as clearly as the one quoted. However, it confirmed the tendency for the research department to be given a higher position in the general organization of a company.

NATIONAL INDUSTRIAL CONFERENCE BOARD. *Organization for Marketing Research*, Part I, 1945, and Part II, 1946.

PASMA, THEODORE K. *Trade Association Opportunities in Marketing Research*, U. S. Department of Commerce, Industrial Series No. 78. Washington, D. C.: Government Printing Office, 1948.

CASE

BLANKERTZ, DONALD F., FERBER, ROBERT, and WALES, HUGH G., *Cases and Problems in Marketing Research*. New York: The Ronald Press Co., 1954, pp. 328–33.

3

TYPES OF MARKETING RESEARCH

The relation of marketing and distribution research to modern business is indicated by the many branches of the field developed in recent years. A wide variety of specific types and applications are found, some of them very specialized and employing highly technical procedures. Each of them is widely used; each makes its particular contribution to better marketing management, and each presents special problems in research method.

The purpose of this chapter is to present a bird's-eye view of the various types of marketing and distribution research. In doing so, a basic structural pattern of types is developed. This pattern is important for understanding the discussion of methods which follows as well as for providing a guide for knowing how, when, and where to employ these methods. Some of the more highly specialized and technical types of research are discussed in detail in Part III of the book.

There are seven basic types of marketing and distribution research, as follows:

1. Market Characteristics Research (Qualitative Analysis).
2. Size of Market Research (Quantitative Analysis).
3. Distribution Research.
4. Sales Research.
5. Advertising and Promotion Research.
6. Product Research.
7. Competitive Position and Trends Research.

Research of Market Characteristics

The most fundamental type of marketing research is that which studies the consumer market for the products of industry or business services. By describing and measuring the consuming market in terms of standard characteristics such as age, sex, and economic class, these studies provide executives with an understanding of the end use of their products which forms a factual foundation for many of the most vital decisions in marketing and distribution. Lack of precise knowledge of the character of the consuming market is one of the most serious handicaps any marketing operation can have. On the other hand, superior factual knowledge of the ultimate buyer provides one of the strongest competitive weapons.

These researches range from basic national studies having a bearing on many phases of marketing policy to small specialized surveys confined to limited geographical areas or designed to answer only one or two vital questions.

Some of the more common subjects studied in connection with market characteristics are discussed below.

Who Uses the Product? It is frequently found that a company does not have an adequate understanding of the types of people who use its product. For example, one company assumed that 80 per cent of its product was being sold for use by adults. A marketing investigation revealed that less than 30 per cent was consumed by adults and that over 70 per cent was being used for infants. Another company found the situation almost exactly reversed. It had been manufacturing a food for infant feeding for many years and assumed that the market was in this field. More and more growing children and adults began using the product, and it was finally discovered that while the use of their product for infant feeding was shrinking, the growing children and adult markets offered the best opportunities for sales expansion. In the case of another company, it was assumed that since it was manufacturing a high-priced speciality, the users of the product would be people in the upper income brackets. A consumer survey, however, revealed that the majority of the people using their product were in the lower income levels, or the mass market. Consumer surveys often reveal startling opportunities for the expansion of the sale of a product by discovering new groups of users either unknown to the management of the company or much more important than the management has believed them to be.

A wide variety of factual information is usually obtained in connection with studies of product usage. In a deodorant market survey, for example, the following topics were covered, along with several others:

1. Number of persons using any deodorant.
2. Types of deodorants used.
3. Possession of deodorant at time of interview.
4. Length of time deodorants have been used.
5. Length of time present brand has been used.

6. Reasons for not using certain brands.
7. How user began using certain brands.
8. Whether users have noticed physical changes in deodorants.
9. Size of package used.
10. Specific purposes for which deodorants are used.

In studies of product usage, it is most important to define "user" accurately. The fact that an individual has at one time or another used a product does not make him a user of any marketing significance. Only as some quantitative measurement of usage is employed, does the term "user" have a significant meaning from the research point of view.

This is the answer to the person who sometimes fails to appreciate the value of studies of product usage, and who may remark, "Everybody uses my product." One would wonder that there are nonusers of canned soups in this modern age, and no doubt there are relatively few families or individuals who have not, at one time or another, had canned soup. However, when the quantitative limit of purchasing one or more cans during a period of six months is set as the definition of a user-family, it has been found that usage is far from universal. When the definition is set at purchase of one or more cans in a period of one month, the proportion of user-families declines very sharply. The value of careful quantitative definition is further illustrated by contrasting the proportion of user-families on the basis of stringent definition between various market segments, such as geographic areas and population groups. This will bring out sharp contrasts in the type and location of users, often leading to radical changes in marketing policies and methods.

Analysis of Relationship Between Buyers and Users. Frequently the distinction between the types of persons who use the product and the types of persons who buy the product is an important one. Housewives are traditionally the "purchasing agents" of families. Sometimes it is important to direct activities toward the buyer, sometimes toward the user.

One special phase of this type of study is the analysis of persons who influence purchasers. For example, the bulk of automobile purchases is made by the male head-of-family. However, automobile manufacturers have learned through study that the wives, children, and friends are important influences affecting the decision to buy a particular make, sometimes more important than the person who does the actual buying.

Consumer durable goods, such as homes, automobiles, and household equipment, as well as important service items such as life insurance and education, present particularly fertile fields for this type of research. Determining the relative importance and relationship between influences such as the owner, building contractor, and architect in the purchase of materials used in building and furnishing a home presents an intricate problem in consumer research.

Why Consumers Buy a Product. Studies of buying motives are common forms of consumer surveys. It is important to the manufacturer to know whether consumers buy the product chiefly because of quality, style, service, or other motives. Marketing research may reveal that a product which on the surface is presumably a health product is bought by the large majority of consumers because of a desire to be beautiful or to advance themselves socially. A mouthwash, for example, as a solution for oral hygiene made little progress, but as a device to win suitors and husbands it was a great success. Some of the most spectacular achievements in marketing have come as the result of aggressive campaigns which have sold products on entirely new appeals. For example, it is assumed that people buy soap for cleanliness, but some of the most successful promotional campaigns in this business have been built on the strategy of selling soap as a cosmetic, tied in with the "beauty" appeal. In this connection a highly specialized field of marketing research, called Motivational Research, has been developed. It is discussed in Chapter 18.

How a Product Is Used. Closely related to the question of why consumers buy a particular product is the question of how they actually use it once it has been purchased. Consumers are great experimenters; they often discover new uses for products which are unknown to the manufacturers. For years raisins had a very restricted use in the American diet. Then a consumer survey discovered that women were using the product in many different ways in their homes, and an advertising campaign stressing new uses proved very successful. Lemons were traditionally used to make lemonade until a marketing research revealed tremendous possibilities in new uses, one example being their use as a hair rinse after shampooing, another as a laxative.

The value of developing new uses for a product can be further illustrated by cleansing tissues. This product was manufactured originally for one purpose, the removal of cosmetics. Today, as a result of changes in cosmetic practices, women use the product so little for this purpose that the manufacturer, had he been content to rest on the original product use, would have had a declining volume. However, the Kimberly-Clark Corporation, pioneers in this product, soon began to develop new uses, especially in the handkerchief field. A large share of advertising was devoted to promoting the manifold uses

BREAKFAST CEREALS
PURCHASE RATE INDEX
1950

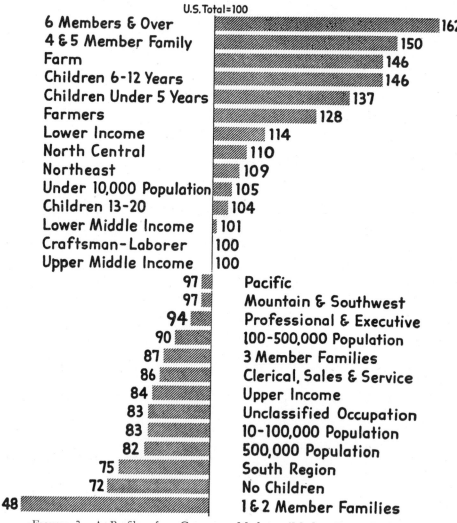

U.S. Total=100

6 Members & Over	162
4 & 5 Member Family	150
Farm	146
Children 6-12 Years	146
Children Under 5 Years	137
Farmers	128
Lower Income	114
North Central	110
Northeast	109
Under 10,000 Population	105
Children 13-20	104
Lower Middle Income	101
Craftsman-Laborer	100
Upper Middle Income	100
97	Pacific
97	Mountain & Southwest
94	Professional & Executive
90	100-500,000 Population
87	3 Member Families
86	Clerical, Sales & Service
84	Upper Income
83	Unclassified Occupation
83	10-100,000 Population
82	500,000 Population
75	South Region
72	No Children
48	1 & 2 Member Families

FIGURE 3. A Profile of a Consumer Market. (Market Research Corporation of America.)

of the product, and many people no longer recall that the disposable tissue they buy today was once exclusively the facial cleansing tissue.

A specific application of studies to develop new uses is for leveling out seasonal sales. Examples are developing the use of coffee as a cold beverage to increase summer sales, and promoting the use of lemons for laxatives to increase winter sales.

The research of new uses has its subtleties, too. For instance, the concept of a "new" use should not be limited to some clear-cut change in the manner or purpose for which a product is used. One study showed that a certain food product was served in great preponderance with a certain type of meal. The market was greatly expanded by suggesting other types of meals with which the product could be served; in fact, almost the entire advertising for several years was devoted to promoting these "new" uses.

Analysis of Consumption Rates. Some of the most revealing marketing researches are those which classify consumers on the basis of the rate at which they consume a given product. Surveys of beverage consumption, for example, classify consumers into "light," "medium," and "heavy" users. When these segments of the consumer market are further analyzed by age, sex, and other classification data, the basic foundation for more accurate direction of promotional efforts and other marketing activities is provided.

A manufacturer of a drug product assumed that his commodity was used rapidly by a relatively small number of users. A field survey showed that the product was used by a very large number of persons, but that the consumption per individual was very small. This obviously pointed to the need for developing some marketing strategy to increase the rate of use by each consumer. On the other hand, a manufacturer of a specialty kitchen cleanser found that the bulk of his sales was to a very few customers who used the product rapidly. His problem was to extend the use, by sampling and other devices, to the large number of prospective consumers who did not use the product at all.

Units in Which the Product Is Purchased. Consumers have definite habits regarding the quantity of a commodity which is purchased at any given time. It is important for the manufacturer to know what the typical quantities are in order that he may offer the product in units most acceptable to buyers. Of interest in this connection is the case of a department store which found that it could sell a much larger volume of shirts by offering them in units of three shirts, at a total price only slightly less than the price of three shirts bought separately. Another analysis showed that a certain type of hosiery was bought in units of one, three, and six pairs most commonly; whereas another type was bought by the vast majority of purchasers in units of twelve.

Some companies have found it possible to increase the unit of purchase by offering multiple units, such as the "Mazda House" package designed by the General Electric Company and the combination packages of individual cereal servings. Buying habits are constantly changing, so the promotion of larger or smaller units from time to time is important. For example, cereal manufacturers who recognized a trend toward large "family-size" packages were able to cash in on it by bringing out larger sizes while their competitors missed the opportunity.

Customs and Habits Affecting the Use of the Product. Just as it is necessary for the sociologist to study the customs which affect the general social behavior, so the marketing researcher must study the customs and traditions which affect the sale of a commodity. Social resistances to the use of certain products, such as chewing gum, may be discovered. Studies which have uncovered the resistance of certain specialized classes of consumers, such as occupational groups, those living in certain geographic areas, and age groups, have proved very productive in showing the way to expand sales by overcoming these resistances.

Many of the important customs affecting the consumption of products are regional in character. The New Orleans market prefers a heavy coffee; morals in certain areas preclude a market for alcoholic beverages; and the relatively cheap household labor in the South cuts down the extensive sale of household appliances. Thus the general living conditions of a region sharply influence markets.

Sociological studies reveal the strength of customs and habits in influencing buying. The importance of class distinctions should not be overlooked. It is claimed that less than 10 per cent of the occupants of any given social stratum will reflect tastes characteristic of a different class. An illustration of the way in which social customs affect marketing is the field of rugs and drapes. A sociological study revealed that upper income families prefer solid color drapes for living-room windows, that middle-class homes generally have drapes with curtains, and that lower income buyers select curtains with intricate designs.

Consumer Attitudes. This type of consumer survey is closely related to the study of the effect of customs on the sale of a product. But it may be regarded as a special field because attitudes toward products change rapidly, in contrast to basic customs built up over many years. Many prejudices, some open and some undisclosed, may exist regarding a product; it is the function of this kind of research to uncover them.

A cigarette manufacturer discovered that consumers in certain sections of the country felt that his product was a "cheap one" because they believed it was consumed by the mass market. A group of public utilities studied the attitude of people toward their services and rates and determined the importance and nature of most common complaints. As a result of the study, it was possible for the utility to engage in a publicity campaign which overcame many of these resistances and to reduce the number of complaints by changing the company's operating methods. A study of consumer attitudes toward competitive products will often reveal advantages enjoyed by some competitors which can be equalized or overcome by a change in marketing policy.

The broader phases of attitude research are covered by the field of opinion and public relations research. A number of firms and university groups specialize in this area and have developed a large body of literature pertaining to it.

One specific application of opinion research frequently used by business is obtaining, usually on a comparative basis, the general rating of a corporation in the public's mind. More specific attitudes, such as those toward the firm's reputation for quality of product, manufacturing skill, research ability, and policies, are likely to be much more revealing. Attitudes toward various institutions in the distributive trade and different types of outlets for merchandise are often very helpful in planning marketing strategy. Opinion as to various types of products is sometimes measured as a means of determining trends in acceptance by the public. Attitudes toward prices, advertising and promotional devices, salesmen, and service organizations are further examples of direct applications of opinion research to marketing policy.

The marketing researcher is also frequently involved in the conduct of opinion research studies in fields somewhat remotely connected with marketing management. The general scope of opinion research has been summarized by Wallace H. Wulfeck as follows:

1. Through periodic nation-wide surveys to determine and plot the changes in public attitudes toward specific corporations.

2. For occasional and trend studies to measure public confidence in business, labor unions, government.

3. For occasional investigations of public opinion toward a specific industry, a philosophy of government, i.e., the New Deal, a particular labor dispute or a special personality, i.e., John L. Lewis or Sewell L. Avery.

4. For investigating stockholders' attitudes toward the management and policies of the corporations in which they share ownership.

5. For finding out what the worker thinks about his job, his company, his foreman and his labor union.

6. For measuring job security attitudes among workers during the war and projected to the postwar period.

7. For determining public attitudes toward and confidence in advertising.

8. For having employees select from among several alternatives the retirement benefit plan they prefer without their knowledge that the survey is being made among the employees of their company.

9. For estimating the competitive position of a given manufacturer against others independently of the product brands made for sale.

10. For predetermining the attitudes of distributors toward the sale of a product which has never been sold, on the basis of the manufacturer's reputation.[1]

Shopping Habits of Consumers. Buyers are constantly shifting in their preferences for different types of outlets as sources for commodities. The manufacturer, wholesaler, and retailer must constantly keep abreast of these shifts. The marketing researcher makes studies to determine the changing importance of such types as super markets, voluntary chains, department stores, and variety stores.

A manufacturer who was not aware of a shift in consumers' buying habits from drugstores to variety stores as a source of certain cosmetics found himself facing restricted sales. On the other hand, one of the most spectacular successes in this field came as a result of recognizing this trend and thereby capitalizing upon it. Shopping habit studies are among the most common and profitable types of marketing research employed by retailers.

Studies of shopping habits of consumers may be divided into three general types. The first embraces those which analyze the flow of trade to certain communities. Examples of this form are the studies conducted by Professor P. D. Converse at the University of Illinois. Professor Converse empirically applied Reilly's Law of Retail Gravitation in number of markets, showing the extent of out-of-town shopping. Development of trading area maps based on shopping habits is an important aspect of these studies.[2]

A second type of shopping-habit study is that which analyzes the type of retail outlet where consumers trade. An increasing amount of research is devoted to determining the types of outlet at which consumers buy different commodities.

[1] Article in Albert B. Blankenship (ed.), *How to Conduct Consumer and Opinion Research* (New York: Harper & Bros., 1946), pp. 88–89.

[2] See P. D. Converse, *Consumer Buying Habits in Selected South Central Illinois Communities,* University of Illinois Business Studies, No. 6, 1948. See also Frank Strohkarck and Katherine Phelps, "The Mechanics of Constructing a Market Area Map," *Journal of Marketing,* April, 1948, pp. 493–96.

A third form of shopping-habit research studies general consumer habits, attitudes toward retail establishments, and services desired. Shopping days, shopping hours, and patronage motives are subjects covered in this form. One of the most valuable researches in this area studies the reasons for purchasing particular types of items at one store and other items at a different outlet, when both establishments are of the same general character. A department store, for example, researched the shopping habits of consumers in its trading area and discovered why it was missing a large volume in the children's apparel line.

Brand Loyalty. A special type of brand-preference study is the analysis of the extent of brand loyalty or disloyalty by consumers. These researches delve into the length of time consumers use a particular brand, the rate of consumer loss, causes of consumer disloyalty to brands, and the direction of brand changes. Sales figures reveal nothing and consumer purchase data only gross information about the undercurrent shifts which are continually going on in consumer use of a product.

Some manufacturers discover that their current sales volume is comprised to a startling degree of relatively new users. After this fact is established, it is the job of research to analyze the factors which contribute to this situation, so that proper corrective steps may be taken. Experience has shown that there are a number of different elements which can contribute to low product loyalty, and these elements must be identified and appraised before such situations can be overcome. On the other hand there are certain industries in which a high rate of brand fluctuation is a normal characteristic. In one such field, a manufacturer had been laboring under the delusion that the leading competitor prospered because he had a great number of loyal users. Marketing research showed that the competitor actually had a rate of user turnover as high as he did, and pointed to the real reason for his continuous sales success: his consistent demand creation had been funneling large numbers of new users to his brand year after year.

Research of Special Consumer Groups. Studies of particular consumer groups which have both a special bearing on the marketing of a product and sufficiently unusual characteristics to make them worth special consideration are rather common. One advantage of this type of study is that it is specific and its value is readily comprehended by sales management. By concentrating on a particular marketing segment, the problem is also generally simplified.

An example of a study of a special consumer group is the Negro market. Many researches in this important field, both by manufacturers and publications, are now being made. Important subjects of special consumer-group research include the farm market, the home-building market, the new-family market, and the juvenile market. A growing number of manufacturers, for example, are making special studies of the market for their products among children from five to nineteen years of age. Because adults operate business enterprises, manufacturers are likely to overlook the importance of children as direct influences in their markets, unless their product is used almost exclusively by children.

Surveys of Local Markets. Surveys of consumers in individual markets provide a source of marketing information which is particularly valuable in connection with correcting weak spots in the marketing and distribution picture and stimulating the sales organization. These studies, which are made continuously by many of the larger business firms, give them a definite competitive advantage. The local market study highlights special conditions. It is usually more comprehensive in the amount of information obtained than the national consumer survey. On the other hand, a number of manufacturers follow a policy of using streamlined local surveys, which obtain a limited amount of data most economically and are thus in a position to cover more key market situations more frequently than they otherwise could.

Examples of local market studies which go into great detail are those employed by the Frigidaire Division of the General Motors Corporation. This firm makes it a regular practice to conduct in each of its key markets extremely penetrating studies which provide management and the district sales organization with valuable ammunition in the form of marketing facts.

Basic Economic Analysis of the Consumer Market. A phase of consumer marketing research growing in importance is the study of broad economic situations affecting markets, such as shifts in income and earning power of various segments of the population. Today, just as management is showing increased interest in general economic and social research, it is paying more attention to the broader economic studies which come within the particular interest of marketing and distribution research.

Perhaps the most significant of these studies are those dealing with the distribution of income and shifts in this distribution. The U. S. Bureau of Labor Statistics and the Bureau of the Census are the basic governmental sources for data on income distribution. In recent years there has been a great amount of interest in this subject, and new data are continually being made available.

The subject of expendable income and analysis of expenditures is a matter of particular interest, particularly in terms of expenditures beyond those for basic cost-of-living necessities. The term "discretionary buying power" is employed to describe the excess of income over the amount needed to maintain the basic standard of living. This provides a measurement of the amount available for purchasing goods in which a considerable amount of option may be exercised by an individual or family.

Basic economic research in marketing goes beyond analysis of income distribution to include studies which broadly analyze the marketing significance of various economic levels. Studies of income groups by area, city-size, age, occupation, and other classifications provide information of help in forming marketing policy.

Quantitative Market Analysis

Quantitative market analysis determines the *amount* of a commodity which the market can be expected to absorb. A study which estimates the amount of breakfast food the entire domestic market, various geographic sections, or different groups of consumers should be expected to buy is an example of a quantitative market analysis.

The term "sales potential" refers to an estimate of the capacity of any given market to absorb a commodity in the light of the general limitations of its past behavior. The theoretical power which might be developed from a gallon of gasoline is greatly in excess of the maximum power which can be developed with present machinery. Just as the engineer must make his measurements of power in the light of the combustion efficiency of machinery now in use, the market researcher must measure the power of markets to absorb commodities in the light of customs and buying habits affecting the expression of that power.[3]

[3] Definitions of some terms used in quantitative market analysis:

(1) Sales or Market Potential—an estimate of the capacity of any market to buy a commodity. This estimate may be stated in absolute numbers of physical or dollar volume, or may be stated in terms of the percentage of the total consumption which any individual section of the market has the capacity to buy.

(2) Sales Quota or Sales Budget—an estimate of the amount of a commodity an individual firm expects to sell in a market within any given period of time. The sales quota may be based upon a sales potential, but it differs from the sales potential in that it sets a goal which should be reached within a specific period of time, taking variations in business conditions, competition, and other factors into account. The sales potential is set for an industry, the sales quota is set for an individual firm or unit within that firm's operation, such as a dealer or salesman.

(3) Market Factor—a statistical series, such as total population, number of persons living on farms, or number of persons filing income tax returns, which is used for setting a sales potential for any section of a market.

(4) Market Index or Sales Index—a market factor in which the data for individual parts of the market have been reduced to a percentage of the total for the entire United States.

The primary activity in quantitative market analysis is the development of sales potentials. Limiting factors, such as demand-creation efforts, competition, and business conditions, should be considered only in so far as they are reflected in definite long-run buying habits. These sales potentials become the foundations for setting quotas and for similar activities. They are a scientific measurement of the power of markets to buy a commodity, and should be used as a basis for market planning.

The results of quantitative market analysis may be applied in many different ways in business operation. In some cases one use may be emphasized, in others a relatively large number. While the following discussion is not all-inclusive, it indicates the most common applications of such studies to different phases of business management.

Total Sales Quotas. The result of quantitative market analysis can be used as a basis for setting the total sales quota for an individual firm. A sales quota is an estimate of the amount of a commodity which a company plans to sell. It may be the share of the total market which the firm expects to appropriate to itself, the amount of sales sought in one of its sales territories, or the sales goal for an individual salesman or dealer.

The establishment of the total sales quota for a company is the chief purpose of long-range trend analyses—which indicate the probable future consumption of a product. With sound knowledge of the future market, a business enterprise can establish a rational sales quota. This quota in turn becomes the basis for production schedules, financing, advertising and sales budgets, plant expansion, and other aspects of business planning.

Quantitative forecasts of the automobile market have long been used as bases for planning by the General Motors Corporation. The retooling of a plant and additional machinery for the production of new models, the planning of demand-creation activities, the hiring of personnel, and the financing of these operations are all predicated on the assumption of a market which will absorb the amount of product to be produced. Companies have gone so far as to use quantitative trend analyses for such an unusual purpose as a basis for bank borrowings.

While estimating the extent of the market for a given product is one of the most difficult tasks of marketing research, it is generally possible to do so within reasonable limits of accuracy. The most difficult situation arises when an entirely new product is involved. The total volume of the market for soap can be established very accurately, but when an entirely new type of soap is introduced it is impossible to forecast with similar accuracy the rate at which consumers' buying habits will change. Even so, marketing research can take much of the guesswork out of such a situation with pretests, consumer surveys, and limited marketing experiments.

Territorial Sales Quotas. A second major use of quantitative market analysis is as the basis for setting territorial sales quotas. These quotas are estimates of what a given sales district should buy and are predicated on measurement of the potential capacity of each territory to absorb the product. The first efforts at quantitative analysis were for this purpose, and this use is probably the most common one to-day.

Quotas for Individuals. A third use is in setting sales quotas for individual salesmen or dealers. In setting this type of quota, the past performance of individuals and dealers and the possibilities of scientific personnel management are very important, but the total capacity of the market to absorb the product should still be a fundamental consideration. There have been many examples of salesmen who were believed to be particularly productive, and then were later found to be relatively weak in the light of the true potential capacity of the market in which they were operating. The opposite condition is equally common.

Quotas for individual salesmen may be applied as bases for remuneration, for special incentives, for promotion or demotion, and for other forms of sales control. Quotas for dealers are used as bases for stimulating dealer activities and selecting channels of distribution.

Boundaries of Sales Territories. A fourth use is in establishing boundaries for sales territories and routing salesmen. In the past, sales territories have been based largely upon the number of dealers to be covered and the transportation facilities available. Quantitative analysis has shown the importance of concentrating sales efforts in the most productive sections of markets and has led to policies of selective distribution. Thus, the sales territories are planned to lead to a concentration of sales pressure on the larger and more profitable markets.

Concentration of Sales Efforts. A fifth use of quantitative market analysis is as a basis for selecting territories in which to concentrate sales efforts, or for dropping territories from the market which a firm cultivates. One of the general results of the increased acceptance of quantitative analysis has been a tendency on the part of manufacturers, especially the smaller ones, to concentrate sales activities in relatively limited markets. The Brockway Truck Company increased sales by 25 per cent by discarding 37 states from its market. The practice of concentrating selling efforts in the more productive markets

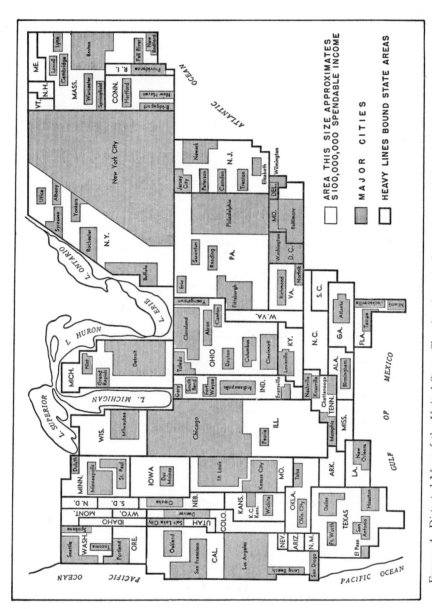

FIGURE 4. Distorted Map of the United States Showing Areas in Proportion to an Index of Spendable Income

in order to balance expenditures against potential is now generally accepted marketing policy.

One of the most profitable uses of market potentials in connection with the concentration of sales efforts is the development of "key markets." Sales potentials for most products are so concentrated in metropolitan areas of larger cities that successful marketing policy generally involves careful scrutiny of a rather limited number of closely knit areas known as key markets. Through quantitative analysis the true significance of each of these markets to sales success is determined, and they become definite target areas for concentration.

Distribution of Sales Force. A sixth use of quantitative market analysis is as a basis for distributing the manpower of the sales force. The Kellogg Company, for example, studied its distribution of salesmen, with the result that additions were made in some territories, while in others the numbers were reduced. It has been reported that the executives of the firm were convinced that such adjustments, in the light of potential markets, considerably increased the efficiency of its selling operations.

TABLE 2

MANPOWER REQUIREMENTS BY TERRITORIES

Territory	Present Manpower	Required Manpower
No. 1	63	33
No. 2	55	13
No. 14	10	3
No. 18	4	2
No. 36	2	5
No. 39	9	33

An example of the use of quantitative analysis in distributing the sales force geographically is that of a large manufacturer of a specialty product. After the sales potentials for each territory had been determined, an analysis of sales records disclosed the sales volume required to support an adequate income for a typical salesman. The sales potentials, in dollars, for each territory were then divided by this volume figure to determine the number of active salesmen which each territory could support. Table 2 shows a comparison of the number of salesmen in some of the territories at the time the analysis was made against the number of salesmen which the sales potentials for the territory warranted. The firm happened to have approximately the correct total number of salesmen, but this study showed that the manpower of the organization was in proper balance in only one out of ten territories. In several areas there were more than twice as many men operating as the territory was able to support. In others, the sales force was clearly undermanned. For the first time the firm was in a position to allocate its sales force on a sound basis.

Distribution of Advertising. A seventh use of quantitative market analysis is as a basis for the distribution of advertising appropriations and the selection of advertising media. Advertisers are keenly aware of the need for some objective measurement of market possibilities so that advertising pressure may be distributed properly.

Quantitative market analysis is particularly useful in the control of an advertising appropriation when a relatively large amount of local advertising is employed. One manufacturer, for example, set up a total budget for advertising in local media, and then distributed this budget among his sales territories on the basis of the potential sales. The budget for each territory was set up in the first column of a control sheet. Each month the expenditures for local advertising in each territory were charged against that territory, and the total for the month was inserted in the second column of the control sheet. In a third column, the difference between the two figures was inserted in black pencil for each territory which had spent less than the budget. This was in the nature of an "open to buy" figure. For those territories in which the expenditures exceeded the budget, the differences were inserted in red pencil. These represented overexpenditures which had to be made up in succeeding periods. By accumulating these data from month to month and obtaining cumulative "open to buy" and "overspent" figures, a careful control on advertising expenditures was maintained.

Appraisal of Efficiency. The eighth major use of quantitative market analysis is as a basis for checking the efficiency of sales and advertising efforts. Effective sales and advertising control is predicated on a sound measuring stick for judging performance. Quantitative market analysis provides such a basis of measurement.

One device for making this checking objective is the use of a method which states sales efficiency in terms of "the penetration ratio." This ratio is found by dividing a firm's sales in a given area by the market potential set for that area. The resulting percentage of attainment is then taken as an index of the efficiency of sales and advertising effort. If a washing-machine manufacturer, for example, sets the potential volume for the Albany territory at 1,000 machines per year, and sells 100 machines during the year, his penetration ratio for that market is 10 per cent. If the potential market for Chicago is set at 20,000 machines and his sales in that market are 1,000 units, his penetration ratio is 5 per cent. Thus, while he sells ten times as many machines in Chicago as in Albany, his efficiency in the latter market is twice as great.

Distribution Research

While the term *distribution research* is often used synonymously with that of marketing research, current practice is to confine it more and more to a specialized type of marketing research. In researching the specialized field of distribution, two broad areas are further separated. The first is research in channels of distribution; the second, research in distribution costs.

Channels of Distribution. The most fundamental research in the channels of wholesale and retail distribution is conducted by the government in its Census of Business. Providing basic data on number and kind of wholesalers and retailers, and their sales and operating practices, this source lays the statistical foundation for a great deal of special analysis.

A number of studies of basic distribution structure are available from time to time from other sources. Bureaus of Business Research connected with large universities report on a state or regional basis. Private firms also gather basic data which are available on a fee basis.

Research studies on channels of distribution are conducted by both manufacturers and distributors themselves, such as wholesalers and retailers. The efficiency of the distributive organization employed by manufacturers is a major factor in marketing success or failure. Manufacturers selling to industrial or institutional markets may have relatively simple distributing structure; yet the effectiveness of the various sales agents, brokers, or institutional wholesalers has a great deal of influence on the sales volume achieved and the cost burden encountered. Manufacturers of consumer goods are faced with wide options as to channels of distribution to be employed. Policy decisions in this respect are vital. Furthermore, there are many problems in connection with how one uses the various channels, relations with individual distributing organizations and outlets and sales policies that are subject to profitable research.

The first problem of the manufacturer is the selection of channels to be employed. After this decision has been made, the manufacturer must know upon which problems to concentrate sales effort. An important consideration is that of the extent of distribution achieved in the market place—that is, the percentage of outlets which have his goods in stock. A great many sales are lost if customers do not find a product available in the places where they normally purchase. Further-more, it has been found that "distribution pressure," the amount of merchandise in the hands of dealers, has a great deal to do with the volume moved. Specialized problems, such as exclusive franchises, operating methods of dealers, dealer attitudes, private labels, and dealer costs and profits are other phases in which research can be profitably applied.

One of the major fields of distribution analysis for wholesalers and retailers is that of defining their trading area to maximize the op-portunity for sales volume at the most profitable level. The analysis of operating and control data is also of vital importance, because of the complexity of lines handled. A most productive specialized form of distribution research by wholesalers and retailers is that of mer-chandise line analysis. Studies of the profit contribution of various goods handled have led to elimination of many items and the seeking out of others, with resulting improvement in the total efficiency of the establishment.

Distribution research is also applied extensively by wholesalers and retailers in the selection of merchandising locations. Studies of physical layout and the handling of merchandise offer fruitful fields for increasing sales on profitable items and reducing operating costs. Research on selling methods, credit policies, store hours, and customer attitudes are further examples of specialized studies employed by wholesalers and retailers in connection with distribution research.

Distribution Costs. Distribution cost analysis is the second broad phase of distribution research. The sheer magnitude of distribution costs, which place an average burden of approximately 60 per cent on the final cost of commodities, is impressive enough evidence of the importance of distribution cost analysis. The tremendous toll taken by distribution costs, the obvious inefficiencies frequently encountered, and the general lack of knowledge regarding the control of distributive activities all point to opportunities for progressive management to make direct reductions in distribution costs.

The problem of reducing the cost of distribution will probably as-sume increasing importance to management during the foreseeable future. In the long run the tendency will probably be for the cost of distribution, in contrast to the cost of production, to become a higher and higher percentage of the total cost of goods and services to the consumer. This expectancy is perhaps the most basic challenge to the profession of marketing research.

The value to the individual enterprise of a bold attack on the cost of distribution is shown by the achievements of companies who have inaugurated a program of distribution cost analysis and put the findings to work in their day-to-day operations. S. C. Johnson & Sons reports that, as a result of its program, total sales and advertising costs in 1947 were 68 per cent of their average for the period 1939–41. Total field sales expense, including warehousing, was reduced to 55 per cent and sales force expense to 42 per cent of the 1939–41 average.

The experience of The Roundup Grocery Company and its chain of retail outlets illustrates the value of such a program in the wholesaling and retailing field. As a result of research, Roundup established a program known as its "X Plan." Significant in this case is the fact that the goal of the program—the reduction of distribution costs so that the company would be in a better competitive position—was achieved with the concurrent goal of increasing total sales volume.

Sales Research

Sales research, often referred to as internal analysis, is one of the most fertile fields of marketing and distribution research. Two general areas are included. The first is *sales record analysis*. It uses as the source of information the records of sales transactions and accounting data on sales accumulated in the ordinary conduct of the business. Sales records are a veritable gold mine for the researcher with a keen analytical mind and imagination. By summarizing, rearranging, comparing, and studying sales data already available in the records of the business, he brings out new facts buried in the detail of day to day record keeping. He establishes new relationships to marketing efficiency. He makes revealing comparisons of performance between units such as sales territories, product lines, dealers, and individual salesmen.

The second area of sales analysis is *sales organization and operation research*. As a result of the scope of modern selling activities, the size of sales departments, and the complexity of markets, there are many aspects of the sales operation requiring application of marketing research techniques. Many of the basic marketing weaknesses of the individual company lie in its sales personnel, its organization, and operation. The importance of developing the greatest possible efficiency in this area is emphasized by the ultimate dependency of all business on sales volume and the relatively large share of marketing expense allocated to the sales function.

The application of marketing and distribution research techniques to the selling operation may range from a basic survey to specialized studies of specific sales problems. (The survey may lead to wholesale revamping of personnel, policies, and procedures.) The specialized studies type is more common, for unless the situation analysis reveals a most serious condition, it is generally much better to improve the effectiveness of the selling organization by a series of progressive developments rather than by sudden reversal of policy or operations.

A qualified, independent marketing research organization is particularly helpful in this type of work, because its objective, impartial point of view provides a proper perspective for cleaning out the dead timber, whether it be personnel or procedures. An outside organization usually makes a broad survey of the sales organization and, on the basis of its experience in similar situations, puts its finger on the critical weaknesses. The value of changes made is proved by performance records for sales control, established as part of the study and used as a check on results.

From an operating point of view, specific decisions in all these activities must be made from day to day by the sales executives. The function of marketing research is to solve the basic problems, establish general policies, and provide proper yardsticks and procedures which guide sales management in specific applications.

A first phase of sales operation research is the development of an efficient sales organization. Important parts of this step are the delineation of authority, definition of jobs, elimination of superfluous functions, and development of key personnel. Aside from sales organization per se, the chief areas in which marketing and distribution research is applied are those connected with the selection of manpower, training of salesmen, definition of sales territories, routing of salesmen, and methods of sales compensation.

Some excellent analyses of nonselling activities have been made. These cover various phases of the work of salesmen which are not shown directly in the sales records, such as sales promotions and display activities of dealers. On the basis of analyses of nonselling activities, some very effective "incentive plans," which provide special rewards to salesmen for this type of work, have been developed by various companies.

Advertising and Promotion Research

Advertising Appropriations. The first broad application of marketing research to the problems of advertising and promotion is in connection with the determination of the total appropriation or budget. The amounts of money to be spent are traditionally fixed by a ratio to anticipated sales. This ratio may be expressed in terms of a percentage of sales dollars or amounts related to physical units such as an allowance per case. The determination of ratios is customarily based upon general practice in the industry or merchandising class to which the company belongs. Frequently the total budget is modified on the basis of the judgment of management, taking into account factors such as general business conditions and the situation of the firm.

Marketing research is used to analyze various types of data which have a bearing on the problem to provide management with better factual information on which to base its policies. A more important research contribution is found when research designs market experiments to determine the optimum rates of expenditure related to building increased sales volume and maximizing profits. For example, certain geographic areas, representing different types of market conditions and levels of sales development, are selected. In these different areas amounts of advertising and promotion moneys which deliberately depart from the general ratios are employed. Sales produced are then related to costs. On this basis it is possible to provide more accurate answers to ever-present questions regarding the profitability and wisdom of "investment spending" in order to increase sales volume. The calculation of "payout," relating the profit obtained to increments of sales volume at various sales levels, is involved. If it is found that an increased amount of advertising or sales promotion expenditure can produce additional sales volume at a profit within one or two years, the extra rate of expenditure is regarded as having paid out.

The basic elements in advertising strategy are the development of (1) the most effective message for print or broadcasting (*copy*), (2) the most efficient vehicles to carry the message (*media*), and (3) the best merchandising devices to stimulate and supplement the general advertising (*sales promotion*). Advertising research makes its greatest contribution when it provides scientific facts which are employed effectively in connection with each of these three essentials of sound advertising. This has led to further specialized fields of advertising research, known as copy testing, media analysis, and merchandising research.

If marketing research is to be used as the basis for the general planning and development of an advertising campaign, it should obtain vital facts about the buyers, their habits, desires, and other characteristics. The creative staff can then use their special abilities to develop the most effective advertising campaign. Facts about the location, reading and listening habits, and other matters which indicate the manner in which the message should be directed, must be made available to the space or time buyer before he can make his fundamental decisions. Full marketing data must also be available to the merchandising department. These facts are necessary for the development of the most effective displays, premiums, or other promotions.

Copy Testing. The greatest amount of specialized research in connection with the creative aspects of advertising is in copy testing.

Copy testing embraces research which is designed to measure directly the relative effectiveness of specific copy themes, individual advertisements, and particular elements within advertisements.

It has been demonstrated that it is possible through research to develop certain bench marks which greatly increase the sales effectiveness of the message put in the white space of a publication or delivered over the air by radio or by television. An advertiser who spends at the rate of $1,000,000 per year, and who through copy research can increase the effectiveness of his message by 10 per cent, has in effect obtained $100,000 worth of extra advertising free. On the other hand, an advertiser who also spends at the rate of $1,000,000 a year, but whose copy is only 75 per cent effective, is wasting $250,000. Studies show that in many fields the best copy can readily be 100 per cent more effective than poorer copy.

Too often too much has been claimed for copy testing. There is no doubt that researchers have frequently worked with shaky data and imputed far too much value to their findings. Furthermore, all too often there have been tendencies to attempt to break down the testing of individual segments of the advertisement much too finely. At present there is a growing tendency on the part of the more experienced analysts to test the total effectiveness of the advertisement rather than to attempt to break it down into the various elements of which it is composed.

One of the needs in copy testing is for a closer association between the researcher and the creative man. Rather than run tests on more or less finished advertisements, the researcher should establish a friendly working basis with those who are responsible for preparing copy and work closely with them during its development. One advantage of this close cooperation is that the researcher knows from experience the kind of copy that can be tested effectively and can aid in the creative development of copy to be tested. Another advantage is that familiarity with the material will enable him to do a much more competent job of designing the test. More important, he will be in a far better position to interpret results so that they are applied effectively in the development of the final advertising copy.

Perhaps the greatest single consideration in the development of successful copy testing is to employ the particular methods which will be most productive in a given situation. Bad copy testing has most often resulted from the tendency of individual researchers and organizations to employ some one method of copy testing more or less automatically, often to the point of promoting the method rather than solving the copy problem. Actually, in most situations, a combination of methods is needed to produce effective results.

Media Research. Until recent years, the buying of advertising media was based largely on a modicum of circulation data, the accumulated experience of individuals, general impressions of the media themselves, and the combined judgments of groups of individuals. In view of the high stakes involved—the expenditures for an individual brand often run into millions of dollars—it has become apparent that a more scientific basis of media selection is needed. Media research measures the relative efficiency of various media in delivering advertising messages to prospective buyers. It substitutes facts for opinion in making decisions.

One aspect is that of cost efficiency. There is wide variance between different magazines, newspapers, television programs, and other media in the cost per thousand delivered messages. Another aspect is the effectiveness with which each medium selects its audience in order to maximize the proportion of genuine prospects for a given product or message. Other considerations include factors such as the mood surrounding the delivery of the advertising message, the size of the delivered audience (advertising weight), response obtained, timeliness, and flexibility.

Sales Promotion Research. Research is applied to sales promotion in a number of ways. It can be used to test or measure the efficiency of various forms, as follows:

1. Dealer displays—shelf, window, combinations of products, merchandising.
2. Deals—special prices, deals for consumers and for dealers.
3. Combination offers—products of same manufacturer or related product combinations.
4. Couponing—through media offers or house to house.
5. Premium offers—consumer and dealer premiums.
6. Sampling—type of sample offer, amount offered, method of distribution.
7. Cooperative advertising—local media.
8. Package devices—cut-outs, etc., to stimulate special sales.
9. Detailing—special demonstration calls to get cooperation of professional men, such as dentists and doctors.
10. Retail sales cooperation—clerk compensation for product push or "spiffs."

A consumer-jury survey, employing essentially the same methods as those used in copy testing, provides a useful pretest base for a promotional idea. It has been found, for example, that consumer choice of a proposed premium when offered against a control premium of known effectiveness can readily forecast success or failure. Surveys of dealers to obtain attitudes toward and appraisal of proposed display devices also have proved helpful. However, a great deal of money is usually spent on a promotion, so more direct evidence of effectiveness is needed. This is supplied either by tests in groups of stores, in selected markets, or by controlled experiments.

Product Research

Three aspects of the product itself have a vital effect on marketing and distribution success: product design, the package, and price. Marketing research is employed extensively by industry for each aspect and specialized research techniques have been developed for each.

Product Design. Product design research determines the preferences of consumers in respect to the physical characteristics of products. Flavor, performance, shape, color, and other features determine the market acceptability of products. This particular type of marketing research has become important because management has learned that having products carefully fitted to the requirements of the buyer and user is a great stimulus to sales.

It is a marketing truism that the product must be sound to enjoy full sales success. While the homely philosophy attributed to Emerson—if a man can make a better mousetrap than his neighbor, you will find a broad, hard-beaten road to his house, though it be in the woods—has been repeatedly attacked, there is a growing appreciation on the part of businessmen that sales success begins with a product which is sound and acceptable to the market. No manufacturer should penalize his activities by attempting to sell a product which will meet unnecessary market resistance.

General Types of Product Design Research. Two phases of the broad field of product design research should be differentiated: (1) technical research, and (2) marketing research. Technical research is the type which is carried on in the research laboratory of a manufacturer, the primary aim being to develop the most efficient product at the lowest possible cost. Marketing research on the product, on the other hand, is basically a study of consumer preferences and habits relating to a given product. Marketing research determines the extent to which it should be changed to meet the existing demands of the consuming market or discovers new products the market desires.

A good example of the distinction between technical research and marketing research on products may be found in the General Motors Corporation. In its large research laboratories in Detroit, the testing and proving grounds, and the smaller laboratories of operating units,

SEAT COMFORT is important

Seat comfort is one of the most important elements in travel enjoyment. Please check the box that best describes your opinion in each case. (These questions do not apply to the movable chairs in the larger accommodations.)

(16)

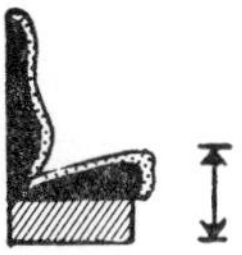

Would you be more comfortable if the seat were higher or lower than it is now?

HIGHER ☐ 1   LOWER ☐ 2

ABOUT RIGHT AS IT IS ☐ 3

Compared to the present seat, would you rather have the seat of the future:

(17)

SOFTER ☐   FIRMER ☐   JUST AS IT IS ☐
1   2   3

Would you change the depth of the seat?

(18)

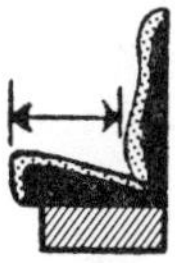

LONGER FROM FRONT TO BACK ☐ 1

SHORTER FROM FRONT TO BACK ☐ 2

ABOUT RIGHT AS IT IS ☐ 3

Would the seat be more comfortable if it had a higher or lower back?

(19)

HIGHER BACK MORE COMFORTABLE ☐ 1

LOWER BACK MORE COMFORTABLE ☐ 2

ABOUT RIGHT AS IT IS ☐ 3

Would you change the angle of the back of the seat?

(20)

STRAIGHTER ☐ 1

MORE RECLINED ☐ 2

ABOUT RIGHT AS IT IS ☐ 3

How important is it to you if you cannot ride facing forward in the daytime?

(21)

DOESN'T BOTHER ME ☐ 1

I'M UNCOMFORTABLE ☐ 2

FIGURE 5. Page from a Product Design Questionnaire. This study dealt with the design of railroad cars. Other subjects in this study included exterior design, windows, lighting, facilities for care of clothes and luggage, sleeping accommodations, air conditioning, and service features. Note the use of illustrations to increase accuracy of data. Small numbers printed on the form are pre-codes for machine tabulation. (F. H. Baird. New York Central System.)

engineers are constantly studying the automobile and other products from the point of view of technical efficiency and cost of manufacture. The prime aim of the technical engineer is to improve the design of an automobile in order to yield more efficient transportation, and to develop an automobile with a body of sound artistic design and a means of transportation which will reduce discomfort to a minimum. Marketing research is carried on in the Customer Research Division. Here the whims and fancies of the consumer, the importance of comfort as opposed to economy, and similar problems are analyzed. As a result of the work of the Customer Research Division, the designers and engineers in the technical research division develop cars which satisfy the measured desires of the public. Glove compartments, the placing of the luggage compartment and the spare tires, and the exterior design of today's automobile are a result.

Sometimes the results of marketing product analysis negate the findings of technical product research. In the laboratories of a mouthwash manufacturer, a new antiseptic ingredient was discovered which was far superior to any on the market. The formula was changed to include it. However, a marketing research showed that this new ingredient had an unpleasant odor which would retard its acceptance, and that it would be folly to attempt to sell the product unless this odor could be hidden. Likewise, in the case of a household appliance it was found that the mechanism would be most efficient if its cabinet had legs which would allow a clearance of at least six inches between the cabinet and the floor. However, market research showed that women preferred a design which would be flush with the floor in order that dirt would not collect easily underneath the cabinet. It was therefore necessary to make an adjustment in design.

Usually the result of the marketing product analysis is merely to introduce modifications of the product which affect its technical efficiency only slightly, if at all. Market analysis will frequently dictate the taste and color of a product, elements which are generally immaterial from the technical point of view. Nevertheless, it is highly important that elements such as taste or color be in exact tune with the desires of users.

Fields Subject to Product Research. That there is no product which is not susceptible to marketing research for its design may be illustrated by the variety of the following examples. The Williamson-Dickie Manufacturing Company has made a study to design an ideal set of work clothes. The Pepperell Manufacturing Company has made studies of sheets and pillowcases, dealing with subjects such as color. In a study for du Pont's Acetate Fabrics Division, Alexis Sommaripa found that the consumer was interested in a cool fabric, but that the consumer's conception of coolness and the manufacturers' did not agree.

The Dobbs Hat Company makes up hundreds of experimental models of women's hats in advance of the season. The company's first step is to show these models to a number of typical women and obtain general preferences in a "consumer jury" type of research. At the beginning of a particular season, the company reduced the number of models to eighteen and placed them on sale in all parts of the country, keeping careful sales records during the early part of the selling season. On the basis of this research simplified stocks were employed, with the result that Dobbs showed excellent sales increases in spite of a generally declining market.

In a classic product study, a manufacturer planned to enter the electric range market. A technical design engineer collaborated with a marketing researcher in planning a product study before the new line was designed. Phases of the product on which consumer preferences were taken included design of base, location of heating units and switches, position of oven and broiler, design of burners, design of oven, and minor features such as work light, time clock, and storage facilities. The result was that the manufacturer entered this new market with a product so clearly in tune with the needs of users that the venture was an instantaneous success.

Firms offering services to the public can also apply marketing research to their "product" successfully. A notable example is the New York Central Railroad's extensive studies in the design of railroad coaches and sleeping cars and in various service features. These studies also gave the management an extremely valuable insight into the attitudes and reactions of the traveling public. Insurance companies and financial institutions also apply the techniques of product research to the specific items of service which they offer the public. For example, insurance policies have definite characteristics to which the public may react favorably or unfavorably, and the methods of product testing provide a means for scientifically obtaining consumer preferences.

An outstanding example of the importance of marketing research on the product is found in the case of the development of the tenderized ham. One of the large meat packing concerns was the first to develop this process in its laboratories, well ahead of competition. The managing executives of the company decided against marketing the new product because their personal opinion, after trying it with their own families and friends, was that it had less flavor and a less appetizing appearance than the traditional smoked hams they were currently selling. Later a smaller food company discovered the process and, instead of taking the opinion of their "ham experts," decided to let the consumer test the product. The tenderized ham proved to be a great success, and the latter company has continued to be the leader in this line as a result of being the first to introduce it to the market.

An unfortunate result of overlooking the requirements of the market is indicated in the report that when the Lambert Pharmacal Company decided to expand its operations and add a tooth paste, it assumed that the large number of Listerine users would welcome a dentifrice which carried a similar flavor. Without any measurement of market preferences, the new product was placed on the market and a considerable sum invested in advertising and selling effort. It was later discovered that taste is one of the chief factors by which the user judges tooth paste, and that consumers did not like the Listerine flavor. The company accordingly changed the flavor of the dentifrice, and it was immediately accepted. A small investment in product analysis would have saved the firm a large loss operation. Examples of cases in which firms have made the mistake of failing to take consumer preferences into account in designing products, whether highly technical or simple consumer goods, can be found frequently.

Package Research. Study of the package is a special phase of product analysis. As a result of the rise of mass merchandising methods, such as the self-service supermarket, package design has become one of the outstanding considerations in marketing. Utility devices, such as a pouring mechanism, have frequently been added to meet the consumers' needs. Reuse packages, such as a coffee package which may be used as a fruit jar, have also been developed as a result of marketing research. The primary use of package analysis, however, is the development of designs which make for better consumer identification, impression, and attitude toward the product.

An example of package research is the series of marketing studies made by the du Pont Cellophane Company. These studies were designed chiefly to demonstrate the influence on sales volume of packaging various types of products in cellophane. Products studied include among others pork sausages, toilet tissues, breads, and condiments. The Beech-Nut Packing Company has done considerable marketing research in package design, segregating elements of general appropriateness to the product, color, and design. In addition to consumer preference tests, package research employs sales tests, observational studies, shelf tests, and use tests.

Price Research. The importance of marketing research as a basis for determining pricing policies can scarcely be overestimated. It is almost universally recognized that, with given production facilities, the most important factor in determining prices in a competitive economy is the market demand for a product. But in actual practice most firms determine pricing policy primarily on the basis of the supply side of the equation. The common practice is to begin with direct manufacturing cost data and add indirect production cost, marketing cost, and a desired profit to arrive at the price to be placed upon a commodity. Only when demand suddenly shrinks to a point where the company consistently loses money or obtains only a very small sales volume, as during a period of depression, do most business executives give major attention to the determination of price from the point of view of what consumers are willing to pay.

This policy is unsound. While it is, of course, obvious that production cost must be taken into account in the final decision of price policies, the first facts which must be determined are the quantities buyers will take at different price levels. When these facts have been determined by a marketing research, they may be brought into relation with production cost at different volumes of output, and the price which will yield the maximum net profit determined.

Competitive Position and Market Trends

The purpose of competitive position and market trend research is to alert the marketing organization to where it currently stands and where it is going. In the past business firms relied largely on their own sales and accounting data to determine the marketing health of the enterprise. In today's fiercely competitive economy any organization which does so is regarded as operating with a blindfold and giving its competitors a tremendous advantage. The modern business firm devotes a great deal of time and money to research which tells it exactly where it and each of its principal competitors stands in the market place.

But it is not enough to know present market position and past history. Business lives continually in the future. Its actions today and plans for the future are dependent on judgments based on the best possible forecasts of anticipated market conditions. Forward planning is a byword in business today. Marketing research has developed methods to take the bulk of guesswork out of forward planning.

Competitive Position Analysis. Competitive position analysis reveals the relative share of total consumer sales obtained by each brand in a given product class or their status in the minds of consumers. The most common forms of such analyses are:

1. Consumer purchases by brands.
2. Number of users by brands.
3. Brand preferences.
4. Brand recognition.

While different marketing researchers will frequently argue in favor of one or the other of these four forms, each of them is important and makes a useful contribution to a full understanding of competitive position. Knowledge of competitive sales (consumer purchases) is, of course, fundamental. However, this does not tell the full story. It is important to know the relative *number of users* of each competitive brand because temporary market positions of high sales may not be based on a sufficiently broad base of customers. *Brand preferences* may also, at any given time, be out of line with current sales figures, and in many fields a separate check on brand preferences may foretell future developments. A fourth measurement, *brand recognition*—that is, the percentage of consumers who can identify a brand name—may shed further light on competitive market standing. Many manufacturers of old, established products are surprised when they discover the relatively small number of consumers who are aware of even the existence of their brand. Measuring the rate of growth of the recognition of a new brand (brand-name penetration) is a vital measurement of the marketing progress of a new product. It is not an infrequent occurrence to find that high identification is coupled with low consumer purchases or vice versa. When all four factors—consumer purchases, usage, preferences, and recognition—are known, they may be related into a pattern which points more clearly to effective marketing strategy than does any one of them alone.

Measurement of Consumer Purchases. It has been demonstrated clearly that a manufacturer's or wholesaler's sales records are inevitably misleading because of the fluctuation of stocks in the hands of dealers. Furthermore, because of cross-distribution of merchandise by various wholesale and retail dealers, the firm's own records are not subject to brand sales analysis by sufficiently refined territorial or city-size units to be fully revealing. The true consumer position of competitive brands and competitive movements from period to period must be known to plan marketing strategy effectively.

Brand position analysis starts at the consumer level. By measuring consumption by families or sales by retailers, accurate brand standing in the market is obtained. The data are most revealing when broken down by package size, price, dollar volume, and unit volume. By measuring dealer purchases simultaneously, the amount of merchandise in stock and turnover rates may be computed. These latter measurements are important in revealing overstocked and understocked conditions.

By breaking consumer purchase data down further by significant market segments, such as geographic areas, city size, and economic class, market planning becomes much more scientific and precise.

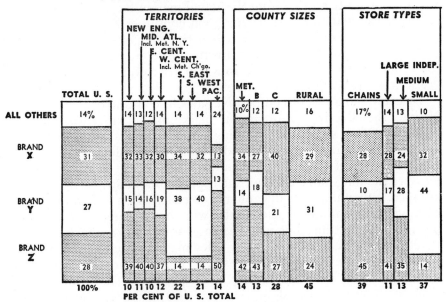

FIGURE 6. Competitive Position Analysis. This chart illustrates the value of competitive position data, particularly when broken down by significant market segments. The figures within the bar show the share of market obtained by each of the leading brands. The figures along the bottom of the chart show the relative importance of each market segment (for example, the New England territory accounts for 10% of total U. S. purchases of this commodity). Note that Brand Z enjoyed 28% of total consumer purchases during this bimonthly period so this manufacturer knows where he stands in the market (regardless of what his own sales figures may show) and how he compares with major competitors. In addition, the analysis by territories reveals that he is extremely weak in the Southeast and Southwest regions where he enjoys only 14% of consumer purchases. The county size analysis shows that his major strength is in the metropolitan and B counties, while he is relatively weak in the more important C and rural areas. The store type analysis reveals weakness in small independent outlets which account for 37% of total purchases of this commodity class. (Courtesy A. C. Nielsen Company.)

Sales policies, the distribution of selling effort, and advertising strategies can be planned to produce much more effective results.

The business firm which has an accurate measurement of competitive sales at the consumer level has a genuine advantage over its competitors. Those who rely on their own sales records are using information quite remote from the actual market facts, so it is literally true that the manufacturer having good consumer brand data knows more about his competitor's sales than the competitor who does not possess this information himself. Furthermore, it is possible to watch the result of every competitive move in marketing strategy—special deals, promotions, price changes, etc.

By careful analysis of competitive sales to consumers over a period of time, the effectiveness of specific marketing activities, such as special advertising campaigns, loading dealers with extra stocks, the introduction of new products, and consumer sampling, is measured. One of the chief values of this information is that it is possible to measure the long-range effect of such special marketing activities. For instance, a manufacturer may offer a special deal on his product, perhaps with a premium. Factory sales will show a large increase for a short period of time, but will give no indication of the long-range effect of the special deal. Factory sales may decline below a normal level shortly after the promotion, so the manufacturer may conclude that the strategy was not effective. Measurement of consumer brand position, however, may show that the deal brought sales to a new plateau; hence it was successful.

Periodic Consumer Surveys. Many firms employ consumer surveys, made at regular intervals, to determine competitive usage of a product. It should be noted that the percentage of individuals or families using a particular brand of a product does not exactly parallel the amounts purchased. However, in some fields, competitive position in terms of users is satisfactory information and is generally desirable as a supplement to purchase data. A great deal has been learned about interviewing techniques to obtain brand usage. These techniques eliminate the hazards encountered in the early days of marketing research which made consumer usage surveys inaccurate. By obtaining data on rates of consumption, it is frequently possible to project usage data into a satisfactory approximation of competitive brand purchases.

The periodic consumer survey is also the form employed for studies of consumer preferences and of brand recognition. These surveys are generally made by the individual competitive firm. For some products syndicated services provide such data. The Psychological Brand Barometer, conducted by the Psychological Corporation, has obtained data on brand preferences i ı a number of fields for several years. The consumer surveys of the *Milwaukee Journal* have provided brand preference data on that market for over twenty-five years. By analysis of changes from year to year, consumer preference and recognition studies show manufacturers how their products are rising or falling in consumer acceptance.

Market Trends. The subject of market trends embraces the study of all changes in the market for a product over a period of time. The object of such analyses is to interpret changing conditions and to forecast future market conditions.

Scientific market forecasting is possible because changes in consumer demand occur as a part of a total social process, and significant social changes move in definite patterns at a relatively slow pace. The reader can probably recall the publicity given to the statement that the brewers were caught entirely unaware by Prohibition, and the complaint that a major industry was suddenly forced out of business by legislative action in 1919. As a mater of fact, the state of Maine went dry in 1850, and from that time the Prohibition movement slowly spread. By the time that the Eighteenth Amendment was ratified, 75 per cent of the population and 90 per cent of the territory of the United States were legally dry by local option.

People in the mass move slowly. From the point of view of technical forecasting, changes which appear on the surface to be rapid and violent usually occur slowly and in a regular pattern. Magazines once printed pictures of a large pile of hairpins which a bankrupt businessman had dumped into a vacant lot when he was confronted with the fact that women's hair styles had changed so there was no longer a demand for hairpins. To the general public, the American woman made a sudden decision to bob her hair. Many businessmen, like the hairpin manufacturer who depended upon the fashion of long hair, held to a similar belief. Had the hairpin manufacturer kept in touch with his market, however, he would have discovered that Irene Castle had bobbed her hair nearly twenty years before. Miss Castle's bobbed hair made front-page news while she was playing in musical comedy in New York at the time. While the play was still running, a few brave New Yorkers followed her style. Very slowly, at first, the fashion spread, and by 1925 a majority of American college girls had their hair bobbed. By 1929 the vogue was common enough to put firms which were not forward-looking out of business.

This example is especially interesting because one manufacturer of hairnets was close enough to his market so that he was not caught unaware by this fashion change. He saw the change coming and did two things. First, he added other products which now provide the major source of income for his company. Second, hairnet production was curtailed enough to maintain a profit, and today he has a line of hairnets which continues to return a profit annually.

Many other examples could be mentioned to illustrate the point that market changes occur at a relatively slow rate and in regular pattern. Women continued to sew by hand for a whole generation after the sewing machine was invented. Zippers were available in 1900, but were regarded as a new invention in the 1920's, and were not in common use until the 1930's. The slow acceptance of the bathtub is still another example. One state even passed a law prohibiting its use.

Many business firms now employ scientific methods to forecast the future market for their products or services. The American Telephone and Telegraph Company, for example, makes many long-range forecasts of the demand for its service in different areas, some confined to sections within cities. Many railroads make careful forecasts of future traffic demands. For several years the General Motors Corporation has made extensive forecasts of the probable future demand for automobiles.

The American Radiator Company is very careful to budget its production in the light of analyses of the future demand for its products. By analyzing the course of such factors as building permits, building contracts, and other data reflecting the amount of building activity, this company can plan production, control both the amount and the distribution of inventory, and in other ways direct its marketing operations more efficiently. This company has been making sales forecasts for many years, and its forecasts have seldom been off by more than 10 per cent.

Another firm which engages in extensive long-range sales forecasting is the General Electric Company. The results of twelve of its forecasts made in 1944, while the war was still on, are compared with estimates of actual industry sales in 1947, in Table 3.[4]

The combined forecasts proved to be approximately 85 per cent accurate. It should be observed that this company has a general policy of being "about 10 per cent on the conservative side." Had the forecasts been made without this element, they would have been even more accurate. These forecasts were made during a wartime period with all the special hazards of transition from war to peace encountered. It is interesting to note that the last two items shown, home freezers and electric blankets, were relatively so new on the market that no market history was available to guide the forecasts; yet they were remarkably accurate.

---

[4] Russell H. Colley, "How Straight Can We Shoot in Long-Range Sales Forecasting?" *Sales Management*, July 1, 1948, pp. 94–100.

TABLE 3

COMPARISON OF SALES FORECASTS WITH ACTUAL SALES

Product	Forecast	Actual Sales
Radio receivers	15,000,000	16,834,700
Refrigerators	3,800,000	3,400,000
Washing machines	2,700,000	3,573,000
Vacuum cleaners	2,390,000	3,704,000
Ranges	850,000	1,200,000
Water heaters	300,000	1,100,000
Ironing machines	335,000	564,000
Mixers	1,100,000	1,450,000
Toasters	4,100,000	3,760,000
Heating pads	1,790,000	1,369,000
Home freezers	500,000	450,000
Automatic electric blankets	450,000	550,000

This example has been presented at some length because it deals with forecasting in a field which is relatively volatile and subject to sharp changes in the market. The forecasting of consumption of more staple products, such as foods and drugs, is much less difficult. The illustration also shows forecasts for individual products, which again is more difficult than forecasting for broader classes.

Single events, particularly those which appear to be exceptional, and short-term changes in sales volume often play too important a part in molding marketing policies. It is unfortunate that business executives do not realize that a single event is but one of a group of similar events differing only in degree. The more unusual or abnormal a single event is, the less likely it is to recur; hence the greater risk in making a business decision on it. Being too close to one's own picture often results in oversensitivity to a sudden change in the sales picture. Only by scientific market trend studies, which place single events in their proper perspective and cause management to think of sales on a base broader than the firm's own immediate situation, can these dangers to sound marketing planning be avoided.

SELECTED READINGS

Automotive Survey, 1953. New York: Crowell-Collier Publishing Co., 1953, 60 pp.

BANKS, SEYMOUR, "The Relationships Between Preference and Purchase of Brands," *Journal of Marketing*, October, 1950, pp. 145–57.

BURCK, GILBERT and PARKER, SANFORD. "The Changing American Market," *Fortune*, August, 1953, pp. 98–105 ff.

CANTRIL, HADLEY, *et al. Gauging Public Opinion*. Princeton, N. J.: Princeton University Press, 1944.

Family Income, Expenditures, and Savings in 1950, Bulletin No. 1097. Washington, D. C.: U. S. Department of Labor, Bureau of Labor Statistics, June, 1953.

GOODMAN, MAURICE E., and RISTOW, WALTER W. *Marketing Maps of the United States*. Rev. ed. Washington, D. C.: Card Division, Library of Congress, 1952.

HOBART, DONALD M. *Marketing Research Practice*. New York: The Ronald Press Co., 1950, pp. 24–34.

Income Distribution in the United States, U. S. Department of Commerce, Office of Business Economics. Washington, D. C.: Government Printing Office, 1953.

NIELSEN, ARTHUR C. "Evolution of Factual Techniques in Marketing Research," *Marketing Research and Business Management*. Illinois Marketing Symposium, University of Illinois, October, 1951.

———. "Technical Research and Marketing Research Must Be Coordinated," *The Nielsen Researcher*, May–June, 1952.

SEE ALSO Chapters 21–26 in this book.

CASE

BLANKERTZ, DONALD F., FERBER, ROBERT, and WALES, HUGH G. *Cases and Problems in Marketing Research*. New York: The Ronald Press Co., 1954, pp. 12–14.

4

SCIENTIFIC METHOD

The essence of marketing and distribution research is the use of scientific method in the solution of marketing problems. The scientific methods which the researcher employs are borrowed from many fields of science, with special adaptations necessary to meet the peculiar requirements of the marketing field. It is important, then, to consider the nature of scientific method before proceeding to an exposition of the special techniques employed in marketing and distribution research.

Much of the superficial work and many of the failures in marketing research may be traced to the lack of an understanding of basic scientific procedure on the part of those in charge. Many of the techniques now employed may be regarded primarily as temporary stopgaps. They are used in lieu of more scientific procedure. With a better understanding of scientific procedure, it will be possible to supplant these temporary techniques with more accurate and reliable methods.

The pioneers in marketing research saw the possible application of scientific methods which have been developed in the many fields of science to the special problems of marketing. These pioneers adapted the basic methods and techniques of other fields to the specific requirement of marketing. While it is possible that entirely new techniques and procedures will be developed, it is clear that this will be the exceptional case, and that the greatest advance will come as the result of the introduction of established techniques borrowed from other fields of science.

What Is Scientific Method? It is impossible to give a categorical statement or definition of "scientific method." Scientists, themselves, are often in doubt as to what constitutes scientific procedure. Some have even gone so far as to argue that there is no such thing as "scientific method." William Graham Sumner is generally considered one of the masters of social science. In discussing the methods used by Sumner, Charles Cooley said:

As regards his technical procedure, there was, so far as I can see, nothing original or distinctive. Like Montesquieu, or Darwin, or a hundred others before him, he simply collected a great mass of relevant material and made what he could of it.[1]

A. G. Keller, in discussing Sumner's methods, said:

Sumner used to laugh at methodology. He had none, except of the sort that is exemplified in Darwin's work; he got myriads of facts and then performed inductions on them. His methodology consisted in toil. I may illustrate his attitude by the advice he gave to a young man about learning a new language: "The way to learn a language is to sit down and learn it."
"The case is one of utter simplicity: Hard work, plus common sense, with no talk about it." [2]

It is impossible to define scientific method categorically, because there is no such thing as merely one scientific method, but rather there are many different scientific methods. An attempt to classify scientific methods met with the following result:

An enumeration of so-called methods was begun by the present writer, but its futility soon became apparent. The number of items in such an enumeration would be indefinitely large. Each subdivision of social inquiry, no matter how small, has its own "methods." Again, the items would be of differing degrees of generality. Sociologists and social workers make use of "case methods," but they also use the "method of the interview" as a subordinate aspect of "case method." "Statistical method" comprises, among others, the "method of least squares," while the latter may utilize the "method of logarithms." [3]

James B. Conant expresses his definition of science as follows:

Science is an interconnected series of concepts and conceptual schemes that have developed as a result of experimentation and observation and are fruitful of further experimentation and observations. In this definition the emphasis is on the word "fruitful." Science is a speculative enterprise. The validity of a new idea and the significance of a new experimental finding are to be measured by the consequences—consequences in terms of other ideas and other experiments. Thus conceived, science is not a quest for certainty; it is rather a quest which is successful only to the degree that it is continuous.[4]

In spite of the confusion as to what constitutes scientific methods, it is possible to differentiate between methods regarded as scientific

[1] Stuart A. Rice, *Methods in Social Science* (Chicago: University of Chicago Press, 1931), p. 4.
[2] *Ibid.*
[3] *Ibid.*, p. 5.
[4] James B. Conant, *Science and Common Sense* (New Haven: Yale University Press, 1951), p. 25.

and those which are not. There are many ways of approaching any problem, some of which are scientific and some of which are clearly unscientific. At the extreme, the differences between scientific and unscientific methods are clear. The solution of a problem by hunch, guesswork, opinion, and isolated examples is clearly unscientific. On the other hand, the solution of a problem by laboratory experiments which eliminate or control all outside variables influencing the results, which employ exact measurements, and which reduce human error and bias to a minimum, is clearly scientific. Between the extremes there are many efforts at the solution of problems which may be said to be in part scientific and in part unscientific.

Scientific method is most clearly expressed in the procedures of the physical sciences. In the physical and chemical laboratory one finds conditions making for exact measurements, objective experimentation, and testing. As one passes from the physical sciences to the so-called social sciences, he finds that it becomes more and more difficult to maintain scientific procedures.

Generalizations in physical science are usually based on controlled observations which are described so explicitly that he who objects may repeat. Social science may look at the same phenomena and draw wholly divergent conclusions, tolerated as legitimate expressions of individual judgment. . . . The demarcation of social science from physical science is a matter of opinion, as is the question whether or not there can be social science in the sense that physics and chemistry are science.[5]

It is in part because scientific method is most clearly found in the fields of the physical sciences that the social scientist or the market analyst must turn to the physical sciences for the foundation of the methods which he is to employ.

Although it is impossible to make an exact definition of scientific method, and although there is no one specific method of solving problems which may be described as the scientific method, there are several standards by which one may judge whether or not a given study has been conducted in a scientific manner.

Among these are the following:

1. *The point of view of the person who conducts the study.* Instead of attempting to define or describe scientific method, it may be explained by examples of the work of men such as Pasteur. The procedure of these masters has the common element of the "scientific mind."

2. *The procedure used in a specific study.* If the procedure employed in a specific study is objective and involves accurate measurements,

[5] Rice, *op. cit.,* p. 3.

it is said to be scientific. The degree to which the procedure employed is adapted to obtaining a sound, verifiable answer to the problem at hand may be regarded as one criterion of the use of scientific method.

3. *The use of generally recognized technique.* This method of explaining scientific method considers the extent to which the basic methods of science—such as the historical, inductive, analytical, or experimental—are employed in an individual study. There are also many generally accepted scientific techniques developed in fields such as statistics, psychology, and sociology, the existence of which indicates that a given operation has employed scientific method.

A further consideration of the first of these—the description of scientific method in terms of the mental attitude or point of view of the person who conducts the study—will be of value. The scientific mind has many basic characteristics:

1. It is primarily *rational* and reasoning rather than emotional. It requires a logical solution to problems.
2. The scientific mind is *free from bias.* The influences of class, religion, ethics, community habits, and tradition are kept at an absolute minimum.
3. The scientific mind *bases its judgment on facts* rather than authority. Nothing is accepted as final, and the scientist constantly seeks new facts in order to confirm the judgment of past authorities in his field.
4. The scientist *deals with probability* rather than certainty. For centuries, mankind has sought final answers to problems. It was assumed that there was a right and a wrong, an eternal truth in all matters. This old bifurcate division of thought, which assumed that people were either good or bad, that things were right or wrong, has given way to a point of view which takes the middle ground, and with this development has come a tendency to express knowledge in terms of probability rather than certainty.
5. The scientific mind is constantly *challenging, weighing, and explaining.* It constantly seeks a "reason why" for the condition studied.
6. The scientist is *objective* rather than subjective. His emphasis is upon the data and facts with which he works, and he strives to eliminate all subjective factors arising from the very fact that he is a human being with human instincts and emotions. The scientist is tough-minded about the facts.
7. The scientist is *selective* and discriminating in the work he does. He probes with keen instruments, constantly seeking that one phase

of the phenomena he studies which will yield an answer to his problem.

8. The scientist is primarily *creative* in his efforts. The thrill of discovery is his great reward. After he has taken things apart, he sees new ways to put them together, new arrangements to make. This is the mark of creative thinking. Without the creative thinking, which carries analysis into the synthesis which produces an integrated result, there can be no true scientific method.

The Creative and Developmental Aspects of Science. The creative aspects of science deserve special mention, for too many persons regard scientific method as being primarily a mechanical operation. The trappings of the scientific laboratory and the tools of the statistician should not be interpreted as signifying that scientific method is at root a mechanical process. Emphasis on the creative and developmental aspects of science is particularly important to the marketing researcher, who toils in a field where there is much room for discovery and where human ingenuity is richly rewarded.

Alexis Carrel has expressed this principle as follows:

Men of genius, in addition to their powers of observation and comprehension, possess other qualities, such as intuition and creative imagination. Through intuition they learn things ignored by other men, they perceive relations between seemingly isolated phenomena, they unconsciously feel the presence of the unknown treasure. All great men are endowed with intuition. They know, without analysis, without reasoning, what is important for them to know. . . . A great scientist instinctively takes the path leading to a discovery. This phenomenon, in former times, was called inspiration.[6]

Beveridge has put it this way: "The most important instrument in research must always be the mind of man." [7]

As Conant points out, science operates on the basis of concepts and hypotheses, rather than blind experimentation. Once a basic concept is achieved, experiments become more fruitful, and new avenues of experimentation are suggested. Hence the greatest advances take place in the practical arts in periods immediately following the emergence of new fundamental theories of wide applicability.[8]

But the development of science in any field is not primarily the work of any one individual. Scientific growth is almost invariably the result of cross-fertilization between groups and laboratories in widely separated parts of the world. Only rarely does one man or group of

[6] Alexis Carrel, *Man the Unknown* (New York: Harper & Bros., 1935), pp. 122–23.

[7] W. I. B. Beveridge, *The Art of Scientific Investigation* (New York: W. W. Norton & Co., Inc., 1951), Preface.

[8] See James B. Conant, "Science and the Practical Arts," *Harvard Business Review*, Autumn, 1947.

men recite a whole important chapter or even a whole important paragraph in the advance of science. Much more often the start comes from some isolated and perhaps timid voice making an inspired suggestion or raising some stimulating question. Then, as various practitioners make their individual contribution, we have a development, say, in marketing research, which truly brings the scientific method to this field.

Obviously, no one scientist is capable of mastering all the techniques indispensable to the study of a single human problem. Therefore, progress in knowledge of ourselves requires the simultaneous efforts of various specialists. Each specialist confines himself to one part of the body, or consciousness, or of their relations with the environment. . . . Each specialty is divided into smaller and smaller parts. There are specialists in glandular physiology, in vitamines, in diseases of the rectum, in those of the nose, in education of small children or of adults, in hygiene of factories and of prisons, in psychology of all categories of individuals, in domestic economy, rural economy, etc. Such a division of the work has made possible the development of the particular sciences.[9]

The important fact which emerges from even a superficial study of the recent history of the experimental sciences (say, since 1850) is the existence of an organization of individuals in close communication with each other. Because of the existence of this organization new ideas spread rapidly, discoveries breed more discoveries, and erroneous observations or illogical notions are on the whole soon corrected. The deep significance of the existence of this organization is often completely missed by those who talk about science but have had no firsthand experience with it. Indeed, a failure to appreciate how scientists pool their information and by so doing start a process of cross-fertilization in the realm of ideas has resulted in some strange proposals by politicians even in the United States.[10]

The importance of the interplay of ideas and the synthesis of factual material from many sources is being stressed more and more in scientific literature. One group has gone so far as to declare that investigations requiring extensive field work and the gathering of masses of quantitative data can be carried out successfully only by organized research agencies. Thus, in marketing research, we must have larger and more competent organizations, and they, in turn, must depend more and more upon the efforts of others.

But at the hub of all scientific work stands the individual scientist, making his unusual contribution as a result of his personal skills, training, and experience. This is particularly true in the development

[9] Carrel, *op. cit.*, pp. 45–46.
[10] James B. Conant, *op. cit.*, pp. 17, 18.

of the generalizations which form the conclusions of a practical research project, and in the development of some new scientific concept or principle.

Such a synthesis cannot be obtained by a simple round-table conference of the specialists. It requires the efforts of one man, not merely those of a group. A work of art has never been produced by a committee of artists, nor a great discovery made by a committee of scholars. The syntheses needed for the progress of our knowledge of man should be elaborated in a single brain. . . . Broad and strong minds are rarer than precise and narrow ones. It is easy to become a good chemist, a good physicist, a good physiologist, a good psychologist, or a good sociologist. On the contrary, very few individuals are capable of acquiring and using knowledge of several different sciences.[11]

The Hypothesis in Scientific Method

The development and verification of hypotheses will be referred to repeatedly in later discussion of marketing and distribution research methods. The selection and development of the single hypothesis or group of hypotheses for a particular study give basic direction to the entire research. This plays such an important role in success that it is essential for the marketing researcher to have a full understanding of the nature and function of the hypothesis in scientific method.

The term "hypothesis" means a tentative statement of the probable basis for the solution of a problem. When a skilled mechanic, for example, examines a motor which is not functioning properly, he does not tear the motor apart and completely rebuild it. On the contrary, he makes a diagnosis of the probable cause of the difficulty, and having decided that the trouble lies in faulty carburetion, proceeds to adjust or rebuild the carburetor. The decision that the solution to the problem lies in carburetion rather than in the ignition or other source is his first hypothesis. The later decision that a certain type of repair will solve the difficulty is a second hypothesis. It would obviously be a foolish waste of time and money to rebuild an entire motor because it does not work properly. Usually one or two factors are the cause of the trouble, and the skill of a mechanic is shown in large measure by his ability to determine wherein the trouble lies. While most garage mechanics have probably never heard of the term "hypothesis" they are using, in fact, a hypothesis every time they decide how to repair a motor, just as the chemist uses a hypothesis in determining what course a chemical experiment should pursue to solve a particular problem.

[11] *Economic Research and the Development of Economic Science and Public Policy,* National Bureau of Economic Research, 1946.

Another example of the use of a hypothesis will be found in the case of medical diagnosis. When a physician diagnoses a case, he does not attempt to apply all the known techniques of remedial or preventive medicine. On the contrary, a good physician makes a very careful diagnosis of the symptoms shown in the individual case in order that he may find the root of the trouble and determine the one or two types of treatment which are required. Many physicians do not think specifically in terms of a hypothesis, yet in casting about for the cause of the difficulty and the probable means of solving it they are in effect setting up tentative hypotheses.

The hypothesis has sometimes been referred to as a hunch or guess on the part of a scientist as to the type of procedure which will yield a sound solution to the problem at hand. The term "hunch" or "guess" is used because hypotheses are usually arrived at in a non-mechanical manner, and often appear to come to the person attempting to solve a problem as a matter of mere chance. When Pasteur, for example, was attempting to determine the means of preventing rabies, it appeared that he suddenly was inspired to inoculate exposed persons with germ cultures obtained from the saliva of dogs suffering from the disease. The idea is reported to have burst on him during a period of meditation after lengthy but seemingly disorderly observation. The event has been dramatized in literature and motion pictures.

It was no accident that Pasteur discovered this solution instead of thousands of other persons who faced the same problem. Years of study and experimentation, much of it apparently fruitless, preceded the development of this hypothesis. When Pasteur finally made use of the idea, he easily concluded his investigation with tests which established a principle that was to change completely the course of medical history.

The place of intuition in the development of a scientific hypothesis has been described by Beveridge as follows: "The most characteristic circumstances of an intuition are a period of intense work on a problem accompanied by a desire for its solution, abandonment of the work perhaps with attention to something else, then the appearance of the idea with dramatic suddenness and often a sense of certainty."[12]

The hypothesis is the hub of scientific method. Everything that is achieved in the nature of a scientific solution revolves around it and is dependent on it. The method of science is based on recognition of the fact that it is only when we approach phenomena with a question that we can expect to get an answer. Scientific method means constant seeking, as opposed to rummaging. Charles Darwin made the following statement in 1861:

[12] Beveridge, *op. cit.*, p. 72.

About thirty years ago, there was much talk that geologists ought only to observe and not theorize; and I well remember some one saying that at this rate a man might as well go into a gravel-pit and count the pebbles and describe the colors. How odd it is that anyone should not see that all observation must be for or against some view if it is to be of any service! [13]

The scientific hypothesis is just as important to the marketing researcher as it is to the scientist or technician in any other field. As will be shown later, the selection and definition of the specific hypothesis or hypotheses is a crucial operation in the third step in marketing research—planning the formal investigation. However, these hypotheses are not developed solely as a result of conscious effort in this third step. They arise more or less automatically as a result of the work which is carried on in the first two steps—the situation analysis and the informal investigation.

The Basic Methods of Science

The Historical Method. The historical method may be defined as that procedure which employs the analysis and interpretation of past historical events as a basis for an understanding of current problems and the prediction of future events.

The value of the historical method as a scientific procedure has frequently been doubted; there are, nevertheless, several concepts or bases upon which a distinct historical method has been built, and this method is scientific in character. These bases are the repetitive idea, the environmental origin of problems, and the environmental application of solutions.

The idea of the repetitive nature of events is most simply stated in the phrase "history repeats itself." For any given current event, historians are able to find analogous events which have preceded it. Depressions follow prosperity, and prosperity in turn follows periods of depression. There is not only a continuous sequence of cyclical business fluctuation, but it is also usually found that the conditions making for one period of depression are essentially the same as conditions which have made for previous periods of depression. In an effort to understand and solve the problems of the business cycle, the historical approach has been most commonly used, since it is believed that discovering what has happened in the past under conditions essentially similar to the conditions of the present situation will foretell to a great extent what is likely to happen in the future.

[13] Charles Darwin, *More Letters*, ed. Francis Darwin (New York: Appleton-Century-Crofts, Inc., 1903), Vol. I, p. 195.

The principle of the environmental origin of problems may be expressed by the statement that each problem grows out of a specific environment and its nature is determined consequently by this environment. Hence, in order to find the fundamental problem at any given time, it is necessary to make an analysis of the environment out of which it arises. Furthermore, in order to determine the essential nature of the problem and solve it, it is necessary to analyze the environment out of which the problem has grown.

The principle of the environmental application of solutions recognizes the fact that the solution to any given problem must be applied in the environment out of which it has arisen. For example, in a marketing research it may have been determined that a certain type of incentive plan for salesmen will increase the efficiency of the sales force. Before such a plan is put in operation, however, the strength and weakness of the sales personnel must be objectively analyzed, since what might otherwise appear to be a sound solution may be of no practical value because of the peculiar make-up of the sales force under consideration. The sales personnel and organization of a company at any given time have been developed over a period of years, and the marketing researcher who does not study the strength and weakness of the sales organization as it stands at the time he has completed his analysis would be likely to make unsound recommendations. The general principle, of course, applies to all types of analyses.

In marketing research the historical method is employed to a certain extent through all stages of the work, but it is used more directly in the following:

1. *Market forecasting and the analysis of market trends.* All work in this field represents basically an application of the historical method.
2. *The situation analysis.* The primary function of the situation analysis is to analyze the environment out of which the specific problem or problems to be solved have arisen.
3. *Interpretation.* When the interpretive stage of the analysis has been reached, all of the facts used in the study have been found. This does not complete the analysis, however, for one is still faced with the question, "What do these facts mean in terms of future policy?" In attempting to formulate a business policy on the basis of the findings of the analysis, one must be fully cognizant of the principle that the solution to a problem must be applied in the environment out of which the problem has arisen.

There are no logical limitations on the soundness of the historical method as a scientific procedure. Its limitations are primarily technical and rest largely upon the lack of sound quantitative measurement of historical facts. So long as the data used in a historical analysis are largely random observations, the materials are loosely woven and lack the precision of accurate quantitative measurements. The nature of the general limitations of the historical method as commonly used are indicated in the following statement:

> General description and general narrative fall short in several respects of meeting the present demand for dependable analysis of social movement. In the first place, they lack precision. Secondly, since they cannot employ precise criteria of relevancy, they tend to select and emphasize particular elements and events which may be striking to the attention, but which are relatively unimportant from the standpoint of later interest. Present-day social scientists would exchange bushels of ancient annals of kings and bishops for a few more authenticated facts concerning such plebeian matters as roads, production, and peasant customs. Thirdly, and to much the same effect, description and narrative tend to deal with individuals rather than with mass situations. The latter may escape recording by virtue of the very fact of universality. Lastly, important relationships may be concealed from casual view, to be disclosed only when the methods of statistical analysis have been developed and applied.[14]

From this quotation it will be seen that the historical method is completely scientific only when combined with other methods, particularly with the statistical methods which provide the necessary quantitative measurement.

The Inductive Method. The inductive method is a scientific procedure by which general conclusions are drawn from an adequate number of properly controlled individual observations or cases. It is sometimes called the method of reasoning from the specific to the general. It is essentially the scientific method of making a generalization.

There are two methods of forming a generalization: by random observations of individual events, and by carefully controlled induction.

Generalizations which are made as a result of the random observations of individual events are not scientific and are subject to considerable error. In the first place, there is the limitation of one man's experience. Although business leaders are often men with amazing capacities for observation, it is impossible for any one person to see enough events to provide a sound basis for the many generalizations which are required for the successful conduct of a business. In the second place, the random observation of individuals is an unsatisfactory basis for generalization because subjective and emotional personal elements are always encountered. Man is essentially an emotional being, and his own feelings, habits, and desires are bound to

---

[14] Stuart A. Rice, "The Historical-Statistical Approach to Social Study," in *Statistics in Social Study* (Philadelphia: University of Pennsylvania Press, 1930), pp. 1–2.

color his observation. Third, the unusual and striking cases are likely to make a strong impression on the individual who observes them. Often the fact of relative unimportance is discovered under such dramatic circumstances that it assumes a mountainous magnitude in the thinking of the individual who has observed it. Fourth, there is a tendency for presumed facts to crystallize and to be repeated by individuals. This condition is commonly met in the reliance of the businessman upon the experience of others. As a result of supposedly "pooling" the experiences of different businesses, habit and tradition are fortified. Traditions, in so far as they are not based upon sound scientific induction, assume a sanctity which brings them close to folklore. Finally, the random observations of individuals do not provide a sound basis for generalizations because they do not involve quantitative measurements.

Generalizations which do not involve sound measurement, and which are not stated in quantitative terms, are likely to be meaningless platitudes. One of the best examples of this is found in some of the principles of orthodox economics, which have in a large measure become merely redundant statements of the obvious. It is perfectly correct to state, for example, that other things being equal, a lower price on a commodity will result in an increase in the amount of the commodity which will be purchased. Such a statement is true but it is meaningless, for unless one knows *how much* of a reduction in price will produce *how much* of an increase in demand, no practical contribution has been made. There is an obvious need for the application of a sound inductive procedure which will provide these measurements.

The second way of forming a generalization is on the basis of carefully controlled induction. By obtaining a sufficient number of properly selected facts it is possible to arrive at correct generalizations. Practically all marketing researches involve the use of induction. If one wishes to determine whether people living in cities buy by mail order in sufficient volume to warrant the cultivation of such markets, the proper thing to do is to go to the people living in cities and determine the extent to which they are actually buying by this method or make an analysis of buying records. Instead of being moved in its business policy by isolated orders which come from people living in cities, or by exceptional individuals who may happen to make large purchases, the use of the inductive process based upon a survey of the proper number of persons or a sales analysis will provide a precise measurement of the extent to which persons living in cities buy by mail. This, in turn, will provide a sound basis for arriving at a decision on business policy.

In spite of the universality of the inductive method in marketing and distribution research, one must not assume that it is the only procedure which must be employed. An attempt to operate solely upon the basis of statistical induction is, in itself, unscientific. Francis Bacon, who was the first great exponent of this method, contended that the essential function of science was to gather all the available facts and on the basis of them to arrive at conclusions and principles. Bacon, himself, could not actually follow this procedure. No individual or organization can obtain all the facts which have a bearing upon a marketing problem. A marketing researcher must, therefore, be highly selective in fact gathering and obtain only those data which are relevant to his problem. Thus, other scientific methods must be combined with the inductive methods, notably the deductive method.

The Deductive Method. The deductive method may be defined as the procedure of arriving at conclusions from generalizations by the use of proper logical processes. It is the function of induction to provide sound generalizations, and the function of deduction to draw sound inferences from these generalizations. For example, suppose that it has been found that 20 per cent of the people living in cities have bought by mail within the past year, and that 70 per cent have bought by mail at some time or other. Assume that this is a sound generalization which has been arived at inductively. We are still faced with the question, "What does this mean to the Jones Mail Order Company?" Shall the Jones Mail Order Company proceed to circularize the residents of cities in an effort to develop mail-order business? It is obvious that the mere statement of the generalization per se does not provide the interpretation which is essential to form business policy.

It is apparent that induction and deduction go hand in hand. Moreover, one does not first induce and then deduce; for after the first deduction it will usually be found that more facts are necessary before the problem can be solved. Further induction is then followed by further deduction. The process may be continuously repeated. One gathers facts and arrives at generalizations (induction), then from these generalizations he draws logical conclusions (deduction). Next the analyst gathers new data and makes new generalizations, followed by new logical conclusions. Whether induction precedes deduction, or vice versa, in a given problem, it is difficult to tell, and is of no more concern to the scientist than the argument as to which came first—the hen or the egg.

Sound deduction is essentially a matter of consistent thinking. The mind has been described as a thinking machine—like a calculating machine. The calculating machine works properly if it produces the correct answer each time that a given set of figures is fed into it. Whether the figures put in the machine are correct or or not makes no difference; the machine is in proper working order if it always provides the same answer from any given set of figures that other machines in proper repair yield. So, too, with the mind and the deductive process. Deduction is not concerned with the accuracy or validity of a generalization from which it proceeds. If the mind arrives at consistent conclusions from given generalizations, it is making proper deductions. It is the function of induction to provide the correct generalization from which to proceed in drawing logical conclusions. To the researcher, therefore, induction and deduction must be coordinated properly, for the correct answer to the marketing problem can come only if the right figures have been fed into the machine, and if the machine is in proper working order.

In marketing and distribution research, deduction is used primarily in the interpretive stage. Having drawn statistical conclusions as a result of tabulation and analysis of the data which have been gathered from the field or other sources, the researcher must interpret these results into business policy. Unfortunately, many make the mistake of assuming that the function of marketing research is solely inductive, and fail to use sound logic in arriving at recommendations for business policy. A research which merely states certain statistical findings about the market is a research which is only half done. If these facts are presented in their raw form to business executives, it will usually be found that many conflicting interpretations will be placed upon them. A researcher must be a logician who will take the facts as found and make these interpretations for the business. Interpretations must, of course, be sound and stand up against the criticism of hardheaded executives.

The use of the deductive method in marketing research is not limited to its application in the interpretation stage. This method is used in other steps of the research, especially in planning the investigation. Before the final plan for the investigation is determined, a test study should always be made. After a small number of field interviews or observations have been obtained, the researcher must project the findings of the test investigation deductively to see if an analysis carried through on the basis of the test investigation will provide a basis for a logical solution to the problems at hand. Usually, such interpretation and deduction will indicate the need for changes in the plan, as a result of which further test data will be obtained. These are then projected deductively, again to make sure that the final analysis will provide a proper solution. This process must be repeated until

finally a basic plan for the final study has been worked out and is put
into execution.

It is an error to plan hastily and to arrive at conclusions which give
no basis for sound interpretation and recommendation. It is much
better to spend more time in the planning stage and to make deductions on the basis of small test investigations. The reason many
marketing researches are never carried into actual business practice
is that the analyst did not properly apply the deductive method in
planning the major phases of the analysis.

The Analytical Method. The analytical method is that procedure
which breaks up the gross and complex facts of observation, which are
often too varied to be understood, into smaller, homogeneous facts.
The best example of the analytical method will be found in the
chemistry laboratory. Suppose that a chemist wishes to study a new
food product which has been submitted to him. By observing the
product he is able to obtain the gross facts which are perceivable by
the senses. He can detect its odor, its color, its texture, and a few other
general characteristics. But it is impossible to determine its composition except by analysis. By the analytical process, the various chemical
elements which make up the product can be separated so that he can
determine the amount of each which it contains. It then becomes
possible to duplicate it or to find methods of improving it.

A market is made up of thousands or millions of persons who are
similar to a degree, but who have many different habits, interests, and
desires. Considered in its entirety, the market for a product is entirely too complex to be understood by even the most penetrating
mind. By the analytical process, it is possible to break a market down
into various elements, such as age groups, sex groups, or geographic
units, each of which is sufficiently homogeneous to be comprehended
and evaluated.

The value of the analytical method as a procedure which clarifies
a complex marketing situation is shown by a breakdown of a large
city. The Bureau of the Census now divides large cities into small
areas, known as *census tracts*, and collects and analyzes market data
on each tract or group of tracts. Cleveland, Ohio, for example, has
been divided into 321 sections, each of which is equivalent to a vil-
lage of 4,200 inhabitants. Facts are now available for these small
units to show the rental value of homes; whether or not the families
own automobiles; where families live who have electric refrigerators,
bathtubs, stoves, and furnaces; how they go to work; the physical conditions of their homes; the sizes of their families; and how they cook.

The whole procedure of marketing research is essentially analytical
in nature. The analytical method is used extensively in the situation

analysis. Sales data and market information are broken down into fine divisions in order that the procedures to be employed in solving the central problems may be determined. Gross facts regarding the market are broken down into fine classifications in order to provide an understanding of the essential nature of the market.

In the informal investigation, the analytical method is employed by questioning consumers and dealers in order to determine the various elements which affect the sale of the product. The method is also used in planning the investigation. In this step the bases of the analysis to be used in the field investigation are determined. Whether marketing facts will be grouped primarily on race, occupation, standard of living, or other facts must be determined. The selection of the proper bases of analysis is vital to the success of the study. The tabulation and analysis step is essentially an analytical process. In it a great mass of data is broken down, grouped, and regrouped to obtain the greatest possible insight into their meaning.

The Experimental Method. The experimental method is essentially the procedure of carrying out on a small scale a trial solution to a problem. This solution is usually arrived at by holding constant all elements which affect the result except the one being measured, which is varied. For example, suppose a chemist wishes to determine the effect of various degrees of temperature upon sulphur. It is not necessary that he study the effect of temperature on all the sulphur obtainable. By a carefully controlled experiment with a very small quantity, he can arrive at a conclusion as to the probable effect of variations of temperature upon any given quantity of sulphur at any time. In conducting the experiment, the chemist would procure a small quantity which has the characteristics typical of sulphur in general. He would then take small quantities of his test sulphur and apply different degrees of temperature to each, recording the results with care. In this experiment, since the element being measured is the effect of temperature, he varies the temperature in order that he may have measurements at all significant levels. All other variables which might affect the result must also be controlled properly. These include all conditions, such as atmospheric pressure, humidity, and other factors in the experiment, which might affect the sulphur.

An example of the application of the experimental method in marketing research is the use of sales area tests. Instead of conducting a general marketing campaign and learning of its effectiveness after the money has been spent, it is possible to conduct small-scale tests within restricted areas and determine its selling power in advance. By using the experimental method in this manner, the weak elements will be revealed and poor campaign ideas may be abandoned. There are many other cases in marketing research in which the experimental method may be used, but the test campaign is one of the most clear-cut examples.

The logical assumption of the experimental method is that the conditions of the test are essentially the same as the conditions which will be found in the "universe" or in the total operation to which the conclusions drawn from the experiment are to be applied. Obviously the conditions need not be identical, but they must be similar in all essential elements. Even in the analyses made in the laboratory, all the test conditions are not identical with those met in the commercial field. For example, after chemists have made experiments which have developed a new type of motor oil, it may be found when actual production is started that certain conditions which were not present in the experiment will arise. In large-scale production, involving large quantities of materials and machinery which are crude as compared with the finer and more accurate equipment of the chemical laboratory, these new elements will be encountered. Sometimes there is so much difference that further experimentation is necessary to adjust the process to the requirements of large-scale production.

It is important to the marketing researcher to realize that the conditions under which the experiment was conducted and those under which the results are applied will never be found to be identical. On the other hand, one must constantly keep in mind the logical assumption that the conditions of the test must be essentially the same as the conditions under which the results of the tests are to be applied.

In many respects the experimental method is the most scientific of all procedures. From the time of Aristotle it had been assumed that two falling bodies approach the earth at speeds in direct ratio to the weight of the bodies. This assumption had been laid down as a scientific law by Aristotle and had been defended for centuries. Galileo did not believe this law to be true. He dropped two balls of different weights from the top of the leaning tower of Pisa. The two balls reached the earth at the same time, and a new law was developed by the experimental method. His ecclesiastical superiors considered this demonstration an attack on authority and had him excommunicated. Galileo's experiment, however, went far beyond the mere development of a single new scientific law. It may be regarded as the origin of the experimental method in science.

To many, the experimental method is the only true method of science. However, it should not be assumed that this method must be employed to make an analysis scientific. There is genuine danger of going through the form of an experiment without an adequate control of variables. An experiment which does not recognize the logical assumption of the experimental method, and which is not properly controlled, will produce results which are unscientific and unsound. The proper use of the experimental method in marketing research and some of the dangers to be avoided are discussed in the next chapter.

The General Techniques of Special Scientific Fields

Statistics. Of all the various social sciences which have developed special techniques, none contributes to marketing research so directly or so extensively as statistics. The study of statistics is concerned chiefly with the methods of collecting and using numerical data. In statistics, the principles which govern the analysis of quantitative data are stated, and the various techniques for such analysis are reduced to a workable basis. Since marketing and distribution research deals with persons and marketing phenomena in the aggregate, these techniques for analyzing quantitative data play a primary role in marketing research methods.

The subjects with which statistics deals indicate clearly the importance of its techniques as a basis for marketing research. The field embraces such matters as the collecting and editing of data, sampling, classification, tabular and diagrammatic presentation, averages, and correlation.

The common use of the phrase "statistical induction" indicates that the field of statistics is of primary value to the marketing researcher in introducing the inductive process into his work. The techniques of statistics are in a large measure those which provide a method for insuring that data are collected in the proper manner to provide the basis for the generalizations representing the end product of induction.

A second important phase of statistical method is the development of the proper technique by which these data may be grouped into sound generalizations. Classification, frequency distributions, averages, and methods of tabular and graphic presentation shape these generalizations into their most usable form. These represent largely the analytical method.

In view of the predominant position of statistics in marketing research, it is important that a word of caution be given. The statistical importance of phenomena is determined solely by the preponderance of sheer quantity. If it is found, for example, that three thousand persons prefer a blue color in a product, while only one thousand prefer a red color, and only a small number prefer several other colors, statistics indicate that the desire of the market is for a blue product. This fact is useful and important. Nevertheless, it is obvious that one should not blindly conclude that the company should produce only a blue product. In such a case it appears clear that the product should be offered in at least two colors in order to obtain a maximum acceptance on the part of the market. Statistics have served a very useful function, however, in indicating the relative importance of the colors which should be employed, and the fruitlessness of attempting to provide the product in too many other colors.

Accounting. Accounting deals with the recording and analysis of all facts which have a bearing on the financial aspects of a business. The facts recorded and analyzed embrace those concerning the external transactions of the company with other firms and individuals and the internal operations subject to financial record and analysis.

It is the function of accounting to give and interpret accurate, up-to-date information on what is happening in the business that affects its financial position and profits. Many of these transactions involve sales, advertising, and other marketing activities; hence, the work of the accountant is, in many respects, of primary importance to the marketing researcher. Techniques developed in accounting, especially those for the analysis of marketing transactions, may be employed directly.

With the increasing complexity of business and the small margins of profit upon which most firms must operate, a specialized field of accounting, which is of particular interest to the marketing researcher, has been developed. This field of cost accounting was developed first as a special procedure for determining the unit cost of goods produced, such as the cost of a barrel of tar or of an automobile part.

Cost accounting for marketing operations has become an important tool in marketing research, because businessmen realize that there are many more wastes in marketing than in production, and hence great opportunities for cost reduction. Standard costs, based on accounting analysis of cost records, may be even more useful for a sales department than for a factory.

Costs may be set for a great number of marketing operations, such as selling, advertising, delivery, inventory maintenance, and collections. Standard costs are also used in setting selling prices. One of the most common uses of standard costs in marketing, as well as in production, is to provide a basis for determining whether performance in specific operations is satisfactory.

A most important application of cost accounting is in decisions as to which of several alternative marketing operations should be employed. Most companies have a number of options with respect to sales methods. For example, one can employ personal selling or advertising, sell through various types of retail outlets, or use different wholesale distributors. By determining the cost and probable return from each of his options, the marketer can determine which one offers the best possibilities.

Engineering. That engineering science has many techniques which are of value to the marketing researcher is attested by the large number of persons with engineering training who play important parts in marketing and distribution research today. In the past the chief emphasis in industrial engineering has been on the production side, especially in the field of technical product research, and in the reduction of costs in manufacturing processes. With the general rise in the importance of marketing, however, engineers have turned their attention more and more to the problem of devising more efficient methods of marketing.

Engineering as a subject concerns itself primarily with the application of the basic principles and laws of the exact and physical sciences, such as mathematics, chemistry, and physics, to the specific problems of the many specialized fields which it embraces. The techniques developed by the industrial engineer are of primary value to the marketing researcher.

Existing techniques of industrial engineering may be said to have developed essentially from two basic principles—the getting of more and better facts, and the relation of these facts to costs. Definite techniques and procedures are developed to solve the special problems faced by the engineer. Such problems as planning, performance, standards, methods of control, and simplification have led to the development of these techniques and of a personnel trained in meeting such situations.

Among these special techniques, the most valuable to the marketing researcher are those employed in time and motion study. As a basis for the elimination of waste, the analysis of time and motion involved in different operations has proved most productive. The researcher who is familiar with the methods employed in reducing costs and eliminating waste from production has a clear advantage in attempting to perform similar functions in marketing operations.

Psychology. Psychology is the study of individual human behavior. Unfortunately, the field has undergone such great transition in recent years, has been marked by so many arguments regarding definition and the various concepts employed in psychological study, and is filled with so many small compartments of specialized psychological inquiry, that it is very difficult to understand the exact nature of the psychological approach. One of the classic arguments in psychology has been developed because of the problem of the mental as opposed to the physical approach. In earlier years, psychology was regarded primarily as a study of the human mind. This approach was attacked largely on the basis of a disbelief in the existence of mind, free will, and consciousness as basic motives in human behavior. With the rise of the so-called "behavioristic psychology" greater emphasis was placed on the physical aspects of behavior, with the result that there is a large branch of psychology called "experimental psychology." In a large measure it entirely disregards the mental aspects and attempts to provide a purely mechanical explanation of behavior.

A marketing researcher is, of course, not interested in the more metaphysical aspects of these problems. What he seeks is a usable basis for analyzing human behavior; whether an analysis from the mental or the physical point of view is philosophically more sound is of no concern to him. He prefers to disregard this issue and to learn all the techniques which may be of value in making it possible to study human behavior.

The chief contribution of psychology to marketing research is in the provision of techniques for analyzing the basic and more fundamental motives which lie behind market behavior. The potential contribution of psychology to marketing research is well indicated in the following statement:

> We recognize fully the present limitations of psychological knowledge. We are not able to offer it as an adequate answer to the market research man's prayers. All that we are suggesting is: first, that market research needs general, orienting, intellectual techniques, even more at the present time than it requires everyday digging tools; and second, that these larger techniques are supplied in a considerable part, though not at all exclusively, by psychology. We suggest simply that a systematic view of how people's market behavior is motivated, how buying decisions are arrived at, constitutes a valuable aid in finding one's way around a thousand and one questions of specific procedures and interpretations in market research. This need for a psychological view grows out of the very nature of market research for that research is aimed predominantly at knowledge by means of which to forecast and control consumer behavior. . . . Sales opportunities exist—or fail to exist—in people's minds. Hence, the task is essentially psychological.[15]

The psychologist has developed many technical research procedures which are of great value to the study of market behavior. From those psychologists who take a more mechanical point of view, we may obtain techniques for recording the facts of market behavior as they are expressed in action. From those psychologists who emphasize the

[15] Arthur Kornhauser and Paul Lazarsfeld, *The Techniques of Market Research from the Standpoint of a Psychologist*, American Management Association, Institute of Management Series 16, 1935, pp. 4 ff.

motives behind behavior, we may obtain special techniques which are particularly valuable in appraising the psychological factors which lie behind the observed facts of market behavior.

Sociology. Sociology emphasizes the analysis of behavior as it is affected by social groups and social relationships. It is obvious that studies of the persons who compose markets must be made primarily in terms of groups and social units. Furthermore, as most marketing activities are directed at groups, the marketing researcher is interested in individuals only in so far as they give him a clearer understanding of group behavior. Marketing and advertising campaigns, for example, are universally directed at people in the mass. Since in most cases it is necessary to determine the marketing policies which will be most effective in obtaining a response from millions of people, it follows that the primary concern of the researcher must almost always be with people in the mass or the social group rather than with the individual.

The following statement indicates the nature of the phenomena which are the primary concern of the sociologist.

Broadly speaking, sociology deals with the behavior of men in groups—a group is any collection of two or more individuals who carry on social relations with each other. Group behavior depends not upon the mere presence of men together, but upon their interaction. . . . In stimulating each other and responding to each other, men develop common modes of thinking and acting. These we call custom, tradition, or mores. More specifically, these include the regulations governing conduct and approved ways of acting, the manners and fashions of a group, and the whole range of social belief, values, convention, social rituals, and the technique of living.[16]

The major contribution of sociology to the field of marketing research lies in its analysis of cultural environment and change. It has been argued that sociological interpretations of many aspects of human behavior are much sounder and more revealing than psychological interpretations. It is claimed that behavior is determined less by the individual's preferences, sentiments, and feelings than by the general cultural pattern in which he fits.

Sociology has developed many techniques which may be used by the marketing researcher in his work. The technique for obtaining the information which must be secured in order to make a proper diagnosis of a social situation will be found especially valuable to a marketing researcher. Complete outlines for a social case history have been prepared. A study of outlines of this type, and the various tech-

[16] Kimball Young, *An Introductory Sociology* (New York: American Book Co., 1934), p. xiii.

niques used by social case workers, is especially useful in revealing the necessity for going beyond broad statistical data and obtaining comprehensive information about individuals who make up the market in order to get the "feel" of marketing problems.

An example may be cited from an analysis of the market for a certain health product. Many researches had been made in this field but none provided a sound foundation for business policy. The customary survey was supplanted by a relatively small number of comprehensive interviews with individuals, conducted in the penetrating and informal manner with which the social case worker proceeds. As a result, habits, attitudes, and other elements which had a vital bearing upon the market for the product in question, and which had been entirely missed in the more usual type of marketing research, were discovered. This "case history" approach gave an insight into the real condition of the market. It resulted in the elimination of many superficial factors which for years had been assumed were important, the development of sound hypotheses, and a new procedure for making a more general analysis which yielded fruitful results.

SELECTED READINGS

ALDERSON, WROE. "Psychology for Marketing and Economics," *Journal of Marketing*, October, 1952, pp. 119–35.

BEVERIDGE, WILLIAM I. B. *The Art of Scientific Investigation*. New York: W. W. Norton & Co., Inc., 1951.

BOAS, GEORGE. *Our New Ways of Thinking*. New York: Harper & Bros., 1930.

BRIDGMAN, P. W. *The Logic of Modern Physics*. New York: The Macmillan Co., 1927, Introduction and Chapters I, II.

CENTERS, RICHARD. *The Psychology of Social Classes*. Princeton, N. J.: Princeton University Press, 1949.

CONANT, JAMES B. *Science and Common Sense*. New Haven: Yale University Press, 1951.

GEE, WILSON. *Social Science Research Methods*. New York: Appleton-Century-Crofts, Inc., 1950.

GOODE, WILLIAM J., and HATT, PAUL K. *Methods in Social Research*. (McGraw-Hill Series in Sociology and Anthropology.) McGraw-Hill Book Co., Inc., 1954.

HOBSON, E. W. *The Domain of Natural Science*. New York: The Macmillan Co., 1923.

JAFFE, BERNARD. Crucibles. New York: Simon & Schuster, Inc., 1930.

JAHODA, MARIE, DEUTSCH, MORTON, and COOK, STUART W. *Research Methods in Social Relations*. 2 vols. New York: The Dryden Press, Inc., 1951, pp. 1–12.

KORNHAUSER, ARTHUR W., and LAZARSFELD, PAUL F. *The Techniques of Market Research from the Standpoint of a Psychologist*, American Management Association, Institute of Management Series No. 16, 1935.

LORIE, J. H., and ROBERTS, H. V. *Basic Methods of Marketing Research*. New York: McGraw-Hill Book Co., Inc., 1950.

MILLIKAN, ROBERT A. *Science and the New Civilization*. New York: Charles Scribner's Sons, 1930.

WILSON, E. BRIGHT, JR. *An Introduction to Scientific Research*. New York: McGraw-Hill Book Co., Inc., 1952.

5

BASIC MARKETING RESEARCH METHODS

Since marketing and distribution research is nothing more nor less than the use of scientific method in the field of marketing, it must be firmly rooted in the basic methods of science. One must recognize, however, the important distinction between the general principles of scientific method and applied science. When one attempts to apply scientific method in a specific field, borrowing techniques which have been developed for other purposes, he must make many adjustments. The chemist, for example, relies largely upon the experimental method. But in solving the problems of chemistry, he must adapt the general method to the specific requirements of the materials with which he must work. So, too, the biologist frequently employs inductive data, using statistical techniques. But he also must make adaptations necessary for the handling of biological data.

The marketing researcher is confronted with many special problems in the field with which he works. He deals with human beings in their economic relationships. He faces a far-flung market, composed of millions of buyers, each making many choices. He deals with a complex marketing structure, designed to bring thousands of competitive products to the market most efficiently. He deals, above all, with human relationships, with fickle desires but forceful opinions. The direct procedures, the exact measurements, and the test tubes of the physical sciences are not at his command.

The fundamental methods of marketing and distribution research are the survey method, the observational method, and the experimental method. These techniques vary greatly in their approach and relative accuracy, and may yield different results when applied to the same problem. In many studies any of the three methods may be used, so that the analyst is usually faced with the necessity of deciding which one is to be employed. Since the results depend in large measure upon the basic method used, it is important that the logical assumptions and implications of these techniques be thoroughly understood.

The Survey Method

In the survey method data are gathered by asking questions. This method is sometimes called the questionnaire technique. The essential element in the survey method is that the data are furnished by an individual in a conscious effort to answer a question.

An example of the use of the survey technique in marketing research is a consumer investigation to determine which of two types of packages is the better. If an investigator shows representative consumers two or more types of packages and asks, "Which of these packages do you prefer?" he is employing the survey method. Note that the investigator asks the question directly so that the respondent must make a conscious effort to reply, and that the data upon which the entire subsequent analysis rests are thus given.

The survey method is a widely used technique in marketing research. Some people go so far as to regard the questionnaire technique as being synonymous with marketing and distribution research. This is a serious error, leading many analysts to use the survey method when the observational or experimental method would be more scientific. In fact, the observational and experimental methods are superior, and occupy fully as important a position in marketing research today as the survey method.

The survey method is used in the three following general forms: factual surveys, opinion surveys, and interpretive surveys. The distinction among these three types is important because there is a difference in the scientific accuracy of information obtained by these forms of the questionnaire method. The position of the respondent in a factual survey question is different from his position in an opinion survey question. Also, different techniques are required to obtain information properly by each of these variations of the survey method.

Factual Surveys. In a factual survey, the respondent acts merely as a reporter. An example is a survey which asks, "What brand of soap do you use?" In this case the respondent simply reports the brand of soap which he uses. The nature of the factual survey is further illustrated by the following questions: "How much did you pay for your radio?" "At what store do you buy most of your groceries?" "How old is your automobile?" "How large a trade-in allowance did you receive on your old washing machine?" "What brands of canned soups do you carry in stock?"

When the survey method is employed in this form, its results are subject to many errors. These include errors of memory, inability to generalize, desire to make a good impression, and various human tendencies which bias the report. Since a human being is reporting an action of himself or someone else, many errors are bound to be injected into the data obtained.

As a result, wherever the survey method is employed in its factual form, one must be especially careful to observe all the fundamental principles of sound questionnaire construction, which are discussed in detail later in the book. It is also important in interpreting the results of factual surveys to recognize all the limitations of the consumer, dealer, or other respondent as a reporter.

Opinion Surveys. In these surveys the respondent is asked to express a personal attitude or opinion, to make an evaluation or appraisal, or to report his judgment on a particular matter. The respondent does not always realize that he is expressing an opinion, but on the other hand often believes that he is making a statement of fact. Unfortunately, researchers sometimes believe that they are obtaining facts when they actually are merely obtaining opinions. This confusion may be avoided if one obtains a clear understanding of the nature of an opinion survey.

An example of an opinion survey is one in which consumers are shown several alternative patterns or designs of a product and are asked, "Which design do you think is the most beautiful?" Other examples are illustrated by the following questions: "Which retail store in this community has the best variety of casual clothes?" and "What major appliance do you plan to buy during the next year?"

The opinion survey is used extensively in marketing and distribution research. It is employed to reflect consumer attitudes, in order that the marketing operations of the business may be planned in the light of a clear understanding of consumer attitudes and beliefs. The method is also used extensively in product analysis. Manufacturers learn how to meet the requirements of the market by obtaining consumers' likes and dislikes of different brands or of test models. Opinion surveys are frequently made in sales and dealer analyses to learn the attitudes of salesmen and dealers toward the company, its products, and sales methods. The consumer-jury method in advertising research is another example of the use of the opinion survey.

Interpretive Surveys. Here the person being interviewed acts as an interpreter as well as a reporter. An example of such a survey is one which asks, "Why do you use this brand of soap?" In this case the researcher relies upon the person interviewed for much more than mere reporting of a fact or stating of an opinion. The answers obtained to questions of this type are subject to all the limitations of the answers to factual and opinion questions, plus the inability of an individual consciously to evaluate his own feelings, motives, and other psychological drives. Even if the person interviewed can introspect effectively, the information sought is of a much more personal and intimate character than that which is usually asked when a factual survey is made. All these elements combine to make the use of the survey method in the interpretive form the least accurate of all procedures in market analysis.

CONSUMER BUYING HABITS SURVEY				
	1	**2**	**3**	**4**
Article	In what store did you last purchase each article?	What was the main reason for your buying there?	If you were to buy a similar article today, where would you shop first?	AND why would you change? (to be asked *only* if store in Col. 3 differs from store in Col. 1).
Silk Hosiery				
Woman's Cloth Coat				
Sheets or Sheeting				
Lingerie				
Woman's Shoes				
Drapes				
Man's Shirts				

FIGURE 7. Part of a Questionnaire Used by a Retailer. Note the use of the survey method in all three forms—factual, opinion, and interpretive.

There is a considerable difference of opinion as to the value of interpretive surveys. The prevalence of questionnaires asking *why* people do certain things, such as why particular brands of a product are bought or why certain types of stores are patronized, indicates that many researchers are inclined to accept the results at their face value.

Psychologists have focused attention on the large number of meaningless and confusing answers encountered whenever "why" questions are asked. In order to overcome this difficulty they have attempted to devise new methods of phrasing questions. For example, instead of asking, "Why do you use this brand?" they ask, "Why did you begin using this brand?" and "What feature of this brand appeals to you most?"

The problem of interpretive surveys cannot be solved by simple changes in the phrasing of questions. It is not a problem in questionnaire technique, but rather a fundamental problem in method. The danger of relying upon phrasing is illustrated by the use of the question "What caused you to begin using this brand?" as a means of obtaining a measurement of the relative importance of external influences, such as advertising and dealer display. In interviewing users of mouthwashes, for example, the majority of respondents would reply on the basis of conditions existing three, four, and five years ago, which may or may not be of value at the time the survey is made.

Because of the difficulties of obtaining accurate and usable information by interpretive surveys on subjects such as buying motives, many researchers have abandoned such attempts. It is now recognized that it is necessary to employ specialized techniques of motivational research to get sound knowledge of the type previously sought in interpretive surveys. These techniques are discussed in Chapter 18.

Limitations of the Survey Method. It is of the utmost importance that the marketing researcher clearly understand the limitations of the survey method. Chiefly, he must constantly bear in mind that a human being, the respondent, is always involved as a reporter or interpreter when the survey method is used. A thorough understanding of the psychology of the respondent in an interviewing situation is necessary to keep bias and errors to a minimum, and every possible expedient must be used to eliminate personal elements in gathering data. The use of the survey method must be restricted to requesting only those data which the individual respondent is in a position to furnish correctly.

In the discussion in later chapters many techniques and practices which overcome the technical limitations of the survey method are explained. In a more general sense, however, there are four specific practices which may be adopted to control the use of the survey method in such a way as to make it as scientific as possible. These are:

1. Careful phrasing of questions.
2. Careful control of data gathering.
3. Cautious interpretation.
4. Restricting the method to obtaining relative facts.

Careful phrasing of the questions employed in obtaining data by the survey method can go far toward overcoming the fundamental weaknesses of the procedure. By changing the question "Do you carry a camera with you when you travel?" to "Did you carry a camera with you on your last vacation trip?" the data obtained are made much more accurate and the whole survey becomes more scientific. A simple question like "How much do you pay for stockings?" may be asked in many different ways. H. G. Weaver has demonstrated the sharp differences obtained by asking, "Why do you prefer a Plymouth?" instead of "Why didn't you buy a Ford?" An experienced researcher can greatly improve the scientific accuracy of an investigation involving such a problem by phrasing the question according to recognized standards.

By carefully controlling the manner in which data are gathered one can also overcome many of the weaknesses of the survey method. The use of specially trained investigators who carefully observe and report on the subtle reactions of persons interviewed can make an investigation much more accurate than one in which investigators obtain answers to questions in a more or less mechanical manner.

Cautious interpretation of the facts obtained by the survey method is also important. A clear recognition of the limitations of the data and an understanding of exactly what they represent enable one to avoid many pitfalls. If one asks the question "What price would you be willing to pay for automatic gas heat?" he has nothing more nor less than the answers, consciously given, of the particular persons interviewed to this question. These answers may or may not be a clue to the price which should be established by a company selling automatic gas heat. If research workers who use the survey method are careful to bear constantly in mind the exact nature of the data which they have obtained, and then interpret them cautiously, one of the chief weaknesses of the survey method, as now practiced, may be overcome.

The restriction of the survey method to obtaining relative facts, as opposed to absolute facts, is one of the most important general principles to bear in mind. A single fact, even if stated in the form of a ratio, can be used only in an absolute manner. If that fact can be interpreted in its relationship to a similar fact, it is thereby placed on a relative basis.

An illustration is afforded by a dentifrice survey. This study showed that 83.3 per cent of the farm families covered used tooth paste. Taken by itself, in the absolute sense, the results of the survey are practically worthless, because the question asked encountered an obvious bias. However, if this finding is placed on a relative basis it may be of considerable value. A comparison of the percentage of farm families using tooth paste against the percentage of urban families using tooth paste may be highly significant, even though the individual figure for each group is incorrect. Absolute data obtained by the survey method may be placed on a relative basis by comparing them with data of different groups of persons covered within an individual study, for different geographic areas, for different occupational or income groups, or for different periods of time.

The difference in scientific accuracy which occurs when data are considered on a relative, rather than an absolute, basis, is clearly illustrated by the tooth paste survey mentioned above. The table below, which shows the results obtained at different periods of time, indicates at a glance that the 83.3 per cent usership found in the fourth study has more value when compared with the result of the three previous studies.

PERCENTAGE OF FARM FAMILIES USING TOOTH PASTE

Study	Percentage
1	86.3
2	88.7
3	84.5
4	83.3

While the survey method is theoretically the least scientific procedure employed in marketing research, it must be remembered that in practice it not only is a prevalent method but, if properly controlled, can be made thoroughly scientific. People in the main are honest; if questions are properly phrased and limited, they can and will respond accurately. Without the vast knowledge gleaned from surveys, marketing research would lack most of its present-day information. Checks on the validity of the survey method continually support the accuracy of its findings when carefully controlled. For example, an ingenious observational test of reading habits showed that, under proper conditions, surveys employing the recall technique can produce essentially valid results. The survey method should be used only when it is appropriate and the specific procedures used should be controlled carefully.

The Observational Method

The observational method relies upon direct observation of physical phenomena in the gathering of data. The observational method of marketing research is similar to the newer psychological approach which studies psychological problems from the physical and mechanical points of view, observing only overt behavior and drawing conclusions from the observed actions or responses. The older psychology relied largely upon introspection and the ability of individuals to describe their feelings, emotions, motives, method of thinking, and similar phenomena. Many psychologists have abandoned this procedure in favor of one which observes only the behavior of individuals and makes no effort to go directly into motives or nonphysical causes of behavior.

An example of the use of the observational method in marketing research is found in a study to determine the brands of food products used. If, instead of asking people what brands they use, the researcher makes a physical pantry inventory of brands actually in the home at the time the study is made or obtains sales data in retail stores, he is employing the observational method. Another example may be cited from studies which determine the extent of substitution. If a study is conducted on the basis of asking dealers the extent to which they can substitute another brand of a commodity for the one which the consumer requests, the survey method is being employed. If an observer is stationed in a store to record the percentage of women who ask for certain brands of the product and the percentage who accept substitutes, the observational method is being used.

In a study of sales efforts exerted by retail clerks, it was decided early in the research that it would not succeed in gathering reliable facts if it were confined merely to questioning dealers. If one were to ask the dealer or clerk whether he suggests the purchase of ties to shirt customers, the answer would invariably be "yes," because every dealer has been told to do so by various shirt and tie manufacturers. Therefore the observational method was the research procedure used to determine the precise extent to which such suggestions were actually made.

Another example is a study of the operations of filling stations. Investigators posed as normal customers, and then recorded what actually happened when they drove into service stations with less than five gallons of gasoline in their tank, their oil down one or two quarts, a tire badly deflated, and a dirty windshield.

The advantages of the observational method over the survey method are apparent. It is much more objective and accurate. It eliminates the human element of the respondent which is present in the use of the survey method. There is still a human element present in the form of the observer. But he is a specially trained individual, who is a reporter of physical behavior, and his work may be controlled and checked.

Furthermore, the observational method records actual market behavior. Expressed market action on the part of consumers and dealers is the ultimate aim of all marketing activities. Since the observational method directly measures some aspect of market behavior, it is in a sense working on the same plane on which the results of the research must be employed.

The observational method is usually much more costly than the survey method. If an observer is stationed in a retail store, for example, the speed at which he can work is limited by the flow of traffic and the frequency with which the phenomenon he seeks to observe occurs. If the observational method is used in consumer analysis, it usually involves gaining an entrance to the kitchen or another part of the home. The observational method is also restricted in its use because there are many phases of marketing research in which it has not yet been found possible to employ this method instead of the survey procedure.

Finally, this method gets at buying motives and other psychological factors only in so far as they are expressed in overt behavior. The method makes the logical assumption, in such instances, that the expressed or observed physical action provides a sufficient basis for interpreting the probable factors causing behavior. This assumption may or may not be true. The observational method shows only what people have done or are doing. One must recognize this limitation and be cautious in the interpretation of the results of the observational approach. It is especially important to keep in mind that inferences as to the motives which lie behind the actions observed should not be made unless they can be justified clearly on the basis of the evidence which has been obtained.

The Experimental Method

The general characteristics of the experimental method as a scientific procedure have already been discussed. In marketing and distribution research, the essentials of the experimental method are the use of sales as the criterion of success or failure, the measurement of the variation of one or a group of marketing activities which are presumed to influence sales in different degree or intensity (the factor being tested), and the elimination and control of other variables and conditions which may influence sales results.[1]

The experimental method is still largely in the pioneering stages of its development in marketing research. Frequently less accurate methods must be used in its place. There are some fields, however, in which its use has become extensive.

One rather common use of the experimental method is in testing marketing campaigns. For example, in order to obtain a more direct

[1] See William Applebaum and Richard Spears, "Controlled Experimentation in Marketing Research," *Journal of Marketing*, January, 1950, pp. 505–17.

measurement of the sales productivity of an advertising campaign than is afforded by other research tools, sales area tests are often employed. While the techniques for these tests are far from perfect, sufficiently accurate results have been found in a number of cases to indicate clearly that the experimental procedure is justified. As more sales area tests are made, the many variables encountered will be understood better, and as a result the proper means of controlling or accounting for these variables will be developed.

A second common application of the experimental method is in testing sales promotion devices. Some rather extensive work has been done in the use of store experiments. An example is a test made in nine Cleveland drugstores:

The method used was the store audit of sales procedure, consisting essentially of a count of sales of the merchandise in question, with and without displays, to determine the relative movement of goods. The hypothesis was that display of the merchandise would produce a sufficient increase in sales to cover the cost of the display, and leave a surplus. The chief variables were thought to be weather, season, special sales effort or display, and unanticipated store promotion in the form of advertising.

Two test stores and one control store were used from each of three major Cleveland chains. Merchandise was inventoried once each week for five weeks, and the weekly rate of flow of merchandise was calculated. In order to cancel out external influencing conditions, displays were kept in each test store for two weeks and then removed for two weeks, according to a prescribed rotation schedule.

At the end of the fifth week, sales for each store were totaled. Total sales increase for six stores with use of displays was 53 per cent, but increases of individual stores varied greatly. Because it was felt that extraneous variables had affected the result, adjustments had to be made on the basis of interviewer's "subjective reports of the conditions he found in the store." After such adjustments were made, sales increase due to display amounted to 31 per cent.

A third major use of the experimental method in marketing research is in determining prices. Tests are set up in which a commodity is offered at different price levels and careful records of the volume sold are made. In this way the marketing researcher takes the theoretical principle of elasticity of demand and translates it into marketing reality. A fourth use is in connection with tests of products and packages.

It was previously shown that a basic logical assumption of the experimental method is that the conditions of the test be essentially the same as those found in the situation in which the results of the tests are to be applied. In the case of the physical sciences, this requirement may be met with comparative ease because the scientist is dealing with relatively stable physical phenomena. In marketing research, however, one is dealing with the least stable of all elements —the human factors. With whims, fancies, and emotions playing an important part in determining market behavior, the whole subject matter of the analysis is exceedingly unstable. Since markets are subject to so many conditions which affect their response to any given commodity, have such wide differences among geographic areas, and are in a state of constant flux, it is very difficult to apply the experimental method. Yet, since this method is in principle the most scientific of all procedures the researcher constantly seeks to develop usable experimental techniques.

As was also shown in the earlier discussion, another assumption of the experimental method is the proper control of all variables except the one which is being measured. In an experiment on temperature, for example, if other variables which may affect the result are not properly controlled, the experiment will not be a success. In marketing and distribution research, there are three ways in which variables other than the one being measured may be controlled properly for experimental purposes, as follows:

1. Holding the other variables constant.
2. Rotation of the experiment.
3. Correction for variations.

The best examples of holding other variables constant will be found in the laboratories of the physical sciences. It is comparatively simple for the chemist, for example, to maintain constant conditions of temperature, atmospheric pressure, purity of materials, quantities employed, and other variables which may affect the result. In marketing experiments, on the other hand, this procedure cannot be employed except in a very limited manner. The habits and activities of the market are not under the control of the researcher. He must take marketing conditions as he finds them, for he has no technique for controlling the behavior of the individuals who make up the market. Some of the difficulties encountered in using the experimental method, including the impossibility of controlling all variables except the one which is being measured, are illustrated by advertising tests based upon the analysis of coupon returns. After a different series of advertisements has been run, the researcher is confronted with the question as to just exactly what has been tested. Among the different elements which have usually varied to a greater or less degree during the period of the experiment are the following items:

1. The media used.
2. The advertising theme.

3. The physical form of presentation, such as size of advertisement and layout arrangement.
4. The illustration.
5. Competitive offers.
6. Changes in retail store operations, particularly displays of merchandise.
7. Changes in market conditions which affect coupon returns, such as seasonal variations in coupon response, effects of weather, local business conditions, etc.

From this brief list it will be seen that there are many variables likely to enter into a marketing research test which cannot be directly controlled. In making an advertising test, such as the one mentioned, the researcher must first be careful to determine what one element is being tested, and then be sure that the others are held as constant as possible. If one seeks to test the sales productivity of different advertising themes, for example, it is possible to use exactly the same physical presentation and the same advertising medium in the test. Unfortunately, many researchers attempt to test several elements at the same time, with the result that they follow the form of the experimental method but are not proceeding scientifically.

The method of the rotation of tests to allow uncontrolled variables to offset each other is frequently employed in marketing and distribution research. It is theoretically possible to work out a plan whereby tests are set up concurrently in different markets and then rotated among the markets in such fashion that the many uncontrolled variables will counterbalance one another. A good example of this method is the sales area test of advertising. A schedule for the insertion of the advertisements in such an experiment is shown below. The reader will note that care has been exercised to provide for an

TABLE 4

SCHEDULE FOR COPY-TEST INSERTIONS

(For three different campaign themes. The numbers indicate the different themes.)

City	1st Period	2nd Period	3rd Period
Albany	#1	#2	#3
Utica	2	3	1
Erie	3	1	2
Elmira	1	2	3
Wichita	2	3	1
Canton	3	1	2
Peoria	1	2	3
Waterloo	2	3	1
Hartford	3	1	2

automatic rotation of both the advertisements and the markets so that differences in weather conditions, competitive efforts, and other uncontrolled variables encountered in the different markets will have an opportunity to offset one another, and the sales made during the period in which each advertisement is run may be attributed directly to the advertising.

The third method of controlling variables is to correct errors in the result caused by the influence of variables which have not been held constant or allowed to offset each other by rotation. In physics, it is not necessary that all factors be held absolutely constant. Certain laws relating to factors like temperature provide a basis on which to make corrections for temperature changes which have affected the results.

Unfortunately, this technique is almost unknown in marketing research. As experience is obtained, however, it will be possible to develop general principles or facts regarding matters such as seasonal sales variation, the effect of temperature on sales, and the effect of display on sales which may be stated with sufficient accuracy to make it possible to correct the results of marketing experiments, just as the scientist makes corrections in the physical laboratory.

The major difficulty in conducting experiments is clearly indicated by the foregoing discussion of the methods of controlling the variables encountered in such study. Differences in weather, advertising media, activities of competitors in local markets, dealer activity, composition of the population of different cities, and variations in buying power are examples of the many variables found. Marketing men, for instance, have listed over one hundred fifty variables which contribute to the difficulty of making dependable sales tests of advertising. The presence of so many elements which affect sales makes the use of the experimental method most difficult. At the same time, it also places a premium on knowledge of scientific procedure and the rare ability to analyze and control the variables. The presence of these variables, furthermore, offers a fascinating field for scientific exploration.

The experimental method is also limited in its application to marketing and distribution research because so many elements which one would like to test have too small an influence on sales to be isolated adequately in an experimental design. Such a multiplicity of factors affect sales volume to such a degree that the one which the experiment seeks to measure is totally obscured by other influences. Results such as those in Table 5, from an advertising test, are frequently encountered. It is obvious that the differences in sales recorded in the test are not sufficient to support any conclusions regarding the effect of the advertising.

TABLE 5

TOTAL UNIT SALES IN TEST STORES

Total Sales (Units)	1,796	100%
E advertising	393	22
A advertising	371	20
D advertising	354	20
C advertising	354	20
B advertising	324	18

The primary purpose of marketing experiments is to employ a more scientific method of solving given marketing problems. However, there are corollary research benefits that are extremely important. The first of these is that the conduct of the experiments leads to a more systematic development of new ideas for improving marketing procedure. To illustrate, an experiment may be set up to determine the relative effectiveness of three types of merchandise display ideas designated as A, B, and C. In the course of conducting the experiment it is quite likely that new ideas, D and E, not thought of in the original design of the experiment, will be developed. Thus experimentation in the market itself can well provide the source of productive innovations. Above all, however, the marketing experiment provides a basis for prediction in quantitative sales terms which can not be done as a result of a survey or purely observational procedure.

The Accuracy of Marketing Research Methods

The general merits and limitations of the three basic methods employed in marketing and distribution research (survey, observational, and experimental) have been discussed. However, a further discussion of the accuracy of the different techniques may prove of value to the researcher.

The contrast between the results obtained by the use of the observational and survey methods is shown in a study of the extent to which consumers specify the brands of commodities asked for, and the extent to which retail salespersons are able to switch customers from the brand requested to another brand. The investigation embraced 609 retail outlets in 5 cities. The salespeople were first asked questions about the extent to which buyers specified brands. The field investigators then personally checked 4,622 customer transactions, observing exactly what happened.

The following table shows the contrast between the results obtained in the two methods:

TABLE 6

PERCENTAGE OF CUSTOMERS NAMING A BRAND

Type of Outlet	Observational Method	Survey Method
Grocery stores	62.1	58.3
Department stores	61.2	64.3
Automotive	85.0	44.4
Drugstores	77.8	61.1
Home furnishings	62.8	40.8
Men's furnishings	35.1	34.3
Appliances, radios	80.0	39.8
Paint	73.0	53.6
Average	67.8	57.5

It will be noted that on this particular question the opinions of all salespeople interviewed by the survey method underestimated the percentage of brand specification by over 10 per cent. In certain lines, notably in automotive, home furnishings, and radios, the degree of overestimation was much greater than this.

Another check on the comparative accuracy of the survey and observational methods sheds light on the degree of inaccuracy injected in the survey method when a question that affects the pride of the person being interviewed is used. The results of the two methods, when used to determine the extent to which salesmen can switch customers from the brand requested to another brand, is shown in the following table:

TABLE 7

PERCENTAGE OF CUSTOMERS SPECIFYING A BRAND WHO
WERE SWITCHED TO ANOTHER BRAND

Type of Outlet	Observation of Customers	Opinion of Salespeople
Grocery stores	5.5	40.5
Department stores	21.6	32.4
Automotive	.5	49.0
Drugstores	6.7	41.7
Home furnishings	25.0	37.5
Men's furnishings	25.8	59.2
Appliances, radios	0.0	39.2
Paint	10.8	36.8
Average	6.9	41.6

The sharp difference between the results which are obtained by the two methods shows the futility of employing the survey method

for certain purposes. Here the observational method is clearly practicable, although somewhat more costly than the survey method. The
results, however, obviously justify the additional cost.

The writer conducted an exhaustive test of the relative accuracy
of the survey and observational methods when applied to a study of
brand preferences for a health product. A large number of persons
were asked, "What brand of —— do you use?" (survey method).
After the answer was recorded, the person interviewed was offered a
new package of the product in exchange for the package in the home,
and, when necessary, was made other offers which would be sufficiently
attractive to induce him to part with the product (observational
method).

The degree of error in the survey method is shown in the following table:

TABLE 8

RATIO OF NUMBER OF TIMES A GIVEN BRAND WAS ACTUALLY
PRODUCED TO NUMBER OF TIMES THE BRAND WAS NAMED

(Percentage of persons stating that they used a given brand who showed it.)

Brand	Ratio	Brand	Ratio
A	43.2%	H	45.5%
B	56.4	I	100.0
C	61.1	J	100.0
D	75.7	K	150.0
E	80.0	L	100.0
F	86.0	M	150.0
G	93.0		

Certain conclusions are very definitely indicated from this investigation. In the first place, there is a very clear tendency for well-
established, national brands to be named by persons who are not
using any brand of the product. By the survey method, less than 2 per
cent of the persons interviewed stated that they did not use the product. On the observational method it was found that over 20 per cent
of the persons interviewed did not use the product. Second, the
persons using brands possessing special qualities or used for special
purposes name the brand most accurately on the survey method.
Third, the brand which sells in very small volume is for the most part
reported accurately in the survey method.

Another indication of the relative accuracy of the survey and
observational methods may be found in the field of measuring radio
audiences. The survey method has been widely used to determine the
size of audiences for radio programs and total station circulation.

In 1936 a mechanical device to be placed on radio sets, which automatically records the station to which the set is tuned, was introduced. This device, of course, represented the observational method. During the period in which it was being tested, the results shown by the automatic recording device were compared with the information which would be obtained by the survey method.

It was found, for example, that the average person was able to report correctly, with unaided recall, the names of only 31 per cent of the programs to which he had listened on the preceding day. When a check sheet which listed the programs broadcast on the preceding day by fifteen-minute intervals was employed, it was found the people could remember 59 per cent of their actual listening experience, as shown by the mechanical recorder. In the latter case unaided recall was supplanted by recognition through the use of the check sheet. With this aid there was a significant increase in the accuracy of the survey method. It is most important, however, to note that under the best circumstances the limits of memory made the survey method highly inaccurate.

An illustration of the superiority of both the observational and experimental methods is provided by results of research on packaging of apples conducted at Cornell University. A national survey of over 3,000 housewives showed that approximately 85 per cent of the respondents preferred to purchase apples in bulk, giving the logical reason that the housewife has an opportunity to select the apples she wants. The University conducted experiments in which identical apples were offered for sale in bulk and in packages. It was found that 95 per cent of the customers chose the packaged apples. Furthermore, in the course of the experiment it was observed that buyers actually did not pick out the individual apples very often, as stated in the rationalization of respondents in the consumer survey.

In general, the survey method is the least scientific of the techniques used in marketing research. The observational method is more objective, and should be used in place of the survey method wherever practicable. The experimental method is theoretically the soundest of all scientific methods. But in view of the many practical limitations on its use and the pitfalls which arise from the difficulty of controlling all factors other than the phenomenon being studied, it is often impossible to employ this method satisfactorily. The marketing researcher is faced with the practical fact that the use of the experimental method may often remain an ideal toward which he should constantly strive, and that he must meanwhile work as effectively as possible with the survey or observational methods. It must also be kept in mind that there are many subjects studied in marketing research for which the survey method is the only proper technique, so this procedure will continue to be a basic one in spite of its limitations.

The Alternative Use of Marketing Research Methods

Earlier in the chapter the statement was made that in many marketing studies one has the opportunity of choosing among the three basic techniques. Frequently practical consideration points directly to the necessity of using one of the three techniques without seriously considering alternative possibilities at length. On the other hand, one of the chief weaknesses of marketing research as now practiced is the tendency to use the first method which comes to mind, without considering other more scientific methods.

In order to illustrate more clearly how one may gain by making an effort to determine the different methods which may be employed, an example from the breakfast cereal field may be cited. In this case the central problem was to determine whether the flavor of the product should be changed to make it more acceptable to the public. While many different approaches might be used in the case of this problem, the three most seriously considered were:

1. Asking consumers who had used this brand of cereal and discontinued its use why they had stopped.
2. Placing an ample supply of this cereal and three others in front of groups of people and making an accurate record of those which were voluntarily eaten.
3. Changing the formula for the product and conducting a test sales campaign.

The reader will notice that the first approach represents the survey method, the second the observational, and the third the experimental. The student will find it an interesting exercise to work out further variations of the different approaches. The important point to notice is that the three approaches are fundamentally different in terms of the scientific principles involved, and that there is a difference in the scientific validity of the conclusions which would be drawn from each of the different methods.

The Combination of Methods

It is often possible to combine the various procedures in a given marketing research. Some phases of the problem may be well adapted to the observational or experimental procedures, while other phases may of necessity call for the use of the survey method. In planning a research one should, therefore, carefully check each aspect to make sure that the best possible method is employed.

There are also occasions on which it is possible to employ two different methods in handling one phase of an analysis, so that the results of the two techniques may be used as a cross-check on reliability. In its product research, for example, the General Foods Corporation combines the survey with the experimental method. When a new product is introduced or when changes are made in packages, the first step is to send the innovation to a group of interested consumers to determine by the survey method whether they like the new product or package. Following this survey test, an experimental analysis is made in which actual sales tests are conducted in different markets.

One should also bear in mind the possibility of introducing some of the elements of the observational or experimental method into any operation, even though the method actually employed is not strictly observational or experimental. An example of an analysis which introduces some of the elements of the observational method, but which is still basically a survey, is found in a study of color preferences. If consumers are shown three samples of a product which are identical except for color and asked which color they prefer, the survey method is used. If on the other hand, the investigator records the order in which the consumers pick up the different products or the length of time each one is held in the hand, some of the objectivity of the observational method has been introduced. As a result, the research is more scientific than it would have been with a typical survey.

A clear understanding of the nature and implications of the three basic marketing research methods is one of the chief earmarks of a truly scientific research worker. Such an understanding far transcends clever manipulation of the minor techniques discussed from time to time later in this book. The researcher must have a keen appreciation of the strengths and weaknesses of each of the basic methods and a subtle understanding of their many vagaries. He must be constantly alert to the possibility of conducting his work on a more scientific basis by shifting to a better method. He must recognize the possibility of combining the methods in order to verify his findings. Where the more scientific methods are not open to him because of practical considerations, he must constantly seek to inject some of the elements of the better methods into the one he must use.

SELECTED READINGS

Holloway, Robert J. "Marketing Research Is More Than Surveys," *Journal of Marketing*, January, 1953, pp. 295–300.

PAYNE, STANLEY L. "The Ideal Model for Controlled Experiments," *Public Opinion Quarterly*, Fall, 1951.
SALISBURY, PHILIP. "Experts Pick Best Test Markets by Regions and Population Groups," *Sales Management*, November 10, 1953, pp. 110–45.

CASE

APPLEBAUM, WILLIAM, and SPEARS, RICHARD. "Controlled Experimentation in Marketing Research," *Journal of Marketing*, January, 1950, pp. 505–17.

Part II

MARKETING AND DISTRIBUTION
RESEARCH PRACTICE

6

MARKETING RESEARCH PROCEDURE

In Chapter 4 it was shown that one way of defining "scientific method" is to describe the specific procedure which is employed in any scientific field or in a specific study within that field. Chemistry, biology, and every other science has its own basic method. A competent scientist in any of these fields knows how to begin solving a problem, what step to take next, and how to proceed in an orderly manner through to the final solution. The purpose of this chapter is to describe briefly the basic procedure of marketing and distribution research which has grown out of the practice of this science. It is recognized today by leading practitioners as the unique procedure of this field of applied science. If this procedure is properly followed, it will insure the solution of a marketing or distribution problem in a scientific manner. In the chapters which follow in this section, each of these steps is discussed in detail.

Marketing and distribution research procedure involves eight basic steps. These are:

1. *The situation analysis (internal research)*. This first step is a complete survey of all available data pertinent to marketing regarding the company, its products, the industry, the market, sales practices and policies, the dealer situation, advertising, and similar matters. The information is gleaned from the internal records of the business and from readily available published material in libraries and trade papers. In this step the researcher seeks to obtain all the information he can about the problems of the company and the environment in which the study is to be made.

2. *The informal investigation*. In this step, the researcher and his assistants talk informally with consumers, dealers, and key men in the industry to get an impartial point of view and the "feel" of the problem. The study director has no notion of the form which the final research will take, but attempts to put his finger on the central problem by informal interviews.

3. *The formal research plan*. The specific procedure for carrying on the remainder of the investigation is determined at this point.

Various hypotheses are considered until the specific purposes for the research have been selected. The types and sources of data which are to be obtained are determined. Decisions are made as to the sample of data to be employed if observational or experimental methods are contemplated, or of people who are to be interviewed if the survey method is used. The various forms and instruction sheets are drawn up. Proposed methods of investigation are tested. The results of this planning work are summarized in a detailed written plan which becomes a basic guide for the conduct of the formal research.

4. *Collection of the data.* In this step the field work or organized collection of secondary data from various sources is carried on. After the practicability of the plan has been tested further the final field survey is made, observations are taken, or the experiments are conducted.

5. *Tabulation and analysis.* The field reports are edited, the sample is tested, and the data obtained are tabulated. The data are manipulated statistically so that they take the form of a series of statistical conclusions.

6. *Interpretation of results.* From the statistical summaries and conclusions which have been developed in the preceding step, the researcher now makes interpretations in terms of business policy. These interpretations may confirm the wisdom of policies already established, or they may point to fundamental changes in the conduct of the business. The final product of this stage is a series of specific recommendations.

7. *Presentation of the results.* This is a separate step in which the results of the research, now in a sense completed, are written in the most effective form for presentation to the executives of the firm and to others. The emphasis is on the preparation of the physical reports which will insure that the results will be clearly understood and the recommendations accepted.

8. *Follow-up.* This final step is most important. While some persons consider the work of the research completed upon the presentation of a good report, the ultimate test of its value is the extent to which recommendations are actually put into practice and the results are achieved.

How to Apply the Procedure. The basic procedure which has been outlined above and which will be discussed in greater detail later has been developed from the experience of many persons engaged in marketing and distribution research work. As in other fields, different researchers will make various modifications. Some steps are at times combined with others, and others added. Furthermore, in any given situation or problem, the procedure will often be altered according to the requirements of the specific case.

On the other hand, a procedure which follows a series of steps similar to those outlined must be followed in any scientific marketing research. Furthermore, the basic procedure explained here will fit most cases. Where a research is being made for a new product, or where the individual conducting the research is working with a specific product for the first time, the procedure will be followed in nearly all of its details. However, once a comprehensive situation analysis has been made, it is, of course, no longer necessary to repeat this step. In certain specific types of marketing and distribution research, such as quantitative analysis, one begins with a clear definition of purpose, then proceeds directly to the gathering and statistical analysis of data. Also, in an established marketing research department, most studies begin with the formal research plan.

In any specific research several of the steps mentioned above will be in progress at any given time. While the situation analysis should be well under way before the informal investigation is begun, it is not necessary that the first step be completed before the second is undertaken. Nor is it necessary that the informal investigation be completed before planning the analysis. Some thought should be given to the plan shortly after the situation analysis is begun. Preliminary field work should be started during the planning stage, and while none of the data obtained may be employed in the final analysis, sometimes information obtained in test questionnaires, observations, or experiments can be used. If the tabulation and analysis of field data are begun as soon as the first reports from the field are received, waste and delay are avoided. The interpretation of results is the sixth step, but the researcher looks forward to the interpretations which will be made during the third step of planning the investigation. Similarly, the work in the last two steps is undertaken before the preceding ones are completed.

The research process consists of a number of closely related activities which overlap continuously rather than follow a strictly prescribed sequence. So interdependent are these activities that the first step of a research project largely determines the nature of the last. If subsequent procedures have not been taken into account in the early stages, serious difficulties may arise and prevent the completion of a study. Frequently these difficulties cannot be remedied at the time when they become apparent, because they are rooted in the earlier procedures. They can be avoided only by keeping in mind, at each step of the research process, the requirements of subsequent steps.[1]

[1] Marie Jahoda, Morton Deutsch, and Stuart W. Cook, *Research Methods in Social Relations* (New York: The Dryden Press, 1951), p. 3.

Under no circumstances should one attempt to complete any step of a research before the preceding one is undertaken and well along. In actual practice one must constantly "back up" at several times during the research, returning to preceding stages. Sometimes errors in planning have been made which appear during the later steps; often it is found that important elements which were overlooked in the earlier stages must be brought into the research; and sometimes it is even necessary to begin a large part of the operation over again as the result of some condition which is not revealed until the study seems to be almost completed.

While several steps in the research are in progress at one time, it does not follow that the order in which the major steps are taken is unimportant. Many marketing researchers fail because the persons in charge have not begun in the right manner and do not proceed from one step to the next in logical order. The most common error is to undertake field work before an adequate plan for the investigation has been carefully prepared. Another frequent error is to attempt to develop a sound plan for an investigation without carrying on the informal investigation as discussed in this book. Without the informal investigation, the person in charge of the marketing research does not have the proper feel of the market, and is almost certain to plan a study which is superficial, impracticable, and unproductive. It is just as great an error to attempt to plan the investigation before conducting the situation analysis. The researcher who does not have an adequate intimate background of the company and the market, provided by the situation analysis, is a tragic figure. He is likely to make blundering mistakes which grow out of his ignorance of the facts to be considered in planning the research. Interpretations carried too far before the tabulations are completed are likely to result in a crystallized point of view which prejudices the researcher against accepting the real facts found in the field work.

A Case Illustrating Marketing Research Procedure. Each of the major steps in marketing and distribution research will be discussed in further detail in the remainder of this chapter. An example of a study of the market for a white floating soap will be frequently drawn on to illustrate the procedure. A relatively simple case has been chosen for this purpose, in order that the various steps in the scientific conduct of marketing and distribution research will be most clearly demonstrated. The case does not represent a model in the sense that the best research techniques were employed; for example, in the construction of the questionnaire. The reader will note several improvements which could be made in the light of discussions of techniques in other parts of the book. However, the case provides a most understandable example of procedure.

Step 1. The Situation Analysis (Internal Research). The objective of the situation analysis is to gather and analyze all available data on the marketing activities of the firm and its competitors which have an important bearing on contemplated research. This exhaustive study of all accumulated data serves several purposes. In the first place, it provides an adequate background for the proper planning and execution of the analysis. Second, it lays a foundation for the development of possible hypotheses for the study. Third, it shows the researcher how to avoid many potential pitfalls which he might otherwise encounter, especially in making his interpretations and recommendations. Fourth, it insures that there will be no useless repetition of work.

In carrying out the situation analysis, an exhaustive search should be made of all company records and other data which may have a bearing upon the company's marketing activities. An example of the value of such information may be found in the study for a white floating soap. It would be impossible to attempt to reproduce all the information obtained in the situation analysis for this product, or even to show all the facts which helped give direction to the study. But a few of the findings will indicate how such data made important contributions to the background of the persons planning the analysis, pointed to certain hypotheses, showed several pitfalls to be avoided, and discovered phases of the problem which had already been adequately researched.

The most important facts gained in the situation analysis for this product included the following:

1. The soap industry employed extremely aggressive sales and promotion marketing, with very large advertising expenditures.
2. The company had had a white floating soap on the market for many years, with very small advertising support, and with a record of constantly declining sales.
3. There was a large established market for white floating soaps.
4. The soap division was regarded as a side-line operation of the company.
5. The selling and advertising methods which had been employed by the division were generally far inferior to those of competitors.
6. Any effort to expand sales would require the addition of a superior product with aggressive promotion.
7. The laboratory had developed a new white floating product which gave genuine promise of market possibility.

Step 2. The Informal Investigation. The purpose of the informal investigation is to obtain an intimate "feel" of the market by making exploratory interviews with consumers, dealers, and key executives. As the name suggests, these interviews are made without any organized questionnaire approach and with as open a mind as possible. The purpose of each of the interviews is to cause the respondent to talk freely about the product, its market, and other related subjects.

The most important single purpose of the informal investigation is to help uncover additional hypotheses for the formal research investigation. The researcher is here mining for important ideas which will give him a clue to the direction which the study should later take. Many possible hypotheses will have been discovered in the situation analysis. In the informal investigation many new ones will be added. In addition, the project director will begin to form a mental appraisal of the relative value of the various hypotheses which have occurred to him.

Since no definite form or schedule is employed in conducting the informal investigation, it is impossible to tabulate its results and prepare a statistical report. Furthermore, such a treatment of the results of the informal investigation would not be desirable. If various persons are involved in this step of the analysis, they usually prepare running reports on the individual interviews which have been made. Examples of the various forms which these reports may take are shown in the discussion of the informal investigation in Chapter 8.

In the study of the market for the white floating soap, many valuable facts were discovered in the informal investigation. In the consumer interviews it was found that a wide variety of brands of toilet and bath soap was used by consumers, that usually several different brands were used within each family, and that individual members of the family frequently used different soaps for different purposes. It was also revealed that there was a considerable tendency to purchase soap at special bargain prices. Consumers were buying in fairly large quantities, and at any given time they were likely to have a considerable stock on hand. It was found that several brands were purchased for specialized uses and that consumers were inclined to be either strongly addicted to their use or strongly prejudiced against them. It was discovered that many consumers objected to the odor of certain brands, and that the size and shape of the bar itself were important considerations.

In the dealer interviews it was revealed that the most important outlet for soaps was the food store, but that certain types of drugstores were recapturing their position in the retail field. The importance of syndicate stores also was brought out. It was found that a vast majority of dealers were actually selling a relatively small volume of soap and that this was made up of many different brands. Dealers clearly indicated that they were not interested in adding a new brand of soap unless given a special incentive, since they believed they were already carrying too many varieties. The dealer investigation further showed that the margin of profit on soaps was very low. A fairly large proportion of the dealers interviewed stated that their largest selling soap was Ivory, which was directly competitive with the white floating soap being studied.

Interviews with key executives were not particularly productive in this study because they tended largely to confirm information already brought out in the interviews with dealers and in the situation analysis. It was found, however, that they recognized the need of intensive promotion of a new item in order to stimulate the activity of the soap division, and that they would be receptive to any practicable ideas.

After a sufficient number of calls had been made on consumers, dealers, and key executives and no important new ideas had been developed, it became clear that further interviews would result largely in mere repetition, and those in charge of the investigation were ready for the third step—planning the formal research project.

Step 3. Planning the Formal Research Project. In many respects this step is the heart of the entire research operation. Here the skill and care with which the situation analysis and the informal investigation have been conducted bear fruit. The plan which is developed at this point determines the course of the remainder of the analysis and hence may be regarded as the most vital part of the entire operation.

In the preparation of the plan, it is important that a specific procedure be followed as exactly as possible. The essential elements in making the plans, in the order in which they should be carried out, are as follows:

1. Determining the purpose of the investigation.
2. Determining the types and sources of data to be obtained.
3. Preparing the forms to be used in gathering data.
4. Planning the samples.
5. Conducting the test investigation.
6. Determining operating plans and costs.

Determining the Purpose of the Investigation. In this phase of the work the researcher carefully weighs the merits of the many hypotheses which have been suggested in the situation analysis and informal investigation. It is probable that there will be many suggested hypotheses, each one of which holds some promise of providing a basis for research that will contribute to the success of the marketing operations of the company.

It is generally recognized, however, that one of the most important considerations in the development of research is the limitation of the study to a small number of workable hypotheses. This means that it is necessary to reject scores of possible hypotheses and to arrive at the very few to be carried through the remainder of the investigation. In this stage of the work it is usually helpful to prepare a list of those hypotheses which will probably be of value and then to challenge the usefulness of each one. The hypotheses finally selected then become the purposes or objects of the analysis.

Sometimes the selection of the hypothesis is primarily a matter of limiting the investigation to a sufficiently small number of hypotheses. The use of a price hypothesis is an example. If it has been decided as a result of the situation analysis and informal investigation that the current price charged consumers is too high or too low for the best marketing results, it is sufficient to state the purpose of the research based on this hypothesis in the following form:

> To determine the effect of different price levels on quantities sold and profits realized.

This may be done because the technique for completing an investigation hinging upon a price hypothesis is rather clearly established.

On the other hand, the subject covered in the hypothesis may lead to many forms of statements and methods of treatment. In such a case it is important in this step to develop the exact statement of the hypothesis which will be of greatest value when solved. An example of a hypothesis of this type is one which relates to the types of advertising media which the company should use. One might state the hypothesis in the following form:

> What types of advertising media should the X Company use?

This statement is entirely too vague and general to be a working hypothesis. The hypothesis should be stated in some form such as:

> The X Company should discontinue its radio programs.

There are many other forms of specific hypotheses which might be used in connection with an analysis relating to the types of advertising media which a given firm should use. The one which has been cited as an example illustrates the point that the exact form in which the hypothesis is stated is an important consideration in this first step in planning the analysis.

After the various possible hypotheses have been carefully considered, the researcher arrives at a small group of carefully stated purposes and is ready for the next step.

In the white floating soap research, many hypotheses were considered and rejected. A good deal of thought was given to problems of distribution as a result of leads developed during the informal investigation with dealers. Consideration was also given to various hypotheses which might have been tested by a consumer survey of usage, preferences, attitudes, etc. However, the findings of the situation analysis led to the conclusion that all other considerations were secondary to that of the marketing possibilities of the new white floating soap which the laboratory had developed.

Accordingly, this research centered around a single hypothesis and therefore a single basic purpose for the balance of the investigation. The hypothesis was *that the new white floating soap, with possible minor modifications, would have sufficient consumer preference so that it could be marketed in profitable volume.* Therefore, the first phase of the planning step led to the following statement of purposes of the research:

1. To determine whether the new variety of white floating soap developed in the laboratory has sufficient consumer acceptance to warrant placing it on the market.
2. To determine what characteristics of scent, size, shape, and color in a toilet soap are most desired by consumers.

Determining the Types and Sources of Data. Two types of data are employed in marketing and distribution research: primary data and secondary data. Primary data may be defined as those data which are obtained directly for the purpose of a specific study. Secondary data are those which have been obtained with some other purpose in mind, and which are available from general sources such as libraries or from company records. In some research investigations, secondary data play an important part. An example is quantitative market analysis, which generally uses a great mass of readily available statistics regarding the market.

In the testing of any given hypothesis, it is possible to employ many different kinds of data. Thus, in the investigation of a price hypothesis the following data may be used:

1. Statements of consumers on what constitutes a reasonable price for the article.
2. Competitive prices taken from catalogs.
3. Competitive prices obtained from retail advertisements.
4. Competitive prices taken from price tags in stores.

5. Published data which show the trend of prices in this and related fields.
6. Estimates of retailers as to the prices which would obtain a maximum volume.
7. Estimates of wholesalers and jobbers as to the best price to be used.
8. Carefully controlled experiments which will yield data on the quantities taken at different price levels.

This list is by no means complete. Many other types and sources of data, both primary and secondary, may be used in testing a price hypothesis. Consideration of the exact nature of the data which could be obtained from each of the eight types and sources listed above will show clearly how important it is to make a careful appraisal of each. It is obvious that they would not yield answers to a price hypothesis which would be of equal value. With some consideration, most people would agree that statements of consumers on what constitutes a reasonable price would be valueless, yet many researches have been made in which such data were employed exclusively. Data from list prices in catalogs would fail to reflect the effects of discounts to particular types of outlets or the effect of price-cutting. Data taken from retail advertisements would probably overemphasize the cut prices placed on items used as leaders.

The list also illustrates the further principle that at times two or even three different types and sources may be combined in a given analysis to produce the best possible testing of the hypothesis. For example, it is clear that data obtained in carefully controlled experiments are far superior to those obtained from most of the other types and sources of data mentioned. However, one would probably find it a valuable contribution to the analysis if he were to obtain published data showing the trend of prices in the field.

In connection with determining the types and sources of data, a decision must also be made as to whether primary data are to be obtained by means of personal investigators, by mail, or by telephone.

In the case of the white floating soap research, the three following types and sources of data for the resolution of the chosen hypothesis were considered:

1. Survey type data, consumers as source.
   (This would involve asking consumers questions designed to obtain reactions to the new soap and preferences regarding size, color, scent, etc., in toilet soaps.)
2. Observational type data, consumers as source.
   (This would involve leaving supplies of different soaps with consumers and observing quantities of each variety used most rapidly.)

3. Experimental type data, retail stores as source.
(This would involve making up quantities of the new soap in different variations of scent, shape, color, etc., and conducting test marketing campaigns, using retail store audits to measure results.

There are, of course, many other types and sources of data which might be employed to meet the purposes of this research. For a variety of reasons, including the impracticability of producing the new product in large quantities and the belief that it would need to obtain marked consumer preference to show promise of potential marketing success, it was decided in the white floating soap case to use survey type data with consumers as the source. It was also decided to use personal interviews.

Preparation of the Forms to Be Used in Obtaining Data. Having determined the types and sources of data which will be the most productive in testing the hypothesis set up for the study, the researcher next prepares the forms or schedules to be employed in obtaining the information. If the survey method is to be used, it will be necessary to prepare a questionnaire. If the observational method is to be employed, forms must be drawn up to provide for correctly recording the exact data which are needed. If the experimental method is to be used, a description of the form of the experiment and a schedule on which the data are to be recorded must be prepared.

In the white floating soap case, since the survey method was to be employed, the preparation of forms centered around the design of a questionnaire. A generalized kind of interview, in which consumers would be asked questions regarding brands of soap used and general preferences regarding specific qualities, such as size and scent, was the most obvious route to be taken. The research director also considered showing samples of the new laboratory soap and obtaining general reactions. However, it was clear that such an approach would be much too loose, providing data of extremely dubious value.

Accordingly, the preparation of forms involved the design of a questionnaire to be used with kits of soap samples. The questionnaire is shown in Figure 8. Two kits, each containing one bar of each of various types of soap, were designed, to be used as indicated by Question 4 of the questionnaire. Kit A contained a new test bar of soap which had been developed in the experimental laboratory. This bar, called "New Soap" on the questionnaire, was essentially similar to the old white floating soap but with some changes in scent, size, shape, and color. A cake of Ivory soap, the outstanding brand in the white floating soap field, and a cake of the old white floating soap ("Old Soap" on the questionnaire), which the company had been

WHITE FLOATING SOAP ANALYSIS

Size of Household .... Nationality .... A ☐ B ☐ C ☐

1. What brand or brands of soap do you use for
    (a) Dishwashing ....
    (b) Regular Laundry ....
    (c) Fine Fabrics Wash ....

2. What brand or brands of soap does your family use for toilet and bath?

	For Face and Hands	For Bath	Why	How Long Used
Husband				
Wife				
Grown daughters (over 14)				
Children (under 14)				
Maid				

3. (a) Did you ever use Old Soap? Yes ☐ No ☐
    (b) If so, for what purpose?....................................
    (c) *Did you ever hear of Old Soap? Yes ☐ No ☐
    (d) *What kind of soap do you think it is?.........................

Investigator: Show each housewife a cake of each of the sample soaps and ask her the following questions:

4. **How do you rank the soaps from the standpoint of:

Kit (A)

Scent	Size	Shape of Bar	Color
New Soap ☐	New Soap ☐	New Soap ☐	New Soap ☐
Ivory ☐	Ivory ☐	Ivory ☐	Ivory ☐
Old Soap ☐	Old Soap ☐	Old Soap ☐	Old Soap ☐
No Choice ☐	No Choice ☐	No Choice ☐	No Choice ☐

Kit (B)

Scent	Size	Shape of Bar	Color
New Soap ☐	New Soap ☐	New Soap ☐	New Soap ☐
Camay ☐	Camay ☐	Camay ☐	Camay ☐
Palmolive ☐	Palmolive ☐	Palmolive ☐	Palmolive ☐
Lifebuoy ☐	Lifebuoy ☐	Lifebuoy ☐	Lifebuoy ☐
No Choice ☐	No Choice ☐	No Choice ☐	No Choice ☐

* To be asked only if question 3a is answered in the negative.
** Indicate rank by numbering the proper squares 1, 2, and 3. If the respondent ranks two soaps equally, indicate the tie by numbering each of their squares with the same number.

FIGURE 8. Questionnaire Used in the White Floating Soap Research

making in the past, completed the contents of Kit A. Kit B contained a bar of the new soap and one each of the three brands on the market which represented variations in scent, size, shape, and color. The two kits were shown to persons interviewed separately, and their selections were recorded as indicated on the questionnaire.

Planning the Sample. At this stage in planning the study, it is necessary to determine the exact nature of the sample which is to be taken. If consumers or dealers are to be interviewed, the researcher must decide how many calls should be made and how they are to be distributed. If the observational method is to be employed, he must determine how many observations must be taken and where they shall be made. If the experimental method is to be used, he must determine such factors as the locations at which the experiments are to be conducted, the length of time they are to run, and the number and types of stores to be checked.

If in the white floating soap case accurate data on brand usage for the total U. S. market or fine measurements of consumer preferences as to characteristics such as color in various geographic areas were required, it would have been necessary to design a national probability sample involving 2,500 to 5,000 interviews, depending on the sampling accuracy desired. However, the situation analysis had revealed that the company already possessed adequate information on brand usage, which in turn reflected general preferences of consumers regarding the physical characteristics of soap. Furthermore, the problem centered about a new product with special characteristics. Therefore the research, from the point of view of sample requirements, fell into the area of product testing, for which samplings of 200 to 300 cases with limited geographic distribution have been empirically established by marketing research practice. The quota method of sampling representative types of users, which has proved adequate for product research, was selected.

It was decided to conduct the research in three markets reflecting various water conditions, and to limit the work to metropolitan areas on the principle that a successful result in this type of market would be essential to marketing success. Approximately 200 interviews were to be made in each market. These were distributed into various areas within each market, by selecting representative blocks on the basis of analysis of statistical information regarding each market. It was also decided to interview every second household on one side of selected streets to assure a random distribution of interviews within each of the subareas of each market. Finally, a complete sampling plan was drawn up, showing precisely how the final sample of qualified respondents was to be obtained.

Conducting the Test Investigation. By this time the research has reached a point where the plan is ready to be tested on a small scale. Ample provision must be made for a test investigation large enough to provide some evidence that the hypotheses are proper and workable. The forms for gathering field data are tested and retested, so that, for example, the various difficulties encountered in the use of the questionnaire are overcome by revision. The preliminary drafts of instructions to interviewers or observers are tested by giving them to new workers and checking their work. Specific problems in sampling, which arise from field conditions, are discovered. New ideas for reconstructing all phases of the plan for the final investigation are developed through repeated testing and retesting of its various phases.

In the white floating soap case, relatively few interviews with consumers, using models of the kits, were necessary. Little difficulty was experienced with the questionnaire, since it called for information which is frequently taken in marketing research. The first models of the kits proved to be workable. Furthermore, the use of the kits themselves provided a physical device which greatly facilitated the entire interviewing process.

Determining Operating Plans and Costs. After the first five steps in planning the research have been completed, a comprehensive written plan is prepared. The plan usually includes a statement of the purpose of the investigation and of the reasons for the operation as recommended. Copies of the questionnaires and schedules to be employed are shown, with a careful explanation of the manner in which they are to be used. A detailed statement of the sample which will be obtained and where the study will be conducted is accompanied by reasons or evidence. Finally, the entire operation is costed as carefully as possible, so that budgets may be set up to cover the total expenses of the study.

The plan which is written at this stage is usually subject to considerable later revision. At this point, however, the progress of the study will be expedited greatly if the plan is written up in the form of a complete guidebook. In the case of one comprehensive study, such a plan embraced fifty-two single-spaced typewritten pages. The final plan should be duplicated so that several persons can have working copies.

Step 4. Collection of the Data. To the extent that the survey method is employed in the research, it is necessary to obtain interviews with individuals, asking them questions. This raises important considerations relating to the technique of interviewing. If the observational method is employed, it is necessary to set up a procedure for making the actual observations. If the experimental method is used, the experiment must be very carefully controlled so as to conform with the scientific principles involved in the application of this procedure.

In nearly all cases, a rather extensive personnel is employed. The primary emphasis in this phase of the work is upon the proper selection, training, and supervision of the persons who are responsible for data gathering.

No matter how carefully the analysis is planned up to this point, conditions which cannot be anticipated are bound to arise when the actual field work gets under way. The test investigation should be carried far enough to make clear that no serious mistakes will be encountered in the analysis and to demonstrate that the study, when carried to its completion, will be successful. Even so, special problems are bound to arise in the conduct of field work. Therefore, adequate supervision and training, constant checking, and close communication during the entire data-gathering process are essential.

In the research for the white floating soap, no secondary data were gathered at this stage. To insure a successful analysis, as soon as the original plan for the investigation had been made, a sufficient number of interviews were conducted in one area to make sure that there were no important errors remaining in the construction of the questionnaire and to insure that the data obtained would be adequate to check the hypotheses which had been set up. The rest of the investigators were then obtained, trained, and sent into the field under careful supervision. Little difficulty was experienced in the field operation.

Step 5. Tabulation and Analysis. Many persons make the mistake of regarding the tabulation and analysis of marketing research work as a routine operation. As will be shown later, tabulation involves far more than mere counting, and the proper analysis of data calls for a very high type of training. Tabulation and analysis should not be turned over to assistants to be carried on without a specific procedure. A very definite order should be followed step by step. Each is important and calls for a thorough understanding of the techniques which should be employed. There are four basic operations:

1. Editing primary data.
2. Validating the sample.
3. Tabulating.
4. Drawing statistical conclusions.

Editing Primary Data. As soon as reports have been received from the field, they are carefully scrutinized by an editor. The purpose of this editing is twofold: to eliminate errors in data, and to prepare the data for tabulation.

In order to eliminate errors found in the data, illogical, doubtful, and obviously inaccurate answers are rejected. Where there is considerable doubt as to the accuracy of the information reported from any one interview, series of observations, or experiments, the entire schedule will be rejected. Sometimes it is possible, by careful scrutiny of the report, to determine the nature of the error and correct the return.

The second purpose of editing—to prepare the data for tabulation—is of equal importance. Many changes which will facilitate and insure the accuracy of the tabulation can be made on the reports. Whenever periods of time or measurement are involved, data will not usually be reported consistently. If a questionnaire reports the size of a room, for example, different linear measurements will be found, such as yards, feet, and inches. In addition, some of the schedules will report in terms of square feet or square yards, whereas others will merely give the data for the length and width of the room. A questionnaire calling for such information will, of course, attempt to standardize the answers as nearly as possible. It will always be found, nevertheless, that a certain number of questionnaires will not conform to the standards set up. It is important to reduce all such reports to a standard unit. If machine tabulation is employed, the original forms are coded or the data are transferred to coding sheets.

The study of white floating soap presents some interesting examples of problems encountered in editing. The field supervisor went over each schedule carefully with the interviewer, checking all doubtful points. Many errors on the part of housewives were detected. It was also found that the interviewers made many mechanical errors in recording data. The most serious mistakes, however, were those which appeared as a result of the prompting which interviewers gave to the consumer in order to facilitate the interview. By challenging results which seemed improbable, it was found that some interviewers had presented questions in such form that they were "leading," hence the answers did not represent the facts. Entire questionnaires were rejected in some cases. In others, the answers to individual questions were thrown out before the tabulation. In this way the errors made in the gathering of the data were eliminated.

The questionnaires were also prepared for tabulation. One problem was to reduce all answers to common units, as in the last part of Question 2 (page 130) which asked, "How long used?" Some of the different units found in answers to this question were days, weeks, months, and years. Several questionnaires showed the month and year in which the family had begun using the particular brand. All these different replies had to be standardized in the single unit of months, which was selected as the basis for tabulation. In Question 3(b), which asked, "If so, for what purpose?" it was necessary to establish classifications to be used in the tabulation. Most of the questionnaires had a different answer to this question, yet 80 per cent of the answers could be grouped into five major classifications. By setting up these major classifications in advance, it was much easier to tabulate consistently and accurately. The answers to other questions were standardized in the same manner.

Validation of the Sample. In the planning of the field work, care has presumably been exercised in determining the exact nature of the sample which will be taken. After the data have been gathered, however, it is necessary that the sample be checked carefully. This is essential for several reasons. In the first place, in planning the sample, it is necessary to estimate the number of cases to be obtained and their distribution. True, this is done on the basis of sound principles, but these principles are subject to severe limitation in practice. In the second place, the many standards and procedures established in order to insure a sound sample may or may not have been closely followed. A third reason for carefully testing a sample is that many unforeseen elements arise in the field which may require the gathering of additional data. For example, the geographic distribution of the sample which was planned may have appeared to be sound. But as the field work proceeds, unexpected strength of regional brands may make it necessary to carry on further field work in certain sections. Fourth, a test of the soundness of the sample based upon the actual cases which are included in the analysis provides specific proof for the final report. Business executives, as well as research men, raise frequent questions about the soundness of the sample employed in marketing research. If one can demonstrate that he has validated the sample involved in the study, he will create confidence in its results.

The samples employed in marketing research are validated in several different ways. If the sample has been designed on a probability basis, statistical estimates of error due to sampling per se are computed. This procedure would be employed, for example, in the case of a large consumer survey, selection of data for a store audit sales analysis, or a sampling of dealer names from company records. If a quota type of sample is employed, it is first tested to determine whether enough cases have been obtained to produce stability, and then certain of the sample findings are checked against outside sources for representativeness. The most common test of stability for a quota sample is to break the sample down into small units and determine whether the addition of groups of data significantly changes the result on certain key items. The most common checks against outside

sources in the case of a consumer sample are on population characteristics, such as the distribution of the sample by age, sex, economic
class, etc., against census data, to make sure that there are no
major distortions in any respect. In the case of an industrial study,
samples are usually checked against census data on size and type of
establishment, geographical location, etc. In case dealers are involved,
the distribution of the data according to size of store, commodity
class, and type of establishment, such as chain and independent
stores, is compared with the distribution of census data.

In the case of the white floating soap example, the questionnaires
were arranged in random order, and tabulations on preferences for the
brands of soap used in the kits were tabulated in groups of fifty. As
these were accumulated, it became clear that no significant change
would occur if interviews were added. The distribution of respondents
according to age and economic class was compared with census data
and since there were no major discrepancies, the sample was acceptable for purposes of this research.

Tabulating. After the field data have been edited and the validity
of the sample has been established, the researcher is ready for the
third operation in tabulation and analysis. This is the actual tabulation of the data. The purpose of the tabulation is to provide a series
of tables which summarize in the most usable form the quantitative
results of the study. While in one sense tabulation is essentially a
counting procedure, it should be borne in mind that effective tabulation involves much more than accurate counting. In the first place, one
is faced with the question of what to count. While it would appear that
the questionnaires, reports of observations, or results of experiments
would automatically indicate what should be counted, there are many
decisions which must be made in the tabulation stage. While straight
counting is often used, as in a simple tabulation of the number of persons using given brands of a commodity, the tables which establish
relationships usually provide the most valuable information. As soon
as one goes beyond a mere counting of the number of persons using a
given brand of a commodity and relates this use to some element such
as sex, age, or economic status, significant relationships begin to
appear.

In the white floating soap case, after the sample had been tested,
the tabulation sheets were drawn up. Several alternative forms for
tabulating the data were considered. Each question might have been
tabulated separately, but this would disclose no significant relationships, except those which were inherent in Question 2. It was, therefore, decided to tabulate all questions by the economic status of the
family and the size of the household, and to tabulate Question 4 by

the type and brand of soap being used by the person whose selections were observed.

To insure accuracy and economy in the tabulation, forms which could be used with a minimum of effort were designed. For example, the work of counting was considerably reduced by transferring the headings of a proposed table from the top of the sheet to the side. The tabulators were separated into groups which specialized in certain phases of the work. Supervisors checked the accuracy of the work of each group at different stages in the tabulation. The results of the tabulation were summarized in a series of carefully headed tables.

Drawing Statistical Conclusions. This is the final phase of the tabulation and analysis step. Here the data which have been tabulated are further manipulated until the best form of statistical summarization has been obtained. Sometimes a well-organized table is sufficient, but usually it is necessary to go further. Frequency distributions, percentages, and averages of many types are examples of forms of statistical summarization which may be used. Great care must be exercised in determining the form of statistical summarization which best fits the data and which will be of greatest value in the interpretive work to follow. Sometimes it will be found that more complex forms of summarization, such as the various measures of dispersion and correlation, will prove of value. The chief problem is to select the type or types of statistical analysis which will state the conclusions in the most useful form.

In the white floating soap research, after the tabulation had been completed, it was necessary to choose the forms of generalization in which the results should be stated. The information obtained on brands in Questions 1 and 2 was grouped into various types of soaps, each of which was further broken down into the leading brands and "all others." The percentage of all families using each major color, shape, size, and scent type of bar soap was then calculated. In Question 2, the data on the length of time used were expressed in a frequency distribution, showing the percentage of families who had used each type less than 12 months, from 12 to 23 months, etc. Question 4 presented some interesting possibilities of statistical generalizations. In addition to the correlation of the answers with other facts, such as type of family, nationality, and brand used, the importance of the various elements of scent and size was determined on the basis of ranks assigned by the persons interviewed. This might have been done by a weighting process which would give three points for every first choice, two for every second choice, and one for every third choice. The total "votes" which each brand or type received would measure its popularity. This procedure is very common, but it would not have been nearly as productive in this case as another which was used. It was found that a direct analysis of the number of first and last choices proved most revealing. Results were stated in comparisons of "positive" versus "negative" rankings.

Step 6. Interpretation of Results. In the interpretation step conclusions of the preceding step are interpreted into a series of recommendations on marketing policies. These recommendations are derived from the generalizations by processes of deductive logic.

Many researchers do not attempt to make specific recommendations. They are content to stop with the drawing of statistical conclusions. Such work, however, is purely descriptive and mere reporting. The interpretive aspects of marketing research appear only when the results of the statistical conclusions are translated into specific recommendations for the company.

As stated earlier in the chapter, in the interpretive stage, one begins with each statistical generalization and asks himself, "What does this mean to the company?" Sometimes the answer is easy. In the case of the white floating soap research, the results were clear, as indicated by two tables. These simple percentage distributions of the preferences of respondents presented no difficulty in interpretation into marketing policy. As shown in Table 9, while the new soap represented some improvement over the old, it was decisively beaten by a brand already established on the market. Table 10 revealed that it made a very poor showing against three other brands. It also showed that consumer preferences were distributed over a wide variety of characteristics of shape, size, color, and odor represented by the various brands. In the light of these findings, it was recommended that the company should not attempt to market the new white floating soap. Also, it was made clear to the executives that minor modifications in shape or other attributes could not improve the product enough to warrant further testing. The only hope would be the development of a new soap which was radically different in characteristics or performance.

TABLE 9

PERCENTAGE OF CONSUMERS PREFERRING NEW SOAP
IN COMPARISON WITH IVORY AND OLD SOAP

(Based on Relative Score, All Characteristics Combined)

Ivory	68%
New Soap	21
Old Soap	9
No preference	2
Total	100%

TABLE 10

PERCENTAGE OF CONSUMERS PREFERRING NEW SOAP
IN COMPARISON WITH THREE SELECTED BRANDS

(Based on Relative Score, All Characteristics Combined)

Camay	31%
Palmolive	26
Lifebuoy	23
New Soap	12
No preference	8
Total	100%

It should be noted in this case that the results of the research were negative. This does not reduce its value in the least, for a negative finding is just as important a contribution of research as a positive one. Business executives are by nature optimists, particularly in the case of a new product development. A primary function of marketing and distribution research is to keep them from making costly and vital mistakes.

Step 7. Presentation of the Results. It is a truism among seasoned marketing researchers that the form in which the results of an investigation are presented is the most important single element in obtaining acceptance of its conclusions and recommendations. Unfortunately, one of the more difficult problems in this field is to write a clear, convincing report, and to develop a dramatic presentation which will obtain the greatest possible acceptance.

In general, there are two types of reports used in marketing research —the popular report and the technical report. While they are usually combined in one physical unit, a more effective report will be prepared if the writer keeps the two essential forms clearly in mind. The popular report, as the name suggests, is developed in dramatic form and briefly shows the highlights of the investigation. It is prepared primarily for the consideration of the major executives of a company in a group meeting. The technical report is a very comprehensive, detailed, scientific document. It contains all the evidence obtained in the investigation, presented in such form that a trained research man will be thoroughly satisfied as to the technical accuracy of the work.

In the white floating soap study a complete technical report was prepared. This report was written on business stationery (8½ by 11 inches) and permanently bound. It contained a statement of the purpose of the investigation and a full description of the procedures employed, including samples of the forms used. Detailed tables as well as charts were included. In addition, the validation of the sample obtained in field interviews was shown in the Appendix. This report was submitted to the firm, and studied by its research division.

The popular report for this study took the form of an easel presentation made up of several large pages, most of which were charts. The report was given a title which established a theme to obtain a continuity in the entire presentation. A series of dramatic charts summarized the most important findings of the investigation and led step by step to the final conclusions and recommendations. This report was presented orally to a meeting of the executives of the firm.

Step 8. Follow-Up. The ultimate test of the value of a marketing research lies in the results which have been accomplished when its recommendations are put into effect. Unfortunately, however, the general impression made on executives, the technical skill with which the work has been done, the dramatic presentation of the findings in conference, and similar superficial phases frequently receive undue consideration. The researcher must appreciate the importance of these more obvious and superficial aspects, but his work is justified only if clearly traceable results are found in the actual operation of the business. What really counts is the degree to which his conclusions are adopted in business practice.

The follow-up stage usually takes the form of carrying out the recommendations of the study on a small scale. By such a test it may be determined whether they are practicable and the best form for translating them into marketing policies and operations may be developed. The results of research often call for vital changes in the marketing policies of a company. Such changes should not be made too rapidly because the disturbances created by the change may in some cases defeat the values to be obtained. A careful testing of the new procedure will clearly indicate the changes demanded by practical considerations.

There are definite advantages in having the researcher take an active part in the follow-up work. In the first place, the knowledge which he has gained through his intimate contact with the marketing problem will prove indispensable in setting up a sound plan for carrying out the recommendations. Second, the actual "road test" of the recommendations of the analysis may lead to a reinterpretation of the findings, and corresponding adjustments in the recommendations. Third, actual practice in carrying the results of the analysis into operation contributes greatly to the skill of the researcher and, in turn, to the value of future studies which he will make for the company. Finally, by taking an active part in the actual marketing operations, he gains the confidence of executives and other employees with whom he will have to work in the future. This confidence is of great value in making it possible to obtain their support in later work.

In the white floating soap case, executive agreement not to market the new laboratory product was first obtained. However, the research director of the company worked over a period of years with members of the laboratory staff and other executives, constantly applying various findings of the study in further product development.

The procedure for conducting a marketing research has been discussed in this chapter in some detail because clear understanding of the complete process, as it has been developed through practice in this field, is essential to sound research. Some aspects are treated rather extensively since they introduce many readers to important concepts for the first time. As each step is discussed in greater detail in succeeding chapters, these ideas will be further amplified.

7

THE SITUATION ANALYSIS

Purpose of the Situation Analysis. The primary purpose of the situation analysis is to obtain an adequate background knowledge of various conditions affecting the marketing operations of a business which may have a bearing on contemplated marketing and distribution research activities. The part which this knowledge plays in the conduct of a research project was discussed in the preceding chapter.

The situation analysis supplies a broad view of the entire business operation. It enables the researcher to understand the relationship and importance of the various activities of the company he is studying. While the final investigation may be limited to only one small field of a company's operation, the researcher, to do a competent piece of work, must have current and comprehensive knowledge of various marketing aspects of the business.

Both finding the central problems and solving them scientifically require that the study begin with a thorough and adequate situation analysis. The researcher must know the product, the company, and many facts learned through internal research to be able to detect the problems whose solutions will be productive. The solutions themselves are not the result of blind guesswork, but are revealed only in the light of an intelligent knowledge of the environment in which the difficulty exists.

Situation Analysis Often Ignored. Despite the fact that it serves as a base or background for all the succeeding steps in the marketing research, the situation analysis often fails to receive proper attention. One reason for slighting it is that it appears to be a dull and routine operation which deals with the assembly of facts which are already obvious to the executives of the business. Such a feeling regarding this stage of the work reveals a misconception of its proper function and its relation to the research as a whole. An adequate situation analysis calls for careful selection of the marketing operations which should be investigated. It is essential, at the same time, that every aspect which may conceivably contain a solution be considered. Omission of a significant element may spell failure. This selection of what is to be investigated demands a keen analytical evaluation since the real creative result of the marketing research may depend upon the correlation of factors which do not, on the surface, appear to have any bearing on the problem. The situation analysis when properly conducted is, therefore, no dull and obvious routine.

A second reason for frequent slighting of the situation analysis is the fact that many analyses are conducted under the pressure of short-time limitations. It takes time to make an adequate situation analysis before planning and prosecuting the formal research project. Those who sponsor and pay for the research may be impatient, and their desire to obtain results as quickly as possible, often coupled with a lack of understanding of the amount of time required for various aspects of the study, causes the researcher to attempt to do his work as rapidly as possible. In his own eagerness to make progress, the researcher, in turn, may omit the situation analysis or make only a hasty, incomplete survey.

There is also too prevalent a tendency to identify marketing and distribution research almost entirely with outside operations, often to the exclusion of internal research based upon study of company records. It is true that the bulk of time and effort devoted to research in this field involves the extensive gathering of external data regarding the market and channels of distribution from sources such as consumers and dealers. Nevertheless, there is a growing appreciation of the value of research employing data available within the enterprise itself, and it is most important that the entire research undertaking begin with a thorough situation analysis, based on internal research.

The situation analysis is sometimes neglected because of the illogical assumption that it will introduce bias and prejudice into the study. One of the common mistakes in marketing research is the supposition that in order to develop a fair and impartial analysis, the researcher should know as little as possible about the company, its past history, and other elements in the environment of the problem which he is attempting first to find and then to solve. This attitude is often expressed in the form of statements to the effect that an outsider who has no prejudices is necessary for the best work. Businessmen often refuse to divulge information about the firm in the belief that such a policy will lead to better research.

Nothing could be further from the truth than such assumptions. Instead of obtaining merely unbiased results, the firm will probably obtain poor results. When the researcher is "kept in the dark," the problem presented for solution exists in a vacuum, as it were, and there is no basis for truly scientific research. As a scientist, the researcher must be able to retain an impersonal attitude toward the whole study. If familiarity with the facts of the case distorts his objectivity, he is not scientifically qualified to conduct marketing research.

How the Situation Analysis Is Made. The situation analysis is primarily the personal work of the individual in charge of the research. Although from time to time it may be necessary to employ assistants in the compilation of data, compilations are not detailed or extensive unless they become a major part of the research itself. In this first step the researcher is primarily concerned with building an adequate background for his own thinking, so the emphasis is placed upon browsing over a wide range of topics. No particular effort is made to assemble the information in any special form other than to gather it at one central point where the project director may refer to it from time to time to help his own thinking in planning the investigation.

The chief sources of information for the situation analysis are company records, libraries, trade and professional publications, and reports of previous marketing research studies.

Reports on past studies, whether available in the files of the company or in printed form from libraries and other general sources, should be examined thoroughly as early as possible. Three things may be gained from studying past investigations. In the first place, the researcher will often learn about certain aspects of the market which may be investigated to advantage. Frequently work which has been done in the past was only partially productive. A repetition of the same operation at a later date may also meet new conditions or yield better results because of comparisons which will be shown over a period of time. A second reason for investigating all previous research is to avoid unnecessary duplication of work which has already been completed and is still adequate. A third reason is to see the results which have been obtained by the application of specific research techniques. A critical perusal of past studies may indicate that certain investigation techniques are fruitless when applied to the field in question. A consideration of the methods employed in the past and the results they obtained may also lead to the development of refinements which will add much to the value of the present marketing research.

Distinction Between the Situation Analysis and the Data-Collection Step. The reader may have some difficulty at first in seeing the difference between the situation analysis and the later step of collecting data. This confusion arises because the topics to be covered in the situation analysis are those which are most frequently made the subject for final analysis. For example, the product is the first subject considered in the situation analysis. If it is not clear as a result of this preliminary step that the purpose of the final analysis should be to determine whether the product should be changed, no further product data are obtained. On the other hand, as a result of the consideration given to the product in the situation analysis, a hypothesis relating to changing the product may be developed. In this case, a procedure would be set up to gather additional data in a formal research project to resolve the hypothesis.

The relationship between the two steps may be further illustrated by a specific case. While looking over sales records during a situation analysis, a marketing researcher noticed what appeared to be an excessively large number of small orders. As a result, when he drew up the plan for the final analysis, his major purpose was to make a study of small orders to determine their profitability and what policy might be instituted to eliminate them if unprofitable. *After* the situation analysis and the informal investigation, a special sales slip was devised to be used in one branch territory and an intensive study made of thousands of individual transactions over a period of a year.

Thus, in the situation analysis, a large number of subjects are given cursory examination. The researcher browses over a wide range of topics, obtaining only readily available facts. In the data-collecting stage, one or a small number of subjects covered in the situation analysis are studied intensively. Routines are set up to obtain a large quantity of data to check the hypotheses regarding these subjects.

The Use of Standard Outlines. Standardized approaches are of considerable aid in making the situation analysis. Many consulting organizations have developed basic outlines for this express purpose. Some of these standard outlines are filled with detail; one embraces nearly 400 pages.

The purpose of these standard outlines is to provide a logical basis for analyzing any given complex business situation. They may, how-ever, have little value, for they usually are so lengthy and complicated that it is almost impossible to obtain all the information indicated, and much of it is likely to have no significant bearing on the research under consideration. The chief practical value of the standard outline is in furnishing a check list which can be turned to as a source of ideas. Used in this manner the standardized outlines may suggest many sub-jects which can be incorporated in the situation analysis for a specific product.

The facts which one might seek to learn about a business in making a situation analysis are almost innumerable. The prime ingredient of a sound situation analysis is careful selection of those points which have a vital bearing upon the marketing problems of the specific company and its products. It is, therefore, essential that the outline for any given situation analysis shall be constructed especially for it.

Nature of Information Obtained in the Situation Analysis. There are six major factors which control the marketing efficiency of a company. These are:

1. The Product.
2. The Company, Industry, and Competition.
3. The Market.
4. Channels of Distribution.
5. Sales Organization.
6. Advertising and Sales Promotion.

In one or more of these factors the marketing researcher will find the clue to recommendations which will improve the marketing operations of the company. The situation analysis, therefore, centers about a survey of the *immediately available* information regarding each of these six elements.

The Product. *Informal Tests of the Product in Use.* The first step in analyzing the product is to obtain samples of the line and become thoroughly familiar with them from the point of view of the prospective buyer. The buyer has certain fundamental demands in regard to features such as quality, flavor, style, and convenience. The researcher usually has a basic appreciation of these demands derived from his own experience. In addition, there is available a good deal of literature as to consumer preferences. The project director should be familiar with this information. By approaching the product in an unbiased, analytical manner, he will often see characteristics which have been built into it as a result of production routine, traditions of the business, or lack of appreciation of basic market demands. Such discovery points immediately toward possibilities for further investigation.

Technical Tests. Having familiarized himself thoroughly with the obvious advantages and disadvantages of the product itself, the researcher next gathers all available data on technical tests of the product. These tests indicate the efficiency of the product in doing its job, and show as well its hidden merits and its hidden weaknesses or limitations. Technical tests reveal the efficiency of the product in relation to such special requirements for its type as, for example, color, taste, solubility, uniformity, stability, or vitamin content.

The Package. The package is next carefully examined. In view of the increasing emphasis placed upon the package as a vehicle for selling commodities, this is often a fruitful source for the researcher to pursue. Every possible aspect of the package which can influence sales is investigated. Its shelf and display value is compared with the packages of competitive products. The convenience of the size and shape is carefully analyzed. The extent to which the package suggests the merits of the product in the subtle use of color and design is observed.

Examination of the container during use is important; frequently a package is quite satisfactory up to the point where the consumer opens it, but proves unsatisfactory when in use because it is hard to handle, spills easily, or otherwise fails to maintain the high standard now demanded of packages. A marketing researcher once made a major contribution to the sales of a cereal manufacturer by developing a new package which was much easier for the housewife to open and reseal than those which were previously used. Another phase of package analysis is the use of consumer utility devices. The adoption of re-use containers, for example, those which can be used as drinking glasses or service dishes, often offers opportunities for stimulating sales.

The adaptability of the package to dealer display, to the dealer's shelf structure, and to the dealer's storage requirements is thoroughly investigated. The efficiency of the package in protecting the product through transportation, storage, and handling in the dealer's store is also considered.

In connection with the review of the package, the researcher should be aware of the fact that technical testing of packages is rapidly increasing. He should check carefully for availability of reports of technical laboratory tests conducted by package design organizations.

Prices. The price of the product is investigated next. The researcher obtains not only the nominal list prices of the commodity, but also the prices which are actually in effect in various types of outlets. The extent of price-cutting and price-maintenance activities is often an important element in the marketing situation. Price variations by different types of outlets may hold the key to the solution of difficult marketing problems. The trend of prices over a period of time should always be reviewed. Comparisons must also be made with the prices of competitive products.

History of the Product. Readily available information regarding the history of the product should be studied by the researcher. A knowledge of the general development of the business, of inventions and patents involved, and of the personality of the organization is important. It is possible, however, for a researcher to waste time in obtaining historical data. He rapidly reaches a point at which there is nothing to be gained by seeking further information.

Methods of Production. Production methods should be studied to a point where the researcher becomes familiar with the general processes and materials involved. It is possible that special methods of manufacture point to marketing opportunities that have been overlooked by the manufacturer. The standards of manufacture and inspection and the limitations on production capacity should be clearly understood.

Manufacturing and Selling Costs of Individual Items. All available data on manufacturing and selling costs should be obtained. These data may be compared later in the investigation to those for similar commodities, and may suggest wastes which can be eliminated. The calculation of the profitability of various items in the line is important in cost analysis. Often the application of simple accounting principles will clearly point to the fact that certain items offer profit possibilities which warrant giving them special consideration.

It is especially important to have the best possible information regarding the cost of production at various volume levels. Many companies strive for as large-scale operation as is possible without knowing at which volume of operation their costs are lowest. When the researcher has information regarding the cost of production at various volume levels, he may have the opportunity to investigate the possibilities of a restricted marketing policy in which the volume of production would be set at a smaller figure than that which had been aimed at in the past. This might be desirable in order to reduce marketing costs, which frequently are not subject to the principle of diminishing costs.

Varieties Manufactured. Special attention should be given to the number of varieties of different items in the lines produced by the manufacturer. One research firm has established its reputation primarily on the basis of simplification of the lines produced. There is a natural tendency in a business to add constantly new products, sizes, and varieties. This policy will sometimes reach the rather absurd point at which a company will have as many as 2,000 different combinations of size, color, and design, yet obtain 80 per cent of its sales from a small number of these items. The researcher, when he clearly demonstrates that the public is concentrating its purchases on a few items, that the dealer can operate at a better profit and faster turnover with a smaller number of items, that the salesmen will be more efficient, and that overhead costs such as accounting and supervision can be reduced, may often point the way to fundamental changes in the operation of a business which will reduce marketing costs and increase profits.

Specific Uses of the Product. Specific uses of the product should be carefully investigated. Most products are designed for some one particular use, but frequently it is found that new uses may be discovered to the advantage of the company manufacturing the product. Often the net result of a marketing research is to recommend the cultivation of entirely new markets by promoting new uses for products.

Seasonal Sales Variations. The seasonal variation in the sale of the product is important in the analysis of the product in relation to its sales. By comparing the ups and downs of the sales curve during the different seasons, an opportunity may be found for developing devices to reduce seasonal changes through the addition of new products to the line, changes in the advertising policy, or changes in the sales operations.

The Company, Industry, and Competition. *General History of the Industry.* In studying the company in its relation to the industry and its competition, one becomes thoroughly familiar with all phases of the industry or group of industries of which the company is a part. In some cases the operation of the company is so dominated by the general characteristics of the industry that it is important to make as broad a survey of it as possible. An example is that of the meat-packing industry. The operations of individual packers are rather definitely standardized by the general practices of the trade.[1]

Sales Trend of the Industry. Careful consideration should be given to the trend of sales of the industry as a whole over a period of time. The trend of the company's sales should be checked against this to determine major departures.

It is important to determine whether the manufacturer is obtaining his proper competitive share of the existing market. The researcher must know whether the chief marketing objective of the company should be primarily competitive or whether it should attempt to convert new users to the type of product which the company makes. This decision is often one of the most basic policy questions.

Sales Trend of Competitors. The sales of important competitors, if readily available, should also be traced against the trend for the total industry. A general knowledge of the standing of the principal competitors and the variations of competitive strength by geographic areas, population groups, and channels of distribution should be obtained.

---

[1] Most of the basic factual data needed regarding the industry may be obtained from the *Census of Manufactures*, published by the U. S. Department of Commerce, Bureau of the Census.

Competitive Products. The chief selling points of each of the competitors should be determined, and comparisons of competitive products made. This step is necessary to determine the principal advantages and disadvantages of the product over its competition, as well as to find possible opportunities for product improvement.

Competitors' Sales Policies. Competitors' policies with regard to different types of wholesale and retail outlets should be thoroughly understood. The minimum orders which will be accepted from various types of outlets, discount plans, price-maintenance activities, and special sales and combination offers made by competitors should be learned. Salesmen and dealers can frequently contribute such information.

The Market. *Geographical Distribution.* Very often one may learn from past studies the variation in per capita consumption of the product in different regions.

Consumption by Population Groups. Available information on variation in consumption by size of city and urban versus rural groups should be obtained.

Influence of Occupation, Income, Age, Sex. All information which may give a clue to the influence of factors such as sex, income, and occupational status on the purchase and use of the product is next investigated. While the accurate measurement of the influence of such factors may become the central operation in the final analysis, it is important to check all readily available data for general background and for possible clues for further study.

Basic Psychological, Social, and Economic Factors. Basic psychological, social, and economic factors relating to the purchase and use of the product should be given careful consideration. The degree to which the purchase is emotional or rational is often important. Changes in habits, attitudes, and customs which affect the position of the product in the social structure should be considered.

Shifts in Brand Preference. Previous studies should be searched for data showing shifts in brand preferences over a period of years and for any clues as to the rate of brand shifting among consumers.

Information on any other subjects regarding the consuming market as such, the types of retail stores at which consumers buy, how the product is used, and the status of the product with special market groups (such as restaurants, institutions, and other large buying units) should be carefully studied, if readily available.

Channels of Distribution. Channels of distribution through which products reach consumers are in constant flux. Because of this continuous shift in methods of distribution, manufacturers are frequently tardy in discovering weaknesses in their dealer organization. By carefully studying company records and competitive methods of distribution, one often may find the principal clue to the solution of a basic marketing problem. Most companies use both wholesale and retail outlets. Each type should be investigated in the situation analysis.

Wholesale Distribution. *Types of Wholesale Units Employed and Trends in Sales Volume by Types.* In considering wholesale distribution, the types of wholesale units employed should be checked first, as well as the trends in the total volume of these different types over a period of years. This information may be readily gleaned from company records. When the data on the trend of the volume of company sales through different types of wholesale outlets are contrasted with census data on the sales of these types of outlets, significant differences may often be discovered.

Trends in Wholesaler Functions and Services. A second phase of the analysis of wholesale marketing is a survey of the trends in wholesalers' functions and services. Discussions found in business magazines will often indicate important trends toward the elaboration or restriction of wholesaler functions and services. These functional changes may have an important bearing on the efficiency with which the product moves through wholesale channels.

Sales of the Company for a Period of Years to Wholesale Accounts, Average Sales per Account. An analysis should be made of the average sales per wholesale account during recent periods. Such an analysis will often prove fruitful as a basis for determining the possibilities of eliminating unprofitable accounts or developing plans for more effective sales promotions through key accounts which contribute a large share of the total volume realized through wholesalers.

Geographic Location of Wholesale Distribution. The researcher should also study the geographic location of wholesalers to determine whether the company is adequately represented in various sections of the country.

Wholesaler-Retailer Relationships, Sales Promotion Activities, Voluntary Group Efforts. With the development of the voluntary chain, the bond between wholesalers and retailers in certain lines has become highly important to the manufacturer. In some fields, for example, it will be found that wholesalers are active in sales promotion for the retail accounts which they serve. The nature and extent of the various activities of the wholesalers in servicing their accounts should be carefully surveyed.

Margins Realized by Wholesale Accounts. Margins obtained by wholesale outlets should be checked. In this connection it is important that the researcher obtain accurate data on the actual margins which are realized by different classes of wholesalers. These margins are often different from the ones indicated by the theoretical discount structure which may have been set up, but which is not actually in effect as a result of the use of special deals and rebates.

Retail Distribution. The retailer has been characterized as the "neck of the bottle" in the marketing structure. While there is some controversy as to the effectiveness of the retailer in controlling the sales of products, there can be no doubt that it is important to the marketing researcher to know the status of retail distribution.

Percentage of Retail Outlets Carrying the Product. In analyzing the retail outlets the extent of distribution of the product should first be determined. By the extent of retail distribution is meant the percentage of all retail outlets handling a given type of product which stocks a particular brand. This ratio is especially important in the case of convenience goods, such as drug and grocery products, where the manufacturer should have as close to 100 per cent distribution as possible. Such complete distribution is realized in the sale of some impulse goods, such as cigarettes, but ordinarily it is merely an ideal toward which each manufacturer strives. Whether the actual distribution of the commodity is found to be 80 per cent, 50 per cent, or 40 per cent, it is important to know if such distribution is adequate for the particular product. This analysis of the extent of retail distribution should be broken down by various items in the line, and wherever possible by geographic areas.

Trends in the Importance of Various Types of Retail Outlets. It is possible that consumers are turning toward new sources for the type of product the company is marketing, and types of retail outlets which are developing in importance should be investigated. The researcher should obtain a clear picture of the relative importance of corporate chains, syndicate stores, voluntary groups, specialty retailers, department stores, mail-order houses, and of all other types which handle the product.

Sales of the Company to Different Types of Retail Outlets. Another phase of the retail situation to be considered is the sales of the company for a period of years to different types of retail outlets. In many instances, especially where the use of wholesalers is prevalent, it is not possible to determine quickly the proportion of the total sales of the company which flow to each type of retail outlet. However, the researcher should seek such information, in order to obtain a clear understanding of the relative importance of each kind of retail outlet, and by comparisons over a period of time, detect significant trends. This information becomes especially valuable when it can be correlated with the general status of individual types of outlets as revealed by the census.

Importance of the Product in Relation to Dealers' Total Sales Volume. The relation of the product manufactured by the company in respect to the total sales volume of each type of dealer is important. If it is found that the particular product being studied contributes a major share to the total sales volume of any given type of dealer, the researcher knows that it will be possible to devise sales promotion plans which will gain the interest and support of the dealers. On the other hand, if it is found that the item is inconsequential, all sales promotion plans must be made simple and automatic if the dealers are to use them.

Profits to Individual Retailers. A fifth phase of the dealer aspect of the situation analysis is the determination of the discount structure in order to establish the margins and profits provided the retailers for the product in question. It is important here, as in the case of wholesale distribution, to distinguish clearly between theoretical margins and those actually realized on the basis of the prices received from consumers. Frequently a company will maintain traditional discount structures based upon theoretical selling prices which, because of price-cutting by retailers, are seldom actually in effect. The dealer is influenced only by the actual margin of profit he realizes.

Turnover of Retail Accounts. The rate of turnover of retail accounts may be very important in analyzing the retail situation. Wherever data on retail accounts are available, it will be possible from the sales records of the company to determine rather quickly the extent to which the company is forced to open new dealer outlets in order to replace those which are lost. While the standards for retail account turnover rates will of necessity vary between different types of business, the researcher should familiarize himself with the rates experienced by the company in order that it will be possible to determine whether this rate is excessively high or satisfactory. Frequently devices for stimulating reorders and keeping accounts active have been of value in maintaining effective retail distribution.

Special Dealer Strategies. Special dealer strategies which have been pursued in the past should be studied. These strategies range from long-run company policies regarding dealers, such as credit policies, to temporary stimulants, such as contests. Among the more important policies with which the researcher should become familiar are those relating to price maintenance, returns and allowances, exclusive representation, contests, premiums, and deals.

The Sales Organization. *General Structure of the Sales Organization.* The first step in the analysis of the sales organization is to obtain a clear picture of the structure of the sales division. This includes an analysis of the number and types of salesmen, their geographic distribution, and the form of sales supervision in central office headquarters and in district or branch offices.

Sales Management Policies. A clear understanding of sales management policies is important. In this connection the researcher should study carefully the basis of selection, training, supervising, and routing the sales force. The basis of compensation, the various incentives which are provided the salesmen, and the turnover in the sales force should be thoroughly scrutinized. Training salesmen in sales promotion work and helping the dealer to be more efficient in selling the product are other considerations. The researcher can often discover means for improving the effectiveness of the sales force through such devices as better selection, training, and compensation methods.

Whether a plan for increasing the accomplishment of the sales force is arrived at as a result of the marketing research, it is important that the researcher understand all these phases of the sales operations thoroughly because some portion of his recommendations will almost invariably find application through the sales force. Obviously the success of the research can be greatly influenced by the care with which the recommendations are made to coincide with the ability of the sales force to help carry them into practice. If the changes resulting from the analysis, for example, center about advertising, it will be necessary to convince the sales force that the new basis of operation is sound and to seek their aid in making effective the new methods of advertising.

Job Analysis of Salesmen's Duties. The next step is to make a job analysis of the duties of the salesman. Frequently it will be found that salesmen operate in a very haphazard fashion, because little thought has been given to the function which the salesman should perform in the marketing operations. The researcher should determine carefully just how a salesman spends his time, learning how regularly he calls on his customers, what he is supposed to do by way of demonstration, dealer service, and display work. He should study the results obtained by the salesmen, how many dealers called upon are sold to, how frequently purchases are made, and the average dollar value of each sale. This information will lead to interest in the cost of sales—information which is likely to prove of great value because later in the investigation it may be found that the addition or subtraction of certain sales functions, outlets covered, or territories will improve greatly the effectiveness of the sales force.

Number of Accounts per Salesman. The number of accounts serviced by each salesman should be determined. It is frequently enlightening to compare the number of accounts handled by different types of salesmen and by salesmen covering different geographic areas. It will often be apparent that certain salesmen are spreading their efforts out too thinly over a large number of accounts; whereas others are not provided with a sufficient number of accounts to show maximum sales efficiency. Thus, a common error is to have too few salesmen in large cities because of the comparative ease of reaching the various retail accounts. The kind of goods being sold will also condition the number of customer calls.

Coordination of Sales with Advertising. The extent to which special sales efforts are necessary to support an advertising campaign should be investigated as a final phase of the analysis of the sales organization. Proper coordination of sales and advertising efforts is usually an important element in marketing success. In studying the sales operations, therefore, the researcher should attempt to form some judgment as to the extent to which the sales force backs up the work done by consumer advertising.

Advertising and Sales Promotion. *Advertising Expenditures in Relation to Sales over a Period of Time.* Consumer advertising expenditures over a period of years should be broken down by different products and related to the sales of these products. It may be found that over a period of time the percentage of sales spent in advertising has shown unwarranted increases, or, on the other hand, that the company has failed to maintain adequate advertising pressure behind certain products in the line.

Media Employed. Analysis of the media which have been employed should next be undertaken. Expenditures by media (such as magazines, newspapers, radio, outdoor, and car cards) over a period of time will show whether the company has pursued a consistent and constructive policy and indicate significant changes in media employed.

Advertising Appeals Used. Analysis of consumer advertising to determine the basic advertising appeals or themes which have been used is highly important, as it is essential that the most effective appeals be employed. Buying motives are subject to change through time, so it is possible that the company is attempting to convert users to their product through the wrong appeal. It is, therefore, necessary to check the timeliness of the appeal.

Seasonal Variation. The seasonal variation in consumer advertising may also be important. The natural tendency of most firms is to concentrate their advertising in the heavy selling season. This policy is usually sound, but it is quite possible that it has been overdone and that the company failed to maintain its representation adequately during the remainder of the year. Again, it may be advisable for advertising to precede rather than coincide with the selling season.

Results of Previous Advertising Tests. Some companies keep careful records of the number of inquiries or of the volume of sales produced by different types of advertisements and media. Scrutiny of such records will provide a valuable background, and may point to further data to be obtained or to experiments which may be set up as a part of the final analysis.

Advertising by Competitors. Competitors' advertising should be thoroughly studied. In addition to obtaining copies of the published advertisements, it is possible through various services to determine the breakdown of competitors' advertising expenditures in different types of media by geographic areas and the individual markets.

Dealer Sales Promotion. The procedures employed in dealer sales promotion should be carefully scrutinized. The researcher should become thoroughly familiar with all materials supplied to salesmen in order to obtain dealer cooperation, such as portfolios and demonstration devices. Examples of direct mail sent to dealers with records of returns, wherever available, should be examined. Store display material may also be collected for analysis.

Consumer Sales Promotions. The researcher should study special consumer merchandising methods which have been employed, and where possible should become familiar with the records of the results of each effort. Among the more common strategies are samples, premiums, contests, and special devices, such as one-cent sales or trade-in deals.

Promotions with Special Groups. In some cases institutional groups are buying units which represent large potential markets and require special promotional methods. Examples are hotels, restaurants, hospitals, state and federal institutions, army units, college dormitories, and Boy Scout camps. With the increase in the importance of social groups, institutional units are becoming more and more significant as markets. Special promotional activities directed toward professional groups, such as doctors and teachers, should also be considered.

The preceding discussion has indicated the nature of the subjects which may be included in a situation analysis. The list is by no means all-inclusive, but is suggestive of the type of information which has been proved by experience to be generally most valuable. Its breadth indicates the importance of emphasizing internal research as a base and background for later activities.

8

THE INFORMAL INVESTIGATION

After the situation analysis has progressed to a point where a reasonable understanding of the product, company, market, dealer structure, sales, and advertising has been obtained, the informal investigation should be begun. This step consists of talking about the product and its marketing with consumers, dealers, and persons occupying key positions in relationship to marketing operations. Observations of marketing methods and practices in various localities and distributing outlets are also made.

Purpose of the Informal Investigation. The primary objective of the informal investigation is twofold: (1) to develop the hypotheses to be used in the final study, and (2) to obtain a "feel" of the market. The situation analysis is in part a source of hypotheses for the marketing research. The informal investigation is even more important in its contribution to the development of these hypotheses. In the first place, the value of any hypotheses suggested by the situation analysis is checked by the information obtained in the informal investigation. Many of them will prove inconsequential as soon as a number of consumer and dealer interviews have been held. On the other hand, these informal calls will usually confirm the importance of some of the hypotheses discovered in making the situation analysis.

The informal investigation may also reveal many new hypotheses not found in the situation analysis. When one talks informally with consumers of a product about what they like and dislike, what their habits are, the motives underlying the use or nonuse of the product, and similar subjects, he is bound to acquire an insight into the vital forces affecting the market for the commodity. Similarly, probing interviews with dealers, salesmen, and key persons in the industry are bound to suggest a variety of ideas which may well become subjects of further research. For this reason the quest for hypotheses becomes the central objective which dominates the informal investigation.

The second purpose of the informal investigation—to get the "feel" of the market—is difficult to explain but is nonetheless important. Too often in research work the analyst closets himself with his thoughts to decide the lines to pursue. The importance of deciding the exact purposes of a research project has been repeatedly emphasized. Many persons will sit down at a desk with no tools other than a good supply of paper and a pencil to plan the study. An investigation begun in this manner may be in large part mere confirmation of already known facts. Such an investigation will usually overlook significant facts which the research should reveal. In developing a genuine "feel" of the market, the informal investigation provides many fundamental and essential ingredients. The planning of fruitful research requires a great deal of insight on the part of the researcher. Only close, personal contact with the dynamic marketing forces in the market place can give a person this insight.

While the first purpose of an informal investigation is to develop the hypotheses for the study, there is no mechanical technique for finding them. They arise automatically as the informal investigation progresses. They may enter conscious thought at the most unexpected moments—while riding in a taxicab, while playing bridge, or while discussing some apparently unrelated subject. One may lie awake at night, suffering from insomnia, and suddenly discover the lines to pursue in tackling the problem. The fact that the hypothesis comes upon one suddenly of its own accord does not mean, however, that it is to be grasped out of thin air. The exact opposite is the truth. To attempt to obtain sound hypotheses while sitting in an office is one form of "thinking in a vacuum." One must dig deeply to find the sources of these scientific hunches or hypotheses.

The informal investigation has important by-product values in addition to its contribution to the development of a marketing research. In the process of making the investigation, it is possible that the reports of individual interviews may have considerable value in themselves. Business executives can frequently learn much from reading a series of such reports. An even more direct application may be found by the advertising and sales departments. A series of fifty or a hundred reports on calls made in an informal investigation may provide a valuable source of ideas to sales managers or to those engaged in creative advertising work. A group of such reports was once assembled under the title "The Pulse of the Market," and furnished to the persons responsible for the preparation of the advertising for the product. The copywriters obtained many ideas and suggestions from a study of these reports. Some of the informal interviews may also be effectively quoted in the final research report, by way of illustration in depth of certain findings of the research. Colorful examples which effectively "make a point" are often found in the dealer or consumer interviews of the informal investigation.

How the Informal Investigation Is Made. In conducting an informal investigation, one should usually plan to make calls on consumers, dealers, and key individuals. There is no particular order in which calls should be made on each of these sources. Sometimes one begins with a few dealer calls, because the dealers are likely to be more familiar with the general subject than the consumers. It usually is most satisfactory to make it a point to intersperse consumer, dealer, and key individual calls in order to check constantly the ideas which have been obtained from one group against those obtained from others.

There is no statistical basis on which to determine the number of calls which should be made in the informal investigation. The best rule to follow is to continue until it becomes clear that one is merely obtaining confirmation of the things which have been learned in previous calls. In some cases it will be found that this point is reached rather quickly, and that the hypotheses which should be laid down for the final investigation have begun to crystallize. On the other hand, it will sometimes be found that over a hundred consumer calls must be made before it has become clear that nothing may be gained by additional informal interviews.

The extent to which the informal investigation may be pursued is almost boundless. New ideas and new facts, seemingly without end, could be obtained by carrying such an investigation on and on. However, since there are practical limitations of time and resources, it is essential to be careful not to overdo the informal investigation. Further informal investigation work should be discontinued when important new knowledge and new ideas cease to appear.

One additional thought should be borne in mind. The informal investigation should be extensive enough to make sure that important regional or local conditions have not been overlooked. This statement means that the investigation should not be confined to one city, but should be scattered somewhat throughout the country. It is especially valuable to have a few interviews with dealers and specialists in several different cities.

Qualifications of Informal Interviewers. When the person in charge finds it desirable to employ assistants to make interviews in the informal investigation, it is essential that they be carefully selected. This type of work calls for certain special skills which demand a higher type of individual than even high-grade field investigators. The first requisite is the ability to interest people in a subject quickly and cause them to talk freely. This ability is especially important in the informal investigation.

A second requirement is the possession of ingenuity and imagination. While the person conducting an informal interview seeks to lead the thinking of the respondent as little as possible, to leave him free to introduce new subjects, it is always necessary to stimulate the discussion. If the investigator has imagination, he will continuously introduce new thoughts into the conversation and thus stimulate the person who is responding to such a degree that the interview will not be confined to the more obvious subjects.

A third requirement is the ability to evaluate the information obtained and to interpret statements to bring out their true significance. Frequently a comment made by a consumer or dealer which appears to be purely incidental will provide the basis for an important hypothesis. In an analysis of the market for furniture polish, one consumer interviewed happened to have recently purchased a new dining-room set. She made the comment that she would not put a furniture polish on this beautiful new piece of furniture. This gave the investigator an insight into an attitude of the public toward the conventional type of furniture polish which laid the basis for the most important single phase of the later research.

A fourth characteristic is the ability to uncover motives behind the habits and attitudes which are found. Most field investigators can be trained to record data accurately once they have been given to them, but the ability to probe into the psychological factors which lie behind the surface facts is rare. Frequently the key to the significant hypotheses is found only after one has dug beneath the surface facts in this manner.

A fifth requirement is the ability to report accurately information obtained in an informal conversation. Since the person making an informal investigation does not have a set questionnaire to follow, there is a temptation to make the report brief and superficial. Reports should be as complete as possible, because a fact which at the time appears unimportant may later be found to be significant.

Finally, an adequate knowledge of the entire research undertaking is important. A person conducting an informal interview should know enough about the subjects covered in the situation analysis to ask intelligent questions and lead the discussion along useful lines. Accordingly, whenever several persons are making these calls, care should be exercised to discuss the findings of the situation analysis with each one so that all of them will have a clear understanding of some of the things to be looked for in the interviews. Sometimes there are technical aspects of a problem which make it desirable to employ trained technicians or specialists for part of the informal analysis. For example, persons with medical, dental, or engineering training have a definite advantage in conducting interviews in connection with certain products. If the study involves a food, home economists are in a position to secure information in an informal interview which other investigators cannot obtain. In conducting informal interviews with farmers, an agricultural agent or extension worker has a technical background and ability to communicate effectively with this type of person which are of great value. There are technicians in nearly every field. Their services may be most useful in making calls in the informal investigation stage of the research.

Results of the Informal Investigation. The most important results of the informal investigation exist in the mind of the one who actually has made the field calls. Some persons believe that in conducting a series of informal interviews one obtains a subconscious grasp of the problems to be resolved in the final analysis. This understanding, it is contended, lies in the subconscious mind of the individual and cannot be directly expressed in words. Hypotheses are often called "hunches" because they are apparently developed in large part by this subconscious process.

Where the individual in charge of the analysis is in a position personally to conduct the informal investigation, there is no need to crystallize its results in any written form. This ideal is, however, seldom reached in actual practice. Usually one is fortunate if he personally can make a reasonable number of these calls. His work must usually be supplemented by informal interviews made by assistants.

Wherever it is necessary to employ assistants to conduct informal interviews, the results must be reduced to writing. The reports of these interviews should be running accounts of the conversations which took place. These reports are best written immediately following each interview. A series of detailed reports of individual interviews is the final form which the results of the informal investigation take.

It is usually desirable that certain basic information about the person interviewed, such as age and economic status, be obtained. The selection of the most important basic types of information to be employed in the final analysis is made from these data. To make sure that such data are recorded, it is a convenience to provide a partially standardized form on which the reports may be written. A suggested form for this purpose is shown in Figure 9. By providing such a form, the results of the informal investigation are reported in an orderly fashion.

It is important to note that no statistical tabulation or analysis is generally employed in summarizing the results of the informal investigation. This is true because the informal investigation is made without any standardized questionnaire form and no effort is made to obtain a satisfactory sample in the distribution of the calls. Where a standardized form for obtaining corollary data regarding such factors as age, sex, and economic status has been used, this information is employed only in relation to other information developed in the individual interview in order to provide a better understanding of the meaning of that information.

Since no comprehensive statistical analysis is possible, there is no purpose in attempting to write a summary report of the informal investigation as a separate step in the analysis. To prepare such a general report might be dangerous in that it would tend to crystallize the thinking of persons who read the report at too early a point.

There is one device which may be of considerable value when several individuals are involved in making the informal investigation. Each person should be asked to write a memorandum interpreting his experiences in a general way. This memorandum should be written after all the interviews have been completed. In it the interviewer expresses his general impressions and beliefs as to what constitute the central problems in selling and marketing the product.

Informal Consumer Interviews. In selecting areas for informal consumer interviews, it is important to scatter the calls as widely as possible. This means that all types of consumers, from low income to high income classes, various race and age groups, and people living in different kinds of communities should be covered. Assuming that no important type of consumer has been overlooked, it is usually wise to make a special effort to make additional calls on the more intelligent and articulate consumers. One can rather quickly obtain all the information of value from the rank and file. Among more intelligent people, however, it is possible to continue to make profitable interviews. Women who are superior homemakers, for example, give more serious attention to the products they use and are much more advanced in their habits and attitudes than others. Consequently, the plan for distributing the calls in the informal investigation among consumers should embrace, first, a broad, general scattering of calls among all types, and second, a deliberate concentration of additional calls among the more intelligent and articulate consumers.

In planning the informal interview, it is important to bear in mind that possible hypotheses for the study will usually emphasize particular market classifications, such as age, sex, nationality, and economic status. The investigator must keep clearly in mind the classifications in which the consumer being interviewed falls. As the interview progresses, he may notice that conditions of age or economic status have direct bearing on the information obtained. If people in the lower economic groups, for example, give a consistently negative reaction to the product, this result immediately suggests the possibility of a study on the basis of economic groups. Similarly, it may be found that certain occupational groups respond in the informal interview in such a manner as to indicate the value of using this basis of classification.

PRODUCT_____

a. Name_____

b. Street and number_____c. City_____

d. Family Structure_____
                                    (Age & Sex)

e. Nationality_____   f. Occupation_____

g. Economic Class_____   h. Persons Interviewed_____

i. Date of Interview_____   j. Interviewer_____

k. Brands Now Used_____

_____

_____

_____

_____

FIGURE 9. Part of a Form for Use in Reporting a Consumer Interview in the Informal Investigation. The material shown in this illustration is reproduced at the top of the first page used for each individual interview. As indicated, the balance of the first page and the succeeding pages are used by the interviewer to record all information obtained in this unstructured interview in depth. The use of the suggested form insures that necessary basic data will not be overlooked.

The interviewer must be constantly on the lookout for unusual experiences with and attitudes toward the product. An apparently incidental comment of a consumer may suggest a line of thought which, if confirmed in other informal interviews, may develop into a basic hypothesis for the study. The investigator should be especially careful to note negative comments on the product for which the research is being made. As certain objections are consistently reported they point to likely hypotheses. The investigator should pay particular attention to statements which indicate what the neighbors are talking about. Attitudes are especially significant when consumers begin to exchange experiences and crystallize their opinions of a product. The location and definition of these new habits, attitudes, beliefs, objections, and experiences may in large measure develop the hypothesis for the investigation.

In conducting the informal interviews with consumers, it is most important to bear in mind that they must be more than doorstep calls. The interviewer must develop a cordial conversation which does not suffer from the pressure of time or distracting influences. The basic approach must arouse the interest of the consumer in the problem to be discussed. The investigator should make it a special point to become as friendly as possible with the consumer and gain her complete confidence.

The investigator should first identify herself, and then, as quickly as possible, make the consumer feel the importance of the interview. A good way for the interviewer to do this is to tell the consumer that she has run into a problem that has bothered her and that she is seeking help in solving it. The interviewer then asks the consumer if she uses the product, and if so, what brands. This forces the consumer to respond and lays her open to the key question, "How do you like it?" From this point on, the interviewer follows the conversation of the consumer. The interviewer, however, is careful to direct the conversation along critical lines by casually raising such direction questions as, "What are your objections to the product?" "Why do you use it?" and "Why do you use this particular brand?"

The conversation should be carried on until it becomes clear that the interviewer has obtained a complete case history of this consumer and has exhausted all possibilities of obtaining new information. The interviewer should have a very modest-appearing notebook or pad of scratch paper on which notes may be made casually during the conversation. It is important that this note-taking should be as unobtrusive as possible. If it appears that the consumer is conscious of the fact that she is answering questions, the interviewer should cease taking notes for the time being. After the interview has been concluded, there are usually many points which have not been written down in the notebook which should be recorded as soon as the interviewer leaves the house. Some researchers make it a special point to make no notes during the interview in order to insure complete informality.

It will usually prove valuable to have different types of persons make informal interview calls. If the person in charge of the analysis is a man of fairly impressive appearance, he usually can obtain valuable information by introducing himself as an executive who has come to seek the advice of consumers. This approach flatters the person being interviewed and causes her to discuss the problems freely. A home economist can obtain a different type of cooperation. A young person who does not appear too sophisticated can often gain the confidence of consumers and extract information which would not be given to others.

Reports on Informal Consumer Interviews. The nature of the informal consumer interview is shown by the following examples from research projects. These reports are in the exact form in which they were written by interviewers. Parts are deleted, but each shows the general nature of the information obtained. Names of brands and persons have been disguised in several cases.

The following was obtained in an informal interview made for a dentifrice.

REPORT 1

Ipana, Revelation, Pebeco, and Squibb's used by family. All give the same result as a cleanser, in their opinion.

Dentist's recommendation that powder is a better cleanser than paste has not influenced this family.

Husband and wife use Squibb's most. Only reason she could think of is that they like the taste.

Purchased these dentrifices originally, because she saw them on the drug store counter and believed that a high-priced article does contain best and finest ingredients. Couldn't remember the number of years these have been used in family.

The son likes Ipana especially for its flavor, thinks it cleans teeth better than the others do and finds a paste more convenient to use than a powder. To him, powder tastes like plaster of Paris.

Their teeth are in splendid condition.

The interview covered in Report 1 illustrates some of the information obtained by informal calls which pointed directly to possible hypotheses for a study. For example, in the case of this family four different advertised brands of dentifrices were being used. The interview showed that in the judgment of these consumers there is no clear-cut difference in the quality or effectiveness of different brands. Notice the effect of the dentist's recommendation. The way in which the importance of taste as a buying motive appeared is also interesting. The importance of dealer display as a brand influence can be readily seen in this interview. The results of a second call in this study follow.

REPORT 2

Family tried a number of pastes and finally settled on Pepsodent and Squibb's—Squibb's because the products of that firm were always trustworthy and Pepsodent because recommended by a dentist and because any product so well advertised must be good. For many years the wife would buy whichever one was on sale. After reading *100,000,000 Guinea Pigs* would occasionally use salt. Was greatly affected by this book and was shocked to learn that some tooth pastes were poisonous. Said she would certainly "steer clear" of them. Found it was difficult to get children to brush their teeth with tooth paste— older girl would gag on it. One month ago man next door who was wholesale druggist gave husband can of Dr. Lyon's as a token of appreciation for a favor. Both families enthusiastic about it. Husband says he brushes his teeth more often now. And children only have to be told once. Wife finds it economical and says that although the children spill quite a good deal, they would smear the tooth paste on the wash bowl just the same. Thinks the powder more efficient than paste. Original can still in house, but next time will buy Dr. Lyon's. Wife buys.

The reader will notice in this report the importance of the general good will of an ethical drug manufacturer in determining the choice of dentifrice. The influence of the dentist is again mentioned. This family is using only one brand of dentifrice, and the way in which they began using it clearly points to the importance of sampling in the marketing of this product. One person, the wife, buys the dentifrice for the entire family.

A careful reading of these reports illustrates the type of information which is obtained in the informal investigation. Over 500 consumer calls were made in the survey from which they have been selected. A careful study of each of these individual reports revealed many possible hypotheses. The consistency with which certain facts appeared pointed clearly to the importance of the ones which later became the purposes of the research.

Results from another informal investigation are shown below in Report 3. This investigation was made in connection with a study for a food product which was sold primarily on a health appeal. Individual brands have been disguised in the report by using capital letters to indicate each of them. Brand A was the one for which the investigation was conducted.

REPORT 3

Using X. Last used three nights ago. Friend recommended it. Used more when girl was ten years old and not very strong. Prefers flavor to other food drinks. Helps children to gain in weight. Has used A, B, and C, but didn't like flavor of these as well as X.

Three months ago used a small bottle of A. Doctor recommended it to grandmother during illness, and mother got some from her. Seems to be very beneficial to grandmother.

Daughters in family are now well and strong and do not need much in the way of food drinks.

Use quite a bit of cocoa. Use on cold mornings and after school. Hershey's. No candy substitutes.

The reader will notice the basis on which the brand used by the family was bought. In spite of the fact that these products are presumably used primarily because they are healthful, the taste of the product is clearly a primary buying motive. This angle was brought out most clearly in negative form in connection with the products which have been used but which have since been discontinued. Notice that the product for which the analysis was being made had been used, as a result of the specific recommendation of a physician, exclusively for health purposes. Reports of this type indicated clearly that a new type of selling and advertising approach would be necessary to expand the market for Product A. This probability became the basis for the chief hypothesis for the final investigation.

Informal Interviews with Industrial and Institutional Users. In a research for an industrial product or in the institutional market, informal interviews with buyers or users are especially valuable. These persons are usually well informed and possess extensive technical knowledge. Furthermore, in view of the fact that industrial products often have a relatively small number of buyers, the informal interviews themselves may provide a sufficient basis for drawing final conclusions. Two reports of informal interviews with users of bearings illustrate the type of information which may be obtained from industrial users.

REPORT 4

This company operates 1,795 trucks of various makes. They do their own maintenance work, using 70 per cent reground bearings which they purchase from the Jones Company. They have no record of their bearing replacement cost, considering it too small an item. Well pleased with service given by Jones Company.

Mr. Smith selects the make of bearing in some cases, but usually gets duplicates of the bearing to be replaced or takes what the Jones Company offers.

He reads *Commercial Car Journal, Fleet Owner, Motor Service, Power Wagon,* and *Brake Service.*

Mr. Smith thinks that advertising keeps the product in mind and probably influences his selection even when he thinks it doesn't. He thought New Departure was out of business until he saw their ads. Formerly thought their product inferior, but now thinks they are among the best.

REPORT 5

Operate 103 trucks of various makes but have more Fords and Chevrolets than anything else.

They do their own maintenance work. Has no idea what his bearing replacement costs might be.

Does not use reground bearings for any truck except the White, but believes reground bearings as good as new bearings.

Buys most of his bearings from truck sales agencies and some from Hanson Bearing Company. Does not specify make of bearing. He merely gives the size and where it is to be used and lets the vendor decide what make of bearing to send. Must be able to get rapid delivery.

Seldom sees any bearing salesmen, but they seemingly have little or no influence.

Reads *Commercial Car Journal.*

He replaces more ball bearings in Ford transmission assemblies than in any other truck and estimated that he bought between 100 and 150 ball bearings a year.

These reports illustrate some of the special types of information which are brought out in informal interviews for industrial products. Notice that the buyers were asked for performance records and cost data. The experience of the individual companies in using the product is a most vital point in this type of interview. The reports also show that the sources of supply are generally important. They also indicate that the investigator was interested in learning the special magazines read by these buyers in order to determine possible sources of influence. In informal interviews with industrial or institutional buyers, the lead question usually relates to the experience of the company with the types of products which have been used. Emphasis is on cost data, performance records, and service furnished by different sources of supply.

Informal Dealer Interviews. In most marketing research it is important to make informal calls on both wholesalers and retailers. The chief advantage of making a number of wholesaler calls lies in the fact that these merchants have a broad picture of the entire marketing operation. Wholesalers make it a special point to keep well informed on the types of products which are currently in demand. The individual wholesaler is also especially well informed about the territory which his firm covers, and he is thoroughly familiar with the retail dealer structure in this area. Finally, the wholesaler is usually an important source of information on general market trends and on current developments.

Two types of persons who are valuable sources of information will be found in most wholesale establishments. First, there is the general executive or merchandise manager type. Such a person is likely to be particularly valuable as a source for obtaining a broad, general understanding of the condition of the market and the merchandising structure which prevails. The second type is the buyer of individual products. In the larger wholesale organizations, these buyers are highly specialized. They are an important source of information in an informal investigation in view of their specialized knowledge of individual types of products.

An example of an informal interview with a wholesale executive follows.

Report 6

Mr. Jackson, buyer for the Anderson Company, believes that there exists a very definite market for an acceptable antiseptic for local skin infections, particularly one to sell at about 50 or 60 cents.

"Hitzit" is the only preparation in this field that is doing a really satisfactory job; but its list price is $1.25, actually selling at from $1.09 to $1.19 in most stores. It has done extensive advertising directed definitely at combating athlete's foot. Mr. Jackson believes that a lower price for an equally acceptable brand would place it in a ranking position among other brands in the field.

However, Mr. Jackson warned against the dangers of too rapid expansion, quoting from his experience the large number of brands which have appeared in this field only to disappear within a short time because of lack of sound financial backing. His recommendation is for such a firm to strive first for sectional distribution by mushrooming around its present locality, supporting this growth, however, with as much local newspaper advertising as the volume of the product would permit.

If the present list price is 50 cents, add 10 cents, making it a 60-cent item, using that differential as the basis for an advertising appropriation.

He also suggested that such a product could be much better sold through a reputable brokerage house than through the manufacturer's own sales channels.

He added that their volume of sales of "Hitzit" would approximate $10,000 annually and estimated that the total annual sales of "Hitzit" would probably not exceed $500,000. Admittedly a small field, Mr. Jackson felt positive that an acceptable and scientifically sound product, popularly priced (suggested 60 cents), and aggressively advertised and merchandised, could attain a much higher volume position than the now existing leader and could reach a higher degree of saturation among potential users than now exists.

This report clearly reveals the breadth of the knowledge of the wholesale executive. The reader will notice the value of this source in reporting general market conditions, competitive positions, prices, and in interpreting the market possibilities for the product. They possess a great amount of trade information as a result of their continuous contact with manufacturers and important retailers.

Informal interviews with executives of central and district head-quarters for chain-store systems should be included in the wholesale calls. While chain stores are regarded as retailing organizations, it should be borne in mind that they are carrying on the functions of wholesalers in their central organization. Frequently it will be found that chain-store executives have a much better grasp of the marketing situation than the executives of wholesaling organizations.

Informal Retailer Interviews. Interviews with retailers are an essential part of the informal investigation. The function of a retailer has been defined as that of a purchasing agent for his customers. He continually meets the consumer face to face when he is making the final decision to buy and presumably reflects the buyer's desires in the conduct of his business. Retailers are an especially valuable source of information about local market conditions. An important phase of the informal interviews with retailers is the observations which the investigator makes while in the store. Since this is the point at which the final influences of advertising and selling work themselves out, a penetrating observation of matters such as display materials, stock on hand, brands, prices, and merchandising devices is most valuable.

In conducting informal interviews with retail stores, the calls should be distributed so as to include all types of outlets in the investigation, but a good share of them should be concentrated in the larger stores. The managers of department stores, supermarkets, and large independent retail stores, for example, are naturally more efficient retailers than operators of small stores, and their opinions are likely to be much more productive in suggesting hypotheses for a later investigation than those of the smaller outlets.

While there is no doubt of the importance of making calls on retail stores in the informal investigation, the researcher should keep clearly in mind the limitations of this source. The retailer usually has hundreds of customers to whom he sells thousands of different items. He is engrossed in the many details of shopkeeping. The time which is spent in supervising personnel, listening to buyers, determining policies, and selling in the store precludes the possibility that he will have a deep understanding of the market for any one product.

It is important to bear in mind that the retailer may be considered from two different points of view in the informal investigation. One purpose of the interview may be to learn how he conducts his business, what his interests and desires as a merchant are, how he regards the product, what brands he pushes, and how the product is displayed and merchandised in his store. Or he may be interviewed as a secondary source of information regarding the consumer. The latter use is less valuable than the first. The retailer is often a very poor reporter or interpreter of the consumer. The retailer should seldom be used for this purpose in the final investigation except in certain specialty lines.[1] In the informal investigation, however, the dealer can sometimes provide a quick clue to facts about the consumer even where he sells a large variety of products, as in the case of grocery or drug stores.

Two distinct types of informal interviews are carried on with retailers. The first is the shopping call, in which the investigator poses as a prospective buyer and observes the way in which the product is offered to the consumer. The second type is the "open" interview, in which the investigator discloses the fact that he is making a research.

The Shopping Interview. The shopping call has the advantage of obtaining objective observation of the manner in which the consumer is influenced by dealers and the shopping environment. The interviewer is careful to make a mental note of the exact manner in which the retail salesman talks with an indifferent consumer, with one who comes into the store with an open mind, or with one who presents specific sales resistances. The order in which products are suggested, the amount of time devoted to each product, and the arguments presented by the retail salesclerk are carefully noted. The interviewer also observes the manner in which stock is displayed in the store, prices shown, and the various display and merchandising devices present to create demand at the point of purchase.

This type of interview is likely to be very productive. Shopping competitive outlets is a well-recognized technique in retail management. In this field emphasis is placed upon prices, styles, and the general efficiency of retail salesmanship. When the researcher makes a shopping contact, he takes a much broader point of view, observing especially the merchandising and display techniques which influence the ultimate consumer. Since most nationally advertised commodities ordinarily do not receive a great amount of direct selling on the part of retail clerks, the more mechanical demand creation devices are given greater consideration. This is, of course, not so true in the case of specialty items such as household appliances, for which the retail salespeople are a much more important sales influence.

Reports 7 and 8 show informal shopping interviews made at the perfume counters of drug and department stores. A reading of these reports will indicate the nature of the facts and ideas which may be obtained by this technique. In this particular study, emphasis was placed upon determining the kind and amount of salesmanship or "counter push" provided different competitive items. Nevertheless,

[1] The retailer of specialties usually handles fewer products and has an opportunity to become much better acquainted with the consumer's desires and habits regarding them.

valuable information was obtained on the items stocked by retailers and prices at which they were offered.

REPORT 7

"Good morning. I was thinking of something in the toilet goods line to give a friend. What do you suggest? Perfume? In sets? What are they giving now?"

"Perfume is our best seller by far now. Have some fine values in gifts today. Lucien Lelong has a new package—three odors in it, etc. (got the story), and also Whisper at $5. They are our best sellers. Then we have Christmas Night, special at $12.95, and Caron's Bellodgia at $7.95"—these being shown off the ad which was well displayed in front of me.

Going to the case he brought out Lelong's Joli at $5 and Whisper at $5. I asked if women buy this for themselves. The clerk said no, they wouldn't spend the money. Women buy in bulk at $1.25, etc. Of the three, he recommended Lelong's Joli because of the new idea of three odors and the hat box.

As a gesture he brought out Dorothy Gray's compact at $3.50. Said it was new. Showed new powder wrinkle. Put it back, and saw no other perfume but Lelong. Got good Lelong workout. Got out Whisper wrapped box. Department looked fine.

REPORT 8

Shalimar at $15. Ciro's Surrender at $15. Showed those. Mentioned Christmas Night special at $22.50 and $12.95, also Caron's Bellodgia and Lelong's Whisper at $5. Gave quite a talk on Shalimar and Lelong. Directed my attention to new idea in Joli at $5—three odors for different occasions. Mentioned Lelong was famous costumer. Showed the Whisper package on ad. Would have bought either that or Joli. Said Lelong is imported—even the bottles. Even charge them for the bottles in the window used for display. Perfume very expensive and exclusive. Good intelligent reasoning used. Knew his business.

Ad well displayed on the counter. The department looked good. The department was 1½ months old, and they are proud of their new department.

One variation of the shopping technique is to station an observer in stores during rush hours to note how customers buy and the way in which salespeople handle them. In some cases it is very revealing to note the kinds of people who purchase specific commodities. For example, a series of observations made at the counter at which dentifrices were purchased completely changed the conception of one manufacturer as to who buys tooth paste and powder.

In the case of specialty products, such as household equipment, the informal shopping interview has special advantages in learning the basis on which competitive salesmen attempt to make sales. An automobile manufacturer who made informal shopping calls learned for the first time about two very vulnerable points attacked by competition. As a result of these informal shopping interviews the final research project employed the shopping technique to test the original hypotheses developed by it.

Report 9 shows the results of an informal shopping interview made for a specialty product. Individual brand names have been deleted. Brand A is the one for which the study was made.

REPORT 9

This store carries the X, Y, and Z. Mr. Bigham showed me the features of each machine and it was hard to determine at first which machine they pushed, but finally learned that it was the Z.

He insisted on showing me the quietness of the motor in the Z and the advantage of having the motor placed so that the bottom shelf was easy to get to.

The very best price he could make me for cash was 5 per cent off on the X and 2 per cent on the other two machines. He said they carry the three kinds of machines so they could satisfy a larger number of people, as some wanted the belt-driven machine while others preferred the sealed motor.

Mr. Bigham states that many times they have people call them for service on their A, sometimes when they have one of the other makes.

The A is a good machine with a good standing and a good service. Reliable and well advertised but can be bought in Jacksonville as low as "nothing down."

It is interesting to notice in this case how the operator sensed an opening and began bargaining with the salesman to determine the extent of price-cutting. Notice also how the effectiveness of competitive selling was indicated by casual reference to the brand for which the study was being made.

The Open Interview. The second type of retailer interview is the open interview. In this type of interview, the investigator introduces himself as an independent researcher making a study in the field. The dealer therefore realizes that he is talking to an investigator.

With the exception of store managers in some chain store systems, dealers will usually talk very freely in an open interview. The disadvantage of this type of informal interview is that the dealer is making a conscious effort to provide information and may take a biased position.

Excerpts follow from two reports which illustrate the kind of information which may be obtained in open informal dealer interviews.

REPORT 10

Handles A, B, C, D, and E. Does not handle any ironers.

C is the leading washing machine in Pittsburgh and B leading nationally.

All the washing-machine companies are interested in volume. B is trying to cooperate and is accomplishing a good deal. Not much money in washing-machine business. The dealers just about make wages. The markup is not big enough. Manufacturers are so eager for volume and there are so many chiselers in the business that you can find washing machines in every basement, hardware, department store, and electric shop in Pittsburgh.

This dealer is distinctly sour on pushing washing machines. His main volume and main profit is on refrigerators. He sells X, Y, and Z refrigerators.

REPORT 11

Xerxes' leading market is in Chicago. The market is currently so strong that the factory is having a hard time keeping up with production. This outlet is not guaranteeing delivery of any orders after July 1. 75,000 machines were sold in the past four months. The new Superb is a seller. This outlet is planning a new campaign for fall. Ironers are selling better than they were. Xerxes new "fold-up" ironer, built like a folding chair or cabinet, is doing a great deal to stimulate sales. All the Xerxes outlets in the Chicago market sell a combined total of 500 units of Xerxes ironers per month. Xerxes is particularly good on servicing, and in backing up guarantees.

This outlet also sells Norge refrigerators and stoves, and Chambers stoves.

Informal Key Interviews. Informal interviews should be made with certain selected types of individuals to take advantage of their special experience and knowledge of particular markets. There are five general classes of persons who occupy key positions which give them such experience and knowledge.

1. *Executives of the company for which the study is being made.* Some of these executives will have been previously interviewed in the situation analysis. However, it is likely that a number of them can be reinterviewed to advantage during the informal investigation. Others not included in the situation analysis are added.

2. *Salesmen and other employees in minor positions with special knowledge.* It will usually be found that it is desirable to make extensive interviews among this group in the informal investigation. Nearly every employee of a company has many ideas which he is anxious to express. Informal conversations with these persons will often be productive in suggesting hypotheses for the study.

The importance of obtaining adequate coverage of the sales force in the informal investigation merits special attention. In the situation analysis one learns a great many facts about the sales organization, management, and policies. It is always a good practice to follow this up by traveling with several salesmen to observe the manner in which they conduct their daily work. By watching the actual selling process where the orders are being obtained or lost, one sees all the elements in the selling operation undergoing their ultimate test. In observing the work of salesmen, one obtains understanding of the effectiveness with which sales policies are executed. The reactions of buyers, the sales arguments which are successful and unsuccessful, and the conditions in retail stores which block sales should be noted. A few days spent with meat salesmen making their routine calls, for example, once led a researcher directly to the development of a most successful research. The study was designed to determine methods by which salesmen could be rerouted and given special training in order to increase productive calls and the frequency with which dealers would be covered.

3. *Competitors.* Some researchers make it a special point to interview key executives with competitive firms. Executives who will talk quite freely about their business and the industry may be found in most companies. Managers of competitors' local sales branches are often very productive sources of information.

4. *Executives of advertising media.* Both the general and business publications have employees who are well informed about the markets for individual products. These media are in constant contact with the different manufacturers and distributors. Most of them have built up a large fund of information over a period of time. In view of the extensive knowledge of these executives, it is desirable to include them in the informal investigation.

5. *Specialists in the field.* For every product, there are certain specialists who possess important technical knowledge. For a drug item, there are doctors, dermatologists, pediatricians, and dentists whose experience and opinions should be considered. For food products, there are dietitians and home economists. For mechanical products, there are engineers, architects, and designers. The specialists who may provide useful sources for informal key interviews range from agricultural agents, airplane pilots, and football coaches to veterinarians.

Reports on Key Interviews. Because of the many different types of persons who may be included in informal key interviews, it would be too laborious to show an example for each type. The following report shows the results of an interview with a speculative builder, made in connection with a research for air conditioning.

REPORT 12

Mr. Clark seemed pretty much disgusted with companies manufacturing air-conditioning units (he refused to mention specific companies for business reasons), because they are using "too much high pressure in their selling— they're pushing too much."

Mr. Clark feels that air conditioning is something new, but it has a most promising future. "It needs a lot of improvement and at present is pretty expensive."

He remarked that the Airtemp and the Carrier Company in particular have good units. The Carrier Company puts out a very complete unit. But most other companies just pick out certain parts of the unit. Most systems which are installed nowadays are a composite of several different companies' equipment. My impression was that he felt the company which put out a complete unit would do a better job.

The Banner Company is particularly interested in schools where they put in washed air. At the present time, also, they are planning on putting in air conditioning in a hospital operating room for more hygienic purposes.

"Air conditioning is purely a cooling device for lessening of temperature for summer conditions." The washed air in schools and hospitals produces this effect, it seems. Window devices are used for air cooling in some office buildings.

The contractor has little to say about the installation of an air-conditioning system becoming one of the specifications of a building. Usually it is the owner and architect who decide upon that and discuss the matter with an engineer who would probably have the final word.

Mr. Clark feels that technical information is unnecessary to him in his business, for the company makes a practice of subletting that part of a job to an engineer.

To illustrate further the type of information secured in informal key interviews, part of the report of a call on a dentist in connection with a research for dentifrices is shown below. The reader will notice the wealth of background information which was obtained from this interview. The interview was made by an experienced physiologist trained for the specific research project.

REPORT 13

He is opposed to tooth pastes that contain an excessive amount of flavor and an excessive amount of bite, because the substances responsible for these effects are irritating to the gums. He has found witch hazel to be useful, particularly in injections for local anesthesia. He thinks that salt and water have a wonderful healing effect on gums. He thinks that salt and soda are satisfactory for cleansing teeth and also that the brush alone is quite effective. He thinks that teeth should be brushed at least three times per day and after eating foods. He thinks it very unlikely that teeth are worn down as a result of excessive brushing. Where excessive brushing does cause wasting away, he thinks it can be attributed to improper brushing.

He thinks it is very important to brush the surface of the molars to prevent food impacts in crevices in the molars that are due to improper closing of the teeth in growth. He thinks that chalk is satisfactory as an abrasive, but does not know what abrasives the manufacturers are using. He thinks that abrasives should not be too hard. He thinks that the use of a soap in a tooth paste is all right, but that an excessive amount should not be used, because it would be irritating to the tissue. He thinks that soap-containing tooth paste penetrates the space between the teeth more satisfactorily than a non-soap-containing dentifrice.

He is not particularly enthusiastic about the use of antiseptics in dentifrices. He thinks that perhaps in some cases it is all right, but in some not necessary. He thinks that sampling dentists by mail is just as effective as sending detail men around, considering the relative cost involved.

This chapter has shown the purpose and the importance of the informal investigation in marketing research. The procedure to be followed and the kind of information developed in this step have been discussed and illustrated. With the results of a comprehensive situation analysis and a penetrating informal investigation at hand, the researcher is adequately prepared for the crucial step of planning the formal research project.

9

PLANNING THE FORMAL RESEARCH PROJECT

The planning of the formal research project is, in a very real sense, the most important single step in marketing research procedure. The success or failure of the entire investigation hinges largely on the care with which the planning step is executed, for all the activities which follow are necessarily dependent upon the skill with which the plan has been developed. Unfortunately, this step is often handled rather superficially for several reasons: lack of a specific program for developing the plan, unwise hurry to obtain the final results, failure to appreciate the importance of exploratory work, and failure to provide adequate funds for this phase of the research.

By carefully following an orderly and logical procedure in preparing the plan for an investigation, the research director may avoid many errors. Care and patience at this stage can contribute a great deal to the success of the final research project. A suggested procedure for the planning stage follows each of the operations listed below in the order given:

1. Determining the specific purposes of the investigation.
2. Determining the types and sources of data to be obtained.
3. Preparing the forms to be used in collecting data.
4. Planning the sample.
5. Conducting the test investigation.
6. Determining operating plans and costs.

Determining the Specific Purposes of the Investigation

Determining specific purposes is the first step in planning the formal research project. At this point, all that has been learned in the situation analysis and the informal investigation is reduced to a few basic hypotheses, which are restated in the form of the specific purposes of the research. The selection of these purposes determines the nature of the entire investigation. If those purposes have not been properly crystallized, it is almost certain that the research staff will wander around aimlessly, obtain unsatisfactory data, and arrive at foggy conclusions. On the other hand, if the purposes have been carefully and wisely selected and are stated as *specifically* as possible, the investigation may proceed to a successful conclusion. At this point the experience, intuition, and skill which mark the outstanding marketing researcher are clearly in evidence.

The final objective of this first step is a clear, concise statement of the specific purposes of the analysis. Therefore, the researcher should take the various hypotheses which have been discovered in the situation analysis and informal investigation, and determine the specific ones which are to become the objectives of the formal research.

Functions of the Hypotheses. The hypotheses serve two functions in marketing research. The first is to limit the investigation to certain specific purposes so that it may proceed scientifically. The second function is to enable the researcher to project his thought to the probable solution of the problem in order that the research may be planned most effectively.

A company once spent a large sum of money for a marketing research. The result was a comprehensive report which went into vast detail regarding methods of merchandising and advertising. After its completion the study was received with considerable enthusiasm. A checkup a year later, however, showed that not one actual change in marketing methods could be traced to this analysis. The work had been done by an individual who was considered a competent marketing researcher, and most of the generally recognized standards for marketing research work had been observed. The study, however, was spread over so many different aspects of the marketing operation and filled with so much confusing detail that it was fruitless.

About a year after this expensive research was made, the company engaged another individual to study its marketing problems. This person spent considerable time in a situation analysis and informal investigation to guide him in planning his marketing research. As a result, he put his finger on one central problem. This was the excessive sales effort which the company placed on products sold in large volume but at a small profit or at an actual loss. The cost of the analysis was much less than the previous one. At its completion it became clear that the company should shift the emphasis in its marketing activities to more profitable lines. As a result, the company changed its marketing operations, with a clear improvement in efficiency. The researcher was able to produce a highly successful piece of work by being careful to limit the study to a workable hypothesis.

The importance of limiting individual research projects to workable hypotheses is generally recognized in all fields of research. One of the most common characteristics of the research novice is that, in a desire to do as complete a job as possible, he fails to obtain the quality of results which comes from intensive concentration. The more experienced a researcher becomes, the more he restricts his work to a few carefully constructed hypotheses. To illustrate the value of concentration from the field of marketing research, the following list of study titles shows a progression from broad to restricted scope:

1. Methods of Marketing Consumer Goods.
2. Methods of Marketing Food Products.
3. Methods of Marketing Dairy Products.
4. Methods of Marketing Cheese.
5. Methods of Marketing Cheddar Cheese.
6. Methods of Displaying Cheddar Cheese.
7. Methods of Displaying Cheddar Cheese in the Chicago Market.

The development in this list follows a concentration in product through the first five stages. In the sixth stage, another concentration factor has been introduced by restricting the study to one phase of marketing. In the seventh phase the subject is further restricted by limiting the geographical area which is researched. With given resources of time and money, a study done at the upper level of this list would probably be superficial. On the other hand, a research on the methods of displaying Cheddar cheese in the Chicago market, for a given amount of research effort, should produce precise results which can be handled in a much more scientific manner than any of the broader studies listed.

Regarding the second function of the hypotheses, one often finds that it is necessary to reject many suggested hypotheses because it becomes clear after some consideration that they could not be proved within the limits of the study. The testing of proposed hypotheses in respect to their probable validity by marketing research methods must of necessity be very general in the early planning stages. Later on, as one progresses to trial data gathering, he has a much clearer concept as to whether the hypotheses can be effectively checked. As the research progresses further through to the interpretation stage, this knowledge is still further advanced. However, in the early planning stage, an experienced researcher has some general notions as to how the project is going to develop. With these in mind, he examines the various hypotheses under consideration according to his best judgment and determines the ease and effectiveness with which each of them probably can be resolved with known techniques.

This statement of the functions of hypotheses indicates the standards which should be set for sound hypotheses. Since the first function is to limit the study properly, the first standard by which a hypothesis should be measured is, "Does it strike at a critical marketing problem of the company?" Since the second function is to crystallize thought as to the practicability of the trial solution of the problem, the second standard for a sound hypothesis is, "Can it be tested by the techniques of marketing research available to me?"

Steps in Stating the Purposes for the Investigation. Unfortunately there are no mechanical devices for the extraction of the hypotheses or purposes for the investigation. All one can do is to make sure that the situation analysis and informal investigation have been conducted with sufficient care so that these hypotheses will arise from a sound background. The ability to select the most important hypotheses and state them in their proper form comes largely from practice.

As a means of avoiding confusion and waste effort in arriving at the final statement of the purposes of the marketing research, however, the following steps are suggested:

1. Prepare a written list of the possible purposes which have accrued from the situation analysis and informal investigation.
2. Select a relatively small number of these hypotheses on the basis of the standards for a sound hypothesis discussed previously.
3. Restate each hypothesis in the best possible form, to make its testing possible.

By deliberately devoting time to each of these three specific steps, the researcher can crystallize his thoughts and write a compact statement of the purposes of the analysis.

An exhaustive written list of possible purposes is the only way to overcome the very real danger of missing fruitful objectives through oversight. It also provides the best environment for reflective thought which is essential to the development and selection of the best possible hypotheses.

The importance of considering as broad a list of hypotheses as possible is expressed in the following classic statement by Venn:

Everyone who has ever had to work out the solution of any little matter in daily life which has puzzled him, knows how many and how wild were the guesses that flitted through his mind before he paused at one which seemed more hopeful. The larger the stock from which he has to draw, the better, other things being equal, is his chance of finding one good one amongst them. And the same holds good of the more serious speculations of the scientific man.[1]

_____
[1] John Venn, _The Principles of Empirical or Inductive Logic_ (London: 1889), p. 399.

The second operation—selecting the few hypotheses to be pursued further—is highly important because the tendency to attempt to solve too many of the marketing problems of the company in one analysis is very common, especially among people who lack a broad research experience. It is the job of the researcher at this point to evaluate carefully all the various possible hypotheses, and to reject those which are impracticable or which do not have a vital bearing upon the marketing success of the company.

In this connection, it is useful to keep in mind the counsel of Darwin: "I have steadily endeavored to keep my mind free so as to give up any hypothesis, however much beloved (and I cannot resist forming one on every subject), as soon as facts are shown to be opposed to it." [2] Many a marketing research has stumbled along its useless path because the researcher has clung to a sterile hypothesis. The facts developed in the situation analysis and the informal investigation must be used to test every suggested hypothesis. The researcher must not allow his pride of authorship to interfere with a cold appraisal of the probable value of a hypothesis on the basis of all the facts at his command.

The third operation merits careful attention, because out of a clear statement of purposes come the ingredients of the successful marketing research. They affect, for example, the sources and types of data required, the sampling decisions, and many other aspects of the final research.

Sometimes a hypothesis is encountered which is so fundamental that the entire analysis is restricted to solution of its related problem. An example of such an analysis is a study made for an automobile manufacturer. During the informal investigation, the researcher found one major negative impression of this automobile which was firmly rooted in the minds of prospective buyers and effectively exploited by competitors' salesmen. An entire investigation was planned around the hypothesis that competitive selling organizations were causing a large number of lost sales by playing upon the vulnerable point that the automobile in question had a very low resale value and would therefore be a poor investment. The result of confining the investigation to this one major hypothesis was an inexpensive and very useful analysis. Investigators, posing as prospects, shopped competitive dealers and observed the salesmen's answer to their statement that they were interested in the brand for which the survey was being made. The investigators later shopped the dealers selling the automobile in question, mentioned this objection, and

---

[2] Charles Darwin, *Life and Letters*, ed. Francis Darwin (New York: Appleton-Century-Crofts, Inc., 1889), Vol. I, p. 83.

observed the skill with which their salesmen were able to meet the argument. The formal research clearly showed the importance of the low resale value claim and the inability of the salesmen to meet the claim. It was a comparatively simple matter to provide dealers and salesmen with the necessary weapons to overcome this sales resistance.

Some of the very best marketing research work is done in those investigations which confine themselves to one hypothesis. In most studies, however, it usually is necessary and profitable to follow a group of hypotheses in one investigation. The following questions indicate the purposes set up for an investigation for a furniture polish manufacturer:

1. Do housewives desire a "high polish" on their furniture?
2. What have been the style trends in furniture finishes, and how do they affect the market for furniture polish?
3. What is the relative importance of different types of outlets, especially the syndicate stores?
4. What price should be placed on the product to produce the greatest net profit, taking into account sales volume in relation to cost of production?

Up to this point emphasis has been placed upon a high degree of selectivity in determining the specific purposes. It should also be recognized that if primary data are gathered in a marketing research, it is often found practical to obtain information on a large number of points which go beyond the primary purposes as originally conceived. Usable by-product information often can be obtained in the field work at no additional cost. These by-products should not be overlooked, but the analyst must be careful that they are at no time allowed to divert attention from the fundamental problems. An example of such a by-product is found in a dentifrice investigation. In this study three major hypotheses were pursued. During the course of the investigation it was found that information about the importance of the dentist in influencing the choice of brands could be obtained as a by-product. This information was very helpful because there had been considerable doubt and confusion in the minds of the executives of the company as to the exact importance of dentists in this connection.

Types and Sources of Data

After the purposes of the analysis have been clearly stated, the next step is to select the types and sources of data which will lead to a scientific appraisal of the hypotheses. The most important principle for the researcher to bear in mind at this stage is that there are many different types and sources of data which may be employed for any given hypothesis. If one is not fully aware of this fact, he is likely to proceed immediately to the collection of data which have an apparent bearing on the hypothesis but may be thoroughly inadequate or even misleading.

There is no certainty that the data that first come to mind will prove to be the best for testing the hypothesis. As a matter of fact, it is usually true that the most obvious, traditional kinds of data are greatly inferior to others which may be obtained. Furthermore, it is frequently found that more than one kind of data is necessary.

Practically all the data of the market researcher are bases for inductions. But these may be classified into three major types: survey, observational, and experimental. The possibilities of using different variations of each of these three types of data should be thoroughly explored. After one has exhausted the possibilities of using the survey method, for example, he may find that he can devise a procedure for using observational or experimental methods which will yield better results.

Sources of Marketing Data. The sources from which marketing data may be obtained are so varied and complex that it is impossible to catalog all of them. In general, however, most of the sources fall into the four following classifications, the first three listed being primary sources and the fourth a secondary source.

1. *Consumers and Buyers.* In many marketing researches, data are obtained directly from buyers or users of a commodity. The distinction between the buyers and the users of the product is an important one to bear in mind in planning the analysis. Thus, in the case of many products consumed within the home, the housewife is usually the purchasing agent for the family. It will be found, however, that the user is more important than the buyer for many products. Deciding the extent to which the use of a product is separated from its purchase is, therefore, an important phase of determining the exact source which should be employed in the analysis.

In the case of industrial products, it is especially necessary to give careful consideration to the individuals who should be interviewed, because there are a number of persons who influence the decision to buy most industrial products. In addition to the purchasing agent, one finds that top-ranking executives frequently exercise a controlling influence. On the other hand, maintenance men and factory workers may prove to have an important influence on the buying of equipment or materials. Sometimes they represent an unusually valuable source of information in a marketing research for an industrial product.

LIST OF SOME POSSIBLE TYPES AND SOURCES OF DATA

Hypothesis—"The flavor of 'X' (a food product) should be changed so it will be sweeter."

Type	Source	Description of Data
Survey	Consumers	Statements of housewives using the product as to whether it should be sweeter.
		Statements of children using the product as to whether it should be sweeter.
		Statements of persons who formerly used the product as to why they discontinued its use.
		Survey of brands used, data to be classified according to "sweetness."
		Make up sweeter samples, give to consumers with samples of product now on market, and ask which they prefer.
		Analyze panel data on switches in brands purchased according to sweetness.
	Dealers	Ask for sales ranking of brands; classify data according to sweetness.
		Ask why people buy leading brands.
	Salesmen	Ask why product does not sell better.
	Domestic Science Teachers	Ask how product could be improved.
Observational	Consumers	Pantry inventory of brands.
		Offer samples of product with varying degrees of sweetness, observe which is eaten in greatest quantity.
	Dealers	Analyze sales records by brands by degrees of sweetness from store audits.
	Company Records	If firm manufactures wide variety of similar products classify sales volume of similar products, according to sweetness.
Experimental	Dealer Sales Records	Test sales campaign on sweeter product in selected markets.

FIGURE 10. Types and Sources of Data for a Marketing Research. The figure illustrates the relationship between types and sources, and the wide variety of data open to the researcher. The reader can undoubtedly think of additional kinds of data which might be employed for the hypothesis.

2. *Dealers.* Dealers are a second important source of data for marketing research. A decision must be reached whether to include both wholesale and retail sources. Furthermore, there are special groups engaged in the distribution of certain products whom it may be wise to include. It may be found, for example, that data from chain-store managers or from owners of small delicatessens will have particular value for a specific research.

3. *Company Records.* A third major source of data is the internal records of the business. In the situation analysis these records are scanned and manipulated to a certain extent. In planning the analysis, it may be found that the solution to a major problem can be made from an intensive analysis of sales data already in the files of the company. If a hypothesis relating to the problem of determining the number of salesmen to be employed in different territories is used, an analysis of the performance of individual salesmen under varying conditions is a source of data which should obviously be included. An intensive analysis of advertising records in the light of a special hypothesis is another example of the use of internal records.

4. *Data from Published Records.* This fourth general source of data is published records. Facts already available through the U. S. Census, for example, may provide the best possible source for testing a major hypothesis in a study. With the development of comprehensive statistics on marketing operations through studies such as the Census of Business, secondary data are becoming increasingly important. Universities and business firms, such as advertising media, also publish large quantities of marketing data in convenient form from time to time.

Sources of Secondary Data. The sources from which a marketing researcher may gather secondary data for his use are almost innumerable. The reader can readily obtain rather complete lists to insure against overlooking possible sources which may be valuable in any given marketing research. The purpose of this brief discussion is to familiarize the reader with the ones he will be likely to turn to most frequently.

Confusion in obtaining secondary data can be avoided by keeping in mind clearly three separate methods of locating them. In the first place, there are several reference books and bibliographies which may be used to locate materials. Secondly, there are various firms and organizations which gather data to which one may turn as a source for the facts to be obtained. Thirdly, there are current publications which may be regarded as source books of generally useful marketing data. A list of the more important and generally used sources, classified according to these three types, is presented on the following pages.

Reference Books and Bibliographies

1. *Monthly Catalog of U. S. Public Documents.* This bibliography lists all the current printed material issued by the federal government. The publications are classified by the various departments. The monthly catalog and the publications which it lists are available from the Superintendent of Documents, Washington, D. C.

2. *Industrial Arts Index.* The *Industrial Arts Index* is a reference book, similar to the *Reader's Guide to Periodical Literature,* but covering technical periodicals in business, engineering, scientific, and industrial fields. It is a complete cumulative index of all the important magazine articles which appear on technical subjects. The index is arranged alphabetically, with many cross-references, so that it is possible to obtain references by industries (such as food, clothing, or automobiles) as well as by subject classification (such as advertising, dealer-display, sales accounting, or salesmen).

3. *Marketing Research Sources.* This publication is a marketing research bibliography which is revised frequently. It is available from the U. S. Department of Commerce, Domestic Commerce Division (Bulletin No. 55).

4. *Public Affairs Information Service.* This general bibliography covering subjects in economics, commerce, and business contains the names and addresses of trade associations.

5. *Government Statistics for Business Use,* written by P. M. Hauser and W. R. Leonard, published in 1946 by John Wiley & Sons, Inc., discusses the various types of statistical data available from sources in the federal government. It includes thirteen chapters written by government employees whose work is directly concerned with the development of certain types of statistics. The book also has a number of practical suggestions as to the uses, interpretations, and limitations of statistical information for business.

6. *A Current List of Selected Information Sources for Businessmen.* This is a regular feature of *Sales Management* magazine. See current issues.

7. *The Journal of Marketing.* This quarterly publication contains a department on "Research in Marketing," which catalogs current studies with brief descriptions of each one.

Organizations Which Gather Marketing Data

1. *U. S. Department of Commerce.* Information supplied by the Department of Agriculture, the Bureau of Internal Revenue, or some other division of the federal government will often be found exceed-

ingly valuable for marketing research work. In general, however, the Department of Commerce is the most important source. This department maintains a comprehensive activity for the gathering of data for use in marketing research.

2. *State Governments.* The governments of all the states are continuously engaged in gathering data on many subjects which are of interest to the marketing researcher. These sources are especially valuable on specialized problems dealing with subjects such as agriculture and retailing. Information on material published by the states may be obtained from *Monthly Check List of State Publications,* U. S. Government Printing Office.

3. *Consumer Advertising Media.* Most magazines gather data which are of considerable value and are made available through their advertising departments. Newspapers are excellent sources for data which have been gathered in preparing the news of the day and for information on local markets.

4. *Business Publications.* The various magazines which make up the business press, particularly industrial publications and trade papers, are each specialists in their own particular fields. The best sources can be located by the lists of business magazines which are classified by industries. These will be found in current issues of *Standard Rate and Data Service.*

5. *Trade Associations.* Every important type of business has its trade association, which nearly always gathers statistics regarding the business as one of its primary functions. The trade association which is likely to have data of use in an analysis for any specific product may be located through *Selected Trade Associations of the U. S.,* published by the Department of Commerce. The names and addresses of associations, with the names of secretaries and managers, are currently brought up to date in a series of bulletins, each of which covers an individual industry. The National Association of Manufacturers and the National Industrial Conference Board maintain extensive business libraries as a service to their members.

6. *Private Corporations.* Several of the larger corporations maintain libraries which will provide data for the public. Each of these libraries is, of course, specialized in its particular industry. Examples are the American Telephone and Telegraph Company, the Metropolitan Life Insurance Company, the Household Finance Corporation, and the Commonwealth Edison Company.

7. *Syndicated Research Data.* There are several specialized research organizations which compile current marketing data. A list of the most important syndicated sources, with an indication of the kind of data each provides, follows:

SOURCE	DATA
Market Research Corporation of America, New York	Continuous consumer panel data, showing purchases by brands of selected commodities
A. C. Nielsen Company, Chicago	Current sales in retail stores for various drug and grocery products; index of television and radio listening
Gallup-Robinson, Princeton	Magazine and television impact ratings
Daniel Starch, New York	Magazine and newspaper readership surveys
Media Records, Chicago Publishers Information Bureau, New York	Volume of magazine and newspaper advertising
International Business Machines Corporation, New York	Data processed on punched cards ready for tabulation according to user's specifications.

CURRENT PUBLICATIONS CONTAINING IMPORTANT MARKETING DATA

1. *Consumer Market Data Handbook.* This volume, published by the U. S. Department of Commerce, brings together in one handbook the most commonly used general statistics about markets. Data on subjects such as population, retail sales, number of wired homes, and income tax returns are provided for states, principal cities, and counties.

2. *Industrial Market Data.* These are booklets published by the U. S. Department of Commerce in the Industrial Marketing Series. They give basic facts on industrial markets, such as steel and paper.

3. *The Census of American Business.* This basic source provides data regarding all types of marketing organizations, including sales of manufacturers' sales agencies, wholesalers, retailers, and service organizations such as banks and hotels. The data are broken down in detail by regions, states, counties, metropolitan areas, and principal cities.

4. *Decennial Census of the U. S.* This publication is the marketing researcher's chief data book. Its use as a source for general population statistics is obvious. However, one should not overlook the many special topics and subclassifications of data included in the census, such as housing and employment.

5. *U. S. Census of Manufactures.* The Census of Manufactures provides data showing the volume of production for all major industries as well as many less important ones. Data are usually given both in dollars and in physical units. This source is particularly useful as a basis for estimating the total volume of commodities consumed and in making market forecasts.

6. *America's Needs and Resources.* A comprehensive source book on vital statistical data of great use to marketing researchers. Edited

by J. Frederic Dewhurst, it is published by the Twentieth Century Fund.

7. *State, Regional, and Local Market Indicators.* A compilation of data useful in quantitative analysis by the U. S. Department of Commerce.

8. *Commerce and Navigation in the United States.* This annual compendium reports the movement of all foreign commerce. Wherever data on imports or exports are required, this is a standard source.

9. *Survey of Current Business.* This monthly publication of the U. S. Department of Commerce currently reports the more important business series, such as production in various industries, retail trade, wages, and financial data. The *Statistical Supplement to the Survey of Current Business* summarizes data for longer periods of time. It is issued every two years.

10. *Federal Reserve Bulletin.* The Federal Reserve Board at Washington issues monthly a general bulletin containing financial data and from time to time other information which is important from the point of view of general business conditions. Each of the Federal Reserve districts issues its own separate bulletin. The bulletins of the individual districts are likely to contain information on some subjects not covered by those of the central board. The bulletin of the Federal Reserve Bank of New York is especially complete.

11. *Monthly Labor Review.* This review is published by the United States Department of Labor, Bureau of Labor Statistics. It is especially valuable for price and cost of living data.

12. *Standard Statistics Service.* This service is primarily financial. It is one of the most complete of the private statistical services furnishing data on general marketing conditions in addition to financial information.

Appraising Secondary Data. While secondary data are frequently used in marketing research work, all are not useful or reliable. Unfortunately, they have the sanctity of print, which leads many to accept them without reservation. One should be careful to scrutinize secondary data thoroughly to make sure that they are sufficiently accurate and useful for his purpose. The following standards are suggested for appraising the value of any information obtained from secondary sources:

1. The organization supplying the data.
2. The authority under which they are gathered.
3. Freedom from bias.
4. The extent to which the rules of sampling have been rigidly upheld.
5. The nature of the units in which the data are expressed.

6. The accuracy of the data.

7. Pertinency to the problem at hand.

The Organization. The first consideration in determining the value of secondary data is the character of the organization which has gathered them. All organizations exist for some specific purpose, and the data which they gather are obtained for some purpose. Some organizations are established primarily for the purpose of obtaining information. With others, obtaining data is purely secondary to some other major function. Data which are obtained for purely promotional purposes, for example, do not ordinarily have the same status as facts obtained by a public body set up for the purpose of providing infor-mation.

There are several other considerations. Some companies have been obtaining information for a long period of time. They have acquired valuable experience and have built an organization which is thor-oughly adequate to the requirements for obtaining the data. Some organizations have individuals who are well-trained scientists to con-trol the gathering of data; others have inadequate personnel. Some are very well financed, while others do not have adequate funds to gather the facts. Some organizations have established very careful standards of research; others have no clearly recognized standards which they follow.

The Authority. Some organizations have the legal right to force information to be delivered to them on the basis of standards which are set out in a carefully prepared plan covering each detail. Exam-ples are the data obtained by the Internal Revenue Department in connection with income tax returns, and by other legal agencies. Other organizations have no authority whatsoever to obtain data and, therefore, the information received may be wholly inadequate.

An example of the way in which authority influences the compil-ing of data is the contrast between reports of the sales of life insurance and those of electric refrigerators. In each case a trade association compiles the figures. The data on sales of life insurance are accurate. The reason is that the sales of life insurance are required by law to be reported by every company operating within the various states. In the case of electric refrigerators, many of the companies reporting to the trade association do not know where sales to consumers have been made and report rough estimates.

Freedom from Bias. The presence or lack of bias, prejudice, and personal interest in data is determined to a large extent by the nature of the organization furnishing the information. Ordinarily public bodies which gather data under legal authority will furnish information which is not influenced by deliberate bias, while some other organizations are much more likely to bias the information.

This rule is not, however, a safe one to follow in any individual situation. Data released by public bodies have been known to be biased. It is, therefore, necessary to examine the data carefully in order to determine whether bias or self-interest has been injected into the facts.

Adequacy of the Sample. Since most secondary data are based upon statistical samples, it is just as important to check the samples taken for any secondary source as it is to plan carefully the sample for primary data. This is rather difficult because it is easy to hide deficiencies in the sampling process. One of the most important considerations to bear in mind in appraising the soundness of the sample used for secondary data is the various subsamples which are included in the study. One should not be satisfied with general statements referring to the gross sample in making this appraisal.

Units in Which the Data Are Expressed. A danger which is ever present in the use of secondary data is that one will not have a sufficiently accurate understanding of the exact definition employed in setting up the units for which data are provided. Even such apparently simple concepts as "house," "apartment," and "automobiles" are subject to varying definitions. The data obtained will depend upon the definitions used in a given study. Composite units, such as "improved house," must be watched with especial care. These involve double definitions, and usually the added factor (such as "improved") is likely to be an important consideration which may be overlooked. Another example of a composite unit is "chain store." In order to understand exactly what is meant by data on chain stores, one must understand, first, the specific definition of the term "store," and second, the specific limitation of the term "chain." To some organizations the word "chain" is limited to five or more outlets under centralized ownership and management; to others, it means three or more outlets, while to still others it means two or more outlets.

One very important consideration in connection with the problem of the units in which the data are expressed is met wherever data are provided in frequency distributions. Data involving ages, for example, are nearly always reported for groups, such as "from 5 to 9 years of age." The classifications which are employed in such cases have usually been set up with some specific requirement in mind. Sometimes the classification will make the data useless for the purpose of a particular marketing research.

Accuracy. All secondary data to be employed should be carefully checked for accuracy. There are three ways in which this may be done most economically.

The first way is to examine carefully for inconsistencies. Errors in addition or in the results of other mathematical processes may appear with sufficient frequency to indicate that the data should not be employed. Tables should be complete; they should show all omissions. Sometimes facts found in two separate parts of one source are directly inconsistent.

A second way of checking the accuracy of the data is to inquire into the manner in which they were gathered, edited, and tabulated. It is often possible to appraise their probable accuracy by talking with some of the people who were involved in the various processes.

A third method of appraising the accuracy of data is to check a part of them against material available from other sources known to be accurate. Most sources of secondary data include some facts relating to subjects which have been previously covered by other sources. For example, a study of consumers' shopping habits may contain a summary table showing the percentage of consumers using different brands of the product. If this table is checked against other studies showing the status of these brands and is found to be clearly out of line with information obtained from a more reliable source, this discovery would cast doubt on the accuracy of all the information obtained in the study.

Pertinency to the Problem. If a researcher has a clear conception of the purposes of the study he is making, he should be able to judge the relevancy of any secondary data to that problem. However, it is very easy to accept data which do not really provide a sound scientific basis for solution of the problem. The fact that their use will avoid the necessity for investing time and effort in the gathering of primary data creates a tendency to accept secondary data even though they are not exactly what is required. Consequently, the researcher should make a special point to challenge them on this score, making certain that they are sufficiently relevant to his problem to warrant their use.

Planning the Means of Obtaining Primary Data. Observational and experimental data are almost universally obtained through auditors or observers closely under the control of the research project director. However, if survey data are used, a decision must be made during the planning stage as to whether to employ a (1) mail, (2) personal interview, or (3) telephone survey. It is especially important to have a clear understanding of the characteristics peculiar to the mail survey, on the one hand, and the personal interview survey on the other. Many researchers are inclined to favor one of these forms and use it more or less habitually, assuming that it has a general superiority over the other. The truth is that each has its own peculiar advantages and disadvantages. The decision as to which type to employ should depend entirely upon the specific problems faced in a given research.

Advantages of the Mail Survey. The mail survey has several advantages, of which four are the most important. The first advantage is that it *avoids the bias which results from the use of interviewers.* By automatically eliminating the personal element introduced by the presence of the field investigator, it is sometimes possible to obtain more accurate data. An example is in certain types of readership studies. It has been found, for example, that many men and women will not admit, in the presence of an interviewer, that they read certain types of advertisements. Readership of treatment to restore health, perfume, and men's store advertisements have been cited as cases in point.

Even with very careful training and supervision, there is a constant tendency for the person conducting the interview to suggest answers in such a manner as to influence the respondent's answers. Another kind of bias is introduced by the tendency of field workers to select certain types of persons to include in the sample, a matter which is very difficult to control. Finally, with the natural turnover in personnel, there is always the danger that personal interviews will be poorly conducted and that the interviewer will make mistakes in filling out the questionnaire, misunderstand the respondent, or even guess at answers. All these difficulties which arise from the presence of the interviewer are automatically eliminated by the use of the mail questionnaire.

A second advantage is the *wide distribution of interviews for a comparatively small expenditure.* A wider geographic spread and coverage of hard-to-reach people, such as families in remote areas, may be obtained easily in a mail survey. This is especially important if one has a limited appropriation and if there is a wide variation in marketing conditions affecting the product. With a limited amount of money to spend, it is often much better to employ a mail survey and scatter the mailing than to use personal interviews which would be restricted to a relatively small number of localities. The mail questionnaire, too, has the advantage of obtaining a wider distribution of interviews even within cities. In large metropolitan cities, such as Boston and New Orleans, it is difficult to spread the work of personal interviewers throughout the city. By use of the mail questionnaire, however, with even a very small number of returns, it is possible to have a distribution which reaches into all sections of the market.

The fact that a wide territory may be covered economically is a particular advantage of the mail survey in industrial and institutional research. The market for specialized industrial equipment, parts, or supplies, for instance, may be limited to a relatively small number of potential users, but these prospects may be scattered all over the country. Similarly, in institutional fields such as state governmental agencies, hospitals, and hotels there is both concentration of important markets and a wide geographic spread. If care is exercised in the interpretation of mail replies and the sample the returns represent, mail inquiry may prove to be a very useful tool in industrial and institutional research.

A third advantage of the mail survey is that *people may take more time and exercise greater care in filling out the questionnaire.* In personal interview work, unless the field force is carefully supervised, a proportion of the interviews are made hastily, sometimes through half-closed doors, and at a time when the respondent is distracted. On the other hand, the people who actually return mail questionnaires usually take time to make out a careful return. If the mail questionnaire has been well prepared, especially with the thought of giving the respondent a real interest in it and making it easy to fill out accurately, it is possible to capitalize on this potential advantage.

The fourth advantage of the mail survey is its *ability to obtain data from certain types of respondents.* Physicians, for example, will respond better to mail inquiries on some subjects than to personal interviews. This is also true of several other professional groups. Busy executives can sometimes be covered more effectively by mail.

Disadvantages of the Mail Survey. There are many inherent weaknesses in the mail survey. The first and most important weakness is the danger of an *invalid, biased sample.* The lists used for mailing often do not, in themselves, provide a representative sample. Furthermore, the persons who return the questionnaires usually represent a highly selective group, which is likely to distort the sample obtained.

No matter how carefully one distributes the sample of persons to whom the questionnaire is mailed, the sample represented by the actual returns will nearly always be distorted. There will be a difference in the percentage of replies received from different areas and other population groups. In general, the middle-class groups are more likely to respond than the high income groups or the low income groups. Certain occupational groups will tend to answer much more than others. People living in smaller cities are more likely to respond than those living in larger cities. A comparatively large share of the total returns actually received may be from habitual "coupon clippers" and children, especially if a premium or other giveaway is used in an attempt to increase the percentage of returns. Finally, the response from users of the product involved will be much greater than from nonusers. All these considerations indicate the first fundamental weakness of the mail questionnaire—a distorted sample.

Another reason for sample distortion is caused by the fact that the lists employed include only certain types of persons. In obtaining mailing lists, reliance is usually placed upon such sources as telephone directories, magazine subscription lists, lists of product owners or users, and membership lists of organizations. The use of such lists clearly affects the sample obtained in the study.

The fact that a questionnaire survey produces a very high rate of return is no guard against sample distortion. For example, in the Broadcast Measurement Bureau survey 43.0 per cent replied to the questionnaire. However, the variations in return by states ranged considerably, as shown in Table 11. These data by states merely

TABLE 11

VARIATION OF MAIL QUESTIONNAIRE RETURNS
BY GEOGRAPHIC AREAS

State	Percentage of Responses
Wisconsin	55.0
Iowa	54.0
Minnesota	53.4
Maine	49.2
Alabama	31.5
South Carolina	30.8
Florida	30.5

illustrate one of the factors which cause different types of people to return questionnaires at different rates. Within each state there were undoubtedly many factors operating to produce still further variations.

Bias resulting from sample distortion in mail questionnaires has been measured in a number of research studies. One of the first was made by the Procter and Gamble Company. This study showed that 92 per cent of the respondents to a mail questionnaire were users of the product with which the survey was concerned while only 40 per cent of those who did not reply to the questionnaire were users.

Franzen and Lazarsfeld concluded from an experiment that mail questionnaires can produce valid samples of comparatively homogeneous groups. In their study 3,000 subscribers of *Time*, taken consecutively from the *Fa* galleys, were used as subjects. These names were divided into three random subgroups of 1,000 each. Each subgroup was again divided in half, and one of these groups of 500 received a different questionnaire from the other half. The questionnaires to the first group dealt with ownership of material goods, readership, and opinions on intangible propositions. Those to the second subgroups dealt with classification data. After the mail questionnaires had been returned, personal interviews were conducted on all subjects included in both mail questionnaires with 1,387 of the original list of 3,000.

Politz and Brumach conducted tests of mail bias for the Broadcast Measurement Bureau. Their conclusions were that persons on the mailing list generally possessed characteristics of a higher income group than the control sample, which was selected at random. An even greater bias in this respect was discovered when only those who answered the mail questionnaire were compared with the control sample.

Brooks made a study in the New York market, a type of area in which mail sample bias would be relatively high. Lists of registered voters were employed, and classification data of the sample obtained by mail were compared with 1940 Census figures. While some differences might be accounted for by differences betwen census data and voting lists, Brooks concluded that the respondent sample was substantially biased with respect to age, income, and education.

A second disadvantage of the mail survey is its potential *high cost*. It is important to bear this in mind because most people assume that a mail questionnaire may be employed at a much lower cost than personal interviewers. This error is made because they think in terms of the cost per mailing rather than the cost per completed return. There are many costs in connection with the use of the mail questionnaire, such as the cost of the mailing list and the mechanical costs of folding, stuffing, and addressing, which may be absorbed as part of the routine overhead of the company making the study. In such cases, the researcher may find it more expedient to use the mail questionnaire. He must, however, figure costs on the mail questionnaire on the basis of actual usable returns received rather than the cost per questionnaire mailed.

A third disadvantage of the mail survey is that the questionnaire *must usually be very brief*. Where personal interviewers are employed, it is possible to obtain a relatively large amount of information in each individual interview. Where the mail questionnaire is employed, however, one must ordinarily limit the number of questions to be asked.

A fourth disadvantage of the mail survey is that it *frequently takes more time to plan and execute* than to employ personal interviews. Researchers are likely to underestimate the length of time required for the compilation of mailing lists, for addressing the mailing, and for the people to receive the questionnaires, fill them out, and return them through the mails. It will usually be found that at least four weeks are required for gathering data by this method. By contrast, it is possible to obtain field data by the personal interview method in less than a week, even where a large number of calls must be made.

The fifth disadvantage of the mail survey is that it *cannot readily obtain certain types of information*. Skillful interviewers can obtain facts in personal interviews which cannot be obtained by mail. Subjects requiring extensive discussion and probing are handled better by personal interviews. Whenever a series of questions must be asked in a special order, because of the particular conditions of the individual interview, an interviewer must be present to direct the interview. Many questions involve careful explanation of the meaning of terms or must be asked in different ways for different respondents. There are some kinds of information which consumers will not give, such as age and economic status, without injecting a great amount of bias into their answers. The personal interviewer can also appraise the quality of the interview. Furthermore, interviewers may report their general observations when making the calls.

Mail Survey vs. Personal Interviewing. The list below summarizes the more important advantages and disadvantages of the mail survey:

MAIL SURVEY METHOD

Advantages	*Disadvantages*
1. Avoids bias of personal interviewer.	1. Sample obtained is likely to be biased.
2. Allows wide distribution of sample.	2. Potential high cost per return.
3. Respondents may take more care in providing information.	3. Usually must be limited in content.
4. Obtains better response from certain types of respondents.	4. Requires longer time to complete study.
	5. Cannot obtain some types of information.

The advantages and disadvantages of the personal interview method of obtaining information are in large measure the opposite of those for the mail survey. The following list summarizes them:

PERSONAL INTERVIEW METHOD

Advantages	*Disadvantages*
1. Sample may be better controlled.	1. Personal bias of interviewer.
2. Better classification data.	2. Costly to distribute sample geographically.
3. Can ask more questions.	3. Interviews may be given hastily.
4. Field work may be completed quickly.	4. Some types of respondents difficult to interview.
5. Can obtain information on subjects which cannot be covered in mail questionnaire.	

In handling mail questionnaires every effort is usually made to produce as high a return as possible, partly in the interest of reducing sample distortion and partly in the interest of economy. The factors governing the rate of return are chiefly the following:

1. Selectivity of the mailing lists.
2. Timeliness of the subject.
3. Prestige of the investigating agency.
4. Quality of salesmanship in obtaining cooperation.
5. Degree of reluctance to reveal confidential information.
6. Interest of respondents in the success of the survey.
7. Amount of work entailed in filling out the questionnaire.

In planning mail survey work, it should always be borne in mind that too great an effort to increase the number of returns may actually increase, rather than diminish, sample distortion. Use of too attractive a premium is an example.

Telephone Interviewing. The use of the telephone as a means of obtaining field data has grown rapidly in the last few years. Its chief advantage lies in the fact that it is possible to obtain a large number of interviews quickly and at a relatively low cost. It is especially valuable in investigations such as those of television and radio audiences in which it is important to obtain interviews at a particular time of day. A further advantage in the use of the telephone is the ease of spreading the interviews within an individual market in a random fashion.

A chief disadvantage is that the telephone interview is limited to telephone subscribers. Limiting an analysis to such a selective group is almost certain to distort the sample. Another disadvantage is that its use is restricted to obtaining a relatively small amount of information, since it is often very difficult to secure the cooperation of the person called. However, if the respondent's interest in the subject matter of the interview is at a high level, it has been proved that telephone interviewing can be used effectively for lengthy interviews. Finally, it is almost impossible to obtain vital classification data, such as the age, economic status, or occupation of the person giving the information.

By carefully considering the advantages and disadvantages of the mail, personal, and telephone survey in the light of the specific problems encountered in a research project, one can arrive at a sound decision as to which type to employ. There are times when it is desirable to combine the methods. Frequently, the mail questionnaire may be used in covering territories which cannot be included in personal interviews. The mail questionnaire or telephone may be used for checking on the accuracy of the work of the personal interviewers. Personal interviews with part of a sample are used frequently to verify mail surveys.

How To Determine the Types and Sources of Data To Be Used. In order to avoid the possibility of overlooking valuable data and to insure that the analysis will obtain the best possible types, the following procedure is suggested.

1. *List all possible types and sources of data.* A list of data should be made separately for each hypothesis. The work will be expedited if the specific kinds of data considered are classified by the type and source each represents. If the various kinds of survey data are listed separately from possible observational data, and these in turn are listed separately from possible experimental data, their relative value will be more readily established. By further classifying these data in the list by the different sources represented (such as consumer and dealer), it will assist in insuring that no important sources are omitted. At the end of this step one has a list of many kinds of data, classified according to type and source.

For some hypotheses it will be found that a number of types and sources of data may be employed. For others, a comparatively short list exhausts the possibilities. It is most important, however, to make every effort to prepare a rather complete list.

An example of a list of different types and sources of data for one research is shown in Figure 10. This list is far from complete, as the reader will notice if he attempts to think of other kinds of data which might be employed for the solution of the hypothesis mentioned. The example also clarifies the distinction between the different *types* and *sources* represented by each kind of data mentioned. Furthermore, it illustrates the value of classifying the data according to type and source as the list is prepared.

Study of the list will reveal almost immediately the infinite possibilities of employing different types and sources of data for a given hypothesis. It also shows how the results of the study may be affected by the choice made.

2. *Determine the relative scientific value of each type and source.* A mental appraisal, from the purely scientific point of view, of the validity of each specific type of data which has been listed will be found helpful when the final selection is made. The different sources which may be used in a given analysis also have varying validity from the point of view of pure scientific procedure. For instance, in the example previously cited, the observational method might be applied to consumers by the pantry inventory, or to dealers by an audit of sales records. It is apparent that the choice of source, even for the same type of data, affects the quality of the facts obtained.

3. *Determine the practicability of obtaining each type of data.* In the operation above, the researcher confines his thinking primarily to a purely scientific appraisal. Other things being equal, experimental data are preferred to observational data, and the latter, in turn, to survey data. As a matter of practical expediency, however, it will be found frequently that it is impossible to employ experimental data. By weighing the practical considerations of the cost and availability of the data against their theoretical scientific validity, one arrives at a conclusion as to which type and source should be used in a given analysis.

4. *Test assumed results.* As a final step in determining the types and sources of data to be employed, it is suggested that the researcher imagine that the study has been completed. By projecting his thought through the end of the data-gathering step to tabulation, analysis, and interpretation, he is in a position to challenge the value of any given kind of data. The time to raise a specific question as to whether the exact data to be obtained will work is at this stage in planning the investigation. It is very embarrassing to find after the data have been gathered that they are not adequate for the testing of a hypothesis.

A helpful device in connection with the fourth step, testing assumed results, it to write down hypothetical percentages or other data which might conceivably be obtained as a result of employing one of the types and sources under consideration. For example, suppose that a researcher plans to obtain observational data on the number of dealers who stock a given commodity. He might at this point make the assumption that he will probably find that 70 per cent of the dealers carry the product in stock and that 30 per cent do not. Assuming for the moment that this is what will be discovered, the researcher then asks himself, "Would this resolve my hypothesis?" He then may make the assumption that he will find that only 40 per cent of the dealers carry the commodity in stock. He then asks the question again, and repeats the process, covering various possibilities. This procedure may demonstrate the inadequacy of the data for the solution of his problem and suggest another type of data which should be obtained. For example, in the case cited, it might reveal that it would be necessary to determine the *amount* of stock which the individual dealers had on their shelves before the data could be meaningful.

5. *Determine the method of data gathering.* In this step the advantages of the use of mail, personal interview, and telephone technique are reviewed in the light of the specific requirements of the research project. A decision is made as to the basic method or combination of methods to be employed.

6. *Prepare a statement of the exact data to be obtained and the method to be employed.* This is merely a summation of the end product of all the five preceding steps. Its value lies in making clear to the researcher the exact data to be obtained in the remainder of the analysis. With such a statement at hand, it becomes easier to prepare the forms which will be necessary, and it helps insure that the data will be properly gathered.

There is one consideration in connection with determining the types and sources of data which calls for special attention at this point. The researcher must at all times keep clearly in mind exactly what his data represent. For example, if he has obtained reasons from consumers interviewed as to why they use a particular product, he must keep clearly in mind that he has statements of consumers and nothing more or less. A common error is to fail to remember the exact nature of the data and to assume that one has facts which will resolve a hypothesis properly. By projecting one's thoughts to the end of the analysis, the exact nature and pertinence of the data which will be obtained usually becomes clear.

SELECTED READINGS

BLANKENSHIP, A. B. (ed.). *How to Conduct Consumer and Opinion Research.* New York: Harper & Bros., 1946, pp. 14–15.

CLAUSEN, J. A., and FORD, R. N. "Controlling Bias in Mail Questionnaires," *Journal of the American Statistical Association,* December, 1947, pp. 497–511.

ERDOS, PAUL L., and EASTMAN, ROY O. "Are Mail Surveys Reliable Marketing Tools?" *Printers' Ink,* August 24, 1951, pp. 34–35.

FERBER, R. "The Problem of Bias in Mail Returns—A Solution," *Public Opinion Quarterly,* Winter, 1948, pp. 669–76.

LUCK, DAVID J., and WALES, HUGH G. *Marketing Research.* New York: Prentice-Hall, Inc., 1952, pp. 127–39.

PARTEN, MILDRED. *Surveys, Polls and Samples.* New York: Harper & Bros., 1950, pp. 48–70.

ROBINSON, R. A., and AGISIM, PHILIP. "Making Mail Surveys More Reliable," *Journal of Marketing,* April, 1951, pp. 415–24.

Standards for Statistical Surveys. Bureau of the Budget, Executive Office of the President. Washington, D. C.: Government Printing Office, 1952.

WALLACE, DAVID. "Mail Questionnaires Can Produce Good Samples of Homogeneous Groups," *Journal of Marketing*, July, 1947, pp. 53–60.

CASE

BLANKERTZ, DONALD F., FERBER, ROBERT, and WALES, HUGH G. *Cases and Problems in Marketing Research.* New York: The Ronald Press Co., 1954, pp. 40–46, 165–67.

10

PREPARATION OF THE FORMS FOR
COLLECTING DATA

After the types and sources of data have been determined, it is necessary to develop standardized forms on which to record them. The importance of exercising care in the development of these forms can scarcely be overemphasized. In the first place, the accuracy of the facts obtained depends to a large degree upon the care with which the forms have been drawn. Secondly, since many people are usually involved in the furnishing and gathering of data, lack of clarity in the forms will lead to various interpretations and misunderstandings which will result in incorrect data. The researcher must bear in mind this important point because by the time he reaches this stage in his work he has become so thoroughly engrossed in his subject that he is likely to overlook the fact that many matters which are perfectly clear to him are not understood by field personnel. A third reason for the careful preparation of forms results from the need of having all the data as completely standardized as possible. This standardization not only aids in obtaining accurate data but also facilitates their handling in tabulation and analysis. Finally, one must be certain that the forms are complete so that all the information necessary for the research will be obtained.

Forms must be developed wherever primary data are gathered by the survey, observational, or experimental technique. If the survey method is employed, a questionnaire must be constructed. Because of the extra human element which is injected where this technique is used, the development of a questionnaire calls for the utmost care and skill.

Forms for Survey Data

The Problem of Communication. The traditional questionnaire approach, consisting of a series of questions and blank spaces for answers, provides only a restricted means of obtaining survey data; it is necessary to take a much broader view of the whole process. The modern approach is to recognize that the problem of collecting data by interviews is essentially a *communication* problem. The researcher must therefore establish an effective means of *communication* between the collector of data and the respondent.

By examining the most essential single element in the process of data collecting, namely, the relationship between the investigator and the individual respondent, the significance of this new approach is made clear. In the traditional survey study, a series of questions is developed, committed to paper in the form of a questionnaire, and then reproduced in quantity. These questionnaires are then placed in the hands of field workers, with verbal or written explanations which seek to make the questions clear in the mind of the field investigator who is going to ask them. The interviewer then proceeds to question the respondent; sometimes the investigator makes various verbal changes in the hope of clarifying the questions or facilitating answers, often with the result of completely changing the meaning of the questions. The respondent then answers the questions, usually to the best of his or her ability. Answers are recorded by the investigator, often hastily lest the rapport with the respondent deteriorate, usually in words which are the investigator's summarization of the answer and sometimes under extremely unfavorable physical conditions. After the questionnaires are returned from the field, editors scrutinize the answers, making such changes as are indicated by their particular understanding of the meaning of the original questions and by the answers which have been recorded on the blanks. By the time the answers have worked themselves back through field investigator, supervisor, and editor, they may change character considerably; yet they become the basic raw material on which the results of the study are wholly dependent.

It is a truism accepted by all marketing researchers that no research result can be better than the original data on which it is based. Many safeguards have been developed to lessen the errors resulting from the inherent nature of the questionnaire process, such as specific rules for wording questions, as well as methods of instructing, supervising, and checking the field workers. However, valuable as these procedures may be, it is necessary in marketing research to rise above the limitations of the traditional verbalized questionnaire. It is now regarded as a somewhat archaic method. The researcher now takes the much broader approach of regarding the whole process as a specific problem in communication.

There are two principal reasons why the traditional verbalized questionnaire is often inadequate: first, because of the problem of semantics in verbal communication; and second, because the questionnaire is limited to only one means of communication—the verbal.

The scope of this book does not make it possible even to summarize adequately the recent findings of students of semantics. However, the marketing researcher should make it a point to follow developments in this field closely, at least to a point where he fully recognizes the limitations of verbal communication. These limitations are particularly acute where the English language is employed, for one characteristic of this language is that most of our words have several meanings, and fuzzy definition is a constant source of difficulty to the marketing researcher. When the simplest of words is used by one person in an attempt to communicate with another, a meaning is often conveyed to the other person which may be quite different from what the speaker intended. For example, take a word such as "dog" or "house," then consider the added difficulties presented by abstract and technical words such as "preference" and "value," which are subject to various and vague meanings among marketing men themselves. Add to these purely semantic difficulties the various "middlemen" who stand between the researcher and his data and who influence the meanings of words—the supervisors, investigators, and editors—and you will see how semantics hinders the marketing research which relies on the traditional verbal questionnaire.

Actually ideas are communicated by various means, and sometimes the nonverbal methods are much more significant than language itself. All five senses—sight, hearing, smell, taste, and touch—come into play when human beings communicate ideas. In a given communication experience the impression received through each of the senses is a complex one. For example, in an oral interview, both respondent and interviewer hear distinctly or poorly, hear tone of voice, hear emphasis on one or another word. Furthermore, there is an interplay between the various senses which affects the transmission of ideas. One cannot dissociate the experience of taste from the sights which accompany it.

In modern research practice, data gathering in a survey is properly planned only when the total communication process is thoroughly explored and all possible means to make communication easy and accurate are developed. The questionnaire is regarded primarily as a form for recording information, even though it contains questions which are presented to the respondent by the interviewer. Questions may be asked verbally, but if the broader view of communication is taken and methods are carefully tested, questions, statements, scales, or illustrations may be printed on cards which are handed to the respondent. As many of the means of communication as possible are brought into play. As a result, the modern questionnaire goes far

A SURVEY OF BAKING PANS AND OTHER EQUIPMENT

This survey is to find out the number, size and shape of ALL the various BAKING (Pie, Cake, Bread, Roll and Cooky) PANS you have. To do this measuring the easiest and best way, we have found some simple steps which save time and really make this one of the most interesting surveys we have sent out.

First—Take ALL of the pans and dishes you use for baking out of the cupboard.

Second—Separate these pans and dishes into 9 groups—All your round pans with sloping sides

(larger across the top than at the bottom); the next group to be the round ones with straight sides

(same across the top as at the bottom); square ones with sloping sides   ; the square ones with

straight sides   ; then the rectangular ones (longer than they are wide) with sloping sides

         and then the rectangular ones with straight sides   ; muffin pans

tube or angel food cake pans   and cooky sheets   Then get out your

measuring cups and spoons because on the back page we ask about these.

Third—Now you are ready to measure with the calipers

Start with the round sloping sided pans and measure the inside bottom diameter (distance from side to side across the center) first and record this measurement in the first space under the drawing, "Round Sloping Sided Pans", on next page. (In measuring all diameters it is well to move the points around a little to make sure you are measuring at the widest point.)

Then spread the points of the calipers so they just touch the INSIDE at the top of the pan and record this measurement in the space reading "Inside Top Diameter".

After recording the "Inside Top Diameter" lay a ruler or some other flat object across the top of pan and using the leg of the calipers that is marked off to be a ruler, measure the depth. (Record this measurement to the closest ¼" in the space marked "Inside DEPTH at center".) Then complete the line, filling in the other information asked for.

Now you are finished with this pan. Use the same procedure and measure the balance of your ROUND SLOPING pans, recording each measurement in the proper column and complete the line BEFORE starting the next pan.

FIGURE 11. Establishing Communication. Part of an instruction sheet used in connection with a study conducted by mail which shows the use of illustrations and physical devices, in addition to language, in order to establish as effective communication as possible. (General Mills, Inc.)

beyond a sheet of paper with a series of questions and is likely to embrace visual exhibits, pictures, diagrams, samples of products, models, and various other physical elements which bring into the process all the senses which will aid in establishing effective communication. Only by employing a variety of devices can the researcher usually effect the recording of responses which most accurately produce the desired information.

The Elements of the Questionnaire

Most questionnaires contain five specific elements. These are (1) the request for cooperation, (2) explanations, (3) sought data, (4) classification data, and (5) identification. Separation of these elements in the mind of the person developing the questionnaire is essential to their proper treatment.

Request for Cooperation. This is one of the most important features of the mail questionnaire, and while it may not appear on each form in the personal interview, it must be developed as part of the questionnaire process for use by interviewers.

The most important factor determining the manner in which the request for cooperation should be handled is the amount of interest on the part of the respondent in the subject covered in the investigation. If the subject is one in which the persons reached by the survey are actively interested, there is no difficulty in obtaining cooperation. A questionnaire to traffic managers on traffic problems will immediately strike a responsive chord. A questionnaire to the same group on their personal habits in the matter of family budgets will find most of them cold to the subject. Because automobiles are a topic for frequent discussion, it is comparatively easy to interest people in a study of this product; a study on furniture polish, on the other hand, must create an interest in the subject.

It must also be recognized that there are groups of people who are particularly interested in certain subjects. The people engaged in any given vocation are naturally interested in subjects relating to their vocation. Housewives are interested in any important problem relating to the management of the household. There are also groups of people intensely interested in subjects such as cooperatives, politics, automobiles, and health movements.

If the persons to be reached by a survey are interested in the subject being studied, it is most effective simply to ask for their cooperation directly and briefly. If they do not have such interest, it is necessary to arouse it.

There are five common methods of gaining cooperation of the respondent. First, one may offer a premium or reward. Premiums are especially effective where children may be used as an entree, or where women or groups are involved. They are less expensive than cash rewards, for it is possible to offer items which appear to have high value at relatively low cost. The chief weakness of using premiums is their tendency to increase returns among certain groups, the "souvenir hunters." Booklets giving recipes or other useful information are often found effective. The Customer Research Division of General

Motors has used extensively booklets containing educational material on automobiles. Sometimes it is necessary to pay cash for respondent cooperation. In one case an offer of merchandise of considerable value was unsuccessful, and the firm had to pay consumers a dollar for each interview. This method was expensive, but it made a sufficient play on the self-interest of the individual to insure cooperation. Premiums, cash, and other forms of direct reward must be used with caution lest they distort results by their tendency to force cooperation.

Second, one may appeal to the instincts, pride, and vanity of the person being questioned. Some questions themselves appeal to the basic instincts, such as beginning the interview by asking about children, a device frequently restorted to in house-to-house selling. We may appeal to pride by saying that we want the opinions of leading authorities, by appointing people to "radio committees," and by other forms of flattery. Telling a woman that she has been singled out of her block for an interview is a play on her vanity. *Time* used a novel appeal to pride when it headed a questionnaire, "Do you own a horse?"

Third, one may use a "begging" approach. This means of securing cooperation was employed when a researcher said in a letter that he was starting in business and needed help to avoid failure. The most coldhearted executive will usually give in to the young chap who tells him that his job depends on getting the interview. One interesting form was used where a letter was sent out over the name of the head of a large corporation, in which the executive began by saying he was "up against it on a problem and needed some help."

A mail questionnaire, using a double postcard, employed the following request for cooperation:

> My boss bet me that I couldn't get the answers to some questions—from a group of people I have never seen. I bet him that you'd be kind enough to help me!
>
> I have no desire to use your name—or sell you anything, so you need not sign the attached card; just answer the questions on the card attached—please.
>
> Amy Swanson

The begging approach must also be used with caution lest it bias the sample.

Fourth, people at times pose as having some sort of authority. By saying, "We are taking a census of . . ." at the opening of an interview, one can often obtain high returns. The ethics of this method is open to question, but it is used because it does get results. Fancy titles on questionnaires, such as "American Survey Council," hints at an authority which some people will respect.

Fifth, one may appeal to interest in the study itself, promising copies of the results. This appeal is especially useful with executives. So many promises to send a copy of the report have been forgotten, however, that this method is less effective than it formerly was.

One should not produce a lengthy, labored approach. It is best to select the one wedge which will be most productive in the specific case, to state it clearly and directly, and do no more.

Explanations. Every questionnaire must have brief and simply worded explanations to clear up all points of likely confusion. For the questionnaire used in personal interviews these explanations are placed in rather detailed instructions to the interviewers. However, it is desirable to place as much explanatory matter as possible directly on the questionnaire as a constant reminder. This is particularly true of directions for sequence or conditional questions and for definition of units in which data are to be taken. The explanatory matter should cover both the general instructions on how to conduct the interview and complete instructions regarding individual questions to insure uniform interpretation.

In the mail questionnaire one is faced with the fact that the very simplest questions are open to misinterpretation; yet there are very strict limits to the amount of explanatory material which can be embodied in the questionnaire itself. At best, perfectly uniform interpretation cannot be secured, but every precaution must be taken to reduce errors from this source.

Completeness and simplicity in the wording of explanations in the questionnaire itself are the major precepts. There are other rules. The proper place for instructions is right next to the specific questions to which they refer. Blanket instructions at the top of the questionnaire should be avoided. The use of pictures as a method of making explanations clear holds great possibilities. The various devices mentioned in the earlier discussion of the communications problem are in themselves forms of explanation.

Sought Data. The treatment of this element will be discussed more fully in the section on General Rules for Constructing Questionnaires.

Classification Data. The term "classification data" means information regarding the respondent himself, or the respondent's family, if that happens to be the unit under study. This information, such as age, sex, and economic status, is used in the analysis of the raw data obtained in the field survey and is the element which makes the answers and other data meaningful.

The classification data to be used depend upon the nature, purpose, and scope of the individual survey. One of the common weak-

ADVERTISING RESEARCH BUREAU

Room 409   955 Eighth Avenue

New York, N. Y.

Dear Reader:—

     We have been asked by several magazines to conduct a survey among their readers — to see just who in the families read the magazine.

     Your name has been given us as a subscriber to Cosmopolitan, and I can assure you that your answers to the simple questions on the attached card will be greatly appreciated, both by us and by the publishers of that magazine.

     As you, of course, realize, it is no easy task to publish a magazine that appeals to more than 1,700,000 families. The tastes and desires of the readers must be very carefully considered.

     Naturally, the first step is to find out exactly who the readers are — that is whether they are men or women, whether married or single, and whether they are above or below certain ages.

     This card asks these questions. There is nothing personal in those questions of course and no one will call on you at any time. In fact, you do not have to sign your name.

     So won't you help us out <u>now</u> by filling out the card? (I have had a sample card filled out to show you how it can be done. Of course, your family will be different, but you can see the general idea of the card and the information that it gives.)

     It is very important that every question be filled out, and that you send the card back as soon as possible. Remember there is no postage to pay (we do that when the card comes back to us) — nothing to buy — no follow-up.

     You will have the satisfaction of knowing that you have greatly helped the magazine, for which we are extremely grateful.

        Yours very truly,

Malcolm E. Rollins

        ADVERTISING RESEARCH BUREAU

mgr/dh

FIGURE 12. Elements of the Questionnaire. This example shows how the various elements of the questionnaire were handled in one survey conducted by mail. The reader will find it a useful exercise to iden 'fy the five basic elements, then to appraise critically the handling of each one.

SAMPLE

1. I am a reader of Cosmopolitan and my status in the home is.
   ☒ Wife ☐ Husband ☐ Daughter ☐ Son
   ☐ Other (Name)----------
   If living alone. check here ☐ Male ☐ Female

2. My family is made up of the following people, (please list all members of your family in relationship to yourself, that is—Wife, Husband, Mother, Father, etc. except children under 13). If living alone, only, fill in line opposite "myself."

		Approximate Ages				Regular Cosmopolitan Reader Note Please check below only if Cosmopolitan is read regularly.	Occasional Cosmopolitan Reader
	under 17	17-24	24-34	34-44	over 44		
Myself	☐	☐	☐	☐	☐	☒	☐
Husband	☐	☐	☐	☒	☐	☒	☐
Daughter	☐	☒	☐	☐	☐	☒	☐
Mother	☐	☐	☐	☐	☒	☐	☐
--------	☐	☐	☐	☒		☒	☐
--------	☐	☐	☐	☐			☒
				☐			☐

3. Number of children in family _2_ Under 5 years _1_
   5-12 _1_

4. Please name the member of your family (Wife, Daughter, etc.) who keeps house i.e. (orders and prepares food, etc.)
   Wife (myself)

5. We own our home ☐   Approx. valuation $_____
   We rent our home ☒   Monthly rental $ _30 00_

Tear off this card on the dotted lines
Fill out each question, then drop in the nearest mailbox – do not stamp.

ONLY FIVE EASY QUESTIONS
Check your answers here
—THEN TEAR OFF AND MAIL
WE PAY ALL POSTAGE
and THANKS A GREAT DEAL

This is how one family would fill out the questions on the post card.

Your family will be different of course, but this suggestion will show you how each question can be answered.

Please send the card back to us as soon as possible.

Remember *you do not pay any postage*—we do that. *Thank you again.*

---

1. I am a reader of Cosmopolitan and my status in the home is:
   ☐ Wife ☐ Husband ☐ Daughter ☐ Son
   ☐ Other (Name)----------
   If living alone, check here ☐ Male ☐ Female

2. My family is made up of the following people, (please list all members of your family in relationship to yourself, that is—Wife, Husband, Mother, Father, etc. except children under 13). If living alone, only fill in line opposite "myself."

		Approximate Ages				Regular Cosmopolitan Reader Note Please check below only if Cosmopolitan is read regularly	Occasional Cosmopolitan Reader
	under 17	17-24	24-34	34-44	over 44		
Myself	☐	☐	☐	☐	☐	☐	☐
--------	☐	☐	☐	☐	☐	☐	☐
------	☐	☐	☐	☐	☐	☐	☐
--------	☐	☐	☐	☐	☐	☐	☐
--------	☐	☐	☐	☐	☐	☐	☐
--------	☐	☐	☐	☐	☐	☐	☐

3. Number of children in family ___ Under 5 years ___
   5-12 ___

4. Please name the member of your family (Wife, Daughter, etc.) who keeps house i.e. (orders and prepares food, etc.)

5. We own our home ☐   Approx. valuation $_____
   We rent our home ☐   Monthly rental $_____

Tear off this card on the dotted lines
Fill out each question, then drop in the nearest mailbox – do not stamp.

FIGURE 12 (*Continued*).

nesses of marketing researches is that scanty classification data are used often when it would be much better to reduce the amount of sought data and to provide for more information about the respondent. Another weakness is to rely too heavily on the traditional and obvious classification data. Frequently a great deal of value is added to a consumer survey by obtaining particularly revealing types of information about respondents; a good deal of ingenuity can often be exercised in this regard.

The following are some of the types of classification data which are most generally used in marketing research.

1. *Age.* People of different ages respond very differently to most products. The consumption of milk, for example, varies greatly between different age levels. A beverage manufacturer found that his sales volume was not satisfactory because he was manufacturing a dark, heavy type, whereas the younger users preferred a light product. Age is so important an influence in the consumer market that it is a standard basis of classification.

2. *Sex.* Analysis of the market on the basis of sex is also standard practice for markets involving both sexes. It will usually reveal an opportunity for market expansion by devices such as changing the package, the product, or the advertising and selling appeals.

3. *Nationality or race.* The differences in living habits between members of different nationalities and races are rather obvious. In the sale of certain commodities, these differences may be important.

4. *Socioeconomic status.* The types of commodities consumed by individuals vary greatly according to the relative income or socioeconomic status of those individuals. In order that marketing activities may be properly directed, it is important to analyze the market for a product by these groups. This classification has been so effective in marketing research that there are many who make it the primary basis of nearly all analyses.

5. *Occupation.* Sometimes the key to an understanding of the market is found by breaking it down on the basis of different occupations. The most essential differences in living habits which affect the sale of some product may be found between different occupational groups—in many respects a painter in Minnesota is more like a painter in Tennessee than he is like a schoolteacher in Minnesota. The segregation of the market into the "class" occupational groups as opposed to the "mass" occupational groups has been employed very successfully in consumer surveys.

6. *Geographic areas.* Because of wide differences in standards of living, customs, buying habits, and brand preferences, it is usually

necessary to break down all facts learned in a consumer study on the basis of geographic sections.

7. *Population groups.* People who live in large metropolitan centers have different living habits from those who reside in smaller cities and towns, and the latter, in turn, have different habits from those who live on farms. An analysis of the market on the basis of various city-size groups usually reveals conditions which point directly to important variations in marketing policy.

There are many other bases on which consumer researches may be analyzed if the classification data permit. Analyses on the basis of religious groups and educational groups, for example, have proved productive. As society develops, there is a constant shifting in the types of social groups, which is significant from the point of view of marketing. One function of the marketing researcher is to keep abreast of these changes in order that any specific analysis may employ the classifications which are most revealing.

In surveys of dealers or industrial buyers, effective classification data are equally important. Type and size of establishment are always taken into consideration and here, too, considerable ingenuity may be exercised in devising novel and revealing bases of classification.

Identification. This last element is very important. In the case of personal interviews, the form should always provide for the name and address of the person being interviewed. Only in this manner is it possible to check the investigator's work. Spaces for identifying the person who is responsible for the interview and the date should also be included on the form.

In mail questionnaires one usually does not ask for the name and address of the individual replying because this request will bias the results and keep many from answering. Sometimes, however, asking people to sign their names can actually increase response. Whether asking for a person's name tends to reduce the number of replies or not is still an open question. One is likely to assume offhand that it will, yet people like to sign their names and doing so makes them feel that they individually are part of the study, not just so many blanks. In one instance respondents were asked to sign their names and then indicate whether they were willing to have themselves quoted. The result was a higher return. Serial numbers or codes on questionnaires are often used to identify the person replying. Provision should be made for tracing the questionnaire geographically. This information may be obtained from the postmark on the return envelope of a mail questionnaire and later transferred to the blank.

General Rules for Constructing Questionnaires

The purpose of the discussion in this section is to state as briefly and clearly as possible the most fundamental rules for questionnaire construction. In a sense, many of the activities pursued up to this point in planning the analysis will help produce a questionnaire which is satisfactory from the technical point of view. For example, some authorities stress the principle that the questions asked must be relevant. This requirement will, of course, be automatically fulfilled if the researcher has carefully followed a sound procedure in the work up to this point. There are, however, ten basic rules which should be kept clearly in mind while actually writing the questionnaire.

Rule 1. Factual questions should be limited to obtaining data which can be clearly remembered by respondents.

This principle is stated first because it is one which is frequently overlooked. Not all persons engaged in marketing research have a full appreciation of the degree to which the memory of most people is limited. If the violation of this rule simply meant that one would not obtain answers from many of the respondents, the situation would not be particularly serious. However, most people who do not actually remember facts will guess. These guesses then appear in the final results as though they were facts properly reported, and may lead to false conclusions.

The following questions are likely to violate this first rule:

Where did you see this advertisment?
When did you begin using this brand?

The first question is an excellent illustration of the principle mentioned above, that people who do not remember will guess. In an investigation which asked this question about an advertisement which had appeared two months prior to the analysis, less than 5 per cent of the people interviewed replied, "I don't know." The advertisement in question was one of thousands which the consumers had seen and it was clearly impossible for many actually to recall the medium in which they had seen that specific advertisement. Department stores which have asked buyers, "Where did you see this product advertised?" have found that large numbers of customers will report newspapers in which the advertisement did not appear.

In order to avoid violation of this first rule, one should follow two procedures. The first is to omit all questions which obviously will tax the memory of respondents; the second is to phrase all questions in such manner as to restrict the time period so as to reduce the demands upon memory as much as possible.

An example of the first procedure would be the exclusion of a question like the second one quoted above, "When did you begin using this brand?" It is obvious that people would not remember, and the question should not be asked, except in the case of a very recently introduced brand. Similarly, one should ask the first question, "Where did you see this advertisement?" only within a very short time after its publication, and then only if it is clear that it is the type of advertisement that has been published in such a manner that people could remember where they had seen it.

The following are examples of the use of the second procedure, restricting the time period:

> What brand did you buy the last time you purchased?
> What radio programs did you listen to during the last hour?

The principle embodied in the first question above is sometimes described as the "theory of the last purchase," although it is obviously applicable to a number of situations other than buying. This technique relies on a random distribution of replies, so that the resulting data reflect the total behavior pattern just as accurately as though the behavior pattern of individuals were completely known. For example, if a respondent replies that her last purchase was Tide, but that she generally uses Dreft and chanced to obtain Tide because of some unusual circumstance, it would be offset by another consumer who chanced to purchase Dreft last but usually used Tide.

It is important to bear in mind that the length of time intervening between the happening of an event and the attempt to remember it is not the only factor in memory. It is erroneous to assume that one cannot obtain data regarding events which have occurred a considerable time before the study is made, or, on the other hand, that if the questions are asked shortly after the event occurred, people will necessarily remember it.

There are several laws of memory. The three most important principles are those of recency of the event, intensity of the stimulus, and degree of association.

The principle of the *intensity of the stimulus* means that if an event has impressed itself very vividly upon the consciousness of an individual, he will remember it clearly for a long time. The importance of keeping this principle in mind in planning a questionnaire can be demonstrated easily by reflecting upon what one is able to remember himself. The first day at school may be distinctly remembered for as long as fifty years as a result of the vividness of the impression which it makes on individuals. Marriage, the arrival of the first child, one's first arrest, the day one first obtained a job, and the day he left a position are examples of events which may remain in the memory for a long time. On the other hand, the purchase of one of the thousands of commodities which are constantly used and the observation of one of the many advertisements which one sees from day to day are very quickly forgotten.

The principle of the *degree of association* is that events which are closely associated with other well-remembered events can be readily recalled. Hundreds of foods served at the table may be quickly forgotten, but the menu of a meal served with distinguished visitors present may be long remembered. Likewise, people have very poor memories for the kinds of oil used in their automobile at any given time, except the day the engine broke down on account of lack of oil.

Year	# New Rackets Bought	Price of New Rackets	# Restring Jobs	Brand of String	Name and Address of Dealer Who Restrung Rackets
1955					
1954					
1953					
1952					
1951					

FIGURE 13. Obtaining Data in Individual Instances

An example of the importance of both the intensity of the stimulus and the degree of association in determining the extent to which people remember can be demonstrated by the case of a market analysis for tennis gut. Among the most important considerations in this study were the frequency with which certain types of tennis players had their rackets restrung and the dealers from whom they obtained the restringing. In order to determine the limits of memory on these subjects, a questionnaire which provided spaces for the recording of individual restringings over a period of five years was devised. An illustration of the technique employed in the design of the questionnaire is reproduced in Figure 13.

At the time this questionnaire was written for testing purposes, the project director assumed that he would be fortunate if he could obtain an accurate record for the two preceding years. He was surprised to discover that in this particular case, because of such factors as association with summer vacations, the length of time devoted to determining whether the racket should be restrung and what type of stringing to purchase (which affected the intensity of the stimulus to memory), the vast majority of persons interviewed could report clearly for the five-year period.

The reader will notice that this questionnaire was deliberately designed to aid in recall by the listing of the seasons and by having the interviewers begin with the last event and work backward in time.

While a knowledge of the general laws of memory and experience in the phrasing of questions are of great value in developing questions so that they will meet the requirements of the first rule, one can be sure that difficulties caused by the inability of respondents to remember will be eliminated only if the questionnaire is carefully tested on this point. In connection with these tests, one must bear in mind that people who do not remember will often guess. Thus, in making the test, it is necesary to make sure that guessing will be avoided.

Rule 2. The data obtained should not involve generalizations.

This rule requires that one should ask for reports of specific events rather than generalizations covering a number of individual events. The following questions violate this rule:

a) Do you use your broiler regularly?
b) How many tubes of Colgate's tooth paste do you sell a week?
c) What brand of gasoline do you use?
d) What percentage of these watches were purchased as gifts?
e) How often do salesmen call on you?

In the case of each of the above questions, it is necessary for the respondent first to remember individual events and then make a generalization. The question "What brand do you use?" is sometimes asked in marketing research. Persons who use one brand exclusively, or almost exclusively, can give a fairly accurate answer. For most products, however, there is a considerable amount of brand shifting, and people who "drift" from one brand to another have no basis on which to make an accurate generalization.

A still more extreme form of generalization is demanded in those questions which, in effect, call for the equivalent of a statistical average. With an accurate series of statistical data available, it is often very difficult for a statistician to determine the proper form to use in arriving at an average. Yet many analysts expect consumers to be able to report accurately the average price which they pay for a commodity. The calculation of a percentage requires some figuring, but people are asked to state the percentage of their total sales which is represented by each brand, or the percentage of income expended for certain purposes. Studies of family budgets which ask people to report their expenditures for different items over a long period of time are further examples which involve faulty questionnaire construction.

In order to avoid violation of this general rule in questionnaire work, the approved procedure is to obtain data on individual events. The use of the panel or diary technique, in which respondents record individual items, is a proper method for overcoming the fault of generalization in surveys. The use of the last purchase or event, discussed above, also avoids generalization. The following questions ask for specific information, which eliminates the necessity of generalization:

a) When did you last shop at Marshall Field's?
b) Did you obtain a premium when you purchased this package of cereals?
c) What brand of oil do you now have in your car?
d) What is the length of your living room rug? The width?

Rule 3. The meaning of every question should be obvious to the less intelligent persons included in the survey.

This rule requires that the questions should be stated clearly and directly. The language employed should be as simple as possible.

There are three ways in which questions commonly violate this rule. These are (1) by complicated statement of the questions, (2) by the use of terms with more than one meaning, and (3) by the use of technical words.

The following question is not clear because of its complicated statement:

How have you found the best way to get a man interested in this idea?

The respondent would have some difficulty in determining whether the investigator is attempting to find out how the best way was found, or which way was best.

An example of a question whose meaning is not clear because it employs words subject to different interpretations is:

What kind of soup do you serve?

The word "kind" is subject to many different interpretations. Some people would think it refers to the difference between canned and home-prepared soup; some would think of different varieties, as vegetable or chicken; some of cream soups or clear soups. It might refer to high-priced or expensive soups as opposed to inexpensive soups, or even hot and cold soups.

Another example is:

Do you use the product frequently, occasionally, or not at all?

The words "frequently," "occasionally," and similar terms have entirely different meanings to different people. Tests show, for example, that people using a commodity with similar frequency will report in all three classifications. A similar term which is almost without exact definition is the word "important." To ask a person whether he regards a certain thing as "important" is almost worthless because of the lack of common understanding as to what this word means.

Another error leading to the inclusion of questions which are not understood is the use of technical terms. In planning the analysis, the researcher becomes thoroughly familiar with many technical terms employed in the business for which the study is being made. Examples of technical words which cause difficulty in questionnaires are "cabinet model," "calrod unit" (on electric stoves), and "markup." One technical term frequently used in questionnaires is "advertising medium." This term has a very clear meaning to advertising practitioners but will be given varying interpretations by dealers and consumers. A further complicating cause is the fact that some technical terms have different meanings in different parts of the country.

The use of words which are misunderstood by respondents or which lead to an excessive number of "no answers" because they are beyond their vocabulary is much too prevalent in questionnaire building. The following words are further examples: "staple groceries," "discriminate," "fabrics," "economist," "diversify."

As a check on the influence of words and the extent to which the meaning of questions is clear, word lists may be employed. The best known is E. L. Thorndike's list of 30,000 words found in literature, from which the most commonly used words may be selected to increase understanding. A number of vocabulary books may be found in any good library.

Three different devices may be employed to eliminate the possibility of violating this rule. These devices are rewording the question, definition, and illustration. The following is an example of a reworded question to avoid the use of a term which is not clear:

If you were buying a new automobile, how much extra would you pay to have safety glass in all windows?

This question was used instead of the question "How important is safety glass to you?"

An example of the use of definition follows:

> What type of dentifrice do you use? (Tooth paste, tooth powder, or other kind.)

This indicates clearly the meaning of the word "type" and will obtain answers which should meet the requirements of the person building the questionnaire.

The use of simple illustrations to clarify technical terms and to make the meanings of words obvious is a very effective technique in questionnaire construction. The most technical subjects can usually be included in a questionnaire if proper illustrations are shown. Examples of the use of illustrations to make the meaning of questions obvious will be found in Figures 11 and 15.

Rule 4. Eliminate leading questions.

A leading question is one which is so worded that it suggests the answer. The most extreme examples of leading questions are found in law courts where attorneys devise questions which will force a witness to answer as the lawyer desires. A classic example is, "Do you still beat your wife?" No matter whether the witness answers this question "yes" or "no" he incriminates himself. If he answers "no," he admits that he has beaten his wife; if he answers "yes," that he is still beating her.

In marketing research one does not encounter such obvious examples of leading questions. However, there are cases in which studies are made by persons whose self-interest causes them to put leading questions deliberately into their questionnaires. Such cases are easily detected and are both unscientific and unethical. Nevertheless, no matter how fair one wishes to be, questions will often be phrased in a manner which suggests the answers. The fact that the suggestion is more subtle does not make the elimination of any possibility of leading or suggesting the answers less important.

The first type of question which suggests the answer is that which is so phrased that it directly leads to a favorable response. Examples of questions which clearly predetermine answers to a degree are the following:

> Did you see this advertisement?

Tests show that people will answer "yes" in about three quarters of the instances, regardless of whether they have actually seen it or not, while other data show that less than 20 per cent have actually seen the advertisement.

> Do you use Ivory soap?

Brand names should never be included in questions of this type. The use of the words "Do you" is also leading, as the natural tendency of most people is to reply "yes."

A second form of leading question includes the use of words which do not admit exceptions:

> Do you always use Texaco gasoline?

The word "Texaco" suggests a favorable answer. However, the word "always" is also leading because it does not admit exceptions. Every respondent can think of instances in which he has used some other gasoline, regardless of how loyal he may be to the Texaco brand.

The third type of leading question is the check list. In order to facilitate answering questionnaires and to make for easy tabulation, it is a common technique to provide a series of answers to the question. The respondent merely checks in appropriate spaces to indicate his reply.

> Which of the following magazines do you read regularly:
> .....Saturday Evening Post
> .....Good Housekeeping
> .....Ladies' Home Journal
> .....Woman's Home Companion
> .....American Magazine
> .....Reader's Digest
> .....Time
> ..... _____
> ..... _____

This type of question greatly stimulates the imagination and causes people to check many more replies than they would give in response to an open-end question without a list. Magazines which are not specifically included in the list will tend to be excluded, in spite of the fact that extra space is provided for their inclusion. A third error in this type of question is that items placed first on the list will tend to receive favorable replies, whereas those placed at the end are put at a disadvantage. The bias which is introduced by the order in which items are listed should be eliminated by rotating the order in different groups of questionnaires. The question as phrased in the example also violates Rule 2 in the use of the word "regularly."

BAKING

1. Have you bought any bakery products in the last week? Yes_____ No_____
   Please write in the number of times in the last week you have bought any of the following bakery products.
   Rolls_____ Muffins_____ Cake_____ Cookies_____ Pies_____ All other_____

2. Have you within the last two weeks baked any of the foods listed below?
   Yes_____ No_____

   If so, please write in what kind:

Yeast bread	Rolls	Biscuits	Muffins	Cookies	Pies	All other
What kind? _____	_____	_____	_____	_____	_____	_____

3. When did you last bake a cake?_____ What kind?_____ Was it for family consumption entirely?_____or for guests?_____or for a special occasion?_____If a special occasion, what?_____

4. How long ago did you bake a cake other than this one?_____ What kind was it?_____

5. What kind were the last two cakes before that?_____

6. Do you bake cakes most often for family use?_____ or for guests?_____ or for special occasions, such as weddings, birthdays, etc.?_____

7. At what time of year do you bake most often?_____
   Least often?_____

8. Do you do more or less baking than you did a year ago? More_____ Less_____
   Same_____

9. Have you a regular baking day?_____ What day?_____

10. What kinds of flour are in your pantry now, and what do you bake with each? (Including quick mixes. Please give brand names.)

Brands of flour and quick mixes	What baked
_____	_____
_____	_____
_____	_____
_____	_____

11. What brands of baking powder are in your pantry now?_____

FIGURE 14. A Well-Designed Consumer Questionnaire. Note the restriction of the survey method to matter which the respondent is qualified to answer and the general observance of many of the rules for questionnaire construction.

In an experiment to determine the amount of bias produced by the use of a check list, the reported readership of publications was studied. The tendency of check lists to lead responses is intensified in this example because of the high-prestige value of certain publications and the low-prestige value of others. The test revealed that when respondents were interviewed and directly asked whether they read a particular low-prestige magazine, a larger proportion admitted readership than when the magazine was included in a check list with high-prestige magazines. The test also revealed that interviewing respondents about just one magazine produced data closely in line with circulation statistics.

A fourth type of leading question, which is most subtle, is the identification of the questionnaire with a specific brand. Persons responding to a questionnaire tend to try to guess the specific brand for which the study is being made. Once the brand has been revealed, the respondent is led toward giving answers favorable to the brand. The identity of the brand may be disclosed by constant repetition of the brand name in the questionnaire, although it is handled on individual questions in such a manner as not to disclose the fact that this is the brand for which the study is being made. The situation may be even more subtle, however, for some elements closely associated in the consumer's mind with an individual brand may disclose it. For example, if a qustionnaire on coffee repeatedly refers to a specific television or radio program, many people will immediately recognize that the study is being made for a certain brand and give replies favorable to that brand. Other ways of subtly revealing the identity of the brand are to keep referring to special features of the product or to advertising slogans.

A fifth form of leading question is the use of particular words which have high emotional content. Examples are "propaganda," "labor union," "fair," and "big business." All questions used should be carefully tested in various forms in order to determine the effect of different wordings of the same question to reveal possible word bias.

Finally, questions which present only a choice between two answers also tend to produce biased results. This practice is so common that it is covered by a special rule (No. 9).

Certain questions also tend to produce interviewer bias, as well as bias on the part of respondents. Those which can be answered "yes" or "no" are most free from this particular source of bias.

The following questions, taken from a single questionnaire, show how easy it is to violate the leading question rule and produce biased results:

a) What is your favorite soft drink?
b) Have you tried 7-Up?
c) About how many times a month do you drink 7-Up?
d) How many in your family like 7-Up?
e) Check any of the following ways in which you have used 7-Up:

    Refreshing drink _____
    With fruit juice _____
    With ice cream _____
    Mixer for gin _____
    Mixer for whiskey _____
    For health _____

The reader will note that this questionnaire is loaded in many ways with leading questions which are bound to produce distorted or biased results.

Rule 5. Omit questions which are too intimate or which raise personal prejudices.

There are many subjects which people regard as very intimate, and it is useless to ask questions relating to them. Questions relating to matters of personal health and morals are examples. There are other subjects where one must be careful that the questions are phrased to avoid personal bias and prejudice. The researcher must be clearly aware of the various customs, mores, or traditions which will affect the answer to questions. Racial and religious prejudices must always be avoided. Examples of embarrassing questions are the following:

Do you brush your teeth regularly?
What is your age?
How often do you drink liquor?

There are times when questions which directly encounter prejudices of the kind cited are asked in marketing research. This questioning is permissible when the purpose of the analysis is to measure the extent of the prejudice. A question on the value of advertising will obtain many personal points of view. Such a question would obviously be worthless as a means of determining the value of advertising, but it would be perfectly proper if the purpose of the analysis was to determine the degree of prejudice against advertising.

The marketing researcher should examine all questions carefully to be sure that none of them is so stated as to hurt the pride of the respondent. Gallup found that an apparently innocuous question, "Have you read *Gone With the Wind*?" was such a question. When the direct question was asked, few people would admit they had not read the popular novel. When the question was changed to "Do you intend to read *Gone With the Wind?*" the response was quite different. The second wording actually flattered people and produced reliable answers to the subject being investigated.

The Indirect Approach. If one wishes to learn about some matters which respondents regard as personal confidences or which would be incorrectly answered because of bias or prejudice, he may employ the indirect approach. By the indirect approach is meant asking one individual to provide information about another. This device is used by house-to-house canvassers, who make it a point to ask neighbors the names of persons upon whom they are about to call.

While many respondents will not correctly reveal their own rent, neighbors are often quite willing to furnish the required information. Many individuals will even hesitate to reply accurately to a direct question as to whether they own or rent their homes. An indirect approach used to meet this situation asked the question, "Do you think rents in this neighborhood are too high?" This question brought forth many answers which voluntarily disclosed whether people owned or rented. If the indirect approach is used, it will often remove the obstacle and produce the desired information, but it should be followed up with a direct question as a check.

Another example of the use of the indirect approach will be found in obtaining confidential business information. For example, dealers may not tell an investigator what their profit margins are, but they are usually quite willing to discuss their competitor's profit margins.

Rule 6. The questionnaire should be limited to obtaining facts or opinions as much as possible.

In Chapter 5 it was shown that in the use of the survey method one may make factual surveys in which the person interviewed acts merely as a reporter, opinion surveys, or interpretive surveys in which the person interviewed attempts to report on his motives. The discussion at that point emphasizes the fact that when people make a conscious attempt to determine the motives behind their actions, they are unable to report accurately. There are some psychologists who are doing work designed to make it possible to devise questionnaires through which people can report accurately on motives. At the present time, however, approved technique calls for the restriction of questionnaires to obtaining factual data or opinion.

Rule 7. The question should be as easy to answer as possible.

This rule refers in part to the physical construction of the questionnaire. Adequate space for the answers and clear instructions to show

just how the answers are to be made should be given. The questionnaire should not be too crowded. Its physical appearance should be
attractive. Wherever possible, especially in mail questionnaires, the
questions should be so worded that the respondent can indicate his
answer by a simple check mark.

This rule has other general applications. For example, questions
requiring long answers should be omitted or broken down into a series
of questions, each of which can be answered quickly.

One violation of this rule, which is frequently met, is asking questions which involve ranking a large series of items in the order of their
importance. People are often asked questions like the following:

Which of the following is most important? (Indicate order of importance by numbering 1, 2, 3, etc.)

.....Price
.....Quality
.....Service
.....Style
.....Durability
.....Economy
.....Safety
.....Trade-in value
.....Dealer's reputation
.....Time payments
....._____
....._____

The question is badly phrased because it is not clear to the average
person as to just exactly what is wanted. Ranking questions, in general, are difficult questions to answer. Most people do not know which
of a series of items is most important and must spend a great deal of
time attempting to make an intelligent guess. The list given is entirely
too long. Most people will not take the time to answer such a question, or will make a superficial answer. Ranking questions should not
involve more than three or four items. Incidentally, some terms involved in the example above, such as the difference between "price"
and "economy," will not be understood by most of the people answering the questionnaire, thus violating Rule 3.

**Rule 8. Questions containing more than one element should be
eliminated.**

Frequently, people will ask questions about an activity which on
the surface can be answered by one reply but which actually involve

two separate activities and, therefore, require two questions and two replies. The following are examples:

Why did you change to Lifebuoy soap?

This question really requires two answers, because in changing, two activities are involved. In the first place, there is a reason for discontinuing the use of the brand formerly used. The reason for adopting the use of the second brand is a separate activity.

Why do you use Lucky Strike cigarettes?

This question also requires two or more answers because the use of a product almost invariably involves at least two elements—a quality of the product (like flavor), and an influence (like advertising).

The detection of multiple-element questions is sometimes rather difficult. The reader should note that this fault does not refer to the inclusion of individual words having more than one meaning, covered in Rule 3, but to the use of a question requiring an answer which reports on an activity involving more than one individual action.

Rule 9. All questions should provide for conditional answers.

This rule is violated very frequently. The most common form of violation is illustrated by the following:

Which liquid has the better flavor?
    Number 1 _____
    Number 2 _____

This question should provide for a third type of answer, "Don't know," or "No choice."

It is a very common error to provide check spaces for answers which force the respondent to vote in the affirmative or negative. The answer to many questions is neither "yes" nor "no," but rather "maybe" or "perhaps" or "I don't know."

All questions seeking a "yes" or "no" answer or asking for any type of choice should provide for a "don't know" column. Where a check list is employed it is also necessary to provide for conditional answers. In such cases, one should always have one or more blank spaces to indicate answers which are not in the prepared list.

The extent to which conditional answers are given is a very important piece of evidence found as a result of the questionnaire study. For example, it is just as important to know the percentage of people who are doubtful as to the comparative merits of two products as it is to know the percentages who are favorably and unfavorably impressed.

Rule 10. The questions should be arranged in a proper sequence.

This rule requires that the questions be asked in such an order that the flow of thought from the first to the last will follow the proper psychological pattern.

It is important to distinguish between what might be termed the psychological order and the logical order. By the "psychological order" is meant the sequence which will best fit the requirements of the interview so that the best possible answers will be obtained. By the "logical order" is meant an arrangement which satisfies the requirements of the logical, orderly handling of the various items in the mind of the researcher. The distinction between the two orders is shown in textbooks. Some books are written with an arrangement of chapters which is determined by the psychological order in which the students can best learn the subject. This is the more modern technique. Many textbooks, unfortunately, are placed in a logical arrangement which satisfies the erudite thinking of the person who has written them.

This distinction is particularly important in questionnaire construction. Unfortunately, many writers in this field have stressed the importance of having a logical flow of thought through the questionnaire. They forget that what may be a logical order to the researcher may be a very poor order to the persons answering the questionnaire.

Beyond a few ground rules, one can determine the proper order only by testing the questions in various arrangements. One can, however, observe the following principles:

1. The first question asked should be the easiest one for the respondent to answer and one which will immediately arouse interest.
2. The order of the questions should proceed from those most easily answered to those more difficult to answer.
3. The necessary transitions between questions should be provided constantly to stimulate interest and to prepare the respondent for the questions which immediately follow.
4. The sequence of questions should maintain a stream of thought throughout the interview.
5. Questions of a personal nature, and those which might conceivably produce embarrassment, should be placed toward the latter part of the interview.

It is obvious that the opening question should not be theoretical, require much thought, or be dependent on previous questions. To open an interview with a question such as, "Which manufacturing firm do you consider outstanding in its labor relations policies?"

would succeed only in baffling respondents. The first question should be one which can be answered with very little thought. Questions such as, "Do you use ————?" or "Do you yourself purchase most of the groceries for your table?" are typical good opening questions.

The conduct of a field interview is dependent on a stream of thought between two parties—the investigator and the respondent. The arrangement of the order of questions in their proper psychological sequence is largely a matter of getting this stream of thought properly started and then maintaining it so that there is as complete rapport as possible between the two individuals involved. A good interviewer contributes a great deal toward maintaining this stream of thought. However, it is vital to establish an order within the questionnaire itself which will help to maintain this stream, for if the questionnaire does not possess this characteristic the ordinary interviewer will become hopelessly lost, attention wanders, and the interview gradually deteriorates.

Frequently questions are inserted in the interview purely to serve as transition devices. Sometimes it is better to have the investigator make a statement to provide a bridge as the subject is changed. In this case, it is important to print the instruction to the investigator directly on the form at the point at which the statement is to be made. This is usually done in the following form, using a bold type face which stands out in contrast to the type in which the question is set:

Investigator: "Now I'd like to ask a few questions about where you buy _____."   or:

Investigator: Show exhibits C and D, saying, "Here are two kinds of _____. Please smell them and tell me if you can detect any difference in odor."

The proper order of a questionnare can be determined only by pretesting the forms under actual field conditions. It is best that these pretests be conducted by two types of investigators: exceptionally good investigators and poorer ones. The former may detect errors in the arrangement of questions during their field work and make suggestions for rearrangement. The latter will encounter difficulties arising from the arrangement of the questionnaire which will be reflected in their reports. By observing the results of their interviews, the researcher can properly plan the order of the questions.

As indicated at the beginning of the discussion in this section, this list of ten rules does not begin to exhaust the many requirements for the construction of a sound questionnaire. The literature on this problem is exhaustive. As one specializes more and more, he finds an opportunity to dig more deeply into the subject. The ten rules discussed, however, summarize the most basic requirements for questionnaire construction.

Among the commonly repeated rules for questionnaire construction with which the author cannot agree is that the questionnaire should be as short as possible. In actual practice, the rule has little practical value and has been so overemphasized that it assumed false proportions. Certainly brevity for its own sake is not a virtue in questionnaire construction, nor is a questionnaire necessarily good because it is short. The length of the questionnaire is limited primarily by the interest of the respondent in the subject and the rapport established by the skill of its design and administration. The interest of the respondent will vary so greatly that some questionnaires containing two or three questions will fail, whereas questionnaires containing over a hundred questions will be highly successful. Furthermore, some questionnaires are made exceedingly interesting, while others are dry and forbidding. The proper length of a questionnaire can be determined only by testing it. In this way the interest of individuals in the subject covered and other factors affecting the length which may be used will be determined.

The most important basic ground rules for questionnaire construction have been discussed at some length. Through experience in the drafting of questionnaires, the researcher learns how to apply these rules more or less automatically. The application of these rules to a specific questionnaire can best be made in a negative rather than a positive manner. In other words, one first draws up a questionnaire and then checks it against the rules to determine whether or not any of them have been violated. After a draft of the questionnaire has been prepared, the researcher should ask himself the following questions:

1. Do I ask for any information which people will not remember?
2. Do any of the questions ask for data which involve generalizations?
3. Is the meaning of this question obvious?
4. Do any of these questions suggest the answers?
5. Will any of these questions stumble on personal bias or prejudice?
6. Do any of the questions ask for motives? (If so, is this a proper exception to the general rule that questions should be limited to obtaining facts or opinions?)
7. How can I change any question to make it easier to answer?
8. Do I have any questions which have more than one element in them?
9. Do I provide for conditional answers in the case of every question where an answer might be forced?

10. Have I an arrangement of questions which follows the psychological flow of thought of the respondent?

Physical Form of the Questionnaire

After the questions to be included in a questionnaire are developed and their order is determined, it becomes necessary to make a layout of its finished form. The physical form of the questionnaire itself may be a great hindrance to the gathering of accurate data, may lead to errors or waste in editing, coding, and tabulation, and may also result in excessive costs. The following are the most important principles to consider in connection with the physical form of the finished questionnaire.

1. Allow Adequate Space. One of the most common errors is to cramp the physical size of the questionnaire in an effort to reduce it to a single sheet of standard dimensions. It is much better to spread the questionnaire over two to four pages and to provide ample space for filling in answers. It should be remembered that the interviewer must fill out the questionnaire under difficult writing conditions at best. Furthermore, if the form is cramped, there will be a tendency to abbreviate, to write in an illegible hand, and to neglect complete answers. When the questionnaires are later processed in editing, coding, and tabulation, failure to allow adequate space will lead to many errors and slow down the work. The main objection to physical form voiced by interviewers is allowing too little space for answers, particularly in "open-end" questions. This principle also applies to mail questionnaires, since restricting the space for answering the questions is uninviting and will reduce the number of responses.

2. Keep Size to a Minimum. On the other hand, too bulky a questionnaire is difficult for field and office workers to handle; therefore an effort should be made to keep the form to a minimum size and yet provide ample space for recording answers legibly and correctly.

3. Provide for Convenience in Handling. The questionnaire should be so constructed physically that it is convenient for handling both in the field and in the office. Odd sizes and shapes should be avoided. Where the questionnaire extends over several pages, a folded form should be employed. A single fold will provide four pages; a double fold, which can be conveniently handled, can be designed to provide six pages of questions.

Where supplementary questionnaires are necessary, paper of a different color should be employed. The supplementary form should be clearly identifiable, so that it will not be separated or lost during handling.

4. Provide for Convenience in Following the Sequence of Questions. The questionnaire should be so constructed that the interviewer can conveniently proceed from the beginning to the end. The arrangement on the page should make for natural transitions as the interview progresses from section to section and as pages are being turned. Instructions should be printed on the questionnaire in distinctive type forms and size.

One major problem in this respect is the matter of the so-called "chain," "filter," or "sequence" questions. In most surveys there is the need for setting up certain conditions under which a question is not asked. This leads to such devices as "If 'Yes' to question 5, ask question 6. If 'No' to question 5, skip question 6, but ask questions 7–10." Many of these sequence situations become very involved and lead to a great deal of confusion on the part of the interviewer. In preparing the final questionnaire form, a great deal can be done to reduce these difficulties by careful physical layout. Sometimes it becomes clear that it is necessary to reconstruct the questionnaire sequence itself.

5. Employ Good Quality Materials and Reproduction. Researchers have learned that it pays to use good reproduction and typography in the finished form. The old practice of running questionnaires on cheap mimeograph paper, loosely held together by staples, is no longer considered wise. With modern methods of offset reproduction, there is no excuse for bad layout, poor typography, or cheap quality paper. Good paper stock, which can be written on easily and legibly, will be of considerable help in the research operation. It will stand the abuse of constant handling in the field and also in editing, coding, and tabulation.

Preparation of Forms for Observations and Experiments

The preparation of the forms to be employed wherever the observational or experimental method is used is not nearly so difficult a problem as the one encountered in the preparation of questionnaires for the survey method. One should exercise care, however, to make sure that the forms are clear and allow plenty of room so that the facts can be recorded easily and clearly. One syndicated service discovered that the principal source of errors in reporting observations in store audits was the design of reporting forms, instead of faulty training of the observers or their human errors in observation.

Furthermore, there are specific kinds of errors which may be made in the preparation of these forms. The following rules are suggested in order to insure against such mistakes:

Rule 1. Forms should provide for complete identification.

The rule for identification requires that the forms should have spaces for all data necessary for proper identification, in addition to items such as the name of the person in charge of the observation, the date, and the name and address of individual stores. The last-named is frequently omitted, but it is essential for checking purposes. In cases of consumer observation, spaces for the identification of each consumer observed should also be provided. In the case of observations made within stores, if the signature of the owner or manager is required, partial check on accuracy will be automatically obtained.

Rule 2. Forms should be self-explanatory.

Wherever possible, all instructions and definitions should be placed directly on the sheet used for making the records. This rule also requires that the use of general instructions be avoided wherever possible. For example, it is common practice to provide a column in which the investigator may record by symbols the type of store involved, explaining the set of symbols to be employed on a separate instruction sheet. It is much better practice to provide separate columns for each type of outlet so that the investigator may place a check mark in the proper place. It is not necessary, then, for the investigator to remember general instructions under the stress of the actual observation. If a check list for the individual type is not employed, the symbols to be used should be clearly explained on each sheet on which data are to be recorded.

Rule 3. Separate spaces should be provided for each specific item.

This rule is best illustrated in the case of a sales or stock check form, in which provision must be made for each separate size and type of the products being checked. For example, in a store audit of cereal sales, one might provide separate places only for the different brands. In this way various size packages of each brand would be lumped together and the accuracy of the data may be completely distorted. The principle also requires that the time period be defined as clearly as possible. One should not use column headings such as "first week," "second week," etc. The column should be headed by designations such as "week ending June 10." This is especially important where work is done in a number of locations because without the more specific data it is difficult to make proper comparisons.

Joe's Market
No.. Main St.
Evanston, Ill.

3

DEC-JAN
1954-55
SHEET
3 of 4

CHECKED BY

A. C. NIELSEN CO.
2101 Howard St.
Chicago, Ill.
FORM 159-10/53

RECORD FULL CASE INVENTORIES SEPARATELY

RECORD FULL CASE INVENTORIES SEPARATELY

P.C. 01	53	52	20	19	17	93		04	03	01
	VEL			TIDE (P & G)					DUZ	
6	Large 15 oz. Case 24	Giant 37½ oz. Case 10	6.8 & 7.2 oz.	18 & 19 oz. Case 24	GIANT 46.6 & 52 OZ. COMBINED Case 9 & 10	5 lb. 3¾ oz.		7.8 & 8 oz. Case 60	20½ & 21½ oz. Case 24	GIANT 50.4 & 56 OZ. COMBINED Case 9 & 10
INVENTORY COUNT UNITS	24 / 3	12		Full Case 72 / 24 (24) (24) (24/1)	Full Case Only 10 / 7 (10)	Full Case Only			Full Case 18	Full Case Only 2 / 10 (10/3)
TOTAL	27	12		96	17				18	15
PREVIOUS	8	10		2	10				0	13
NET CHANGE (+ —)	+19	+2		+94	+7				+18	+2
PURCHASE UNITS	144	30		600	190				120	50
PURCHASE VALUE	4074	2037		16975	12901				3395	3395
CONSUMER SALES	125	28		506	183				102	48
SELLING PRICE UNIT	29	69		29	69				29	69
SELLING PRICE MULT	/	/	/	/	/	/	/	/	/	/
2 MOS. AGO	143	23		384	150				109	25
4 MOS. AGO	134	28		432	142				107	32
SPCL. OBS. DISPLAYS COU NFI / ADV NDI	CDS Ods AO (ADV) PRE M N O			CDS Ods AO (ADV) PRE M N (O)					CDS Ods AO ADV PRE M N (O)	
SPECIAL PRICE UNIT	21 ¢	21 ¢	21 ¢	21 ¢	21 ¢	21 ¢	21 ¢	21 ¢	21 ¢	21 ¢
SPECIAL PRICE MULT	/	/	/	/	/	/	/	/	/	/
RE-ORDERS PURCHASES				72	10				0	

GROSS PURCHASES — JOBBERS AND OTHER SOURCES

	Large		Giant		6.8 & 7.2 oz.		18 & 19 oz.		46.6 & 52 OZ.		5 LB. 3¾ OZ.		7.8 & 8 oz.		20½ & 21½ OZ.		50.4 & 56 OZ.	
	UNITS	VALUE	UNITS	VALUE	UNITS	VALUE	UNITS	VALUE	UNITS	VALUE	UNITS	VALUE	UNITS	VALUE	UNITS	VALUE	UNITS	VALUE
	24	XXX	10	XXX			72	XXXX	20	XXXX					24	XXX	10	XXX
	24	XXX	10	XXX			72	XXXX	20	XXXX					24	XXX	10	XXX
	24	XXX	10	XXX			72	XXXX	20	XXXX					24	XXX	10	XXX
	24	XXX					72	XXXX	20	XXXX					24	XXX	10	XXX
	24	XXX					72	XXXX	30	XXXX					24	XXX	10	XXX
	24	XXX					72	XXXX	20	XXXX								
							48	XXXX	20	XXXX								
							48	XXXX	20	XXXX								
							72	XXXX	20	XXXX								
TOTAL	144		30				600		190						120		50	

FIGURE 15. Form for a Sales Audit. This example illustrates the care with which store audit forms are designed to provide for individual observations. The complete form provides separate spaces for the recording of purchases direct from manufacturers, and returns, credits, nonconsumer sales, etc. It also provides for additional information on special prices and displays.

Rule 4. Forms should provide for the recording of individual observations.

The rule which requires that the form be so constructed that individual observations are recorded is a particularly important one. If one is making records of sales, for example, one should never use a form in which the field worker himself records the sales figures. In order to arrive at the sales of a store during a given period, three individual observations must be made: (1) stocks at the beginning of each period, (2) purchases during the period, and (3) stocks at the end of the period. On the basis of these three individual observations one can accurately calculate sales. The computation of the sales, however, should never be left to the field worker. The importance of this principle will be seen immediately if one notices the frequency with which errors are made by field workers who attempt to calculate sales.

Another example is afforded in the case of stock checks. The field worker must make separate counts of the amount of stock on the shelves, in displays, and in the stockroom. If one merely provides a total column inventory, he will not obtain as accurate results as he will if he provides separate columns in which to record the amount of stock on hand at each different location.

In studies of consumer behavior, the form should provide for separate recording of each item to be observed (if more than one) about each individual consumer.

As in the case of the preparation of questionnaires, these rules become most valuable if the researcher uses them as a basis on which to challenge the skill with which an individual form has been drawn. For example, bearing in mind the general principle that individual observations should be recorded separately, he may find that he has called for data which represent a combination of two or more separate observations. The researcher should then alter the form to provide for reporting separately each individual observation or item recorded.

SELECTED READINGS

Bauer, E. J. "Response Bias in a Mail Survey," *Public Opinion Quarterly*, Winter, 1947, pp. 594–600.

Blankenship, Albert B., *et al.* "Questionnaire Preparation and Interviewer Technique," *Journal of Marketing*, October, 1949, pp. 399–433.

Clausen, John A., and Ford, Robert N. "Controlling Bias in Mail Questionnaires," *Journal of the American Statistical Association*, December, 1947, pp. 497–511.

Ferber, Robert. "Order Bias in a Mail Survey," *Journal of Marketing*, October, 1952, pp. 171–78.

Hubbard, Alfred W. "Phrasing Questions," *Journal of Marketing*, July, 1950, pp. 48–56.

Jahoda, Marie, Deutsch, Morton, and Cook, Stuart W. *Research Methods in Social Relations.* New York: The Dryden Press, Inc., 1951, pp. 431–62.

METZNER, CHARLES A. "An Application of Scaling to Questionnaire Construction," *Journal of the American Statistical Association*, March, 1950, pp. 112–18.

PARTEN, MILDRED. *Surveys, Polls and Samples.* New York: Harper & Bros., 1950, pp. 177–217.

PAYNE, STANLEY L. *The Art of Asking Questions.* Princeton, N. J.: Princeton University Press, 1951.

SLETTO, R. F. "Pretesting of Questionnaires," *American Sociological Review*, April, 1940, pp. 193–200.

SUCHMAN, EDWARD A., and GUTTMAN, LOUIS. "A Solution to the Problem of Question Bias," *Public Opinion Quarterly*, Fall, 1947, pp. 445–55.

CASE

BLANKERTZ, DONALD F., FERBER, ROBERT, and WALES, HUGH G. *Cases and Problems in Marketing Research.* New York: The Ronald Press Co., 1954, pp. 106–10; 173–80.

11

THE PRINCIPLES OF SAMPLING

All marketing research depends upon the collection of information. In practically all cases this information is only a fraction of all the facts which might be obtained. This is true whether the sources of information are consumers, dealers, or company records. It is also true whether the basic method used for the collection of information is the survey method, the observational method, or the experimental method. A sample in marketing research is that fraction of all elements—whether consumers, dealers, or company records—that are actually employed in the research.

The Importance of Sampling. Over the past decade, marketing research practitioners and the users of the results of research studies have become increasingly aware of the fact that sampling is one of the most important and difficult aspects of the science of marketing research.

There is abundant recent evidence of the awareness of the sampling problem and its importance in research. First, and very important, is simply the ever-growing number of sample surveys being conducted in the United States. These surveys are being conducted by all kinds of agencies: business firms with their own marketing research departments, advertising media, independent research organizations commissioned by private firms, and advertising agencies on behalf of their clients.

The second indication of the growing importance of sampling is found in the fact that an important subcommittee of the United Nations has seen fit to publish a document setting up standards for satisfactory sample surveys.

Third, it has become commonplace for published reports on marketing research to include detailed explanations of the sampling methods used in collecting the data upon which the report is based. This trend is indicative of not only the importance of sampling itself, but also the recognition by the business community that such a report is only as valuable and defensible as the sampling methods which underlie it. Furthermore, promotional studies have come to capitalize on the quality of the sample employed in soliciting acceptance of their results.

Fourth, the growing importance of sampling is indicated by the degree to which sampling terminology has entered into the vocabulary of marketing research. Whether this terminology is properly or improperly used, it is important to note that certain sampling concepts have become an active verbal tool in the effective communication of businessmen on marketing research facts.

Fifth, the extensive sampling work done by the U. S. Bureau of the Census and other government organizations has both stimulated the growth of the use of sampling surveys and contributed greatly to the development of sampling theory and practice. Marketing research especially owes much to the Bureau of the Census. The dependence of this government body on sample measurements and the tenacity with which its personnel has developed sampling methodology have been of major importance in the development of sampling.

Finally, and most important, the use of sampling is the only practical method of obtaining the information required within a span of time which will permit the data to be practicably used for the purpose of helping the businessman make better decisions. Furthermore, sampling is the only method of procuring information at a relatively reasonable cost available to the typical business concern using marketing research. In fact, if sampling were not feasible, it would not be possible from a practical standpoint to conduct most marketing research as it is now practiced.

As sampling has grown in importance, it has, of course, grown in complexity. As recently as fifteen years ago, the typical marketing researcher was considered competent enough to prepare the sample design for any research he might be planning. However, the day has now arrived where the marketing research practitioner must rely to a considerable degree on sampling experts. Sampling theory and sampling methodology have progressed to the point that they have established their own specialized domain. Sampling is now recognized as a technical subject for technicians.

The discussion of sampling in this book does not attempt to make the reader a sampling expert. The chief purpose of this chapter is to place sampling in its proper perspective and to relate sampling methods to the whole field of marketing research. It is also designed to provide the reader with a sound understanding of elementary sampling principles needed by the general marketing research practitioner. Finally, it builds a foundation for those who are interested in pursuing the technical subject further and provides guides to more advanced and specialized literature.

It is very important that the marketing researcher recognize that a little knowledge about sampling can be a dangerous tool. Therefore, this chapter will attempt to provide enough sampling knowledge so that the reader can recognize the pitfalls and complexities of sampling and realize those situations where his sampling knowledge is inadequate to meet the situation. In this way, he will consult a sampling technician when necessary, just as the business executive, at the proper time, might consult a lawyer or an auditor.

Sampling Accuracy

No research technique is perfect in its design, and, therefore, the very collection of this information necessarily involves certain inaccuracies—no questionnaire is impeccable, all field workers are subject to human frailties, marketing experiments have pitfalls in design and execution, and most company records are not complete. However, careful planning and effective designing of the research will help keep such inaccuracies to a minimum.

In addition to inaccuracies due to other sources, the process of choosing only a fraction of the total sources of information introduces other inaccuracies of a different nature. There are two kinds of inaccuracies inherent in the process of sampling; one is called *sampling error* and the other is called *sampling bias*. These sampling inaccuracies will be discussed in detail later in this chapter, but it is very important to recognize—at this point—that the sampling methods used to choose the specific units to be included in the research are susceptible to inaccuracy. Thus, in marketing research, it is apparent that the confidence placed in the final results of a piece of research is dependent to an important degree on the sample used in the research.

Sampling Errors Not Only Source of Research Inaccuracy. In the final analysis, the value of marketing research information depends on the accuracy of the data produced. The accuracy of the data is in turn dependent on the entire design of the research—on all elements entering into the research job. Sampling is only *one* of the contributions to inaccuracies; it is only *one* element in the research design, and, as such, it should not dominate marketing research thinking.

As a guide for understanding the relative importance of sampling in the complete marketing research operation, the following hypothetical diagram may be helpful:

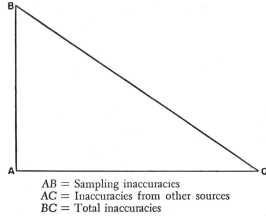

AB = Sampling inaccuracies
AC = Inaccuracies from other sources
BC = Total inaccuracies

FIGURE 16. Marketing Research Inaccuracies

This triangle indicates that the typical contribution of the sampling process is markedly less than the contribution of the nonsampling elements in the research design in terms of total survey inaccuracies. Thus, the diagram emphasizes that the development of techniques for the control and reduction of sampling inaccuracies does not necessarily mean that the total inaccuracies in a marketing research survey are substantially reduced. This does not mean that sampling is not important; it simply acts to place sampling in proper perspective to the totality of marketing research methodology. This is important because it is easy to get the impression that once sampling inaccuracies have been controlled and measured, there is little else to be concerned about. The fact of the matter is that more progress has been made in the scientific application of sampling than in other areas of marketing research, and therefore more emphasis has been placed on the contribution made by sampling inaccuracies where marked progress in measurement and control has been achieved.

The importance of this concept is effectively underlined by Howard C. Grieves, assistant director, Bureau of the Census.

Sampling error in almost all surveys is not the only source of error, and often not the primary source. Hence, if greater accuracy [in the survey] is needed, it may be possible to reduce the total error, e.g., by correcting some other weakness in the total project. . . . This brings under review such things as response error; deficiencies of enumerators; coding or classification errors; processing errors; definitional weaknesses; and other aspects of the operation, which through faulty functioning, incomplete communication, or other defects can contribute error to the final statistical product. These factors may be the cause of large errors, and until they are measured and brought under control, it becomes logically impossible to determine how much of the total survey resources should be devoted to reducing sampling error and how much should be devoted to the control of other sources of error. This should be a major concern for all who are responsible for the *management* of surveys or their financing.[1]

A leading marketing research practitioner, Alfred Politz, calls this concept "Balanced Accuracy":

From the technical viewpoint, the objective of any study is to produce specified data with a maximum of accuracy within a given administrative structure. Aside from the mechanical factors of coding, editing and tabulating, the accuracy of a sample survey depends upon (1) the reliability of the response on the part of the person being interviewed, (2) the execution of the field work and interviewing, and (3) the sampling error.

A sample survey consists of a series of operations (such as field training, questionnaire-testing, instructions, etc.), and the experimenter, in his design, has considerable choice in the utilization of those operations that meet the purpose of the study. He should select those operations which, in combination, contribute to the maximum over-all accuracy. The difficulty arises in that one particular operation may be most efficient for one of the above components of accuracy and yet may be highly inefficient for the other two components. For instance, a factor that would increase accuracy of field operation might decrease reliability of response and decrease the sampling reliability. The selection of one operation may consequently force the inclusion of another operation which, from a standpoint of over-all accuracy, is undesirable.[2]

The tendency to confuse the inaccuracies in a survey with sampling inaccuracies is often present. For example, it is not uncommon when differences are noted between two surveys ostensibly designed to measure the same factors to hear the casual remark: "Oh, there must have been some sampling error working the wrong way against us." However, in actual practice, it is soon learned that many inaccuracies other than those attributable to sampling affect the end results.

To illustrate: It is most common in marketing research surveys, as part of the questionnaire, to ask respondents to tell how old they are. Such data are used for a variety of purposes. For instance, it may be important to find out what specific age groups are the most important consumers of a company's products. Frequently, comparisons of the data, broken down by age groups, with some other accepted secondary source—such as the Census—reveals marked variation. There is the immediate tendency for a relatively uninformed person to conclude that the differences are due to sampling inaccuracies.

---

[1] M. H. Hansen, W. N. Hurwitz, and W. G. Madow, *Sample Survey Methods and Theory* (New York: John Wiley & Sons, Inc., 1953), Vol. I, p. viii.
[2] A. Politz, *A Study of Four Media* (New York: Time, Inc., 1953), Technical Appendix.

However, such variation may well be due to any one of a large number of causes such as:

1. Differences in the form of the question. Two possible alternatives are "How old were you on your last birthday?" versus "Please tell me how old you are."
2. Differences in the sex of the interviewer. A woman's response to a question on her age directed to her by another woman may well be different from her answer when the same question is put to her by a man.
3. Differences in the manner in which the results are classified in tabulation. One grouping might classify all women under 35 in one section, while the other might use two groups to handle the women under 35, such as 16 to 25 and 26 to 34.

Thus, in placing sampling in its proper perspective, a critical point to be kept constantly in mind is that the value of marketing research information depends on the *total* accuracy of the data produced; even though most nonsampling inaccuracies are normally not subject to accurate measurement and cannot be described with figures, tables, and charts.

Probability Concepts

It is unnecessary for the marketing research man to be an advanced mathematician. Nevertheless, it is critically important to realize that sampling is based on mathematical theory in order effectively to understand its principles. The branch of mathematics from which sampling derives its theoretical background is called the theory of probability, or the science of chance. The purpose of this section is to develop— from the viewpoint of common sense rather than by using the symbolic logic of mathematics—the connection between the theory of probability and actual sampling problems in marketing research.[3]

There are two links between probability theory on the one hand and practical sampling methods. These links are:

1. The link of experience.
2. The link of intuition.

The Link of Experience. In everyday life one is constantly faced, either consciously or unconsciously, with the necessity of making decisions in terms of expectations. In other words, every day of our

[3] See especially in this regard: M. H. Hansen, W. N. Hurwitz, and W. G. Madow, *op. cit.*, p. viii, and F. Yates, *Sampling Methods for Censuses and Surveys* (London: Charles Griffin & Co., 1949).

lives we make decisions which actually depend on our past experience with the *theory of probability*. For example, you may commute to your place of work on a railroad. You may have read in your newspaper this very morning that a major train crash occurred on the same railroad the day before, injuring hundreds of commuters. Nevertheless, you are not dissuaded from taking the train to work this morning. In fact, you continue to take the train to work in preference to other available means of transportation. Why do you take the train to work? Because your experience indicates to you, regardless of what happened yesterday, that the chances of a similar train wreck today on your own particular commuter train are so slight that you can afford to take the train. To put it another way, the risk of making a mistake in this situation is so small that it is worth your while to assume that risk. Having weighed the risk against the cost, namely, the alternative of taking a less convenient and familiar method of transportation, you regarded the cost as relatively high compared with your evaluation of the risk. This evaluation of risk vs. cost has been done subconsciously, but you are, in effect, applying *probability theory*.

To take a second contrasting example, you have worked a full morning and are on your way to an important business lunch. You are late. When you get to the corner of First Avenue and Main Street, you find the traffic light against you. Since you are in a hurry, you can cross this busy intersection against the light, or you can wait another minute or two for the light to change. You want to cross the street immediately, but you stop after looking at the traffic and wait for the light to change. Why did you stop and wait? You have decided, based on past experience, that the chance of being struck by an automobile is too great to warrant taking the risk of crossing against the light. Thus, you are saying—in this case—that the potential risk of crossing the street against the light is greater than the cost to you of annoying an important sales prospect.

How have you really evaluated these two different situations so that split-second decisions were unconsciously reached? On what basis have you decided that the probability of injury in a train wreck is relatively slight and the probability of being struck by an automobile is relatively large? In neither of these cases has there been a conscious formulation of the exact mathematical odds which can be applied to the two situations. You know the odds only imperfectly, but in your subconscious you are aware of them.

What has all this to do with sampling in marketing research work? Marketing research studies are made to accumulate data which can help management make more accurate business decisions. Researches are conducted by taking small groups (samples) of consumers, stores, sales data, or other sources and collecting specific kinds of data about them. The specific question which must be asked about all marketing research studies is: What confidence can be placed in the information gathered from this small sample? In this connection, the mathematical theory of probability makes two major contributions to marketing research:

1. It permits researchers to have confidence in results based on relatively small samples.
2. It provides a basis for estimating the degree of confidence which can be placed in the sample results.

Therefore, in the same way that the commuter's past experience permits him to make a decision subconsciously on the basis of probability, the theory of probability tells the marketing research man what risks are involved in making a business decision on the basis of the sample of data he employs.

The Link of Intuition. Common sense tells us that it is possible and necessary to think in terms of probability in connection with many situations in life.

The terms PROBABLE and PROBABILITY are used in ordinary language in many different connections; and the reader will agree that, in a great many instances, it is useless to attempt a numerical estimate of the probability under consideration. For instance, we cannot give a numerical value to the probability that a certain man's political or religious beliefs are correct, or that a statement by a perfect stranger is true. There is, however, a very large group of questions in connection with which a numerical estimate of probability may be attempted with very useful results.[4]

Marketing research is concerned with situations which, in the main, lend themselves to a numerical estimate of probability. In fact, one of the great contributions of the mathematics of probability is the finding that probability can be numerically estimated in both social and physical scientific research. The practical result of this fact can best be illustrated by a specific example.

Suppose that you are the owner of a chain of 1,000 food stores. You want to find out, on the average, how many cars use the parking lot of each store on each day of the week in order to determine whether your parking facilities are adequate.

Seven hundred of the food stores are small two- to four-clerk stores. The other 300 are large supermarkets. You decide it would be both

---

[4] C. E. Weatherburn, *A First Course in Mathematical Statistics* (Cambridge, Mass.: University Press, 1949), p. 20.

too expensive and time consuming to make a traffic count in each parking lot for each of the 1,000 stores so you decide to pick 100 stores to represent your entire food chain. You select a sample of 100 stores.[5] After the sample is drawn, you decide to inspect it to see what size of stores you have in the sample you selected. You find that there are 20 single-clerk type stores and 80 large supermarkets!

You know, simply on the basis of intuition, that your sample is not a "good" sample because it does not represent all your stores in terms of store size. Your sample is far out of proportion. You simply would not expect a result as far removed from the 70–30 per cent division (700 to 300) as your result of 20–80 per cent, just on the basis of your own common sense or your intuition. You would expect that your sample would approach, in composition, a proportion of 7 to 3 in favor of small stores. You might not expect your sample results to be exactly in the proportion of 7 to 3, but on the basis of simple logic, you would expect your sample results at least to approach the 7 to 3 proportion closely.

The contribution which the mathematical theory of probability makes to sampling in marketing research is this: It permits the researcher to know precisely, in exact numerical terms, the chances that a given sample result has of deviating from the true value which would be obtained if it were feasible to take a census.

In the example just given, you found that the sample result was in the proportion of two small stores to eight supermarkets. You note that on the basis of common sense, this is an improbable result. The mathematical theory of probability tells you exactly how improbable this result is; in other words, it tells you how many times out of 100 you could expect a result which deviated from the actual situation (seven small stores to three supermarkets) to occur. In this particular case, any one of many results would have been obtained in the sample of 100 stores you picked. You actually could have found no supermarkets and 100 single-clerk stores or you could have found a sample in which there were no single-clerk stores and 100 supermarkets. Probability theory therefore tells you how often each result can be expected.

Thus, the mathematical theory of probability makes this fundamental contribution to sampling in marketing research: It tells the researcher that in the vast majority of cases a sample will produce results sufficiently close to the actual situation to provide a valid and realistic basis upon which the data supplied from the research can, as far as sampling considerations are concerned, act as a sound guide in the making of business decisions.

[5] The problems of method of drawing and sample size are not considered at this point.

Sample Adequacy and Representativeness

Experience and intuition can provide a grasp of the fundamentals of the sampling process. However, it must be kept in mind that these fundamentals compose only the embryo of sampling theory as applied to problems in marketing research. It must be realized that an intuitive grasp of these fundamentals does not create a knowledge of sampling.

Intuition can be misleading if it is not supported and channeled by a proper understanding of the important concepts of more advanced sampling theory. Two core concepts in sampling theory are *sample adequacy* and *sample representativeness.* Before getting into the details of sampling methodology itself, it is critically important to understand the meaning of and the difference between *sample adequacy* and *sample representativeness.*

Sample Adequacy—Errors. Strictly on the basis of intuition, it might be inferred that the larger the sample for any survey, the more faith could be placed on the result. For instance, if you wanted to find out how many people owned Ford automobiles in the United States, you could interview 5,000 car owners or 25,000 car owners. On the basis of common sense, alone, it might appear that a sample of 25,000 car owners would produce a demonstrably more accurate result than a sample of 5,000 car owners. It might even be thought, on the basis of intuition, that the sample of 25,000 should be five times as good as a sample of 5,000.

Actually a basic principle of sampling theory is that there is a sample size which is large enough to mirror the group from which the sample is drawn accurately (within stated limits). A sample size larger than the adequate size is inefficient because we are sampling more people or other units from the group being sampled than is necessary. Increasing the sample size beyond this point reduces the chances of error more than is necessary. Furthermore, additions to the desired accuracy as a result of the increase in size beyond a reasonable point are slight relative to the cost of making these additions.[6]

For any marketing research problem the researcher has normally made some decision about the chance he is willing to take by accepting the results. If the situation with respect to the marketing decisions to be made is such that the researcher can afford relatively large deviations in sample results, which is to say that the sample does not need to be too accurate, then an excessive sample size is simply a waste of money.

[6] The relationship of sampling costs to size of sample is discussed in Chapter 12.

Deviation in sample results is called *sampling error*. This sampling error can be said to spring from the general sampling process itself—regardless of the particular sampling *method* used, although different methods yield different amounts of sampling error.

In any given marketing research problem, larger sampling errors will result from smaller sample sizes, and conversely, the larger the size of the sample, the smaller the sampling errors will be. When the researcher decides what range of sampling errors are permitted by the decision-making requirements of his problem, he can determine approximately an *adequate* sample size. If he uses a smaller sample size, he is taking a greater risk than he can afford to take. If he chooses a sample of larger size, he increases his cost by reducing the sampling error past the necessary point.

Sample Representativeness—Sample Bias. There are two other kinds of inaccuracies in sampling besides sampling error. The first is bias from improper sample design. The second is incorrect definition of the universe. If either an improper sample design or an incorrect definition of the universe is used, then the resulting sample will not be *representative*.

Sample design may be defined as the method by which the sample is physically chosen. There are many types of sample design. The selection of any particular design depends primarily on the specific research problem confronting the researcher. The final choice of any sampling design to be used on a specific research project is not only a function of sampling theory but (as will be shown in detail in the sampling methods section) also depends on practical experience. No sampling concepts can be arbitrarily used in a vacuum.

When a sample is improperly designed, the unrepresentativeness is due to what sampling men refer to as sampling bias. To illustrate an unrepresentative sample resulting from a biased method of selection, consider the following example. Suppose you were interested in finding out what proportion of the people in the New York metropolitan area use the subway system to get to work. It has been decided that a sample of 2,000 people, if properly drawn, will be adequate to represent the universe. The universe in this case is made up of men and women who earn their living in the New York metropolitan area.

With a relatively limited budget and in light of time pressure, it is important to adopt a method which is both rapid and inexpensive. Therefore, it is decided to restrict interviews to the five major boroughs of New York. This will keep transportation costs to a minimum and also result in more completed interviews per day for each field interviewer.

Unfortunately, by restricting the geographical distribution of the sample, a sampling bias has undoubtedly been introduced. This is owing to the fact that the commuting habits of the large group of people who live on the periphery of the New York area differ from the habits of the people living in the five boroughs. Thus, you would most probably find that in the course of their daily commutation, there may be less subway usage on the part of the working people living in the outlying areas. Sampling more people in the boroughs themselves will not solve the problem. In fact, it will merely result in giving the impression of more reliable information but, as a matter of fact, it would merely be compounding a critical error.

This example demonstrates clearly a severe case of bias where what is measured in the survey is very obviously related to the specific bias introduced. In other words, it is quite apparent that sampling the city areas will result in a subway usage figure which does not clearly portray the commuting habits of all working people in the universe. However, in many instances the bias introduced by ineffective representation is not as striking and as obvious as in this case. In such situations it is not uncommon to find important bias quietly creeping in and destroying the basic validity of the research study.

The example just cited would be considered a severe case of bias, but it serves to demonstrate the extent of sample bias possible as a result of improper sample design.

Normally, the researcher's objective is to reduce sample bias to a minimum. However, in any practical marketing research situation, if alternative sampling methods available differ in very small degree with regard to the amount of bias inherent in each method, then the choice of methods depends less on consideration of the bias factor than on other factors, such as the ease of administration and the ultimate cost of the procedure.

Sample Representativeness—Definition of the Universe. The second kind of inaccuracy in sampling besides sampling error also leads to an unrepresentative sample. However, it actually has nothing to do with the sample itself, but rather concerns the universe from which the sample is drawn, the whole group from which the sample is taken. If the sample is drawn from a universe different from that which it is supposed to represent, then the sample, regardless of the presence or absence of sampling error or sampling bias, cannot be representative of the population it is designed to measure.

The researcher must be constantly aware of the universe problem. The first reason is that he may unwittingly choose some segment of the universe which can be easily measured without realizing that he is not measuring the whole universe.

Suppose that you want to determine the proportion of homes owning automatic washing machines in one city. You decide to determine this proportion by selecting names at random from the telephone directory.[7] You will call each of the names you select and simply ask whether or not an automatic washing machine is owned. After calling 1,000 housewives, assuming that every dialing results in a completed call, you find that 73 per cent of all the homes you contacted own automatic washing machines. Suppose, after the survey is completed, some one says: "This is very interesting, but did you know only half the homes in this city are equipped with telephones, and that nontelephone homes have an average income much lower than the homes owning telephones?" Your first reaction would probably be to say to yourself, "Well, I'm sure the homes with higher incomes would be more likely to own automatic washing machines." If there is a significant relationship between telephone ownership and income on the one hand, and a significant relationship between income and washing-machine ownership on the other hand, you would probably be concerned about the results of your survey. You might say to yourself: "I guess my 73 per cent figure is definitely high!"

Thus, your survey figure has not told you much about automatic washing-machine ownership in this city. It has told you only what proportion of telephone homes own automatic washing machines. Yet, your sampling method left nothing to be desired. What happened?

The list from which you drew your sample did not include the entire population but was rather only a selected or an atypical portion of that population or universe. A common cause of unrepresentativeness in sample surveys is the fact that the sample is frequently drawn in such a way that the universe which it actually measures differs in very important ways from the universe which one really wants to measure.

The second reason for the researcher being alert to the universe problem is that it is sometimes impossible actually to measure the universe that you should be measuring. An excellent illustration of the second kind of problem is the situation confronting the pollsters when they try to predict the outcome of an election. Although the pollsters know that most adults can vote, the problem that is difficult to solve—if not impossible—is to determine which of the franchised adults actually will vote at election time. Since, typically, only about one-half of franchised America goes to the polls, the pollsters find themselves measuring the total franchised population to represent the

---

[7] This example ignores the problems of not-at-homes, busy signals, and lines disconnected.

part of the total which will eventually take action at the polls on election day. Regardless of the sampling method employed or the sample size used, the fundamental problem confronting the pollsters is this universe problem. It is for this reason that the pollsters are now attempting to predict future voting behavior by asking a series of questions about the past voting behavior of the people they interview.

Sampling Methods

The Importance of the Language of Sampling. We are now ready to consider the actual methods which are used in the selection of marketing research samples. First, it is most important to realize that the words which are used to describe sampling and sampling methods must be as clear and precise as possible. Unfortunately, as the science of sampling has developed, there has been a tendency to use the new phrases which came into being with the new science indiscriminately. This has had the unfortunate effect of inducing a certain looseness of thinking in the field of sampling. This, in turn, has tended to inhibit the understanding of sampling both among researchers themselves and also, and most importantly, among nonresearch people.

Words and phrases like "probability method," "modified random sample," "scientific sample," and "sample of area design" have come into common use among market research technicians and nontechnicians alike. They have been used and misused to the point that even if the phrases were once capable of precise definition, it is now almost impossible to define them adequately. The result is that now when such phrases are used, it is virtually impossible for anyone really to know exactly what they mean. Many misinterpretations and misconceptions are prevalent.

In the following pages a categorization of the better known and most widely used methods of sampling in marketing research will be made. The basic objective of this grouping is so to define and differentiate sampling methods that the basic ones can be easily understood. An attempt will also be made to give simple, yet precise, labels to each of the methods of sampling so that the labels themselves will help describe the methods which they title.

The Two Basic Sampling Methods. Basically, the sampling methods which are now used in marketing research can be divided into two broad groups. The first of these groups can be called the random sampling approach or *probability* method. The second broad group can be called the nonrandom sampling approach or the *quota-sampling* method. In the preceding pages of this chapter, the random sampling frame of reference has been assumed. The concepts of adequacy and representativeness, as they have been developed above, have assumed specifically that the sampling method used is based on some sort of a random sampling procedure.

Probability sampling method may be defined as follows:

> Probability sampling is a method of choosing for investigation a number of units or individuals according to some mechanical or automatic principle unconnected with the subject or purpose of the inquiry, the selection being arranged so that each unit or individual in the universe has an equal or known chance of being included in the sample.

A nonrandom sampling method may be differentiated from a random sampling method as follows: The nonrandom method does not have some sort of mechanical or automatic principle of selection, and most importantly, the individuals are not selected in such a way that each individual has an equal or known chance of coming into the sample.

Quota sampling may be defined as follows:

> Quota sampling is based on the assumption that if cases are selected from the universe according to a predetermined design which provides for specified proportions of various types of cases, based on known characteristics, the sample will be representative in terms of unknown characteristics.

In practice, random and nonrandom sampling methods are both used frequently. The selection of any particular sampling design depends upon many factors, such as cost, experience, the problem to be solved, the need for determinable accuracy, and the time requirements of the research. It is not the intention of this description of sampling to imply that a random method is always superior to a nonrandom method in every situation. However, in terms of sampling theory, *if all other factors are equal*, a random sampling method must be considered superior to a nonrandom sampling method. To use an analogy: expensive and inexpensive watches both tell time. There are circumstances, rough and ready though they may be, in which the inexpensive watch is to be preferred to the expensive watch. However, if one were given the free choice of either an expensive or an inexpensive watch, he would most certainly choose the former. The inexpensive watch usually tells time with fair accuracy but sometimes it is fast, sometimes it is slow, and sometimes it stops altogether. The expensive watch has one major virtue—it almost always tells the time with a high degree of precision, and it is very unlikely that the expensive watch will stop if it is properly wound. It is extremely important for the researcher to recognize the existence of the expensive watch, and to know, intimately, the differences and superiorities of performance which it possesses relative to the inexpensive watch. This is not to say that the expensive watch is always to be preferred, but it is most important that its existence be known and considered in the selection of a sampling method for any given research.

Random and Nonrandom Sampling—General Considerations. In a quota sample the final responsibility for selecting the individuals who will compose the sample rests with the interviewer. The interviewer is supplied with certain quotas of personal characteristics which must be represented by the sample which she selects. These controls broadly define the individuals which may be selected for the sample and try to guarantee that the sample will reflect certain population characteristics with precision. Thus, the typical quota sample will have certain proportions of males and females, certain proportions of different age groups, certain proportions of different income groups, and so on. Each of these stated sample proportions will presumably be the same as the population which the sample is designed to reflect.

The basic assumption of the quota method is that if the sample accurately reflects certain known population characteristics, it will then mirror the population with regard to characteristics which are unknown. In this assumption can be seen a basic flaw of the quota method. "Quota sampling is widely condemned on the grounds of this inverse logic." [8]

Two other criticisms are important. The characteristics of the total population upon which the controls are based may be inaccurate. This is especially true when the population has been subject to great change. Another criticism is that the success of the survey depends almost completely on the degree to which the enumerator is able or disposed to select an ideal and thus representative group of respondents. These two criticisms will be developed in terms of their effect on the sampling error below.

The probability sample, in its pure theoretical form, involves the concept of the "ideal bowl." [9] Thus, picture a bowl containing marbles, each one representing an individual in the universe. These marbles are all of equal size. The marbles in the bowl are thoroughly mixed and one individual is removed. Then they are thoroughly mixed a second time and another individual is removed, and so on

[8] Stock and Hochstim, "Commercial Uses of Sampling," *Journal of the American Statistical Association*, December, 1948, p. 519.

[9] W. E. Deming, *Some Theory of Sampling* (New York: John Wiley & Sons, Inc., 1950), pp. 135–65.

until a sample of the required size has been drawn.[10] The random sampling design method, as noted above, has the following characteristics:

1. Every individual in the population has an equal or known chance of being selected.
2. The chance of selecting any particular individual is independent of the characteristic which is being studied.

Thus, in a pure random sample the researcher has absolutely no control over the particular units or individuals which appear in his sample. It is here that we find a critical distinction between the quota and the probability methods of selection. In the latter instance the interviewer has absolutely no choice as to which individuals are interviewed.

Of course, in the practical application of random design sampling, the "ideal bowl" is somewhat modified. For instance, a primary application of probability sampling in market research is found in so-called "area" sampling, one method which is frequently usable in marketing research. In this method it is assumed that the individuals in the universe are uniquely associated with certain small land areas and the dwelling units located on these land areas. The total sampling area (e.g., the United States) is conceived as consisting of a variety of groups of areas, each one of decreasing size. At successive stages in the sampling process certain of these land areas are selected. Thus, at the first stage a group of counties may be chosen. Within these counties a group of townships, for example, is drawn in the second stage. Within these townships smaller areas such as census enumeration districts are selected. This process of successive selection at random continues until certain small areas, such as city blocks or small rural areas, have been chosen. Within these blocks or areas dwelling units are selected at random and interviews are conducted with the residents.[11] The area sampling design is in a sense unrelenting in its working; no substitution is allowed. All specified individuals must be interviewed and no individuals other than those specified can be interviewed.

Of course, in practical field situations, it is not possible to interview everybody that falls into the sample as selected. There are three alternatives for handling this situation. The first alternative is to set

[10] The question of whether such sampling is done with or without replacement is here ignored: In practice there is seldom replacement. Thus, in any event, the question is largely academic.

[11] The sampling design described here consists of random selection of units at different stages. This is known as multistage sampling.

up a procedure for minimizing the possibility of not reaching each specified respondent. Here, one or more callback interview attempts are made. If there is still some percentage of originally specified people who have not been reached, it is common practice to replace them with other persons according to some predetermined plan.

The second alternative is simply to interview as many of the originally specified persons as possible with a series of callbacks. Here, no replacement procedure is used; rather, the number of callback attempts is extended, and the sample is tabulated without any adjustment. Thus, while the first alternative involves a small number of callbacks and a replacement procedure, the second alternative involves a maximum number of callbacks and no replacements. Naturally, this latter method is not usable unless the survey organization is willing to spend the time and money required to make extensive callback interviews.

This procedure was used in "A Study of Four Media" conducted by the Alfred Politz Research:

The extensive field requirements for this study necessitated prodigious efforts by the field staff, probably never before demanded in a national audience study. Each interviewer was instructed to make up to eight calls, if necessary, on each respondent in each wave. (There were special occasions where efforts had to be extended up to 12 calls.) Most interviewer visits were made in the evening, but if any one particular respondent preferred to be interviewed at another time or place, then the interviewer returned to him at the time and place specified by the particular respondent. No substitutions of any kind were permitted. The principal consideration was that once a respondent was specified . . . that person and no other had to be interviewed—no matter where or when.[12]

Another method which has from time to time been used with success to meet this problem is described by Simmons and Politz. This approach substitutes a weighting procedure in tabulation to account for interviews not completed.[13]

It is virtually impossible in practice to follow the concept of pure randomization, in terms of the "ideal bowl," since the time and money required are excessive. Fortunately, the area plan produces comparable results at a fraction of the cost, and the mathematical probability framework attaching to pure random samples can be largely carried over to samples drawn with an area design.

[12] "A Study of Four Media," Life Magazine, 1954.

[13] See W. Simmons and A. Politz, "An Attempt to Get the Not-at-Homes into the Sample Without Callbacks," Journal of American Statistical Association, March, 1949, pp. 9–31, and W. Simmons, "A Plan to Account for 'Not-at-Homes' by Combining Weighting and Callbacks," Journal of Marketing, July, 1954, pp. 42–53. As the title of the latter article suggests, its plan involves both the use of callbacks and a weighting procedure.

The problem of measuring sampling error follows logically from these essential differences between the quota and probability sampling plans. In the probability sample the researcher is able to state unequivocally that in a given number of cases out of 100 (usually 95 or 99) the results obtained from his sample differ from the true values of the universe being sampled by no more than a stated percentage.

No prior assumptions are made about the population under investigation in a pure random sampling design. If such assumptions are made, as they are in quota sampling, and if the sample is drawn according to these assumptions, the sample can be no more valid than the assumptions. But no underlying set of assumptions can perfectly reflect particular characteristics of a population which is always in a state of flux. Such assumptions must be based upon past censuses or surveys. Such prior studies tend to be obsolete as soon as they are made and are themselves subject to all the errors of any data-collecting project. When they are applied to a later study, the later study is subject to an indeterminate amount of bias.

For example, assume we are conducting a survey of beer drinkers in the United States. An important objective of this survey is to determine the in-home consumption of beer by state. Let us also assume that it is 1949 when the survey is being planned and that the researcher allocates his interview quotas by states according to the 1940 Census of Population. In 1940 the state of California had a population of 6,907,387, and this population represented 5.2 per cent of the total population of the United States. In 1950 the population of California was 10,586,223, representing 7.0 per cent of the total U. S. population. Therefore, a survey in 1949 which allocated interviews by states on the basis of the 1940 Census would underrepresent California.

The bias introduced through this source may be great or small, but it cannot be measured. In a strict random sampling design, randomness is depended upon rather than prior information about the population. Therefore, the sampling errors inherent in random sampling can be measured. We see here one of the elements which may predispose the quota method to uncertain results.

In addition, we must also consider the effect of allowing the interviewer discretion in choosing respondents. In the probability method no such discretion is allowed. If it could be demonstrated that the interviewer in the field could independently choose a random sample, this matter would not be serious. Yet it follows from the very fact that quotas are given to field workers that these interviewers cannot be depended upon. Further, there is the problem of whether the individuals who show up in a quota sample, even if selected by chance, are representative of the entire population. The units in a quota sample are selected as the opportunity presents itself.

As previously noted in this chapter, the preceding paragraphs do not mean that quota sampling should never be used. Situations in which quota sampling is appropriate will be examined in the next chapter. However, it is extremely important to understand the basic nature of the quota design before it can be used by the marketing research man with any confidence.

Neither, as previously indicated, is there any intent to imply that the problem of sampling error is the only one faced by the researcher. "Objection . . . on the ground of sampling errors can be sustained only if after consideration of other inaccuracies the elimination of sampling errors seems a wise investment . . . they are controllable through the size and design of the sample . . . , but they are often the least of the errors present." [14]

In practical situations, it would seem that, in consideration of these other sources of bias and error, the quota method may often produce a quality of results not significantly different from those attained with a random design. Hansen and Hurwitz make the following comment in this regard:

> Generally it should be considered worth while to take a probability sample where results of higher precision are needed or where objective and unbiased results are wanted, because important decisions or courses of action will be determined on the basis of the sample results.[15]

The only reason that quota sampling is used to such a great degree is that it is considerably less expensive than probability sampling. A consideration of sampling efficiency (i.e., What design produces the most reliable results for the lowest price?) cannot be precisely made with existing theory since the precision of a quota sample cannot be assessed. Thus, the ultimate decision as between these alternative designs must be based arbitrarily upon some criteria such as those suggested by Hansen and Hurwitz.

In summary, then:

1. Only a random or probability design will produce results of assessable accuracy. This is because cases are chosen at random, no prior assumptions are made about the nature of the population, and

[14] W. E. Deming, "On Errors in Surveys," *American Sociological Review*, August, 1944, pp. 359–69. The author refers to inaccuracies due to factors such as sampling bias, response variability, interviewer bias, bias of auspices, imperfection of questionnaire construction, imperfection in tabulation plans, bias due to late reports, and unrepresentative data for the survey.

[15] M. H. Hansen and W. M. Hurwitz, "Dependable Samples for Market Surveys," *Journal of Marketing*, October, 1949, p. 364.

no substitution is allowed.   When a nonrandom selection is used, it is based on prior assumptions about the population; selection of respondents is left to the discretion of the field workers, so there are many potential sources of bias and error. We do not know how to assess the weight which they may have upon sample results.

2. Estimates of population values based on sample results can be valid only when the sample has been drawn according to a random or probability design.

3. Sampling error is not the only important factor impinging upon results obtained from sample surveys. Its significance depends largely upon the use to which the sample results will be put. *The probability design will not always produce results which are sufficiently different from a quota sample design to affect any decision which might be based on the findings.* However, the researcher will be able to know the sampling error exactly when he uses a probability sample.

SELECTED READINGS

BIRNBAUM, Z. W., and SIRKEN, MONROE G. "Bias Due to Non-Availability in Sampling Surveys," *Journal of the American Statistical Association*, March, 1950, pp. 98–111.

COCHRAN, WILLIAM G. *Sampling Techniques.* New York: John Wiley & Sons, Inc., 1953.

CROSSLEY, HELEN M., and FINK, RAYMOND. "Response and Non-Response in a Probability Sample," *International Journal of Opinion and Attitude Research*, Spring, 1951, pp. 1–19.

DEMING, W. E. *Some Theory of Sampling.* New York: John Wiley & Sons, Inc., 1950.

HANSEN, M. H., and HAUSER, P. M. "Area Sampling—Some Principles of Sample Design," *Public Opinion Quarterly*, Summer, 1945, pp. 183–93.

HANSEN, MORRIS H., and HURWITZ, WILLIAM N. "Dependable Sample for Market Surveys," *Journal of Marketing*, October, 1949, pp. 363–72.

HANSEN, MORRIS H., and HURWITZ, WILLIAM N. "The Problem of Non-Response in Sample Surveys," *Journal of the American Statistical Association*, December, 1946, pp. 517–529.

HANSEN, MORRIS H., HURWITZ, WILLIAM N., and MADOW, WILLIAM G. *Sample Survey Methods and Theory.* New York: John Wiley & Sons, Inc., 1953.

MANHEIMER, D., and HYMAN, H. "Interviewer Performance in Area Sampling," *Public Opinion Quarterly*, Spring, 1949, pp. 83–92.

POLITZ, ALFRED. "Can an Advertiser Believe What Surveys Tell Him?," *Printers' Ink*, April 5, 1946, pp. 23–25.

SIMMONS, WILLARD R. "A Plan to Account for 'Not-at-Homes' by Combining Weighting and Callbacks," *Journal of Marketing*, July, 1954, pp. 42–53.

SIMMONS, WILLARD R. "Prelisting in Market or Media Surveys," *Journal of Marketing*, July, 1953, No. 1, pp. 6–17.

STEPHAN, FREDERICK F. "Sampling," *American Journal of Sociology*, January, 1950, pp. 371–75.

"What Are the Odds?" *The Neilsen Researcher.* Chicago: A. C. Neilsen Co., January, 1954.

BIBLIOGRAPHY

Bibliography on Sampling Procedure. New York: Business Information Division, Dun & Bradstreet, Inc., 1949.

12

PLANNING THE SAMPLE FOR MARKETING RESEARCH

The preceding chapter has discussed the fundamental theory and principles of sampling. This chapter is concerned with applications of this theory as presently practiced in marketing research. An example of the selection of an actual sample is given in the Appendix, page 525.

The objective of sample planning is to produce the most accurate information for the least amount of money. To put it another way: the practical goal of the sample is to produce data of the desired degree of accuracy necessary for a business decision, for a given expenditure of funds. It is very important to understand those factors which have the greatest effect on sample accuracy in terms of the theory developed in the preceding chapter. However, there are a great many decisions to be made in sample planning, and most of them affect the costs of the research significantly. Therefore an efficient sample design in marketing research recognizes and minimizes burdensome cost factors and, at the same time, emphasizes those aspects of sampling theory which have greatest bearing upon increases in accuracy.

Planning a Probability Sample

Defining the Universe. As has been indicated in the preceding chapter, an important preliminary step in the planning of the sample is definition of the universe. In a sampling sense the universe is that collection of units which are to be sampled. The universe, or population, is composed of people, stores, business firms, sales transactions, inventories, etc., in short, of whatever specific group of items or people about which data are to be collected.

The objectives of each research project will serve as the most important basis for defining the particular units which will compose the universe. For example, let us assume that the objective of a survey is to measure the attitudes of owners of television sets about their receivers. The *universe* is then defined as owners of television sets, and a sampling *unit* in this case would be defined as any owner of a television set. Our interest might, on the other hand, be only with owners of television sets with screen sizes of 16 inches or over. In this case, our universe would be defined as owners of sets with large screens, and the sampling unit would be anyone who owned a television set with a 16-inch or larger screen.

It is quite possible, at this stage in planning the sample, to fall into difficulties caused by faulty definition of the universe. For example, assume that you desire to draw a sample of all television owners. Assume further that a list of owners is available to you. If this list includes all owners of television sets, a satisfactory sample of television owners can be drawn if an unbiased method of selecting units is used. However, if this list includes only owners of television sets purchased after January, 1953, it would be impossible for us to draw a sample of all television owners: our sample could, in this case, include only owners who bought in 1953 or later.

It is therefore most important to emphasize that it is quite easy to introduce bias into one's sample in defining the universe to be sampled. Such bias results from selection of a list of sample units which does not include all the sample units which have been, by definition, included in the universe.

The Sample Frame

The sample frame is a list which includes, in one form or another, *all* the sampling units which are included in the defined universe. In marketing research three kinds of sample frames are generally used:

1. *The Direct List Frame.* A sample frame which is a direct list includes all those sampling units which are in the defined universe but does not include other units not in the universe. For example, suppose we desired to sample all owners of television sets who purchased a television set during or after 1953. If a list which included only persons who purchased sets during 1953 or later were available, it would be a direct list frame. If, on the other hand, the only available listing of television owners included all owners of television sets without reference to date of purchase, it would not be a direct list frame.

2. *The Too Inclusive Frame.* The too inclusive frame is a frame which includes not only those units which are included by definition in the universe, but also includes other units which, although similar, are not defined as part of the universe. Thus, in the example above, if we are interested in persons who purchased a television set during or after 1953, any list which includes persons who purchased sets

during 1952 or before would be *too inclusive*. Note that such a *too inclusive* list may still be used as a basis for drawing a sample. In such a case it is possible to select a sample from all the units included in the list and then separate out those units not included in the universe by use of a filter question on the questionnaire. In the example given above, a sample of all television owners would be selected and then the first questions on the questionnaire might take the following form:

a) Do you own a television set?
b) In what year did you purchase your television set?

3. *The Indirect List Frame.* The indirect list frame is a frame of some kind of unit which is different from the units which compose the defined universe. Therefore the indirect list frame is not a listing of the sampling units in the defined universe at all—rather it is a list or grouping of other units or elements. For an indirect list frame to be usable, one condition must hold: *all* of the units which compose our universe must be directly associated or connected, in one way or another, with the units in the indirect list frame.

A commonly used type of indirect list frame employs the various decennial census materials available from the U. S. Bureau of the Census. The census releases describe the population and its characteristics in relation to the various civil and census *land areas* such as states, counties, townships, cities, census tracts, city blocks, etc. If, for example, we are interested in taking a national sample of cracker eaters, or a sample of cracker eaters in a particular state or city, we may use the census data as an indirect frame in the selection of sample units. Since the census provides a count of dwelling units and people within small areas, this count can be used as a basis for drawing the sample. Note that the basic frame, in this case, is of land areas—not of cracker eaters or people. Therefore, in proceeding to draw our sample we will proceed *indirectly* by first drawing, let us say, city blocks, then selecting homes within the city blocks, and finally finding cracker eaters among the people living within the homes. Such a procedure is called area sampling.

The Area Sample. Area samples are very commonly used in marketing research at the present time simply because the census data provide an extremely usable frame for many kinds of marketing surveys. A basic area sampling plan for a national sample follows this pattern: Areal units are drawn in a series of steps or *stages*. For example, in the first stage a fraction of all the counties in the United States may be drawn. Then from within these counties, a series of townships may be drawn from the rural areas and a series of census

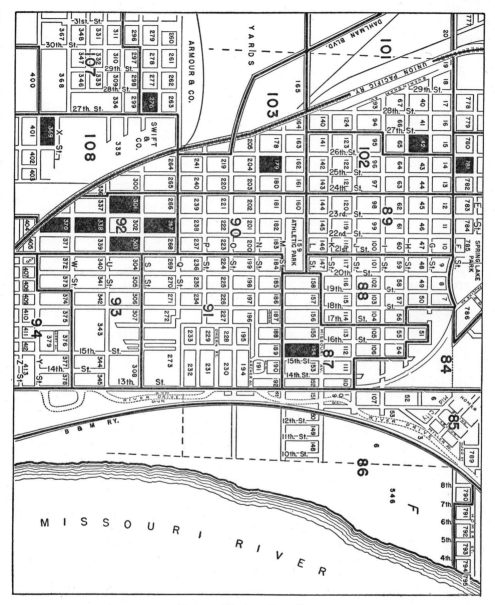

FIGURE 17. Area Sampling

This figure reproduces a section from a block map of a large city. Note that the city has been divided into census enumeration districts, indicated by the large numbers on the illustration. Each block has been assigned a block number. From the entire city, blocks in the selected enumeration districts have been chosen by random sampling methods to provide the locations for interviews and are shown in solid black. The next step is to provide a means of taking a random sample of individual households within each of the designated blocks.

263

enumeration districts may be drawn from the cities or towns which fall within the counties selected. At the third stage city blocks are drawn from within the census tracts, and smaller land areas such as hamlets or voting districts may be drawn from within the townships. At the final stage, specific households are selected and, from within these households those people with the characteristics of defined sampling units are selected. The details of a typical area sample are shown on pages 525–537.

The Importance of the Frame. Unfortunately, in most marketing research work it is impossible to find in some readily convenient form a listing of the sampling units which compose the universe which one intends to survey. It is not possible to isolate all those people who drank frozen orange juice in the last month, or all persons who have regularly used (according to some exact definition) Saltine crackers in the past year. We know that drinkers of frozen orange juice and regular consumers of Saltines are all around us, that we pass them on the street every day, but nowhere is there a register of these persons.

Yet, recalling our definition of a probability design sample, it is critical that each sample unit have an *equal* or *known* chance of coming into the sample and that the selected units be drawn into our sample according to some mechanical principle. If we were just to go out into the street and interview people passing by about their orange juice or Saltine consumption, then these critical elements of a probability sample would not be part of our sample plan. We would be interviewing only those drinkers of frozen orange juice who just happened to be in the street at that particular time. This would eliminate all other persons who drank frozen orange juice but did not also happen to be in the particular street at the particular time that we were conducting our survey.

Our method of selection would therefore be biased in that it would not provide all drinkers of frozen orange juice an equal or known chance of coming into our sample. Our method of selection would, additionally, not be in accordance with any automatic principle: we would be forced to take people as they came and, within the limits imposed upon us by juggling questionnaires and asking questions on a crowded thoroughfare, as we could handle them. In addition, the ultimate choice of respondents would be left to the interviewer. Therefore, on-the-street interviews in such a situation would most likely have heavy possibilities of bias.

Thus, it can be seen that in order to meet the conditions of *all* probability designs, it is most important to have some sort of frame which includes *all* the sampling units which compose our universe. However, as indicated above, it is not necessary, and most frequently not possible, that this frame include *only* those units which are included in our universe; it is usually simple to exclude the additional units which do not qualify for interviewing in terms of our survey objectives at an early stage in the interview by means of filter questions. In addition, it is not necessary that our sampling units actually be listed, just as long as they are associated with some other kind of unit which is listed.

Thus, these two factors—that the list can include units which are not items to be sampled and that the list can be composed of items that are not units to be sampled but are directly associated with them—in large part make it possible to apply probability techniques to marketing research problems. It is, for example, not necessary that we have a complete and exclusive list of frozen orange juice drinkers; any list of people which includes all drinkers of frozen orange juice will do. Furthermore, it is not even necessary to have a list of all people. Since people live in houses and since houses are associated with small land areas which are completely described in terms of the number of people and houses which occupy them by the decennial census, census lists will do.

The critical point to remember is this: in order to draw a true probability sample, it is most important that some sort of listing or frame be available from which the sampling units which compose our universe can be drawn.

Yates classifies available frames into six general groups as follows: [1]

1. Lists of individuals in the population, or parts of it.
2. Aggregate of census returns resulting from a complete census.
3. Lists of households or dwellings in given areas.
4. Town plans.
5. Maps of rural areas.
6. Lists of towns, villages, and administrative areas, often with supplementary information of various types.

In connection with the over-all importance of the frame in drawing a probability sample, Yates comments,

The whole structure of a sampling survey is to a considerable extent determined by the frame. The methods of survey which are suitable for a given type of material (or group of sampling units) may be radically different in different territories because different types of frames have to be used. Consequently, until particulars of the nature and accuracy of the available frames have been obtained, no detailed planning of the survey can be undertaken.[2]

[1] F. Yates, *Sampling Methods for Censuses and Surveys* (London: Charles Griffin & Co., 1949), p. 63.
[2] *Ibid.*, p. 60

The Influence of Cost Factors upon the Sample

Once a suitable frame has been found, our next problem is to find a sample plan by which a sample may be drawn from this frame. The sample plan will provide that each unit included within the frame will have an equal or known chance of being selected, and the plan will provide that automatic principle which is to be used in making the actual selection from the frame.

In most cases it will be possible to select any one of several alternative sampling plans. The actual design which is selected must satisfy the specific aims of the survey and the characteristics of the frame with which one is to work. Nevertheless, in most cases it is possible to make a selection between alternative plans simply in terms of the cost advantages which one has over another.

The importance of cost elements related to sampling plans is illustrated by the survey type of research. Survey costs spring from five principal sources:

1. Direct hourly costs of interviewers at work in the field.
2. Interviewer expenses while working, including transportation, food, and lodging when it is necessary for the interviewers to use an automobile and/or travel any considerable distance from home.
3. Field supervisory expenses.
4. Office expenses incurred in setting up sample designs, preparing maps, and other materials needed by the interviewers in executing the sample design.
5. Miscellaneous material charges for maps, lists, and other necessary items.

From this listing of survey costs, it becomes apparent that there are several ways in which survey costs can be increased or reduced, depending simply upon the nature of the requirements of the sample. Any sample design which tends to increase the amount of traveling required by the interviewing staff will directly increase survey costs because transportation costs will be increased, and in addition, more interviewer time will be required to fulfill assignments. On the other hand, any sample design which tends to concentrate interviews within a particular geographic area will tend also to reduce cost both in terms of direct travel expense and in terms of time charges.

Furthermore, designs which maximize time and travel expenditures will also tend to increase supervisory and other expenditures. It is usually required that the actual field work be conducted over a relatively short period of time. This is true because it is often important, as much as possible, to eliminate time as a variable affecting the data collected, and also because considerable urgency usually surrounds the need for the results of the survey itself. Therefore, a design which maximizes interviewer time and travel usually requires considerably more interviewers than does a design which reduces the amount of time required in execution. As the number of interviewers working on a particular job is increased, the amount of supervision required is also directly increased, with attendant cost increases.

There are many other survey elements which can, if included as part of the design, contribute heavily to survey cost. For example, if it is impossible to obtain a frame which directly lists the units to be sampled, it may be necessary to fall back upon some sort of area design. In this connection it has been argued by some statisticians that existing census information is inadequate to achieve a satisfactory selection of homes without the possibility of bias due to interviewer selection of sampling units.[3] In many area designs, prior sample selection is carried out down to the block or rural section in which the interviews are to be made. Interviewers are then sent to selected blocks and required to select dwelling units or individuals in each block themselves, or to carry out such a selection in accordance with some sort of assigned selection procedure. For example, an interviewer may be told to start at the third house from the northeast corner of the block, and to proceed around the block selecting every third dwelling unit on the block. Some sampling experts contend that such procedures actually leave dwelling unit selection too much within the interviewers' hands and also argue that it is quite possible for the interviewer to make substantial errors and omissions if left on her own actually to find the block to be surveyed and to proceed around it in accordance with any particular plan. They therefore suggest that a substantial bias can be introduced by such procedure. They conclude that a true probability selection of dwelling units can be made, under an area design, only if a thorough listing of all the dwelling units on selected blocks is made prior to the actual interviewing. These pre-listings are then returned to the supervisory center and a random selection of dwelling units is made from the lists in the office. At the time interviews are made, interviewers are actually assigned specific dwelling units through the use of actual street addresses and even detailed descriptions of the location of obscure dwelling units.

Unless it is possible to amortize the cost of such prelisting over several surveys, this process can be extremely expensive, adding greatly

---

[3] W. Simmons, "Prelisting in Market and Media Surveys," *Journal of Marketing*, July, 1953, pp. 6–17.

to the over-all cost of a survey, since it requires that each interviewing area be visited at least two times—first for prelisting, and later for the actual interviewing process. However, it is sometimes possible to combine the prelisting operation with the actual interviewing procedure. Although such a practice may tend to introduce some dangers of errors and omissions and interviewer choice into the field work, nevertheless it also tends to reduce costs considerably. The Bureau of the Census has found that under certain circumstances it is possible to combine the prelisting and interviewing phases of the work.

It is also necessary, in the use of most frames, to set up some procedure for "callbacks." As previously noted, a probability design involves the selection of specific individuals from a frame consisting of all the individuals or households in the universe which is being studied. We often find that no one is at home on our first call, or that if someone is at home the specific individual to be interviewed is not. In order to carry out the sampling plan it is necessary to call back at a later time to contact these dwelling units or individuals. In theory, it is necessary to continue calling back until every one of the individual households which were originally specified have, in fact, been contacted. In the practical situation, one of several alternatives have been outlined above on page 255. In any event, as soon as the "callback" element is made a part of the sample plan, an additional cost factor of considerable size has been injected.

A particular sample plan will, in most cases, be applicable to whatever sample size is required. On the other hand, it is possible that some types of plan will require, for equivalent accuracy, considerably greater sample sizes than will alternative designs. It is also possible that a plan which requires many fewer cases for equivalent accuracy may be more expensive to execute than an alternative plan which requires many more cases. For example, following our discussion of cost functions above, we know that a plan which calls for wide geographic dispersion of interviews is likely to be considerably more expensive to execute than is a plan which requires more concentrated interviewing. This follows directly from the economics of field force operation. On the other hand, it is often true that a sample which is very widely dispersed will, for equal accuracy in results, need many fewer cases than will a sample which is highly concentrated. Therefore, it is important to recognize that any particular sample plan must be evaluated in terms of its cost per unit of information delivered. If the cost per unit of information is high, then, for equivalent accuracy, it may be more efficient to choose an alternative plan which requires more interviews but which will deliver these completed interviews at lower cost.

Sample Adequacy

One of the first questions put to the marketing research man by the business executive is: "What was the size of the sample for this study?" As has been previously shown, the question of how big the sample should be is only one consideration in any evaluation of the sampling part of a research. However, sample size is very important because it is directly related to critical aspects of the business problem confronting the researcher.

The four following elements must be taken into consideration in planning the size of a sample:

1. The permissible sampling error.
2. The assumed risk that the sample results might fall outside the permissible error.
3. The budget situation.
4. The degree of variation in the characteristics being measured.

Permissible Sampling Error (Sample Tolerance). The first business consideration which must be resolved in determining sample size is, "How are the results of the research going to be used in connection with the specific problem involved?" This question is critical because the answer to it determines the degree of *sampling error* that can be accepted without leading to an incorrect business decision.

For example, you may wish to measure the average income of families in two different groups of communities in order to determine whether or not these communities have about the same average income level. Let us assume that the characteristic of income is of great importance to you in deciding whether the two groups of towns are closely matched. You may, for instance, wish to conduct a marketing test with two alternative products in these towns, and you know that the purchase pattern for the particular product you are selling is directly related to income level. Business judgment itself would dictate that it would not be necessary for the sample of families taken to be large enough to allow you to have confidence in the results within, let us say, a $10.00 limit. In fact, if the two samples taken in the two groups of markets had a sampling error of $100.00 in average income, it would not seriously affect your evaluation of whether the two areas had about the same average income level. Only a large difference between the two market areas would have any important effect on our decision to choose the areas for test purposes. Suppose the average income in one area were $4,000 and in the other area $3,950, based on the sample results. Even if a complete census showed that the true income levels were $4,100 and $3,850 respectively—that is, even if your sample estimate were off by $100.00 from the actual income average of either community—it is reasonable to assume that your decision based on the sample figures would not be changed. In both instances average income level would be looked upon as close enough to warrant using the markets for testing purposes, in so far as the income factor was concerned.

On the other hand, suppose you are conducting a sales test of two alternative package designs for a wax product. In this case, instead of a sample of people, you are dealing with a sample of stores. Suppose that mangement would make the package change if the difference in consumer's purchases of one package over the other was as little as 55 per cent for package A to 45 per cent for package B, since they felt sure that even this small expressed preference would be sufficient to make a change in package design a profitable one for this particular company.

In such a situation, the sample of stores would have to be large enough so that a difference as little as 55 to 45 per cent could be reliably measured. If the sample size were too small—if, for instance, the sample measure could vary as much as ten percentage points from the true measure, it would be possible to get an actual reversal because of sample size. In such a case, the results might be 45 per cent for package A to 55 per cent for package B. In this situation management could be misled and make an incorrect decision on a critical packaging problem.

Assumed Risk (Sample Confidence). The second aspect of the business problem confronting the research and sampling man is this: Since *all* samples necessarily involve some sampling error, what risk is the businessman willing to assume that the sample results are, indeed, within the limits regarded as permissible? Does he, for instance, wish to be 99 per cent sure, 95 per cent sure, 66 per cent sure, or only 50 per cent sure? The less risk he is willing to take—even within the permissible error limits—the larger the sample size will have to be. Naturally, the more serious the problem or the greater the amount of money involved, the less risk the businessman likes to assume.

For example, suppose a businessman is contemplating a critically important product change in order to broaden the market appeal of a product which is already quite successful. He would want to be very sure indeed that he is not jeopardizing an already successful market situation. On the other hand, a man with a product whose share of market is nominal and which had been relatively unsuccessful in building sales might be willing to take more than a slight risk.

The Budget Situation. The third vital business consideration in connection with sample size is: How much money does one have available for the research? If the cost of meeting the requirement of Point 1—the permissible sampling error—and Point 2—the desired degree of confidence—is unrealistic, then some compromise between accuracy and cost must be made. Often it is better to have the research information to help guide business judgment in making an important decision even if less certainty can be placed on the results than is desired. On the other hand, on occasion, it may not be wise to compromise with tolerable error or confidence limits although the cost of the research may be very high in order to meet these criteria. In such a situation, it might be wiser not to do the research at all rather than to do an inadequate job which might, in fact, actually be misleading.

In this connection, it must always also be kept in mind that a selected sample size may actually be too large. It may be too large in the sense that unnecessarily close precision, from a decision-making standpoint, is being obtained and therefore too much money is being spent on the research. Accuracy is not an academic factor; it is not achieved purely for the sake of scientific precision in marketing research. It is a very practical concept. In addition, it is just as important that management be convinced that a relatively small sample size is really sufficient in much research as it is to point out in other cases that a very large sample has been used in the research.

Size of Variation in Characteristics Being Measured. The size of sample needed is not constant even if permissible error limits, accepted confidence limits, and the monetary factor are constant. There is another critical variable—the basic nature of the research being conducted. Is a product test being run among consumers? Is a measurement of television-viewing habits being made? Is the relative share of market of a series of competing brands being estimated? Is a copy test on the extent of consumer familiarity with a brand's slogan being conducted? Is research into basic consumer motivations the problem at hand? Is a measurement of movement of merchandise out of supermarkets being taken?

The fundamental nature of the research problem is intimately tied in with the sample size problem. For instance, how many brands are competing in the market we are trying to measure and how loyal are consumers to these brands? In the product test, is there a marked observable difference in the products being researched, or is there only a small hidden difference between the two products? Is the supermarket store audit research on a brand with a large sales and frequent purchase or on a brand with relatively small sales and infrequent purchase?

From the viewpoint of the sampling aspects of marketing research, the reason that the basic nature of the research and specific aspects within the research structure influence the sample size problem is fundamentally this: that the sample size necessary to meet the three basic factors just discussed will change with the degree to which the factor being measured varies in the universe being measured—this consideration is called *variance* by sampling men.

For instance, we would be inclined to believe that the variation in people's opinions on the physical flavor of alternative margarine products measured in a product test would be less than the variation in their actual purchasing behavior in selecting brands of margarine. This would appear to be true because a physical reaction of the taste buds in a product test situation would tend to be affected by fewer variables than actual purchasing behavior. Purchasing behavior is influenced not only by the actual physical values of the product but also by promotion, advertising, competitive activity, and other dynamic elements in the market situation.

To take another instance, if we wish to measure the share of market of brands within a product group by store audits, we might anticipate needing more stores for one product than for another to get as reliable a measurement of share of market. This is true because the variation in consumer behavior in one industry may be greater than in another. If, for example, we are measuring the relative share of market for a product group where three brands dominate the business almost completely, there is less anticipated variation (other factors being equal) in movement out of stores than if we are measuring another product group where fifteen brands all have significant shares of the available business.

Sometimes, a reliable picture of the nature of the variation can be obtained by using available data directly related to the problem at hand, or at least related closely enough so that a general notion of the variation can be obtained. For instance, if a survey of the market for regular ground coffee has already been complete, a statistical measurement of the variation of any characteristic, usually measured in terms of the standard deviation, can be computed from this completed study. Then, if you are going to do a study of the instant coffee market, you have some information to go on, some approximation of the kind of variation you might expect. In addition, it is often possible to obtain good estimates of variation through pretest or pilot studies.

An Example of the Estimation of Sample Size. From the standpoint of the sampling statistician, each type of sample plan has a distinct mathematical formula for relating these four key characteristics determining sample size so that the actual size desired can be computed. Derivation, usage, and correct interpretation of these formulas fall into the province of the professional sampling statistician who is equipped to deal with this highly technical subject. However, in order to illustrate just how these considerations interact to influence the necessary sample size, a relatively simple example is presented.

Suppose you wish to obtain an up-to-date estimate of the average years of education of subscribers to a certain magazine. Assume that it is important for you to know this accurately because the educational level of prospects is a significant factor in the sale of products which might be advertised in your magazine. Also, assume there is a general feeling that in recent years your magazine has appealed exclusively to the very well-educated people. Let us presume that the four critical sample size considerations are as follows: [4]

1. The *permissible sampling error* which you feel can be allowed is half a year (0.5 year). It is important to you that no question be raised about the accuracy of the educational level measurement. In addition, you wish to break down the educational data to show the distribution of education within subgroups of the sample— grade school, high school, and college—and you know if the overall permissible error is relatively large, there will be too large an error within the subgroups, each of which make up only part of the total sample size selected.

2. The *assumed risk* that the sample results might fall outside the possible error must be kept very small—you wish to be more than 99 per cent sure. In a statistical sense you are saying that the true value of the universe will be included within 3 standard errors on either side of the sample value in more than 99 cases out of 100. In other words, there is only one chance in a hundred that the results will be due to chance.

3. As far as *cost* is concerned, with the probability sample design and the questionnaire you intend using, you estimate that it will cost you $7.00 to locate and make a personal interview with a subscriber. This allocated cost covers sampling, interviewing, coding, and tabulation results.

4. The *variation* inherent in measuring this factor is estimated from previous studies to be about 5.0 years of education. This is known statistically as the standard deviation.

Here are the essential facts, other than cost:

1. The permissible error limit: 0.5 year.
2. The allowable confidence limit of 99 per cent, or 3.0 standard error.

[4] This example does not consider the problem of the finite multiplier.

3. The variation of the characteristic being measured (the standard deviation): 5.0 years.

The appropriate formula [5] is:

$$\frac{1}{n} = \frac{d^2}{t^2 s^2}$$

where:

		Actual value
d = error limit	....	0.5 year
t = confidence limit	....	3.0 standard errors
s = standard deviation	....	5.0 years
n = sample size	....	(?)

Substituting in the formula:

$$\frac{1}{n} = \frac{(0.5)^2}{(3.0)^2(5.0)^2} = \frac{0.25}{9(25)} = \frac{0.25}{225}$$

$$\frac{1}{n} = \frac{0.25}{225}$$

$$0.25n = 225$$

$$n = 900$$

By this mathematical procedure we arrive at a sample size of 900 subscribers. This means an estimated total cost of 900 × $7.00 or $6,300.00. Now, cost enters the picture. This may be too much money for the publication to spend on one survey at this time. If management decided that the somewhat detailed breakdown data on age would not be critical, and, therefore, a permissible error limit of 1.0 year rather than 0.5 year would be satisfactory, then the sample size necessary to get a result which will conform to the criteria set up is 225 subscribers. The total cost of the survey would obviously decline markedly. Suppose another of the basic considerations is changed. If, for example, the variation inherent in the characteristic being measured was 7.5 years rather than 5.0 years, then the necessary sample size to meet the original set of criteria—including the 99 per cent confidence limit initially set—would be about 1,800 people. It is apparent that a change in any of the factors involved has an important effect on the size of sample necessary.

The general problem of sample size together with its relation to cost leads directly into the problem of specific sampling plans and the relationship between alternative sampling designs. If money can be

---

[5] The specific formula relating the sample size considerations other than cost will vary with the sampling method the satistician employs. However, for the purpose of illustration, it has been assumed that a simple random sample is employed.

saved by the use of a certain sample plan, then additiona'
be available to increase the size of sample and conseque.
cision of the sample. On the other hand, the cost factors anu
can often be manipulated in such a way that more accuracy can be
produced for less cost through an increase or decrease in sample size.
In either case, greater efficiency can be achieved by carefully investigating a number of alternatives.

Simple Random Sampling

The discussion of probability sampling thus far has referred entirely
to simple random sampling, often called pure or unrestricted random
sampling. This kind of probability sampling involves the selection of
sampling elements drawn from the totality of cases in the universe
being sampled. In other words, the units to be sampled are not
organized in any systematic fashion. The units are selected directly
from the frame, and the frame is not first organized according to any
principle.

As a matter of practice, simple random sampling is not often used.
It is possible to modify this fundamental approach in certain ways
which increase the efficiency of the sample in terms of cost while still
adhering to the mathematical principles behind the sampling process.

Suppose you wish to sample from a universe of drugstores in order
to determine the average price of a series of drug items throughout
the country. Let us say that there are 6,000 drugstores in the country
that meet the definition of your universe in so far as items carried, size,
and other qualifying factors are concerned.

You arrive at a necessary sample size of 100. Now, you know that
of the 6,000 stores in total, about 3,000 are outlets of drug chains, and
the other 3,000 are independent drug outlets. Thinking back to our
example in the first chapter on sampling theory, you would expect
intuitively that a random selection of drug outlets would result in your
getting about 50 independent stores and 50 chain stores in your sample
of 100. It would be important to you that you did not get too many
independent stores or, on the other hand, too many chain stores in
the sample because you know that the price structure of some drug
items varies significantly as between chain and independent outlets.
However, as we noted before, and as we now realize, drawing a pure
random sample might possibly result in your getting proportionately
more or fewer chain stores than exactly 50.

Looking at the situation in the statistical sense, you always know
that there may be some possibility of getting a sample, when you
make a pure random selection, that is unrepresentative. In any ran-

dom selection process, you are always confronted with this possibility, and this possibility increases the chance of error inherent in your sample.

To take another example, if you wish to make a survey among consumers, based on a simple random sample, you know that you will tend to get people in all economic groups in your sample. However, again, there is some chance that you might get too many people in one income group when you simply choose people as they fall into your sample.

Suppose, to take a very simple instance, the weekly income of three families where the head of the household is 35 years of age or older is:

Family A	$150
Family B	200
Family C	180

On the other hand, the weekly income of each of three families whose head of household is less than 35 years of age is:

Family D	$60
Family E	80
Family F	70

Now the average income for all six families is $123.33 ($740 ÷ 6). If we took a sample of *two* families from this small illustrative universe, using a simple random sample, we could get any one of the following samples of two families:

Family	Average Income for the Two Families Selected
(1) A & B	$175
(2) A & C	165
(3) A & D	105
(4) A & E	115
(5) A & F	110
(6) B & C	190
(7) B & D	130
(8) B & E	140
(9) B & F	135
(10) C & D	120
(11) C & E	130
(12) C & F	70
(13) D & E	70
(14) D & F	65
(15) E & F	75

Although the average income of all possible samples is $123.33 ($1,850 ÷ 15), the range of sample results produced by alternative simple random samples is quite large.

The example of simple random sampling demonstrates clearly that it is possible to get an "unusual" sample with this kind of sampling.

Note that, even in this oversimplified situation, the *chances* are that the sample extremes would not be drawn; in the more realistic situation of a large universe, and a sizable sample, the chances are even smaller that a relatively "unusual" sample will be selected. However, such an eventuality is possible, and thus the sample size might need to be increased—at an increased cost—in order to minimize this eventuality.

Stratified Sampling

Proportionate Stratified, or Restricted, Random Sampling. A stratified, or restricted, random sample takes into consideration certain *known* characteristics of the population being sampled, in the selection of the sample units. For instance, in the example given above, suppose we divided the total universe into two groups—one group with heads of households more than 35 years of age or over, and the other group with heads of households less than 35 years of age. Then in choosing our sample of two families, we randomly selected *one* family from each of the two groups of families—known in sampling terminology as *strata*. In such a case, instead of fifteen alternative sample possibilities, we could only get nine possible samples, and in the process, as you will note in the table below, the *extreme* possible samples have been eliminated:

| Families: | | | Average Income for the |
35 and over		Under 35	Families Selected
A	&	D	$105
A	&	E	115
A	&	F	110
B	&	D	130
B	&	E	140
B	&	F	135
C	&	D	120
C	&	E	130
C	&	F	125

Now, the income of all the samples selected still averages $123.33 ($1,110 ÷ 9), which we know is the exact figure obtained when we discussed the pure random method. Here, however, there is less variation among the averages; in statistical terms, the standard error is less. We know from our section on sample size that, other things being equal, with less variation we can achieve comparable accuracy with a smaller sample, and thus, from a budget efficiency standpoint, save money. If stratification is possible, it permits us to get more value for our sampling dollar.

It is important to remember that stratification is most effective when it is possible to assume some direct relation between the groupings or strata which are set up and the characteristic which is to be measured. In the case noted above, it was possible to assume that income was associated with the age of the head of the household. In this same example, it is quite probable that stratification of the sampling units according to the religion of the head of the household would not necessarily have accomplished much reduction in sampling error. This is true because it does not appear that religion and income are very closely related. Therefore, stratification is most helpful when a real association can be assumed between the characteristics being measured and the groupings employed.

A second limitation on the use of stratification is that often, although a relationship can be assumed, there is not sufficient information available upon which to arrange the sampling units into subgroups or strata. It would, for example, be impossible to arrange housewives into groups according to the brand of household soap or detergent which they used if we had no basic list of housewives giving their brand usage of soaps and detergents.

Disproportionate Stratified Sampling. The situation just covered is a case of what is known as *proportionate stratified sample* because the number of sample elements selected from each of the two age strata set up was in proportion to the number of units each stratum had to the total population. Each stratum had three units, or half of the total of six units in the universe; the sample of two which was chosen came equally from each stratum—one element from each representing half of the total sample selected.

A disproportionate sample is one in which the sample units are allocated in proportion to the variance, or other criteria, within each stratum. Thus, the number of sample units selected from each stratum is not proportionate to the number of *units that each stratum is to the population* (except in a case where the variance, or other criterion, and the population characteristic of a stratum are coincidentally the same proportion of the total population). In the example on page 275, it was known that the variance in prices was much greater among independent drugstore outlets than among chain store outlets. Thus, instead of stratifying the stores on the basis of affiliation and selecting half the sample from each of the two groups, it would be better to select proportionately more stores from the independent group because the price variance is greater in that group (stratum).

This fits in with the logic of getting the most from the sample selected because, naturally, fewer chain stores are needed to provide a reliable picture of the chain store price situation where variance is relatively small than for independent stores where the variance in pricing policy is apparently marked. Thus, to take an extreme case, if all the chain stores had the same price, one chain store would be all you would need in your sample. If, on the other hand, each independent store had a different price, you would need a relatively large sample of independents. If half chain and half independent stores are selected, the sample size would be inefficiently used because one store is all you would really need to represent the chain segment of the universe.

In disproportionate sampling, you must weight out your sample results if you sample proportionately more in one group than in another so that the total result represents the total universe. Thus, in the previous case, the average chain price would be weighted by the total number of chains in the universe, and the average independent price by the total number of independents in the universe so that no bias in the final result is introduced.

Stratification, whether proportionate or disproportionate, is an important tool used by the sampling statistician in his attempt to achieve maximum reliability at a minimum cost. The basic advantages of sample stratification are summarized by Hansen, Hurwitz, and Madow, as follows:

> . . . the essential characteristics of stratified sampling, . . . are:
> (1) Certain samples possible under simple random sampling are impossible with stratified sampling, and with effective stratification these tend to be the more extreme samples that contribute more heavily to the sampling variance.
> (2) The variance is smaller when we are able to classify the units into groups so that the differences within each group are relatively small, while at the same time differences between groups (measured by the differences between their averages) are large.
> (3) Stratification can be particularly effective when there are extreme values in the population which can be segregated into separate strata.[6]

The introduction of stratification into a sample plan therefore can often reduce survey costs by reducing the size of sample required to produce a desired accuracy. This greater efficiency is due to the fact that stratification can effectively reduce variance.

Cluster Sampling

Cluster sampling is another aspect of sampling which grew directly out of the need for controlling survey costs when probability sampling

[6] M. H. Hansen, W. N. Hurwitz, and W. G. Madow, *Sample Survey Methods and Theory* (New York: John Wiley & Sons, Inc., 1953), Vol. I, p. 47.

methods are used. Clustering involves the intensive sampling of certain concentrated groups of sampling units instead of selecting sampling units which are widely dispersed throughout the population. Clustering is most widely practiced in area sampling. Instead of selecting individual households which are widely scattered throughout a city, it is common practice to select blocks which are widely scattered through a city and then to sample households intensively within the selected blocks. This procedure can accomplish a substantial saving in costs.

However, it should be noted that clustering also tends to reduce the efficiency of sample plans. This is because, as a general rule, people living within a particular cluster tend to be quite a bit alike with regard to most characteristics. For example, in most blocks the income level is about the same; it is unusual to find wide deviations in income within the same block. If the characteristics which one is measuring also happen to be quite similar among all the families on the block, then clustering will reduce sample efficiency because the use of clusters tends to introduce groups of similar elements into the sample. It can be seen intuitively that the more variations of a particular characteristic (say, income) which are introduced into the sample, the more likely is the sample to reflect the total universe adequately. The only way in which such a range of variations can be introduced into the sample is to contact as many dissimilar families or individuals as possible. Obviously, clustering tends to impede this process.

Therefore, the use of a cluster sample means that, for equivalent accuracy, a larger number of sampling units must be included in the sample. Even so, it is often possible, through clustering, substantially to reduce the survey costs. It has been noted above that appreciable savings may be realized through the use of any method which tends to reduce the geographic dispersion of the sample units selected; clustering certainly accomplishes this result. It is quite easy to recognize the cost savings which are introduced when clustering is used on a national survey which involves 5,000 or 6,000 interviews.

It is often possible to achieve substantial savings through the use of a cluster sample which is substantially larger than a noncluster sample that might be alternatively used in the same survey. In other words, it often is possible to achieve such substantial reductions in cost through clustering that the increased costs due to sample size required by the use of clusters is offset by field economies of clustering.[7] This is particularly true when it is possible to select clusters

---

[7] Even more substantial savings can often be achieved when both stratification and clustering are used.

which have within them relatively heterogeneous groups of peopl
with regard to the characteristics measured.

Permissible Bias

Permissible Sample Bias: Use of Ratio Estimate. It has been a basic
assumption of these chapters on sampling that sample bias is to be
reduced at all reasonable cost. It has been continuously pointed out
that sample survey results are particularly vulnerable to gross error
through the use of sampling plans and methods which are biased in
one way or another. It has been suggested that there are many recognized areas of sample bias, and methods of controlling bias have been
indicated at several points.

However, there are instances in which the introduction of some
slight bias into either the sample plan or the estimating procedure
used in the sample can greatly improve the accuracy of the estimate.
In a sense this situation is analogous to that sketched above in which
it was pointed out that less acurate cluster samples were often substantially more efficient than nonclustered sample plans, and that it
was therefore often most practical to use a cluster plan. The use of
slightly biased estimating procedures which achieve substantial increases in the over-all accuracy of survey results can often increase
substantially the efficiency of a sample design.

In this connection, it is common practice to use sample values in
conjunction with known population values to produce population
estimates of higher accuracy than if the population estimate had been
projected directly from the sample values. Use of such a method may
introduce some bias, but it tends to overcome the greater risk that the
particular sample which is drawn differs from the true population
value by a relatively large amount.

Assume, for example, that it is desired to find the average 1955
income of wage earners in Omaha, Nebraska. Let us assume that we
draw, according to some probability design, a sample of 100 in Omaha.
Let us also assume that the mean income of this sample in 1955 is
$4,000. We could take this as an unbiased estimate of the current
mean income of Omaha wage earners. But suppose that in 1950, as a
part of the Census, the income of all Omaha wage earners was obtained. If we compare the 1950 records of our present sample of wage
earners with the average for the total wage earner population in 1950,
it may be possible for us to improve this current estimate. Let us
assume that in Omaha in 1950 the Census shows a mean wage of
$3,700. In addition, a special tabulation of the 100 wage earners shows
that they then earned, on the average, $3,900. In other words, in

1950, our current sample of wage earners was above average in respect to income.

It can be seen that, unless the income of our particular sample of 100 has been affected in some very peculiar way relative to all Omaha wage earners since 1950, then our present estimate can be improved through the use of this available information. Our new estimate would be produced by multiplying the current mean income of our wage earner sample by the *ratio* of the mean income of all Omaha wage earners in 1950 to the mean income of the sample in 1950. Thus, we would multiply the original unbiased estimate of $4,000 by $3,700 (1950 income of the total Omaha wage earner population) divided by $3,900 (1950 income of the sample):

$$\frac{3,700}{3,900} \times 4,000 = 3,795$$

The result, $3,795 is the new income estimate. This new estimate, due to the application of known data to the original sample estimate, is more reliable than the first estimate; that is, the total variance has been reduced.

Since the 100 wage earners were above average in mean income in 1950, it is assumed, when using the ratio estimate, that they are also currently above average. Thus, the ratio estimate procedure uses available data, from a complete census with high reliability, to adjust upward the current estimate, which is based on the sample alone.

Such adjustments can be made only if it can be assumed that the characteristic being measured has undergone the same changes in the sample as in the total population. Since this is not literally true, some slight bias is introduced into the estimate. However, in most cases, it is true that this bias is slight relative to the reduction in the effect of sampling error upon our population estimates. Therefore, the use of such a ratio-estimating procedure can increase the accuracy of the sample estimates in many instances.

The End Product of Sampling: Estimates of Universe Values. It is important to recognize the end product of sampling. A research is undertaken to find something about the characteristics of a universe. The objective is to describe this universe through the use of the values which the sample produces.

These values can come directly from the sample itself. For example, sample percentages are assumed to hold for the universe generally. Likewise, it is often desired to find the mean value of some characteristic in the universe, and the mean value of the characteristic in the sample is taken as the universe value. In such instances the sample measure serves directly as a measure of the population. For example, if 13 per cent of all males in a sample are found to smoke filter-tip cigarettes, it is assumed that 13 per cent of all males (within certain limits of sampling error) smoke filter-tip cigarettes. In the same manner, if a sample indicates that the mean income of milk delivery-men interviewed is $6,180 per year, it is assumed that the mean income of all milk deliverymen is $6,180 per year.

It is also common to project sample values to the entire population. In such a case we may find that in a sample of 1,000 homes in a given city, 100 housewives regularly read a certain Sunday Supplement Section. If there are, in total, 100,000 housewives in the city, we estimate that in the universe a total of 10,000 housewives regularly read the Sunday Supplement Section being studied.

It is important to note that, as an important phase of the planning operation, the precise estimating procedures to be used and the precise end figures desired must be considered. In planning the sample it is possible to anticipate these requirements and sharpen research objectives to a considerable degree.

Planning a Quota Sample

Quota sampling is based on the principle that if cases are selected according to a predetermined design, the sample chosen will be representative in certain known and measurable characteristics. A sample design is established on the basis of selected controls, such as age, sex, and economic class. The total number of cases is spread to the various cells in this design so that the number in each classification for each of the controls is in the same proportion to the total number of cases in the sample as it is to the total universe being sampled.

In quota sampling, proportionality is obtained by distributing the sample according to a limited number of controls. The first step is to select these controls. Let us assume that a distribution study is to be made among retail druggists in a limited territory, and the total sample calls for 100 drugstores. Sampling controls which might be employed are geographic location, size of store, and whether they are chain or independent outlets. Let us say the Census of Business shows that 20 per cent of the druggists in the territory being studied are located in city A, 12 per cent in city B, and so on. Quota sampling would then require that 20 interviews be made in city A, 12 in city B, etc. The total of 100 interviews would be similarly distributed according to the other controls. Distribution of interviews in a typical quota sample is shown in Table 12.

The implicit assumption of the quota method is that if the sample is representative of the universe, or total population, with respect to a

DISTRIBUTION OF A QUOTA SAMPLE—FAMILIES IN TOTAL CHICAGO MARKET AND IN SURVEY SAMPLE

(By income classes and type of dwelling)

Income Class	Chicago Families — By Type of Dwelling				2,036 Families Surveyed				
	Total Families No.	%	1-Family Homes	2-Family Homes	3 or more Family Homes	Total Families No.	%	1-Family Homes	2-Family Homes	3 or more Family Homes
"A"............	105,204 100.0%	11.1	26,238 25.0%	29,083 27.6%	49,883 47.4%	224 100.0%	11.0	64 28.6%	32 14.3%	128 57.1%
"B"............	209,811 100.0%	22.1	52,239 24.9%	57,904 27.6%	99,668 47.5%	452 100.0%	22.2	97 21.5%	93 20.6%	262 57.9%
"C"............	291,241 100.0%	30.6	72,331 24.8%	80,174 27.5%	138,736 47.7%	627 100.0%	30.8	182 29.0%	196 31.3%	249 39.7%
"D"............	199,048 100.0%	21.0	49,639 24.9%	55,022 27.6%	94,387 47.5%	429 100.0%	21.1	107 24.9%	157 36.6%	165 38.5%
"E"............	144,000 100.0%	15.2	35,929 25.0%	39,825 27.7%	68,246 47.3%	304 100.0%	14.9	50 16.5%	77 25.3%	177 58.2%
Total Families.......	949,304 100.0%	100.0	236,376 24.9%	262,008 27.6%	450,920 47.5%	2,036 100.0%	100.0	500 24.6%	555 27.3%	981 48.1%

TABLE 12

limited number of characteristics employed as controls, it will also be representative with respect to all the various items studied in the research. To put it another way, it is assumed that people are sufficiently alike so that if some sort of nominal dispersion is achieved in the sampling plan, a sufficiently representative cross section will be obtained for the purpose at hand.

Such a plan is, of course, inconsistent with probability sampling. However, many practitioners feel that their experience is sufficiently broad so that they can choose those situations in which the risk involved in using a quota sample is so slight as to justify its use. The lore of marketing research is filled with outstanding successes and failures which have come from quota samples. It is undoubtedly true that quota samples can be used successfully under many circumstances. It is important to realize that the experience of the market researcher is most important in determining just when these circumstances are present.

The place of quota sampling in marketing research has been summarized by Lester R. Frankel, technical director of Alfred Politz Research, Inc.:

The principal argument against the use of quota sampling is that this method violates the assumption of randomness in the final selection of respondents, and because of this, inferences drawn from such a sample are not valid. This argument is sound and logical, but, on the other hand, we know from actual experience that quota sampling usually works. . . . Business and marketing decisions made on the basis of a quota sample are, for the most part, correct. Market research agencies that have used quota sampling exclusively have not gone bankrupt. Quota sampling cannot be as bad as it is thought to be.

Let us attempt to rationalize. According to statistical theory, quota sampling is unreliable. But let us use the theory to show why it sometimes works. In doing so it is necessary to go back to some basic statistics. As you recall, the purpose of sampling is to estimate some unknown characteristic in the population. A ramdom sample is selected, and on the basis of this sample an estimate is made. *It is not expected that the estimate will be in perfect coincidence with the true value, but the average of all possible samples will equal the true value. Such an estimate is known as an unbiased estimate.* If a nonrandom method of selection is employed, the sample estimate will be biased in the sense that the average of all possible samples will not be true value. This difference is known as the bias of the sample. In random sampling the bias is zero. In sampling where the probability of selecting an individual is not known, the bias has some value, but this value is unknown. The unconscious aim of quota sampling is to eliminate or minimize the bias through the proper selection of controls, through the use of detailed interviewing instructions, and other such devices. Now, it often happens that this bias is small in relation to what is being estimated. Suppose, for example, a presidential election poll is taken in South Carolina. Quota sampling is used, and because of a tendency of interviewers to reach only certain segments of the population, there is a two percentage point bias in favor of the Democratic candidate. Now, suppose the results indicate that 72 per cent of the voters will favor the Democrat. There is a bias here, but the decision that the state will go Democratic is perfectly valid and sound.[8]

Suppose a survey is to be conducted to determine if the readership of a magazine is in the order of magnitude of 25, 50, 75, or 100 per cent. If quota sampling is used and one can be reasonably sure that the bias is in the order of about 5 per cent, some degree of confidence can be placed in the findings.

In conclusion, if precise estimates are required with a statement of the reliability of the estimates, the researcher has no other choice but to use area sampling. Suppose a survey is conducted to compare the relative popularity of different brands of tooth paste. An error of one percentage point may shift the ranking of one brand from first to third place. Here a large-scale area sample is indicated.

If on the other hand broad estimates are required where a range of ten percentage points would not materially affect any decisions made upon the findings of the survey, a small-scale quota sample may very well serve the purpose.

Current Practice. The use of quota samples is most common in the following marketing research situations:

> Product design tests
> Package research
> Advertising copy tests
> Readership and impact surveys
> Psychological tests
> Merchandising and sales promotion experiments
> Industrial market research

Probability sampling methods are employed most frequently in the following situations:

> Consumer surveys
> Dealer surveys
> Sales analysis
> Brand position analysis
> Opinion and attitude research

[8] From an address before the Chicago Chapter of the American Marketing Association, December, 1947.

Selection of Quota Sample Controls. If a random sampling method is used, it is assumed that, through its random element, the various segments of the market will be represented in the sample in the same proportion in which they occur in the universe.

However, if a quota sample is used, it is necessary to construct a sample design, based on certain preselected market characteristics—or controls—and depend on interviewers to find people who fall into these chosen quotas. The use of these quota controls is designed to insure a better distribution of the sample among marketing segments than if interviewers were given absolute autonomy over the individuals selected for interviewing.

There are three important principles which should be kept in mind so far as selecting quota sample controls is concerned:

1. *The most important rule to remember is that controls should be considered only for those market characteristics which have a significant bearing on the study.* For example, in a survey on the use of various types of soaps and detergents, water hardness would be an important quota control; however, in a study of automobile ownership or flour usage, the water hardness factor would not have any significant bearing on the study. Routine controls should never automatically be applied in a study. Past experience and pilot test results should be consulted before the final controls are chosen.

2. *Controls finally selected should be limited to the few characteristics which it is judged are most highly correlated with the specific subject matter of the study.* The use of a large group of controls is unwise for two reasons: First, they lead to added costs since honest filling of a very rigidly defined quota means less interviewer efficiency, that is, fewer interviews completed per day. At the same time, from the standpoint of achieving sample representativeness, statistically speaking, diminishing returns set in quickly. Thus, the fifth control adds much less to the sample's proportionality to the universe than the second control. Second, using too many controls is likely to lead to a drop in the standards of the interviewers. When the number of controls reaches the stage where the interviewer must find a southern European male aged 35 to 45, married, with no children, owning a medium-priced automobile, in the "C" economic class, living in a small community, and reading one or more of a designated list of magazines, it is little wonder that the field worker throws up her hands and does a little substituting.

3. *The key controls finally selected should be carefully defined and practicably applicable in the field.* For instance, if economic status is a selected control, the characteristics of the various economic strata used should be carefully outlined for the investigator; those particular

factors which will be used for economic classification (such as size of and location of home) should be spelled out in detail for the interviewer.

In addition, it must be remembered that a control which cannot be applied by the interviewer just does not work no matter how logical it is from a theoretical standpoint. For instance, religion may be closely related to the subject of the survey, but it is sometimes difficult to get an accurate answer to a question on religion. Under such circumstances, it has only surface validity as a sample control and should not be used if impractical to apply in an interviewing situation.

One question which always arises in connection with quota sampling is whether the controls should be applied individually or concurrently in arriving at the distribution of the sample into its various cells. Suppose that a sample is to be controlled by age, sex, and economic status. Individual application of controls means that the total sample includes the proper proportions of age groups, sex groups, and economic classes, without considering the relationship of one factor to another. Concurrent control means that cells are set up in such a manner that each unit reflects age groups by sex and by economic status.

The latter method is much more complicated, particularly if a large number of controls are employed. However, it is obviously a much more accurate method, for a sample might well be proportional for each of three or more controls considered independently, but quite disproportionate in relation to one another. For example, too many of the interviews with males might run in the younger age categories with those of females being in the older. The controls would check out individually, but the end result would be a distorted sample.

Where a large number of controls is employed, the complete concurrent application to sample design is impracticable. The most common procedure, therefore, is to apply certain controls concurrently, but to allow some of them to be applied independently.

Determining the Size of a Quota Sample. None of the relationships on sample size previously discussed apply unless a sample of some probability design is used because only with probability design can sampling errors be computed. The mathematical formulas used in computing sampling errors have meaning only for probability designs. If a quota, or a sample of nonprobability design is employed, the sampling error and the necessary sample size must be determined on a judgment basis. In other words, with a quota design, experience in the field with surveys of varying kinds will, over time, dictate in a rough way the sample size which is required. For instance, experience itself may indicate to the marketing research practitioner that a few hundred interviews suffice to get trustworthy results in normal blind product testing, while many more will be needed in order to measure other kinds of consumer behavior, such as buying habits. The stability tests described on page 329 give some clues as to quota sample sizes to be employed on the basis of experience.

Quota Samples Not Projectable. It is not possible to make population projections from a quota sample because with a quota sample we do not know the persons from which our sample is drawn (we have no frame) and each sample unit does not have an equal or known chance of being drawn.

This limitation of quota sampling is not only to be found in terms of projections to the total population. It is only most obvious in this case. There is a deceptively thin line between sample percentages and means and the assumption that these sample percentages and means hold for the total population. We have noted that, in the case of quota samples, we have no measure of sampling error, and that certain types of sample bias are difficult to control. The possible sampling error and biases attaching to percentages, means, etc., produced from quota samples often tend to be forgotten in the use of quota results. With quota sample results it must be remembered at all times that these data reflect the people that were interviewed, and it is assumed (with greater or lesser certainty, depending upon experience) that these individuals are representative of some larger group or universe.

SELECTED READINGS

CORDELL, WARREN N. "The Commercial Use of Probability Samples," *Journal of Marketing*, October, 1949, pp. 447–49.

FERBER, R. *Statitical Techniques in Market Research.* New York: McGraw-Hill Book Co., Inc., 1949, Chaps. 3 to 9.

GREENBERG, ALLAN. "Matched Samples," *Journal of Marketing*, January, 1954, pp. 241–45.

HAUSER, PHILIP M., and HANSEN, MORRIS H. "On Sampling in Market Surveys," *Journal of Marketing*, July, 1944, pp. 26–31.

KISH, LESLIE. "A Procedure for Objective Respondent Selection Within the Household," *Journal of the American Statistical Association*, September, 1949, pp. 380–87.

PETERSON, P. G., and O'DELL, W. F. "Selecting Sampling Methods in Commercial Research," *Journal of Marketing*, October, 1950, pp. 182–89.

Report to the Statistical Commission on the Third Session of the Sub-Commission on Statistical Sampling. New York: United Nations Economic and Social Council, 1949.

SMITH, E. R., *et al.* "Design, Size, and Validation of Sample for Market Research," *Journal of Marketing*, January, 1946, pp. 221–34.

STOCK, J. S., and HOCHSTIM, J. R. "Commercial Uses of Sampling," *Journal of the American Statistical Association*, December, 1948, pp. 509–522.

WARNER, LUCIEN. "Estimating the Character of Unsampled Segments of a Universe," *Journal of Marketing*, October, 1947, pp. 186 ff.

YOELL, WILLIAM A. "How Big a Sample In Qualitative Research," *Advertising Agency and Advertising & Selling*, July-December, 1950, pp. 62, 63, 139.

CASES

BLANKERTZ, DONALD F., FERBER, ROBERT, and WALES, HUGH G. *Cases and Problems in Marketing Research*. New York: The Ronald Press Co., 1954, pp. 130–36.

JENKINS HAROLD L. "An Application of Probability Sampling to Retail Store Customer Analysis," *Journal of Marketing*, April, 1954, pp. 399–401.

KISH, LESLIE. "A Two-Stage Sample of a City," *American Sociological Review*, December, 1952, pp. 761–69.

13

THE FINAL PLAN

The Pilot Study

Before a manufacturer goes into full-scale production on a new product, he sets up a pilot plant, which is a small-scale replica of the intended production method. No matter how carefully the machinery and processes are designed in advance, there are always unforeseen problems in production which can only be discovered in pilot plant operation. By proceeding in this manner the manufacturer avoids many costly mistakes.

Similarly in marketing research, no matter how carefully the project has been planned, there is no certainty that it will run smoothly. Therefore it is essential that a pilot study, which carries the project through to completion on a small scale, be conducted before going into full-scale data gathering. This pilot study is sometimes referred to as a test investigation or an exploratory study. Whatever it may be called, it is necessary that such a small-scale research be made in order to confirm the soundness of the planning up to this point and to make any adjustments found to be necessary under actual operating conditions.

The specific purposes of the pilot study are as follows:

1. To develop and verify the final forms to be employed in collecting data.
2. To develop and verify the instructions to field workers.
3. To discover problems in connection with the sampling plan under field conditions, including obtaining quotas for the various strata involved in quota sampling and control of randomization in probability sampling.
4. To discover the various mechanical problems which arise in connection with the field work, and provide a basis for proper supervision and handling of the field force.

5. To provide an opportunity for trial editing and tabulation so that procedures for the later processing of field data may be developed in advance.
6. To gear up the entire organization for the handling of the major project.
7. To develop cost data for later operations.

In addition to meeting these specific purposes, the pilot study provides the researcher with final confirmation of the value of the total research undertaking. This proof of the essential validity of the research is most essential before final commitments for the bulk of the project are made. It is therefore paramount that a sufficiently formalized and extensive test investigation be made at this point in the planning operation.

Actually the testing of methods is a more or less continuous procedure. Effective research is earmarked by the amount of testing and retesting to which the various operations are repeatedly subjected. One question to be asked in a survey, for example, may be tested in various forms several different times to determine the specific wording which will yield the most accurate replies.

Such testing and retesting, however, is applied to individual elements of the project, such as the questionnaire and instructions. These tests are very informal in nature and limited in scope. Before the final operating plans are developed, however, it is necessary to conduct a more organized test of the entire research project in order to uncover all possible difficulties which may be encountered later in the study and to verify the appropriateness of the basic procedure.

The scope of the pilot study is quite limited. If the sample plan calls for 5,000 completed interviews, the test investigation may be restricted to 200 to 500 interviews. In observational or experimental studies, the test may be limited to observations or experiments set up at one or two points. Statistical quantities obtained in the pilot study are not significant. What is necessary is that all the important elements which will be present in the final project be represented in the test and that the conditions of the test simulate those of the formal investigation as closely as possible.

This simulation means, for example, that the interviewers or observers employed to conduct the field test work must be of a caliber similar to those who will be doing the bulk of the data collecting later on. It is a common error to rely upon tests made by supervisors or high-quality interviewers. In the pilot test average field workers must be employed, and it is generally good practice to select some of the lowest-grade investigators. Similarly the instructions should be tested in their final form, subject only to minor editing, and given to investigators in exactly the same manner as they will be employed later. For example, if the field force is to be contacted by mail rather than by central-office supervisors, the instructions should be handed to the test field workers without comment. The forms, likewise, should be identical with those to be used in the final investigation.

After the test field work is completed, the forms are processed by editing, coding, and tabulating, just as the reports received in the final field work will be handled. This work is most important, as it provides the final check on the forms and field procedures themselves and also provides a basis for preplanning the later stages.

The pilot study must be followed carefully by the project supervisors and by others associated with the research. On this proving ground problems which will arise in later stages are first encountered. Solving these problems by small-scale tests in advance of the more costly expanded operations saves money, time, and trouble. Few operations pay greater practical dividends to the researcher than careful handling of the pilot study.

Determining Operating Plans and Costs

The next step in planning a marketing research is laying out a set of operating plans and costing the remainder of the work. The factors which control the operating plans and costs for any given research are determined by the circumstances under which the specific job is carried out. It is, therefore, impossible to apply too general standards to this phase of the work.

The importance of planning a specific operating schedule for a marketing research can scarcely be overemphasized. By the time the plan has been completed and tested in the pilot study, it is possible to work out an accurate time program and cost estimate which will make the progress of the research orderly and avoid confusion, unnecessary delays, or excessive costs.

Costs of Marketing Research. Costs vary greatly and are dependent upon the character of the problem. Hence no detailed statement or listing of costs which should be anticipated can be made here. However, the importance of carefully costing the various operations and setting up an adequate budget should be recognized. It is very easy for the costs of staff time, supervision, field work, tabulation, and the physical preparation of reports to get out of hand. A budget based upon past experience and pilot study results should be worked out and a routine established for currently recording commitments.

Cost Elements in the Particular Problem. There are several pitfalls in costing marketing research work to avoid. One of the chief errors is the failure to recognize the various cost elements dictated by the character of the problem which must be solved. There is an unfortunate tendency to assume that any study of a given general type, such as a product research, a consumer survey, or a market test, should involve total expenditures which are more or less standard for each of these types.

That such an assumption is erroneous is illustrated by an analysis of the costs incurred in seven different product researches made by an independent research organization. While these studies were of one general class and made by one organization, hence elements in costs such as salary rates were constant, the total expenditures for each of the seven studies ranged from approximately $800 to $13,000. The wide variation in total cost arose from differences in the kind of products being tested, variations in marketing conditions, contrasts in developmental problems encountered, and other specific research requirements. Differences in the difficulty of locating qualified respondents, sampling requirements, the amount of exploratory work required, and many other factors which affect research costs are encountered in each type of marketing and distribution research.

Understanding the Scope of Work Involved. A second pitfall in estimating and judging research costs is the failure to understand the scope of the work involved. This is illustrated by the common tendency to emphasize the more physical aspects, such as field work and tabulation, without recognizing the many other phases of marketing research which are necessary and which therefore take time and cost money. The practice of comparing costs on the basis of "cost per interview," which is rather prevalent in some quarters, is proper as a basis of appraising interviewing and tabulation costs, but only when limited to comparable operations. It is a completely erroneous practice when applied to the total expenditures involved in different research projects because the amount of time and money required in planning, testing, analyzing, and interpreting, and in other phases of the work, vary greatly as between projects. Experience has shown that these less physical elements determining the ultimate value of a given project are sometimes the most costly part of the job.

Keeping Cost Records. An important consideration is the keeping of adequate cost records. Many research organizations fail to keep accurate records of cost items so that they may have usable data on studies made in the past. These records should be maintained and analyzed from time to time to establish standards for marketing research work, just as cost standards are developed in other phases of business operations. Various cost ratios, such as the cost per interview and tabulation rates under various conditions, should be developed for purposes of internal control.

The most helpful device in estimating and controlling marketing research costs is the use of a cost analysis sheet such as that illustrated by Figure 18. This form shows the breakdown of research costs into the important standard elements. Additional columns may be inserted to record percentages which will show the distribution of cost among the different elements for various types of research projects. These percentages are very helpful ratios for use in estimating when a large number have been accumulated. The actual form should be larger than that shown and should provide ample space for figuring cost estimates.

By keeping accurate records of cost experience in various projects, it is possible to arrive at standard costs or ratios. If this information is accumulated, a proposed undertaking can be estimated with surprising accuracy unless some exceptional, unforeseen circumstance arises. Leeway must be provided for such contingencies. Under any circumstances it is important to have a carefully prepared cost estimate as a budgeting device and as a control on the major research project.

Allowing Adequate Time and Funds. One of the most common causes of ineffective marketing research is the failure to allow adequate time and sufficient funds. It is a long-established scientific truism that good research takes time and costs money. Unfortunately, due largely to the fast tempo of many marketing activities, a time pressure is sometimes placed on the research which makes it impossible to conduct an adequate analysis and solution of the problem. Likewise, because of faulty practices developed in its early beginnings, there is insufficient appreciation of the costs which are inherent in producing high-quality research.

There is no excuse for unnecessary delay or for wasting funds. On the other hand, it is an injustice to sacrifice the quality of the research to the two enemies of quality: speed and false economy. If the nature of the problem does not warrant the necessary time and expenditures, it is often better to forgo the research because bad research may be misleading and disastrous.

A great deal of misunderstanding exists about the cost of marketing research work. All too often executives who do not know the various cost details of research attempt to protect themselves by looking for bargains, not realizing that cheap research, like a cheap machine, is likely to be more costly in the long run. The benefits resulting from effective research accrue over a period of many years. In relation to the financial importance of the decisions based on it, the cost of research is

COST ESTIMATE

Job No. _____   Date _____   Department _____

Description of Project_____

_____

Operation	Time or Quantity	Direct Costs	Indirect Costs	Total Cost
Research Staff		$	$	$
Planning............				
Sample development.....				
Field supervision........				
Field work by staff				
Editing and tabulation				
supervision.				
Analysis and report time.				
Travel expense..				
(Subtotal).........				
Field Costs				
Procuring staff...				
Testing				
Urban interviews........				
Rural interviews.				
Other field help........				
Field travel..				
Checking returns........				
(Subtotal).........				
Editing, Coding, Tabulation				
Planning............				
Editing and coding......				
Tabulating...........				
Outside tabulation... ...				
Computing				
(Subtotal)..				
Report Preparation				
Typing				
Art work.....				
Binders..				
(Subtotal)				
Misc. Outside Costs				
Postage and express ...				
Printing and offsetting...				
Consulting services......				
Participation fees........				
Other......				
TOTAL COSTS				

FIGURE 18. Cost Estimate Form. This form, or one similar to it, is of great value in controlling costs of marketing research. It should be used both for the preparation of estimates in planning projects and for analyzing actual costs incurred in work which has been completed, in order to develop standard costs.

negligible. At the same time an unnecessary contributing factor to high costs is the lack of care in determining operating plans, proper budgeting in advance, and the maintenance of adequate analytical cost records. As people understand marketing research better, both the researcher and the businessman who uses his services will appreciate that marketing research work need be neither too costly nor wasteful, but that adequate time and money to meet the specific requirements of the problem must be provided.

The Formal Plan

The research director is now ready to prepare the formal plan for the investigation. This formal plan should be a written document which brings together in one place the results of all planning and sets forth the specifications for the balance of the work.

A great deal of confusion, delay, and error can arise if time is not taken to reduce the formal plan to writing. The plan should not exist in the form of scraps of paper, memoranda limited to individual phases of the research, and in the minds of various people connected with it. Several persons are usually involved in the direction of a project, whether it is a large one or a small one. The research can proceed to an orderly and effective conclusion only as a written plan guides their thinking and action uniformly.

The formal plan may be an extensive document; sometimes it runs into many pages. Length and detail depend on the complexity of the research and the experience of the organization in conducting similar projects. The plan must be as complete as is necessary to insure against slip-ups which may do damage to the undertaking.

It is a mistake to assume that a formal written plan is unnecessary for a small or routine research project. In an established department some plans can be reduced to a single typewritten page. However, good research requires that there must be a written plan for every project, regardless of its size or complexity.

The formal plan should be reproduced so that copies can be made available to all individuals involved in the direction and use of the research. By circulating copies to management one can often avoid embarrassing questions at a later date regarding method or costs. There is also a real psychological value in broadly circulating the plan. Executives are given the feeling that they are actively participating in the research. Since they are a part of it, they tend to give it more personal support. With a carefully prepared written plan covering detailed specifications for the formal research project, the researcher can proceed with confidence.

14

COLLECTING MARKETING DATA

Most marketing research projects involve collection of *primary data*—those which must be obtained directly in the course of the study. Because it is extremely important that the field force obtain accurate and useful facts in accordance with high quality standards, this chapter discusses the gathering of original marketing data in some detail.

However, the importance of secondary data—those which have already been obtained by some other source, such as a governmental agency, the accounting department of the individual firm, or from published sources—must not be overlooked. A list of sources and criteria for determining their usefulness has already been presented.[1]

Supervision

The success of the entire data-gathering operation depends largely on the quality of field supervision. The first consideration should, therefore, be providing an adequate number of well-qualified and trained supervisors. Unfortunately there is a tendency to skimp on this part of the work because it is an overhead burden. However, payment for high-grade supervision is a good investment which will more than carry itself in the savings resulting from more efficient work of investigators and from improved quality of the field reports.

The first qualification of the good supervisor is successful experience as an investigator. One of the primary duties of the supervisor is to train investigators. This training can be effectively accomplished only if the supervisor can make good demonstration observations or interviews. Furthermore, experience as an investigator teaches the problems likely to be encountered and therefore makes it possible for the supervisor to control better the persons placed under him. Not all qualified investigators, however, make good supervisors because they do not possess some other necessary characteristics.

[1] See pp. 185–93.

A second qualification for a supervisor is the ability to handle other people. His patience will be constantly tried by the unsatisfactory work of many investigators. He must have a sufficiently commanding personality to persuade investigators to carry out his instructions when he is not present. He must be able to communicate instructions to others and to train them effectively for specific jobs.

A third qualification is thoroughness and attention to detail. There are many routine administrative functions which must be performed in organizing and directing investigators, even if only a few assistants are employed.

A fourth qualification of a supervisor is a willingness to work hard and spend long hours at his task. A great deal of time must be spent in checking the work of individual investigators, making out reports, and mailing forms to the central office. Much of this work must be done in the evening and on holidays. It is, therefore, important that the supervisor be one who is prepared to work hard and spend long hours.

A final important qualification for supervisors is honesty. There are many points at which investigators can be dishonest. The supervisor must be careful to check them and report fairly. There is a tendency for supervisors to attempt to cover the mistakes of investigators. There are also many temptations in making out time sheets and reports of expenses. Since most supervisors will be far removed from the control of the central office, honesty is a primary requisite.

Some people stress the importance of general education, knowledge of marketing principles and research procedures, understanding of the purposes of the particular study, and various other qualifications for supervisors. While these abilities are desirable, they are not nearly so significant as the five qualifications which have been discussed above.

Building the Field Force

Selecting Investigators. Syndicated services gathering data on a regular basis and a few very large companies can maintain at least a core of full-time, salaried investigators. However, the bulk of marketing research data are collected by part-time investigators who work for various research organizations in localities in which they reside. The variation in volume of field research and the necessity for covering so many different markets make it uneconomical for most firms to attempt to maintain full-time field staffs. In fact, relatively few commercial organizations maintain even a modicum staff of full-time field supervisors. Most of them rely on established local organizations and local supervisors who work for different companies from time to time.

There is a national pool of local investigators, spread throughout hundreds of communities, who are generally known to most research organizations. Some of them devote their full time to observation and interviewing as a career, but most of them work on a part-time basis. Furthermore, the bulk of these field investigators work for a number of different research organizations. A survey of 695 local interviewers revealed that they worked for an aggregate of 438 different concerns. Three out of ten of these interviewers had worked for ten or more concerns, and more than half of them had worked for five or more.

In the principal cities there are also local or regional organizations which provide field coverage on a flat fee or cost-plus basis. In several sections of the country these organizations have considerable experience and extensive facilities. There are few research projects, however, in which it is not necessary to select individual local investigators from the general pool.

Sources of Field Investigators. Once a research organization has operated over a period of time, it acquires a list of part-time field investigators. However, it is necessary to recruit a new field staff constantly, both to keep field resources up to full complement and to cover new markets.

New investigators are obtained chiefly from these sources:

1. Letters of application.
2. Academic institutions (student and faculty).
3. Women's organizations, key citizens of the community.
4. Newspapers.
5. Other marketing research organizations.

Qualifications of Investigators. The importance of skillful and careful selection of investigators is emphasized by a number of studies of interviewer bias and inaccuracies. Controlled tests have demonstrated a great variation in personal bias, degree of success in eliciting information, accuracy in reporting answers, and ability to follow instructions.

One should guard against forming a crystallized notion of the "ideal investigator" and judging applicants on any such standard. It is entirely too easy to set too high standards of appearance, dress, manner, and experience. To have such a stereotype in the minds of the supervisor or other person responsible for hiring investigators may often lead to employing individuals who lack more important qualities.

All general characteristics of a good investigator must give way to one basic consideration: the special requirements of the particular research. If the field work involves interviewing business executives, it obviously calls for an entirely different type of interviewer from that needed to interview retail grocers. For calls made in high-income neighborhoods, still another sort of person may be required from that needed for calls in the low-income groups. Depth, exploratory, and interpretive surveys can be successfully made by only a very exceptional type of interviewer. A person who is making interviews among the rank and file of passers-by at a street corner does not need the qualifications of one who must gain access to the kitchen or bathroom. A good observer for store auditing may be a very poor personal interviewer for a survey, and vice versa. The first consideration in selecting investigators should, therefore, be the exact job which they must perform.

Bearing in mind the primary importance of the requirements of the work to be done, there are several points on which general standards may be set.

Age. One is most likely to find the best type between the ages of twenty-five and forty. Those who are too young lack tact and the ability to approach people properly. Those who are too old are usually not willing to follow instructions carefully and are not sufficiently aggressive. Generally speaking, a person about thirty years of age is ideal for field investigation work.

Sex. Some researchers prefer women investigators; others, men. It is common practice to employ women for consumer calls and men for store observations, executive interviews, and dealer calls. Some men, however, are very capable of conducting consumer interviews, and some women are superior to most men for dealer work. Certainly it is a mistake to employ a mediocre person because of a preconceived notion that one of the sexes has an advantage over the other. Sex, therefore, is a relatively minor matter which should give way to other qualifications, except in so far as unusual demands of a particular analysis require the employment of either men or women.

Occupation. Persons who make field work their entire source of income are not necessarily the best type of interviewers. Housewives who find it necessary to supplement the incomes of their husbands and younger widows are generally among the best occupational sources of field investigators. Schoolteachers often make excellent interviewers. One danger in using teachers as investigators is that they are sometimes inclined to turn the actual field work over to inexperienced students who are too busy with their school work. Graduate students specializing in marketing or social sciences are an excellent source. Undergraduate students are frequently used as field investigators, but they are not generally satisfactory. Most of them are too young, do not take the work seriously enough, lack previous experience, and are entirely too busy in their school work to devote the necessary time.

Voice and Appearance. Most people assume that a good investigator should be brimming with personality and present the best possible appearance. Experience shows that one who is rather plain-looking and not too well dressed is much more satisfactory. The investigator's voice and manner of speaking should be pleasant, clear, and firm. Some researchers prefer that investigators do not appear too intelligent or sophisticated, as these qualities may put the person interviewed on guard and make it difficult to obtain the desired information.

Experience. The importance of experience on the part of interviewers depends largely on the amount and quality of supervision which is provided. If the analyst has no organization in operation, it is important to obtain investigators with wide experience. If an efficient organization which provides adequate training and supervision is doing the research, the amount of past experience possessed by field workers is less important.

It is desirable to require some field experience, but its value may be greatly overestimated. After six months to one year of training there is usually very little increase in investigating ability as a result of the additional work.

Willingness to Work. A large share of field work must be done when it is impossible to provide direct supervision. Also, the nature of the work is such that there are many temptations to "soldier." Field investigating is also hard and sometimes unpleasant work. It involves travel, being on one's feet, night work, being rebuffed, and being in undesirable neighborhoods. Investigators who are not nearly so well qualified as others on some points are often much more satisfactory because they are willing to work hard. Many researchers make this quality a primary consideration in employing investigators.

Honesty. There are many opportunities for dishonesty in spite of the care with which supervision and systems for checking the work of field interviewers are developed. Personal reliability is regarded as one of the most important single qualifications for field investigators.

Ability to Follow Instructions. The ability to understand and follow instructions is one of the most significant qualifications. Age, appearance, experience, and various other qualifications are not nearly so important as the ability to understand and the willingness to follow instructions carefully. By the time a research project has reached the field, the data-gathering operation has been tested and retested so that it is usually reduced to a largely standardized operation. If an ordinary investigator carefully follows the prepared instructions, a satisfactory job is bound to result. Yet the careless or deliberate violation of specific instructions is one of the biggest problems met in field work. If a research employs quota sampling, it is particularly vulnerable to failure of investigators to follow sampling instructions.

Freedom from Personal Bias. Analyses of marketing research studies and controlled experiments constantly demonstrate that results are unduly influenced by the personal biases of individual interviewers. An extreme example is found in the field of social work. In a case study of 2,000 applicants for lodging, one investigator consistently found that those whom he interviewed met their downfall from one cause—liquor. He was a prohibitionist. A second interviewer found that more cases were caused by economic conditions. He was a socialist.

Personal bias is present to a degree in all interviewers and will be brought to the surface to some extent in almost any kind of marketing research. In product tests, for example, interviewers are likely to try the test products themselves, often later warping reports. Another kind of personal bias frequently encountered arises in connection with sampling. In spite of instructions for quota sampling, a good deal of personal interpretation as to whether to include a given respondent or how he should be classified is necessary. The tendency of individual interviewers to upgrade or downgrade in the matter of economic status is an illustration of a specific form of personal bias which may influence the quality of the distribution of a sample.

Interest in Field Work and Reason for Working. A final qualification of a good investigator is a lively interest in doing field work. If an assignment is accepted as a dull, necessary chore or stopgap, the quality of field work is not likely to be very high. The field director usually makes an effort to determine just why an individual applicant wishes to do field work. The desire to supplement another source of income or to obtain experience in marketing work indicates that a prospect is likely to do a good job. Some understanding of the broad field of marketing research also reflects interest. But the most significant indication of all is evidence of belief in the crucial importance of the quality of field work to the success of research.

In connection with the 1951 Surveys of Consumer Expenditures, a division of the U. S. Bureau of Labor Statistics administered a battery of aptitude tests in the process of selecting 1,200 field interviewers. Experimentation with the test on 130 investigators showed a high correlation between test scores and interviewing efficiency. The tests measured the following aptitudes:

        Intelligence—general learning ability.
        Verbal aptitude.
        Numerical aptitude.
        Spatial aptitude.
        Form perception.
        Clerical perception.
        Aiming, or eye-hand coordination.
        Motor speed.

In addition, the test battery included 359 interest items and 48 personality items.

These experiments emphasize the importance of basic mental and physical skills in interviewing success. They also suggest the value of formal screening tests for the selection of investigators. On the other hand, the National Opinion Research Council, based on an analysis of its interviewer experience, concluded that there is low correlation between aptitude tests and interviewing skill. They believe that special tests for selecting interviewers must be developed.

Handling the Field Force

Investigator Relations. In the past, marketing researchers have paid too little attention to their personal relations with field workers. Too often members of the home office have looked down on field work as being beneath their dignity and relatively unimportant.

Progressive organizations have now instituted programs for building field morale. Regular visits from home-office personnel aid greatly. Interviewers appreciate being given notebooks or other materials which they can use on the job, and the materials can be used as training devices. Small gifts from time to time also help to build morale and loyalty to a particular organization.

The investigator is a human being and, above all, wants to be treated like one. Many have suffered from difficult personal or economic conditions at one time or another. Their task involves a great deal of drudgery and hard work. Unfortunately, they have been given very little personal consideration by too many organizations. There has been too common a tendency to exploit field personnel by a low rate of pay and by assigning unreasonable quotas. The idea that field work is purely a production matter, and that costs must be reduced by every conceivable device, must disappear. A long-range morale-building program among interviewers is just as important to marketing research as an enlightened personnel program is to any industry.

Training Field Workers. There are two aspects to the work of training field investigators. The first is the general, continuing training activity which any research organization should maintain to improve the quality of its field staff. The second is on-the-job training for a specific assignment.

It should be emphasized that continual training of investigators must play an important role in the research operation. Too often the field worker is thought of only when there is a specific job to do and forgotten as soon as it is completed. Actually, there should be a continuous relationship, regardless of the immediacy of specific assignments, if one is to have a field force available to do a competent job when the time arises. This maintenance work costs money and is too often ignored through a shortsighted financial policy.

Well-handled correspondence is one of the most important elements in the general training. Calling the attention of interviewers to mistakes they have made, showing them how they can improve their own performance, and generally maintaining friendly relations are all important.

More and more attention is being paid to the development of field manuals or handbooks as the basis of the general training procedure. These handbooks are usually organized in loose-leaf form so that they can be continually revised. They deal with general research procedures of concern to the field worker, give specific information about the policies of the firm which prepares the manual, and provide specific instructions for handling certain situations according to the standards of the organization. The most important points covered in a typical field worker's manual are the following:

1. Sampling procedures.
2. Selection of respondents.
3. Judging economic class.
4. Approach and manner of interview.
5. Question phrasing and order.
6. "Don't know" answers.
7. Reporting verbatim responses, voluntary comments, etc.
8. How to probe.
9. Checking questionnaires immediately after interview.
10. Other technical points.
11. Administrative section. (How to make out time reports, expense policy, etc.)
12. Job reports and questions during the survey.

On-the-Job Training. The importance of adequately training investigators for each individual job cannot be overemphasized. This special training should be provided for all investigators, regardless of their previous experience or skill. A system which has been established for on-the-job training is outlined in the discussion which follows.

1. Meeting of Supervisors and Investigators. The first step in training is to have a meeting of the supervisor and all persons involved in the gathering of data in any one market or investigating unit. At this meeting the chief supervisor or other person most familiar with the purpose and scope of the study should carefully go over the forms and instructions word by word with the group, allowing ample opportunity for questions and answers.

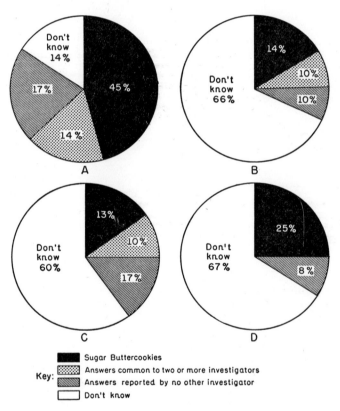

FIGURE 19. Influence of the Investigator on Survey Data. Responses reported by four different investigators (*A, B, C,* and *D*) to the question, "What name would you call this cookie?" Note particularly that A reported 45 per cent of respondents saying "Sugar Buttercookies" in contrast to 14 per cent and 13 per cent, respectively, for *B* and *C*. Also note the extreme variation in "Don't know" responses. (National Biscuit Co.)

2. Experimental Interviews Within the Group. Just as nurses learn to handle hypodermic needles by practicing on each other, the investigators should be given an opportunity to try the questionnaire on one another immediately after the meeting. It is usually desirable to have each interviewer go through a complete interview from approach to departure with the chief supervisor at this time.

3. Supervisor's Demonstration. To demonstrate the proper way in which to handle the calls, the supervisor should conduct two or three observations or interviews in the presence of the field worker. This demonstration should be done for each investigator before he starts out, but it is obviously impractical in all cases. Usually the supervisor should allow the more experienced ones to begin their field work while he conducts individual demonstrations before the less experienced undertake their work. However, the supervisor should later conduct demonstration interviews for other members of the staff, including the most experienced ones.

4. Supervised Interviews. After the supervisor has conducted two or three demonstration interviews, he should have the investigator being trained make a number of calls under his direct observation. After each of these calls, the supervisor makes suggestions for improvement.

5. Spot Supervision. Throughout the period of field work, the supervisor should make a limited number of observations of investigators while they are making calls. This spot-checking is necessary to complete the training process as well as to keep the field force at maximum efficiency. It will often be found that field workers have developed undesirable habits, such as injecting personal bias into the study, after they have been working for a day or two. The frequency with which this happens is in itself sufficiently important to warrant spot-checking interviewers throughout the progress of the field work.

6. Checking Completed Returns. At regular intervals, usually every day during the period of the field work, the supervisor should check over all the reports of calls made by the investgator. Each report should be gone over carefully to give it a preliminary editing and to show the investigator errors which have been made.

While the method for training and supervising field work which has been outlined above will insure maximum efficiency, it is neither difficult nor expensive to follow. A well-qualified supervisor can readily handle five or more investigators without slighting any of the steps mentioned.

Instructions to Persons Gathering Data. Each person engaged in gathering data, whether for survey, observational, or experimental research, should have complete written instructions. These instructions are usually written to field interviewers or observers, with supplementary instructions (often handled in a covering letter) to supervisors. These written instructions are very important, regardless of the amount of personal supervision which is provided.

The preparation of proper instructions is one of the most commonly neglected aspects of marketing research. Carelessly written instructions, or those which do violence to certain basic rules, are bound to depreciate the quality of any research. They may also lead to inordinate costs, for faulty instruction often necessitates the repetition of some field work which has already been completed.

A group of field workers were once asked to analyze instructions in a variety of surveys. These were the most common criticisms: "too wordy," "omissions," "too fussy," "ambiguous," and "insults intelligence."

A number of general considerations regarding instructions to interviewers must be kept in mind. These considerations center around one principle: the instructions should be prepared with a basic knowledge of the problems that the interviewer will encounter in connection with the specific project. Every study has its own peculiar characteristics and problems requiring that the instructions be specially written for each job. However, there are certain basic rules for written instructions which should be carefully followed in any given case.

Rule 1. The instructions should be written so that they tell the interviewer exactly what to do.

A common error in writing instructions is to explain at great length the information desired and why the questions are asked, rather than to show the interviewer just how to obtain the facts desired.

The following excerpt from a questionnaire will illustrate this point. This information relates to the desirability of certain features on automobiles.

(1) Accessory	(2) Value	(3) Would Buy at This Price	(4) Would Pay
1. Glove compartment	$4.00		
2. Spotlight	6.00		

In order to get a specific indication of the importance of these items to the individuals interviewed, a value was affixed to each of them as shown. The investigator was to write in the third column whether people would the pay the standard price set, and if they said they would not pay this price, he was to put in the fourth column the amount they would pay.

The instructions covering this question might have been written as follows:

In the third column indicate whether people would pay the price shown in the second column or not, and if they would not pay the price, show how much they would pay in the fourth column.

Instructions written in this manner violate the first rule because they do not show the investigator exactly what to do. The proper way to word these instructions follows:

Say to the person you are interviewing, "Suppose you were buying a new car which did not have a glove compartment in it, would you pay $4.00 extra for it?" If respondent says "yes," write "yes" in the third column on the first line, and proceed to the second question (about the spotlight). If the person says "no," write "no" in the third column and then say to him, "Well, how much extra do you think you would pay for a glove compartment?" If the respondent gives a dollar-and-cents figure, write the exact amount in column four. If respondent says, "I don't know," write "Don't know" in the fourth column. If respondent says, "Nothing," write "Nothing" in the fourth column.

After you have obtained the correct answer to the first question (on the glove compartment) ask the person you are interviewing, "If the car did not have a spotlight, and you could get one for $6.00, would you buy it at this price?" Record the answers exactly as instructed for question one (relating to the glove compartment).

The reader will note that the instructions as rewritten tell the investigator exactly what to do. The first instructions are perfectly clear to the person who wrote them and would be understood by any intelligent person who took the time to study them carefully. They would not, however, result in standardized reports, which are essential. Furthermore, in many instances, most interviewers will not read instructions carefully enough to interpret properly general statements of what is wanted.

An important application of Rule 1 is in that part of the instructions which discusses the opening of the interview. Sometimes the instructions will go into a rather involved dissertation of the various ways of opening an interview. This violates the first rule, for the instructions should be written in the following form:

Begin the interview by saying, "Good morning, I am Miss Jones of the National Health Bureau, which is making an investigation of . . . ."

The researcher, of course, realizes that there are many different ways to open an interview and that the form which should be used in any given case is a matter for special decision. Once he has decided the best general form, however, he should write his instructions as suggested above. If one form will not suffice for an investigation, alternative forms should be written. The alternative forms should be handled as suggested above, by telling the investigator exactly what to say.

Rule 2. Tell investigators to report on all interviews or observations.

This rule, frequently overlooked, may cause much difficulty if not followed. Most investigators will submit only those reports which in their opinion represent completed and satisfactory interviews. The rejected cases may be more pertinent to the study than the ones included.

An example may be found in a study of mail-order buying habits. The most important single bit of information required in this study was the percentage of people of different types who bought by mail. All the interviews made in one vicinity had to be discarded because the supervisor and investigators did not report on people *not* buying by mail. This was a perfectly natural mistake on their part because the first question was, "Have you bought anything by mail in the last year?" If the answer to the question was "No," the interview was completed. The investigator, however, thought this represented an incomplete report and did not include it.

Another reason for requiring that reports on all interviews be submitted is that the number of refusals and incomplete interviews sheds light on the abilities of the investigator and the care with which the job was performed. These reports are also very important in connection with sample validation, particularly in connection with determining the significance of noncooperators.

Rule 3. The instructions should be brief as possible, yet sufficiently complete.

This is a rather obvious rule, yet it is both difficult to follow and frequently violated. The importance of brevity can scarcely be overestimated, because investigators will never devote the time the project director would like to have them give to studying instructions. It does not help to tell them, "Read these instrucions carefully" or "Read these instructions three times." The only solution is to make the instructions simple enough to be read as quickly as possible.

The rule for brevity requires primarily that wordy sentences, involved instructions, and repetition be eliminated. It does not mean that any phase of the work should be omitted. If the instructions relate to a questionnaire, for example, the investigator should be told exactly how to ask every question and fill in the replies. They should not, however, be given a philosophical discussion of the reasons for each question.

Rule 4. The instructions should be broken up into a series of short paragraphs.

One common error in writing instructions is to write a general essay composed of many long, involved paragraphs. The instructions should be arbitrarily broken up into a series of very short paragraphs, each usually containing only a few sentences. A good way to determine whether this rule has been properly followed is to check each paragraph to see if it contains only one clearly expressed idea. If a paragraph contains several ideas, it should be broken up into a series of paragraphs, each containing only one clear thought.

Rule 5. The instructions should be written in simple language.

After the instructions have been written, a careful review should be made to determine whether simpler words can be used. Nothing is more confusing than to use polysyllabic or uncommon words in instructions. The use of words like "interviewee," "establishment," "personality," and "intrusion" should be avoided and more generally used words substituted, even though the rules of good English may be violated.

Rule 6. All terms must be clearly defined.

No matter how clearly and simply the questions are written, there will be many terms which must be included that are subject to definition. The instructions should be carefully checked for such words. An example is "upper-class family." Unless the meaning of the term "upper-class" is clearly defined, one will find almost as many interpretations as investigators.

Rule 7. The investigators should be told exactly where and when to call.

One of the common errors in preparing instructions is to send investigators into a market without telling them exactly how to distribute their calls. These instructions should not be vague and general, such as "obtain a representative cross-section of the city," but should tell the specific streets or blocks to be worked, where to begin and where to stop interviewing, and exactly which houses to take. Sometimes it is necessary to rely upon local supervisors for specific assignments, but under no circumstances should the distribution of calls be left up to the interviewer. Sometimes there is a reason for the investigator not calling at certain times of the day or on certain days of the week. The instructions should be perfectly clear on this point.

Rule 8. The investigators should be told that their work will be checked and edited.

The work of all investigators should be carefully checked to make sure that they have carried out the instructions. If no system for regularly following up the field work is installed, some investigators may falsify returns or even report interviews which have not been made. A system whereby the supervisors will check a portion of the calls, or some other method of checking, should be set up and enforced.

The investigators should be informed of this in the instructions. In the first place, it is only fair to them to tell them that their work will be checked. Furthermore, this will cause them to do a better job. If they understand in the instructions that their individual reports will be carefully edited, they will also fill them out much more carefully.

Rule 9. The instructions should be tested.

After the instructions have been written as carefully as possible, following the rules previously discussed, they should be tested on a few investigators who have had no experience whatsoever with the particular job to be undertaken. In selecting the investigators on whom the instructions are to be tested, it is a good policy to choose those who are known to be among the less intelligent and capable ones. If the instructions are clear to the poorer grade of investigators who are not familiar with the study, one can feel assured that they are correctly written.

Interviews with Executives and Other Important Persons. Whenever persons like business executives or professional men are to be interviewed, special problems arise. Such interviews are usually more difficult to obtain than ordinary dealer or consumer interviews, and the success of each individual interview has a more important bearing on the success of the investigation. These interviews are, therefore, usually planned carefully in advance so that they may be handled most effectively. The following rules cover this type of interview:

1. Make a definite appointment in advance by letter or telephone.
2. Learn as much as possible about the man to be interviewed before you approach him.
3. Know the subject of the interview. The best interviewer is one with whom the respondent can talk on equal terms.
4. Do not expect the respondent to volunteer information. Take the lead in conducting the interview.

5. Frame in advance some pertinent questions that will stimulate the interest of the respondent.

6. Do only as much talking as is necessary to keep your subject talking.

7. Keep some leading questions in reserve with which to bring the interview back to its subject matter and restimulate interest on the part of the respondent.

8. Observe the courtesies of your position—don't argue—don't contradict—don't insist. Discuss the points that require some comment in order to bring out their meaning or to keep the interview moving.

9. If the information obtained involves statistical references, figures, mathematical formulas, or other exact statements, it is generally best to submit the report for checking by the respondent before sending it to the central office.

Checking the Field Force. Checking on the work of the field force has been mentioned in connection with the writing of instructions. This is a part of their general supervision which is so important that it can well be given special attention. Every call should be accurately identified and a reasonable sample of each man's work spot-checked in the field.

There are five methods of checking the work of field investigators in common use. These are:

1. Personal callbacks by supervisors.
2. Postcard, letter, or telephone checks.
3. Stability curves.
4. Analysis of consistency.
5. Use of battery of questions.

The first two procedures may be considered direct checks, and the latter three indirect, as they rely on analysis of the completed questionnaires themselves.

The use of a postcard checking questionnaire is an inexpensive method of checking field work. The replies received are compared with field reports for inconsistencies. The number of cards or letters returned by the post office indicate the validity of the work.

The following is an example of an authenticating letter:

Our representative has told us of her recent visit with you and we take this opportunity to thank you for your cooperation in testing the two new hair tonics for us.

As our interviewer told you, she will call on you again in a few days to ask for your opinion of these two new hair tonics.

In the meantime, we would like to get some advance information and will greatly appreciate it if you will supply the information requested on the enclosed card. Please check it at your early convenience and drop it in the mail. It is stamped and self-addressed.

Thank you for your assistance.

> Yours very truly,
> BLANK RESEARCH COMPANY

A postcard was enclosed, with the following copy:

Blank Research Company
12 Main Street
Middleville

Gentlemen:

I am now using ——————————— brand of shaving soap.

Before starting to use the test hair tonics supplied by your interviewer, I had been using ——————————— brand.

> Yours very truly,
> Name ———————————
> Address ———————————

In this postcard check, the shaving soap was a product in which the research organization could naturally have been interested. This device made it apparent that new information was being requested. The second question provides a check on a report from the interview. The percentage of cards returned for each interviewer is an additional clue to the care with which the field work is being done.

The stability-curve check is applied by tabulating answers to selected questions as reported by an individual interviewer. Questionnaires are tabulated in a sequence order, usually in the order of the days during which the interviewer worked. The percentage of "yes" answers should stabilize according to a regular pattern. If they are too consistent during the early interviewing period, it is concluded that the interviewer is not reporting accurately. The findings of different investigators are compared. If those of an individual are too far out of line from the general result, the work is challenged and investigated further.

The analysis of consistency is based on the examination of individual questionnaires by a skilled editor. When field work has been done dishonestly or is grossly inaccurate, the reports are bound to show definite evidence through answers to certain parts which are inconsistent with answers to others. An excessive number of unanswered questions or "don't know" answers is also suspect. Frequently a too standardized pattern of answers, for example, in the use of certain words, will give away the interviewer. By examining questionnaires for consistency, a skilled editor can often detect bad field work.

The use of a battery of questions involves deliberately constructing a questionnaire so as to provide a multiple check on the accuracy of certain answers. By asking a sequence of questions in different form, or by reintroducing a given subject later in the questionnaire, also in different form, it is possible to check on the accuracy of individual answers and obtain the true facts regarding the respondent's report or opinion.

Collecting Data by Mail

The essential problem in the mailing of questionnaires is to select lists which will yield an adequate and representative sample. Very often the lists most readily available and those which will yield the highest returns at the lowest cost are the poorest ones from the point of view of the accuracy and reliability of the results.

The most common sources and types of mailing lists for questionnaire work follow.

1. *City Directories.* Where it is desired to obtain a cross-section of all walks of life, the city directory often offers the best source. It can be used only when the study is restricted to cities large enough to have rather frequent issues of directories. Because of inaccuracies and the number of "dead" names, however, it is often not advisable to use this source.

2. *Telephone Books.* If the study will not suffer from the selective nature of the telephone list, these offer a highly accurate and "live" source. One difficulty is that the commercial phones must be eliminated if consumers are being surveyed. The classified sections offer valuable lists for dealers and select business and professional groups.

3. *Rating Books.* Dun and Bradstreet's credit-rating books offer good lists for business firms. The ratings facilitate selection.

4. *Trade Directories.* In many business lines, where a particular industry is to be covered, the trade directories give useful lists.

5. *City and County Records.* Many governmental records which are open to the public provide good lists. These are particularly valuable where selected groups are desired. Chief among these types are city and county tax lists, automobile registration lists, license and permit lists, school lists, corporation lists, and vital statistics lists.

6. *Organization Lists.* For certain select groups, organization lists may be of value. Commercial, civic, golf club, professional, fraternal, and religious groups are typical of the lists which may be obtained.

7. *Mailing-List Dealers and Addressing Companies.* There are several organizations, such as R. L. Polk & Co. and the Buckley-Dement Co., which make a business of maintaining mailing lists. These are

classified by various types, on bases such as occupation, income, or club membership. If a large mailing is to be made, it is often more economical to employ the lists or complete services of these organizations.

8. *The Company's Own Records.* Customer and dealer records may be used to obtain lists where the specific survey is concerned only with the restricted groups which such lists represent.

Collecting Observational Data

The most important consideration to bear in mind in connection with observational work is that the human factor is still present. The best way in which to appreciate the difficulties which beset the observer is to note the care with which checks are established in the laboratories of the physical sciences. Here, in spite of the objective manner in which the work is controlled, errors on account of the failure of the observer properly to record data, such as temperatures, are constantly encountered.

Making observations appears to be a simple matter. Most people, however, are poor observers. If one makes it a point to notice the things which he has failed to observe previously in walking to his office, or during a meal, he can quickly appreciate some of the difficulties involved in making penetrating observations. The weakness of the average person in observing conditions about him is further shown by the popularity of parlor games based upon this frailty. Casual looking does not represent the scientific use of the observational method. The proper items must be seen and recorded correctly if the work is to be scientific.

A few specific rules especially important to the successful application of the observational technique follow.

1. *Be sure conditions are favorable to accurate observations.* If one is making observations in a retail store, there are many unusual conditions which may make it impossible to obtain the type of information required for the study. The same is true in making observations in a home. The observer must constantly be on his guard against circumstances which distort conditions or actions which he is attempting to watch. Even more important, the condition of the observer may make it impossible to obtain accurate observations. If a person is tired, in a careless mood, or has poor eyesight, he is not in a position to make good observations.

2. *Assume an open mental attitude.* The observer must, of course, be free from bias and prejudice in order to make accurate observations. As one notices the results of the first observations made, he begins to

form an opinion of the findings of the study. As this opinion grows, he may find that his recordings are becoming very similar, as a result of a prejudice based upon what he has learned from earlier observations. The elimination of such bias is in part a problem of checking the observer and in part a problem of self-discipline by the observer.

3. *Observe one thing at a time.* This point has been previously mentioned in connection with the problem of preparing forms for observations. In observational work it is especially important that the attention of the observer be concentrated on only one type of observation at a time. If it is necessary to make several different types of observation, it will be found that errors will rapidly creep into the study. The observational field work should therefore be planned so that investigators observe only one type of item during a given time period.

4. *Obtain all essential facts.* While the observer must concentrate his attention upon one or a very few types of specific observations, it is most important that he be alert to record all conditions which may have an effect upon the phenomenon being studied. Every fact having a bearing upon the central problem of the analysis must be carefully noted. A whole series of observations may be entirely thrown out because the observer failed to note some general condition, such as the type of store in which observations are being made, or special display features, unusual traffic, or other external conditions.

5. *Record observations immediately.* One should never attempt to make a series of observations and then try to remember them later or record a generalization. Provision must be made on the forms for easy recording of each individual observation as it is made, and the observer must be carefully checked to make sure that he is following the instructions to record immediately.

Collecting Experimental Data

Difficulties of applying the experimental technique in the social field point to the need for very careful supervision of marketing experiments. One must bear in mind above all else the essential requirement of experimental work, namely, that all conditions and variables aside from the one being measured must be properly controlled. It is not good scientific judgment to rush into experiments when it is impossible to control them adequately. The theoretical advantages of the method can be more than offset by the errors introduced by uncontrolled marketing conditions.

Some of the points which must be watched in marketing experiments follow.

Selection of the Markets. In view of the cost of conducting marketing experiments, they are usually made in a small number of markets, often from only two to five, especially if a sales and advertising campaign must be conducted. Even if twelve or twenty cities are employed, one can immediately see the danger of applying the results of test work to the country as a whole.

Efforts to find a market which is representative of the entire United States have been frequently made. But there is no such thing as a "typical" or "average" city. Every market is different from every other market. Only by careful selection of a group of markets, which together provide most of the conditions which will be encountered in a large number of other markets, can an experiment be successfully conducted. Having selected a representative group of cities, the analyst must be careful to keep in mind their characteristics, such as size and economic structure, and notice the conditions present in the rest of the country which are not reflected in the test markets. New York City, rural areas, and the "Old South" are examples of markets not usually paralleled in a selected list of test markets.

Length of Time. One of the most important considerations in connection with the handling of experimental studies is to allow ample time for the tests. One should allow at least two months, and sometimes even a longer period, for a controlled experiment. A full-scale market test, involving sales and advertising activities on a broad market coverage basis, needs six months to a year or more.

One common error, caused by the desire to obtain results quickly, is to rotate advertisements or other marketing strategies being tested between markets and then to credit sales to them before adequate time has been allowed for the preceding activities to produce their total effect. Some researchers, for example, will insert a single advertisement in a newspaper, and then check sales five days to one week later, crediting all the sales in this period to that advertisement. A second advertisement is then inserted, and the sales immediately following the insertion of this second advertisement are credited to it, without an allowance being made for the influence of preceding advertisements. It is very important to allow a breathing spell between individual advertisements or campaigns so that there is no confusion in the proper assignment of sales to the advertising responsible for creating them. Allowing adequate time also helps to even out minor disturbances caused by unusual factors such as changes in weather and special retail sales drives.

An example from a company which tested different types of selling displays may be cited to show the necessity for allowing plenty of time in experimental studies. Experimental displays were installed in fifty

stores in one market for a period of one year. In the test, all information which might have a bearing upon the result of the experiment—
sales volume, the general movement of business conditions, sales by
competitors, and many incidental facts—was obtained. After the conclusions from the first year of experiment were drawn, 500 displays
were installed and tested in another market for a period of six months.
The experiment was, therefore, conducted for a year and a half before
final conclusions were drawn. Display experiments need not usually
take such a long time as this. The example is of a special case which
warranted a long period.

External and Internal Controls. Usually, in conducting experiments, it is considered desirable to set up external controls which
provide a "normal" standard against which to interpret the results of
the test. In a copy test, for example, if advertisements are tested in
four markets, and sales data are gathered only for those four markets,
the only evidence obtained is of the relative strength of the advertisements, with no external evidence indicating the general value of the
campaigns. To provide the latter, control markets, in which no advertising is run, are usually set up. The sales in these control markets are
then taken as "normal" sales without advertising and used as a basis
for evaluating the productivity of the advertising which has run in the
test cities. The same principle applies to any other type of marketing
experiment, such as one involving new products, sales methods,
changes in distribution, advertising media, or promotions.

Two types of controls are commonly used. These are control markets, described in the preceding paragraph, or control periods before
and after the experiments are made. Neither of these is entirely satisfactory. The use of control cities, often limited to one or two, is particularly open to question. There are so many conditions which cause
sales to fluctuate in an individual market for a short period of time
that the sales in one or two control cities are usually far from "normal." Unusual conditions may also be encountered in a control period
preceding the experiments in the test markets. The use of control
periods after experiments is, of course, questionable because it is often
difficult to determine when the effect of the experiments conducted
has dissipated itself. Temporary activities on the part of important
retailers, wholesalers, the manufacturer's sales force, or competitors in
control markets or during control periods have often influenced sales
more than the activity being tested in a marketing experiment.

In view of the difficulties of obtaining "normal" markets or "normal" sales periods for purposes of external control, it is often far more
scientific to use internal controls, that is, sales data obtained in the
test markets during the period of the test. Sales of other products

similar to the one for which the experiments are conducted or of competing brands are examples. The conditions affecting the sales of selected products or of competing brands, during the experiment, usually parallel the conditions (other than the factor being tested) which affect the sale of the product studied closely. Weather, business conditions, and other disturbing elements are the same in the test markets during the test, but may vary at other times or places.

Allowing Variables to Offset One Another. It is impossible to control mechanically the many variables encountered, as the chemist controls conditions in the laboratory. It is also very difficult to establish external controls, as is shown in the preceding discussion. The researcher must, therefore, rely largely on conducting his experiments so that the uncontrollable elements may offset one another. When these other influences are identified as far as possible, the remaining problem is to carry the experiments through in such a manner that the other conditions themselves will be varied so as to offset each other. The rotation of tests between markets is designed to accomplish this. Weather will offset itself in time. The influence of special advertising drives may be offset by continuing through periods of little advertising. Seasonal influences are offset by repeating experiments. The effect of the type of store is offset by repeating in other types. The conditions under which the experiments are conducted should be altered until all external variables have offset themselves as far as possible.

Records of Variables. In any experiment there will always remain some variables which cannot be controlled and which do not offset one another. In order that they will not ruin the experiment, careful observation of all significant conditions must be made. If weather conditions can seriously affect the experiment, they should be recorded. Special sales efforts or advertising campaigns by competitors should be noted. As no statistical means of correcting the results of marketing experiments for these remaining variables are available, the problem of estimating the remaining influence of these other factors is one of interpretation. Keeping accurate records during the gathering of the experimental data is required to provide the basis for this interpretation.

SELECTED READINGS

Bader, Carolyn F. *The Interviewer's Guide.* Institute of Market Research, 1947, pp. 35 ff.

Beckman, R. O. *How to Train Supervisors.* 3d rev. ed. New York: Harper & Bros., 1952.

Bevis, J. C. "Interviewing with Tape Recorders," *Public Opinion Quarterly,* 1949, pp. 629–34.

BORDEN, NEIL H., FRAME, STANLEY, GORDON, WILLIAM C., JR., and SMITH, CHARLES W. "An Appraisal of Census Programs for Marketing Uses," *Journal of Marketing*, April, 1954, pp. 331–60.

CLARKSON, ELEANOR P. "Some Suggestions for Field Research Supervisors," *Journal of Marketing*, January, 1949, pp. 321–29.

COMAN, E. T. *Sources of Business Information*. New York: Prentice-Hall, Inc., 1949, Chap. 10.

DVORAK, BEATRICE J., *et al.* "Tests for Field Survey Interviewers," *Journal of Marketing*, January, 1952, pp. 301–6.

FERBER, ROBERT, and WALES, HUGH G. "Detection and Correction of Interviewer Bias," *Public Opinion Quarterly*, Spring, 1952, pp. 107–27.

HYMAN, HERBERT. "Problems in the Collection of Opinion-Research Data," *American Journal of Sociology*, January, 1950, pp. 362–70.

JAHODA, MARIE, DEUTSCH, MORTON, and COOK, STUART W. *Research Methods in Social Relations*. New York: The Dryden Press, Inc., 1951, pp. 465–92.

MOSER, C. A. "Interview Bias," *Review of the International Statistical Institute*, Vol. 19, No. 1, 1951, pp. 1–13.

PARTEN, MILDRED. *Surveys, Polls and Samples*. New York: Harper & Bros., 1950, pp. 124–49.

RANDALL, LOIS E., and SHARPNACK, DOROTHY M. *Market Research Sources—A Guide to Information on Domestic Marketing*, Domestic Commerce Series No. 20. Washington, D. C.: U. S. Department of Commerce, 1950.

RAYNOLDS, E. M. "How to Get the Most from Sales Tests," *Printers' Ink*, September 4, 1953, pp. 35–37.

REED, VERGIL D., *et al.* "Selection, Training and Supervision of Field Interviewers in Marketing Research," *Journal of Marketing*, January, 1948, pp. 365–78.

SHEATSLEY, PAUL B. "An Analysis of Interviewer Characteristics and Their Relationship to Performance," *International Journal of Opinion and Attitude*, Winter, 1950–51, Part 1, pp. 473–98.

SKELLY, FLORENCE R. "Interviewer-Appearance Stereotypes as a Possible Source of Bias," *Journal of Marketing*, No. 1, July, 1954, pp. 74–75.

SMITH, HARRY, and HYMAN, HERBERT. "The Biasing Effect of Interviewer Expectations on Survey Results," *Public Opinion Quarterly*, Fall, 1950, pp. 491–506.

CASES

ANDERSON, DALE. "Roper's Field Interviewing Organization," *Public Opinion Quarterly*, Summer, 1952, pp. 263–72.

BLANKERTZ, DONALD F., FERBER, ROBERT, and WALES, HUGH G. *Cases and Problems in Marketing Research*. New York: The Ronald Press Co., 1954, pp. 180–84; 184–92.

FELDMAN, J. J., *et al.* "A Field Study of Interviewer Effects on the Quality of Survey Data," *Public Opinion Quarterly*, Winter, 1951–52, pp. 734–61.

15

TABULATION AND ANALYSIS

In tabulation and analysis, the field reports are processed in order to arrive at meaningful statistical conclusions. Frequently much of the usefulness of a study is lost through inadequate handling of this operation. The danger of taking raw data as they are received from the field, mechanically counting them, and computing obvious percentages or crude averages can scarcely be overestimated. Often studies undertaken with high hopes have resulted in a series of meaningless generalizations which fail to solve the problems to which the research has been addressed because of faulty handling of the tabulation and analysis step.

To insure proper tabulation and analysis, four separate operations should be carefully followed:

1. Editing and coding the data.
2. Validating the sample.
3. Tabulating the data.
4. Drawing statistical conclusions.

Editing and Coding Data

The purpose of editing the questionnaires or schedules is twofold: to eliminate errors in the data, and to prepare the data for tabulation.

It is a good plan to have both a field edit and a central office edit of each report. The field editing is done by the supervisor, preferably in the presence of the investigator who obtained the information. This field editing is limited to making direct changes on the returns to eliminate all possible errors. A separate central office edit should be made after the reports are received from the field. A person who has had special experience in this type of work may be employed. His duties are to catch errors overlooked in the field editing and to prepare the data for later tabulation.

If the number of interviews is not too large, it is desirable to have one person do all of the central office editing, as this will tend to insure more standardized work. Usually, however, it is necessary to have a group of people editing the individual schedules. In this case it is especially important that a set of editing instructions be drawn up and posted where it is readily accessible to all persons engaged in editing. Separate editing specifications must be drawn for each job because special problems will always be encountered. These specifications should be drawn jointly by the person in charge of the research and the individual who is to be in charge of the tabulation which follows. The two persons should go over a representative group of questionnaires to familiarize themselves thoroughly with the problems to be encountered.

Special Qualifications of an Editor. It is most important that the editing of field reports be entrusted to experienced individuals, for the editors must exercise important judgments. A properly qualified editor should be:

1. *Experienced in field work.* Editing must always be assigned to people who have had considerable experience in field interviewing, never to an inexperienced or temporary clerk.
2. *Familiar with the subject.* The editor must be familiar with the subject of the investigation. Although this type of work is closely supervised, the editor should know the possible range of answers.
3. *Conservative.* The editor must not be too ready to change or revise answers which seem extreme, but which *may be possible.* Most answers must be accepted as correct.
4. *Observant.* Nothing should escape the editor's notice. He may find a great deal that is significant in comments which clarify answers.
5. *Alert to supplementary statements.* The editor must study carefully any notes penned on the questionnaires, for these may contain very significant statements.
6. *Acquainted with machine tabulation requirements.* If machine tabulation methods are to be employed, the editor also becomes a coder, assigning proper code numbers to all answers which have not been precoded.

Rules for Editing. In editing field reports one should not make erasures or destroy the original data received from the field. Editing marks and changes should be made with colored pencil or colored ink which is adopted as standard for this purpose by the organization. It is then possible to check the work of the editors, and the original data are available for later reference.

While each research project raises special problems in the editing of the data, certain conditions arise so frequently that it is possible to adopt standardized practices to be used as a basis for preparing the editing instructions for an individual study. The rules which are explained below cover the most common requirements for editing.

Rule 1. The returns of individual investigators should be examined.

An important phase of editing is to scrutinize the reports of each investigator to appraise the care with which the work was done. The reports from each market should also be reviewed and compared with the others. As a result of such examination and comparison, it may be found necessary to throw out all the work of some investigators and to carry on additional field work in some markets.

Such necessities are usually indicated by the general appearance of the questionnaires or the inconsistency of one group related to the general averages observed in the others. For example, it was found in one study that about 25 per cent of the families interviewed were using a certain product. Examination of the reports from one investigator showed, however, that almost every family she interviewed used the commodity. It was immediately apparent that the investigator was in some way so biasing the interviews that it was necessary to reject all of her work.

This general checking of the returns of the individual investigator and by cities also is an important element in appraising the supervision of field work. It gives the project supervisor an indication of the general quality of work which is being done.

Questionnaires which are based on persons who should not have been included in the study, such as children and servants, are also rejected at this point.

Rule 2. Inconsistent answers should be rejected or changed.

It will frequently be found that the answers to two different questions are inconsistent. The following is an example:

5. What kind of program do you like best? "Symphony Orchestra."
6. Indicate in order of preference three of the following classifications of programs:

    1 Dance orchestra
      Symphony orchestra
    2 Drama
      Children's program
    3 Grand opera
      Classical music

The answers to these two questions are obviously inconsistent, as "symphony orchestra" should have been given the first rank in the sixth question, in view of the answer to the fifth one.

Appliance	Now in Use				Formerly Used			
	Type	Brand	Year Bought	Owned or Furnished	Type	Brand	Year Bought	Owned or Furnished
Range	Elec. ✓ Gas ✗	Hotpoint	✗ *(1945)*	Owned	Elec. ___ Gas ✗	Don't *(D.K.)*	Know— Too *(D.K.)*	Long Ago *(D.K.)*
Washer	Elec. ✗ ___ ___	Easy	✗ *(1944)*	*Owned*	Elec. ___ ___ ___		None	
Ironer	Elec. ___ Gas ___ ___ ___	*None*			Elec. ___ Gas ___ ___ ___	*None*		
Refrigerator	Elec. ✗ Gas ___ Ice ___	Frigidaire	6 Mo *(1947)*	Owned	Elec. ___ Gas ___ Ice ✗	D.K.	D.K. *(very old)*	Owned

FIGURE 20. Section of an Edited Questionnaire. The encircled information indicates the editor's corrections, which are usually made in colored pencil. Note that the editing corrects errors and prepares the questionnaire for tabulation.

In case of such an inconsistent error, the editor must determine whether the real intent of the respondent is clear. If the editor is certain of the true intent, he then changes the inconsistent answer to make it consistent with the answer to the other. If the intention of the respondent is not perfectly clear, however, the answers to both questions should be deleted, as in the case shown above.

An example of an inconsistent answer which may be corrected by changing the one obviously incorrect is the following:

3. What brand of radio do you own? "Philco DX."
8. How much did you pay for your radio? "$300."

When the model of the radio is given in answer to the first question and the editor knows that the price of this radio is $110, the answer to the second question can safely be changed to that figure.

Rule 3. Incomplete answers should be filled in where possible.

Frequently the answer to a question will be omitted, in whole or in part, yet the editor can fill in the correct answer on the basis of other information obtained from the schedule. The following is an example:

7. What television programs can you associate with advertised products? "Arthur Godfrey with Chesterfields."

12. What television programs advertise cigarettes? "<u>I Love Lucy for Philip Morris.</u>"

It is obvious that the respondent associates "I Love Lucy" with Philip Morris cigarettes, and this should be included in the answer to question 7. The answers, of course, do not show the entire range of association, but they do clearly show that this one should have been included.

Rule 4. Obviously inaccurate answers should be rejected.

In examining any given set of questionnaires it is comparatively easy, after one has had experience in editing, to locate answers which are extremely doubtful and should be discarded. An answer may be rejected because it is clear that it has been given carelessly or unintelligently. A certain number of "jokers" will be found in the answers on some of the questionnaires and should be eliminated.

Rule 5. Answers involving units of measurement should be standardized.

Wherever units of measurement are involved in the answer to questions, such as periods of time, the answers will be given in varying units on different questionnaires, even if the questionnaire does specify one particular form. An example is shown below.

12. How long have you used the product? (In months) "<u>2½ years.</u>"

The tabulation will be greatly expedited if all answers of this type are reduced to one standardized unit and properly coded.

Rule 6. Questions to be tabulated by classes should be converted to the proper classification.

The answers to questions are often tabulated on the basis of frequency distributions. An example is the following:

4. How long have you used this product? "<u>13 months.</u>"

In such a case it is entirely too cumbersome to make a separate tabulation for every possible answer. The editor therefore usually sets up class intervals, such as "less than six months," "six months, but under one year," "one year, but under two years." The class intervals should be accurately defined and mutually exclusive. Persons making the tabulation cannot be relied upon to convert a specific answer to the proper classification. Furthermore, even though the tabulators would not make mistakes in so doing, time will be saved by having the classification indicated in the editing. In the example cited, therefore, the editor should write in "one year."

Rule 7. General answers should be properly classified.

Many questions will obtain a wide variety of answers which call for proper classification. Types commonly encountered are opinion answers, occupation answers, and brand data.

In such cases it is necessary to indicate the proper group in which the individual answer should be tabulated. An example of an opinion question calling for such treatment is the following:

3. Why do you use this product? "Mild Tasting."

In answer to such a question the respondent may express the general attribute "flavor" in many different ways. It is necessary to decide whether certain variations in the expression are significant for the particular analysis at hand. Individual answers should then be assigned to those groups by proper codes. In the example cited it might be valuable to tabulate separately answers which represent special variations of one general quality. On the other hand, this answer may be of most value as a reflection of the importance of flavor as opposed to other factors, such as price. The interpretation of answers of this type cannot be left to the tabulators, for it will be found that each one will have his own notions as to the proper classification of different answers.

Any one occupation may be described in many different ways. Even though occupational classes are listed on the questionnaire, a certain number of persons will give a detailed description of their occupation rather than a direct answer. In such cases the editor must decide the classification into which the report falls and code accordingly.

Where questions relating to brands or types of products are asked, such a large number of different ones are usually reported that it is necessary to set up general classifications, such as "other brands," "other liquids," and "other powders." If such classifications are to be used in the tabulation, the editor should indicate the proper classifications for all brands not tabulated separately. This will make for accuracy in tabulation and eliminate a great amount of waste effort. In some studies, for example, it would be necessary to tabulate over 200 brands if each were listed separately.

Validating the Sample

In planning the sample, every effort is made to insure that it will be sufficiently accurate for purposes of the research. However, after the field work is completed, it is necessary to take steps to check on the actual sample obtained to be certain that the data are adequate from a sampling point of view.

The process of validation for a probability sample is entirely different from that for a quota sample. The procedure at this point therefore depends on which type of sample has been taken.

Validation of Probability Samples. Returns from the field are first scrutinized to make sure that sampling instructions have been carefully followed. In cases of error or omission, it is necessary to carry on additional field work to fill in the gaps. If prelisting has been employed, this is a relatively simple matter, as the field workers have specific instructions regarding each individual case to be included. If some general system of randomization has been used, it is necessary to spot-check the field work to make sure that instructions have been carried out.

The second step in validating a probability sample is to check the proportion of returns successfully completed against the ideal sample specifications. Some standard must be set for an acceptable minimum proportion of cases which were planned to be covered but were not actually included. In areas where the number of failures exceeds this minimum standard, further callbacks must be made to bring the sample up to it. Sometimes it is necessary to send new investigators into an area to insure satisfactory sample accomplishment.

The third step is to compute sampling tolerances. Since probability sampling is based on mathematical formulas, it is possible to compute the actual tolerances, or the degree of error due to the sample itself. These tolerances are computed by mathematical formulas. They reflect the influence of sample size and representativeness in one operation, although the matter of representativeness is basically dependent upon the sample design and the degree to which individual cases have been obtained in strict accordance with chance probability. Since each probability sample has its own design, the formulas for computing tolerances must be constructed for each sample. In other words, standard formulas for computing tolerances of probability samples are no longer used.

Validating a Quota Sample. Strictly speaking, it is impossible to obtain mathematical validation of a quota sample. This is one of the chief weaknesses of this type of sample, as has been shown in Chapter 11 on principles of sampling. However, there are many situations in marketing research in which quota sampling is employed. Furthermore, it is just as important to check the actual sample obtained if the quota method has been employed as it is to validate a probability sample. In validating a quota sample two separate operations are necessary. First the sample size must be checked to determine if a sufficient number of cases has been obtained. This characteristic is commonly referred to as *reliability* or stability. Second, the sample must be checked to determine if its distribution provides an adequate representation of various classes or items. This characteristic is commonly called *proportionality*.

Testing for Reliability. The problem of reliability is simply that of making sure that enough cases are included in a quota sample to reduce the possibility of distortion by its being too small. There are several different methods which may be used to determine the reliability of a quota sample. Some of the methods involve rather complicated statistical manipulations; others are short-cut methods which do not provide such exact results but which may be quite satisfactory for a given purpose.

One fact should be kept clearly in mind. All methods for testing the reliability of a quota sample rest upon the same basic, logical assumption. This assumption is that the reliability of a sample is determined by its relative consistency or stability.

The terms "consistency" and "stability" mean simply that the addition of more cases or interviews will not significantly increase the accuracy of the conclusions. Suppose as a result of a study of a proposed change in the flavor of a product, after 500 calls have been made, it is found that 82.6 per cent of the interviewed prefer the new product. If one were to make 500 additional calls, and found that the percentage of people preferring the new form was approximately the same as that found in the first 500 calls, he would conclude that the first sample of 500 interviews possessed stability. The test which is described in the following discussion is a practical method for determining whether it is necessary to obtain additional cases for any given quota sample.

The Cumulative Frequency Method. The procedure for testing a sample by this method may be described as follows.

1. *Arrange the data in random order.* In the case of a market survey, shuffle the questionnaires so that they are in chance order. Some persons give each return a serial number as it is received and keep them in this order for purposes of testing. This plan is unsatisfactory, however, as the order of receipt at the central office is not necessarily a chance order, because mail from certain geographic sections will always be received ahead of others. Where personal interviewers are used, the returns are received by markets. If all the New York questionnaires are placed together, and are then followed by Des Moines, Pittsburgh, Atlanta, etc., they will not be arranged in chance

order. Chance order is essential to the correct application of this short-cut test for reliability.

2. *Divide the data into separate groups.* The number of groups into which the data should be divided is flexible. If one has a total of 400 questionnaires, he will ordinarily divide them into eight or ten groups. If he has 5,000 questionnaires, he might divide them into twenty-five or fifty groups. If the sample is relatively small, one must be satisfied with a comparatively small number of groups. The number of groups into which the questionnaires are divided has no theoretical bearing on the validity of the method, but the use of too large a number makes for unnecessary handling.

In determining the number to include within each group, it is usually more convenient if 100 questionnaires are in each class, as this facilitates the calculation of percentages. If there are not enough questionnaires to provide at least ten groups of 100 each, the number in each group should be reduced to 50, which is also a convenient number to employ. With less than 500 questionnaires, however, it is best to divide them arbitrarily into ten groups.

It is not strictly necessary that each group contain exactly the same number of data. Likewise it is not necessary that all data be included in the groups to be tested, provided that those excluded are only a very small number and represent merely the last few which remain after all the reports required to complete the groups set up have been sorted.

Let us assume, for example, that we have 2,016 completed questionnaires. These might be divided into twenty groups of 100 each, or ten groups of 200 each. The remaining 16 questionnaires may be omitted from the test or added to one of the groups. Let us assume that the remaining 16 have been omitted from the test and that we have divided the questionnaires into ten groups of 200 each. We now have ten piles of schedules, distributed as follows:

Groups	Interview Numbers
1	1– 200
2	201– 400
3	401– 600
4	601– 800
5	801–1000
6	1001–1200
7	1201–1400
8	1401–1600
9	1601–1800
10	1801–2000

3. *Determine the bases on which the test is to be made.* It is necessary to select from a questionnaire or schedule reporting observations

one or more items to be used for the test for reliability. If only one question is asked in a survey, the sample must obviously be tested on this basis alone. However, most surveys ask several questions, and the analyst must decide which ones are to be used for purposes of the test. Theoretically one might test the reliability on every question included in the survey. This energy would be wasted, however, for one can readily select a few key questions which will provide an adequate basis for testing the entire job.

On the other hand, one should not assume that because the data pass the test for reliability on one question, the sample for the entire study is satisfactory. Each subsample must be tested separately for reliability. The decision as to the bases on which the test is to be made is, therefore, represented in the data at hand. In the case of a survey one should carefully check the questionnaire to determine which questions represent different universes, and then make a separate reliability test for each universe.

For example, assume that the following questions were asked in a survey:

1. Do you have a television set?
2. What brand is it?
3. How many times has it been serviced in the past year?

Every person who was interviewed in this study had an opportunity to give an affirmative or negative answer to the first question. Therefore, this question adequately reflects the total sample taken in the study. If it is tested for reliability, it establishes the fact that enough persons have been asked this question to determine the extent to which people own television sets. This procedure could, therefore, be accepted as a basis for a test for covering the total sample.

In answer to the second question, however, it is obvious that only those people who answered "yes" to the first question have a chance to reply. They represent a subsample of owners. Those who reply "General Electric" represent a further subsample. If conclusions regarding service experience (from question 5) are to be drawn for General Electric owners, it is obvious that the reliability of this group as a subsample must be tested independently of tests of the total sample.

It is of the utmost importance that the analyst guard against statements regarding the reliability of samples which purport to prove the accuracy of an investigation but which are limited to tests covering only the total sample. Significant subsamples should be tested separately and must stand on their own feet so far as their reliability is concerned.

Let us assume for the illustration that we have decided to test the total sample first on the basis of the answers to the question "Do you have a television set?"

4. *Prepare a table of cumulative frequencies.* The next step is to count the frequency with which the phenomenon being measured occurs, and to calculate the cumulative percentage of occurrence. The necessary data should then be inserted in a table similar to Table 13.

TABLE 13

TELEVISION SURVEY—TABLE OF CUMULATIVE FREQUENCIES

(1)	(2)	(3)	(4)	(5)
Group Number	Frequency of Occurrence	Cumulative Frequency of Occurrence	Cumulative No. of Cases	Cumulative Per Cent of Occurrence
1	138	138	200	69.0
2	163	301	400	75.3
3	189	490	600	81.7
4	150	640	800	80.0
5	165	805	1000	80.5
6	149	954	1200	79.5
7	158	1112	1400	79.4
8	185	1297	1600	81.1
9	141	1438	1800	80.0
10	159	1597	2000	79.9

In the first column the numbers identifying each of the groups of 200 questionnaires are inserted. The frequency with which any given answer occurs in each of these groups is inserted in Column 2, as indicated. For the question "Do you have a television set?" this would be either the number of questionnaires in each group answering "yes" or the number answering "no."

It is important to notice in this connection that questions which do not provide a for a "yes" or "no" answer may be used as a basis for the test for reliability. An example is the question "When did you last view television?" In this case the answers may be divided into several groups, such as "today," "yesterday," "two days ago," "three days ago," or "four days ago." If such a question is used as the basis for the test, one simply selects arbitrarily the number of answers falling into one or more of the classifications; for example, the number answering "today," or a group including both "today" and "yesterday."

In Column 3, the cumulative totals from Column 2 are inserted. The table shows, for example, that in the first four groups, 640 persons reported owning a television set.

In Column 4 the total cumulative number of cases (in this instance the questionnaires) which are included in each group is inserted. Since there are 200 questionnaires in each group, the table shows that the cumulative total for the first six groups is 1,200 questionnaires.

In Column 5 the cumulative percentage of occurrence of the item being measured is obtained by dividing Column 3 by Column 4.

5. *Chart the cumulative frequency.* The decision as to whether the sample is valid or not is based upon the stability or consistency of the cumulative percentage of occurrence as one progresses from the first to the last group. By an examination of Table 13, it will be seen that in the first 200 questionnaires, 69.0 per cent of the families owned television sets, and that this percentage increased rapidly to 75.3 per cent for the first 400 questionnaires and 81.7 per cent for the first 600 questionnaires. Running down the column, however, one notices that

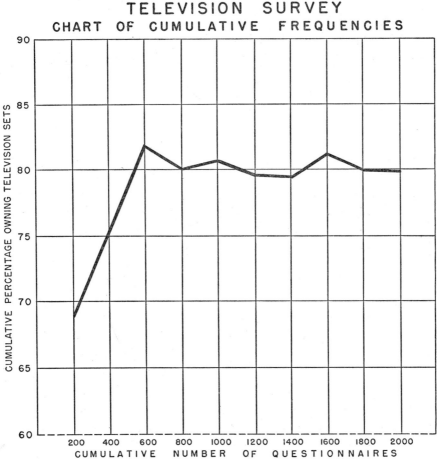

FIGURE 21. Chart of Cumulative Frequencies Used in Testing a Sample for Reliability. (Based on data from Table 13.)

the cumulative percentage does not vary as each additional group of 200 is added nearly so much as it does toward the top of the column. By the time the sixth group, which represents 1,200 questionnaires, is included, it is found that 79.5 per cent of the families own television sets. This percentage does not vary greatly from that shown for the entire group of 2,000 questionnaires, which is 79.9 per cent. It will also be noticed that the fluctuation in this percentage from the sixth through the tenth group is not very great. On the basis of this consistency in the latter part of the cumulative percentages, one may decide that the size of the sample is adequate for his purposes.

It is usually helpful, however, to draw a simple line graph showing the cumulative percentage of occurrence. Examination of this chart makes the degree of stability obtained by the cumulation of these individual segments clear. Noticing that the variation in the last half of the cumulation is only about 1 per cent, most researchers would readily assume that the sample is adequate.

This method of testing a sample for reliability is the most simple. Its use depends to a considerable extent on the experience of the researcher, which gives him a basis on which to exercise his judgment in determining whether the evidence is sufficient to warrant the acceptance of the sample.

Testing for Proportionality. The principle of proportionality requires that each significant class or group must be represented in the sample in the same proportion as it occurs in the total universe. In testing a quota sample for proportionality, one must first go over the study to determine the classifications which have a significant bearing upon the conclusions of the study and which must, therefore, be checked for proportionality. The classifications which are usually most important from the point of view of proportionality are the following:

1. Economic groups.
2. Geographic groups.
3. City-size groups.
4. Users and nonusers of the commodity.
5. Age groups.

It is not always necessary to test every sample on all of these five points. Furthermore, they do not necessarily provide the most significant groups to be used in testing any given sample for proportionality. For example, in a study of the market for electrical refrigerators, having the proper proportion of refrigerators of various ages in the sample would be one of the most important considerations.

The actual test for proportionality in a quota sample is very simple. One compares the distribution of the sample with the distribution of the total universe which is obtained from some reliable source for significant classifications. Suppose, for example, that one wishes to test a sample for proportionality of the distribution of people in different age groups. By turning to the U. S. Census he can find the percentage of people in each of these groups. The tabulation below shows a comparison:

Age Group	Distribution of "Universe"	Distribution of Sample
Under 20	38.7%	25.2%
20–39	31.8	42.8
40–59	20.9	23.7
60 and over................	8.6	8.3
Total	100.0%	100.0%

It is apparent that too few cases in the youngest group and too many cases in the group from twenty to thirty-nine years of age are included in the sample. There are also too many in the age group from forty to fifty-nine. The difference for the group sixty years of age and over is not important.

A quota sample is corrected for proportionality in one of three ways. In the first place, one may gather additional data. In the example cited above, it would be necessary to obtain more interviews. In the second place, one may discard some data. Providing that the sample is large enough, part of a group which is too large for proportionality may be omitted from the tabulation. This solution is not usually practical, however, and must be watched very carefully. It is, of course, of the utmost importance that if parts of the questionnaires are discarded, they be taken in an absolutely random fashion, lest the results be distorted. A third alternative is to adjust the sample for proportionality.

Adjustment for Proportionality. This procedure is very frequently practicable and is generally preferred to obtaining additional data, since the latter involves some extra time and expenditure. It is also preferable to the rejection of some of the data, as this procedure is dangerous. The adjustment for proportionality is accomplished by taking the conclusions obtained in the tabulation and weighting them by the true proportions which exist in the total universe. An example is shown in Table 14.

In the first column of the table the various classifications for which proportionality is desired are inserted by age groups. In the same study one might set up similar tables for economic groups, city-size groups, or any other base for proportionality. The data are tabulated and separate averages struck for each of the groups shown in Column 1. The example is taken from an analysis of the consumption of milk.

TABLE 14

ADJUSTMENT FOR PROPORTIONALITY
Milk Consumption by Age Groups

(1) Age Group	(2) Milk Consumption in Pounds	(3) Per Cent in Each Age Group in Universe	(4) Weighted Consumption
Under 20	300	38.7	116.10
20–39	180	31.8	57.24
40–59	160	20.9	33.44
60 and over..............	70	8.6	6.02
Total		100.0	212.80

In those questionnaires covering people under twenty years of age it was found that the average consumption of milk for the period studied was 300 pounds. This figure is inserted in Column 2. The averages for each of the other groups are inserted in this same column.

The percentages of each age group existing in the total universe are next inserted in Column 3. In this case the percentages were obtained from the U. S. Census.

Column 4 is the product of Columns 2 and 3. While whole percentages are shown in Column 3, Column 4 shows the results of multiplying Column 2 by the proper mathematical expression of the percentages in Column 3. For example, the mathematical expression of the whole percentage (38.7) is .387. This figure is multiplied by the figure in Column 2, which in this case is 300. Three decimals are pointed off in the product, giving the result 116.10. This computation is made separately for each of the groups and the figures inserted in Column 4, as shown. The sum of Column 4 (212.80) is the correct per capita milk consumption after the data obtained in the study have been adjusted for proportionality.

The milk consumption figure which would have been arrived at by a straight tabulation of the returns in the sample would have been 196.47 pounds. The difference between this figure and the true figure shown in the table above is the amount of error existing in the sample because of its lack of proportionality.

Tabulation

After editing and testing the sample, the field data are ready for statistical manipulation. The statistical treatment involves two separate operations: tabulating the data and drawing statistical conclusions. The process of tabulation, per se, is essentially that of counting the data. The process of drawing statistical conclusions is that of manipulating the data to bring out the best possible forms of quantitative summary.

The two processes of tabulation and drawing statistical conclusions are closely interwoven. The research director has in mind the types of statistical generalizations most likely to be drawn when he plans the forms and procedures for tabulation. He then sets up the tabulations in such forms as will be most efficient for the anticipated summarizations. However, it is important to challenge the value of these conclusions after the basic tabulations have been made to see if there are other ways of manipulating the data which will lead to more revealing conclusions. Therefore, it is necessary to look on the process of tabulation as essentially a separate step from that of drawing statistical conclusions.

The counting of data may be done by manual or machine methods. The decision as to which of these two alternatives should be used is based upon several considerations discussed at the end of this section. The basic principles which govern tabulation, regardless of method, can best be explained in terms of hand tabulation procedure. The discussion below, while it applies in large part to the more commonly used manual tabulation, covers all the basic considerations met if machine methods are used, except the technical details of machine operation.

Types of Forms Used. In the tabulation of primary data two separate types of forms are employed—the counting sheet and the summary tables. The counting sheet, in hand tabulation, is the form on which the tabulators record the number of items found on the questionnaires or schedules. Its form is determined largely by the tables which are ultimately to be produced. The counting sheet should be kept as simple as possible, preferably the equivalent of not more than a two-dimension table, explained below. To attempt to obtain too many classifications in the original counting of the data will lead to a great amount of error and will defeat the effort to save time and expense.

One should not regard the counting sheet as an unimportant form. Most of the errors made in the tabulation process will occur at this point. Speed and economy in tabulation depend on the clarity and arrangement of the counting sheet. Furthermore, its form determines the classifications and cross-classifications of the data which will be available for analysis at a later time.

Summary tables are tables which summarize the results of the counting and may be classified into three major types. The first type is the simple or one-dimension table. An example is one which shows only the number of persons using different brands of dentifrices. This type is very common, but it usually has very little analytical value.

The second type is the correlation or two-dimension table. An example is a table in which the brand used is related to the age of the persons included in the research. This type is much more illuminating than one which shows merely the number of persons who use different brands or only the ages of persons included in the study.

#4069 - Question 4. "How was the sample used?" Atlanta - 84 families who did not buy		
		TOTAL
WITH CHILDREN		
Cereal only	HHT HHT HHT HHT HHT HHT ///	33
Raw confection	HHT HHT ////	14
Cooked candy	//	2
General Cooking	///	3
With cottage cheese	/	1
Salad	/	1
Fed to dog	/	1
No answer	//	2
		57
No. of interviews		50
WITHOUT CHILDREN		
Cereal only	HHT HHT HHT HHT HHT ///	28
Raw confection	HHT /	6
Cooked Candy	//	2
General cooking	//	2
In soup	/	1
No answer	/	1
		40
No. of interviews		34

FIGURE 22. Counting Sheet for Hand Tabulation

It is possible to set up tables which show more than a two-dimension relationship. These are the third type, which may be called complex tables. An example is one relating brands used to ages, sex, and income. Such tables are sometimes of value as a means of compressing a large amount of information in a small space. They should usually be avoided in marketing research work, however, as they are likely to become so confusing that the true significance of the data becomes obscured or is lost.

Standards in Tabulation. Two standards should be kept clearly in mind throughout the tabulation stage. The first is that the necessary routines must be set up to insure accurate counting of the data from the original questionnaires or schedules. The second standard is that the tabulation forms should bring out the most significant meaning of the data. Frequently this standard is not given the attention it deserves. Each of these two aspects of tabulation will be discussed separately.

TABLE 16—DISPOSAL OF SAMPLE

(Based on 84 Atlanta Families Who Did Not Purchase the Product)

	All Families		Families With Children		Families Without Children	
	No.	%	No.	%	No.	%
Total	84	100.0	50	100.0	34	100.0
Cereal only	61	72.6	33	66.0	28	82.4
Raw Confection	20	23.8	14	28.0	6	17.6
General Cooking	5	6.0	3	6.0	2	5.9
Cooked Candy	4	4.8	2	4.0	2	5.9
Other Uses	4	4.8	3	6.0	1	2.9

NOTE: Percentages do not add to 100 because 13 families (7 with children and 6 without) used sample both as cereal and for some other purpose; 3 families did not answer.

FIGURE 23. Table Drawn from Counting Sheet

Rules for Obtaining Accuracy in Tabulation. In order to insure accuracy in tabulation work, as well as to conduct the work with a maximum of speed and a minimum of expense, there are several general principles which may be followed.

These principles are summarized in the discussion of a series of twelve rules for tabulation which follows.

Rule 1. The data should be tabulated separately by major groups and by individual tabulators.

By separating the tabulation work into major groups is meant the division of the tabulation into units such as cities, or parts of the questionnaire. If separate counting sheets are set up for each market included in the study, an extra opportunity for checking the accuracy of the tabulation, as well as keeping a clear record of the progress of the tabulation work, is made possible. Separation of the tabulation by different questions or parts of the schedule is also sometimes employed for this purpose.

In planning a tabulation one must decide whether the most convenient major groups to employ for this division are markets or parts of the questionnaire. Sometimes a tabulation is broken down on both bases. As individual tabulators specialize on certain questions or parts of the schedule, they gain a facility which speeds up the tabulation and helps make for accuracy.

Separating the tabulation by individual tabulators is necessary when hand tabulation is employed in order that the accuracy of the work of each person may be checked. Even when only two or three different tabulators are employed, it will often be found that one is not sufficiently accurate for the work. By separating the work by individual tabulators, one can also check the rate of speed at which each is progressing. This check will make it possible to forecast quickly the length of time the tabulation will take and indicate whether it is necessary to increase the size of the tabulation force.

The fact that the data should be tabulated separately by individual tabulators does not preclude the possibility of setting up teams of tabulators for certain questions. Frequently, greater speed can be attained if two people carry on a tabulation operation, one reading the schedules and the other making a record on the counting sheet. In this case, the team takes the place of the individual tabulator as the unit for which the work is to be checked.

Rule 2. Base totals should be established at the beginning of the operation.

The first step in tabulation is to make a count of the total number of schedules by markets and by several other classifications, such as age groups, economic groups, or population groups. This series of numbers, representing the total number of schedules in each class, becomes the first basis on which the accuracy of the work of the tabulation is checked. If there are 326 questionnaires from Cleveland, for example, every tabulation involving that city should total 326, regardless of the subject tabulated. If proper provision has been made for a "no answer" column and for tabulating duplication or multiple answers, the totals will always check against the base total.

Rule 3. A chief tabulator should be put in charge of the operation.

It seems hardly necessary to point out the importance of having one person in complete charge of the tabulation operation. However, it is common practice to divide the authority, with the result that errors are not caught quickly and a great deal of time is wasted.

In a tabulation involving more than two or three persons, one individual, who is himself an expert tabulator, should be placed in complete authority. This person can often very well devote a major share of his time to assigning work to individual tabulators, keeping records of the progress of the tabulation, checking on the accuracy of the work, and assembling the completed tables as developed. It is a very simple matter for field reports to be mixed up or lost in a tabulation operation. Unless a central depot for the clearing of work to be done and work completed is established, very serious mistakes may be encountered.

Rule 4. A routine for regular checking of tabulation against base totals should be set up.

The work should be assigned to individual tabulators in as small quantities as possible. This means, for example, that an individual tabulator would be given the questionnaires for one market to make the tabulation on, say, "Question 3." As soon as this has been completed on the counting sheet, the results should be totaled for the market and checked by the supervisor against the base total which was earlier established. As a general principle, at least one check against the base total should be made on each occasion when a tabulator completes a unit of tabulation.

Rule 5. Counting sheets should be standardized.

Often a group of questionnaires is given to a tabulator, with some blank tabulation paper and some oral instructions as to how the counting sheet should be set up. This practice is not satisfactory, because errors in column and line headings will be made, sheets may be too crowded, or variations introduced which will make the comparison of counting sheets for different markets or units of the job difficult. The person in charge of the tabulation should decide the exact form which should be used for each counting sheet, and then prepare these forms so that when the tabulator begins his work on any unit he is provided both with schedules and a complete counting form.

One common error is to make these counting forms too small so that it is necessary to run the check marks over into the wrong column. This fault, of course, leads to inaccuracy.

Rule 6. All forms should have clear, complete, descriptive titles.

This rule applies both to the counting sheets and to the tables which are later drawn from them. It seems a very simple rule, but in actual practice it is necessary to check constantly to make sure that the titles are satisfactory. The title placed at the top of a counting sheet or table should indicate clearly the exact nature of the data recorded thereon. Completeness of the title is something which must be constantly watched. For example, it is very common to omit dates, and sometimes the individual units, such as the market or economic group, covered will be forgotten.

Rule 7. Serial numbers should be assigned to schedules and other forms used in the tabulation.

It is not always necessary to assign serial numbers to individual questionnaires or schedules, but it is usually desirable as a means of keeping a more accurate record of the progress of the tabulation and of locating misplaced schedules. The assignment of proper numbers to counting sheets and tables is especially important where more than one sheet is used to record the same kind of data. Sometimes it will be found necessary to have three or four separate sheets to cover one tabulation. If these sheets are not properly numbered, they may easily get out of order, very much to the embarrassment of the person in charge of the tabulation work. By assigning serial numbers to the counting sheets and tables it is also easier to determine just how much work has been completed.

Rule 8. Forms should provide for all possible classifications.

Counting sheets and tables should make provision for all cases so that the totals derived for them are complete and correspond with the totals found at other points in the tabulation. To insure completeness, spaces should be allowed for the tabulation of "No answer," "Don't know," etc.

Rule 9. Class intervals should be mutually exclusive.

This is a very simple rule but one which is frequently violated. An example is shown below.

Rental Value of Home	Number of Families
$ 0 to $30	223
30 to 40	257
40 to 50	165
50 and over	79
Total	724

These classifications are not mutually exclusive and it is impossible to tell the exact distribution of the rentals of the homes included. Having mutually exclusive class intervals is especially important in handling survey data because people tend to report data in even numbers. In such cases the even numbers should be made the midpoint of class intervals, for in this respect the distortion of the original data through summarization is held at a minimum. A correct form for the rental data follows.

Rental Value of Home	Number of Families
Under $25	206
$25 to 34................................	279
35 to 44.................................	142
45 and over.............................	97
Total	724

Rule 10. All tables should be complete.

In drawing summary tables from the counting sheets or from a run of machine cards, the tables do not usually record all the information shown. Frequently, from one counting sheet it is possible to construct more than one table and also to combine class intervals set up in the original counting sheet. The rule for completeness, however, requires that all data necessary to a thorough understanding of the information which a table purports to show should be included in the table. One important phase of this is that "No answers" or "Don't knows" should be included in the summary tables. Another requirement is that the totals should always be shown wherever percentages are given. Unless one knows the total on which a percentage is based, he has no basis on which to determine the significance of that percentage.

Rule 11. Classifications used on counting sheets or original tables should be narrow.

In summary tables one usually has rather broad class intervals for the various data which are shown. For example, a table showing magazine readership by income groups would perhaps have all the data classified into four or five income groups.

It is a grave mistake, however, to set up the original counting sheet or summary table on the basis of a small number of arbitrarily assigned classifications. One can determine the proper limit for class intervals only on the basis of an examination of the data themselves. Therefore, one should set up the narrowest classifications which are compatible with reasonable speed and ease of tabulation. In tabulating age data, for example, the counting sheet should theoretically provide for individual ages, such as 8, 9, and 10. If one is familiar with the vagaries of age data, however, he may set them up in five-year intervals. If single years are used, perhaps seventy-five different class intervals will be found on the counting sheet; while if five-year intervals are employed, fifteen class groups will suffice.

Rule 12. Data should be arranged in a table in the order which best reveals their significance.

The question of the order in which data should be arranged in a table may appear unimportant, but it is possible to gain a great deal in clarity by carefully planning the order in which they are presented.

The top position in the column receives the greatest attention; therefore, the most significant data should be placed at this point. It is now the policy of the Census Bureau to show the total of each column on the first line, rather than at the bottom of a table. By this arrangement the total, which is usually the most important single figure, is given the position in which it will receive the greatest attention.

Frequently the order in which the column headings or lines of the table are arranged is a matter of tradition. If the data deal with geographic units, for example, one may follow the traditional arrangement of the Census Bureau by census regions. Sometimes, however, it may be better to follow another traditional and arbitrary arrangement—the alphabetical. The advantage of alphabetical arangement is, of course, that it makes for quick identification of individual units.

Data involving periods of years or months are traditionally arranged from the first point in time to the most recent. Sometimes a table will be more effective by reversing this process and showing the most recent data first. Age data are also traditionally arranged so that the youngest age group appears first.

There are times when an alphabetical or other traditional arrangement can best be eliminated and an arrangement according to the size or frequency of the item substituted. The Census Bureau, for example, tabulates data such as the value of products of manufacturing industries in a descending order of magnitude. This method of presentation is much more emphatic and emphasizes the most important parts of the table.

Obtaining the Most Significant Meaning from the Data. The bulk of the preceding discussion was related primarily to the matter of obtaining accuracy in tabulation. Setting up the tabulations so that they will best reveal the meaning of the facts is even more important.

The proper classification of data by using cross-tabulations, such as the relation of brands used to age, is the key to accomplishing this objective. Presumably, in planning the investigation one has kept clearly in mind the bases for analysis which will be most important. Once the data have been gathered, however, there is ample opportunity for exercising ingenuity in employing other classifications to show the relationship of one part of the findings to another.

The correlation aspects of tabulation should not be overlooked. Unfortunately the term "correlation" has been commonly associated with advanced mathematical and statistical techniques employed to arrive at measurements of the degree of association, such as the co-efficient of correlation. As a matter of fact, one is making a correla-tion when he employs a two-dimension table just as when he calcu-lates a coefficient. In the first case he is presenting a tabular relation-ship; in the latter he is measuring the degree of concomitant variation. To the analyst a tabulation is chiefly a means of expressing corelation-ships. To illustrate, when we prepare a table showing the number of persons of different ages who use a product, we are not just counting. We are in effect measuring the relationship here between two variables —age and consumption.

Some research directors make it a point to tabulate personally a small number of the returns in order to familiarize themselves thor-oughly with the exact meaning of the data which have been obtained. Sometimes it will be found that it is possible to discover entirely new methods of breaking down the data and developing significant facts and relationships by going back to a few of the individual schedules after the tabulation process has been largely completed.

Machine Versus Hand Tabulation. One must usually choose be-tween machine tabulation and hand tabulation for counting the data. If machine tabulation is to be employed, the data are transferred to punched cards. Tabulating machines sort the cards into various clas-sifications, mechanically count the data, and may print the totals. A wide variety of types of tabulating machinery is now available, the latest development being the electronic calculator.

Some companies have a sufficiently large volume of regular tabu-lating work to warrant maintaining their own tabulation equipment. Service organizations in the larger cities supply machine tabulation facilities on a job basis for companies which cannot afford to lease the machinery.

Both machine tabulation and hand tabulation have advantages and corresponding weaknesses.

Advantages of Machine Tabulation. *Low Cost in Large Opera-tions.* The first advantage of machine tabulation is its low cost if a large volume of data is to be counted. Operations such as the U. S. Census and the analysis of life insurance records are examples of situations in which it is obviously economical to use machine tabula-tion methods only. In marketing research, machine tabulation is more economical than hand tabulation when a reasonable number of fairly complex schedules is involved.

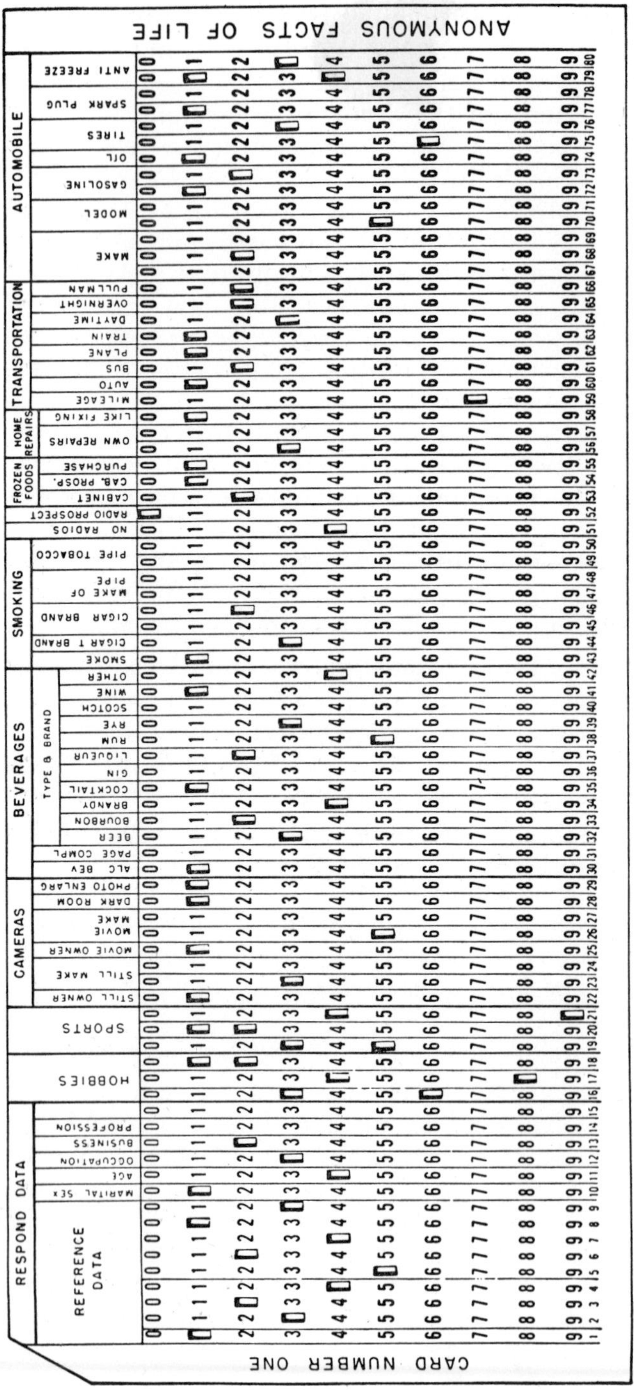

FIGURE 24. Machine Tabulation Card. Columns 1 through 14 are for the punching of classification data, the balance for sought data. The rectangles represent holes punched in the card, which are counted by a card sorter. The punching of item 1 in Column 43 indicates that the respondent is a smoker. The punching of item 3 in Column 44 indicates that he smokes the brand of cigarettes which has been given the code number 44–3.

Speed. For work which involves a large number of items, counting can be done more rapidly by machine than by hand. However, in machine tabulation three specific operations must be employed: coding the schedules, punching the cards, and running the cards through tabulating machines. While the final counting may be done at the rate of several hundred cards a minute, the two preliminary steps may require considerable time. Except in rather large or complex jobs, therefore, the use of machine tabulation may not save time. In small or relatively simple operations it may be slower than hand tabulation.

Cross-Classification. Machine tabulation probably has its greatest advantage over hand tabulation in cases where a number of cross-classifications are desired. If the facts obtained in a research are to be broken down on several different bases, such as age, sex, time periods, and brands used, these various cross-classifications can be very quickly and economically established. In hand tabulation, the data must be recounted over and over again if a large number of such cross-tabulations is desired. Many people make the mistake of thinking of the advantages of machine tabulation largely in terms of cost, speed, and accuracy, whereas its most fundamental advantage is the ability to obtain an endless degree of cross-classification and tabulations.

Accuracy in Counting. In the mechanical phases of punching and running the cards through the tabulating machine, machine tabulation is more accurate than hand tabulation. The accuracy of the card-punching operation may be established by having the cards run through a verifier, so that errors in punching will be caught. The coding work which is necessary for machine tabulation, however, is not a mechanical process and is fully as subject to error as any phase of hand tabulation. If the hand tabulating is carried on with the type of checks and controls recommended in this chapter, the possibility of error should be no greater than in the machine tabulations.

Ease of Retabulation. Another advantage of machine tabulation, frequently overlooked, is the speed and low cost at which it is possible to obtain special tabulations after the original tabulation has been completed. Frequently one will find that a certain type of fact overlooked in the original tabulation is desired in the process of interpretation, or when writing the report, or even after the report has been presented. For example, one might discover at a very late stage of the research that a special breakdown of magazine readership by users of certain brands and by income groups is desirable. If hand tabulation has been used, this requirement would necessitate locating the original schedules and setting up entirely new tabulation operations. If machine tabulation has been used, it would merely be necessary to run the cards through sorting machines, a process which could be completed in a few hours.

Disadvantages of Machine Tabulation. While machine tabulation is frequently more desirable than hand tabulation, one should keep clearly in mind the disadvantages of using the machine methods while determining which process to employ.

High Cost in Small Operations. If a comparatively small number of questionnaires or schedules is involved in the study, or if the quantity of information or number of questions on each schedule is small, machine tabulation is more expensive than hand tabulation. There is no economy in machine methods unless a large number of operations is involved.

Confusing the Analysis. This disadvantage of machine tabulation is met under those conditions most favorable to it, namely, where many questions are asked in an individual survey or many cross-classifications are desired. Unfortunately the danger of confusion is not too generally recognized. In view of the flexibility of machine tabulation, it is common practice to set up as many different cross-classifications as possible. The result is that one may be faced with a large number of sheets showing thousands of different facts. In attempting to carry on the study from this point, the researcher is likely to have his thinking confused by the sheer complexity of his facts. There is, of course, no reason why he should not be able to separate the wheat from the chaff. As a matter of practical fact, however, the writer has seen a number of cases in which researchers have lost significant findings of a study because they became entangled in the large quantity of details obtained by the use of machine methods.

When to Use Machine Tabulation. From the discussion of the comparative advantages and disadvantages of machine tabulation above, one can readily determine the conditions under which machine tabulation is justified. Machine methods should be used when a large quantity of data is involved. For questionnaire studies, a rule commonly followed is that machine tabulation is justified if there are approximately 1,000 average-length questionnaires. It is important to note that the complexity of the questionnaire is the chief guiding factor. If only a few pieces of information are obtained on each individual report, there is little advantage in machine tabulation, regardless of the number of reports. On the other hand, machine tabulation may well be indicated for only 200 to 300 schedules if extensive cross-tabulation is indicated.

Wherever information is obtained currently in connection with the general routine of business, or a certain type of study is repeated at regular intervals, machine tabulation is obviously indicated. A mail-order company, for example, may select a group of 50,000 customers and tabulate the facts regarding their orders from day to day as the mail is received. In such a case machine tabulation is obviously the better form. If a company wishes to make a regular analysis of its sales, machine tabulation should also be used. A manufacturer, for example, can usually well afford to employ machine tabulation equipment for the purpose of recording the various facts about orders received. Some retailers have also found that analyses of individual sales slips, which would require the use of machine methods in any but the smallest stores, are desirable.

The mechanics of machine tabulation is not discussed in detail at this point for several reasons. It is a highly technical procedure and requires specially trained personnel for its most effective use. The development of the specific method which should be employed in handling any given market research study by machine tabulation is a special task. Those companies which lease the machines or do machine tabulation on a fee basis have specially trained servicemen to lay out each individual job. If machine tabulation is contemplated, these specialists should be consulted in planning the analysis, as considerable time and expense may be saved by precoding the forms to be used in gathering data and planning the tabulation at an early stage of the project.

Drawing Statistical Conclusions

The distinction between the process of tabulation and that of drawing statistical conclusions was made earlier in this chapter. It was shown at that point that, while in practice the two processes are interwoven, it is essential to keep clearly in mind the special problem of the final statistical conclusions. This caution is necessary to insure that the statistical generalizations will be cast in the most enlightening and useful form.

While there are many possible ways in which statistical generalizations could be drawn from any given body of raw data, the researcher is limited by cost and time considerations to relatively few of them. Furthermore, there is almost always a great difference in their value for any given marketing research. If he allows himself or his organization to get into the statistical rut of automatically applying certain forms of generalization, he is blind to many opportunities to improve the quality and value of his research by employing those forms of generalization which are most appropriate and will contribute most to the analysis.

The drawing of statistical conclusions should never be regarded as an automatic result of the tabulation process. The researcher is faced with a variety of options providing many opportunities for skillful creative judgment. If he is unimaginative he can draw his statistical conclusions by merely summarizing the data in neat tables. He may go a step further and show simple relationships by the use of percentages. He may conclude that the data can best be summarized by using arithmetic means (the common average). He may employ weighted means. Instead of arithmetic means he may use medians, modes, or harmonic means.

Possibly the data will be most revealing if cast in frequency distributions. Cross-tabulations, relating two or more elements such as consumption to family size, may be most enlightening. More abstruse statistical devices, such as coefficients of correlation or measurements of deviation or dispersion may be employed. At times analytical charts, such as scatter diagrams, are the best form of generalization.

It is important to bear in mind that, no matter how carefully the tabulations have been planned, the most significant facts and relationships are not usually evident after the first routine tabulations have been made. The summary tables should be carefully examined with the thought of discovering new types of generalizations which may be more revealing. In studying a table showing the brands of a product used by different income groups, for example, it may occur to the analyst for the first time that a special tabulation should be made to break down the data on the basis of the length of time the product has been used. An examination of the results of taking arithmetic means may reveal the necessity of employing other averages, such as the median, or perhaps the need of working with frequency distributions. Sometimes it will be found necessary to run a special tabulation to obtain the best form of statistical conclusion. Sometimes it is not necessary to retabulate, because the problem is merely one of drawing a different form of conclusion from the original tabulations.

The decision as to the statistical conclusions which should be drawn from a given set of data must be based upon a thorough understanding of statistical method. The meaning, characteristics, and limitations of all forms of statistical summarization and generalization, such as the median and frequency distribution, must be kept clearly in mind during this process.

There are no peculiar conditions in marketing research which call for special techniques in drawing statistical conclusions, nor is there any place for unsound statistical jugglery or manipulation. There are, however, two considerations, frequently overlooked, which the analyst should bear in mind when drawing his conclusions. The first of these is the importance of establishing relationships. The second is the danger of overgeneralization.

Importance of Establishing Relationships. Relationship is the fundamental of all science. Absolute facts, by themselves, are likely to be meaningless. The fact that a given share of the market buys a particular brand of a product, by itself, has little or no significance. It is important only when related to other facts, such as its share during preceding periods of time, in different geographic areas, or by economic groups. The share of market for one brand also becomes more meaningful when related to shares of competing products and to the marketing activities of manufacturers, wholesalers, or retailers. The value of a statistical conclusion is in large part determined by the extent to which it establishes significant relationships. In drawing statistical conclusions, therefore, attention must be focused on the possibility of establishing all important relationships within the data. In the final stages of tabulation and analysis, the researcher constantly re-examines his data for new relationships.

Dangers of Overgeneralization. A fundamental purpose of statistical analysis is to make generalizations. We begin with a vast mass of data. Perhaps we have the results of 10,000 interviews, which as a group reflect the characteristics of our total population. By employing this sample, we have in effect reduced our number of cases to a point where we have a manageable group. Yet we must go much further. The limits of the human mind are such that we cannot merely read and reread these individual schedules. We must find some means of further reducing our data to arrive at some generalizations which can be applied in our marketing policy.

By properly classifying data we are further generalizing, for it is now possible to select certain phenomena for consideration. The frequency distribution, by which we lump together all cases falling within certain established class limits, is another step in generalization. By use of the various means we reach an ultimate reduction to one single concept. Thus there is no limit to the extent to which we may generalize statistically. Our raw data may begin with 160,000,000 cases (for the United States alone). By the use of simple averages we reduce the facts regarding these 160,000,000 cases down to one, as, for example, if we were to say the average age of persons in the United States is 30 years.

The process may be carried further. By the measurements of deviation (average or standard deviation) and by the measurements of error (standard error or probable error), we have produced further generalizations. A correlation coefficient is an average—a generalization. We may even measure, and sometimes do measure, the probable error of a coefficient of correlation.

Thus we see that fundamentally we are engaged in a process of successive generalization, illustrated as follows:

```
                         1. Total poulation .......... (160,000,000)
(reduced to)............. 2. Sample ................. (10,000)
(further reduced to)...... 3. Classification ............. (5,100 male; 4,900 female)
(further reduced to)...... 4. Frequency distribution ..... (0–4.99 years...1,112)
                                                          (5–9.99 years... 978 etc.)
(further reduced to)...... 5. An average .............. (Median age, 30.2 years)
```

By thus making generalizations possible, statistical method is of inestimable help in marketing research. But the very process is fraught with danger. We constantly forget that our various forms of averages are really substitutes. That fact must constantly be kept in mind.

Since these generalizations or averages are substitutes for the total population, the prime test in applying them statistically is the accuracy with which they reflect the characteristics of the original population. Every abstraction loses detail while it gains in clarity. It is important to make sure that you have lost nothing vital.

The danger of losing vital facts in the process of generalization is illustrated by the discovery that some single incident or case is much more important than statistical generalizations. To illustrate—some time ago a group of women was interviewed to determine resistances to the buying of shoes. Only one woman of several thousand mentioned that when she went in to buy shoes, she first had to take off her shoe, which was embarrassing and placed her at the mercy of the clerk. The unskilled researcher would have overlooked this fact, for the preponderance of evidence made this objection unimportant. Yet a further investigation adopted this as its hypothesis and used techniques which made it possible to obtain a real appraisal of this resistance. The second study showed that this was the most important single resistance to be overcome.

The danger of carrying statistical analysis too far is further illustrated by the following data taken from a cost accounting study of selling expenses for a rubber manufacturer.

The contrast between the results of the analysis if one were to consider only the average expense for each group of accounts, and the results obtained if one were also to consider the expense range, clearly indicates the danger of the use of ordinary "averages" without other forms of statistical description. It will be noticed, for example, that there are individual accounts in every class above $2,000 which are as costly to sell as some accounts which are found in the $500 and $1,000 class.

TABLE 15

COST OF SELLING TO ACCOUNTS OF VARYING SIZE

(Expense expressed as percentage of sales)

Size of Account	Average Expense	Expense Range *
$ 100..........	24.0	15.0 to 33.0
500..........	15.0	10.0 to 20.0
1,000..........	13.5	11.0 to 16.0
2,000..........	10.0	7.0 to 13.0
3,000..........	11.5	6.0 to 17.0
5,000..........	8.9	5.4 to 12.5
15,000..........	9.0	7.0 to 11.0

* Exceptionally high and low extremes were omitted to obtain a constant expense range.

If one were to think solely in terms of the average cost of selling different groups of accounts, he would conclude that there was a complete correlation between the size of account and the expense of handling it; that is, as the size of the account increases, the cost of selling the account declines. Consideration of the expense range column, however, indicates that each account is individual and that the factors which determine the cost of selling vary considerably between accounts of about the same size. If one's thinking were limited to the showing of average sales, he might rush into a very radical recommendation of marketing policy, such as the complete elimination of accounts of a minimum size or an arbitrary set of discounts completely out of line with the requirements of true selling costs.

In general it is probably safe to say that the present tendency among most researchers is to push the process of abstraction entirely too far. By habit, often from our early arithmetic, we constantly look for means. These means are usually the least important product of our investigations. Of what significance is information such as the *average* size of stores, the *average* age of automobile buyers? The increased use of frequency distributions which tell us the characteristics of various classes is to be greatly encouraged.

In a study made at automobile shows some years ago it was found that by far the largest number of votes was cast for the then revolutionary Chrysler. But to conclude that the public preferred this style was erroneous, for a checkup on votes for the least attractive car showed that the Chrysler was also given a preponderance of negative votes. When these negative votes were deducted from the positive, it was found that the Chrysler had very poor acceptance. Packard, on the other hand, did not have nearly as many votes as the best-looking car; inasmuch as very few mentioned it unfavorably, it was concluded that this car had a much better general acceptance than the Chrysler.

The important fact, in the last analysis, is not an average vote of popularity. What is needed are the statistical conclusions represented by frequency distributions which show the relative numbers voting each way on all makes. Thus, while Chevrolet may average high, medium, or low; from the point of view of marketing policy, we are chiefly concerned with obtaining an accurate picture of the number of people who rated it high, medium, or low. This form of statistical generalization points directly to the nature of the acceptance of the public.

Thus we have gained the benefits of statistics—we have abstracted a picture of attitudes toward the styles of current models from the vast mass of millions of car owners. At the same time, we have been careful to avoid losing the really vital characteristics of those attitudes. That represents sound development of statistical conclusions.

SELECTED READINGS

BOYAJY, JOSEPH S., et al. "Tabulation Planning and Tabulation Techniques," *Journal of Marketing*, January, 1949, pp. 330–55.

DEMING, W. E. *Some Theory of Sampling.* New York: John Wiley & Sons, 1950, Chap. 10, Estimation of the Precision of a Sample, pp. 329–55.

DURBIN, J., and STUART, A. "An Experimental Comparison Between Coders," *Journal of Marketing*, July, 1954, pp. 54–66.

GREENBERG, ALLAN. "A Method of Coding Questionnaires in Market Surveys," *Journal of Marketing*, October, 1949, pp. 456–58.

HOBART, DONALD M. *Marketing Research Practice.* New York: The Ronald Press Co., 1950, pp. 105–19.

JAHODA, MARIE, DEUTSCH, MORTON, and COOK, STUART W. *Researching Methods in Social Relations.* 2 vols. New York: The Dryden Press, Inc., 1951, pp. 259–69.

KROEGER, ARTHUR. "A Device for Simplifying Tabulation," *Journal of Marketing*, January, 1954, pp. 285–87.

LUCK, DAVID J., and WALES, HUGH G. *Marketing Research.* New York: Prentice-Hall, Inc., 1952, pp. 301–22.

PARTEN, MILDRED. *Surveys, Polls and Samples.* New York: Harper & Bros., 1950, pp. 425–43.

VOIGHT, ROBERT B., and KRIESBERG, MARTIN. "Some Principles of Processing Census and Survey Data," *Journal of the American Statistical Association*, June, 1952, pp. 222–31.

ZEISEL, HANS. *Say It with Figures.* New York: Harper & Bros., 1950.

CASE

BLANKERTZ, DONALD F., FERBER, ROBERT, and WALES, HUGH G. *Cases and Problems in Marketing Research.* New York: The Ronald Press Co., 1954, pp. 208–11, 223–31.

16

INTERPRETATION

After drawing conclusions of a purely statistical and objective nature, the researcher must interpret these conclusions into specific marketing recommendations before making any effort to produce a formal report. Statistical conclusions and evidence from surveys, observations, and experiments, per se, prove nothing. They are merely evidence. Having marshalled his evidence, the researcher still faces the problem of using these results logically so that he may determine the best policy for his company.

Interpreting Research Findings into Business Policy

One of the chief issues in the problem of interpretation is determining how far the researcher should go in attempting to put his findings into practical use. There are four common attitudes on this problem, each representing varying degrees of interpretation. The first attitude is represented by those who contend that the job of the researcher is finished when he has marshalled his facts in presentable form. These people believe that the researcher, being of a scientific turn of mind, should concentrate on the development of correct conclusions, such as those statistical assemblages of facts discussed in the preceding chapter, and give no thought to the interpretation of these conclusions into business practice. They argue that the best scientist is an impractical type of person, and that he can do his work best if he is completely relieved of any necessity for moulding his results into policy.

A second group believes the person in charge of the work should go further than a mere statement of factual findings but that he should give his facts only general interpretation. For example, this group would have the researcher draw such general conclusions as "The sales managers should check carefully on the number of calls and number of displays set up. . . ." This procedure is considered going slightly beyond the mere assemblage of the data but does not look to specific statements of recommended policies or practices. Those who hold to this view recognize that the person who has been intimately associated with the study is in the best position to draw general conclusions in relation to the company's problems.

A third group would have the researcher go much further. They would have him, for example, work out a specific marketing plan or program based on his findings. In this case the conclusions are transferred into specific recommended actions, and all the firm has to do is to implement the proposals which are contained in the report.

There is a fourth group which would go even further. They contend that research work is not done until the analyst has supervised the working out of his recommendations in actual operation. They would have him cooperate with the sales department, travel about from branch to branch, set up his system, and see that it works. This group contends that there are two important reasons for this policy. First, there is a common tendency among business executives to receive a report and do little or nothing with it. Marketing research studies often cut across departmental lines, and each executive is therefore inclined to wait on others for action. Also, there are always some individuals in an organization who will believe that an obstructionist policy on their part will further their own individual interests. Second, it is contended that the researcher, in making his study, has gained a great amount of valuable experience which will be of use in making sure that the proposed changes are carried out successfully.

It has now become a generally accepted principle in marketing research practice that it is desirable for the researcher to make interpretations and recommendations unless he is specifically instructed to the contrary. There are, of course, a number of research jobs of a purely fact-finding and mechanical nature, such as continuous store audits. In these cases, the research function for the particular organization charged with gathering the data ceases once the facts are properly presented. However, in a complete marketing research study, which begins by setting forth a specific problem and then proceeds through to its solution, it is highly desirable for the researcher to extend his activities through the interpretation and recommendation stages.

That such activity is now considered a legitimate province of research is shown by the following statement by a committee of the American Marketing Association:

This commitee believes that the recommendation function, far from being inherently inimical to the research function, is a logical component of it, and that the arguments against its inclusion are in reality indications that there may be some instances in which recommendations may not be appropriate to the assignment or to the capacity of a particular research person. . . . It seems clear that the researcher, as such, does not make policy decisions of management based on his recommendations, nor can he assume responsibility for execution of policy. If he shares in these activities as a participant in top management, he does so not as a researcher but as a well-informed executive.

It is assumed that in cases where the client requests the research organization to make recommendations, these recommendations are accepted as research counsel. The researcher thus takes the responsibility of giving good counsel but management takes the responsibility of deciding whether or not to act on the counsel.[1]

The Problem of Interpretation. The function of the interpretive stage in marketing and distribution research is to interpret the factual conclusions developed in tabulation and analysis into a set of specific recommendations regarding the marketing practices of the company. The two fundamental requisites for the proper development of these interpretations are:

1. Using sound reasoning from facts to recommendations. (Making logical interpretations.)
2. Constructing the recommendations so that they will be adopted. (Making practical interpretations.)

The first problem in interpretation is to reason logically from the facts found in the analysis to a set of recommendations. This procedure is seen to be merely a matter of straight thinking.

The establishment of the statistical conclusions in the tabulation and analysis represents the end of inductive work. But no company can make a profit from the statistical conclusions of facts found in the research, per se. The gain arises only when the facts have been logically interpreted into marketing techniques and policies which will in turn contribute to increased profit. Thus the inductive facts must be converted into specific recommendations by deductive logic before their value can be realized.

The second basic problem in interpretation—developing the recommendations in such form that they will be carried into actual practice—requires keen appreciation of many practical considerations. While it is generally conceded that faulty presentation is one of the chief reasons why some research work is disregarded by executives, the lack of a clear-cut policy statement which fits the specific requirements of the business is likely to be equally important.

[1] Committee of the American Marketing Association, "Preparation and Presentation of the Research Report," *Journal of Marketing*, July, 1948, pp. 64–65.

Making Logical Interpretations

It is beyond the scope of this book to discuss the many ramifications of the problem of straight thinking or logic. The ability to keep within the bounds of sound logic is something which is acquired from experience as well as training and becomes an integral characteristic of an individual rather than a matter of hard-and-fast rules.

There are many handicaps to straight thinking which should, of course, be avoided by the researcher. One of the most important is the desire to be spectacular. The tendency to overemphasize the revolutionary nature of their findings and recommendations is especially common among less experienced analysts and those who find it necessary to impress clients or individuals with the value of their work. Marketing and distribution research can never be a panacea for all business ills, nor is it the most important single aspect of the complex and many-sided operations of a business. In the desire to impress others with the importance of his work it is not uncommon for a researcher to read into the statistical findings entirely unwarranted interpretations.

A second prevalent handicap to straight thinking is the fear of being forced to admit that one does not have a complete solution to a problem. Unfortunately, the researcher is too frequently confronted with a demand by businessmen for absolute finality and certainty. As a matter of fact, this desire for a complete solution to a problem is most unfortunate because experience shows that there is no absolute and complete solution to most business problems.

In order to avoid raising doubt in the minds of others as to the adequacy or accuracy of the analysis, the marketing researcher is usually forced to cast his recommendations in very positive form. He should not, however, allow this circumstance to cause him to make unwarranted interpretations. People are afraid to admit that they "don't know." This fear becomes an underlying reason for a great amount of loose and illogical thinking in an attempt to convert the facts found in a marketing and distribution research into a recommendation for a business policy.

A third logical fallacy frequently met is the tendency to believe that if one is unable to prove a given proposition, the opposite must be true. If one attempts to determine whether a company should open a sales branch in a certain city and cannot prove that the branch should be opened by his marketing facts, he may assume that the data prove that the company should not embark on the proposed course of action. Likewise, if one is unable to prove that a certain advertising medium should be used, he may assume that his evidence shows that it should not be used. One might also study a proposed marketing campaign and be unable to show clear-cut benefits which have accrued from a small test. He is likely to conclude that the proposed campaign would not be successful.

The results of many marketing operations are so intangible that it is impossible to obtain final and complete evidence which establishes their exact value beyond the shadow of a doubt. The research man must not allow himself to overlook the many unmeasurable factors present in any given situation. A list of the probable benefits to be derived from a national advertising campaign by a mail-order house showed that it would be possible to obtain a statistical measurement of only two out of twelve objectives set up for the advertising. These objectives were the value of mail orders received and the number of new customers gained. Since two of them were subject to dollars-and-cents appraisal, the company attempted to judge the value of the campaign solely on the basis of the two measurable factors. The test was doomed to failure because ten of the twelve benefits could not be directly measured. It was unsound logic to assume that failure to establish the success of the campaign on two grounds proved that it was not successful.

Standards for Interpretation. Since interpretation is primarily a problem of straight thinking, it is impossible to develop a mechanical formula by which any given type of statistical conclusion can be interpreted into a specific recommendation. The researcher can, however, test a proposed interpretation, once it has been made, to determine to a certain extent whether the facts warrant the proposed recommendation. It is suggested that the following criteria be used as a basis for testing the logical foundation of any interpretation.

1. *Is the relationship between the facts and the recommendation real or imaginary?* The most important danger to be guarded against in this connection is the fallacy of apparent similarities. Because the data gathered in the study have the same word description as the problem with which the analyst is wrestling, it must not be assumed that they present a satisfactory basis for direct interpretation.

For example, one may have obtained from a large number of consumers statements as to whether they received a premium in connection with the purchase of a certain product. It was once found in a survey that 20 per cent of the buyers of a certain product stated that they had obtained a premium in connection with its purchase. It does not follow that one can jump to a recommendation regarding the use of premiums on the basis of such facts. In the first place, the analyst has only the statements of consumers, which may or may not be accurate and are, therefore, an inadequate factual basis for his interpretation. In the second place, the mere fact that 20 per cent of the purchases involved the obtaining of a premium may or may not represent a sufficient basis on which to make a policy recommendation concerning the use of premiums because we have no standard against which to measure its significance.

Above all, one must be careful to avoid the fallacious assumption that merely because the facts gathered in the analysis deal with "premiums" they necessarily warrant his making direct recommendations regarding the "premium" policy of the company.

The whole process of research is essentially a "thinking" process. Everything that is done as the research project unfolds must be controlled by clear-headed and tough-minded thinking on the part of the researcher. In the interpretation stage, he must, in effect, review this entire thinking process to make sure that unwarranted assumptions do not destroy the basic chain of the logic of the research.

This problem is particularly acute in a science like marketing research which deals with human matters. Its importance is emphasized by the fact that the problem is acute in the physical sciences which are able to rely upon controlled experimentation:

A whole chain of reasoning connects a conceptual scheme with the experimental test. More than one false step has resulted at this point; hidden assumptions as prickly as thorns abound; these may puncture a line of reasoning. What was observed in an experiment may not be actually related to the conceptual scheme in the way the experimenter had believed.[2]

2. *Is the interpretation supported at several points by the evidence?* If the recommendation of a certain marketing policy is based upon only one piece of evidence discovered in the research, it is much less likely to be logically sound than if evidence from several different parts of the analysis points unmistakably in one direction. If, for example, facts obtained from consumers, dealers, technicians, secondary sources, technical experiments, and cost accounting analyses *all* point toward the advisability of adding a lower-priced item to the cultivator line of a farm implement manufacturer, the analyst may confidently make such a recommendation. If his evidence is restricted to one source, however, he is in a less fortunate position.

In making a crucial interpretation, it is always advisable to check the evidence carefully to see if the general conclusion on which a given interpretation is to be based is true in different localities, for different types of dealers, or for different periods of time. The more uniform the evidence and the more points from which it converges in the

[2] James B. Conant, *Science and Common Sense* (New Haven: Yale University Press, 1951), p. 74.

direction of one recommendation, the more confident the researcher can be in making such a recommendation.

In connection with this general principle, that the interpretation should be confirmed at as many points as possible, it is well to remember that one can seldom base a safe interpretation upon only one type of evidence. For example, suppose one were making an analysis of the productivity of salesmen of different ages. If it were found that the annual sales per salesman consistently declined after the age of forty, this would be an important bit of evidence but not in itself sufficient for proper interpretation into a specific recommendation. Questions might arise, such as: "Should salesmen over forty years of age be discharged?" "Should they be reassigned?" "Should they be pensioned?" "Should their pay be decreased?" One cannot logically determine, solely on the basis of the evidence cited, which of these courses is the correct one. Other facts must be made available. It might be determined that none of the recommendations mentioned is the proper one. Other facts, when combined with the data on productivity by age groups, might show that the real cause of the difficulty is the lack of adequate sales training and supervision for those in the higher age groups.

One of the most important ideas for a marketing researcher to bear in mind in interpreting his work is the fallacy of straight-line thinking. One is likely to acquire the habit of attempting to solve problems in a "straight line." Such expressions as "building a chain of evidence," "thinking straight," and "arriving at a direct solution" indicate the prevalence of the straight-line idea.

One source of confusion is the traditional method in which logic is taught. The subject of logic is usually introduced in terms of the syllogism and fallacious forms of syllogistic thought. The author has no quarrel with syllogistic logic, but he has observed that it implants the notion that logical thought is a process by which one reasons from a major premise through a minor premise to a conclusion, with the implication that by a series of individual steps one progressively arrives at a conclusion.

The idea of straight-line thinking is also implanted in the more elementary courses in mathematics. A mathematical equation, which is nothing more than a special form of symbolic logic, implies that solutions are obtained by a series of straight-line steps. As a result, many people acquire the habit of thinking in oversimplified straight-line relationships.

Another notion which contributes to this misunderstanding is the old idea of cause and effect. Unfortunately, most people look for some one cause which has produced a given effect, in spite of the fact that scientific thought has demonstrated for some time that the old notions of causal relationship are unsound. For example, some physicians, in making a medical diagnosis, seek to find one direct cause rather than considering the problem as a whole.

So far as marketing is concerned, there is no simple parallelism such as that found in logic, in mathematics, and in isolated cases of cause and effect. Any given condition has many causes. Many paths must be followed in the solution of a marketing problem. Nor can the marketing researcher hide behind the theoretical dodge "other things being equal," because in marketing *other things are never equal*. A marketing problem represents the sum total of many influences. Its solution must, therefore, be many-sided.

The tendency to straight-line thinking causes many people entirely to overlook multiple relationships. The chief contribution of multiple correlation in the field of marketing is not merely that it may provide a more scientific solution to a problem. A major contribution may be said to be that it inculcates an appreciation of the fact that marketing conditions represent multiple relationships which must be investigated both separately and jointly. The researcher should abandon the idea of reasoning in a straight line from one set of facts about a market to a logical conclusion. He should develop the habit of bringing all possible knowledge about the problem to bear in its general solution. One is usually helpless with a limited number of inductive facts. Only by bringing together all the available evidence bearing upon a proposed interpretation can one feel on safe logical ground. For this reason, the researcher is particularly careful to see that a proposed interpretation is supported at many different points by the evidence.

In judging a proposed interpretation, it is good practice to cast about for confirmation from sources outside the specific study. It will usually be found that some phases of the evidence obtained parallel information already available from other sources. An interpretation of information obtained from retailers, for example, might lead to the conclusion that the margins offered on a given product should be increased. It is helpful to determine what evidence available from external sources tends to confirm this need. If it is found that the data on gross margins by various types of retail organizations reported by the Harvard University Bureau of Business Research show that the present margins offered by the manufacturer are out of line with the general standards, the interpretation is given further support.

3. *Are any crucial exceptions to the proposed interpretation found in the evidence?* When one has hit upon a suggested recommenda-

tion, he does not usually find that all the evidence bearing upon it points clearly in one direction. In a study for a washing machine, it may be found that the vast majority of consumers prefer a machine which washes clothes as rapidly as possible. This fact, confirmed by other evidence, may point directly to the recommendation that a machine which will wash clothes at a rapid rate of speed should be produced. However, a close examination of the evidence may show that an important group of consumers regard speed as an undesirable factor.

In such a case the researcher is presented with the problem of determining whether the exceptional cases destroy his proposed interpretation, or merely modify it. In the case of the washing-machine analysis, the exception cited points to the need for modification of the recommendation by requiring the production of a second type to meet the demands of the minority of the market.

A case of finding one sort of evidence which completely negatived a proposed interpretation is afforded in a study for a breakfast cereal. From many sources it was determined that a certain cereal should be packaged in a box larger than the one previously used. The company apparently was faced with an opportunity to make a master strategic move which would give it a great competitive advantage. Fortunately, it was found that the majority of consumers' cupboards were so constructed that they could not accommodate the proposed package. This finding represented a crucial exception which completely negatived all the other evidence pointing toward the desirability of the proposed change in the size of the cereal package.

4. *Does the evidence satisfy the requirements of the hypotheses?* When one is making interpretations of statistical conclusions, it is wise to go back to the original hypotheses set up in planning the research to make sure that the data obtained provide a sound basis for testing them. As the study progresses and one becomes immersed in the details of gathering and analyzing data, it is easy to forget that the evidence obtained may not prove to be adequate.

As a matter of fact, one must bear in mind that many hypotheses are untenable. One may attempt to determine whether a certain radio program should be abandoned and obtain all the evidence available. This evidence, however, may not be sufficient to make such a decision. In such a case the researcher is tempted to bolster it by positive statement and dramatic presentation, an unscientific procedure to be avoided.

One must also recognize that it is quite possible that the facts obtained have led to important conclusions on points which were unanticipated at the time the study was planned. If the data point clearly to a recommendation not anticipated by any of the hypotheses, the recommendation should, of course, be made.

5. *Do the data point to the opposite recommendation?* A very important step in proper interpretation is testing the validity of the opposite conclusion to the one being recommended. Thus, if the researcher's conclusion is that "the X company should abandon radio advertising," he would do well to state his conclusion: "The X company should *not* abandon radio advertising." Then he should go back and check the evidence to make sure that it does not point just as logically to the second conclusion as it does to the first. This apparently naïve process will often show that a false interpretation has been read into data, possibly influenced by personal interests and prejudices.

The problem of making sound logical interpretations calls for the deepest kind of sound thinking. While no certain means for arriving at the proper recommendations from a given set of data may be provided, the five tests discussed above will frequently make it possible to avoid violating the requirements of sound logic.

Making Practical Interpretations

It is not enough to be a sound logician to interpret the findings of a marketing and distribution research into recommendations. There are many practical considerations which the analyst must recognize in order to be sure that his recommendations will be carried out into the operations of the business. A purely theoretical interpretation usually must be greatly modified by these practical considerations. The discussion which follows presents considerations which will go far toward insuring practical interpretation.

1. *The condition of the company and the market should be taken into account.* A purely logical interpretation of the findings of a marketing research in any given field usually will point to a recommendation which could be followed theoretically by all companies in the industry. It is obvious, however, that what might be a good policy for one company might be a very bad one for another. The facts obtained in the situation analysis should be recalled at this point to make sure that the recommendation is modified as required by the situation of the company for which the study is being made. While a research may show the need for developing an additional specialty sales force, it is obvious that a flat recommendation for such a change should not be made if the company does not have sufficient funds.

At the time the research is made the company is geared for a certain type of marketing operation. This operation involves tradition, personnel, finances, dealer structures, production policies, and many other established factors. Each recommendation must be properly qualified in the light of all characteristics of the company's operation.

In some fields, custom or agreement within the industry affects the marketing operations of individual members. This practice is becoming more, rather than less, common and should be watched carefully by the marketing researcher. He may discover a rather obvious opportunity for the aggressive marketing of a certain product only to find that an industry practice on raw materials makes it impossible to carry the recommendation into practice.

It is especially important to check a proposed recommendation to make sure that it is acceptable to dealers. The researcher must be careful not to recommend a marketing policy which will encounter the opposition of a sufficient number of dealers to offset its value.

The condition of the market at the time the recommendation is made must also be taken into account. If the industry is depressed, the time may not be ripe for a proposed policy. It is even possible that business conditions have changed since the research was undertaken so that a proposed change cannot immediately be put into effect.

In connection with this first principle of keeping the condition of the company and the market in mind, the researcher should remember that most important changes are usually costly. Furthermore, during the period in which the new policy is first instituted, the gains from following it are not rapidly obtained. For these reasons, the analyst should be careful to estimate the costs of following a proposed recommendation before it is submitted.

2. *The probable opposition of executives should be analyzed.* Most marketing research recommendations involve a change in marketing policy. Any proposed change is likely to be interpreted by some executives as a reflection on the efficiency with which they have been performing their functions. One should not submit a plan without first determining the opposition likely to be encountered and then taking the necessary steps to overcome this opposition. Executives who believe that a recommendation affecting marketing operations under their direction is a reflection on their efficiency will usually make a personal issue of the recommendation, and sidetrack it by any means at their command.

It is, of course, impossible to avoid all opposition. On the other hand, one should not omit a sound recommendation merely because it is likely to encounter resistance. It is simply good strategy to determine the probable resistances to a proposal in advance and erect fences before recommendations are made.

3. *Company officials should be given an active part in the interpretation.* The most obvious way to overcome successfully resistance to a proposed policy is to enlist the aid of those who are likely to oppose it while it is being developed. Many researchers make it a policy to show individual findings from the field work to executives as they are received and to suggest interpretations which the latter may well come to regard as their own.

Giving officials an active part in interpretation has additional practical value. Their experience is an important factor in developing recommendations which will result in successful marketing practices and policies.

The answer to the question as to how far the researcher should go in interpretation lies largely in this principle. If executives are brought into the interpretation, there will be no danger of impracticable recommendations. Furthermore, there should be no criticism of the researcher for taking an active part in carrying the results of the analysis to fruition.

One of the problems of the outsider, such as an independent marketing consultant, is the difficulty of obtaining the cooperation of company officials in making interpretations. Usually, where an outside organization is employed, it is expected that it will prepare a final report independently. It is for this reason that many such firms do not attempt to carry their work beyond the stage of supplying marketing data, allowing the company to make its own interpretations and application.

4. *The required course of action should be clearly stated.* Many research projects fail to be as effective as they should be because the recommendations are stated so vaguely that the executives of the company do not know what specific marketing operations to follow. If any research is worth its cost, it should point directly to a course of action. Unless this is stated in such form that the executives understand it clearly, the benefits of the study are likely to be lost in a maze of general discussions.

It is not sufficient to submit a well-written statement of a general plan of action. One should develop workable methods for putting it into effect.

One should remember that businessmen tend to think in terms of concrete instances and specific cases. They distrust abstractions and generalizations. Recommendations stated in general terms lead to involved discussions of reasons why they are or are not true. A specific course of action, such as a proposal to set up a test grocery-store demonstration program, suggests immediate action.

5. *A series of progressive changes should be recommended.* Sometimes the final result of research leads to a recommendation which is carried out at a single stroke, such as the dismissal of a sales manager or the addition of a new type of product. Usually, however, it is possible to state the recommendations in such form that the ultimate goal is reached by a series of progressive steps.

One of the most dangerous practices in marketing and distribution research is to recommend sweeping, violent changes. Some executives are greatly impressed by such recommendations, and no one can deny that they have dramatic power. Sometimes the company is in such poor condition that violent change may be needed. Such a case, however, should be treated as exceptional.

A proposal which recommends a comparatively simple step at the outset, without losing sight of the ultimate goal, is relatively easy to put into effect. Disturbance and confusion will be avoided. The recommendation will have a fair opportunity to demonstrate its merit without being counterbalanced by such handicaps as inexperienced personnel and inadequate routines. The most successful businesses do not usually have violent fluctuations in policy. Rather, they slowly adapt themselves to changing marketing conditions.

An advantage of recommending a series of progressive changes is that it tends to minimize the danger of having the results of the research handicapped by the overenthusiastic executive. The researcher must constantly be on his guard against officials who become excited over his findings and rush into a radical change in marketing policy. This danger is illustrated by the large number of companies who have suddenly decided to eliminate wholesalers from their distributing organizations. Many of them have been forced to take the hard and slow path back to their former channels after a hasty decision to eliminate this middleman. The wise companies were those who gradually set up direct-to-retailer selling operations only as they clearly proved to be more efficient.

The final recommendation of many research studies is a specific plan for testing out a proposed course of action in the market place. Where the research is based upon survey or observational data, a good deal of rather broad interpretation is usually necessary before the results can be translated into recommendations. In such cases, if it is at all possible, the first step should be a test of the proposed course of action on a reasonably large scale. Even where the study has employed the experimental method, it is usually good judgment to recommend the extension of the experiment on a somewhat broader scale, to obtain verification.

6. *Recommendations should be interpreted into concrete gains.* The researcher should attempt to determine, in as concrete terms as possible, just what the company may gain from following his recommendations. The number of additional outlets, number of new customers, additional business, potential size of new markets, savings in marketing expense, or other results should be estimated if practicable.

Estimating the results of following a recommendation in profit terms is most desirable. Businessmen are basically interested in greater profit. They are immediately interested if the amount of potential profit is laid clearly before them.

Estimation of concrete gains also has value in helping to insure logical interpretation. It is not always possible to make even a rough estimate of the specific gains which should accrue. Where such an estimate can be made, however, one may find that the proposed recommendation has little or no practical value and should therefore be discarded. There is always the danger of recommending a change when the proposed marketing method really has no measurable advantage over the one in operation.

17

PRESENTATION OF THE RESULTS AND FOLLOW-UP

Importance of the Reports. It is generally recognized that many marketing and distribution research studies, costing large sums of money and resulting in most significant conclusions, fail to yield full value because the results have not been properly presented. Sometimes the presentations are too long, sometimes too short. Many reports are too technical, too intricate in their arrangement, or just dull. The analyst often fails to understand the capacity and circumstances of those who must read the report and put its recommendations into effect. It is perhaps safe to say that in the typical case a large share of the effectiveness of a marketing research depends on how skillfully the report is written.

This statement is, of course, particularly true of the report which comes to the attention of the business executive. It is perhaps unfortunate, but the researcher nevertheless must recognize the fact that some businessmen judge a study more on the appearance and clarity of the report than on the merit of the research itself. A researcher may spend considerable time and much of the firm's money in doing a job. He is enthusiastic because the findings point very definitely to important conclusions. Much effort is spent in producing a really worth-while report. The results are sent to the head of the organization, and the analyst waits for comments. Then he is called into the office and is greeted with the question, "Who read proof on this job? I've found three errors in spelling in the report." When one has had experiences similar to this, he begins to appreciate the importance which the executive attaches to the presentation form of the results.

Many a research which is pure scientific nonsense is considered outstanding and the results are accepted because a board of directors has been swayed by skillful presentation. Many another study which is scientifically sound is cast aside because the executive has concentrated his attention on some minor error in presentation, or for some other reason is not "sold."

The importance of effective reporting of marketing research is emphasized in the following quotation:

Market research will continue its development only if it can improve its service to management. Market research men will move into top management positions and top management men will move into market research on the plane of the same two abilities: the ability to see what answers to management problems can be brought by research, and the ability to simplify the findings of research so they show the answers to these problems of management.

Every time you try to get across a plan, a finding, or a recommendation to officers of your own firm or to a customer, you need salesmanship. No matter how sound and important a report or presentation seems to you, to the other man it is just something else that demands some of his money or his life, and he learns to guard both.[1]

In view of the fact that research is a thoroughly objective process, as has been stressed repeatedly in this book, one may wonder that the popularization of reporting is recommended. Certainly the use of salesmanship must be closely restricted to the reporting phase of research and complete objectivity maintained at all other times. That it is considered legitimate, however, to promote the acceptance of research findings, once they have been obtained scientifically, is shown by the following statement by a committee of the American Marketing Association:

The process of research is largely one of the impact of facts and ideas on one mind (the researcher's), and is one of penetration. The process of communication, on the other hand, is one of presenting these facts and ideas to other minds; it is a process of interpretation by the written and spoken word aided by the graphic arts. One may not always expect to find equal facility in both processes in every mind. It is therefore of great importance to the marketing researcher to study the needs of reporting as well as of fact-finding itself, and to devise means of achieving good reports, perhaps in spite of his own personal limitations. A persuasive attitude of mind is very helpful to research reporting, and while it may be true that people engaged in selling and promotion as a career should not engage in research, it does not follow that researchers should not use honest salesmanship based on tenable research methods. The fact is that this is just what they should do.[2]

Determining the Reporting Form to Be Used. It is desirable that an organization develop certain standard practices in the preparation of reports. These practices may relate to matters such as the outline followed, the use of certain methods of graphic presentation, and the

---

[1] Frank R. Coutant, "Market Research Must Hold Executive Attention," *Journal of Marketing*, January, 1946, pp. 288–89.

[2] Committee on Reporting of the American Marketing Association, "Preparation and Presentation of the Research Report," *Journal of Marketing*, July, 1948, pp. 62–63.

size and physical characteristics of reports. At the same time, it must be recognized that the differences in the character of research projects, their importance, their uses, and their audience must be taken into account in planning a presentation, and standard practices must be varied to meet the specific needs of each research project.

The Committee on Reporting of the American Marketing Association has prepared the following list of factors which affect the form of the report: [3]

1. The instructions from the authority or client may indicate purely a statistical report on the one extreme or a fully elaborated recommendation on the other.

2. The nature and complexity of the problem will certainly dictate the manner in which the report must be presented.

3. The nature and variety of readers for whom the report is intended will vitally affect its form and content. If a report on the habits of buyers and users of a product is intended for the company's salesmen, it must certainly be less formal and technical, and perhaps briefer and more fully pictorialized than if it is solely for use of the sales manager.

4. The size of the report will influence its format, binding, and even the nature of the exposition of the findings.

5. The number of copies to be made will determine the types of reproduction and therefore the nature of the illustrative material.

6. The length of the useful life of the report may influence the expenditure of money and effort that is to be invested in presentation.

Primary Principles of Presentation

All the essentials of sound presentation apply in the preparation of reports. Good English is a first essential. The researcher should choose words which are vivid and make the findings clear. General principles of organization and arrangements which make for unity, coherence, and emphasis are important. All the principles of correct statistical presentation, such as the proper use of charts and graphs, should be carried out. Marketing research presentations, however, while embodying all these general principles, must have special qualities.

The primary fact for the researcher to bear in mind is that there are two distinct groups of executives to be satisfied. The first group includes the individuals in management positions outside the research department. They are generally not trained research men. They cannot, or will not, follow detailed technical reports. Yet they are the ones who are responsible for investing the money which is required for conducting the research, and they are the ones who must translate

[3] *Ibid.*, p. 68.

the conclusions into actual operation. Accordingly, the development of a report to meet the demands of this group is absolutely essential.

The second type is the research man. He may be a trained marketing researcher, a general statistician, or a technical scientist. But he knows scientific methodology. He will take time to mull over the most detailed and technical material. He may even take a delight in checking over work to find flaws. He will not be satisfied unless every minute detail of the job is carefully explained.

Most firms either have a technical man on their staff or will see to it that a technician checks the work. While there are still business houses which do not recognize the importance of having such a person go over the results of the research as they are reported, their number is decreasing, and the analyst must always be prepared to meet the technician.

Types of Reports. It is usually impossible to serve the demands of both these groups in one style of reporting. Their interests and capacities are so different that if the researcher tries to satisfy both in one form he will find that he has satisfied neither. Accordingly, the marketing researcher makes it a standard practice to think in terms of two types of reports: (1) the "popular" report, and (2) the "technical" report.

In the actual preparation of the report, the material should be worked up first in technical form if time permits. This report is the logical, scientific, and complete one. Having developed the basic report, the researcher then abstracts from it, concentrating on the special techniques of popular presentation.

Generally a single report, combining both the popular and technical elements, is produced. The researcher usually begins with a complete assembly of tables, arranged in a logical order under five or more major headings. Within each group those findings which are most significant are selected for popular presentation, with the balance set aside for the statistical appendix to the report. Then a series of charts illustrating the more important findings is constructed. The final step is the writing of the verbal copy which, with the charts and tables, represents the entire report. Some researchers make it a practice to concentrate the popular elements of the reporting in the first section of the report, devoting the balance to technical reporting. Others intersperse tables throughout the popular presentation of charts and interpretive copy, although detailed tables on less significant findings should always be confined to the appendix.

In the case of some marketing research studies, however, separate technical and popular reports are prepared. For a large and comprehensive analysis, the basic report may consist of a brief bound in several volumes. The popular report may involve easel presentation, a series of large cards, film, or slides projected on a screen, as well as considerable supplementary material. On the other hand, it may consist of merely a small number of large maps and charts for visual presentation.

Regardless of the length of the reports and whether they are physically separated, the distinction between the technical and popular forms must be kept clearly in mind. Even in a single fifteen-page report, covering a very small study, the writer must recognize the difference between the technician and the businessman and write with the requirements of the two groups in mind.

The Technical Report

The technical marketing research report should have the following definite characteristics:

1. *It should be complete.* Nothing should be omitted. Detailed tables, samples of questionnaires or other forms used, a complete exposition of methods, description of the sample, and all other material which will make the basic report a complete scientific document should be incorporated in it.

2. *It should be arranged logically.* Each step in the procedure should be unfolded exactly as it was done. The procedure should have been scientific, which means that the work is divided into specific steps, each step leading logically to the next one. The background and the problem come first, the conclusions and recommendations come last.

3. *It should be impersonal.* The basic report, throughout, should be a clear exposition of what has been done. A statement of facts, without color or bias, is required. It must be unemotional. Weak points must not be covered up.

4. *It must be accurate.* Facts must be accurately stated. Conclusions and recommendations must be sound.

5. *It must contain only pertinent matter.* There should be no padding of the basic report. While it is to be complete, there should be no extraneous material introduced to create an impression.

In order to achieve these characteristics, it is important that the material in the basic report be properly organized. A good outline would take a form similar to the one shown on the next page.

The technical report on a marketing research may take one of several physical forms, depending on its extent and character. The simplest form appears on standard typewriter sheets (8½ by 11 inches). Because this limits the space ordinarily required for charts

OUTLINE OF THE TECHNICAL REPORT

TITLE PAGE.

1. Subject.
2. For whom prepared.
3. By whom prepared.
4. Date of report.

PREFACE.

1. Brief statement of occasion for the study.
2. By whom authorized.
3. Statement or letter of transmittal.

I. PURPOSE OF THE STUDY.

A clear statement of the problem or problems for which the answer is sought. This should take the form of a clear organization of hypotheses used.

II. METHODS EMPLOYED.

1. Description of the conditions under which the study was conducted. A running account of how the study was made, step by step.
2. Statement of sources of data. Full description of the sample.
3. Samples of schedules and questionnaires. (May be placed in Appendix.) Description of procedures employed in data gathering.
4. Description of any special methodologies employed with reasons for their use.
5. Statement of limitations from the point of view of scientific methodology.

III. FINDINGS.

The body of the material on which conclusions are based. This should include significant tables and charts showing all statistical summarizations, whether in table or chart form.

IV. CONCLUSIONS.

A summary of the most significant conclusions brought out in the study.

V. RECOMMENDATIONS. (If authorized.)

A statement of specific business policy recommendations to which the conclusions point.

APPENDIX.

1. Detailed tables, showing data and breakdowns by groups.
2. Details of the sample, with validation.
3. Other detailed matters, such as bibliography, etc.
4. Exhibits of forms used.

and complex tables, a form gaining in favor employs pages which are 11 by 15, or 11 by 17 inches in size. Charts and tables in this basic report can then be blown up to a larger size for popular presentation if desired.

Many reports are so long that it is good practice to break them up into small volumes. This fact is particularly true if a large amount of technical appendix material is required. The reports are usually bound in a simulated leather binder in loose-leaf form in order to provide for efficient assembly and to facilitate inserting or deleting pages.

The Popular Report

Frequently a marketing researcher has occasion to prepare a separate popular report for presentation to group meetings. It is assumed that the technical report on the research has been prepared. Attention is now concentrated on the problem of selecting such materials from the basic report as will be best for popular presentation and devising means of dramatic presentation to laymen.

The qualities of the group to whom the popular report goes indicate the nature of the report. They are the general business executives—heads of companies; directors, who have only sporadic glimpses into the business; general managers, whose minds are filled with myriad details of all aspects of the business; sales managers, whose primary concern is to keep the sales force producing; advertising managers, whose time is taken up largely by copy and media conferences; the treasurer; the comptroller; perhaps the production manager. These men are busy. To them, marketing research may be a side issue, as compared with the routine of their own jobs.

The American businessman is a man of action. He does not like to ponder problems; he is not a philosopher. The chief characteristic of the executive is his ability to make sound decisions quickly. He sometimes has little patience with time-consuming research and often works on the basis of first impressions. Unless his attention is held completely, his mind will wander to other things.

Forms for Popular Reports. The exact form of the popular report will depend on whether it is to be read by an individual or to be seen visually and listened to by a group.

If the popular report is to be read by a few persons, it is best put up in a convenient reading size. This type of popular report may well be preceded by "feelers," short letters which present the most dramatic findings. The purpose of these "feelers" is to get the man who really controls final decisions to request further information.

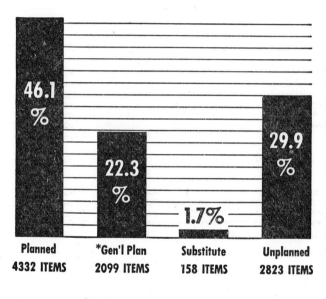

THE *Results*

1,448 shoppers were interviewed, and a total of 9,412 items purchased were analyzed. The four types of purchases are shown below.

46.1 %

22.3 %

1.7%

29.9 %

| Planned | *Gen'l Plan | Substitute | Unplanned |
| 4332 ITEMS | 2099 ITEMS | 158 ITEMS | 2823 ITEMS |

*Classification planned, but no specific item.
Regarding clerk's suggestions see page 9.

FIGURE 25. Popular Presentation Form.

This procedure is good psychology, for if one can get these men to ask for the findings, they are half sold before they ever see them.

There is an increasing tendency for the popular report to take the form of visual group presentations. The least expensive, hence rather common, method for these presentations is to use photostatic blow-ups of typewritten copy and large maps and charts. The research man then delivers his report orally, illustrating from time to time with this material. The material is set up on a table or on racks which make for ease in handling the large sheets. There are definite disadvantages to this type of presentation. The research man must be a good speaker—he must be at his best and make a good speech. Thought is often broken by the difficulty in handling material.

Where money and facilities are available, the popular presentation is usually bound in a loose-leaf easel, with the pages hinged at the top so they can be turned over as the report is given—the standard professional form. In preparing such a presentation, each page should be a unit by itself and have a continuity in the presentation which will hold attention. Above all, copy (statements in words) extending beyond three or four sentences on each sheet should be avoided. Pages must be turned fairly rapidly to retain attention.

These verbal presentations are difficult to make. The speaker often loses his control of the conference, or the thought is interrupted by nonessential questions. When one must turn back five or six pages, much valuable time is lost.

As the result of these difficulties, slides or photographic stills are often employed. Sometimes a motion picture projector with sound accompaniment is used. This form of presentation has many advantages: the "speaker" is always at his best, everything can be timed properly for attention, and there is no interruption. It is possible to introduce caricatures or characters and plot to set a tone to the story and dramatize it. By setting a presentation into narrative form based on a theme such as "Livetown and Sleepytown," and unfolding a running story of the contrast between results embodying the recommendations of the research and the present situation, the analyst can effectively present his findings.

The contents and arrangement of the popular report are shown on the next page. This arrangement may be used if the report is made in small form or if a more elaborate group presentation is used. It will, of course, need to be modified for different presentations.

How to Write a Popular Report. Writing a successful popular report, whether for individual or for group presentation, is largely a matter of following a few well-recognized principles. The chief qualities which it should possess follow:

1. *Personal characteristics of the persons who are to act on the reports should be taken into account.* Businessmen differ greatly in the type of reports to which they will give the most favorable reception. Some are greatly impressed by extreme dramatic devices, such as large maps, lengthy listings of comments from individual interviews, extensive use of art work and color, or a presentation which obviously seeks to "sell" them. Others will be much more receptive to a more restrained form of presentation. It is important that the

OUTLINE FOR A POPULAR REPORT

TITLE PAGE. This should keynote the remainder of the report.

I. WHY THE STUDY WAS MADE.

In from one to three pages the practical importance of the research is quickly established. A brief summary of the objectives of the study may be sufficient.

II. HOW THE STUDY WAS MADE.

A brief summary of the conduct of the study should be presented as quickly as possible and should not cover more than four or five pages. A map showing the markets used, how calls were distributed in a sample city, and pictures of typical homes interviewed may suffice. The details of questionnaires or other forms should not be discussed.

III. CONCLUSIONS AND RECOMMENDATIONS.

A brief summary of the final conclusions of the analysis and the recommendations based on them is often introduced at this point. This insures that attention will be given them and heightens curiosity in the evidence which will be shown in greater detail later. Sometimes the pages in this section can be divided vertically; hence, conclusions can be summarized in "1, 2, 3, . . ." order on the left side and the parallel recommendations summarized on the right side of the page. If this is not practicable, the conclusions should be summarized on one or two pages followed by a general statement of the recommendations.

IV. CHIEF FINDINGS OF THE STUDY.

This section should show in visual form the outstanding facts brought out in the investigation. The sample page shown in Figure 25 is from this section of a report. The reader will note that only one fact is presented on each page, thus concentrating attention on a single subject. It is clearly titled, the facts are presented graphically, and continuity with preceding and following pages is established. Only the chief findings are presented in the body of the popular report. If qualifying details are necessary, they may be shown in small scale at the bottom of appropriate pages. Tables are not shown in the popular report if the data are summarized graphically, as the data necessary to support the chart are shown on the form suggested. This section may contain twenty-five or more pages. If it is long, it should be broken into sections, with appropriate title pages.

V. SUMMARY OF RECOMMENDATIONS.

In this section the recommendations are stated in greater detail, especially if a decision is to be reached when the presentation is made. If the recommendations require an involved plan, they should be written separately and introduced at this point.

researcher gauge his audience just as carefully as a speaker or actor must, to avoid using techniques in presentation which will distract attention. He must, of course, play on the personal whims of the more important people to whom the presentation is directed. A most valuable consideration is that of properly timing the report so that it will be neither too short nor too long. The majority of business executives prefer a popular report which will give them the essential facts in as short a period of time as possible. The researcher must always be prepared for the executive who wishes to "get over the report in five minutes." On the other hand, there are many businessmen who are slow and deliberative in their thinking. The latter type of person will regard a report which moves too quickly as reflecting a superficial study. In planning the presentation of the results, one must thus size up his audience and develop the report in the light of his best understanding of the personal characteristics of the people to whom it is to be presented.

2. *It should be brief.* The popular report "high-spots" the outstanding findings of the study. Usually, however, it is a complete presentation of the most important results. Even though the presentation may last an hour or more, brevity should characterize the writing so the reporting moves at a fast pace. Reference is made to the technical report for those who wish to check further into details.

3. *Emphasis should be placed on the practical use of the findings.* The businessman can understand a recommendation which is stated in terms of some change in policy or the organization of his business. He may be able to understand a general conclusion and make his own interpretation into policy, but not nearly so clearly. The report should talk in terms of action and use conclusions and data as evidence to support recommendations.

4. *Statistical terminologies and concepts should be avoided as much as possible.* There are many important executives who cannot read even a slightly complex chart. The researcher should use only the simplest of devices and explain them carefully. He should avoid the use of such terms as "sum" or "mean." They are kindergarten terms to the statistician, but they are new to the businessman. Many a popular presentation has lost much of its effectiveness because of interruptions caused by the necessity of explaining some statistical technicality.

5. *It should have a definite sales slant.* The researcher should employ persuasive devices to obtain acceptance of the research. He should be positive in his statements; the businessman expects it. The researcher should write the report with the assumption that he must sell both his research and its recommendations.

6. *The arrangement should be psychological, rather than logical.* The researcher should use an arrangement that will get his story over most effectively, thinking in terms of attention value. He should begin with material which will immediately arouse interest, cover less important material, and then work up to a climax with the most significant findings.

7. *It should be dramatized.* Dramatization is the most important single characteristic of the popular report. The researcher strives to obtain as enthusiastic a reception of his work as possible. To do this, he employs many so-called dramatic devices. As long as there is no violation of the truth or distortion of facts, there is no reason why he should not go far in this direction.

How to Make a Popular Presentation Dramatic. 1. *Have a Central Theme.* The popular presentation should have a central idea or plot, like a good motion picture or stage play. Sometimes an effective theme may be merely a word summary of what the analyst set out to determine. Examples are, "What Mrs. Consumer thinks of our product," "A sales program for 1950," or "A new type of outlet for Jones' products." Another form of successful theme is that which injects personality into the story of the results of the analysis. Examples are, "Mrs. Smith tells us," "Livetown versus Sleepytown," or "The three little piggies who went to market." Since most of the listeners are primarily interested in how to increase the profits of the company, a form of theme such as "How to increase profits 20 per cent," is often successful.

Regardless of the type of central theme which is developed, it is most important that the results of the study be presented in an effective psychological order which will unfold step by step, as the plot of a play moves to its conclusion. There are several schemes which help in effective theme development. One person who has been very successful at building dramatic presentations of marketing research first compliments the executives by showing the favorable results of the analysis and then presents the unfavorable side of the picture, finally leading to the solution of a critical problem. This method is quite effective.

2. *Use Visual Devices Liberally.* In the popular presentation, words should be kept at a minimum. Here the researcher applies the Chinese proverb, "One picture is worth ten thousand words." The results of the analysis should be presented in simple but interesting charts with a minimum of words used for continuity. Very often rather expensive art work is employed to make some of the examples as dramatic as possible. "Blow-ups" (very large pictures, charts, and maps) are often freely used.

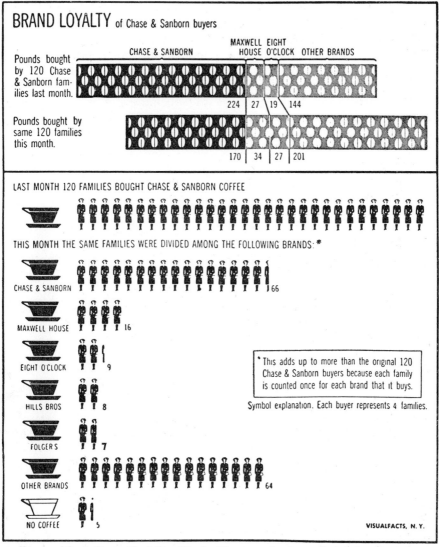

FIGURE 26. A Dramatized Bar Chart. The example shows that it is not necessary to violate the rules of graphic presentation to make a chart interesting.

It is possible, however, to use entirely too many pictures. Researchers who try too hard to be dramatic are likely to make the mistake of using too many illustrations and decorations in the presentation. It is possible to make the popular presentation too pictorial, and thereby give the entire study a very superficial effect. A good rule to remember is that a visual device should never be used if it tends to distract attention from the point being presented.

An undesirable result also may be produced by using too expensive or too carefully prepared material, such as artistic hand lettering or typography. If the charts and illustrations have a certain degree of crudeness about them, it often will be found that a more favorable impression will be created.

3. *Use Specific Examples.* As mentioned before, the average businessman tends to think in terms of specific cases rather than in generalizations. The researcher should constantly bear this in mind when developing the popular presentation. Where possible, it is a good idea to supplement charts or other generalizations with a few specific examples.

For instance, if a page shows the sales increases obtained by a certain type of display, it should be preceded or followed by a picture of such a display in a specific store, with the increased sales obtained in that store. Many of the listeners will clearly understand the specific illustration, agree with it, and accept the generalization as a consequence.

One important application of this principle is in the part of the presentation which explains how the field work was done and how the sample was distributed. Instead of general statements and laborious explanations, pictures of individual field workers, a large map of one of the markets, a map of a specific street showing actual homes or stores included in the sample, or a series of photographs of a typical area covered may be used.

4. *Use Illustrations and Analogy Freely.* This principle, which is closely related to that of using specific examples, means that one may inject into the popular report references to the experiences of other companies and other industries or even more general analogous illustrations.

The businessman is greatly impressed if he can be shown that a principle being demonstrated for his company holds true for other companies and industries. Suppose, for example, that the chief point in a research for a watch manufacturer is that the market has shifted so that his most important buyers are the members of the mass or wage-earner market. If evidence is introduced which shows that the same situation confronts the manufacturers of radios, electric clocks, high-priced fountain pens, and other commodities, the listener is impressed. In spite of the traditions of business leadership, the fact is that some businessmen are primarily followers and imitators, and the quickest way to get action is to indicate what competitors are doing. For this reason, a carefully handled reference to a competitor in a popular report may go far toward injecting drama into the presentation.

The use of concrete analogy to dramatize theoretical ideas is a common practice. An analyst wished to show the relationship between the functions of general advertising, direct-mail advertising, and the salesman in the marketing of automobiles. Instead of a theoretical discussion, he drew for an analogy upon the manufacturing process used in finishing a cylinder block. The first crude process—boring, which was rapid and inexpensive—was compared to general advertising, which reached a maximum of people (few of whom were real prospects) at a minimum cost. The second step—sand blasting—was still crude, but finer and more expensive than the first. This procedure was likened to direct mail, which sought out more likely prospects at a higher cost than general advertising. The final step—machining—is the most costly process in finishing a cylinder block. The work of the salesman was compared to the work of the machinist.

The relationship between the three marketing methods was thus developed in understandable terms. The main point, that one would no more rely upon salesmen to do the rougher work of demand creation than he would use a machinist for all the operations in finishing the cylinder block (although one could at very high cost), was quickly and effectively established.

The liberal use of analogy in developing the popular report can be an effective application of the psychological principle of leading from the known to the unknown. If the analogies are drawn from the industry of the company for which the study is made, they will immediately obtain attention and understanding.

5. *Write in Headline Style.* The copy (words) which is used in the popular report should be similar to the headlines of newspaper articles or advertisements. The writing of each phrase or sentence should be as brief and clear as possible; the words and sentence structure should be simple. Most of the findings are established by charts and other visual devices. The purpose of the written material is to provide continuity and necessary explanations. The writing is sketchy and largely elliptical; short phrases rather than complete sentences are often relied upon.

6. *Use Physical Demonstration Devices.* In order to relieve the monotony of going through the pages of a presentation and to introduce more vivid dramatics, special demonstration devices or more spectacular displays are sometimes introduced. The simple form is the jumbo map or chart, which by its size secures emphasis. Frequently several large displays are arranged about the walls to provide a "stage setting" for the basic presentation.

The accordion folder is another variation. In this device a series of photographs or illustrations is mounted on cards which are joined so that one person may hold each end of the series and the individual cards appear in order as the two individuals separate. As many as twenty-five units may be thus mounted. The accordion fold is best used when a large number of units, which all demonstrate the same point (like pictures of typical store displays used in a test), are shown rapidly to impress the listener with the breadth and intensity of the investigation.

Another display device is the use of a street map which is on a roller so that it may be unrolled as desired by the person making the presentation. The listener is asked to walk down a typical street with the investigator. Information such as the various brands found in homes is shown for each individual call. This procedure applies the principle of showing specific examples in a form possessing much drama.

The variety stores are a veritable gold mine of materials which can be used as demonstration devices. If one is presenting the results of an analysis of trends in the automobile market, for example, he may lay a number of toy cars on a large table in such a form that they can be moved about to represent the findings in animate chart form. Dummy cartons of a product may be piled up before the listeners to represent crude charts which visualize the results of the analysis.

Another excellent device for popular presentations is that of introducing some sort of mechanical device which in its operation illustrates your point. A very ingenious presentation was made by an analyst who had been studying profit results from stock turn. He had a machine built to illustrate the conclusions of his studies. In a hopper at the top 100 pennies were dropped. There were two compartments below; one was marked "X products—low margin, rapid stock turn," the other "Competing products—high margin, slow stock turn." A crank, when turned, distributed the pennies into two receptacles, one marked "Profit from handling X products," the other "Profit from handling competing products." Gears in the machine distributed the pennies in the ratio determined, which forced more pennies at each turn into the "Competing products" compartment, but which sent pennies more rapidly into the "X products" compartment. Thus, after the 100 pennies were run through the machine, the "X products" showed the larger profit. This device was excellent because it was visual and had motion in it. Furthermore, it showed the executives how salesmen, equipped with similar machines, could dramatize the story to dealers to make more sales.

Having two or more persons share in the oral presentation of the popular report often provides a desirable change of pace and also introduces another visual device—in the form of personalities.

Standards of Report Presentation

In preparing the report for a marketing research, it is necessary to keep in mind certain basic standards which must be followed. Adhering closely to these standards is an earmark of professional competency. Their consistent presence in the report will insure greater acceptance of the findings and conclusions and will also guard against criticism by technicians.

Charts and graphs, which present statistical facts in visual form, are used very extensively in the presentation of marketing research. Adequate general treatement of this subject is readily available in general textbooks on statistics. However, in the production of charts it is very useful to have a list of standards which will guard against the danger of resorting to unsound practices. Such a check list has been prepared by the Joint Committee on Standards for Graphic Presentation of the American Society of Mechanical Engineers. Excerpts from these rules which cover the points most generally applicable to marketing research charts are given in the following check list:

1. *General Rules.*

   a) The general arrangement of a diagram should proceed from left to right.

   b) Where possible, represent quantities by linear magnitudes, as areas or volumes are more likely to be misinterpreted.

   c) For a curve, the vertical scale, wherever practicable, should be so selected that the zero line will appear on the diagram.

   d) If the zero line of the vertical scale will not normally appear on the curve diagram, the zero line should be shown by the use of a horizontal break in the diagram.

   e) It is advisable not to show any more coordinate lines than necessary to guide the eye in reading the diagram.

   f) The horizontal scale for curves should usually read from left to right and the vertical scale from bottom to top.

   g) Figures for the scales of a diagram should be placed at the left and at the bottom or along the respective axes.

   h) It is often desirable to include in the diagram the numerical data or formulas represented.

   i) The title of a diagram should be made as clear and complete as possible. Subtitles or descriptions should be added if necessary to insure clearness.

2. *Curve or Line Charts.*

   a) Units of measurement should be selected which will allow desired curves to be plotted without exaggeration.

   b) When the chart covers a long space of time, it is well to place the vertical scale at the right as well as at the left. Similarly, it may be advisable to put dates at the top as well as at the bottom.

c) Reading matter should not appear in the body of the graph.

d) Whenever it is desired to represent rates of increase or decrease, the ratio or logarithmic chart should be used.

3. *Bar Charts.*

a) Bar charts may be used to show relative values between two or more factors.

b) Bar charts may be used to show component parts.

c) Figures and descriptive matter should preferably be placed at the left of the bars.

d) Bars should always be of the same width.

e) Bars should be wide enough to prevent optical illusion.

f) When horizontal bars represent years, the earliest years should be shown at the top; vertical bars, at the left.

g) Spaces between bars should represent equal periods. Where it is necessary to represent unequal periods, there should be a proportionate amount of space between the bars.

h) When certain facts are emphasized because of importance, they should appear at the top, or from left to right.

4. *Circle Charts.*

a) The use of circle charts should be confined to the showing of component parts.

b) Circles should not be used to compare more than a few component parts.

c) When descriptive matter is incorporated in the circle, it should be readable without turning the illustration.

d) If two or more circles are used, comparison should be based upon area rather than diameter.

5. *Pictorial Charts.*

a) The unit should be as simple as possible.

b) The comparison should be on one dimension only and that dimension mentioned in order that the reader may determine the actual relation if supporting statistics are not included.

c) The reading matter should be especially clear and complete to compensate for the difficulty in judging correctly from the pictorial chart alone. In all cases the description should be closely associated with the diagram.

6. *The Ratio or Logarithmic Chart.*

a) In general, the rules for constructing ratio charts follow those given for arithmetic charts.

b) Primarily, a chart should be upon one-zone paper if it can be so arranged.

c) Vertical scales should be placed on both sides of the coordinate area.

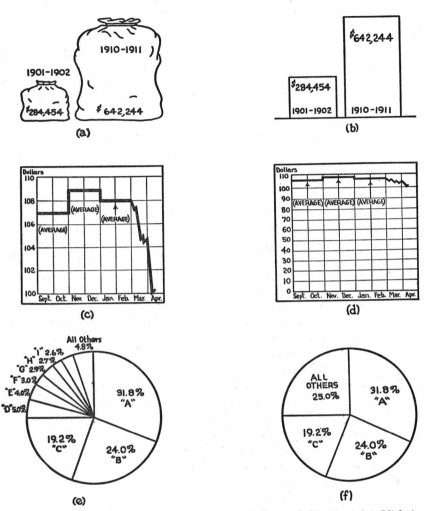

FIGURE 27. Examples of Incorrect and Correct Methods of Charting. (a) Violation of Rule 1(b). (b) The bar chart shows the proper relationship. (c) Example of distorted effect caused by omitting base line. (d) The chart to the left redone in accordance with Rule 1(c). (e) Violation of Rule 4(b). (f) Correct treatment of pie chart shown on the left.

The three left-hand charts show the distortion or confusion caused by faulty charting; the three right-hand charts are drawn according to accepted standards. Note especially the contrast in the two line charts—the incorrect one shows great exaggeration of a decline which is actually less than 8 per cent.

Intermediate coordinates should be clearly labeled where they indicate important points.

7. *Map Charts.*

    a) The localities of areas to be emphasized should be marked with the heaviest shadings, or otherwise made to appear prominent.

    b) Density of distribution should be shown by the dot method. (The relation between size of dot and value represented must be constant on any given map.)

    c) Color should be used wherever it serves to show relative values between various portions of the map.

    d) Descriptive and reading matter should always be large enough to be plainly legible.

Checking the Reports. After the materials for presentation have been completed, it is usually beneficial to go over them carefully, checking against some list of generally undesirable characteristics of reports such as the following:

1. No clear statement of the problem—this should be stated at the beginning of the reports.
2. No concise summary.
3. Poor organizaiton—the reports should be divided into sections clearly related to one another.
4. Lack of continuity from page to page.
5. Lack of thorough analysis.
6. Failure to describe methods carefully, including pretesting, how investigators were selected and trained, details of instructions, methods of interviewing, observation, or experiment employed.
7. Lack of complete description of the sample employed, how it was prepared, its limitations, and validation.
8. Failure to show relative importance of factors.
9. Hasty generalization.
10. Reasoning in a circle.
11. False analogy.
12. Unjustified argument from authority.
13. Irrelevant material introduced.
14. Lack of proof.
15. References not given.

The Oral Presentation. It is standard practice for research reports to be presented orally to groups of executives. A great deal of the acceptance of marketing research depends on the skill with which these oral presentations are made, and here the researcher must most literally be a salesman of the findings of the research.

The following standards for oral presentation have been prepared by the Committee on Reporting of the American Marketing Association: [4]

a. See to it that physical facilities are adequate and well planned. Check ventilation and have sufficient lighting arranged to focus attention on the charts. The audience must be comfortable but not too comfortable.

b. Keep the meeting free from interruptions and distractions. The speaker should control the situation and command respectful attention.

c. The person making the presentation must have a full grasp of the report and of its implications with respect to the problem.

d. Avoid confusing technical jargon and translate concepts into terms and images that are readily understood.

e. The oral delivery may be informal, but there must be good choice of words and word images, with pleasing voice.

Statement of Limitations and Restriction. Every research report should contain, in a prominent place, a clear statement of the extent to which the results of the research are dependable. This calls for a careful consideration of the validity of the actual evidence which has been obtained. After such consideration, a statement of the limitations of the research must be brought to the attention of the reader, generally along with the statement of the reliability of the findings.

It is also standard practice to place some restriction on the use of reports. This restriction may consist of a statement that the report is limited to the confidential use of the executives of the firm or firms concerned. In case the research is conducted by an independent research organization, it is good professional practice to incorporate a statement limiting the publication of the findings to exact reproduction from the report or subject to the approval of the research firm.

There is always danger that some ambitious executive will take parts of a research report, reinterpret them, and use them for promotional purposes. Too often this process involves garbling data, presenting only part of the findings, or employing charts and other statistical devices which distort the facts. This practice does marketing research a great deal of harm and must be controlled as much as possible. A clear statement on restriction of the use of research findings for promotional purposes is the first remedy.

The Follow-Up

The last step of marketing research is carrying the recommendations into practice. The success with which the researcher will take an active and effective part depends upon the degree to which he pos-

[4] *Op. cit.,* pp. 70–71.

sesses experience and ability in marketing. One who attempts to put an advertising recommendation into effect must be a qualified advertising man as well as a marketing researcher. One who makes a change in a sales operation must have the abilities of a sales executive. The practical side of the analyst and his work meet an acid test when the final recommendations are transferred into operations.

Observation of the general practice of marketing and distribution research in the United States reveals that neglect of the follow-up to the research—seeing to it that the individual firm effectively translates the conclusions into its day-to-day operations—is an outstanding weakness. Too often business executives are content to read reports, agree with them in principle, and then retain the old, inefficient marketing practices. Too often the researcher feels that his responsibility ends with the delivery of the final report. Too frequently fear of hurting the feelings of company personnel, failure to delegate responsibility, and the inertia of the complex business organization rob marketing and distribution research efforts of their full value.

The *ultimate test of the value of a marketing research* lies solely in the results which have been accomplished by carrying its recommendations into effect. But unfortunately, the general impression made on executives, the technical skill with which the work has been done, the dramatic presentation of the findings in conference, and similar superficial phases of marketing research frequently receive undue consideration. What really counts is the degree to which its conclusions are adopted in business practice. The marketing researcher can feel sure that his work is justified only if clearly traceable results are found in the actual operation of the business.

There are definite advantages in having the market researcher take an active part in the follow-up work. In the first place, the knowledge which he has gained through his intimate contact with the marketing problem will prove indispensable in setting up a sound plan for carrying out the recommendations. Actual practice in carrying the results of the research into operation also contributes greatly to the skill of the researcher and, in turn, to the value of future studies which he will make for the company. Finally, by taking an active part in the actual marketing operations, he gains the confidence of executives and other employees with whom he has to work.

The follow-up stage in marketing research should, if practicable, first take the form of carrying out the recommendations of the study on a small scale. By such a test the researcher can determine whether the recommendations are workable, and also the best form in which they may be carried into effect. The results of the analysis often call for vital changes in the marketing policies of a company. Such changes generally should not be made too rapidly because the disturbances created by the change may defeat the values to be obtained. A careful testing of the new procedure will also indicate clearly any modifications demanded by practical considerations.

Insuring the Success of Follow-Up. The foundation of successful follow-up is the development of policy interpretations which will be followed by business executives. The general rules for adapting interpretations to their requirements have been discussed in detail (see pages 364–68). After the final report has been prepared, it is usually good practice to review the recommendations to make sure that they are in accord with these principles.

After the researcher has reviewed his recommendations to be certain that they are adapted to the requirements of the executive, he may further insure the success of his follow-up work by employing the following principles:

1. Get thoroughly acquainted with the business—know its marketing operation in detail.
2. Cultivate the personal friendship of *all* the personnel you possibly can—from top management executives to salesmen on the firing line.
3. Honestly create the impression in your every action that you have one interest at heart—the welfare of the company, rather than your own personal advancement.
4. Show operating personnel how the research makes their job easier —how they can use it to grow in stature.
5. Don't be afraid to stand on your facts, but recognize the limitations and any deficiencies of your research—be the first to admit an error or weakness, and don't claim too much.
6. Keep any discussion of the recommendations on the main and critical issues—don't quibble over technique or minor points.
7. Review progress in the application of the results of the research constantly and regularly—find the specific improvements, then be sure everyone knows about them.

In other words, the researcher must live and sell the application and success of marketing and distribution research all the time. Only as a result of such constant pioneering and persuasion will American business take full advantage of this tool of management.

SELECTED READINGS

CORDELL, WARREN. "Six Ways to Appraise the Reliability and Usefulness of Marketing Research," *Printers' Ink*, July 1, 1949, pp. 36–38.
FROTHINGHAM, ROY S., *et al.* "Preparation and Presentation of the Research Report," *Journal of Marketing*, July, 1948, pp. 62–72.

Luck, David J., and Wales, Hugh G. *Marketing Research*. New York: Prentice-Hall, Inc., 1952, pp. 337–66.

Modley, Rudolph, and Lowenstein, Dyno. *Pictographs and Charts*. New York: Harper & Bros., 1952.

Moore, C. W. "How to Write a Report," *Printers' Ink*, July 22, 1949, pp. 32–33.

Nelson, J. Raleigh. *Writing the Technical Report*. New York: McGraw-Hill Book Co., Inc., 1952.

Spear, Mary E. *Charting Statistics*. New York: McGraw-Hill Book Co., Inc., 1952.

Standards for the Publication of Statistical Data. Washington, D. C.: Bureau of the Budget, Executive Office of the President, 1952.

CASE

Blankertz, Donald F., Ferber, Robert, and Wales, Hugh G. *Cases and Problems in Marketing Research*. New York: The Ronald Press Co., 1954, pp. 290–92; 312–16.

Part III

SPECIALIZED FIELDS AND TECHNIQUES OF MARKETING AND DISTRIBUTION RESEARCH

18

MOTIVATIONAL RESEARCH

Motivational research, which seeks to determine *why* people act as they do, has recently received the most attention of all specialized areas in marketing and distribution research. In the past, marketing research has been largely concentrated on factual studies employing quantitative statistical methods. A great deal of work has been done in "nose-counting" to determine how many and what kind of people use a product or service, where they live, where they buy, what they prefer, how they are reached, and how they respond to marketing activities. These established tools of marketing research have revolutionized marketing practices, but they have largely failed to answer one of the most vital questions in marketing—Why do people buy my competitor's product instead of mine? They have also failed to provide adequate answers as to the motivations behind other forms of market behavior.

The primary application of motivational research to marketing is for the discovery and evaluation of the drives which cause people to buy a particular kind of product or to select a specific brand. There are, however, other important applications. A number of magazines have employed motivational research in an effort to establish their influence on readers, a better definition of the type of readers they select, a more effective description of the mood created by editorial matter, and the potential transfer of this mood toward making advertising more effective.[1] Motivational research has also been employed in connection with the measurement of attitudes toward industries and corporations. Still another example is the use of these techniques in studies of a corporation symbol such as Betty Crocker, in order to determine its marketing values, strengths, weaknesses, and implications.

Importance of Motivational Research. Current marketing literature contains an increasing amount of material devoted to motiva-

---

[1] *Women and Advertising, A Motivation Study of the Attitudes of Women Toward Eight Magazines* (New York: Good Housekeeping Magazine, 1954).

tional research. However, the most striking evidence of its growing importance in marketing research is an annotated directory of organizations practicing in this field.[2] This directory is based on a survey made in 1954. It lists 82 different companies and individuals practicing motivational research in marketing. A number of them are leading independent marketing research firms. Others are psychological and sociological groups associated with universities. The balance is made up largely of individuals who regard themselves as competent to undertake a motivational research project on their own.

Another recent evidence of the rise of motivational research applied to marketing is the development of a guidebook to the terminology employed in this field by a committee of the Advertising Research Foundation.[3] Motivational research is so characterized by confusing terminology that this document was prepared to help executives and researchers communicate more effectively among themselves in connection with motivational studies relating to advertising and other phases of marketing.

The primary reason for the rapid development of motivational research in marketing has been the recognition by business executives that one of their most critical needs is for an understanding of the hidden motivations of potential buyers. In advertising, for example, it is a universally accepted principle that appealing to the strongest buying motives is the most important single element in a successful campaign. Historically, it has been observed that the classic examples of effective advertising have been identified with headlines which tapped the most basic desires of the consumer. Similarly, in personal selling, it is generally recognized that appeals to the strongest buying motivations are most successful. Because they realize that the most basic and dynamic motivations are often hidden and obscure, there is a constant feeling of insecurity on the part of businessmen as to whether their marketing is in tune with those motivations. As a consequence, businessmen are highly motivated in their own desire to learn more from motivational research.

The Wall Street Journal reports:

The businessman . . . is devoting increasing attention to such bizarre things as airline passengers' "fears of posthumous guilt," the spankings industrial pipe buyers received in childhood and the psychological characteristics of beer drinkers. . . .

[2] *Directory of Organizations Which Conduct Motivation Research* (New York: The Advertising Research Foundation, 1954).
[3] Joseph W. Wulfeck and Edward M. Bennett, *The Language of Dynamic Psychology as Related to Motivation Research* (New York: McGraw-Hill Book Co., Inc., 1954).

Godyear Tire & Rubber, General Motors, General Foods, Jewel Tea, the Book of the Month Club, Columbia Broadcasting System, Regal Amber Brewing, and Lever Brothers are only a few of the outfits that have made use of motivation research studies.[4]

A second reason for rising interest in motivational research methods is the failure of ordinary marketing research techniques to provide satisfactory answers on the "why" of human behavior. As pointed out in Chapter 5, a great deal of work has been done in the past in an effort to develop interpretive survey techniques which will produce meaningful results. The more marketing researchers have experimented with various types of interpretive interviews and different forms of question construction, the more they have come to realize that respondents are often unable consciously to reveal their own motivations. Meanwhile, work in psychology and psychiatry has continuously proved that human beings are sometimes least able to verbalize their strongest motivational drives. The sense of failure to evaluate motivations through ordinary research methods is thus another motivating force in causing researchers to seek new approaches to the problem.

No psychologist believes it is possible to really get at motives by simply asking people why they do something. The human being is so complex, and so much of our behavior is governed by emotions and quirks of personality that we just don't know the real underlying causes of so many actions.

In the first place, no one is going to admit he ever did anything from derogatory motives. We just don't tell people we are cowards or social climbers. All kinds of people buy Cadillacs as a symbol of worldly success, but they never admit it to other people.

Below this level of conscious motives are all the unconscious forces that sway us. One individual is different from the next one because of experiences that go all the way back to infancy.

Of course we would like to have people think that everything we do has a well thought-out logic. So we rationalize our behavior by giving all sorts of possible reasons so that we always look good in other people's eyes and in our own eyes. It is the perfectly human thing to do.[5]

A third contributing factor to the rise of motivational research has been the sheer novelty of many of the methods in current use and the intriguing terminologies employed in connection with them. The theory of games, association techniques, group interviewing, and projective techniques are in themselves fresh and exciting concepts. Words such as ambivalence, cultural anthropology, apperception,

---

[4] *The Wall Street Journal*, September 14, 1954, p. 1.

[5] *Automobiles—What They Mean to Americans*, A Study for The Chicago Tribune by Social Research, Inc., 1954, p. 6.

reaction-formation, rapport, ego-ideal, wish-fulfillment, fantasy, and trauma are stimulating symbols. Names such as those of Freud, Jung, and Dichter are intriguing; the clinical environment and the scientific background excite the novice. Articles expounding new types of motivational research studies in marketing and advertising trade journals provide a great stimulus to interest on the part of the layman.

A fourth element which has helped to arouse interest in motivational research has been the expanding interest of businessmen in broader fields of science. They have seen the magic which has been brought to their enterprises through their own technical laboratories. They have had the profit value of pure research in the physical sciences demonstrated in their own companies. They no longer think within the confined focus of their own business, but realize that their enterprise is one small part of a broad social, economic, and political organism. They are generally reaching out into newer and broader fields for knowledge which can contribute to the success of their own corporation.

Definition of Motivational Research. Motivational research in marketing may be defined as *the use of social science techniques to discover and to evaluate the fundamental motivating forces or drives which impel human behavior in the market place.* Motivation has been defined as the "why" of behavior, the "triggers" to action.

The academic field most directly drawn upon for motivational research in marketing is psychology. Motivational psychology is concerned with the reasons and laws underlying learning, thinking, and acting in specific ways. The findings and methods of experimental psychology have been adapted to use in marketing research. The techniques embrace procedures such as attitude scales, word association, and thematic apperception.

Sociology, particularly the combined field of social psychology, is a second area making major contributions. Whereas psychology deals largely with the individual, sociology deals with mass behavior. Since marketing is concerned with mass behavior, the contribution of the sociologist is of primary importance. This contribution comes in two general ways. The first is a structural contribution. An example is the concept of social classes. This concept is applied to marketing research in terms of the study of the contrasting behavior of various classes such as the "upper-upper class" as opposed to the "lower-lower class" in response to marketing stimuli. The analysis of social classes has shown, for example, that at any given time we have very rigid social classes in America, each with its characteristic behavior patterns. These studies have also shown that there is considerable fluidity for individuals to move from one social class to another over a period of time. This rigidity-fluidity, incidentally, is a fundamental basis of democracy in America. Furthermore, the behavior patterns of social groups change over long periods of time. All of this social structure analysis is highly significant to the marketing researcher.

Secondly, sociologists contribute specialized techniques for measuring motivations of individuals and combining them into group motivations. In this connection, for example, the studies of leadership influence in groups have great potential meaning for the marketing researcher.

While the disciplines of psychology and sociology are the major immediate contributors to motivational research in marketing, the fundamental background of much of this work lies in the field of psychiatry. The clinical work done in this field has demonstrated the degree to which motivations lie beneath the surface of human behavior and can be brought out only by penetrating analysis. The work of the psychiatrist deals with the prevention, diagnosis, and therapy of mental disorders and diseases. Its techniques have therefore been developed in connection with abnormal individuals suffering from conditions ranging from minor neuroses to complete lack of mental, emotional, and social adjustment. The transfer of these techniques to situations dealing with normal people in the aggregate raises serious questions regarding their appropriateness. On the other hand, since the researcher is seeking to penetrate hidden motivations, the methods which have succeeded in abnormal circumstances give most promise of penetrating beneath the surface and revealing the true motivations of normal persons.

Every individual has his own complex personality controlling his motivations. He interprets situations and adjusts his behavior to them in terms of his total past experience and temperament.

Personality, however, operates on at least three levels. First, there is the outer level which one shows to the world. When we speak of a person as being blustery or calm, we speak of this level. Second, there is the conscious inner level of personality. This level is the private world of wishful thinking, secret plans, and daydreaming. Third, there is the subconscious level. Here there are strong motivating forces which the individual himself does not recognize. All of us have had the experience of being surprised, or possibly shocked, by our own unexpected reactions to many situations. The basic problem of motivational research is to penetrate into the conscious and subconscious inner levels of personalities.

A large variety of methods are employed in conducting motivational research. The procedures used in any specific project depend upon the training and background of the individuals conducting the research as well as on the nature of the problem. A great deal of experimental work is also being conducted to develop more effective techniques.

In the discussion which follows, the principal methods found most useful in marketing research are explained. These methods are:

1. Depth interviewing
2. Focussed group interviewing
3. Projective techniques
   a) Free word-association
   b) Sentence completion
   c) Picture responses (frustration)

Depth Interviewing

The depth interview is an adaptation of the basic practice of clinical psychiatry. The psychiatrist places the respondent in the most relaxed and comfortable position possible, asks many questions, and makes statements to stimulate reactions. The psychiatrist works over a long period of time, usually from six to eight months in weekly sessions. Voluminous notes of the patient's answers to questions and free associations are made. He then spends a great deal of time studying these notes and other data obtained in the case history. The analysis is often supplemented by study of the results of various psychiatric tests that have been administered. Out of all this, he draws conclusions which provide a foundation for the therapy he will recommend. In depth interviewing, a similar procedure is followed. However, it is vastly compressed in time, the typical depth interview with a consumer lasting from one to two hours. The common elements are the following: the work is done by a person trained in the techniques of probing, the interviewer asks questions he considers appropriate as the interview progresses, the questions are asked in an order developed during the interview, and the interviewer is alert to make observations of subtle reactions of the respondent. The questions are largely indirect in nature, but are centered around the product or problem involved.

A good example of the contrast between the depth interview and the ordinary questionnaire process is the following: The interviewer is attempting to determine the respondent's true feelings with respect to his position in a corporation. In a depth interview he casually mentions the name of one of the respondent's associates who has recently been promoted. He then observes reactions. After the respondent has indicated for the third time that he is not jealous of his associate's progress, the depth interviewer concludes that the truth is precisely the opposite, namely, that the respondent is motivated by deep feelings of jealousy. In the ordinary questionnaire process, a direct question would be asked, such as "How do you feel about X?"

The following quotations from depth interviews illustrate the sort of penetrating raw material produced by this technique. The name of the product is deleted for obvious reasons.

I'd really feel like a lazy slob to serve canned _____. The kind of woman that uses it lays around in a housecoat all day, or is the kind of person that doesn't care about their home at all, or someone who knows or cares nothing about food. . . . The woman who serves canned _____ for lunch to her kids I get the feeling that the kids aren't the least bit important to her. There's no feeling of family. It's a kind of ersatz living.

I don't know what kind of a woman would serve canned _____ to her family. Some kind of a sluttish person. . . . It shows an utter disregard for the pleasure of her husband and children. . . . She just doesn't care if she'll serve them canned _____ as an entree.

Now it stands to reason. When you fix a dinner at home, you cook it at the last minute. You don't want it standing around, and you don't want it overcooked. You want it to have some body. But if you've got it all cooked in the cans and then have to reheat it, well, it's like anything would be when it's twice cooked. Especially something that should not be overcooked and soft. . . . I should think that the packaged _____ dinners where everything is packaged separately—and you cook it yourself at the last minute—is better. I like it better anyway.

In this research the analyst interpreted the depth interviews illustrated above into the following conclusions in part:

"The Negative Stereotype." We find a series of relaxed images underlying what seems to be the present block.

Consumers tend to consider this product:
   . . . An uninteresting, take-it-for-granted food.
   . . . A fill-in-the-gap when you're in a hurry.
   . . . An economical, poverty-associated food.
   . . . More filling than nutritious.
And, at a deeper level, they feel that it is addressed to the lazy housewife kind of woman, not to the thoughtful, considerate wife and mother that they picture themselves as being.

Because all the principal basic motivations are rooted in fundamental and common psychological characteristics of people, a researcher employing the depth interviewing technique relies on a small number of interviews, generally from 50 to 200. After the interviews are completed, a psychologist with psychiatric training or a team of analysts studies the reports to determine the threads of common responses and reactions running through them. Applying their specialized knowledge, a team of psychologists prepares an analytical report itemizing and evaluating the motivations on the basis of their psychological training, clinical experience, insight, and experience gained from previous work in marketing research.

The primary advantage of the depth interview technique is its ability to discover unsuspected new motivations. In the marketing operation, traditional patterns of selling and advertising appeals evolve and are generally followed. These appeals frequently depart from the motivations which really determine consumer behavior. Another consideration is that the relative importance of various motivating drives changes over a period of time. Through depth interviewing, one frequently discovers the strength of a new appeal so that an entirely different approach to the market can be made.

A second advantage of the depth interview procedure is that it lends itself effectively to the development of a motivational pattern with respect to the selection of a brand or other action under study. This pattern is particularly well structured in case the work has been done by people who have been trained in the comprehensive and systematic Freudian approach. Even though many of Freud's theories have no bearing on a marketing situation and some of his ideas have been greatly modified, the Freudian school has a relatively complete theory of human motivation, which relies basically on the depth interview, and people trained in this school are particularly skilled in developing a pattern of motivation. Once developed, this pattern is generally supported by logic and common sense.

A third advantage of the depth interview is that it provides a tremendous stimulus to the insight of the interviewer. In most marketing research based on interviewing, the knowledge gained is limited to that which comes from the respondent. In a depth interviewing study, so much of the final conclusion depends upon the beliefs and judgment of the people who do the interviewing that we have in effect a two-way street where both interviewer and interviewee are contributing to the knowledge gained. Experience with depth interviewing in marketing research has demonstrated time and again that the major contribution to the solution of the problem has often sprung from the clinical insight of the people conducting the research rather than from the answers and observations recorded in the interviewer's notebooks.

There are a number of important weaknesses in the depth interviewing approach. The first of these weaknesses is the tremendous compression of time the depth interview receives in contrast to the psychiatric interviewing process on which it is based. While there has been repeated demonstration of the validity of psychiatric therapy, there is little or no proof that the depth interview as practiced in marketing research does actually define basic motivations with similar accuracy.

A second weakness of the depth interview in marketing research is the lack of a systematic structure for interpretation of the information obtained. Persons trained in the psychoanalytic school do have a systematic approach to the study of motivation. This approach, however, is with respect to the problems met in clinical psychiatry. No systematic approach adapted specifically to marketing research has been developed. Furthermore, the bulk of people who practice depth interviewing do not have the advantage of psychoanalytic training, hence have no systematic structure for interpretation.

A fourth difficulty is that no quantifiable data are obtained in the depth interviewing process. This means that human judgment is involved in summarizing the findings. Different results will often be obtained by different people in the same situation. As a result, there is little or no opportunity for verification.

A final weakness of depth interviewing is the lack of trained persons who are competent to do the interviewing work. The importance of this deficiency is exemplified in the case of one very successful organization practicing in this field. There is no doubt that the head of this organization can conduct extremely productive depth interviews himself. However, it is found that other staff interviewers are unable to develop the same quality of penetrating information, in spite of the fact that they have studied extensively in the field of psychology. Depth interviewing is often a self-reflection of the one or two key individuals who have the primary responsibility for the project. It is a highly personal matter.

Furthermore, there are a great many people who purport to practice depth interviewing but who do not actually employ the technique as it is understood in the fields of psychiatry and psychology. It became fashionable to employ the term "depth interview." People without training conduct unstructured and fairly lengthy interviews. These are no more than the informal type of interviewing discussed in Chapter 8 in connection with the informal investigation. Yet they are frequently advanced as true depth interviewing.

Focussed Group Interviewing

In the focussed group interviewing method a small number of representative consumers, usually from 6 to 12, is brought together for an informal group discussion of the matter under consideration. The discussion leader is a trained psychologist experienced in group interviewing techniques. He has an outline of specific topics to provide the focus of the research. However, he allows the session to follow its natural course, bringing the discussion back to his topics as he feels the need to do so.

In addition to subjects for discussion, the group leader may also introduce various stimuli, such as products, packages, pictures, and advertisements. The entire discussion is recorded on a wire or tape recorder. Comparisons of recordings of one session with those of another often show great contrast. After sessions with several groups have been conducted, the discussion leader listens repeatedly to the recordings. He then analyzes their content against the background of his psychological training and draws his conclusions with respect to the motivations uncovered.

Some similarities may be seen between the focussed group interviewing procedure and the depth interviewing technique. The order of the subjects discussed in the group interview and the form of questions are completely unstructured. A large amount of time is given to probing and stimulating questions. A typical group session, for example, lasts about three hours. Also, reactions to various stimuli introduced by the group leader are observed carefully.

However, there are fundamental contrasts between focussed group interviewing and depth interviewing. The principal contrast is that group interviewing depends primarily on the interaction of ideas, attitudes, emotions, and beliefs among the various members of the group. The theory is that motivations rise to the surface most effectively in the process of action and counteraction produced by various statements made by group members. For example, when one woman says, "I find ——— Soap is terribly hard on my hands," other members of the group are bound to respond strongly, to expand this thought considerably, and to disclose their own reactions. In the depth interview, we rely upon one individual for this response, expansion, and reaction. In the group interview, we rely on discussion and often obtain heated debate. This process is called social facilitation.

The general nature of a focussed group interviewing session is shown by the following outline of the principal topics used in a study of motivations in the purchase and use of ketchup:

Before beginning the interviewing, a number of problem areas were isolated for special study. With these areas in mind, we developed an interview guide which was used with some variations at all sessions with women, and in suitably modified form with men and children. The following topics were covered:

1. What are some of your meal planning problems? What things concern you most? How do you try to solve these problems? Where does ketchup fit in? Is it important to you in cooking and serving meals, or not so important? Why would that be so?

2. What are some of the specific ways in which you use ketchup? What are some specific foods you put it on? Do you use it in cooking? How? What are some recipes that you especially like?
3. What do you look for in ketchup? How important is taste? Color? Describe the taste which you find in your present brand of ketchup. How would you improve ketchup to make it more useful to you, more enjoyable?
4. Does brand or company name seem to influence your selection of ketchup? In what way? How do you feel about _____ both as a company and as a brand of ketchup?
5. How great is the influence of men and children in your selection of the brand of ketchup which you use? How do the other members of your family feel about ketchup? What are their criticisms?
6. What about the presentation of ketchup in advertising? Can you recall some ads you have seen? What about these we have here—how do they make you feel, what associations come to mind?

Advantages of Focussed Group Interviewing. The advantages generally claimed for the focussed group method are:

1. *Interstimulation broadens the base of communication.* People in groups share ideas . . . more points emerge to think about, discuss, and evaluate than is true of a two-person conversation.
2. *The threshold for personal revelations is lowered.* One person makes a "daring" or intolerant statement which is accepted by the others, someone else feels encouraged to speak more personally, and so on, until the participants as a group move toward a mutually sanctioned standard of frankness which one respondent talking privately to an interviewer cannot achieve so readily.
3. *Social inhibitions cause individuals to respond more nearly in line with their behavior.* The exaggerator, the fabricator, the irresponsible respondent is considerably "toned down" when talking for group consumption.
4. *Respondents in groups try hard to contribute.* Esprit de corps usually develops, which means that a high percentage of the respondents are motivated to give as much information, to express as many views, as possible.
5. *Note-taking is facilitated.* The tape recordings provide a reservoir of realistic communication which may be studied from many points of view. Recordings catch the "flavor" of words used by participants—the emphasis and nuances of oral expression.

Projective Techniques

One of the most interesting developments in motivational research is the use of projective techniques for penetrating the conscious and subconscious motivations of human behavior. Projective devices operate on the principle of confronting an individual with a purposely ambiguous situation which he must interpret and structure. The ambiguous situation may just be a word, such as candy, an incomplete sentence, or a picture. The subject is simply required to respond to the materials in some manner which seems appropriate to him. For example, he may be asked to tell a story about a picture. Within the framework of such flexible directions, complete freedom is allowed. In his response to such stimuli, a person discloses his private world of attitudes, feelings, and values. The projective devices tend to remove the inhibitions of the individual because he is responding in terms of other people rather than thinking of himself.

An illustration of the basic principle of the projective technique in very simple form is found in a slight change in wording of a preference question. Housewives were shown two statements, each of which described a laundry product in a different way and asked, "Which of these two products would you prefer to use?" Their responses to this direct, subjective questioning were 20 per cent in favor of statement A and 80 per cent in favor of statement B. A comparable group of housewives was shown the identical statements but with only a very slight change in the wording of the question to "Which of these two products *do you believe most women* would prefer to use?" Their responses to this indirect, projective questioning were 53 per cent in favor of statement A and 47 per cent in favor of statement B.

It is seen that this slight change in the wording of a question actually reversed the preference vote. The nature of the change was to shift the frame of reference from the respondent herself to an outside situation (other women); hence, in principle the second question form was an application of the projective technique. When confronted with the direct question, housewives would not admit a preference for statement A; by the projective device a large proportion displayed their actual preference for that statement.

Projective techniques are designed to tap the deeper strata of personality in terms of unconscious motivation. In any direct question situation, even the most cooperative subject who has no intent to falsify can tell only what he knows about himself. It is generally accepted that we are inclined to deny many of our true motives and to rationalize impulses in order to make our behavior more socially and personally acceptable. The material brought forth by means of projective methods goes beyond these superficial defenses. For example, it is often very difficult to get a true evaluation of housewives' attitudes toward various home service personalities because of women's apathy or reluctance to say unfavorable things about them.

Projective tests make use of what a person selects for response to a planned stimulus and of his characteristic manner in organizing and deriving meaning from the ambiguous field confronting him. How a person responds to an idea or condition depends upon his own needs, wishes, and preoccupations.

There are several dangers in the use of projective techniques. They must be administered and interpreted by trained, experienced practitioners. Since the tests are largely unstructured, their administration by unskilled persons can cause serious biases. The interpretation of the results can be misleading or meaningless unless undertaken by those who know what to look for and how to do so.

The key to the successful use of projective devices lies in three areas. The first requirement is the development and selection of materials (stimuli) which are most successful in obtaining responses that project beyond the conscious surface level. The second requirement is that the stimuli evoke responses which are related to the motivational problem being researched. The third requirement is that the responses can be interpreted into a logical motivational pattern.

Free Word Association

Word association is one of the oldest of projective techniques. The respondent is read a list of words, one at a time, and asked to respond with the first word that comes to mind. In this way, by careful planning of the order in which the test words appear, the replies become almost automatic.

The data-gathering procedure for word association is standardized. The investigator makes a preliminary statement such as the following to the respondent: "I am making a study of the way different words are put together in people's minds. I will read you a list of words one at a time, and I want you to tell me the very next word you think of. Any word is all right—the main thing is speed. For example, if I said PAPER, you might say BOOK; do you understand?"

The interviewer then reads a list of words carefully selected to reveal motivations with respect to the subject of the research and records word responses. An example of such a list for a study of a food product is the following:

1. Bread	7. Guarantee
2. Garden	8. Economical
3. Home economist	9. Kitchen
4. Wish	10. Old-fashioned
5. Modern	11. Sweet
6. Hungry	12. Health

13. Promise	21. Frosting
14. Honesty	22. Trust
15. Season	23. Advertising
16. Need	24. Diet
17. Lazy	25. Pledge
18. Confidence	26. Cake Mix
19. Fresh	27. Gift
20. Money	28. House

Word association data are usually judged in three ways: by frequency with which any word is given as a response; by analysis of the amount of time that elapses before a response word is given to a test word (hesitation); and by the number of respondents who cannot give any response at all to the test word after a reasonable period of time (blocking).

Common Responses. An analysis of the frequency with which a particular word is given as a response is an analysis of common responses. Although it might seem that the unconscious attitudes of an individual would be so different from those of any other individual that no two could be grouped for analysis, the opposite is usually the case. When unconscious attitudes are tapped, they are strikingly similar for most people. Thus, the number of times that a word is given as a response to a test word shows a basic attitude toward the test word.

Hesitation. The respondent is timed from the moment the test word is spoken until he gives a response. In laboratory work a calibrated stop watch is used. In home interviews investigators count seconds for recording hesitations, after practicing their estimates with a watch. When the respondent takes more than three seconds to respond, it is called a *hesitation*. A hesitation indicates that the respondent is involved in some way with the test word or what it symbolizes; his response is not immediate and automatic. He may, for example, be substituting a second response for his immediate reaction, which he feels is not acceptable. However, he is able to respond to the word in some fashion, even though he hesitates. Hesitation shows the comparative emotional involvement for each word.

Nonresponse. In some cases the test word or what it symbolizes is so charged with emotion for the respondent that he "blocks" so that he can give no response at all. It has been demonstrated that in the case of such words, little if any consistent communication is possible. These words simply do not convey a conscious message and are charged with strong emotional inhibition.

These methods must be used in combination for anything more than the most simple word association analysis. Among the most useful combinations in indicating emotional involvement with a word is the combination of the *hesitation* and *no response* rates. For example, if a word shows a high *hesitation* rate and a low *no response* rate, we can assume that although there is concern about the area that the word symbolizes (as shown by the high hesitation rate), the low *no response* rate shows that the word does convey its message. This type of response often indicates an attention-attracting word for conveying a message. However, when a word has both a high *hesitation* rate and a high *no response* rate, the word is usually a bad word for conveying a message. When a word or group of words with high *hesitation* and *no response* rates are presented in a message, the meaning of the message is usually highly distorted in its transmission or simply not transmitted at all.

Successive Word Association. This technique is similar to single word association except that the respondent is asked to continue to give single word responses to the same test word as long as he can. As single word association gives the most common response, successive word association continues through several levels of attitudes. This method shows which words and attitudes are in the process of becoming common and indicates the growth of favorable or unfavorable attitudes. Successive word associations are judged in ways similar to single word associations with the aid of common responses and no response rates.

Sentence Completion

Closely akin to word association is the sentence completion technique. In this method the respondent is presented with a series of statements which express incomplete ideas but direct his attention along a predetermined path. The respondent is asked to complete each of the sentences with whatever thoughts first come to mind. Thus, he finishes each sentence with his own interpretation of what the beginning means to him. An example is shown in Figure 28.

The sentence completion method operates on the principle that the associations revealed by responses to the incomplete stimuli reveal hidden motivations. In the construction of the incomplete sentences the researcher deliberately varies the nature of the ideas presented so that the respondent is not aware of the specific sentences which are inserted to obtain data directly related to the problem at hand. The sentences are kept as simple as possible to encourage rapid completion so that the respondent will shift his thoughts back and forth between different subjects as he completes the series of sentences.

SENTENCE COMPLETION SURVEY

Complete these sentences to express your real feelings You can write anything you like as long as it is your true feeling. Try to do every one. Be sure to make a complete sentence.

1. The future_____

2. Atomic warfare_____

3. The Army_____

4. The draft _____

5. The reason most men enlist in the Army _____

_____

6. When I am old I hope that _____

7. Back home_____

8. The main difference between a civilian career and a career in the Army is_____

_____

9. My greatest worry is_____

10. My greatest fear _____

11 The one way in which the Army helps most men is _____

_____

12. I regret_____

13. The best thing about the Army_____

14. I hate _____

15. Army discipline_____

16. The best way a man can serve his country_____

_____

17. People_____

18. The worst thing about the Army _____

FIGURE 28. Section from a Sentence Completion Test

Sentence completion is used primarily in conjunction with other projective methods to amplify the data obtained by other means. The results produced by this technique are also valuable as a basis for verification of interpretations and conclusions.

Picture Responses (Frustration)

In the picture response technique the respondent is shown an illustration which may be interpreted in many different ways and is asked to interpret or tell its story. The pictures are purposely made quite vague in order to provide the greatest possible opportunity for a variety of responses. The Rorschach ink-blot test is used in clinical psychology. These "pictures" are literally made by ink blots so that only an apparently meaningless form is shown. However, it has been

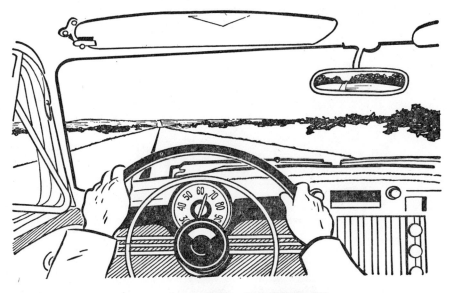

Put yourself HERE

FIGURE 29. Picture Response. One of a series of pictures used in a motivational study of automobiles.

found that when people are asked to describe what such "pictures" convey, they do project their own personality traits into the pictures. The Thematic Apperception Test presents a subject with a series of social situations which he tries to explain, tells how the situation came about, and describes the outcome of it.

An example of the picture response technique, based on an adaptation of the Thematic Apperception Test, is afforded in a study of motivations with respect to automobiles made by Social Research Incorporated. They used a picture of the road seen from behind the steering wheel position. Only the hands grasping the wheel were shown, the respondent was told to put himself in that position, and

FIGURE 30. The Picture-Cartoon Technique

asked to tell what kind of things came to his mind. The speedometer
was shown in the picture—set between 60 and 70 miles per hour.

Although the instructions told the person to put himself in the
driver's situation, most people did not do this because they did not
want to think of themselves as going so fast. The picture clearly
elicited contradictory attitudes about speed. Respondents told stories
about how much fun it would be going this fast somewhere on the
open road, but it was always someone else doing it; he should not be
doing it. Social Research translated this to mean that a car must be
capable of high speed, but high speed is wrong. Speed involves both
pleasure and fear. The manufacturer must therefore convince prospects that his automobile is both fast and safe.

In marketing research the picture response technique usually employs illustrations of situations involving the use of the product or service under study. One of the most effective forms is the picture cartoon. In this device the picture usually shows two persons. One of them is making a statement in the speech balloon. An example would be a picture of two housewives talking over the back-yard fence. The first housewife is saying, "I just served my family Swift's new precooked sausages." The balloon for the second housewife's response is left blank and the respondent is asked to tell what she said. Psychologists interpret these responses in terms of the attitudes, reactions, doubts, fears, and other motivations revealed with respect to this new product.

Experience in marketing research with picture response devices clearly indicates that they succeed in getting people to respond impersonally to the situations confronting them. There is no question that these responses are quite different from those which are obtained by direct questioning. Also, there is little doubt that this device gets much closer to inner motivations.

One of the advantages of the picture response method is the control of the researcher over the situations presented to the respondents. It is possible to explore many different aspects of motivation and to relate them rather directly to the specific problem.

Another advantage of this method is that it is particularly applicable to situations in which the respondent is most likely to hide his real feelings because of social pressures. An example is found in a study of motivations for enlisting in the army. It is not socially acceptable for one to give avoidance of the draft as a reason impelling enlistment. However, in response to a picture cartoon which confronts the respondent with the statement, "I hear Bob has enlisted. Why do you suppose he did that?" it is perfectly proper for a young man to ascribe the draft as a motivating force for an anonymous Bob.

Another important advantage of the picture response technique is that a relatively large number of respondents can be covered economically in the research, and responses to a variety of situations can be obtained from each one. The responses also tend to pattern themselves. As a result, analysis into basic motivational themes running through responses from different subjects is facilitated.

Limitations of Motivational Research

As more and more motivational work is being done, leaders in the field are raising questions as to the precise scope which should be assigned to it. Because of the intense desire to obtain sound answers as to basic motivations, there is a natural tendency to assume the existence of some single dominating motivation or drive behind any given form of market behavior. However, there is a growing feeling that there is no such thing as one most important motivation in the market place, but rather that there is a variety of motivations toward which markeing efforts may be directed. Furthermore, researchers are coming to the point of view that the differences in the power of the drives represented by a number of motivations are not as great as might be assumed. A number of leading practitioners now believe that motivational research is primarily a verbalizing device which helps make respondents more articulate in expressing their reasons for buying a product or selecting one brand over another rather than a mystical procedure for discovering some one all-embracing hidden motivation.

There is also a growing caution against automatic acceptance of motivational devices developed in other fields. These devices have been *individual-centered,* dealing with a single person, rather than *mass-centered.* The problem of the psychiatrist is to develop a tremendous mass of data covering the entire life of an individual. Out of this mass of data he arrives at certain conclusions regarding factors motivating the patient's current behavior. In applying motivational techniques to the masses of individuals who compose a market, we must work with a relatively small amount of data regarding each individual who is studied. These relatively thin data on many individuals must then be combined into a general rationalization regarding large social groups. Whether this is a legitimate transfer is a moot question.

Related to the preceding difficulty is the question as to whether motivational data on individuals are even additive. In a market survey, we can learn facts about the behavior of individuals with respect to phenomena such as brand preferences and add them up to arrive at conclusions regarding the total market and its various subdivisions. It is doubtful whether the motivations compelling one individual toward a certain type of behavior and the motivations impelling another person to identical behavior are sufficiently homogeneous so that we can add them together.

A fourth concern regarding motivational research is that the data are not usually quantified. Since quantification is generally regarded as an essential element in scientific method, its absence in motivational research removes a key process creating confidence in a result. There is always room for doubt as to the true significance of any given finding. This lack of quantification also leads to questions regarding sampling structure. While it is generally accepted that motivational research can work effectively with small samples, just how one is to determine how many and which individuals are to be included in a motivational study is largely a matter of opinion.

A fifth problem is that of interpretation. Since the results are not expressed in quantitative form, interpretation becomes a personal matter. This means that the results of a motivational study largely reflect the frame of reference of the individual who is responsible for its interpretation. Obviously, his own motivations, training, attitudes, beliefs, and desires constantly tend to influence the results. In order to minimize this difficulty it is a standard practice to have the field findings analyzed and interpreted independently by two or more individuals. If their interpretations coincide, it is assumed that the conclusions are correct. However, analyses and interpretations should always be in the hands of trained social psychologists with a great deal of experience in this area. Unfortunately, much of this work is done by amateurs and laymen, who do not have the advantage of training, experience, and the resulting objective and cautious point of view which is essential to sound interpretation of motivational data.

Motivational research is also plagued by major problems of semantics. In developing its own vocabulary, terminologies have arisen which tend to be complicated. Worst of all, there are many different schools of thought in the various disciplines represented in this field; many of them have their own unique terminologies and, at the same time, use the same words with different meanings. A common difficulty in all the social sciences is a lack of precise symbols such as those employed in chemistry, physics, and mathematics. Furthermore, instead of using completely coined words or a dead language such as the Latin used in medicine and law, many of their words are similar to those in common English usage. This leads to vagueness and considerable difficulty in communication.

A seventh major problem is the lack of positive validation of conclusions. The closest approach to validation has been verification by obtaining similar interpretations of parallel situations by different analysts. Motivational research therefore suffers from the lack of any outside criteria which can be employed to validate its conclusions. As a result the question is frequently raised, "Does this test measure what it sets out to measure?" The fact that many of the methods produce clear-cut behavior responses does not necessarily mean that these responses are to be interpreted as a direct reflection of the motivations and drives they purport to measure. All motivational research makes the assumption that there is a direct and definable relationship between what is observed in the research and the motivation the researcher is seeking.

In spite of the difficulties discussed above, there is no doubt that the current techniques of motivational research have taken us a long way down the tortuous road toward understanding human behavior. The actual experience in its applications to marketing problems is still quite limited. As more experience is obtained, many of these questions will be answered and the failures overcome by more effective and dependable methodology.

SELECTED READINGS

ABRAMS, MARK. "Possibilities and Problems of Group Interviewing," *Public Opinion Quarterly*, Fall, 1949, pp. 502–6.

ABT, LAWRENCE E., and BELLAK, LEOPOLD (eds.). *Projective Psychology*. New York: Alfred A. Knopf, Inc., 1950.

ANDERSON, HAROLD H., and ANDERSON, GLADYS L. (eds.). *An Introduction to Projective Techniques*. New York: Prentice-Hall, Inc., 1951.

BELL, JOHN E. *Projective Techniques*. New York: Longmans, Green & Co., Inc., 1948.

BERNAYS, EDWARD L. "Why Understanding Human Motives Is Essential to Business Success Today," *Printers' Ink*, September 19, 1952, pp. 44–45.

BRITT, STEUART HENDERSON. "The Strategy of Consumer Motivation," *Journal of Marketing*, April, 1950, pp. 666–74.

CHESKIN, LOUIS, and WARD, L. B. "Indirect Approach to Market Reactions," *Harvard Business Review*, September, 1948, pp. 572–80.

COBLINER, W. GODFREY. "On the Place of Projective Tests in Opinion and Attitude Surveys," *International Journal of Opinion and Attitude Research*, Winter, 1951, pp. 480–90.

DICHTER, ERNEST. "Case Histories in the Study of Motivation," *Research Topics*, 1951 A.A.A.A. Annual Meeting Transcipts, Part III, p. 1. New York: American Association of Advertising Agencies.

DICHTER, ERNEST. "Psychological View of Advertising Effectiveness," *Journal of Marketing*, July, 1949, pp. 61–66.

GARBER, C. W., JR. "Play Techniques for Interviewing on Durable Goods," *Public Opinion Quarterly*, Spring, 1951, pp. 139–40.

GREEN, HAROLD E. "Top Executives Tell How to Use Social Sciences in Advertising," *Printers' Ink*, February 27, 1953, pp. 35–37.

HARE, MASON. "Projective Techniques in Market Research," *Journal of Marketing*, April, 1950, pp. 649–56.

HENRY, WILLIAM E. "A Study in the Application of Socio-Psychological Research to the Problems of Business and Industry," *Journal of Social Psychology*, February, 1948, pp. 37–61.

MERTON, ROBERT K., et al. *The Focussed Interview*. New York: Bureau of Applied Social Research, Columbia University, 1952.

"New Techniques in Questioning, Part of Proceedings of the American Association for Public Research," *Public Opinion Quarterly*, Winter, 1951–52, pp. 788–93.

NEWMAN, JOSEPH W. "Looking Around: Consumer Motivation Research," *Harvard Business Review*, January-February, 1955, pp. 135–44.

PARADISE, L. M., and BLANKENSHIP, ALBERT B. "Depth Questioning," *Journal of Marketing*, January, 1951, pp. 274–88.

SANFORD, FILLMORE H. "The Use of a Projective Device in Attitude Surveying," *Public Opinion Quarterly*, Winter, 1950–51, pp. 697–709.

SHAPIRO, EMORY P. "The Group Interview as a Tool of Research," *Journal of Marketing*, April, 1952, pp. 452–54.

SMITH, GEORGE HORSLEY. *Motivation Research in Advertising and Marketing*. New York: McGraw-Hill Book Co., Inc., 1954.

Vicary, James M. "How Psychiatric Methods Can Be Applied to Market Research," *Printers' Ink*, May 11, 1951, pp. 39–48.

Warner, W. Lloyd, *et al. Social Class in America*. Chicago: Science Research Associates, Inc., 1949.

Wechsler, Irving R. "Problems in the Use of Indirect Methods of Attitude Measurements," *Public Opinion Quarterly*, Spring, 1951, pp. 133–38.

Wood, Albert J. "Word Association Tests Help in Product and Copy Research," *Printers' Ink*, October 11, 1946, pp. 48–49.

Woodward, Julian L., *et al.* "Depth Interviewing," *Journal of Marketing*, April, 1950, pp. 721–24.

Yoell, W. A. "The Depth Interview Reveals Attitudes Toward New Products," *Printers' Ink*, February 7, 1949, pp. 50–52.

CASES

Automobiles—What They Mean to Americans. Chicago: The Chicago Tribune, 1954.

Brown, William F. "The Determination of Factors Influencing Brand Choice," *Journal of Marketing*, April, 1950, pp. 699–706.

Weiss, Edward H. "Why Do Consumers Really Buy Your Products?" *Advertising Age*, November 24, 1952, pp. 48–49.

19

OPERATIONS RESEARCH

During World War II, first in England, then in the United States, the most baffling military and naval strategic problems which arose were solved by an entirely new research technique. Teams of scientists, representing a variety of disciplines, were organized to concentrate on the development of a quantitative basis for solving these major problems. The specifications of their assignment required essentially the discovery of the means for making the best and most efficient use of military forces and weapons then available with the least loss of life. Problems of early warning radar, air-borne rockets, anti-U-boat offenses, mine warfare and more efficient logistics and supply are examples of areas in which these teams worked very effectively. The new development, from a research point of view, was to take scientists out of their laboratories and combine them into groups working against specific problems in conjunction with the operating commands in the military and naval forces. The name "Operations Research" was given to this technique.

A generally accepted formal definition of the concept of operations research has not been developed as yet. One investigator, who has made a thorough study of the problem of definition, has arrived at the following statement:

Operations research is a movement toward the unification of the tools of the sciences, where teams of scientists of various abilities, making use of the scientific method, employ these tools at top levels of management, in order to provide management with a quantitative basis for decision. The primary tool is statistical analysis and probability theory. The teams act in an advisory capacity to management, unhampered by controls of the industry.[1]

Because of their great accomplishments in solving the most critical problems in the war, the use of operations research in solving peacetime problems of government and of industry has rapidly developed. It is particularly effective in dealing with complex problems involving

[1] Alfred Jan Kana, An unpublished paper, November, 1953.

many influencing factors which cannot be reduced to a common measurable denominator. Since marketing is a very complex activity, operations research gives great promise of future development in this field. Because of the impetus given to operations research by its wartime success, its widespread use in government, and a growing acceptance in industry, an understanding of this approach is of vital interest to market researchers.

As will be seen from the definition above, marketing and distribution research themselves constitute a form of operations research in many respects. When "O.R." is discussed as a means of solving marketing problems, people frequently mean a comprehensive marketing research as expounded in this book. While one researcher is "in command," most marketing research involves several top-flight researchers. There is also a growing trend toward employing persons with specialized training in outside fields, such as psychologists, on major projects. If a group of researchers trained in different scientific fields is given the opportunity to solve a marketing problem as a team, the marketing research is, in effect, operations research.

In marketing, an operations research team might well represent a combination of scientifically trained persons from the fields of statistics, mathematics, psychology, sociology, economics, engineering, and business management, and even from physics or biology, depending on the nature of the problem. It can be said that operations research techniques are being applied in marketing and distribution research when the following conditions prevail:

1. A team rather than an individual is in control.
2. The team is composed of scientists trained in different fields.
3. The team is working with top management.
4. The team is concentrating on a basic marketing problem.
5. The team is given freedom to define the problem and develop novel techniques for its solution.
6. Quantitative data and analysis used extensively as a basis for the final solution of the problem.
7. The solution to the problem is placed in the hands of management for executive decisions.

There are great differences in the way in which people trained in different scientific fields think. Therefore, a major contribution of operations research is bringing minds trained in separate disciplines together to think rigorously about a common problem. Also, each scientific field has its own procedures for handling data. Thus another advantage of operations research is the increased opportunity to develop the novel procedures and new types of data which are most effective in the solution of complex problems as a result of combining different disciplines.

The Model. The concept of a "model" is often a key part of the operations research process. Operations research assumes that there are alternative courses of action from which choices can be made. Measures of effectiveness of various alternatives must be obtained in order to determine which course of action will best achieve the explicit goals which have been set up by the operations research team. A model of the operations is particularly helpful in this connection.

The operations research model may be a physical model which diagrams the results to be anticipated from various courses of action. It may be a stack of punched cards containing sales data. It may take the form of a series of mathematical equations. It may be an aspect of probability theory. The model is, in a sense, an explicit expression of hypotheses.

Under any circumstance, an operations research team must rely heavily upon the marketing researcher and his materials when it undertakes to find the solution to a marketing problem. The bulk of the quantitative data employed by the operations research team is of the type provided by marketing research. These may be internal data such as those obtained from sales analysis, or they may be external data such as those obtained from surveys, dealer records, or marketing experiments.

Operations Research Methods

Many tools are employed in the computational aspects of operations research. The most prevalent tools are simple arithmetic, linear programming, the queuing theory, and the symbolic logic method. The latter methods are rather involved. The reader is referred to the list of references at the end of this chapter if he wishes to pursue them.

An example of the simple arithmetic approach is the following: Suppose your automobile is unavailable for transportation to work. A problem immediately arises concerning which method of transportation you should take. You know that a train takes one-half hour each way and costs $1.25 per round trip. You also know that a bus takes an hour each way and costs 50 cents for a round trip. Immediately your decision is to take a bus and save 75 cents. However, an operations research team would analyze the problem more deeply and put values on the intangibles, making it possible to arrive at a more all-inclusive decision. Suppose your spare time is worth 60 cents an hour, the desirability of having a seat on the train vs. no seat possible on the bus worth 20 cents, and the extra half-hour sleep in the morning worth an additional 15 cents. Adding these values to the 50 cents fare by bus, you would have 50¢ + 60¢ + 20¢ + 15¢, or $1.45 as the total real cost by bus as compared to $1.25 by train. In this case it would be worth while to take the train.

Probability theory is a basic tool of operations research. Many complex problems involving the appraisal of alternative actions can be solved by the application of mathematical formulas of various probability functions. The construction of these formulas lies in the province of the mathematician or statistician. However, the value of this procedure in operations research has been illustrated frequently by another hypothetical example:

A newsboy buys newspapers for 2 cents and sells them for 3 cents. He cannot return any of the papers. He sells an average of ten papers per day although he often sells more or less on any one day. However, it is found that he sells 11 as often as he sells 9; 12 as often as 8, etc. The problem is, "How many papers should he buy to maximize his profits?"

In solving this problem, first a table of profit is set up as shown by Table 16.

TABLE 16

NET PROFIT REALIZED AT VARIOUS LEVELS
OF PURCHASES AND SALES

Number of Customers	Number of Papers Bought						
	8	9	10	11	12	13	14
14	8¢	9¢	10¢	11¢	12¢	13¢	14¢
13	8	9	10	11	12	13	11
12	8	9	10	11	12	10	8
11	8	9	10	11	9	7	5
10	8	9	10	8	6	4	2
9	8	9	7	5	3	1	− 1
8	8	6	4	2	0	− 2	− 4
7	5	3	1	− 1	− 3	− 5	− 7
6	2	0	2	− 4	− 6	− 8	−10

Next a table showing the "profit by alternatives" to relate various purchase levels to various rates of sale is set up, as shown in Table 17. The sum of each of the columns in this table clearly demonstrates that buying nine newspapers per day would be most profitable for the newsboy. This kind of finding, applied against the many thousands of transactions in a marketing establishment, would have significant profit results.

TABLE 17

NET PROFIT REALIZED BY EVENLY DISTRIBUTED COMBINATIONS
OF PURCHASES AND SALES

Demand	Number of papers bought						
Possibility	8	9	10	11	12	13	14
10 demanded	8¢	9¢	10¢	8¢	6¢	4¢	2¢
9 or 11 demanded	8	9	8½	8	6	4	2
8 or 12 demanded	8	7½	7	6½	6	4	2
7 or 13 demanded	6½	6	5½	5	4½	4	2
6 or 14 demanded	5½	4½	4	3½	3	2½	2
Total Profit	35½¢	36¢	35¢	31¢	25½¢	18½¢	10¢

Marketing Research Applications

A classic example of the application of operations research to a marketing problem dealt with the problem of the amount of sales time which should be placed against prospects for a manufacturer of portable tools. This company had limited its promotional selling expenses to a fixed percentage of sales and their salesmen called on only about 40 per cent of the accounts in any one area.

The operations research group assigned to work with this company set as its objective the problem of getting an explicit and quantitative description of customer behavior and the effect on it of the company's promotional effort. It was expected that this would make it possible to construct a measure of relative efficiency of the existing promotional sales activities and to determine a measure of the amount of sales increase resulting from a given amount of promotional activity.[2]

The solution of this problem was found in a statistical analysis of the frequency with which customers ordered in relation to whether they had or had not been exposed to sales promotion. The team discovered that customers, regardless of the total value of their purchases or the average value of their individual orders, tended to buy the same types and assortments of products and tended to have the same average order value. Mathematical equations which described the distribution of the frequency of purchase of customers in various areas were found to coincide with their actual behavior in ordering. Promoted and nonpromoted customers were then separated. A comparison of observed and calculated numbers of each type of customer

[2] John F. Magee, "Application of Operations Research to Marketing and Related Management Problems," *Journal of Marketing*, April, 1954, p. 362. The article describes this example in detail.

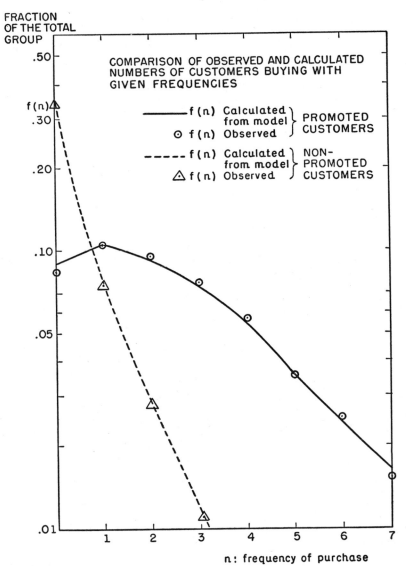

FRACTION
OF THE TOTAL
GROUP

COMPARISON OF OBSERVED AND CALCULATED
NUMBERS OF CUSTOMERS BUYING WITH
GIVEN FREQUENCIES

——— f(n) Calculated from model } PROMOTED CUSTOMERS
⊙ f(n) Observed

----- f(n) Calculated from model } NON-PROMOTED CUSTOMERS
△ f(n) Observed

n: frequency of purchase

FIGURE 31. Comparison of Observed and Calculated Numbers of Customers Buying with Given Frequencies. (John F. Magee, *Journal of Marketing*, April, 1954, p. 364.)

buying with various frequencies showed sharp contrast between the promoted and nonpromoted customers (see Figure 31).

As a result of this analysis it was found that the expected business from a customer was reduced by 50 per cent if a promotional salesman did not call on him. Customers were then classified on the basis of the number of orders placed during a period of one year. An ideal allocation of promotional time was developed, based on projections of increased volume which could be anticipated from sales promotion of customers with varying ordering characteristics. The system was tried out on a small scale and proved successful. When it was spread to all sales areas, phenomenal sales and profit increase were obtained.

Operations research holds great promise of future growth in its application to the solution of the most baffling marketing problems. It has already been used successfully in connection with problems in the amount of promotional effort which will maximize profits, the more efficient use of salesmen's time, the establishment of inventory policies in the face of business fluctuations, the evaluation of trade advertising, and remuneration of chain store managers. There appears to be no phase of marketing to which this technique cannot be potentially applied. As more experience is gained it should be anticipated that marketing research will draw more and more on operations research techniques for the solution of critical problems.

SELECTED READINGS

GOLDSMITH, MAURICE. "What Is Operations Research?" *Discovery*, January, 1948.

HERMANN, C. C., and MAGEE, J. F. "Operations Research for Management," *Harvard Business Review*, July, 1953, pp. 100–112.

HORVATH, WILLIAM J. "Operations Research: A Scientific Basis for Executive Decision," *The American Statistician*, October, 1948, p. 6.

KITTEL, CHARLES. "The Nature and Development of Operations Research," *Science*, February 7, 1947, pp. 150–53.

LEVINSON, H. C., and BROWN, A. A. "Operations Research," *Scientific American*, March, 1951, pp. 15–17.

MORSE, P. M. "Operations Research," *Technology Review*, February, 1951, pp. 191–94.

MORSE, P. M., and KIMBALL, GEORGE E. *Methods of Operations Research*. New York: Chapman & Hall, Ltd., 1950.

SOLOW, H. "Operations Research," *Fortune*, April, 1951, pp. 105–7.

STEVENS, R. "Operations Research Is Common Sense," *Business Week*, December 1, 1951, pp. 62–64.

CASE

MAGEE, JOHN F. "Application of Operations Research to Marketing and Related Management Problems," *Journal of Marketing*, April, 1954, pp. 361–69.

20

THE PANEL TECHNIQUE

Applications of the survey method in marketing research may be classified in terms of whether a single interview is used or whether the same respondents are interviewed a number of times. The latter procedure is known as the panel technique.

Participants in the panel are selected on the basis of regular sampling methods. Their willingness to act as respondents in the research for an extended period of time is determined before any research data are obtained. Panel data may be obtained through personal interview or by mail. Participants, except in panels which are used to study subjects in which they have a vital personal interest, are usually secured by offering them cash payments or premiums for their cooperation.

One continuous national purchase panel maintained by the Market Research Corporation of America is available on a fee basis to different manufacturers on a syndicated basis. A continuous national panel used for special projects, such as product tests, is conducted by National Family Opinion Company. Some manufacturers operate their own panels on a limited scale. Magazines, newspapers, and some retailers, particularly large chain organizations and department stores, now use panels extensively. Advertising agencies also operate consumer panels, an example being that of the J. Walter Thompson Company. Temporary panels are established from time to time for specialized research projects.

The most common form of panel consists of a group of consumers who report purchases and other marketing data at regularly stipulated intervals. In addition to consumer panels, there are studies employing dealer panels, panels of executives, panels of experts, and panels for public opinion research. Panels are also used in television and radio research, particularly in connection with audience measurement by means of mechanical devices recording the use of radio sets or diaries in which viewing or listening is entered. No matter what the composition of the panel, its essential characteristic is that the same group of persons is interviewed or observed over a period of time.

PAGE FOUR

FRUITS: (PACKED IN CANS OR GLASS JARS)

WHEN PURCHASED	BRAND	DESCRIPTION	QUANTITY	WEIGHT	PRICE	WHERE PURCHASED

FIGURE 32. A Panel Diary. This page from the questionnaire used by a consumer purchase panel illustrates one method employed to obtain continuous data from panel participants. (Market Research Corporation of America.)

RECORD YOUR PURCHASES OF FROZEN FRUITS ON PAGE 5 — FRESH AND DRIED FRUITS ON PAGE 6

Of course, no panel is composed of the same individuals throughout its existence. In addition to the natural losses from deaths, removals, etc., many panel members lose interest and drop out. One of the chief problems of panels, particularly those which attempt to maintain a continuous sample of the national consumer market, is the turnover of panel participants. Substitutions are made from time to time. Utmost care must be taken that the sample proportions of various geographic areas, family characteristics, etc., are maintained.

Consumer Purchase Panels. The most common types of data acquired in consumer purchase panels are illustrated by the following questions:

> "How many units of a specified product did you buy during the reporting period?"
> "How much did you pay per unit?"
> "What brand did you buy?"
> "What size package, what style or design of that product did you buy?"
> "Where did you make your purchase?"

Other subjects often included concern newspapers and magazines read, television or radio programs received, and general questions regarding other family habits and activities. Sometimes questions such as "If you made a change in brand preference, please state why the change was made," and "What and how much do you expect to buy during the next reporting period?" are asked.

Advantages of Panel Research. Panel research has its own particular characteristics which differentiate it from other applications of the survey method. There are five features of panel studies which can be real advantages in marketing research:

1. A panel provides a continuous record of the behavior of the individuals composing the panel. Thus it is possible to make special behavior studies over a period of time, such as studies of brand loyalty, which cannot be made accurately by one-time interviewing. Furthermore, the data acquired are based on the continuous record of the respondent's behavior rather than on his memory.

2. A panel provides opportunities for measuring changes over a period of time, as well as changes brought about by specific influences. The members of the panel actually may serve as "guinea pigs," whose behavior in response to various influences may be observed in much the same manner as the biological scientist observes results of controlled feeding or applications of drugs. In this connection it should be borne in mind that marketing influences are extremely complex, and there is a great temptation to attribute change in a panel to

some single element. Actually the change may have come about as a result of many factors, some of which may not even be known to the researcher. An example is the attempt to measure the influence of an individual advertising medium on family purchases.

3. A panel may offer special opportunities for deep-probing analysis. Since the panel participants have established their willingness to cooperate and proved this willingness by their continued presence in the panel, the "stranger" influence present in one-time survey interviews is eliminated.

4. The panel technique has advantages from a sampling point of view. Since the group being used is a relatively stable population, smaller numbers are required for measurements of change through time.

5. A consumer panel obtains information on buying from all sources, whereas store-auditing procedures may miss important purchase sources, such as large chain organizations and mail-order and house-to-house purchases.

Disadvantages of Panel Research. The advantages of panel research, discussed above, are realized only if the panel is properly constructed and administered for the specific purposes for which it is designed. All the advantages do not apply to every type of panel. For example, a consumer purchase panel is of no value for deep-probing analysis, as the ability of the participants to contribute is exhausted by the amount of effort involved in accurately reporting family purchases.

There are also specific weaknesses of panel research, some of the most important of which are the following:

1. All panels have a drop-out problem. In a panel constructed for a special purpose to be used only for a limited time period, this difficulty is overcome by deliberately overloading the panel when it is established. Even in this case, there is always the danger that the individuals or families who drop out during the course of the study will represent particular types, so heavy overloading and careful reconstruction of the sample are necessary. In panels operating over a very long period of time, the turnover and the replacement of participants are a problem. A special difficulty arises with the participants who nominally continue but whose cooperation has become so stereotyped and inaccurate that they are not effective members of the panel. The difficulty of detecting such cases and determining their extent is obvious.

2. There is danger of attempting to obtain too much information from panel members. Establishing and conducting a panel operation

is expensive. There is always the temptation to use names of co-operators for special mail questionnaires and to extend the scope of subjects included, with the result that the validity of the information obtained in the total operation is seriously impaired. Syndicated panels, which distribute their information to a number of clients, must exercise special caution in this regard.

3. The incentive may produce distorted results. In practically all panels it is necessary to offer either a cash payment or premiums as rewards for cooperation. There is danger that the sample will be distorted by overselecting those individuals who are particularly susceptible to premium offers. As any advertiser with premium experience knows, there are particular classes of individuals who are responsive to premium offers. It is much less costly to retain an individual or family in a panel than to find a new replacement, so there is a temptation to offer extra bonus premiums, tending to produce further selectivity.

4. Panels are susceptible to distortion in sampling. Persons who are willing to participate in any long-range research activity tend to compose an unrepresentative sample.

5. Participants may report data inaccurately. This reporting is a special problem of the panel technique when individuals or families are required to keep records of daily or frequent occurrences. Purchase panels require participants to keep a diary in which purchases and other data are recorded. It is obvious that many persons fill out their diaries some time after purchases have actually been made. Furthermore, if a large number of items is covered in the diary, fatigue will cause many omissions of entries or inaccurate reporting.

6. Panel operations are expensive. This fact is not a disadvantage in the case of syndicated services, where the individual company subscribing to the service pays only a part of the total cost.

In spite of the limitations outlined above, there is no doubt that the panel technique is one of the important forms of consumer survey work. Special panels designed to solve difficult but limited problems are especially valuable. Various devices to lessen the dangers inherent in the panel method are being developed; this procedure has now thoroughly established its place in marketing and distribution research.

SELECTED READINGS

BLACK, THOMAS W. "Using the Consumer Panel to Measure Department Store Buying," *Journal of Retailing*, December, 1948, pp. 151–57.
Establishing a National Consumer Panel from a Probability Sample, An Agricultural Marketing Act of 1946 (RMA, Title II), Contract Report, Marketing Research Report No. 40. Washington, D. C.: U. S. Department of Agriculture, June, 1953.

FERBER, ROBERT. "Observations on a Consumer Panel Operation," *Journal of Marketing*, January, 1953, pp. 246–59.

HOBART, DONALD M. *Marketing Research Practice*. New York: The Ronald Press Co., 1950, pp. 222–34.

J. WALTER THOMPSON'S CONSUMER PURCHASE PANEL. *Advertising Agency and Advertising and Selling*, December, 1950, pp. 56 ff.

JAHODA, MARIE, DEUTSCH, MORTON, and COOK, STUART W. *Research Methods in Social Relations*. New York: The Dryden Press, Inc., 1951, pp. 588–609.

REED, V. D. "Good News and Bad About Sales: How Panel Studies Reveal It," *Sales Management*, March 15, 1948, pp. 58 ff.

ROLLINS, M. "The Practical Use of Repeated Questionnaire Waves," *Journal of Applied Psychology*, December, 1940, pp. 770–72.

RUCH, F. L. "Effects of Repeated Interviews on the Respondent's Answers," *Journal of Consulting Psychology*, September–October, 1941, p. 179–82.

CASE

BLANKERTZ, DONALD F., FERBER, ROBERT, and WALES, HUGH G. *Cases and Problems in Marketing Research*. New York: The Ronald Press Co., 1954, pp. 56–62.

21

METHODS OF QUANTITATIVE MARKET ANALYSIS

Many different methods of quantitative market analysis are now used. These methods differ both in fundamental philosophy and in techniques employed. The most important methods are:

1. Direct data method.
2. Corollary data method.
3. Single index method.
4. Arbitrary factors method.
5. Multiple correlation method.

Direct Data Method

The direct data method relies upon sales statistics for a commodity as the best method of measuring its potential market.

The automobile industry is an outstanding case in point. Because of the licensing system in force, automobile manufacturers are able to obtain monthly figures by counties of new-car sales (registration) for each make and model. This accurate information is essential in any quantitative analysis in the automobile field and precludes the necessity of other methods, except in very special cases.

There are several types of direct sales data employed in quantitative analysis. In the first type, the sales data appear as a by-product of some licensing, inspection, or tax system. Data employed by automobile, gasoline, and insurance companies are of this type. A second type is that in which the data are gathered by trade associations for the benefit of members, or through direct exchange of data by members of the industry. Examples are the data provided by the Washing Machine Manufacturers' Association, the Electric Refrigeration Bureau, and the Radio and Television Manufacturers' Association. A third type is the data provided by service organizations. These organizations maintain retail store audits or consumer panels to report the flow of merchandise into various sections of the market. The A. C. Nielsen data, for example, are sufficiently adequate and reliable for sales-potential purposes. Other methods of quantitative analysis, however, are necessary to adapt the facts to marketing units finer than those reported.

TABLE 18

APPLICATION OF THE DIRECT DATA METHOD

(1) Territory	(2) Total Gasoline Consumption (000 omitted)	(3) Relative Potential (% of U. S. total)	(4) Market Potential * (000 omitted)
Alabama	140,513	0.91	154,700
Arizona	66,396	.43	73,100
Arkansas	117,352	.76	129,200
(etc.)	(etc.)	(etc.)	(etc.)
U. S. Total	15,440,919	100.00	17,000,000

Explanation of columns:

1. Territorial units: states, counties, sales territories, etc.
2. Latest available data on sales, covering a period of one to four years.
3. Column 2 converted to percentages.
4. Column 3 times total anticipated sales (17,000,000) during period for which the potentials are being set.

* The reader will note the potential varies from the sales data only by the difference between the total sales and the total potential.

The primary advantage of the direct data method is that it works with actual facts regarding the amount of the commodity which the market has consumed, and it therefore gives an accuracy which no other method provides. Another advantage is that the data on the market are usually provided rather speedily, so that the lapse of time between the taking of the data and their use is much shorter than in cases where general market factors are employed. The method is also easy to use, since the sales data reported represent the sales potential.

There are, however, several limitations which keep this method from being universally applied and which caution against its hasty acceptance. First, its use is confined to relatively few commodities. Second, data needed for individual areas, such as sales territories, are often not available. Information on most commodities is available only by states or regions. This fact necessitates the use of some other method of quantitative analysis before data can be fitted to manufacturers' sales territories or used for smaller geographic units. A third weakness is that the facts may be inaccurate. Statistics on sales gathered by trade associations are sometimes open to question. A fourth limitation is that the method is restricted to past performance.

Market conditons may change between the time the data are gathered and the results of a quantitative analysis are put into use. Finally, and most important, the method gives no weight to the potential purchasing power of a community beyond that which had been shown in past sales. These past sales may have been influenced by special temporary situations, such as the weaknesses of demand-creation methods.

Corollary Data Method

In this method it is assumed that the sales of two commodities parallel each other so closely that the direct data for the sales or the consumption of one gives the market potential for the other. For example, we have no geographically distributed data on the sales of automobile tires. However, the possibility of the use of this product in the replacement market is determined by the use of automobiles. Hence, where we have such a direct causal relationship between the sales or use of one product (for which we have accurate data) and the sales of the product for which the market is being measured (for which we have no direct sales or consumption data), we assume that the first data measure the market possibilities of the latter.

The use of horses, for example, points to the use of many products— feeds, ointment, saddles, riding clothes, etc. But the relationship of some of these things is very direct; in the case of others it is very indirect, representing only a general tendency. Provided that the factors of the specific case warrant the assumption of a close relationship between two sets of sales data, the corollary data method automatically carries most of the advantages and disadvantages inherent in the use of the direct data method discussed above.

The chief limitation of this method is that the relationship between the sales of the two commodities involved may not be sufficiently direct to give accurate results. In most cases some sort of adjustment is necessary. Often the relationship is so indirect that the use of one series of sales data in setting sales potentials for another product will yield false results.

Single Index Method

The single index method employs a general measurement of purchasing power as the basis for estimating the market potential for a given commodity. Usually a number of market factors, such as population, retail sales, and spendable income, are combined to produce the single index. However, sometimes one series of data, such as total retail sales, is employed as a single index. Regardless of the manner in which these indexes are built, they all make the basic assumption that some general indicator of purchasing power may be used as the basis of market potentials, either alone or as the basic series to be modified with special factors.

The single index method is one of the easiest methods to use. The following example shows the use of a single index to establish market potentials for gasoline.

TABLE 19

APPLICATION OF THE SINGLE INDEX METHOD

(International Magazine Co. Index)

(1) Territory	(2) I.M.C. Index	(3) Market Potential for Gasoline
Alabama	1.19	202,300
Arizona	.28	47,600
Arkansas	.88	149,600
(etc.)	(etc.)	(etc.)
Total	100.00	17,000,000

Explanation of columns:
1. Territorial units: states, counties, sales territories, etc.
2. International Magazine Company Index.
3. Column 2 times total anticipated sales (17,000,000) during period for which the potentials are being set.

The Retail Sales Index. While the Census of Business reports sales by types of outlets, it cannot be used effectively as a basis for the application of the direct data method or the corollary data method. The data for total retail sales by geographic divisions must be considered only as a general sales index which is composed of a heterogeneous assortment of commodities. The data by types of outlets, such as food stores, cannot be used as direct data because of the many types of commodities handled by different types of retailers.

The chief advantage of the use of total retail sales as a basis for the application of the single index method is that the data are based on actual purchases of commodities rather than relatively static population or wealth factors.

Several objections have been raised to the use of census data on total retail sales as a single index. In the first place, it has been contended that they do not measure the total power of people to buy, because people do not spend all of their incomes in retail stores. Approximately 60 per cent of the total national income is spent in retail establishments. Also, retail sales on a county and city basis understate the total buying power of counties and towns adjacent to large cities. A major objection is that people in some parts of the country spend a relatively larger share of their total incomes in retail stores than do people in other sections.

Sales Management Index. Probably the most widely used single index at the present time is that prepared annually by *Sales Management*. Each year this magazine publishes an exhaustive "Survey of Buying Power," in which current estimates of retail sales, effective income, and population are presented for all counties and cities with retail sales of $10 million or more.

Between census periods the Department of Commerce prepares current estimates of total retail sales for the United States. These estimates are apportioned by *Sales Management* to counties and cities largely on the basis of sales tax data, Department of Commerce surveys of sales of independent retailers, department store sales, bank debits, and other factors.

The Department of Commerce also prepares estimates of effective buying income, based on wages, salaries, dividends, interest, government income, and miscellaneous items of income. These estimates are available on both a national and state basis. *Sales Management* spreads these estimates to counties and cities.

Population estimates of the nation and the states are furnished by the Bureau of the Census and are apportioned to counties and cities largely on the basis of sample surveys of metropolitan areas by the bureau, state surveys of population, and estimates of local chambers of commerce.

The Sales Management Index is presented in the form of "% of U.S.A. Potential." This is a weighted average of three of their estimated factors: per cent U. S. Effective Buying Income × 5; per cent of U. S. Retail Sales × 3; and per cent of U. S. Population × 2. The magazine presents charts and tables summarizing the findings of the survey and lists suggested procedures for applying the index.

A special feature of the Sales Management Index is the publication each month of revised estimates of retail sales for "high spot" cities. For nearly 300 market centers the magazine compares current figures with the previous year and shows relative position on a national basis.

A number of other single indexes [1] have been published, including the following:

> Batten, Barton, Durstine, and Osborn Index—based on population, number of retail outlets, and income tax returns.

---

[1] For a further exposition of index factors and the single index methods, see R. Parker Eastwood, *Sales Control by Quantitative Methods* (New York: Columbia University Press, 1940), pp. 240–61, and Lyndon O. Brown, *Market Research and Analysis* (New York: The Ronald Press Co., 1937), pp. 427–37.

Curtis Index—based on circulation of Curtis magazines.

Crowell Index—based on an adjustment of retail sales data to estimate consumption by each county.

International Magazine Index—based on an average of 21 factors.

McCann Index—based on number of income tax returns, domestic lighting customers, bank deposits, and combined circulation of four magazines.

The chief advantage of the single index method is the simplicity of its use. The indexes are pre-prepared and readily available. They are usually stated in terms of the percentage of the total potential which each geographic section of the market should buy. The analyst can then immediately prepare sales quotas or distribute advertising budgets. This method is also superior to the direct data method in that it makes allowances for general purchasing power.

The most fundamental weakness of the single index method lies in its failure to account for differences in the markets for individual commodities. This weakness is now frankly admitted by the most aggressive sponsors of this method. Weld, who developed the McCann Index, pointed out the serious dangers arising when analysts and businessmen adopt such indexes as a measure of the market for individual commodities. He believed that one of the most glaring fallacies in market evaluation work has been due to the assumption that one single index can be used to measure the market for any and all commodities.

Even if analysts and businessmen can be educated away from the early propaganda which advanced the merits of the single index method, there still remains the problem of how to modify it. If the analyst merely guesses that certain combinations of factors should be used, he is no longer using the single index method but the arbitrary factors method. In this use, the single index ceases to exist as a method of market evaluation but is simply a predigested series of data which are taken into a study as a group of factors. Some labor may be saved in using an index which has already averaged the factors, but such use of the prepared combination is not a special method of quantitative analysis.

A second criticism of the single index method is that most forms are based on the assumption that the all-important element in quantitative analysis is general buying power. Such an assumption fails to recognize other elements which may be more important than buying power itself, chiefly buying habits. With given buying power, people in some markets buy more freely than those in others. Furthermore, markets vary greatly in their preferences for individual kinds of products. The quantity of ham or chicken consumed in two markets is primarily a matter of habits and desires rather than of purchasing power.

Arbitrary Factors Method

The arbitrary factors method is one of the oldest techniques used in quantitative market analysis. As the first step, those who are conducting the analysis select a group of market factors on the basis of their experience and judgment. These statistical series, such as population, total retail sales, spendable income, age, education, housing data, weather data, and automobile ownership, are known as market factors.

Part of the skill of the quantitative market analyst is knowing the sources of data which may be employed in a given analysis and using ingenuity in experimenting with various factors. The government, the chief source of these data, prepares source books from time to time. Considerable market factor data are also available from other sources in connection with prepared single indexes.

Sometimes these factors are compared with the past sales of the firm for which the analysis is being made, or with total retail sales. However, the distinctive characteristic of the arbitrary factors method, indicated by the term "arbitrary," is that personal judgment is used in the selection of the factors and their weighting rather than any scientific technique.

After the factors to be used in the analysis have been selected, they are next weighted. If in the judgment of the analyst they are of about equal importance, no weights are assigned. If some of the factors appear to be more important than others, they are given special weights. Thus, in combining three factors, factor A might be weighted three times, factor B twice, and factor C once.

The factors are set up in terms of the percentage of the total units of each one which are assigned to each market. These percentages are then weighted, an average is struck, and the resulting figure is used as the market potential index (see Table 20).

The chief advantage of the arbitrary factors method is that it takes into account the conditions peculiar to each individual product. Each analysis is constructed specifically for the commodity for which the market is being measured. The method is also easy and inexpensive to apply. It is simple to understand; hence it has had wide acceptance by businessmen. The basis of selecting and weighting factors is usually agreed to by the persons who are to use the analysis, thus furthering its acceptance.

TABLE 20

APPLICATION OF THE ARBITRARY FACTORS METHOD

(1)	(2)	(3)	(4)	(5)	(6)	(7)	(8)	(9)	(10)
	Population		Dwellings		Occupations				
Territory	% U.S. Total	Weight-ed % (× 3)	% U.S. Total	Weight-ed % (× 1)	% U.S. Total	Weight-ed % (× 2)	Sum of Factors	Market Index	Market Poten-tial
Alabama	2.16	6.48	2.20	2.20	.99	1.98	10.66	1.745	8,725
Arizona	.36	1.38	.39	.39	.34	.68	2.45	.409	2,045
Arkansas	1.51	4.53	1.66	1.66	.52	1.04	7.23	1.205	6,025
(etc.)									
Total U.S..	100.00	300.00	100.00	100.00	100.00	200.00	600.00	100.000	500,000

Procedure:

a) List territories or other units in Column 1.

b) List percentages of total United States or area being studied for each factor used in Columns 2, 4, and 6.

c) Multiply each factor by its weight, placing result in appropriate columns.

d) Add items horizontally in Columns 3, 5, and 7, placing totals in Column 8.

e) Divide Column 8 by the sum of the weights, placing result in Column 9. This is your market index, that is, the percentage of total sales possibilities assigned to each territory.

f) Multiply the products in Column 9 by the total anticipated sales volume for the entire market, pointing off two places (since the index is expressed as whole percentages). This is your market potential, in terms of dollars, cases, or other units used in the total.

The fundamental weakness of this method lies in its arbitrary nature. What is called judgment is largely guesswork. There is no scientific basis for the selection and weighting of the factors; all this is left to human intuition. The dangers of this method are readily seen when one has studied quantitative analysis thoroughly enough to see how very different the true relationship between individual factors and commodities may be from the apparent relationships which persons often assume to exist.

An analysis of the relationship between income factors and the market for specific commodities will illustrate this latter weakness. Some measure of income or buying power is nearly always employed in the arbitrary factors method.[2] Studies of the consumption of lard, however, show that the market runs directly opposite to incomes. The lower the income in a section, the greater the potential market for lard; in the higher income brackets, very little lard is consumed. In such an apparent case, the analyst who is applying the arbitrary factors method should not be misled. However, there are many instances in which all logical reasoning might appear to point to the use of an income factor in an arbitrary factors analysis; yet this fact is not necessarily true. A study of the market for washing machines is a case in point.[3] Here is a high-priced specialty. Yet an analysis of washing-machine sales showed that once one gets beyond the range of extra-

[2] Since single indexes almost invariably include some measure of purchasing power, the same criticism applies to them.

[3] The illustrations are from multiple correlation studies made by the writer.

marginal income groups—those who do not have money to buy the product even on an easy-term basis—the extent to which washing machines are used runs quite directly opposite to the amount of income.

Multiple Correlation Method

Market analysts have long sought a procedure eliminating the guesswork involved in most of the methods discussed above. Statistical methods of correlation provide a mathematical means of measuring variation in buying power. The theory of correlation analysis is thoroughly discussed in books on statistics. The method has long been used in the study of relationships between variables in other fields, notably medical biometry, agriculture, and engineering. Its use in quantitative market analysis work has been a more recent development.

Stated in its simplest terms, the theory on which multiple correlation is used in quantitative market analysis follows. There are certain known facts regarding sales or consumption of the product studied. These facts may be in the form of an individual company's past sales, the sales of groups of companies or the entire industry, or consumption rates in various sections of the country which have been determined by store audits, purchase panels, or field surveys. If any of these are set up in a series for various geographical areas, they provide measurement of a known variable—sales. It is presumed that the market conditions which make for easy sales have been operating in past sales or consumption data. True, this information reflects many things other than sales possibilities, such as competitive conditions and selling and advertising effort. But the chief general force at work is market potential and, since the correlation process measures the general variance, individual exceptions do not disturb it significantly. The market conditions causing sales to be high or low may be described by statistical data such as total retail sales, number of income tax returns, and number of automobile registrations.

In the multiple correlation method, the analyst uses his sales (or consumption) data as the control series, or dependent variable. He then measures the general variance in market potential by correlating it with different market factors, his independent variables. He selects any market factors which he desires, with the result that he knows statistically whether a suggested factor influences the sales of the commodity. If a simple correlation is made between sales and spendable income, and a positive relationship is found, the conclusion is that there is a tendency for sales possibilities to be highest where spendable income is highest, and vice versa. If, on the other hand, no correlation is found between these two variables, the presumption is that this factor is not a satisfactory means of measuring the sales possibilities. If a negative correlation is found, it is concluded that there is a tendency for sales to be lowest where spendable income is highest in the market for the commodity under study.

By the statistical manipulations in the multiple correlation process, the selection or rejection of a number of factors and their weighting are accomplished scientifically and objectively. The use of the coefficient of multiple determination gives an indication of the relative accuracy of the results. The use of coefficients of part or partial correlation makes it possible to reject factors having no particular value in the analysis. Furthermore, the relative strength of each factor in influencing sales is determined, so that the group of factors used to set potentials is weighted with mathematical precision. The analyst finally arrives at an estimating equation by which the market potentials for each geographic unit are established.

The primary advantage of this method lies in its objective, scientific nature. It eliminates elements of judgment and substitutes mathematical and statistical methods. Another important advantage is that it reflects buying habits as well as purchasing power and other elements which influence actual sales.

One of the first limitations on the multiple correlation method is that it is complicated. Some business executives may refuse to have confidence in it because they cannot understand its technique. Since the method is complicated, the persons responsible for such an analysis must be thoroughly familiar with the various phases. Like any statistical device, multiple correlation is merely a tool. The effective use of such a tool presupposes that it will be placed in skilled hands. The dangers of spurious correlation must be recognized and avoided. It must not be assumed that high coefficients prove causal relationships.

The method also presupposes that adequate sales or purchase data are available by geographic divisions sufficiently numerous to lessen the danger of chance correlation. Data for an entire industry should be employed, if available. In practice, multiple correlations have more frequently been based on the experience of a few companies or only one firm.[4] The questions of trading areas and channels of distribution become problems in the development of the control series. If sales are

---

[4] The inexperienced observer is likely to come to the conclusion that the ideal sales series is one prepared for the entire industry and that to use sales data for only one manufacturer or a small group is wrong. As a matter of fact, the latter has the advantage of giving some weight to competitive conditions and may therefore be superior.

made directly to retailers this limitation is not important. In lines in which wholesaling establishments are employed, some adjustment of the sales data must be made to account for wholesale territories which cross state boundaries.

In applying the multiple correlation method, there are several points at which sound judgment must be employed. The general danger of chance correlation has already been mentioned. The analyst must also bear in mind that he is making the correlation for the purpose of setting sales potentials; he should, therefore, be guided at all times by logical as well as correlative relationships.

However, the multiple correlation method is the most advanced and scientic method of quantitative analysis. It should be used whenever possible in preference to less accurate procedures.

SELECTED READINGS

Analyzing Markets and Setting Sales Quotas. Philadelphia: Research Department, The Curtis Publishing Co., 1954.

AUBLE, ARTHUR G., and BOYD, HARPER. "An Analysis of Purchase Rates by City Size," *Journal of Marketing,* April, 1953, pp. 411–16.

The Basics of Sales Quota Making or *The Trading Area Method of Sales Control.* New York: International Magazine Co., 1938.

COWAN, DONALD R. G. *Sales Analysis from the Management Point of View.* Chicago: University of Chicago Press, 1938.

EASTWOOD, R. PARKER. *Sales Control by Quantitative Methods.* New York: Columbia University Press, 1940, pp. 234–61.

EZEKIEL, MORDECAI. *Methods of Correlation Analysis.* New York: John Wiley & Sons, Inc., 1950, Chap. 1.

GROSS, JACK L. "Measuring Correlation with a Short-Cut Method," *Journal of Marketing,* April, 1952, pp. 447–49.

HOBART, DONALD M. *Marketing Research Practice.* New York: The Ronald Press Co., 1950, pp. 391–95.

MAYNARD, HAROLD H., and NOLEN, HERMAN C. *Sales Management.* New York: The Ronald Press Co., 1950, pp. 186–206.

"The New Look in Quota Setting," *Sales Management Survey of Buying Power,* May 10, 1954.

WHITE, JOSEPH H. "Discretionary Spending Power at Multiple Levels," *Journal of Marketing,* July, 1948, pp. 1–11.

WOLFF, REINHOLD P. "Estimating the Market Potential of a Floating Population," *Journal of Marketing,* July, 1954, pp. 12–17.

22

DISTRIBUTION RESEARCH

While the term *distribution research* is sometimes applied broadly to include all phases of marketing research, it is best confined to those specialized fields dealing with the physical distribution of commodities from the producer to the consumer. Marketing research techniques are applied in three major areas in connection with distribution problems. They are:

Channels of distribution analysis by manufacturers.
Distribution analysis by wholesalers and retailers.
Distribution cost reduction.

Channels of Distribution Analysis by Manufacturers

Selection of Channels of Distribution. Most manufacturers have a series of options as to channels of wholesale and retail distribution which may be employed. Products generally fit into a normal pattern of distribution, such as building materials which traditionally move through lumberyards and drug products which naturally flow through drugstores. However, the development of nontraditional channels has paid huge dividends to alert manufacturers. The use of marketing research makes it possible to insure that the most effective channels are employed, as well as to detect channels expanding in importance.

By way of example, the distribution of major electric appliances may be cited. The appliance dealer at one time played a much more important role than he does today. Public utilities, department stores, furniture stores, and other types are of varying importance from time to time. Another example is the expansion into nonfood lines by supermarkets. For instance, they account for over 50 per cent of total sales of some products formerly regarded as drugstore items, such as shampoos and cleansing tissues. A current national survey shows that over three-fourths of grocery stores stock nonfood items, such as toothpaste, shoe polish, cigarettes, insecticides, and lamp bulbs. A research of the various channels open to any particular product shows where emphasis should be placed to obtain the greatest total sales result.

The new manufacturer, or an established one bringing out a new product, is faced with the primary job of determining the types of wholesale and retail outlets into which his sales efforts are to be directed. One manufacturer decided to produce and distribute lawn sprinklers. An extensive study of channels of distribution surveyed

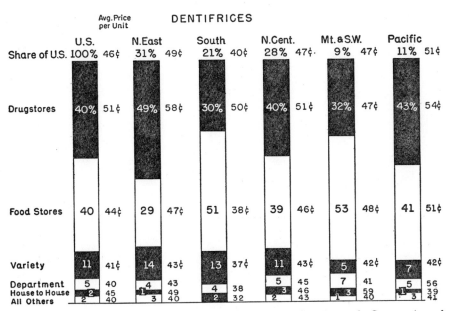

OUTLET SHARE WITHIN REGIONS

Avg. Price per Unit — DENTIFRICES

	U.S.		N.East		South		N.Cent.		Mt.&S.W.		Pacific	
Share of U.S.	100%	46¢	31%	49¢	21%	40¢	28%	47¢.	9%	47¢	11%	51¢
Drugstores	40%	51¢	49%	58¢	30%	50¢	40%	51¢	32%	47¢	43%	54¢
Food Stores	40	44¢	29	47¢	51	38¢	39	46¢	53	48¢	41	51¢
Variety	11	41¢	14	43¢	13	37¢	11	43¢	5	42¢	7	42¢
Department	5	40	4	43	4	38	5	45	7	41	5	56
House to House	2	45	1	49			3	46	3	59		39
All Others	2	40	3	40	2	32	2	43	1	40	3	41

FIGURE 33. Channels of Distribution Analysis. (Market Research Corporation of America.)

competing manufacturers, manufacturers' representatives, and whole-sale and retail dealers. The study also developed information about comparative prices, features, selling terms, and selling methods of similar products. The types of distributors best suited to handle the product were recommended, and a pattern of recommended cities in which distributors were to be appointed was worked out.

A common error of an established manufacturer introducing a new product is to assume that it can be most effectively distributed through his regular trade contacts. One manufacturer of electrical products introduced a new product similar to his old line. He naturally employed his regular channels of distribution. When sales on the new product were unsatisfactory, a marketing research revealed that his established wholesaling channels were not logical suppliers of the new product. Changing to new channels brought an immediate increase in sales to normal expectancy and turned a potential failure into a marketing success.

One of the findings of a survey of independent tire dealers shows the type of basic information obtained in an analysis of merchandise lines handled by retailers [1] (see Table 21).

TABLE 21

PERCENTAGE OF ALL INDEPENDENT TIRE DEALERS AND U. S. AND FIRESTONE INDEPENDENT DEALERS SELLING DIFFERENT COMMODITIES

	All Dealers	U. S. Dealers	Fire- stone Dealers
Tires and Tubes			
New tires	99.4	100.0	100.0
Used tires	90.6	96.4	94.9
Vulcanizing	80.9	80.2	69.2
Recapping	71.0	77.8	65.4
Automobile Supplies			
Batteries	87.4	95.8	93.6
Spark plugs	71.8	80.2	89.7
Accessories	62.9	63.5	65.4
Heaters	41.7	13.8	74.4
Electrical Appliances			
Radios	47.0	19.2	74.4
Electric toasters	31.5	24.6	70.5
Electric irons	31.2	13.1	71.8
Refrigerators	26.9	15.6	74.4
Phonograph combinations	25.3	6.6	61.5
Deep freeze units	24.0	16.7	60.3
Other electrical appliances	16.1	12.0	24.4
Miscellaneous			
Phonograph records	6.2	16.7	23.1
Sundry products (automobiles, bicycles, sporting goods)	33.6	31.7	70.5

Selection of Individual Dealers. There was a time when industry sold its products indiscriminately to dealers, but manufacturers have learned that policies of selective selling produce greater volume and profits. Dealer research sorts out the most efficient units and establishes policies making it possible to develop a most efficient dealer program within a given type of channel. The result is usually a key dealer pro-

[1] A. F. Schalk, Jr., "Significant Merchandising Trends of the Independent Tire Dealer," *Journal of Marketing*, April, 1948, p. 465. This article gives more data than are shown in the table.

gram for primary outlets to insure that an efficient organization is obtained.

The most important form of research designed to provide a basis for selecting individual units to be included in a manufacturer's distribution pattern is the analysis of the profitability of accounts by order size. Such an analysis may be made on the basis of total volume obtained from a given outlet during a sales period. However, the most revealing basis is to analyze sales in terms of the size of the average individual order obtained from each customer or prospect.

An illustration of the technique and results obtained in one study of the profitability of accounts on the basis of weekly purchases is shown in Table 22.[2]

TABLE 22

PROFITABLENESS OF DIFFERENT CUSTOMERS CLASSIFIED
BY AMOUNT PURCHASED WEEKLY

Amount Purchased during Week	Percentage of Total Customers	Percentage of Total Sales	Percentage of Total Expenses	Percentage of Average Sales per Customer	Gross Earnings per Sales Unit	Direct Expense per Sales Unit	Net Profit per Sales Unit *
Dealers unsuccessfully solicited	27.0	...	3.9	...	...	...	...
Less than $5.00	12.0	0.8	2.1	6.5	$1.50	$2.95	$−1.45
$ 5.00–10.00	10.1	1.6	2.8	15.5	1.38	1.92	−0.54
10.00–15.00	7.3	2.0	2.5	27.4	1.33	1.33	0.00
15.00–20.00	5.8	2.1	2.3	36.7	1.16	1.16	0.00
20.00–25.00	4.9	2.4	2.2	49.0	1.09	0.97	0.12
More than $25.00 ...	32.9	91.1	37.1	276.6	0.76	0.44	0.32
Average	100.0	100.0	52.9	100.0	$0.80	$0.57	$ 0.23

* Gross earnings minus direct expenses only.

Dealer Distribution. The term "dealer distribution" is commonly used to designate the proportion of logical outlets which carries a given manufacturer's product in stock at any given moment. The first step in successfully marketing a packaged consumer product is to have the largest possible number of outlets. This problem arises in the case of a new product, for obtaining 60 to 70 per cent distribution requires a great amount of effort. Many a new product must struggle along for a considerable period of time with a much smaller proportion

[2] Donald R. G. Cowan, *Sales Analysis from the Management Standpoint* (Chicago, University of Chicago Press, 1938), p. 135.

of retailers stocking it. This problem also exists for established products, as serious out-of-stock situations develop for many old products. Manufacturers all too often fail to realize the marketing penalty they pay when even a small proportion of outlets normally handling their type of product does not have their brand in stock. Generally speaking, all marketing, selling, and advertising effort which has been put behind the product fails to the extent that potential buyers do not find it on hand when they are buying in the retail store.

The dealer distribution analysis should include data on the completeness of the product line represented. A given brand of any product is generally sold in a number of different package sizes or varieties. One food manufacturer, who is so well known that anyone would be likely to assume that he enjoyed 100 per cent distribution, found that the percentage of food dealers handling different varieties of his product ranged as follows:

Variety	In Stock Percentage
A	85.1
B	51.1
C	49.3
D	12.1
E	8.8
F	3.7
G	0.2

Exclusive Franchises. A common marketing policy in many fields is to limit competition among dealers in order to obtain additional dealer support by some sort of exclusive selling arrangement. This procedure may vary from an exclusive territory contract with one distributor to a policy of selling only a limited number. Regardless of the extent to which the exclusive feature is emphasized, the general problem of the value of exclusiveness is present. Research procedures analyze the benefits from restricting the number of outlets in order to determine the optimum number to obtain maximum sales results under any given situation.

Operating Methods of Dealers. In order to obtain maximum effectiveness from individual dealers, it is important that manufacturers know in detail the various operating methods of different types of dealers so that sales policies may be kept in tune with dealer requirements. The manufacturer is interested in a variety of operating methods, such as commodities handled, factors considered in selection of brands for promotion, reaction to display materials, store remodeling plans, advertising policies, merchandise display, and pricing. Only by careful analysis of dealer operating practices can the manufacturer be assured that his merchandising program is sound.

Basic changes in operating methods and sales policies of dealers naturally affect sales of manufacturers' goods. It is important to keep abreast of trends so that marketing policy is kept up to date and capitalizes on current changes in operating methods. The trend to self-service is an illustration of such an operating policy at the dealer level. During the past ten years, the percentage of retail grocery sales on a self-service basis increased from 18 per cent to 60 per cent. The proportion of self-service varies greatly by product class, type of outlet, geographic area, and city size. The manufacturer needs to know the pattern for each type of product he makes, because commodities sold by self-service require marketing policies different from others.

Attitude of Dealers Toward Manufacturers and Wholesalers and Their Products. Even if a dealer will not make sales success by pushing a product, he can do a great deal of damage by diverting consumers away from products. Having the good will of dealers is always desirable. Marketing research measures the degree to which their good will has been obtained and the ways to increase it. Cases in which dealers have refused to stock or display brands of certain manufacturers are rather common. For this reason companies frequently study dealer attitudes toward the company and its products. It is usually not enough to rely upon reports from the sales organizations because these reports are colored by the interest of the salesman. If a question of the attitude of the dealers toward the company is important enough to warrant study, the appraisal of this attitude should be made in a thoroughly detached manner by a marketing research.

Status of Private Labels. In most lines wholesalers and retailers sell products under their own trade name or a special brand name. Since this private label merchandise usually offers wider margins, dealers often push it at the expense of the brands of national manufacturers.

A research into the problem of private labels should be comprehensive. It is all too common for manufacturers to become unduly alarmed as a result of general trade reports, field reports from salesmen, or stories in the trade press. Actually, it is necessary to obtain precise data regarding the distribution, sales movement, pricing, and other factors relating to private brands in order to obtain a sound conclusion. It is also highly desirable to have data over a period of time which can be analyzed from a trend point of view.

Dealer Stocks. Marketing men hold to the belief that a manufacturer will obtain greater sales volume if he loads the dealer with the maximum quantity of stock commensurate with a reasonable rate of stock turnover. Some special researches have shown the amount of a product that dealers should carry in stock in order that the manufacturer may obtain the maximum sales volume. As a result of some of these analyses "model stock" units have been devised for different types of dealers. A. C. Nielsen, in an article entiled "The Battle of the Shelf," says:

> For a grocery manufacturer to maintain his basic retail display position is a tough job—and it's getting tougher every day. Relative to sales, retail inventories for established grocery lines are at the lowest level in history. . . .
>
> A number of powerful forces have combined to cause this situation, including:
>
> 1. The continuing growth in importance of large, self-service stores—stores built on the principle of fast turnover.
> 2. The tendency of these large stores to stock more and more lines of merchandise without correspondingly increasing their total shelf space.
> 3. The inflation of capital requirements and store operating costs, making it necessary for the retailer, in effect, to put a price tag on every inch of his shelf space—and then endeavor to realize that price. . . .
>
> Adequate shelf representation is vital to the *manufacturer*—particularly with self-service stores doing as much as 70% of the business in some lines. And the *retailer* has a basic interest in adequate displays, too, because all of our records show that consumer sales are keenly sensitive to mass displays and adequate shelf representation.[3]

Dealer Costs and Profits. Another form of dealer analysis is the study of the costs and profits obtained on competitive lines of merchandise. The Coca-Cola Company made one of the most extensive analyses of this type, analyzing the net profits of various items sold at soda fountains. With the development of accurate cost accounting, it has been possible to make some very fine analyses of net profits on individual items. The margins dealers realize on competitive products, the extent of returned goods and spoilage, and rates of stock turnover as they affect profits are examples of specialized research in this field.

Distribution Analysis by Wholesalers and Retailers

Wholesaling and retailing concerns use marketing research in many of the forms discussed elsewhere in this book. Consumer surveys, sales organization research, and market trend studies (for example, fashion forecasts) are a few illustrations. There are, however, certain types of studies discussed in this section particularly within the province of the merchandise distributor.

Wholesale and Retail Trading Areas. One of the most important uses of marketing research by distributing organizations is measuring

[3] A. C. Nielsen, "The Battle of the Shelf," *The Nielsen Researcher* November, 1952.

the natural boundaries of the trading area to be served most profitably. In the desire to increase sales volume, many distributors expand their territories to a point where more and more submarginal customers are added. While additional sales volume is obtained, the marketing costs are increased to a point where an actual loss accrues from serving certain customers. Many retailers find it important to define their trading area carefully in order to avoid waste in advertising and promotional materials. The control of delivery service is another use to which trading area research is put by merchandising organizations.

The goal of trading area analysis is to define the area to be covered by a wholesaler or retailer so that the geographic distribution of sales will bring maximum return at the lowest cost. Research in trading areas generally employs a considerable amount of data available from secondary sources such as the economic structure of the territory, traffic flow, transportation facilities and rates, location of competitors, location of various buying units, and circulation of advertising media. Distribution data from the Census of Business are used to show the competitive situation and the trade facilities available. The Bureau of the Census makes detailed data for smaller political units, such as wards or enumeration districts, available for the larger cities.

Field surveys of dealers, in case a wholesale area is being analyzed, or of consumers, in the case of a retail analysis, are also frequently employed in trading area analysis. An example of retail trading analysis based on consumer surveys is one made for the town of Jefferson, Iowa, with a population of only 4,326 in 1950. Fifty-three different goods and services were covered in this research. They included various items of apparel, convenience and bulk goods, durable goods and services, professional and institutional services, and recreation facilities. Personal interviews were conducted in nine counties contiguous to Jefferson. Figure 34 reproduces one of many maps which were prepared and shows the geographic distribution of purchases of major appliances among trading centers.[4]

A series of maps of the territory under consideration is drawn. Each of them visualizes the distribution of an element affecting the problem, such as population, location of retailers, and location of buyers. From this series of maps, a general pattern soon becomes more or less clear, and trial contours are drawn to indicate the boundaries of the trading area. By a process of trial and error, evaluating the significance of each item of data, the researcher finally produces the common contours which define the trading area.

[4] Bureau of Business and Economic Research, State University of Iowa, *Retail Trade Area Analysis—Jefferson*, 1952.

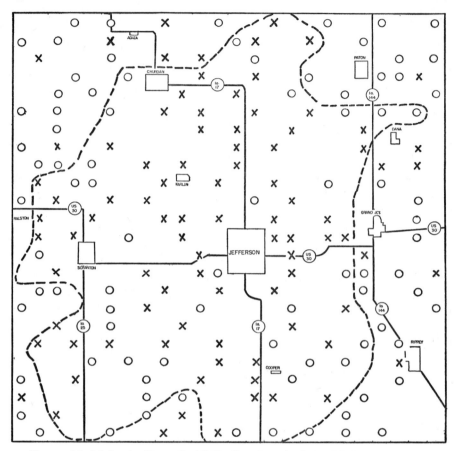

FIGURE 34. Major Appliance Retail Trading Area Analysis of Jefferson, Iowa. One family living in each section of land covered by the above map was interviewed. The symbol X represents a family which made its last purchase of a major appliance in Jefferson. The symbol O represents a family which made its last purchase of a major appliance in some other city. The dotted line shows the limits of the general trading areas of Jefferson, based on similar analyses of the purchase patterns for a large number of goods and services.

The simple outside outline of the trading area is merely the beginning. Trading area analysis becomes more useful to the merchandise distributor when a series of contour lines is drawn to designate varying degrees of intensity with which parts of the area should be cultivated. For example, the map may show three types of areas: A—those prime areas in which the merchandiser concentrates his major aggressive work, B—those good areas which receive more than minimum cultivation, and C—those areas which are still within the total trading area but warranting only minimum effort. It should be observed that while these contours generally flow outward from the wholesale house or retail store, they are irregular and contain "pockets" which do not conform to the general pattern of grading.

At the present time most trading area studies are based on observation of market data and field surveys. Several approaches toward developing mathematical bases of trading area delineation are being developed. One of these is Reilly's Law of Retail Gravitation, tested and developed by P. D. Converse. It establishes the breaking point between two shopping areas on the basis of the following formula: [5]

$$\frac{\text{Proportion of Trade to City A}}{\text{Proportion of Trade to City B}} = \left(\frac{\text{Population City A}}{\text{Population City B}}\right) \left(\frac{\text{Distance to B}}{\text{Distance to A}}\right)^2$$

Analysis of Operating and Control Data. Because of the variety of items handled, the large number of sales transactions, and narrow margins of profit, both wholesale and retail establishments have established elaborate accounting and control systems. The data produced by them offer rich opportunities for solving many management problems.

The most useful research form of operating data is the operating ratio. By using net sales as the base, a series of indexes may be developed for any of a number of factors which significantly affect the efficiency of the marketing operation. The following are examples of common operating ratios:

$$\frac{\text{Total Operating Costs}}{\text{Net Sales}} \qquad \frac{\text{Net Sales}}{\text{Accounts Receivable}}$$

$$\frac{\text{Cost of Goods Sold}}{\text{Net Sales}} \qquad \frac{\text{Wages and Salaries}}{\text{Net Sales}}$$

$$\frac{\text{Net Sales}}{\text{Average Inventory}} \qquad \frac{\text{Advertising Expense}}{\text{Net Sales}}$$

It is common practice to develop these operating ratios for the total enterprise. They become much more meaningful when they are broken down by smaller units, such as branches, departments, merchandise lines, or specific products. The more detailed the breakdown, the more revealing such ratio figures become. For example, it is useful to a merchandiser to know that his over-all sales cost is 22 per cent. However, if his line embraces items selling for $2 and others selling

[5] See Frank Strohkarck and Katherine Phelps, "The Mechanics of Constructing a Market Area Map," *Journal of Marketing*, April, 1948, p. 493, and P. D. Converse, *Retail Trade Areas in Illinois*, Bureau of Economic and Business Research, University of Illinois, Business Studies No. 6, 1948.

for $4, it is obvious that the sales cost is not identical for these items. Food and apparel chains have made notable progress in allocating costs so that much finer ratios, many for individual products and relatively small product lines, are obtained.

Ratio analysis becomes even more meaningful when ratios for any given wholesale or retail operation are compared with those for other firms. It is important to limit such comparisons to comparable situations. Any special conditions limiting comparability must be clearly understood and taken into account.

Merchandise Line Analysis. In a merchandising establishment there is a constant tendency to increase the number of lines handled as well as the number of varieties within each line, such as brands, sizes, and prices. Because of the desire to have as wide an assortment as possible to meet the varying demands of customers, a broader and more complicated product line is gradually accumulated. These products burden the efficiency of the operation, with the danger that many items will be unprofitable because of standard markups, slow movement, and obsolescence. The solution to this problem requires the development of unit costs and profit data for each item under study. This information, when related to sales volume, provides a basis for weeding out lines and items that do not properly contribute to net profit.

Merchandising Location. The selection of the location of wholesaling or retailing establishments has long since passed the stage when it was determined by the experience of individuals and by a cursory examination of the territory to be served. One factor which stimulated the general adoption of research as a basis of choosing locations was the experience of the large mail-order companies. When they went into the retail store business, they found that faulty store location led to serious drains on the resources of the business. Many large national retail chains now maintain established departments which specialize in merchandising location research.

The techniques for merchandising location analysis have now become generally standardized. The scientific selection of store location is based on a detailed survey of the territory to be served. Population data are broken down into the smallest possible divisions of the areas. Economic and social data reflecting sales opportunities are analyzed. Traffic flow maps are obtained, usually from local governmental sources. Surveys of shopping habits may also be made. After these steps a series of traffic counts is made for several optional locations. These various factors affecting the desirability of locations should be studied on a trend basis if possible.

Physical Layout and Handling of Merchandise. Marketing research is being applied increasingly to the problems of physical layout of the merchandising establishment and the physical handling of commodities. The design of retail store layouts, including decoration and customer facilities, is being based more and more on consumer surveys. The arrangement of stock and displays in order to produce maximum sales is based on studies of customer traffic. While the ingenuity of the designer is still a major factor, he now works on the basis of research data, just as the building architect works on the basis of the findings of the engineer.

Management is coming to realize that one of the best means of reducing the cost of distribution is in analyzing the costs and man-hours involved in the physical handling of goods. While studies of warehousing, packing, stock handling, and delivery procedures call for the application of engineering techniques, they are quite properly part of the province of marketing research.

Other Types of Marketing Research by Merchandising Establishments. In addition to the major uses discussed in this section, there are a number of special applications of marketing research in current use by wholesale and retail merchants. Studies of effective selling methods are one example. There is always the danger that the wholesale salesman or the retail clerk will turn into a mere order-taker. The distributor's salesperson generally handles a large number of customers in a day and sells a wide variety of products. As a result, there is a tendency for the buyer to assume control of the sales situation. Research studies prove that by following certain methods the salesperson will increase his performance.

Studies of credit policies, sales training methods, and the development of merchandising methods are other examples of the use of marketing research by merchandising establishments. A study of store hours can be very useful to the retailer. Knowledge of customers' attitudes may even be helpful in connection with personnel relations. Finally, special problems in inventory and stock control are solved by the techniques of marketing research.

Distribution Cost Reduction

Many techniques which have been developed in the analysis of production costs may be employed in cost analysis of some of the more mechanical aspects of distribution. However, approaching the problem of distribution costs from the limited point of view of the production engineer is inadequate and may be positively dangerous.

It is of primary importance to recognize that the problem of reducing distribution costs is infinitely more complex and difficult.

Cost elements in distribution are much more intangible than production costs. Furthermore, distribution activities are spread over the entire marketing area rather than being concentrated in comparatively few locations and tied down to a specific area within a plant. Distribution costs are associated largely with human effort rather than with physical machine production. These human activities generally cannot be reduced to mechanical, repetitive operations. The materials, parts, and processes involved in the production of a mechanical refrigerator, for example, are nothing compared with the multitude of activities involved in their distribution from factory door to the consumer's home. The sheer multiplicity of persons, efforts, and activities involved in distribution makes the determination of costs an extremely complex operation.

In a program to reduce factory costs, one begins with specific materials and operations for which costs are usually well established. The problem is to discover means of directly reducing the cost of various operations from previously established levels. In the field of distribution there are a number of areas in which this approach is fruitful and appropriate. For example, when costs of travel or physical transportation are found to be excessive, rerouting of salesmen or goods can effect important direct reductions in costs. On the other hand, the arbitrary reduction of a sales commission, a distributor margin, or an advertising budget may lead in the long run to sharply increased distribution costs.

One must distinguish between a distribution expenditure and a distribution cost. Distribution costs are the product of accomplished sales effectiveness achieved at a given expense. An increase in sales effectiveness may vastly offset an increase in gross distribution expenditure, with the ultimate effect of a reduction in distribution costs per unit of production. Only after the assembly of all the facts can the marketing researcher determine whether the wisest course of action designed to reduce distribution costs will be attended by an increase in distribution expenditure or by an immediate decrease.

Program for Reducing Distribution Costs. In planning a program for reducing distribution costs, it is important to appraise all factors bearing on a given operation before taking radical action. There is a tendency to eliminate ruthlessly some cost element without fully analyzing the results of such action. One manufacturer arbitrarily discarded all of his small customers without analyzing this group by individual accounts. The result was a substantial loss of business from a number of small customers whose potential was overlooked. They would have been retained had the research been conducted with sufficient care to eliminate those without real potential while retaining those who could be developed by proper cultivation. The *temporary* reduction of distribution costs is not the proper approach to the problem. Only through a long-range program can one develop the optimum balance between adequate market development and efficient operation from a cost point of view.

The following is suggested as a seven-point program which can be adapted to almost any business enterprise:

1. Know your distribution costs accurately, and in as much detail as possible.
2. Provide an adequate accounting procedure for reporting data on distribution costs.
3. Evaluate costs in relation to functions performed.
4. Find wastes in internal distribution costs.
5. Find wastes in outside channels of distribution.
6. Obtain comparative data for distribution costs from comparable fields.
7. Establish a specific program to reduce distribution costs.

Knowing Distribution Costs. The lack of understanding of true distribution costs by management is appalling. Some years ago, a manufacturer of industrial products was under the impression that distribution was not one of his major problems. The president of the company, when asked what distribution costs were chargeable against his product, replied, "Very little, about 5 per cent." Inquiry revealed that his concept of distribution costs was limited to his own salesmen's compensation, salesmen's expenses, and advertising. He did not include many internal costs, such as salaries of a number of high-priced executives who spent all or a major portion of their time in selling and distribution activities, any portion of general administrative expense, or credit and invoicing costs. He also failed to include any outside distribution costs, such as margins allowed his exclusive distributors, not realizing that these were cost burdens against his product. His true total cost of distribution was in the neighborhood of 28 per cent.

Providing Adequate Accounting. The accounting systems of many business enterprises are a great handicap to marketing executives. Because they are the product of traditional needs for financial operating purposes, they fail to reveal current operating data vital to the efficient conduct of distribution.

Accounting procedures should be revised if they fail to provide needed marketing data. A case in point is that of a large food manufacturer. A tremendous volume of accounting data regarding a certain product line failed to provide a basis for some of the most significant marketing decisions. Several months of digging in the records revealed that he was losing money on one large volume product. The same research discovered another product with possibilities of increased sales at a much lower distribution cost. This analysis was then employed as the basis for a marketing program for the latter product; it has since become the most profitable item in the manufacturer's entire business.

Another case is the recently reported experience of a retail shoe store chain, which has changed its accounting procedures in order to allocate sales costs properly to various individual items in the line. The accounting system now differentiates between styles and price lines as well as product groups.

The starting point in applying accounting procedures is to measure direct costs and assign them to products, customers, or other control units. Indirect expenses are then established for functional cost groups. These expenses are assigned to products or customers on the basis of the extent to which they utilize the activities giving rise to them. One scheme for analysis is shown in Table 23.[6]

In setting up a procedure for the allocation of distribution costs, one should guard against the establishment of an elaborate cost accounting system which in itself becomes an exorbitant cost factor by producing a maze of confusing detail. The best procedure is to select a small unit, a minor product, or a small territory, and to experiment with different methods of analysis and control until a definite pattern has emerged and justified itself. Cost allocations are relative rather than absolute, and good judgment and experience are necessary to produce results which are effective in the long run.

Evaluating Costs in Relation to Marketing Function. After distribution costs have been determined, it is most important to analyze the functions performed in relation to their cost. Merely to seize upon an apparently high cost and force a reduction is extremely dangerous. An illustration of this point is the attempt to eliminate some link in the distribution chain. Time and again manufacturers have decided to cut a corner, only to discover that distributors were performing functions which fully warranted their existence. On the other hand, analysis often reveals that established distributors are no longer performing vital functions but are exacting too high a toll from the products they handle.

[6] Charles H. Sevin, "Some Aspects of Distribution Cost Analysis," *Journal of Marketing*, July, 1947, p. 97.

TABLE 23

FUNCTIONAL COST GROUPS AND BASES OF ALLOCATION TO PRODUCTS AND TO CUSTOMERS

Functional Cost Groups	Bases of Allocation	
	To Products	To Customers
1. *Investment in finished goods* Taxes, insurance, and interest on inventory of finished goods.	Average inventory value	(Not allocated)
2. *Storage of finished goods* Warehouse rent, or taxes, insurance, depreciation, maintenance and repairs on warehouse buildings. Heat, light, etc.	Floor space occupied	(Not allocated)
3. *Inventory control of finished goods* Salaries—stock record clerks. Overhead charges.*	Number of billing lines	(Not allocated)
4. *Order assembly* Salaries—warehouse receiving and shipping clerks. Packing and shipping supplies. Overhead charges.*	Number of standard handling units	Number of billing lines
5. *Transportation* Freight, truck, express, parcel post, etc.	Weight or number of shipping units	Weight or number of shipping units
6. *Sales solicitation* Salesmen's salaries, commissions, and traveling expenses. Sales clerical salaries. Sales correspondents' salaries. Sales engineers' salaries. Sales executives' salaries, and travel. Overhead charges.*	Time studies or estimates	Time studies, number of sales calls or estimates
7. *Advertising* Advertising space and media costs. Advertising production costs. Advertising executives' salaries. Overhead charges.*	Direct, i.e., cost of space, etc., of specific product advertising †	Direct, i.e., cost of space, etc., of specific customer-class advertising †
8. *Order entry* Salaries. Overhead charges.*	Number of invoice lines	Number of invoice lines or orders
9. *Credit extension* Salaries. Overhead charges.*	(Not allocated)	Number of invoices
10. *Billing* Salaries. Overhead charges.*	Number of invoice lines	Number of invoice lines
11. *Accounts receivable* Salaries. Overhead charges.*	(Not allocated)	Number of invoice lines

* Includes portions of space, equipment, supplies, and supervision charges which may be divided among the functional cost groups on the basis of total direct salaries of function, amount of space occupied by function, value of furniture and equipment, etc.
† Institutional advertising not allocated.

The experience of one manufacturer illustrates the importance of functional analysis extremely well. He was beset by price competition from integrated, low-margin competition on the one hand and by the high distribution costs of his own distributive mechanism on the other. It seems that he must either place himself at the mercy of certain powerful distributors or fight a losing battle because the sheer economics of the situation were against his traditional distribution system. A careful analysis of costs related to functions performed by all factors of distribution in his line was made. Two keys which solved his problem were revealed. First, he found that the costs of his own system were not out of line with those of his toughest competitors for certain vital functions performed. Second, he discovered that with careful streamlining he could eliminate costs not associated with necessary functions so that his total cost differential was comparatively slight. As a result, the distribution of his products was sufficiently superior in terms of functions performed to more than justify his pattern and yet enable him to compete fully with anyone.

Finding Internal Wastes. One of the chief handicaps to progress in the reduction of distribution costs has been a rather widespread lack of appreciation of the importance of internal costs burdening the product before it is placed in the hands of a distributor or retailer. The high percentage margins required by retailers and other distributive agencies have drawn the attention of management and students to these external costs. However, experience has shown that the hidden distribution costs within the manufacturer's or wholesaler's own organization frequently provide great opportunities for cost reduction.

One interesting case which illustrates the importance of internal wastes is that of a wholesale house which in one year went from a 7 per cent loss on sales to a 12 per cent net profit. One of the chief wastes found was in the sizes and varieties in the line. The analysis showed rather quickly that this firm had accumulated a number of side lines, several of which would not have justified their inventory cost even if the full requirements of all the customers in these items had been sold. It was also found that a great deal of sales time was being spent on customers who either were too small to bother with or were largely buying these side-line items. Sales costs were greatly reduced by the simple process of listing all accounts for each of twenty-seven sales territories and showing for each account the following basic information: city, purchases for two accounting periods, returned goods, markdowns, credit status, number of times called on by salesmen, estimated total purchases from all sources, and estimated total requirements in lines sold.

Approximately 3,000 of the firm's 9,000 active accounts were thrown out as a result of this analysis. An important element in this case history is that the specific recommendations, account by account, were reviewed with the salesmen so that there was complete agreement as to which to eliminate. In the process of this review, sales education was also achieved. Another interesting result was the discovery that in one sales territory the sales costs were 48 per cent of gross sales, compared with an average of 17 per cent for the company. One city was found in which sales costs were over 80 per cent of sales volume in the current period. This case is a dramatic example of the results achieved by finding internal wastes.

Finding Outside Wastes. Very few business enterprises are involved in all the distribution processes from producer to consumer. Characteristically, the manufacturer's product is handled by a large number of distributors. The retailer, at the other end of the chain, handles products against which many distribution costs have been placed before he receives them.

By and large management fails to appreciate the fact that the burden placed against products at any point in the distribution system is of direct concern to each factor. The view must be adopted that whatever one's immediate concern in the distribution process may be, he cannot escape responsibility for doing something about the total burden against the products or merchandise from which he makes his livelihood.

Obtaining Comparative Data on Distribution Costs. One of the problems in the effort to reduce distribution costs is the lack of comparative cost data. A basic need of marketing today is for a greater body of specific information on distribution costs in various fields. The interest of the government in distribution costs has led to a number of studies by various branches. Most of them provide useful data on costs for various industries and functions. These studies also suggest specific cost items which the marketing researcher can investigate further in connection with a particular problem. For example, one study calls attention to the fact that the principal factors accounting for high distribution costs for biscuits and crackers are the high expenses for salesmen's salaries and for advertising per dollar of sales. On the other hand, in the case of beet-sugar manufacturers, the high amounts paid for storage are a principal factor in their relatively high costs.

Establishing a Program to Reduce Distribution Costs. The final step in reducing distribution costs is to establish a definite cost reduction program so that, as each sales period passes, specific progress in the reduction of costs will be achieved. To attempt to cut distribution costs at all points through one general analysis can serve only to dissipate effort. Furthermore, the greatest progress can be made by selecting the areas which offer the greatest opportunity for immediate improvement and concentrating on them. If the program is to succeed, it is essential to define these areas and to establish a time schedule for attacking the critical problems.

SELECTED READINGS

CLEWETT, RICHARD. *Marketing Channels for Manufactured Products.* Homewood, Ill.: Richard D. Irwin, Inc., 1954.

COOLSEN, FRANK, MYERS, WILL S., and MARTIN, JAMES W. *Paducah and Western Kentucky Income, Labor, and Retail Trade Patterns.* Frankfort, Ky.: The Agricultural and Industrial Development Board of Kentucky, August, 1952.

CULLINTON, JAMES W. "The Management Challenge of Marketing Costs," *Harvard Business Review*, January, 1948, pp. 74–88.

ENGLAND, WILBUR B. "Automatic Merchandising," *Harvard Business Review*, November–December, 1953, pp. 86–94.

FINE, I. V. *Retail Trade Area Analysis.* Madison, Wisc.: University of Wisconsin Bureau of Business Research and Service, 1954, p. 46.

HANSEN, RALPH F. "Before You Claim Distribution Costs Are Too High," *Sales Management*, April 1, 1953, Part 1, pp. 86–87.

HECKERT, J. BROOKS, and MINER, ROBERT B. *Distribution Costs.* New York: The Ronald Press Co., 1953.

HORN, JOHN D. "Merchandising Non-Food Items Through Super-Markets, *Journal of Marketing*, April, 1954, pp. 380–86.

JONASSEN, C. T. *Downtown Versus Suburban Shopping.* Columbus, Ohio: The Ohio State University, 1953, pp. 99 ff.

LOCKLEY, LAWRENCE C. "A Measure of Retail Efficiency," *Journal of Marketing*, April, 1951, pp. 482–83.

LONGMAN, DONALD R. *Practical Distribution Cost Analysis.* New York: Dun & Bradstreet, Inc., Business Information Division, 1953.

"Putting Safeway in the Right Places," *Business Week*, December 26, 1953, pp. 90–98.

RASMUSSEN, E. GUY. "Hardware Wholesale Trading Centers and Trading Territories in Nine Southeastern States," *Journal of Marketing*, October, 1943, pp. 165–71.

REYNOLDS, ROBERT B. "A Test of the Law of Retail Gravitation," *Journal of Marketing*, January, 1953, pp. 273–77.

SEVIN, CHARLES H. *How Manufacturers Reduce Their Distribution Costs.* Washington, D. C.: United States Department of Commerce, Economic Series No. 72, 1949.

STEDMAN, G. H. "Customer Viewpoint as a Guide to Store Operation," *Journal of Retailing*, Summer, 1953, pp. 135–44.

STROHKARCK, FRANK, and PHELPS, KATHERINE. "Mechanics of Constructing a City Market Map," *Journal of Marketing*, July, 1950, pp. 61–64.

TOUSLEY, RAYBURN D. "Some Aspects of the Spokane Wholesale Market," *Journal of Marketing*, January, 1952, pp. 321–31.

CASES

BLANKERTZ, DONALD F., FERBER, ROBERT, and WALES, HUGH G. *Cases and Problems in Marketing Research*, New York: The Ronald Press Co., 1954, pp. 10–12.

DOUGLAS, EDNA. "Measuring the General Retail Trading Area: A Case Study," *Journal of Marketing*, April, 1949, pp. 481–97, and *Journal of Marketing*, July, 1949, pp. 46–60.

TOUSLEY, RAYBURN D. "Reducing Distribution Costs in the Grocery Field," *Journal of Marketing*, April, 1948, pp. 455–61.

23

SALES RESEARCH

Marketing research methods are applied in a specialized manner to the sales problem in two ways. The first is sales record analysis. The second is research of sales organization and selling operations.

Sales Record Analysis

The term "sales record analysis" includes those phases of marketing and distribution research dealing with the analysis of internal sales records. These records offer a veritable gold mine of information on which marketing policies may be developed.

Because there are so many possible ways in which sales records can be analyzed, most business firms now use machine tabulation methods so that data are readily available. The details of every sales transaction are recorded on a punched card. With tabulating machinery it is possible to draw from these cards every conceivable combination of data recorded thereon. One firm prepares 196 different types of reports from one card form recording the details of each sales transaction. The following list shows some of the data which another company can obtain currently from the machine tabulation system which it has installed:

1. Date of each sale.
2. Plant (factory).
3. Commodity classification.
4. Item—style, size, color, etc.
5. Size of order, in units or pounds.
6. Dollar value of order.
7. Customer.
8. Customer classification—size, type of business, etc.
9. Customer credit rating.
10. City.
11. State.
12. Sales territory.

13. Discounts allowed.
14. Trade-in allowance.
15. Salesman.
16. Sales commission.
17. Bonus classification.
18. Price.
19. Cost.
20. Net profit.

With such a comprehensive record of every sales transaction, the marketing researcher can readily make cross-combinations which will reveal opportunities for more effective marketing. A comparison of net profit (Item 20) by customer classification (Item 8) or size of order (Item 5) is bound to reveal opportunities for concentrating demand creation efforts on the most productive prospects.

Sales analysis should be established as a regular operating procedure, with constant comparisons of performance and costs to keep the marketing mechanism as efficient as possible. Where a current system of sales analysis has not been installed, a special comprehensive research which digs into past records will often prove most revealing. The Allis-Chalmers Company, for example, did not have data which could properly relate sales to costs. All sales costs except direct field selling expense were buried in profit and loss statements of individual product departments. Costs of operating a field warehouse were spread among four or five different product departments. The company's experience with a comprehensive sales analysis is reported as follows:

We analyzed our past sales over a four-year period. This information was organized on the basis of customers, industries, method of sales, and territory. We established a sales analysis system which would provide current information. We use IBM punch-card accounting machines to give us as elaborate or as simple reports as we need. Sales analysis information has played a big part in development of our sales plans. Since we manufacture a wide range of products, many of which have to be custom engineered, we have a serious problem.

The cost of paper work is a cause for concern to many companies. It became evident that some of our orders were unprofitable just on the cost of handling, even before manufacturing costs. We made two separate studies, one on cost of processing orders, the other on how many orders there were. Results were disturbing—so much so that we decided to expand our dealer organization to handle the major portion of the sale of small apparatus. This program alone will effect savings sufficient to support market research for years.[1]

---

[1] J. L. Singleton, "When the Controller Says 'Costs Are Too High,'" *Sales Management*, May 20, 1948, p. 38.

Bases of Sales Analysis. A sales record analysis may be made from any one of three different approaches: sales, costs, and profits. An example of the difference between the three types of analysis may be shown in the case of a territorial breakdown. One might analyze sales volume by territories, the costs of selling by territories, or the profits per dollar of sales by territories. The analysis of sales results is a common starting point, and often that is as far as the work is carried. Analyses of the cost of selling have been developed more recently and are proving very valuable. Analysis of profits related to various marketing operations is a field which has been barely scratched, but one which should grow.

The key to successful sales analysis lies in the proper selection of the basis for analysis. There are many ways in which sales data can be broken down. The total sales, costs, or profits for the company may be analyzed over a period of time to discover significant trends. Analyses separating individual products and items in the line are likely to prove very productive. Some of these analyses break down the sales records by individual styles, sizes, and packaging units. A breakdown of such data by territories is common. Comparative data for individual salesmen and dealers are also likely to prove enlightening.

The data in Table 24 illustrate an analysis of sales, expenses, and profit contribution by individual salesmen.[2] From the data it can be seen that while Seewall sold $21,416 and Bristol sold $15,753, Seewall's profit contribution was only $2,637 in contrast to Bristol's profit contribution of $3,473. This illustrates the error in using sales volume as the sole indicator of sales performance. When the analysis is extended to incorporate average sales, sales by class of merchandise, performance against quota, and other factors, then close control on sales activities of individual salesmen is obtained.

Performance Data. An important form of sales analysis is the development of detailed data on sales performance which are used as an incentive to stimulate management and individual salesmen. Total sales production is a first and universal standard, but modern research has developed much more detailed data which further highlight performance and also inform the sales organization more specifically what to do to obtain better results. Examples of such data are:

1. Frequency of customer contact.
2. Orders per man-day.
3. Average order size.
4. Sales by type of customer.

[2] *Sales Research*, the Policyholders Service Bureau, Metropolitan Life Insurance Company, New York, undated, p. 23.

TABLE 24

ANALYSIS OF SALES—EXPENSES AND PROFITS BY SALESMEN

April

Salesman	Gross Sales	Returns and Allowances	Net Sales	Cost of Goods	Gross Profits		Expense		Net Profit	
					Amount	% to Net Sales	Amount	% to Net Sales	Amount	% to Sales Net
Seewall, A.	$ 21,416.83	$ 5,716.80	$ 15,700.03	$11,272.60	$ 4,427.43	28.2	$ 1,789.83	11.4	$ 2,637.60	16.8
Heywood, H. M.	17,497.30	3,873.20	13,624.10	9,577.74	4,046.36	29.7	1,171.70	8.6	2,874.66	21.1
Bristol, E.	15,753.81	1,160.21	14,593.60	9,135.56	5,458.04	37.4	1,984.75	13.6	3,473.29	23.8
Hilton, W. J.	12,227.83	2,116.08	10,111.75	6,613.15	3,498.60	34.6	879.72	8.7	2,618.88	25.9
Lawrence, T.	10,110.70	310.40	9,800.30	6,713.17	3,087.13	31.5	774.21	7.9	2,312.92	23.6
Stewart, A.	9,572.81	1,987.49	7,585.32	4,839.41	2,745.91	36.2	963.37	12.7	1,782.54	23.5
Rice, W. R.	8,242.18	3,416.20	4,825.98	3,373.34	1,452.64	30.1	690.08	14.3	762.56	15.8
Drummond, A.	7,731.50	140.10	7,591.40	4,919.39	2,672.01	35.2	1,169.14	15.4	1,502.87	19.8
Combs, A. B.	7,270.21	373.20	6,897.01	4,655.43	2,241.58	32.5	737.98	10.7	1,503.60	21.8
Richmond, S.	6,413.71	715.20	5,698.51	4,034.80	1,663.71	29.2	695.62	12.2	968.09	17.0
Brennan, H. A.	5,837.02	336.08	5,500.94	3,487.07	2,013.87	36.6	720.13	13.1	1,293.74	23.5
Reynolds, H.	5,102.60	284.26	4,818.34	3,309.65	1,508.69	31.3	506.21	10.5	1,002.48	20.8
Total	$127,176.50	$20,429.22	$106,747.28	$71,931.31	$34,815.97	32.6	$12,082.74	11.3	$22,733.23	21.3

5. Sales by type of product.
6. Sales expense.
7. New customer production.

Data of this type are particularly valuable when placed on a comparative basis. Selling is above all a competitive activity. Performance data which compare one district against another, one sales team against another, or individual salesmen against one another are a primary force of sales stimulation. Comparisons for various time periods, particularly those which measure a salesman's or a sales group's growth in performance, are also valuable contributions to sales management.

Establishing Standards from Sales Analysis. Sales record analysis provides a vast fund of data regarding sales volume, cost of sales, and profitability of sales. These data in themselves are very useful aids in managing the marketing operation. By developing ratios of costs and profits to sales by various products, lines, territories, and other units, meaningful comparisons can be made from time to time.

However, the greatest value of sales analysis comes when standard performance ratios are developed. By establishing typical yardsticks of performances for various functions, then applying them to different units, the individuals responsible for management and control are provided with a realistic understanding of the quality of the job they are doing. In setting these yardsticks average performance is most frequently used. For example, the cost of sales ratio for the entire company is developed; then the corresponding figure for each territory is related to the average. In interpreting these results, it should be borne in mind that the sales problem varies greatly from district to district, depending on the market potential, density of customers, size of customers, business conditions, and other factors.

Sales Organization and Operations Research

There is scarcely any single phase of sales organization or sales operations to which marketing research may not make a valuable contribution. However, selling activities are extremely complex and their human nature gives rise to a tremendous number of problem situations. It is most important that the marketing researcher be highly selective in defining areas where he will concentrate on the most vital problems.

Job Analysis. One basic application of marketing research to the sales function is the analysis of the specific duties which salesmen should perform. It has been found that too much of the salesman's effort is devoted to simple order-taking, with only a limited amount of time devoted to presenting sales arguments for the product he is attempting to sell. Actually, the sales process is so complicated that field observation of sales interviews should be employed as a basis for selecting those selling methods most productive.

Some of the questions answered by marketing research through field observations in which the investigator contrasts the performance of strong with weak salesmen are suggested by the following list:

1. For consumer goods:
   a) Who in wholesaler and retailer outlets should be seen?
   b) What facts should be presented?
   c) What services should be performed?
   d) Time to be spent on particular types of calls.
   e) How many calls per day can be made?
   f) How often should calls be made?

2. For industrial goods:
   a) Who makes the buying decision?
   b) What buying reasons should be presented to him or them?
   c) Time to be spent on particular types of calls.
   d) How often should calls be made?
   e) What selling aids are needed?

In exploring these and related activities which make up the selling job, the experience of successful salesmen should be studied closely. *Why* have they been successful? What have they said? What have they done? [3]

Time and Duty Studies. By observing the activities in which salesmen engage during the normal course of their selling, it is found that an undue amount of time, hence of sales expense, is usually spent on nonselling activities. Sometimes this is the fault of the salesman; more often it is caused by faulty training, direction, or lack of guidance. Relating the amount of time spent in selling certain products in the line to sales results will usually lead to a more productive direction of sales effort. Contrasts between the operations of the best sales producers and those of the poorest generally show that sales results are more a consequence of *what* salesmen do than of *how* they do it.

A time and duty analysis introduces the engineering approach to sales management. Just as the industrial engineer observes operations in the factory, noting the amount of time required to perform certain operations, in a marketing time and duty study an observer with a stop watch accompanies a salesman on his regular calls and records

[3] Marvin Bower, "Throwing the Sales Program Into High Gear," *Nineteenth Boston Conference on Distribution*, 1947, p. 49.

the amount of time devoted to specific activities. The observer must be well trained and the operation set up so that the salesman conducts himself in normal fashion and accepts the value of such a study. It has been found that the salesman soon becomes accustomed to the observational procedure and ceases to be particularly aware of the observer's presence. Showing these results to sales groups arouses their interest, helps them to apply this tool to make their own work more productive, and assures further cooperation.

The results of a large number of observations are summarized to develop a general pattern for the sales operation. Table 25 shows such a summary from a study of wholesale drug salesmen in Ohio: [4]

TABLE 25

DISTRIBUTION OF WHOLESALE SALESMEN'S TIME
PER DAY AND PER CALL MADE

| Time Elements | City Salesmen | | | Country Salesmen | | |
| | Minutes | | | Minutes | | |
	Per Day	Per Call	Per Cent of Time	Per Day	Per Call	Per Cent of Time
Idle	60.0	6.3	13.5	92.4	11.3	14.7
Travel	79.0	8.3	17.5	123.4	15.1	20.4
Await interview	48.1	5.2	10.7	44.0	5.1	6.9
Broken interview	30.4	3.3	6.8	36.8	3.6	4.8
General conversation	50.5	5.0	11.1	68.0	8.0	10.9
Collecting	8.3	0.8	1.8	20.2	4.0	4.7
Making adjustments	5.3	0.9	1.7	12.7	1.7	2.3
Miscellaneous	30.8	3.2	6.5	34.0	4.0	5.4
Order taking	32.8	3.4	7.6	99.8	12.2	16.1
Selling	99.0	11.3	22.8	83.1	10.2	13.8
Total	444.2	47.7	100.0	614.4	75.2	100.0

From a time and duty analysis, a number of norms for performance are obtained. The general average for all salesmen of a given firm is only a starting point. Norms should also be developed for various types of salesmen, as in Table 25, and for various sales units, such as different branches.

Perhaps the most useful end product of the time and duty analysis is the comparison of the performance of an individual salesman against norms for his particular group. An illustration of the variance of individual performance is given in Table 26.[5]

[4] Herman C. Nolen, "Time and Duty Analysis of Wholesaler's Salesmen," *Journal of Marketing*, January, 1940, pp. 274–84.
[5] Donald R. G. Cowan, *Sales Analysis from the Management Standpoint* (Chicago: University of Chicago Press, 1938), p. 3.

TABLE 26

PERCENTAGE OF SALESMEN'S TIME DEVOTED TO VARIOUS ACTIVITIES

Activity	Average	Salesmen				
		I	II	III	IV	V
Travel betwen stores	23	26	27	25	13	23
Waiting in store	14	7	15	16	18	13
Selling and collecting	31	31	32	26	31	34
Miscellaneous	17	17	12	25	23	10
Detail work	15	19	13	8	15	22

A refinement of the time and duty analysis is to extend the observations so as to record more specific activities engaged in by the salesman in connection with the selling function. For example, the type of sales presentation made may be related to average order size. Another illustration is to make a record of the specific products the salesman has attempted to sell in each interview. This form of study has proved to be particularly fruitful where salesmen have a line of products to sell. The results of such studies have inevitably indicated that the failure to mention products has contributed much more to low sales per interview than has faulty sales presentation. Still another application of time and duty analysis is to record the amount of time actually spent by salesmen in the use of various sales aids furnished to him by sales management. The results of some of these studies have proved rather startling to sales directors who had been unaware of the spotty use of their sales materials.

Selection and Training of Salesmen. Marketing research is being used more and more to provide a basis for the selection and training of salesmen. The foundation is provided by job analyses or time and duty studies. In addition, specific research in methods of selecting salesmen is frequently conducted. A correlation study relating personal characteristics, such as age, experience, and response, to sales performance establishes standards against which applicants may be measured. That such studies are far from purely theoretical is attested by the accuracy with which some companies are able to predict sales success of applicants on the basis of their tests.

Sales training has passed the stage where it is based primarily on the ability of senior salesmen to pass on general principles gleaned from personal experience. Marketing research, by establishing the importance of various specific sales functions, provides a more scientific basis for preparing the novice salesman and stepping up the performance of those who are more seasoned.

Sales Compensation. One of the chief problems of sales management is to establish a method of sales compensation which will insure maximum sales performance and properly reward those salesmen who make the greatest contribution. The methods employed are becoming more and more complex. Instead of a fixed salary or a commission, many companies have rather elaborate compensation plans. Some of them provide incentives for activities not always immediately reflected in sales volume. Some notion of the complexity of the problem of establishing an effective compensation plan is given in the following statement of the requirements which must be met according to one writer: [6]

> Increasing gross *sales.*
> Pushing sales of *profitable lines.*
> Pushing sales of *all* lines.
> Providing definite *incentive.*
> *Increasing* salesmen's *incomes.*
> *Decreasing* salesmen's *expenses.*
> Performance of special *tasks.*
> *Standardizing* incomes between men.
> Eliminating violent *income fluctuations.*
> Making the plan *simple.*
> Getting more *new calls.*
> Getting more *general cooperation.*
> Re-establishing *morale.*
> Cutting down *turnover.*
> *Reducing* the percentage of field selling expense.

Marketing research, through sales analysis, quantitative analysis, and field observation, establishes both sales quotas and standards for the performance of supplementary sales activities. These, in turn, provide a scientific basis for many decisions in building a sound compensation plan.

Measurement of Manpower Requirements. Analysis of the selling operations of almost any concern will reveal a considerable lack of balance between the requirements of the sales job to be done and the manpower assigned to the various territories. It is impossible to achieve perfect balance, but there is no reason why certain territories should be oversupplied with manpower while others are being inadequately covered. One of the most common types of unbalance, for example, is that between city and rural areas.

To obtain the proper amount of manpower, it is first necessary to make a job analysis which will reveal the specific functions required

[6] J. B. Lathrop, *Compensation Adjustments in a Period of Uncertainty,* American Management Association, Marketing Series No. 70, 1947, p. 41.

ANALYSIS OF SALES COVERAGE AND
SALES EFFECTIVENESS

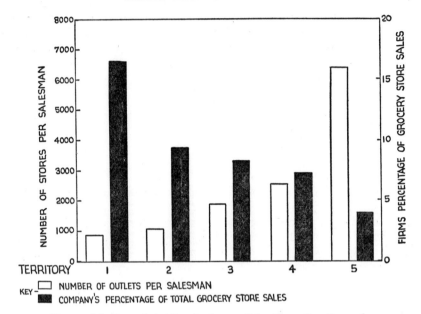

FIGURE 35. Part of the Results from a Sales Operation Research

The purpose of the study was to determine the optimum number of accounts to be assigned to each salesman. First, the number of grocery stores in each sales territory was obtained from the Census and divided by the number of salesmen assigned to the territory to determine the ratio of salesmen to total number of prospective dealers. Then the company's sales volume for each territory was divided by the total dollar grocery store volume to obtain the ratio of sales performance to an index of sales possibilities.

The chart compares these two ratios for five selected districts. It shows the general principle, confirmed by an analysis of all territories, that sales performance was in inverse ratio to the number of stores each salesman was forced to cover in his regular routine. Before a final policy decision could be safely made, however, it would be necessary to carry the analysis further on the basis of selling costs and profitability. It might be found, for example, that the addition of salesmen in territories like No. 5 would increase sales costs and reduce profits per salesman to a point which would offset the potential gain in sales volume indicated by the chart.

The example illustrates the importance of selecting the proper basis for a sales analysis by showing a novel breakdown, and also the need for considering the cost and profit approach as well as that of sales volume.

of each salesman in relation to various types of customers and prospects. After standards of work performance are established, time standards for their performance are obtained. Next, a detailed analysis of each sales territory is made, showing the number and location of customers and prospects by type. These data, taking into account travel time, can then be used as a basis for developing the number of man-hours or man-days required for each territory. Such an analysis is insurance against wasted dollars. This type of research also results in a general toning-up of the morale of the sales force.

Another basis for determining the amount of manpower required is obtained by a comparison between sales costs and sales performance by individual salesmen for different territories. The Johnson Wax Company found a variation of from 67 to 149 per cent of the national average in the sales return per man in its different sales districts. A comparison between this result and sales strength and sales cost revealed that although the company had high performance in some territories, there was also high sales cost and low yield per man. An undermanned condition was indicated in other cases, where the district had low performance with a low sales cost ratio and high yield per salesman. By carrying these data below the district level to individual salesmen or to groups, sales management learns how to deploy its sales resources more effectively.

SELECTED READINGS

FOULKE, ROY A. "Fourteen Important Ratios for Twenty-Four Wholesaling Lines and Fourteen Important Ratios in Twelve Retail Lines," *Dun's Review and Modern Industry*, November, 1953, pp. 68–70, 73–74.

MAYNARD, HAROLD H., and NOLEN, HERMAN C. *Sales Management.* New York: The Ronald Press Co., 1950, pp. 616–27.

McNAIR, MALCOLM P., and MAY, ELEANOR G. "Department Store Expense Control," *Harvard Business Review*, May–June, 1953.

Operating Results of Department and Specialty Stores in 1953, Operating Results of Limited Price Variety Chains in 1953. Boston: Graduate School of Business Administration, Harvard University, 1954.

RUSSELL, JACK. "A System of Sales Analysis Using Internal Company Records," *Journal of Marketing*, April, 1950, pp. 675–90 (see also p. 140).

CASE

MAYNARD, HAROLD H., and NOLEN, HERMAN C. *Sales Management.* New York: The Ronald Press Co., 1950, p. 648.

24

ADVERTISING RESEARCH

Advertising deals with many imponderables. Its aim is to influence the minds and emotions of millions of prospective buyers. It is a mass demand-creation device, so its messages must be standardized. Furthermore, conditions in the market are constantly changing. It is also expensive and highly competitive. In view of the many difficult problems which beset advertising, a great deal of attention is devoted to the development of research techniques to provide better knowledge on which to base advertising decisions. The two areas embracing the most pressing problems are those of advertising copy (the message) and advertising media (the carriers).

Copy Testing

Many different methods have been developed for copy testing. A great deal of controversy develops from time to time regarding the validity of these techniques, and frequently some new and presumably unique device is developed. However, all copy-testing procedures fall into the following major types:

1. Consumer-jury surveys.
2. Coupon-return analysis.
3. Recognition tests.
4. Impact tests.
5. Psychological analysis.
6. Sales area tests.
7. Controlled experiments.

Consumer-Jury Surveys. The consumer-jury test is based on consumers' preferences under controlled conditions in which they are presented with alternative choices. The consumer rates themes or advertisements according to his opinion by direct comparison. This type of rating, fundamental to much experimentation in psychology, has been effectively adapted to advertising copy research.

In using the consumer-jury method to evaluate advertising themes, two methods are most commonly employed. The first, known as the theme preference technique, involves the preparation of a series of statements regarding the product. Each statement presents a distinctive basic theme for a campaign. The following are examples of theme statements in a research for men's shoes:

1. This brand is worn by leading professional men, actors, and business executives.
2. This brand is the most comfortable on your feet.
3. This brand wears the longest.
4. This brand is made of the finest English-type leather.

These statements are then typed on small cards. Two at a time are placed in the hands of a prospective buyer of the product and the respondent is asked a question similar to the following: "Please read each of these two statements carefully, and tell me which one would be most likely to cause you to buy this product." After the choice has been made, the respondent is probed for reasons for his selection.

The second method of evaluating advertising themes by the consumer-jury method is to prepare a series of advertisements, each of which reprsents a different basic campaign theme. Usually these are in the form of identical layouts, with identical illustrations, so that the only variation is in the headline or in the headline and a paragraph of copy. These are then shown to consumers, who indicate their preferences.

The consumer-jury method is also used to evaluate various elements of advertisements. Consumers are shown two or more sample advertisements and asked which advertisement interests them the most, which headline appeals to them, which illustration they like best, etc.

In conducting consumer-jury tests there are three aspects to be handled with utmost care. The first is the selection of individuals to be interviewed. This is a problem in sampling control. The most important principle is to be sure that the test is limited to genuine consumers of the product and that various types of consumers are adequately covered. It is much too common practice to run consumer-jury tests among the employees of an advertising agency or of the advertiser, to place an interviewer near Grand Central Station, or to send interviewers out at random to make street interviews. The sample must be distributed carefully by the various market segments, such as age, sex, and economic status. Unless this element is properly controlled, the results may be quite erroneous.

A second important factor in consumer-jury tests is the preparation of the materials to be used. A properly conducted consumer-jury test requires much effort and patience in the development of the theme statements or sample advertisements to insure that they are properly constructed for the research. Before the final survey is made, the materials themselves must be tested.

Finally, interpretation is most important. There is a tendency to take the opinion rankings obtained in a consumer-jury test without carefully appraising the meaning of these rankings by thoroughly analyzing the reasons for choice.

The consumer-jury method has one outstanding advantage: it can be employed before advertisements have been run and a large sum of money spent. Since it is the most flexible of all forms, a wide variety of ideas can be tested economically. One of its greatest values is that it can warn an advertiser against some basic mistake which might be made through failure to understand the reaction of consumers to a proposed advertising effort.

Coupon-Return Analysis. In coupon-return analysis various themes, advertisements, or elements are measured on the basis of the number of inquiries received in response to an offer contained in the advertisement. In the case of products sold by direct mail, this method is generally the sole copy-testing procedure applied, since the number of sales produced by an advertisement is a direct guide to its efficiency.

However, coupon-return analysis is often made for products which are not sold on the basis of direct orders from the advertisement. It is therefore necessary to resort to premiums offered in the advertisements as the yardstick. A continuous controversy arises over whether the number of inquiries for booklets or other premiums is a true measurement of the sales power of an advertisement. One school aggressively contends that the correlation between direct response and indirect response to an advertisement is so high that coupon returns can be almost universally used as the most efficient guide to advertising effectiveness. Others contend that the function of most advertisements is long-range and indirect action, that there are many variables affecting coupon returns, that a special class of persons responds to answers, and that the offer itself is such a distorting influence that coupon analysis can be used only in a limited fashion.

Various devices for employing coupons in a copy test are available. The first is to make an open coupon offer of a standard premium in a series of test advertisements. An example of this technique was the test of the cartoon-strip technique by the Pepsodent Company. The strip was run in black and white in newspapers in two cities and in color in two other cities. The offer was a free sample of the product. The giving of the sample was considered a more accurate gauge of the selling power of the advertising copy than an unrelated premium, such as model airplanes or live turtles.

A different device is the so-called "hidden offer." In this technique no coupon, as such, is employed. Instead, a premium offer is buried in the copy, usually near the end of the advertisement. This device is directed to those persons who are sufficiently attracted by the advertisement to read it completely. It also eliminates the "coupon hounds" who glance through media for free or inexpensive offers. One must be cautious in using this method because of the comparatively small number of returns received as a result of hiding the offer in this way.

Another device employed in coupon tests is the split-run technique. In most coupon analyses comparisons must be made between different media and different time periods. The result is that one is always in doubt as to the extent to which the media and time of insertion, rather than the copy, have influenced results. A number of magazines and some newspapers offer the split-run service, in which different advertisements may be inserted in one issue. Thus, the influences of the medium and of time are held constant.

Recognition Tests. A large volume of copy testing is devoted to readership of published advertisements. One research technique is to obtain the recognition of advertisements by interviewing readers of magazines or newspapers. First the interviewer makes certain that the respondent has read the issue of the magazine or newspaper being used. Then he turns the pages of the publication and determines the specific parts of advertisements and editorial copy which the respondent claims to have read. These data are then analyzed to yield figures such as "per cent seeing (or noting)," "per cent reading some," and "per cent reading most."

Readership data are provided continuously on magazines by the Starch Readership Service and for selected newspapers by the Bureau of Advertising. Special studies are made from time to time by advertising agencies, advertisers, media, and foundations. The recognition technique has also been applied to outdoor and transportation advertising.

An analysis by the Bureau of Advertising of 902 food advertisements in newspapers, for example, showed that skill in copy was a more important influence than size of advertisement, and that advertisements employing editorial techniques such as news photos, cartoons, and comic strips were 249 per cent more effective than conventional display advertisements in attracting reader attention. Studies of display advertisements showed that a single illustration was superior to multiple illustrations, that a dominant illustration was better than an incidental one, and that photographs were superior to wash or line in obtaining high readership.

A further illustration may be found in the industrial field. The results of an analysis of readership data by the Advertising Performance Laboratory of the McGraw-Hill Publishing Company indicate that informative advertisements, telling a reader what the product will do for him, attract a greater readership than either inquiry copy or institutional advertisements. They also analyze the results obtained by various illustrations and length of copy.

A number of technical problems arise in connection with the conduct of readership studies. The chief problem is that of confusion on the part of the respondent. Because the typical consumer is confronted with thousands of advertising mesages from many sources and most reading is done very casually, he is usually unable to recall individual advertisements accurately. Studies of reader confusion point to many elements which cast doubt on the validity of much readership data. Another weakness is the obvious tendency of some respondents to overclaim readership.

However, some experiments designed to measure the accuracy of readership studies under controlled conditions, where the reader was observed by a hidden observer and later interviewed by the normal readership-survey procedure, indicate a high ability of readers to recall accurately what they have read. These tests establish the validity of the readership survey in principle, provided that it is properly conducted and interpreted.

The judgment of the best practitioners is that the test of readership research is primarily the quality of the field work. It is difficult to locate qualified respondents and the readership interview is usually a long one. There is an ever-present tendency for the interviewer to rush through the interview, to influence results by hints and assumptions, and in other ways to do sloppy work. Careful supervision of sample selection and of field workers is the primary technical concern in readership studies.

Impact Tests. Impact tests measure the residual amounts of advertising copy remembered by readers, listeners, or viewers. In post-testing applications of this method (after advertising has been run) consumers are first qualified as to their exposure to the medium. They are then cued with names of commodity classes or brands and "play back" to the interviewer all that which can be remembered about individual advertising messages. The Gallup-Robinson Company maintains a continuous impact service for advertisements appearing in three national magazines. They measure the percentage of readers who are able to prove that they can recall an advertisement and report verbatim everything the respondents are able to remember from it. They also report similar information for television advertising.

The impact method is also employed in pretesting copy which has not yet appeared. The Schwerin Corporation, for example, exposes groups of people to radio or television programs in which test commercials are inserted. After exposure, the respondents write down all that they can remember from the commercials, yielding remembrance of brands advertised and remembrance of selling points. In doing impact research of magazine copy prior to publication, respondents are exposed to test advertisements along with a group of control advertisements of known impact value. This exposure may be conducted in a single interview or through a dummy magazine which is left with the respondent.

The primary merit of impact testing is that it is based on the objectivity of experimental psychology rather than relying upon readers' claims of recognition. The data are thoroughly objective. There is no doubt that this procedure produces an accurate measurement of the ability of the advertisement to communicate its ideas to the consumer. There is disagreement whether the method gives any clue as to the effectiveness of different sales appeals in an advertisement. One school of thought holds to the position that in the process of selecting ideas to be remembered and others to be rejected, the consumer retains those which are most meaningful. He thus indicates those advertisements which are most effective in creating a desire for the product depicted. Since there is no clinical evidence to support this hypothesis, there is room for those who contend that impact studies are entirely limited to measurement of communication effectiveness.

Psychological Analysis. The studies of the psychologist and the experimental work in psychological laboratories have provided a considerable amount of material on copy testing. Since the whole process of advertising is psychological in character, it is natural that certain psychological procedures have been adapted for copy testing.

Four psychological testing techniques are most commonly used: tests of readability and comprehension, tests of believability, attitude tests, and triple associates tests (theme penetration). Every book on copywriting emphasizes simplicity of presentation, yet examination of a set of current advertisements makes it clear that the writers are continually tending to stray from this dictum. We also know that the ability of individuals to read is severely limited, for even at the college level reading difficulties are a chief cause of failure. Recently a great deal of work has been done in psychological laboratories to devise more effective methods of testing individuals for ability in reading and in comprehending written materials. These identical methods can be

Mister, you may look like
a thoroughbred in front...

but...

How's the view from the rear? Wrinkles are o.k. for elephants, but not for the human male. Yet that's the way your suit or slacks often look in hot, sticky, summer weather.

What a man needs is Milliken's Visa, the tropical fabric that "stands up" where you sit down. Visa is blended of enough Dacron (55%) to retard wrinkles and hold its trouser crease, even in the rain ... enough luxurious worsted (45%) to absorb moisture

and provide summer weather comfort. What's more, Visa keeps you cooler than any tropical, because it's 20% lighter and twice as porous.

To enjoy all the extra benefits of this blend, insist on Visa, the only Dacron-Worsted that's been worn and proven over the past 3 summers. You'll cut pressing bills ... travel light ... and look right all the time, rear as well as front!

Milliken's **Visa**® TROPICAL FABRIC

THE ORIGINAL 55% DACRON*—45% WORSTED BLEND

*DuPont's polyester fiber

DEERING MILLIKEN & CO., Inc., *Men's Wear Division,* Dept. L, 1407 Broadway, New York 18, N. Y.

◄ *See opposite page for information on how to be sure you get Suits and Slacks made of Milliken's VISA*

FIGURE 36. Results of Impact Research. These advertisements for the same type of product appeared in one issue of *Life* magazine. Only 1 per cent of the readers were able to "play back" (recall) any part of the message of the advertisement on the left-hand page, in spite of the use of tricky illustration designed to force attention. On the other hand, 25 per cent of the readers could play back the advertisement on the right-hand page. (Based on adjusted Proved Name Registration scores. Gallup-Robinson, Inc.)

HOT DAY doesn't keep this young executive from leaning back and relaxing. The Viracle tropical suit he's wearing resists "chair wrinkles" even on the muggiest days. And he finds his Hart Schaffner & Marx Viracle as cool and comfortable as it looks.

HOW TO RELAX WITHOUT WRINKLING

Viracle tropical stays cool, crisp and creased on muggiest days

Time was when a man who had a dinner date during the summer months either had to dash home after 5:00 and change his wrinkled suit or spend the day cautiously avoiding comfortable chairs. Now the Viracle tropical by Hart Schaffner & Marx has come to his rescue. This handsome summer suit looks as fresh and crisp at dinner as it did at morning coffee. So does the man who's wearing it, for Viracle's exceptionally light weight and open weave are designed for cool comfort on the hottest days.

A blend of 55% Dacron and 45% fine worsted*, the Viracle tropical virtually refuses to wrinkle—even on the muggiest days. Its trousers retain their press even through a downpour. It requires fewer trips to the cleaners because most spots can be sponged right off without harming its finish. It's a wonderful traveler, too. Occasional wrinkles from packing and day-after-day wear hang out overnight. Moreover, the Viracle wears and wears.

To make your summer a more relaxing and comfortable experience, ask your nearest Hart Schaffner & Marx dealer about the Viracle tropical suit. For the address of the dealer most convenient to you, write Hart Schaffner & Marx, Department L4, 36 South Franklin Street, Chicago, Illinois.

*Fabric by MILLIKEN.   VIRACLE—Reg. U.S. Pat Off.

HART SCHAFFNER & MARX

GRAY DAY brings a shower right at luncheon time, but his Viracle tropical keeps its trouser crease even in the rain.

HOLIDAY from the office with an afternoon at his club. His suit, gray-on-gray Viracle, is in the tall, trim Trend styling.

BUSY DAY ENDS WITH A LIVELY SAMBA AND WITHOUT A WRINKLE ➜
. . . at the Savoy-Plaza, Fifth Avenue, New York

employed in copy testing to determine, in advance of publication, the ease of readability and comprehension of proposed copy.

The second type of psychological analysis applied in copy testing is the test of believability. Most people agree that an advertising message must have a high degree of credibility for readers or listeners. Measurements of credibility may employ a scale technique, in which various statements or product claims are rated by consumers. A more effective method is to ask respondents what parts of an advertisement they find hard to believe after they have been exposed to it.

A third form of psychological analysis measures attitudes produced by proposed advertising copy. Various types of attitude tests have been developed by psychologists and applied to copy testing. Typical consumers are exposed to sample advertising messages, either printed or oral. The attitudes produced by these various messages are then determined by means of a series of penetrating questions. This type of research promises to yield a great deal of value in copy testing as it is further developed. Current applications stress the psychological reactions created by the cues given in the advertising, such as ego involvement, the type of person who would use the product, and the personality of the product reflected by the advertising being tested. The researcher looks especially for elements in the advertising which create hostility. It is an amazing fact that many things done in advertising actually arouse psychological hostility. Since the purpose of advertising is to create favorable attitudes and desires on the part of the reader, listener, or viewer, the detection and elimination of such elements is of vital importance.

A fourth type of psychological analysis is known as the triple-associates test. In this procedure the consumer is given an advertising theme or slogan, the commodity class of the product advertised, and is asked to identify the brand. The question might be phrased: "What brand of cigarettes advertises 'For a treat instead of a treatment?' " The percentage correctly identifying the brand is computed and then compared with similar ratios for other brands. This procedure is sometimes known as "theme penetration." A series of studies is often made periodically to determine the increase in correct identification during the progress of a new campaign.

Sales Area Tests. Sales area tests apply the experimental procedure to copy testing by making sales results the yardstick of the effectiveness of advertising copy. Trial campaigns employing different themes or copy presentation techniques are run in a group of local markets, and sales are then measured by store audits.

This method is believed by many people to be the best procedure for measuring the over-all effectiveness of advertising because the testing standard is sales results. It is not employed extensively, however, because of the difficulty of controlling the many variables likely to distort results, such as differences between markets, competitive activities, sales efforts, weather, and media. Furthermore, sales area tests are very expensive, take a long time to run, and tip an advertiser's hand to competitors. Nevertheless, those who carry out a properly controlled program of sales area testing have a measurement of advertising effectiveness which gives more confidence than any other type of test.

Controlled Experiments. Controlled experiments are similar to the sales area test in general character but are conducted on a much smaller scale. This method promises a great deal for copy testing. One form of the controlled experiment is to erect standard displays in a series of retail stores, varying only in the copy theme presented on a card. Sales in a series of outlets during a given period are recorded as the basis for measuring the effectiveness of the various themes tested.

Another variation of the controlled experiment is to place a salesperson in a high traffic area in a large store. This individual, operating like a demonstrator, stops persons and tries to sell the product with carefully worded statements of various themes. A further variation of this method is to attempt to sell the product door to door. The percentage of successful sales is recorded as the basis for measuring the value of each theme. This method is not used extensively because of the difficulty of standardizing the sales presentation.

The use of door-to-door circulars is another type of controlled experiment. Handbills, which are adaptations of proposed advertisements, are distributed in saturation quantity in neighborhoods surrounding selected stores. Store audits of sales are employed to measure the effectiveness of the various copy presentations of the handbills.

Media Research

The four principal types of media research are:

1. Circulation analyses.
2. Media audience measurement.
3. Advertising audience measurement.
4. Qualitative media appraisal.

Circulation Analyses. With the development of the Audit Bureau of Circulations, the problem of obtaining accurate data regarding the circulation of printed media has largely been solved. The work of the media analyst is now primarily that of breaking down circulation data on the basis of geographic areas and other market groupings which are most appropriate to the problem of a specific advertiser. This work is now done largely on a "coverage" basis, in which the proportion of families or individuals in different groups covered by the circulation of a given medium or combination of media is determined.

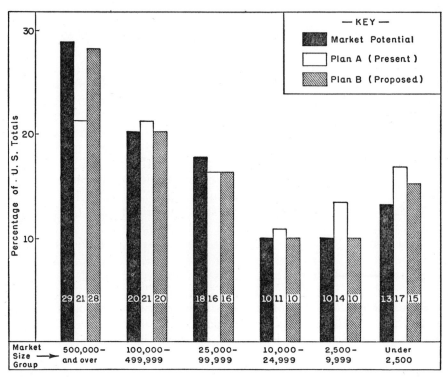

FIGURE 37. Balance of Circulation of Two Media Plans Against Market Potentials for One Product. (Data rounded to nearest whole percentage.)

Coverage analyses do not play such an important role in television and radio broadcasting as they do in print media. Because of the wide variation in the number of people reached by individual programs and the magnitude of the changes in these numbers from time to time, broadcasting research has focussed much more attention on individual program audiences. However, coverage studies which report the general circulation of stations and networks are made periodically. These studies are used chiefly in connection with reviewing proposed station line-ups to insure that no important areas are uncovered.

The analysis of circulation against potential sales is a very useful device. Where a sound quantitative analysis is available, the circulations of various media can be related to potential sales by geographic areas, sales territories, or population groups. This type of study can be one of the most important forms of media analysis, for it insures against overspending or underspending in markets. Such analyses for campaigns not previously planned in this manner invariably show that the distribution of advertising dollars has been seriously out of balance with the market.

Media Audience Measurement—Print Media. For many years advertisers have not been satisfied with circulation data as the sole yardstick for buying advertising media. It has been clearly demonstrated that the number of readers of a given copy of a publication not only significantly exceeds circulation but also varies from gross circulation figures as between various publications. An increasing amount of research has been applied in recent years to the measurement of actual reading audiences. Techniques for measuring reading audiences are now sufficiently perfected so that these data are generally accepted and widely employed. The value of print audience measurement is shown by Table 27.[1]

TABLE 27

COMPARISON OF MAGAZINE AUDIENCES WITH CIRCULATIONS

Magazine	Total Circulation	Total Audience	Readers per Copy
Life	5,210,000	26,450,000	5.1
Look	3,180,000	18,050,000	5.7
Saturday Evening Post	3,980,000	14,050,000	3.5
This Week	10,070,000	23,000,000	2.3

The crudest type of audience measurement is the survey which asks respondents what publications they read, sometimes with a check list. This method produces a large amount of distortion, overrating the "prestige" publications and likewise underrating certain publications which readers do not care to admit they read. The accepted method of obtaining audience data is on the basis of identification of editorial material in a specific issue of a magazine or newspaper. The reader is led through a copy of the publication and required to recall specific editorial items which he had read prior to the interview, or he is taken through a special kit which contains reproductions of enough editorial items to establish readership or nonreadership of a given issue.

[1] Based on *A Study of Four Media, Their Accumulative and Repeat Audiences* (New York: Time, Inc., 1954).

A recent study of the audiences of national magazines yielded the data contained in Table 28.[2]

TABLE 28

TOTAL AUDIENCE REACHED BY MULTIPLE ISSUES OF MAGAZINES

	People 10 Years of Age or Over Covered	
	By 1 Issue	By 4 Issues
Life	22.1%	44.0%
Saturday Evening Post	11.8	25.0
Look	15.1	34.8
Ladies' Home Journal	9.6	20.2
This Week	19.2	32.0

Audience studies are applied to various types of printed advertising media. While special problems in measurement are involved, the method is used in connection with farm magazines, newspapers, and outdoor advertising. In addition to measuring the total audience, these studies generally make rather extensive breakdowns of the families or individuals reached. Typical classifications include geographic area, city size, age, sex, economic status, and education. They may also include marital status, composition of household, employment, type and size of home, ownership or rental of home, and stability of residence. By showing the comparative structure of the audiences of different media, these data are of great help to the individual advertiser.

Media Audience Measurement—Broadcast Media. The most extensive research in connection with broadcasting media is the measurement of listening and viewing audiences. The following methods are commonly employed:

1. The recall method.
2. The diary method.
3. Coincidental telephone surveys.
4. The audimeter method.

The Recall Method. The recall method obtains its data through listener surveys in which the respondent is asked to report the television or radio programs he heard during a specified period of time

[2] See "A Study of Four Media, Their Accumulative and Repeat Audiences," *Life Magazine*, 1953, and "Duplication of Magazine Audiences," *Ibid.*, 1954. See also "National Study of Magazine Audiences," *Look Magazine*, 1952. For a research of the audiences of a newspaper, see *A Study of the Des Moines Sunday Register Audience in Iowa* (New York: Advertising Research Foundation, 1953). For an audience study of transportation advertising, see *The Continuing Study of Transportation Advertising, No. 14, Los Angeles* (New York: Advertising Research Foundation, 1952).

30

N Y T	6:00	6:15	6:30	6:45	7:00	7:15	7:30	7:45	8:00	8:15	8:30	8:45	9:00	9:15	9:30	9:45	10:00	10:15	10:30	10:45	11:00
HOMES THIS RPT.	299	337	348	378	410	439	462	511	563	595	627	648	671	677	616	599	563	549	509	458	
USING LAST RPT.	267	289	300	333	373	400	432	468	522	551	578	603	623	632	583	583	554	534	482	434	

PROGRAM THIS RPT. / COVERAGE LAST RPT.

% THIS REPORT / % LAST REPORT

Senator Irving Ives (Independent) / Chicago Periods Amer. Homes [Wk 1]

Doug Edwards & the News (Hdqp. & Myers) [Wk 1] — 87.5 / 86.3 — 88.0 / 86.4

Perry Como News — 22.6

IR — 1,844 / 5,847 / 4,734

Burns & Allen (Goodrich) [Wk 1] (OP) — 73.3 / 93.9 — 30.2 (93.7)

8,284

Godfrey's Talent Scouts (Thomas J. Lipton) — 91.8 / 91.2 — 34.6 (93.7)

9,339

I Love Lucy (Philip Morris) — 96.3 / 92.3 — 52.0 (95.7)

14,721

December Bride (Gen. Foods) — 92.2 / 90.1 — 34.7 (94.3)

9,407

Studio One (Westinghouse) — 95.7 / 93.9 — 30.4 (94.0)

8,375

NIELSEN RATING (30 / 15 / 0)

PROGRAM STATION BASIS

HOMES (000)

| AVERAGE THIS RPT. / AUDIENCE LAST RPT. | 17.0 / 16.0 | 21.4 / 18.8 | 27.8 / 19.9 | 30.7 / 26.3 | 48.2 / 50.9 | 31.5 / 32.9 | 24.0 / 22.7 |
| SHARE OF THIS RPT. / AUDIENCE LAST RPT. | 34.0 / 35.8 | 37.9 / 36.4 | 43.4 / 34.3 | 44.0 / 43.8 | 66.7 / 71.7 | 50.1 / 54.6 | 46.1 / 45.3 |

31

PROGRAM THIS REPORT / COVERAGE LAST RPT.		

% THIS REPORT / % LAST REPORT

Tony Martin (Gene) — 86.8 / 89.4 — 15.7 (77.5)

4,007 / 4,804

Camel News (Reynolds) — 92.3 / 92.0 — 17.7 (7.7)

Sid Caesar Show (Participating) [Wk 1] (OP) — 92.0 / 89.1 — 34.3 (87.5)

9,076

The Medic (Dow Chemical) [Wk 1] (OP) — 91.1 / 92.2 — 22.8 (89.8)

6,106

Robert Montgomery Presents (Amer. Tobacco) [Wk 2] (OP) — 95.6 / 95.0 — 31.7 (95.7)

8,911

NIELSEN RATING (30 / 15 / 0)

PROGRAM STATION BASIS

HOMES (000)

| AVERAGE THIS RPT. / AUDIENCE LAST RPT. | 15.2 / 16.3 | 17.6 / 17.7 | 23.8 / 26.5 | 21.7 / 23.4 | 24.7 / 19.7 |
| SHARE OF THIS RPT. / AUDIENCE LAST RPT. | 28.0 / 32.8 | 29.7 / 33.2 | 35.8 / 42.7 | 30.0 / 34.8 | 42.8 / 35.0 |

(OP) OTHER PROGRAM. SEE PAGES 50-53   (IFR) INSUFFICIENT FOR REPORTING

FOR DEFINITIONS OF RATINGS AND TERMS SEE PAGES 6-7

U.S. TV HOMES: SEPTEMBER 29,400,000

FIGURE 38. Part of a Television Audience Report. All data except homes are percentages of total U. S. television homes. For example, the Nielsen Rating of 34.3 for the Sid Caesar Show means that 34.3% of TV homes tuned to this broadcast for at least six minutes.

previous to the interview. Generally speaking, the day is divided into three units—morning, afternoon, and evening—on the assumption that each represents a time span over which the respondent can recall programs to which he listened. The information may be obtained by unaided recall or by the use of a roster which lists programs broadcast during the period being covered in the interview. This method tends to produce inflation, particularly as regards well-established and very popular programs. It also deflates viewing or listening during early morning and late evening hours.

The Diary Method. In the coincidental diary method a form listing broadcasting stations and time periods is left with the respondent, who makes notations of programs received. The diaries are usually designed so that they can be attached to the radio or television set for convenient recording. Sometimes a mechanical reminder device which rings a bell when the set is turned on is attached to the set in order to reduce omissions from the diary form.

The chief advantage of the diary method is that the respondent records his listening or viewing at the time, thus eliminating the burden on memory. It also has the advantage of making it possible to obtain classification data regarding the listener or viewer. Furthermore, it provides a relatively inexpensive method of obtaining a broad sample, particularly in rural areas, since the diaries are usually mailed to a central research office. The primary weakness of this method is inaccuracies of reporting because there is a constant tendency to neglect to make entries at the time the set is actually in use. This neglect leads to deflation through omissions and inflation of reporting certain programs when the respondent attempts to fill in parts of the diary on the basis of his memory.

Coincidental Telephone Surveys. In the coincidental telephone survey, investigators call telephone subscribers according to a predetermined sampling pattern. The number of "not at homes" is recorded. When a telephone is answered, the respondent is asked if the television or radio is on at that moment, and if so what program or station is being heard. It provides more accurate data than other survey methods, since it eliminates the necessity for memory or entries in a diary. Also, it is based on a report of actual viewing or listening, rather than mechanical evidence that the radio set was operating. The method has two weaknesses. First, it is limited to telephone homes. Since not all families possess telephones, this is a selective and unrepresentative sample. Second, the coincidental rating covers only an instant of the broadcasting period for any one subject. As a result, since there is a considerable turnover of listeners during the time a broadcast is on the air, the method tends to understate the total audience and is limited to average audience comparisons.

The Audimeter. The audimeter is a mechanical device attached to a receiving set which automatically records the station to which a set is tuned when it is in use. A variety of designs have been developed and constant improvements which reduce the cost of operating and servicing the units are being made. The most extensive use of the audimeter is in the Nielsen Television and Radio Index Service.

TABLE 29

TYPES OF INFORMATION FURNISHED BY NIELSEN RADIO
AND TELEVISION INDEX

1. Homes Using:
   a) By Months and Seasons
   b) By Days of the Week
   c) By Quarter-Hours
   d) By City Size
   e) By Time Zone
   f) By Income Class

2. Audience Size:
   a) Average Audience
   b) Total Audience
   c) Six-Minute Audience
   d) Full-Coverage Audience
   e) Commercial Audience
   f) Cumulative Audience

3. Audience Type:
   a) By Territory and Time Zone
   b) By City Size
   c) By Income Class
   d) By Use of the Brand
   e) By Use of the Commodity
   f) By Education, Children, Age, etc.

4. Minute-by-Minute Audience

5. Audience Flow:
   a) Sets Turned On or Off
   b) Competing Programs
   c) Adjacent Programs

6. Holding Power

7. Holding Power Analysis

8. Turnover (1, 2, and 4 weeks)

9. Frequency of Listening (1, 2, and 4 weeks)

10. Duplication Between Programs

11. Coverage Factor

12. Homes per Dollar

13. Share of Audience

14. Audience for Network Sustainers

15. Network Audience—Each Unsponsored Quarter-Hour

16. Audience for Large Non-network Programs

17. Audience for Spot Announcements

18. Station Audience and Other Data:
    a) New York Primary Area
    b) Chicago Primary Area
    c) Los Angeles Primary Area

19. Special Reports

One advantage of the audimeter is that it is a mechanical device which eliminates the use of interviewers in recording the raw data and reporting by respondents, hence eliminates human error. Another advantage is that, since it makes a continuous record of set usage by individual families, it yields data which can be broken down in many different ways to produce a variety of measurements. One example is the minute-by-minute variation of the listening audience from the beginning of the program to the end. With the audimeter it is possible to measure the actual audience listening to commercials, the in-and-out flow of audience between programs, and the accumulated audience over a period of time. The list in Table 29 shows the completeness of data available for both radio and television from audimeter analysis.

There are limitations on the use of the audimeter as a basis for measuring audiences. One is that the actual measurement is of mechanical tuning, not of viewing or listening. Another is the high cost of the mechanical units, their servicing, and the machinery of analysis. The fact that there are so many possible breakdowns of audimeter data sometimes presents the temptation to analyze the data beyond the point justified by the adequacy of the sample. However, these limitations are minor in comparison with the much higher accuracy of audimeter data in comparison with those produced by other methods.

Analysis of Advertising Audience. Studies of media audiences show the number and kind of persons reached by a given medium. Media analysis may be carried one step further to measure the number of people reached by the advertising carried by the medium. This measurement may be done in terms of all advertising, advertising of a particular product class, or the advertisements of an invidiual advertiser.

Studies of the general advertising audience of a publication are based on readership or impact of advertisements. The percentage of total readers who are effectively reached by advertisements is projected against the total audience of the publication to obtain the total advertising audience. These data may then be analyzed further in terms of the cost of advertising space, to arrive at an estimate of advertising audience per dollar. The following data show part of the results of one such analysis:

Magazine	Total Readers	Advertising Audience (4-color)	Audience per Dollar
A	4,269,281	1,080,128	158
B	2,518,394	1,631,919	286
C	3,869,510	1,478,153	123

This study shows the value of going beyond media audience analysis, for the tendency to read or listen to advertising varies significantly among publications or broadcast media. It also indicates the importance of considering advertising rates in any media analysis.

In the broadcasting field, analysis of advertising audience measures the number and kind of individuals who actually see or hear the commercials that are broadcasting the advertising message. Measurement is made by coincidental personal or telephone interviews. This is a relatively new type of media research but one which is highly productive. Large differences have been found between the number of persons who are reached by advertising messages and the number of sets tuned in to a program.

Qualitative Media Appraisal. In addition to knowledge regarding circulation and audience, the advertiser is anxious to obtain facts regarding the quality of a given advertising medium as a vehicle for the advertising message. Measurements of quality are made in many different ways, and the development of new techniques is constantly sought, for this aspect of media selection is fraught with personal prejudices and is difficult to bring under factual measurement. A number of techniques, however, are now available and are of considerable help in taking the qualitative appraisal of a publication out of the realm of guesswork.

Buying and Usage. One measurement of the quality of an advertising medium is the extent to which a particular commodity is bought by the typical reader or listener. Consumer purchase panels have been employed in an effort to produce such a measurement, but the methods of obtaining audience data are inadequate.

The closest practical approximation to such a measurement is based on the proportion of readers, listeners, or viewers who use a particular product. Manville has developed a particular device for this measurement, which he calls the audited "customer quotient." As a result of considerable experimentation he has demonstrated that the number of prospects for a given product among the readers of various publications differs significantly. By correlating these data with readership for specific advertisements, a further refinement is possible.

It is important in these studies to distinguish between the buying of a commodity and the use of a commodity by the readers of a particular medium. High usage may reflect a high degree of saturation, which may make for less actual buying of the commodity than would be found among the audience of another medium. This consideration is particularly important in the case of durable consumer goods.

Measurements of Reading Interest. Another form of qualitative appraisal of print media is research to determine the degree of interest which readers have in various publications.[3] One study, for example,

[3] For a detailed discussion of certain qualitative aspects of magazine circulations, see *Measuring the Impact of a Magazine* (Philadelphia: Curtis Publishing Co., 1951), pp. 19 ff. Subjects covered in the research include time spent reading a typical issue, times picked up, reliability, attention to advertisements, and confidence in products advertised. See also *National Magazine Readership Survey, No. 1, Depth of Reading* (New York: Crowell-Collier Publishing Co., 1952).

questioned female readers between the ages of sixteen and thirty-five to determine which of 26 magazines were "read regularly," which were rated "most interesting," and which were considered "most useful."

Some studies measure the amount of time spent in reading a publication or the amount of editorial content read in individual issues by individual readers. Approximations of the time factor are often obtained by measuring the so-called life of a publication, that is, the time period over which the reading of a publication is spread. Certain publications are kept by readers for a much longer period of time than are others, affording greater opportunity for rereading, thus increasing the advertiser's opportunity to impress a larger audience.

Analysis of the type of editorial content read in specific publications and the use to which it is put provides a further basis for qualitative measurement. One magazine, for example, asked its readers which editorial features they preferred, which feature writers in different publications they preferred, and whether they clipped the magazine. The analysis of "clipping" was particularly enlightening, for it showed the extent to which readers clipped and saved recipes and other items gleaned from the magazine.

Media research also concerns itself with a number of specific problems in connection with the scheduling of advertising. Typical considerations are the size of advertisements, frequency of insertion or broadcast, use of color, and timing of the advertising. It has been shown that the efficiency of advertising can be greatly increased by relating the size of the advertisement or length of commercial to number of readers or listeners obtained at a given cost. The selection of the day of the week on which to make newspaper insertions is another example of a field in which research has been employed to assist in scheduling. The relationship of the advertising audience to the number of pages of an individual issue, as well as to the position within the issue or on the page, is a further example of media research which provides important facts to guide the space-buyer in his scheduling decisions.

SELECTED READINGS

The Continuing Study of Transportation Advertising, No. 14, Los Angeles. New York: Advertising Research Foundation, 1952.

CROSS, JAMES S., ELDRIDGE, ROSWELL E., and BARBAROSSA, ROSEMARY. "The Consumer Jury Method of Measuring Advertising Effectiveness," *Journal of Marketing,* April, 1952, pp. 435-39.

How to Increase the Effectiveness of Television Commercials. New York: The National Broadcasting Company, 1954.

LUCAS, DARRELL B., and BRITT, STEUART H. *Advertising Psychology and Research.* New York: McGraw-Hill Book Co., Inc., 1950.

LUCAS, DARRELL B., and BRITT, STEUART H. "Measurement of Advertising Audiences," *Harvard Business Review*, September, 1950, pp. 90–101.

More Power in Newspaper Ads, Parts 1 and 2. New York: Bureau of Advertising, American Newspaper Publishers Association, 1948.

NAFZIGER, RALPH O. "Problems in Reader Interest Surveys," *Journal of Marketing*, April, 1945, pp. 359–63.

National Magazine Readership Survey, No. 1, Depth of Reading. New York: Crowell-Collier Publish Co., 1952.

OGILVY, DAVID. "How Research Aids Copy at Hewitt, Ogilvy," *Advertising Agency and Selling*, July, 1952, pp. 56–59.

RASMUSSEN, ARNE. "The Determination of Advertising Expenditure," *Journal of Marketing*, April, 1952, pp. 439–46.

A *Study of the Des Moines Sunday Register Audience in Iowa*. New York: The Advertising Research Foundation, 1953.

A *Study of Four Media, Their Accumulative and Repeat Audiences*. New York: Life Magazine, 1953.

TWEDT, DIK W. "A Multiple Factor Analysis of Advertising Readership," *Journal of Applied Psychology*, June, 1952.

ZEISEL, HANS, and HARPER, VIRGINIA EPES. "The Advertising Value of Different Magazines," *Journal of Marketing*, July, 1948, pp. 56–60.

CASES

BLANKERTZ, DONALD F., FERBER, ROBERT, and WALES, HUGH G. *Cases and Problems in Marketing Research*. New York: The Ronald Press Co., 1954.

HOBART, DONALD M. *Marketing Research Practice*. New York: The Ronald Press, Co., 1950, pp. 246–77.

25

PRODUCT RESEARCH

Specialized marketing research techniques have been developed for the solution of two types of problems in connection with product research: The first type of problem is that of product design; the second problem is one of pricing policy.

Types of Product Design Research

Adapting Products to Market Preferences. Many an existing product is severely handicapped because one or more of its characteristics are not in tune with current demand. The consuming public is extremely sensitive to relatively minor variations in taste, color, and shape. Only through comprehensive product tests is it possible to discover precisely the product characteristics which make a market winner. Since consumer preferences are constantly changing, progressive manufacturers periodically subject their products to marketing research.

Minor product changes are made from time to time in the normal course of business. Sometimes it is necessary to change a formula or specification because of a shortage of a particular raw material; sometimes a change in manufacturing methods occurs; often products are changed in order to keep up with competition. No product change should be made without a marketing research on the new variation, for the public is uncannily sensitive to the smallest change. To illustrate, an apparently unnoticeable variation in the consistency of a dentifrice, resulting from a substitution in one raw material, resulted in an immediate and severe loss of market position for one manufacturer.

On the other hand, when sales lag, marketing research will often find some product change which makes it posisble to revitalize sales with a campaign based on a new and improved product. In some cases it is size, shape, or color which is the important problem. In others, the chief issue may be taste or texture. Often ease of use or operation is a dominant consideration. At other times the package offers the best opportunity for change to stimulate sales.

Marketing New Products. Manufacturers and merchants find that adding new products provides a constant opportunity for expanding sales and increasing profits. Many companies begin with the manufacture of one product or a small number of specialized products; as they grow, they feel the restriction of a market limited by the number of products manufactured. Marketing and distribution research investigate the potential markets for products which are not fundamentally different from those being marketed by the company and can indicate the type of commodity which it would be most advantageous to add to any given line of products. Also, they can discover the demands of the market for new types of products to fill needs which have not yet been met.

In making marketing studies for new products, it is important to concentrate on fields closely related to the one in which the manufacturer is currently engaged. Nielsen Index records show a much higher percentage of failures than successes where companies established in one field have attempted to invade a nonrelated field. A toothpaste manufacturer, for example, has a much greater chance of success in bringing out a new type of dentifrice than he does of invading the hair tonic field. Manufacturers are all too likely to fail to analyze competitive conditions accurately or to appraise properly the power of entrenched products. The Nielsen records, which have measured competitive sales progress of a large number of new products attempting to invade established fields, also indicate that it is better to introduce a new product of improved or different characteristics than to imitate a successful competitor.

Sometimes consumer research goes beyond the normal "new product" study, which generally deals with products new to the manufacturer but already in use by consumers. The purpose of a study to determine unsatisfied needs is to learn what entirely new type of product, not now in use by consumers, would be in demand if made available to them. As consumers themselves are not aware of them, these needs can be discovered only by careful study of what people now have, how they use present products, and their reaction to products now available. One company undertook to find out how well satisfied housewives were with their kitchen duties. Each housewife recounted every task performed in her kitchen, indicating which tasks were difficult or took too long. Promising market opportunities for a number of new products grew out of this study. This technique can also be applied to industrial products.

Analyzing the Product Line. A specialized aspect of product research which is frequently a fruitful source of increased marketing
efficiency is the analysis of the line of products which a firm manufactures or sells. The term "line of products" embraces all varieties
which are sold, including the various product types, brands, sizes,
colors, designs, and other variables. If an organization must sell four
different grades in twenty different colors, thirty patterns, and twelve
sizes, it is easy to see how the line will wind up in a maze of complexity, even for one product.

In the normal growth and operation of a business enterprise, there
is a natural tendency to add new items in order to expand volume.
Frequently these items are added without sufficient study of whether
the total gain represents a significant contribution to profits or what
the effect of the extra item will be on the sales and profits of the balance of the line. Additions are often made to meet the special requirements—real or imagined—of small geographic areas, specialized
distributors, or individual customers, whose importance or special
needs are magnified by sales personnel. Then, too, market requirements change from time to time, yet obsolete and outmoded items
are often retained long after they have served their purpose. Blind
following of competition, habit, tradition, sentiment, lack of courage
to prune out dead items, and many other irrational practices lead to
lines which are so cluttered that they greatly impair the efficiency of
the selling operation. The ability of dead items to survive is amazing.
Only through application of the sharp tools of marketing and distribution research can the line be scientifically pruned down to the most
efficient combination of items.

Streamlining the line is only one aspect of the application of product line analysis, for marketing and distribution research also usually
reveals serious gaps in the line from the point of view of market
requirements. Producing a new package size which meets the needs of
a significant segment of the market has increased volume and profits
for many firms. The marketing researcher who is making a line
analysis, therefore, works simultaneously in the directions of streamlining the line and discovering important new additions which should
be made.

Technical Procedure for Product and Package Research

1. Laboratory Development of Test Varieties. The first operation
in product research is the development of a series of variations of the
product itself. A great deal of basic research should precede this
specific operation. Sometimes management decides hastily to make

a product study and attempts to have test units of the product prepared without an adequate background of physical research. This
danger is to be guarded against carefully. Good products, no matter
how simple, are based on painstaking laboratory research. If the company has been neglecting its technical product research, many months
of work on the product in the laboratory may be required before any
work in the market is undertaken. Experienced marketing researchers
have often found a deficiency in the basic laboratory work.

The laboratory should produce a wide number of product variations
in this stage, as there is always great danger that the best marketing
opportunities may be overlooked because the product experimentation
has stopped short in the scale of values covered. For example, a food
product test, in which the degree of flavoring to be used is being
tested, should include samples which deliberately overflavor and others
which deliberately underflavor the product beyond limits considered
reasonable. The number of different variations developed for market
testing will vary according to the nature of the problem. In one
dentifrice study, over twenty different products were developed in the
laboratory; in a hair tonic study, six; and in a syrup test, eighteen.

In the case of a larger product, such as an electric refrigerator or a
piece of industrial equipment, it is obviously impracticable to produce
a large number of test models for marketing research purposes. In
such cases, the problem is solved by isolating different elements or
features of the product. When the marketing investigation is later
made, a great deal of ingenuity is often employed in simulating the
products through scale models of sections, folding dummies, and
illustrations.

It is highly desirable that the marketing researcher and the laboratory scientist work closely together during this first step, because personal experience and good judgment are essential factors in the process
of developing the best product variations for market testing. Many a
product research has failed to yield results because the products being
tested were inadequate rather than because of faulty testing procedure.

2. Exploratory Consumer Survey. After the first group of product
variations has been prepared, the marketing researcher makes a number of informal exploratory interviews with users of the product. He
shows the new variations and has the consumers use them. The general technique is similar to the procedures of the *Informal Investigation* (see Chapter 7).

This step is very important for three reasons. First, it provides a
basis for reducing the large number of test variations to the smaller
number which will be submitted to formal research. Second, the
marketing researcher often obtains ideas which lead to further modifi-

cation of the original test products in the laboratory. Third, this exploratory work provides a basis for designing the questionnaire forms and field procedures for the formal testing.

3. Selection of the Control. In all product testing the best results are obtained by employing a control product against which different product variations can be tested in paired comparisons. A common practice is to use established competitive brands for controls. The use of competitive brands has the advantage of more directly indicating whether the new product will stand up on the market. In such a case, it is important to remember that it is not necessary that the test product receive an absolutely higher preference than the control product, for the established brand usually has the advantage of many years of intensive promotion and an established preference on the part of the consumer through habitual use.

Sometimes it is more effective to employ one of the test variations as a control unit. This procedure is particularly valuable in the early stages of product testing, during which the objective may be to determine which new product should be checked later against established brands.

4. Determining the Testing Series. Most marketing product tests do not involve research confined to one variation of the product or to a single factor, such as color, flavor, design, or package. A common mistake is to employ two or more test variations which contain more than one factor of difference, then to attempt to interpret results which are not subject to proper interpretation.

For example, a test of two hair tonics, one green in color with a relatively oily consistency, and another neutral in color with low oil content, would be inconclusive. In product testing all variables except one should be held constant in each unit of the test. Thus, in the hair tonic test, the two colors should be tested while the degree of oiliness is held constant, and the oiliness should be tested separately.

As a result of this requirement, a formal product test is likely to involve a series of two to four variables, with two to three different test products representing differences within each of the variables. When these are thrown against control units of established brands, some very complicated varieties of individual comparisons are sometimes set up in a comprehensive product research.

For this reason, and also because any product test is likely to lead to new ideas for further product development, it is becoming increasingly common practice to plan a number of tests over a period of time. In fact, some firms make it a practice to engage in continuous product testing. There is no doubt that the best results are obtained when it is possible to do this, instead of hoping to obtain final results in one product research operation.

5. Preparation of Test Units. After the product variations to be submitted to the final tests are selected, the final form in which they are to be used in the field is determined. While this step may appear to the uninitiated as relatively minor, there are a number of specific problems which arise.

One of these problems is the amount of each test product to be furnished each tester. A sufficient amount should be provided to make a fair test under normal use conditions, yet the amount must be kept reasonably small to avoid difficulty in physical handling in the field and to keep costs down. Another problem is that of providing control products, usually an established brand currently in use by the individual tester, in unidentifiable form. A third question is the means of identification, usually accomplished by the use of random letters from the alphabet. However, these letters must be selected so that there is no danger that they will influence choice. This means avoiding the first and last three letters of the alphabet and letters which may be regarded as a clue to identity, such as the first letter in the name of a known brand. Affixing identification to each unit of the test products so that there is no danger of its becoming removed or illegible is also necessary. The package or other container in which testing units are to be placed must be designed. Finally, a kit which contains test products in the right combination, and in such form as will be most effective from the point of view of both the use of the product by the tester and economical handling by the investigator, must be prepared. All these problems usually provide opportunities for ingenuity and call for considerable experience in product research on the part of the research organization.

The most common field technique in product and packaging research is obtaining consumer preferences through paired comparisons. The essential characteristic of paired comparisons is that the respondent is exposed to only two variations of test products or packages at a time. In the case of product research, this means that separate individuals or families must be used for each comparison because they must be consumed. In the case of package or label design, it is possible to make several comparisons with each respondent. In a study of design for a beverage container, for example, seven alternative package designs were produced and identified by letters "A," "B," "C," etc., in such manner that the respondents could not see the identification marks. Individual respondents were shown two designs at a time, and asked to make a selection. The various designs were rotated through a series of interviews with 350 men and women so that a total of 1,050 comparisons were made, with the results given in Table 30. Multiple paired comparisons with individual respondents, as illustrated in Table 30, may be used sometimes with studies of single product elements, such as appearance, color, or odor. This is most useful in preliminary testing. Before final marketing decisions are made, it is wise to conduct a single paired comparison research, in which individual respondents make a choice between only two alternatives.

TABLE 30

INDICVIDUAL COMPARISONS AND TOTAL VOTES

(50 votes in each comparison)

Number of Votes for	When Compared with							Total Votes
	A	B	C	D	E	F	G	
A	–	33	18	38	24	39	38	190
B	17	–	23	37	19	29	25	150
C	32	27	–	32	19	39	35	184
D	12	13	18	–	13	26	28	110
E	26	31	31	37	–	24	40	189
F	11	21	11	24	26	–	15	108
G	12	25	15	22	10	35	–	119

6. Selection of Consumer Testers. Inexperienced product researchers frequently make the mistake of failing to exercise proper care in the selection of consumers who are to participate in the final tests. Taking individuals in more or less random manner as they happen to come in the population will not produce proper results. Testers must qualify on the basis of stringent specifications. The first of these is that they must be typical users of the type of product being tested. In addition, matters of age, sex, brands habitually used, and similar marketing characteristics must be carefully considered in selecting the actual participants in the test if the conclusions are to be valid.

Here is a point at which possession of good consumer market data is of great value. Knowing the basic characteristics of the consumer market is essential for successfully selecting test subjects.

The number of consumer testers to be included in the study is also determined at this point. It should be noted that in product tests the size of the sample is much smaller than in general market surveys. Usually one hundred testers of each pair of products compared is adequate, although some firms require two hundred.

7. Preparation of Forms and Field Instructions. The preparation of forms for recording consumer preferences and field instructions in a product test follows the general principles of other field investigations.

In product testing, however, it is particularly important to keep adequate control sheets which show placements and recalls. This practice is necessary because such research involves two or three different interviews. Detailed classification data, such as age, sex, brand use, and economic class, are taken in the first interview. These data provide the basis for determining whether the respondent qualifies properly for making the tests. If he qualifies, a supply of two test variations of the product, for example, "N" and "T," are left for normal use. The next callback obtains preference based on use of these two variations, with reasons for preference. The number of days which elapse between these two interviews, and possibly succeeding ones, is very important. It is essential that proper controls be set up so that the timing of the calls is correct.

8. Controlled Consumer Choice. Most product researches end with the completion of the seventh step. However, it is frequently desirable to carry on two more phases.

The controlled consumer choice involves a technical procedure which goes beyond the stated preference of the respondent and simulates market conditions. The first form of controlled consumer choice is observation of quantities consumed when respondents are given large supplies of two or more test products. The second form offers free test products in different quantities to persons who have already participated in a regular product test.

In using the first form, the investigator calls upon the consumer several times, observes the order in which the various units are used, and measures the rate at which each variation is consumed. Adequate quantities of the test products must be provided so that each may be used freely. The test must continue over a long period of time, sometimes several weeks, so that the testers may become thoroughly used to the product. Sufficient quantities must be consumed so that the difference in amounts of each product used is statistically adequate to reflect product preference.

If the second form of controlled consumer choice is used, the tester is offered varying amounts of two products free as a means of observing preference. For example, if the product test up to this point indicates a preference for "F" over "O," the respondent may be offered a choice between one package of "F" or two packages of "O." If "F" is still chosen, her stated preference is confirmed; if not, it is modified. By offering different relative amounts of the test products, a quantitative measurement of the degree of preference is indicated. Some attempts have been made to adjust these amounts in such manner as to obtain a measurement of how much more a consumer would be willing to pay for one product variation as against another.

9. Sales Testing. A final step in product research is to make a controlled sales test in order to provide conclusive evidence of the degree of market acceptance. Care must be taken to select representative markets. In interpreting results it must be borne in mind that the sales obtained are also a test of the advertising, distribution, and promotion as well as of the new product. Collateral advantages of the sales test are that retailer resistances to the new product are uncovered and effects of display, pricing, and distribution influences on sales volume may be disclosed.

A sales test should be used in addition to the consumer tests discussed above and not be regarded as a substitute for consumer product research. Certain limitations of sales testing of new products must be kept in mind:

1. They are very costly.
2. Only one, or at most, two variations of the product can be market tested.
3. Competitors are given an opportunity to copy product features and to build up their defenses against the new product.
4. Sales data during a test period are not entirely a reflection of consumer acceptance of the new product.
5. Sales tests provide no qualitative data regarding reactions to the product.
6. It is difficult, often impossible, to give proper consideration to various factors affecting sales, such as weather, promotion, competitive conditions, and the many other variables which complicate all experimental work in marketing.
7. Sales tests take considerable time.
8. It is necessary to go into pilot-plant production of the product.

Methods of Price Analysis

Marketing research may be employed as a basis for establishing price policies in several ways. The most useful methods embrace the following procedures:

1. General price research.
2. Price surveys.
3. Analysis of sales-price trends.
4. Controlled experiments.

Generally a combination of these approaches is most effective. Any one approach is likely to overlook important factors or fail to provide necessary data.

General Price Research. Before beginning a detailed statistical analysis or setting up controlled experiments, it is usually desirable to conduct a general study of the price situation. A number of elements should be explored as a foundation for later research and taken into account in interpreting the results of more specific pricing studies. The following is an outline of typical elements which should be covered in this phase of the study:

1. Take a complete inventory of your current prices and make a systematic, up-to-date comparison with competitors' prices.

2. Get down on paper an exact description of your present pricing methods and policies. (In many companies . . . this policy inventory in itself is highly valuable.)

3. Define explicitly both the general and the specific objectives of each of your pricing policies. (Price policies are not an end in themselves but a means to an end.)

4. Determine whether your prices and policies are tuned to your company's economic environment (to the economic nature of the product and the structure of competition).

5. Check your prices and policies for consistency with relevant costs.[1]

Price trends must be taken into account in any pricing study, even though they will not provide a direct basis for price setting. A leading washing-machine manufacturer, for example, priced himself out of business primarily because he was unaware of the general trend of prices on household appliances, although a study of the general price level over a period of twenty-five years clearly indicated the necessity for radical downward price revision.

Current price data, related to an increasingly extensive history of price behavior, are made available by various government agencies. The Current Survey of Business regularly reports price information. General analyses of price behavior by economists may be studied. In addition to their conclusions regarding price behavior one may frequently obtain useful price data for his specific problem from these sources.

Price Surveys. The price survey is the simplest approach for obtaining market information applicable to a particular pricing problem. These surveys are made for two purposes: (1) to obtain accurate current price data, and (2) to obtain opinions regarding what constitutes the most effective price for a given product.

One of the chief causes of bad pricing is ignorance of actual market price as opposed to listed prices. Large-scale production generally

---

[1] Joel P. Dean, *Research Approach to Pricing*, American Management Association, Marketing Series No. 67, 1947, p. 5.

involves standardized prices, and national manufacturers usually set uniform prices at which their products are to be sold. Actually, prices vary considerably between territories, types of outlet, and periods of time. Price cutting becomes prevalent during a period of declining business. Too often manufacturers have no idea of the actual market prices paid by consumers for their products. The price survey which obtains realistic data on market prices is an important element in constructing a price policy.

Another form of price survey measures the attitudes of consumers and distributors toward various price levels. This procedure has some value as a preliminary to more scientific tests and in situations where products are not available on the market. However, it is extremely dangerous, because respondents are notoriously not qualified to estimate their reaction to a given price situation.

Analysis of Sales-Price Trends. Conventional price studies follow the pattern of relating competitive sales volume to competitive prices on a trend basis. One national manufacturer observed the relationship of his competitive share of market to competitive prices over a period of time. He found that when the consumer price of his product was no more than 4 cents per unit above the average price of competitive products, he could obtain satisfactory sales volume. As soon as the consumer price differential exceeded 4 cents, however, a sharp decline in his volume occurred. This led to a policy of pricing which generally produced a differential of 3 to 4 cents over competition at the retail level.

The chief problem in securing a historical measure of the effect of price changes on sales volume is to take into account the various other elements of the pricture which may have changed. Statistical methods may be applied to eliminate variables and to distill a pure demand curve.[2] Prices and quantity changes are correlated by multiple-correlation procedures to produce data which are generally much more useful than cruder statistical methods or mere observation of trend data on sales and prices.

Controlled Experiments. The most scientific application of marketing research to pricing problems is in the measurement of quantities of a given product which will be absorbed by the market at various price levels. Most manufacturers hope to obtain the highest possible price consistent with reasonable volume of sales. However, many overlook the possibility of obtaining a much greater net yield as a

[2] See Frederick C. Mills, "Elasticity of Physical Quantities and Flexibility of Unit Prices in the Dimension of Time," *Journal of the American Statistical Association*, December, 1946.

result of the increased volume which could be gained by a reduction in price. A utility system which fought rate reductions for years found that price reduction stimulated demand to such an extent that net profits were greatly increased, even in a monopolistic situation.

In these experiments the amount of product sold at different price levels must be correlated with production and marketing costs to arrive at the price which will yield the greatest net return to the manufacturer or merchant. The following example illustrates the method of analysis:

TABLE 31

EFFECT OF VARYING UNIT SELLING PRICE ON TOTAL EXPENSE AND NET EARNINGS

Selling Price per Unit	Number of Units Sold	Total Sales Made	Cost of Goods	Gross Profit	Variable Expense	Fixed Expense	Total Expense	Net
10.........	600	$60.00	$40.00	$20.00	$3.60	$10.00	$13.60	$ 6.40
9.........	800	72.00	48.00	24.00	4.32	10.00	14.32	9.68
8.........	1,200	96.00	66.00	30.00	5.76	10.00	15.76	14.24
7.........	1,300	91.00	71.50	19.50	5.46	10.00	15.46	4.04

By conducting controlled pricing experiments, the marketing researcher is simply translating the theoretical economic principles of demand elasticity into realistic practice. Where the study reveals an elastic demand, it will generally point the way to greatly increased profits as a result of expanding demand under lower unit prices. Studies of the price differential which should be charged for Ethyl gasoline showed that it was possible to take it out of the luxury class and make it a large volume item by narrowing the margin over regular grades.

Controlled pricing experiments may also lead to the discovery that greater returns will be obtained by increasing the unit price. Manufacturers who use instinct or casual observation as a basis for pricing often price themselves out of the market by cheapening their product in the eyes of prospective consumers. The experiments conducted on Perstiks, a deodorant in the shape of a lipstick, are an example of how controlled pricing can lead to comparatively high prices. Prices were tested in representative neighborhoods at 25-, 35-, and 50-cent levels, and it was found that the 50-cent price brought the best return. One must be careful to consider possibilities of higher prices as well as lower ones in setting up a market experiment on this subject.

Marketing research may be brought to bear on decisions regarding pricing policy in many different ways, as has been shown in the discussion of this subject. However, its most effective contribution is in the conduct of pricing experiments in the market place.

SELECTED READINGS

BLANKENSHIP, ALBERT B. (ed.). *How to Conduct Consumer and Opinion Research.* New York: Harper & Bros., 1946, pp. 12 ff.

BROWN, GEORGE H. "Measuring Consumer Attitudes Toward Products," *Journal of Marketing,* October, 1950, pp. 691–98.

Buyer Preference for Cranberry Packaging in Boston and Topeka. Washington, D. C.: Bureau of Agricultural Economics and Farm Credit Administration, Department of Agriculture, Marketing Research Report No. 34, May, 1953.

DEAN, JOEL P. "Pricing Policies for New Products," *Harvard Business Review,* November, 1950.

DEAN, JOEL P. *Research Approach to Pricing,* American Management Association, Marketing Series No. 67, 1947, p. 5.

FRANK, HERB. "Modernized Product, Not Needs Alone, Make Successful Seller," *Advertising Age,* July 12, 1954, p. 3.

HAWKINS, EDWARD R. "Price Policies and Theory," *Journal of Marketing,* January, 1954, pp. 233–40.

HOUFEK, LYMAN J. "How to Decide Which Products to Junk," *Printers' Ink,* August 1, 1952, pp. 21–24.

"How Lever Markets a New Product," *Tide,* October 29, 1948, pp. 33–36.

MILLS, FREDERICK C. "Elasticity of Physical Quantities and Flexibility of Unit Prices in the Dimension of Time," *Journal of the American Statistical Association,* December, 1946.

MOULTON, RICHARD H. "The General Foods Check List for Development of New Products," *Sales Management,* May 1, 1948, pp. 37–39.

26

MARKET TREND ANALYSIS

Marketing research for forecasting purposes is divided into two types. The first is quantitative forecasting, for the purpose of estimating future sales. The second is qualitative forecasting. This type predicts changes in the nature of consumer demand in regard to matters such as product characteristics, colors, fashions, and shopping facilities.

Sales Forecasting

The most extensively used form of market trend analysis is the development of sales forecasts. The function of such research is the determination of sales-volume objectives in units or dollars on the basis of the anticipated trend of the size of the total market. Many companies maintain a large staff for sales forecasting alone. Sometimes it is called an economic research department and separated from the one performing other marketing research functions. However, the sales forecasting work is more frequently done by a unit in the marketing research department. In either case, the forecasting group works closely with general management, production, finance, engineering, and other departments in planning sales by products and individual items in each product class. It keeps a large amount of current information regarding business conditions, consumer purchasing power, sales trends, and other data on hand at all times. The group makes periodic sales forecasts for management and individual operating units within the company. Revisions of forecasts are issued as necessary.

A variety of technical approaches to sales forecasting have been developed. Some of these methods are very simple to apply. Examples are the jury of executive opinion and the sales force composite. These are essentially the pooling of individual estimates of future sales made either by groups of executives or by members of the sales force. Other methods are highly complex, such as correlation analysis and trend and cycle forecasts. Each approach to the technical aspects of forecasting has its own advantages and limitations.

Special Methods of Market Forecasting. A number of special methods to forecast market trends have been developed. The most important of these methods will now be discussed.

Surveys of Buying Intention. This method employs consumer survey techniques to determine the intentions of buyers to purchase specific goods in the future. This procedure cannot provide precise data because consumers are often vague about their future plans and their intentions are always subject to change. On the other hand, there have been many evidences that surveys of buying intention help to shed light on the forecasting problem. This is particularly true in connection with major purchases, such as housing, automobiles, and appliances.

The Survey Research Center at the University of Michigan has done a great deal of pioneering experimental work on surveys of buying intentions as a forecasting tool. The Federal Reserve System has also employed the method extensively. There is much further experimentation and verification to be done. However, enough progress has been made to date to establish the basic soundness of the method in situations to which it is applicable.

Structural Analysis. An entirely different approach is structural analysis. This procedure is limited to analysis of the market for industrial products. The essential operation in this method is to analyze statistical data on the level of activity of different industries.

Various industries, such as ferrous metals, textiles, and rubber, are arranged along the top and side of a two-dimensional table. The distribution of sales of each of the industries to all other industries in the analysis is spread along the rows. In each column the purchases of an individual industry from all other industries are shown. Based on the theory that the sales outlook of any one industry is inseparably connected with the level of output of other industries, this method thus makes a simultaneous analysis of input and output of all industries. The Bureau of Labor Statistics assembles the original data which are available for ninety-four separate industries.

Income Distribution Analysis. Another special method of market forecasting is based upon analysis of the distribution of income payments to individuals. These data are provided regularly by the Departments of Labor and Agriculture and current estimates are prepared by *Sales Management* magazine. The Consumer Purchase Study and other researches provide data on the relationship of various income classes to the purchase of different types of commodities so that projections based on total income payments are possible.

These data are used in analysis in the following steps:

1. Estimates of population growth.
2. Estimates of total income trends.
3. Estimates of future purchasing by income classes.
4. Summation to obtain total sales forecast.

Comparisons of the results of this approach with known sales of different textile products by years from 1935 to 1941 show a very close correlation in trend. This approach has advantages in developing sales budgets for territories and local markets because sales trends can be computed directly for each unit for which local data are available.

Pooled Forecasts. Another approach to the forecasting problem is pooling forecasts of individual members of an industry. The methods employed by any individual industry member may vary considerably, ranging from pure guesswork to scientific forecasting. However, this method has worked very well in some industries. An example is the National Electrical Manufacturers' Association. Individual members report their sales forecasts by months to the association, which prepares a total industry forecast for different types of appliances.

The Sales Budget. After the quantitative trend analysis has established the total sales forecast for the company or for major product lines, it is necessary to make a detailed breakdown in order to establish a complete sales budget. A great many marketing policy decisions can be made directly on the basis of the over-all sales forecast. However, the most effective control of marketing operations from a trend point of view arises from the development of detailed sales budgets.

These budgets are essentially breakdowns of the total sales forecast. The most common units for which anticipated sales budgets are developed are the following:

1. By products.
2. By sales territories.
3. By months.
4. By class of trade.
5. By class of market.

The extent to which these are further broken down—as, for example, to show forecasts of sales by territories by months—depends on how far the firm wishes to go in sales budgeting. Theoretically, it would be desirable to have these budgets broken down in great detail in order to provide complete control over marketing operations in the various units. Practically, the amount of expense and paper work often militates against too fine a budgetary breakdown. A detailed breakdown should not be attempted until the company has obtained enough experience in forecasting work to be sure of its ground. A few bad experiences with forecasts will do great harm to the morale of the organization and make it extremely difficult to obtain acceptance of future forecasting or other research work.

Qualitative Forecasting

The discussion of market trends up to this point has dealt with the *quantitative* aspects of the problem, namely, the volume of a commodity to be sold during some future period. Another important aspect of market trend analysis is the *qualitative* forecast dealing with changes in the nature or character of the market.

Almost any market phenomenon can be observed in its relationship to time, so qualitative analysis can be applied to all forms of marketing research. Changes in the attitude of consumers toward product design, changes in buying habits, shifts in brand preferences, changes in their reaction to advertising or prices—all these are specific examples of the breadth of the field of qualitative trend analysis. The marketing researcher should consider the time-dimension aspects of any problem on which he is working.

Shifts in Market Patterns. One aspect of qualitative forecasting deals with anticipated changes in the relative importance of various consumer groups in the market for a product. By comparing market patterns over a period of time, those elements which are growing and those which are declining in significance are delineated. For example, the data in Table 32 show the per capita consumption of a certain food product by population groups during two successive years (data in dollars per 1,000 families):

TABLE 32

CHANGES IN PER CAPITA CONSUMPTION OF A FOOD PRODUCT

Size of City	Year A	Year B
Over 100,000	1,032	958
10,000–99,000	858	914
Under 10,000	683	712
Farms	321	367

This trend analysis indicates that the big-city markets are declining in importance for this product and that the farm market is growing at

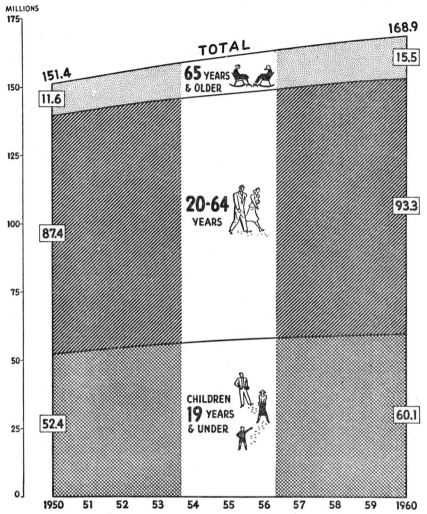

MILLIONS

175 —

168.9

TOTAL

15.5

151.4

65 YEARS & OLDER

150 —

11.6

125 —

20-64 YEARS

93.3

100 —

87.4

75 —

50 —

CHILDREN 19 YEARS & UNDER

60.1

25 —

52.4

0 —

1950   51   52   53   54   55   56   57   58   59   1960

FIGURE 39. Population Forecast Estimates by Age Groups. (U. S. Census Bureau.)

the fastest relative rate. In this case the largest market segment happens to be the declining one, a challenging problem for management. Of course the data above are inadequate as a basis for making a major change in marketing policy and the apparent trend in the example would have to be substantiated with more information.

One of the most common applications of shifts in market patterns is the analysis in trends of consumption by geographic areas. One such study, for example, revealed that consumption in certain areas had begun a declining trend although total sales were showing a fine increase. The manufacturer was provided with forecasts for these areas which helped him decide whether to attempt to reverse the trend by increasing promotional efforts or to accept it as a changing market pattern and conserve his resources for more promising segments of his market.

Fashion Forecasting. One of the most interesting fields of qualitative trend analysis is fashion forecasting. Changes in style and fashion are of great importance in many lines of business. Both producers and dealers concerned with products subject to fashion trends require scientific information to guide manufacturing, buying, or merchandising policies. Manufacturers of products which are not generally considered strictly fashion merchandise, such as automobiles, floor coverings, and home equipment, are interested in fashion forecasting because changes in appearance in such products are important to successful marketing. The principles of fashion forecasting have been most fully developed in connection with fabrics, colors, styling, and items such as the length of women's dresses.

In spite of the general impression that fashions and style preferences are highly volatile, actually they are relatively stable in the course which they run. There are, of course, wide variations in the rate at which different fashions rise and fall in public favor. Occasional fads appear and disappear so rapidly that they cannot be forecast effectively. However, the vast bulk of fashion changes is predicted with amazing success. Manufacturers or merchandisers no longer rely on personal observation or instinct to guide them. Several fashion services now provide forecasts on a subscription basis.

There are three general methods of fashion forecasting. The first is based on the principle of the fashion cycle. It involves statistical analysis of the frequency with which particular styles, colors, etc., are worn or purchased. Counts of the frequency with which styles or fashion features occur are made wherever people representative of the market may be found conveniently in large numbers. Favorite locations for such counts are streets, hotels, football games, and the like.

The specific type of information taken in a fashion count is illustrated in a study of women's hats. Various types of hats, such as sailor, breton, beret, classic brim, off the face, and pillbox, are listed on a counting sheet. Columns opposite each style are provided for checking the basic colors, such as black, navy, and brown. The result is a two-dimensional table showing the frequency of occurrence of two of the basic elements of hat fashion. By making a series of such counts through time, the rising and declining interest of the public in various types of hat design and color is plotted. Since basic fashions run in regular cycles, the forecast is made on the basis of the point in the cycle reflected by the current count.

A second basis of fashion forecasting is leader-group analysis. This method is based on the psychological theory of emulation ("keeping up with the Joneses"). Certain classes of people are known as fashion leaders. It is possible to forecast the likely course of future public acceptance far in advance by observing the styles worn by these people. The social set at Palm Beach, the country-club crowd, and college students are examples of key groups which are studied in applying this method. A specific illustration of the use of this method is that of a manufacturer of men's belts. He suddenly discovered that his complete inventory was obsolete because the demand for narrow belts had disappeared almost overnight. This change of style brought the firm close to bankruptcy. When the cause was investigated it was discovered that the fashion for wide belts had originated on the campuses of certain universities. Since then, this manufacturer has been able to anticipate demand for various fashions in the products he sells by carefully following style trends among collegians.

A third method of fashion forecasting is based on consumer jury opinion. A group of typical users of the product is shown a number of sketches or models of proposed designs and indicates its preference. This method has been extensively employed in connection with the styling of refrigerators, the determination of designs and patterns for rugs, and the planning of television cabinet designs.

SELECTED READINGS

"Annual Statistical and Marketing Issue," *Electrical Merchandising*, January, 1954.

BACHMAN, JULES. *Price Practices and Price Policies—Selected Writings*. New York: The Ronald Press Co., 1953.

BLISS, PERRY. "Price Determination at the Department Store Level," *Journal of Marketing*, July, 1952, pp. 37–46.

BRITTAIN, R. L. *Sales Forecasting and Marketing Cost Control*, National Association of Cost Accountants, Bulletin 35–300, November 10, 1953.

1954 Buying Intentions of Farm Families in Eight Midwest States. St. Paul, Minn.: Midwest Farm Paper Unit, The Farmer, 4 pp.

"The Changing American Market, 1954–59," *Fortune*, August, 1954, pp. 82 ff.

COWAN, DONALD R. G. "Management and Business Forecasting," *Journal of Marketing*, October, 1950, pp. 215–18.

COX, GARFIELD V. "Forecasting Expenditures for Plant and Equipment," *Journal of Business*, January, 1954, pp. 22–31.

CRAWFORD, MERLE. *Sales Forecasting: Methods of Selected Firms*. Urbana Ill.: Bureau of Economic and Business Research, University of Illinois, 1955.

DEWEY, EDWARD R., and DAKIN, EDWIN F. *Cycles*. New York: Henry Holt & Co., 1949, pp. 43, 46.

FERBER, ROBERT. "Sales Forecasting by Correlation Techniques," *Journal of Marketing*, January, 1954, pp. 219–32.

GOULD, JAY M. "Sales Forecasting," *Journal of Marketing*, January, 1951, pp. 357–61.

Lansing, John B., and Whitney, Steve B. *Analysis of Consumer Demand from Repeated Interviews and Re-interviews.* Ann Arbor: Survey Research Center, University of Michigan, 1952.
Lorie, James H. "Forecasting Demand for Consumer Durable Goods," *Journal of Business,* January, 1954.
MacGowan, A. C. "Techniques in Forecasting Consumer Durable Goods Sales," *Journal of Marketing,* October, 1952, pp. 156–62.
MacGowan, T. G. "Forecasting Sales," *Harvard Business Review,* January, 1949, p. 27.
Newbury, Frank D. *Business Forecasting Principles and Practices.* New York: McGraw-Hill Book Co., Inc., 1952, pp. 273 ff.
Scherer, M. "Fashion Forecasting," *Journal of Retailing,* October, 1941, pp. 69–77.
"Streamlining the Sales Forecast," *Dun's Review and Modern Industry,* August, 1953, pp. 42–45.

CASE

Forecasting Sales, Studies in Business Policy No. 25, National Industrial Conference Board, September, 1947.

27

INDUSTRIAL AND INSTITUTIONAL
MARKETING RESEARCH

The importance of marketing research to companies selling products to industry and to institutions is emphasized by the growing appreciation of the fact that this type of business is going more and more to those firms which study the rapidly changing requirements of their customers. Because of the large amount of direct selling involved in the marketing of industrial and institutional products, it is sometimes erroneously assumed that distribution costs are necessarily low. Experience has shown that opportunities to improve the efficiency of marketing and to eliminate distribution wastes are plentiful. When the research is skillfully conceived and executed, results have often been more decisive and immediately profitable in the industrial and institutional field than in that of consumer goods.

The Industrial and Institutional Research Program

In applying marketing research to industrial or institutional products, it is important to have a well-planned program whereby the particular aspects of the marketing problem to be researched are identified and a plan for assigning time and effort to the various phases is definitely established. The complexity of industrial and institutional markets makes this approach mandatory.

Of course, a general market survey is an essential part of such a program. For example, a market survey for industrial pumps might embrace subjects such as the types of pumps being offered to the market, their uses, buyers, channels of distribution, policies of the various manufacturers, buying influences, and the competitive position of the larger manufacturers.

This type of general survey may be restricted to a particular segment of the market, such as a survey of power industrial trucks in the metalworking industry. Such a survey provided one manufacturer with a basic starting point. The number of industrial trucks used in metalworking and metal-producing plants was determined and classified according to type of power employed and by type of industry. Similar restrictions are also desirable in studies of the institutional market. For example, a research of lighting requirements of food supermarkets made separately from one for filling stations would give much sharper detail.

An indication of the various elements which may well be considered for the industrial marketing research program will be found in the results of a survey which shows the most important functions of marketing research in the industrial concern, ranked in order of importance (see Table 33). A research program for the institutional market follows the same pattern.

TABLE 33

MOST IMPORTANT FUNCTIONS OF THE INDUSTRIAL
MARKET RESEARCH DEPARTMENT

Estimating potential sales (general)	Estimating demand for new products
New product development (nonengineering)	Market analysis by customer
	Price structure
General analysis of market	Improvement of present products
Competitive position of company's products	Relative profitableness of markets
	Choice of advertising media
Customer preferences	Relative distribution costs and profits of products
Competitive conditions in markets	
New uses for old products	Market analysis by areas

There are six specific areas of industrial and institutional marketing research which generally require special attention. They are:

1. Product research.
2. Classification of markets.
3. Measurement of sales potentials.
4. Channels of distribution.
5. Analysis of buying factors.
6. Buying motives.

Industrial and Institutional Product Research

The application of product research to industrial products lagged for some time because industrial products are presumably bought on the rational basis of objective standards of efficiency. Now manufacturers have seen how marketing research of industrial products has achieved these results: discovery of unsuspected sales opportunities, of unknown needs of buyers, of special features which lower sales resistance; reduction of sales costs through the elimination of unprofitable items; and increased profits through line simplication. Comparatively slight adaptations in product design, resulting from marketing research, have greatly expanded the market for a number of industrial manufacturers.

A study of electronic heating equipment, for example, obtained data on performance records in actual use, disclosing the advantages, disadvantages, and technical limitations of products. An example of industrial product research which emphasized simplification of the product line is a study made by the General Electric Corporation. The research showed that the number of models of one product could be reduced from twenty-eight to four, including both domestic and foreign requirements and two special applications. As a result, 950 employees in 216,000 square feet of floor space were able to turn out 2,500,000 units per year. With the old line, it would have required 120 per cent more people and 75 per cent more floor space to turn out a similar volume. With only four models, dealers had much less of an inventory problem, selling was made easier, and turnover increased all along the line from company to user.

Institutional product research related to equipment has the same characteristics as that for the industrial field. However, a large share of sales to institutions consists of products essentially the same as those sold to the consumer market, such as foods. Nevertheless, it is still necessary to be sure that special institutional needs are met, such as form, quality, and size of container.

Industrial and institutional product research frequently shows that there is not a large enough market to warrant the production of a proposed new product. An example is a case in which a manufacturer expanded facilities for making specialized precision instruments during World War II. Planning in terms of the future, he developed a new wire recorder to market in peacetime, engaged an industrial designer, and set up a complete sales and advertising structure. The parent company insisted that a marketing research be conducted before it would invest the large sum of money required for going into production. The resulting study proved that the proposed new product could not stand up against competition and could not hope to achieve a volume which would warrant its production. Analysis of competitive products, interviews with potential users, and demonstration of the product provided the evidence. In this case it was unfortunate that marketing research was not called upon sooner because much time and money could have been saved, and the firm could have been directed to products for which there would have been profitable marketing opportunities.

Classification of Markets

Manufacturers of industrial products frequently overlook sales opportunities because they are not aware of the relative importance of different industries which can use their products. Sometimes entire industries, relatively minor as individual units but offering rich market opportunities, are missed because they are hidden in the broad picture. Similarly, the marketing opportunities in the institutional field vary greatly as between specific types of institutions. Classification researches seldom fail to uncover important new marketing opportunities.

Another value of classification studies is that through their appraisal of industry potentials they show how sales effort should be apportioned to each class of customer. Frequently those types which are traditionally considered important turn out to be relatively minor factors in the market for an industrial or institutional product.

A study of industry classification determines the type and size of establishments in all categories which are potential users of various products. Classification studies develop specific limits of marginal customers and show the size of firm below which cultivation is not warranted in any given type. In many cases it is possible to develop precise classifications and to estimate the amount of sales and advertising effort which can most profitably be put against each classification.

After the users of a given product have been identified by type and their potential value determined by the research, the next step is *classification analysis*, which breaks them down by geographic area or marketing units. When compared with actual sales performance, this analysis measures the amount of effective sales coverage of various types of prospects by specific geographic markets. It often reveals rather startling facts, as suggested by the following:

On the wall of many a sales executive's office hangs a map of sales territories. Studded with map-tacks, it pin-points distribution. At LeTourneau, such a map was changed one day to pin-point product-in-use data. A glance told the story of spotty distribution in terms of owners. Closer scrutiny provided real shocks. Prepared from owner lists, the map revealed that geographic areas in which no LeTourneau sales had been made outweighed the areas where sales had been made.[1]

A final step is the analysis of individual firms. In any given industrial or institutional market there is a great variation in the potential

---

[1] Robert C. Judd, "How LeTourneau Sweetens Sales Trainee Investment," *Sales Management*, June 1, 1948, p. 118.

sales prospects represented by individual customers. Generally relatively few prospects account for a large share of potential volume. An effective classification study identifies these specific prospects and develops detailed information regarding each firm which can be of great value in building sales among key prospects.

A good deal of reliance must be placed on published sources of information as well as field surveys because of the complexity of these industrial markets. The basic source of data is the U. S. Census of Manufactures. The McGraw-Hill Publishing Company provides market identification charts which help to analyze market classifications in connection with identifying and rating various fields, determining buying influences, and defining outlets of distribution.

Measurement of Sales Potentials

Classification of markets is the foundation of sales potentials for industrial and institutional products. It is an arduous task to go through the complicated fabric of American industry and institutions and pick out those fields which offer a significant potential for any given product. After the fields have been identified, it is then necessary to evaluate the potential in each one. This identification is done either by field surveys or by statistical analysis. The field surveys are conducted by investigators who interview representative prospective firms to learn their requirements for a given product. Figures are then projected from this sampling to obtain total potentials for various types of users. If statistical analysis is relied upon, certain data, such as number of employees, are used as an index factor, to set potentials by industries, institutional types, geographic areas, etc. The methods of applying these index factors are described in Chapter 21. Generally the most satisfactory method of establishing industrial or institutional sales potentials is to use a combination of the field survey method and the statistical analysis method.

The detailed analysis of sales potentials for industrial or institutional products is one of the most fruitful forms of marketing research. The Sterling Tool Products Company, for example, found that it was necessary to obtain greater cooperation from distributor salesmen in promoting the company's products. The key to the problem was found by obtaining sales potential data which established realistic sales quotas. Using a study of the distribution of industrial supplies, made by the American Supply & Machinery Manufacturers Association, the company found the following situation: [2]

[2] John I. Dean, *Establishing Sales Quotas*, Industrial Marketing Case Study No. 2, Industrial Marketing Committee of the American Marketing Association, 1948.

To start with, they made a test case of the state of Illinois. In the survey, they noted that 89 other manufacturers reported they did an average of 6.2% of their industrial business in the state of Illinois.

. . . In the city of Chicago, 86 of the total 89 manufacturers reported that they did approximately $5,000,000 worth of industrial business, which represented 5.26% of the total nation's industrial business.

In looking up their sales figures for the state of Illinois, for the year 1945, they found that this state represented 8.75% of their total industrial business. In the city of Chicago, on the other hand, they actually did only 4.20% as compared to the Association's 5.26%. When comparing the Survey figures to their own, it became evident that they did more of their business in the state of Illinois than the average of other industrial manufacturers, but they did proportionately less in the city of Chicago.

In analyzing the results this company obtained from the preliminary analysis for the state of Illinois, it was revealing for them to find that while their sales were below average in the larger industrial cities, they were above the average for the state as a whole. . . . This situation clearly showed that they were expending too much effort in the smaller industrial areas and not enough in the larger ones. Their conclusion was a logical one. Through the system of sales quotas they increased their sales emphasis in the larger areas.

Armed with quantitative forecasts of his future markets, a manufacturer or merchant has removed one of the most dangerous threats to his business. To be either far under or far over in sales anticipations is equally dangerous. These risks are minimized by market trend analysis. Furthermore, continuous forecasting instills confidence in all personnel involved in marketing. This knowledge in turn helps stimulate the enthusiasm so essential to marketing success.

Research of Channels of Distribution

The importance of dealers and other middlemen is frequently overlooked because of the large volume of direct sales in industrial and institutional marketing. The emphasis on personal contact has led to archaic distribution channels in many lines. Meanwhile the increasing complexity of American industry has brought increasingly complex distribution procedures. For these reasons the analysis of channels of distribution has become a fertile field for marketing research. Many dealer organizations need thorough renovation on the basis of facts instead of continuing to rely on traditional selling channels.

Distributors in the various industrial and institutional lines have distinctive characteristics, not only for the various types of products handled but also by geographic area, type of market covered, and various other factors. To employ a traditional type of distributor, based on the general type of merchandise they handle, will usually result in a very weak organization. Furthermore, individual distributors vary a great deal in aggressiveness, in their selling resources, and in their ability to work effectively on individual products.

This field is extremely complex. It is possible to weed out the inefficient ones and have a lively distributing setup only by painstaking research which probes deeply into the business methods of individual distributors. In the mill-supplies field alone, for example, there are some 1,678 main-house industrial distributors, with 508 branch houses. The lines handled by these distributors make a complex pattern which illustrates the difficulties in properly planning the distributing organization for a given manufacturer.

In spite of the vast knowledge regarding distributors which its personnel usually possesses, the operating sales department is in no position to undertake an analyis of industrial channels of distribution. The day-to-day pressure of calling on the trade, of performing the many auxiliary functions with which selling is now burdened, and the constant pressure for sales accomplishment keep the regular sales organization fully engaged. Any broad analytical effort made by them is done superficially as a distasteful odd job by persons not trained in this function.

The typical manufacturer makes a variety of products. There is a common tendency to use traditional channels of distribution employed for their main line of products for all products they make. The result is that some products fail to obtain their full potential sales volume. A manufacturer of paper products, for example, sold the bulk of his volume through a certain type of paper distributor. As new products came along, the easiest selling means was through the established trade connections. Distribution research, however, showed how direct selling was necessary for certain items and where different types of distributors were necessary for others. This manufacturer was not even aware of the existence of one important type of distributor uncovered in the research. The basic distributing problem was resolved by an organized pattern for various products which gave the manufacturer clear channels to his markets.

An analysis of channels of distribution for industrial and institutional products should include the following basic steps:

1. Review of the company's present methods of distribution.
2. Review of competitors' present methods of distribution.
3. Field survey of selected distributors of the company and leading competitors to determine sales volume on products under study, organization, operating practices, man power, sales coverage, and distributor attitudes.

4. Analysis of sales development in relation to potential by distributor territories.

5. Plan for intensive cultivation of selected territories, including programs for company salesmen, distributor eliminations and additions, improvement in distributor practices, changes in policies relating to product sales and pricing, and consumer advertising. This program should be set up on a progressive timetable in order to concentrate resources and to prove its value from territory to territory.

Analysis of Buying Factors

One of the more important forms of marketing research peculiar to the industrial and institutional field is determining the types of individuals who influence the purchase of equipment and supplies.

A machinery or equipment manufacturer, for example, finds that many different persons are involved in the decision to buy his product. The purchasing agent has his ideas. Many executives holding different titles are also interested. The treasurer of the company, for example, must be convinced that a proposed machine is a good investment. In many cases his opinion may be the most important individual factor. But the operator of the machine, the foreman, the maintenance man, and others may have a good deal to say about the purchase of a machine from the point of view of production or operation.

The following quotation indicates the frequency with which a number of persons influence the buying decision.[3]

The number of persons in buying organizations who function in the purchase of plant equipment and supplies ranges from one to nineteen. The average for all transactions studies in this survey is practically five (4.8). In less than one per cent (0.7%) of the transactions were all of the buying functions performed by one individual. In only 9 per cent of the transactions were two individuals involved. Three persons functioned in 29 per cent of the transactions, four in 26 per cent, five in 13 per cent, and six or more in 22 per cent.

In the purchase of products costing more than $1,000 the number of people who functioned in buying ranged from one to 19 and the average is almost six (5.8).

These buying factors cannot be properly appraised by tradition or by some arbitrary classification. Both the degree and the manner in which each type influences buying vary from industry to industry and from institution to institution.

There are three steps in an analysis of buying factors in the market for industrial or institutional products, as follows:

[3] *Who Buys for American Industry?* a survey made by R. O. Eastman, Inc., 1927.

1. Make a survey of representative prospects to determine the types of positions held by persons who influence buying and the relative importance of each type.
2. Build a list of individuals in key prospect firms who enter into buying transactions, with information regarding the part each one plays in decision-making.
3. Develop a sales plan to reach these firms and individuals most effectively and economically.

Such an analysis provides salesmen with direction, with answers to their most important problem—which is that of seeing the right man in order to consummate the sale. The salesman can concentrate his effort on his specialty—selling. Management knows that sales are not being lost because of failure to provide full coverage of all important factors in buying.

Buying Motives

In the industrial and institutional markets, the application of research to the analysis of buying motives provides a much-needed foundation for sales presentations, advertising, and promotional material. One reason for the importance of such studies is that motives for buying a given product or service vary greatly among different buyers and buying influences. A piece of machinery which is used in a variety of markets must usually be sold to different industries or institutions on the basis of differing appeals. Furthermore, the president of the company, the engineer, and the treasurer have different attitudes and interests when they consider the purchase of an industrial product.

An example is a study for the Ingersoll Koolshade Sun Screen, a device designed to keep out direct rays of the sun as well as insects. Twenty-five sales appeals were analyzed to determine their relative strength in different segments of the market. The results are illustrated in Table 34. This example is chosen because it contrasts the effectiveness of identical appeals to two groups, residential architects and hotel managers.[4]

A well-known principle of effective selling is to gear the sales presentation to the fundamental interests of the prospect. Research of buying motives provides the sales manager with a basis for preparing an effective basic sales presentation and aids greatly in training salesmen to use the proper sales approach. Salesmen make more

[4] Roland D. Doane, "The Role of Research in Launching a New Product," *Industrial Marketing*, April, 1940.

effective sales solicitations when they understand the relative importance of various motives to the different types of customers.

TABLE 34

PERCENTAGE OF RESPONDENTS RATING APPEALS IMPORTANT

	Residential Architects (Per cent)	Hotel Managers (Per cent)
Shades window from sun	52	*
Saves expense of awnings	52	*
Keeps room cool	50	90
Smart appearance	48	85
No summer air conditioning needed	43	100
Lowers cost of air conditioning	39	80
Saves inconvenience of awnings	40	*
Wire will not sag or bulge	38	*
Good vision looking out	22	*
Added privacy	5	85
Prevents fading of furnishings	*	80

* Relatively unimportant in their opinion.

Analysis of buying motives together with research on buying influences provides the basis of broad advertising strategy planning for industrial and institutional manufacturers. Research is also applied to industrial advertising in other ways. Studies are designed to provide the basis for media selection and to increase the effectiveness of individual advertisements. For example, a machine-tool manufacturer set up a program of advertising research with the following objectives:

1. What direct mail copy was most profitable?
2. Which trade paper copy was most productive?
3. Which mailing lists were most productive?
4. Which publications were most profitable?
5. How did direct mail compare with magazines in profitability?
6. What is the mean time lag between inquiries and orders?
7. Are accounts opened with the aid of advertising as profitable as those opened by other means?

SELECTED READINGS

ARIES, ROBERT S., and COPULSKY, WILLIAM. "Determination of Area Market Potentials for Chemical Process Raw Materials," *Journal of Marketing*, October, 1949, pp. 730–32.

HUMMEL, FRANCIS E. "Market Potentials in the Machine Tool Industry—A Case Study," *Journal of Marketing*, July, 1954, pp. 34–41.

JURASCHEK, F. "Will Sampling Techniques Work for Industrial Sales Research?" *Sales Management*, April 1, 1950, p. 48.

LEWIS, HOWARD T. "Marketing Research from the Standpoint of the Industrial Buyer," *Journal of Marketing,* July, 1950, pp. 14–20.

STANLEY, E. M. "Can You Safely Rely on Titles to Indicate Purchasing Influence?" *Sales Management,* April 1, 1953, pp. 62–64.

CASE

BLANKERTZ, DONALD F., FERBER, ROBERT, and WALES, HUGH G. *Cases and Problems in Marketing Research.* New York: The Ronald Press Co., 1954, pp. 127–30.

APPENDIX

EXAMPLE OF A PROBABILITY SAMPLE OF A SINGLE MARKET

(Using Stratification, Clustering, and Area Design)

The purpose of this Appendix is to show an actual area sampling plan. This simple plan, which will produce satisfactory results in many marketing research situations, illustrates the basic problems which must be faced in using a probability design. Although it is of a true area probability nature, it is not necessarily the most efficient nor best plan to be used for any particular marketing research problem.

This example is the plan used in a study of housewife readers of a magazine in Omaha, Nebraska. This problem has been outlined on pages 273 through 274. You will recall that a primary purpose of the research was to determine the average education of readers.

A sample size of 900 interviews was required under a simple random plan because the variance of the years of education of readers was estimated to be five years, the error in sample results was to be limited to 0.5 year, and the sample results were to be reliable at the 99 per cent confidence level.

This sampling plan, however, involves the elements of stratification and clustering, both of which have a very important effect upon the determination of sample size. If a sample plan involves stratification, the required sample size will in general be smaller than that required for a simple random design to produce results of equivalent accuracy. If it involves clustering, the required sample size will usually be larger than that required for a simple random design. In the Omaha research, it was decided that these two factors would roughly offset each other. Therefore, the sample size of 900, determined on the basis of a simple random design, was employed.

Step 1. Definition of the Universe and the Sampling Unit

At the outset, the researcher must decide the scope of his study in terms of geographic limits. Will the study be a national one, or will it cover only one state or one market? The answer to this question springs directly from the research problem. This research was limited to Omaha because a purpose of the research was to make an intensive study of one community.

For purposes of this survey, the universe was defined as all housewives eighteen years of age or older in the Omaha market who regularly read the magazine. The *sampling unit* would therefore be any housewife eighteen years of age or older who regularly reads the magazine.

This definition of the sampling unit suggests two questions:

1. *Why should the universe be limited to housewives eighteen years or older?* The magazine has an editorial content of such a nature that it appeals primarily to housewives over eighteen years of age. In such a situation, a certain efficiency in field operation can be gained by setting a specific lower age limit in defining the universe.

2. *How shall we define a "regular" reader?* In this survey the questionnaire defines a regular reader as any housewife who can identify and recall, without prompting, at least one editorial item in any of the three most recent issues of the magazine.

Step 2. Selection of the Frame

An indirect list frame was used in this research. By definition, an indirect list frame is composed of units, other than the survey sampling units themselves, which *represent* the survey sampling units. The survey sampling unit is any housewife who regularly reads the magazine. The indirect list frame is occupied dwelling units. Almost every occupied dwelling unit in Omaha will include one housewife— that is, one female who is primarily responsible for the purchase of food and the planning of meals. Since each occupied dwelling unit is very likely to contain such a female, an occupied dwelling unit can be regarded as equivalent to one housewife for practical sampling purposes. Therefore, a sample of occupied dwelling units can be drawn directly to obtain a sample of housewives. From within the primary sample of housewives a final sample of housewives who regularly read the magazine can be obtained by means of filter questions on the questionnaire.

However, the basic sample must be of housewives without regard to whether they are regular readers of the magazine. Nine hundred readers cannot be drawn directly because a direct list frame of these readers is not available. Therefore, a sample of housewives large enough to include 900 regular readers must be drawn. At this point, it is necessary to fall back on already existing knowledge or conduct a pretest to determine how many housewives must be interviewed on the average to find one regular reader of the magazine. Knowledge from prior readership studies indicated that approximately one out of every four housewives is a regular reader of the magazine. Therefore, approximately 3,600 housewives must be contacted in order to find 900 readers of the magazine in Omaha.

Step 3. Classification of Blocks and the Stratification Plan

The first units to be selected under this plan were city blocks. They were drawn directly from the 1950 Housing Census Report (Vol. 5, Part 136; Block Statistics for Omaha, Nebraska), which formed the primary indirect list frame for the sample. All city blocks in Omaha were separated into three strata, as follows:

Stratum   I: All blocks having no occupied dwelling units according to the 1950 census: These are called "zero blocks."

Stratum II: All blocks having between 1 and 99 occupied dwelling units according to the 1950 census: These are called "small blocks."

Stratum III: All blocks having 100 or more occupied dwelling units according to the 1950 census: These are called "large blocks."

The choice of 100 dwelling units as the dividing line between small and large blocks was influenced by the general Bureau of the Census recommendation favoring this size. In general, these three strata were used for the following reasons:

1. There were no occupied dwelling units on the zero blocks in 1950. In many cases these blocks are completely unsuited to residential homes of any kind: they may be completely devoted to industrial plants, municipal buildings, city dumps, or be otherwise unsuited to residential building. On the other hand, some of these blocks may have developed into residential areas since 1950. It is most important, if new homes have been built on any of these areas since the census of 1950, that these homes be included in the sample.

2. The division between large and small blocks was made on the basis of experience and judgment. In general, the families found on those blocks which have a large number of dwelling units are relatively homogeneous with regard to factors such as income and education. Blocks having more than 100 dwelling units are very often blocks with apartment buildings or some kind of housing development.

At the same time, the "small blocks" tend, in general, to be less homogeneous internally than do the large blocks. Therefore, under this sample plan the large and small blocks were separated into two strata, and different sampling fractions were applied to these different strata. A larger proportion of homes was selected from each of the less homogeneous small blocks but a smaller proportion of small blocks was included.

3. This stratification plan depends largely upon experience and the assumption that the families on large and small blocks are differentiated, in general, with regard to income and education, two factors closely related to the characteristic being measured: the average education level of readers of the magazine. Under this area plan different stratification could be accomplished through a finer division of block size. In addition, other bases of stratification such as by geographic area of the city, could be used. In the absence of specific evidence to the contrary, it is *judged* that the stratification plan outlined above will produce, relative to both cost and sampling considerations, as accurate information as any alternative plan.

Step 4. Organizing the Block Statistics for Sampling

At this point is is necessary to process the basic Omaha block statistics into the three strata. Table A shows a specimen page from the Omaha block statistics. Table B shows the way in which the block statistics were broken down into the three strata. Note that the city blocks are grouped into census tracts, convenient units in which to process the census data. Table B shows the number of blocks and dwelling units in each census tract which fall into each of the three strata. In addition, cumulative totals are shown for the number of blocks by strata and by tract. These cumulative totals simply represent the total number of blocks included in any stratum in a particular tract and all the preceding tracts in the listing. The use of these cumulative figures will be explained in Step 6.

The total number of dwelling units in Omaha which fall into each stratum can be obtained by adding together the number of dwelling units for the tracts in each stratum. These totals are shown at the bottom of Table B. They are essential to the computation of sampling fractions.

Step 5. The Computation of Sampling Fractions

A key tool in sampling procedure is the *sampling fraction*. By this term is meant the proportion of total units in any given segment of

TABLE A.

SAMPLE SECTION OF BLOCK STATISTICS

OMAHA, NEBR.

CHARACTERISTICS OF HOUSING FOR CENSUS TRACTS, BY BLOCKS: 1950

[Detailed statistics not shown for blocks containing fewer than 3 dwelling units, nor for dwelling units not allocated by blocks (designated by NR)]

Census tract	Block	All dwelling units by occupancy and tenure					All dwelling units by condition and plumbing facilities			Occupied dwelling units				Contract monthly rent¹		Value of one-dwelling-unit structures	
		Total	Owner occupied	Renter occupied	Vacant non-seasonal not dilap., for rent or sale	Other vacant and non-resident	Number reporting	No private bath or dilap.	No running water or dilap.	Total	Persons per room — Number reporting	1.51 or more	Occupied by non-white	Number reporting	Average monthly rent (dollars)	Number reporting	Average value (dollars)
1	1	1															
2	3	48	4	5			45	4		48	45			4	59.00	37	18,548
	4	5	3	2			5	5		5	5					5	7,760
	5	3	1				2	2	1	3	3			2		1	5,250
	6	10	2	8			9		3	10	10			8	12.00	1	
	8	6	3	3			6	1	1	6	6	6		1		1	5,125
	9	3	3				5	8		3	3			1			
	11	1	2	2			2	18		2	2			2		4	
	13	7	3	2	2		7	2	1	7	7			7	53.57	2	
	14	14	7	7			14	14		(14)	14		6			6	6,316
	15	7	6	1			7	7		7	7			1		6	6,250
	16	15	4	6	1		14	1	1	7	7			6	47.50	13	6,166
	17	12	15	1	2		15			15	15			1		16	4,500
	18	11	6	2	2		12	3	3	12	12			2		9	6,383
	20	11	9	1	1		11			11	11		1	1		9	6,900
	21	8	12				8			8	8					7	5,588
	23	4	7				7			7	7					7	6,471
	24	12	10				10	1		(12)	10			1		9	6,625
	25	5	5	1	1		5	5	2	5	5		2	3	21.66	5	6,311
	26	7	7		4		7	7		7	7			4	27.50	6	6,400
	27	4	4	1	1		4			4	4			1		4	6,183
	28	9	9	2	1		9	3	1	9	9			2		2	5,625
	29	11	12	1	3	1	11	4		11	10						9,100
	30	11	12	2			11	1		11	11			3	53.33	5	8,727
	31	7	7	1			7	5		7	7					11	4,333
	33	5	5	1			5	4		4	4					1	5,375
	34	4	4			1	4			4	4						
	35	9	9	1	1		9	3	1	(9)	9			2		7	10,000
	36	9	9	2	2		9	9		9	9			1		1	7,000
	37	6	6	1	1		6	6		6	6			1	50.00	5	7,200
	38	8	8	1	4		8	8		8	8			1		5	7,500
	40	10	7	1	2		10	7		10	10			3		5	6,500
	41	7	6	2	2		7	1	1	7	6			2		5	7,700
	42	7	5	2			9	3	3	6	6			2		4	7,625
	43	9	4	4			3	1	1	9	9			3	22.33	4	5,250
	44	6	5				6	1		9	9					6	4,583

9th block → (at Census tract 2, block 14)

Skip to 10 (at Census tract 2, block 15)

Skip to 11 (at Census tract 2, block 35)

TABLE B
SUMMARY WORK TABLE
BLOCK STATISTICS FOR OMAHA, NEBRASKA

Tract	STRATUM I			STRATUM II			STRATUM III		
	No. of Blocks	Cumulative Blocks	No. of Dwelling Units	No. of Blocks	Cumulative Blocks	No. of Dwelling Units	No. of Blocks	Cumulative Blocks	No. of Dwelling Units
1	1			0			0		
2	29	30		92	92	1,526	0		
3	2	32		37	129	1,081	0		
4	34	66		48	177	598	0		
5	1	67		1	178	5	0		
6	1	68		54	232	1,219	0		
60	3	635		87	3,063	1,434	0	33	4,775
61	36	671		74	3,150	622	0	33	4,775
62	51	722		100	3,224	1,300	0	33	4,775
Totals	722			3,324		67,575	33		4,775

the universe that is to be included in the data gathering. For example, a sampling fraction of 1/60 applied to dwellings for a total market means that one out of every sixty dwellings is included in the sample drawn; a sampling fraction of 1/10 for a series of sales data means that every tenth sales transaction is included in the sample.

The basic sampling fraction in any probability sample is:

$$\frac{\text{Number of sampling units in sample}}{\text{Total number of sampling units in the universe}}$$

The numerator of the basic sampling fraction from Omaha is 900×4, or 3,600, because the sampling plan calls for 900 readers and it is necessary to interview four housewives to obtain one reader. The denominator is 72,350, which is the total number of occupied dwellings in Omaha. The basic sampling fraction is therefore:

$$\frac{3,600}{72,350} = \frac{1}{20.97}$$

This fraction rounds off to 1/21 when the decimal is eliminated.

The next problem is the conversion of this basic sampling fraction into "working sampling fractions" for each of the strata. The basic sampling fraction is expressed in terms of occupied dwelling units. The basic data are, however, expressed in terms of city blocks and then in terms of occupied dwelling units. Some method of selecting city blocks and also of selecting dwelling units within those blocks must be found.

It is possible to equate the block fraction and the within-block fraction to the basic sampling fraction as developed above. Let $\frac{1}{a}$ represent the block sampling fraction, and $\frac{1}{b}$ the within-block sampling fraction. They can be equated to $\frac{1}{a \cdot b}$, which represents the basic sampling fraction as follows:

$$\frac{1}{a} \times \frac{1}{b} = \frac{1}{a \cdot b}$$

Since the basic fraction 1/21 is already available, if we can decide on either the proper within-block fraction or the proper block fraction, the equation can be solved for the remaining fractions. Therefore, it is now required that we determine either the block sampling fraction or the within-block sampling fraction. These values can be determined mathematically for any given problem by a complex method beyond the scope of this book. However, a great many applications of these formulas to a wide variety of sampling situations makes it possible to construct a *within-block* sampling fraction on the basis of experience and judgment with reasonable confidence. In small blocks, an optimum number of interviews, from the point of view of both sampling and field efficiency, ranges between five and ten per block or cluster. If interviews can be made in almost every home contacted, it is advisable to obtain a somewhat smaller number per cluster (four to six). If, on the other hand, complete interviews will be made in only a small proportion of the homes contacted, then more contacts can be made efficiently per cluster (ten or twelve). In the Omaha study we expect to find a "regular reader" only in every fourth dwelling unit which is contacted. Therefore, it is advisable to employ ten or twelve dwelling units per cluster. The average small block (cluster) should then produce somewhere between 2.5 and 3.0 completed interviews. How is the actual within-block fraction determined?

Determining the Sampling Fractions for Small Blocks. First, the average number of dwelling units per small block must be found. From Table B it can be seen that there were 67,575 dwelling units on 3,324 small blocks in Omaha in 1950. Therefore, there were, on the average, 20.3 dwelling units per small block. It is decided to contact ten dwelling units per small block in Omaha. The within-block sampling fraction is:

$$\frac{1}{b} = \frac{10}{20.3} = \frac{1}{2.03}$$

Rounding off this result to even numbers, we have a within-block fraction of 1/2. Now we can solve easily for the block sampling fraction:

$$\frac{1}{a} \times \frac{1}{b} = \frac{1}{21}$$
$$\frac{1}{a} \times \frac{1}{2} = \frac{1}{21}$$
$$2a = 21$$
$$a = 10.5$$

Determining the Sampling Fractions for Large Blocks. A slightly different approach is used in determining the working sampling fractions for the large blocks. A smaller proportion of dwelling units is drawn from the large blocks because these blocks have, on the average, higher internal homogeneity with regard to income and education than do the small blocks. Therefore, these large blocks can be adequately represented with a smaller proportion of interviews than is necessary for the small blocks.

The optimum lowering of this within-block proportion is assured through the use of the following formula:

$$\text{Large block fraction} = \frac{\sqrt{\text{Number of dwelling units contacted in each small block}}}{\text{Denominator of small block fraction}}$$

The numerator of this fraction for Omaha is 10, the average number of dwelling units contacted in each small block. The *small block fraction* is 1/10.5 and, therefore, 10.5 becomes the denominator of this fraction. Thus:

$$\text{Large block fraction} = \frac{\sqrt{10}}{10.5} = \frac{3.15}{10.5} = \frac{1}{3.3}$$

By rounding off to even numbers, the working large block fraction becomes 1/3.

The computation of the within-block fraction for large blocks is obtained by substitution, as follows:

$$\text{Block fraction} \times \text{Within-block fraction} = \text{Basic fraction}$$
$$\frac{1}{3} \times \frac{1}{b} = \frac{1}{21}$$
$$3b = 21$$
$$b = 7$$

Thus, the within-block fraction for large blocks is 1/7.

It is important to note that a larger proportion of large blocks is selected than was the case for small blocks (1/3 vs. 1/10) and a lower proportion of dwelling units is selected within each of the large blocks than within the small blocks (1/7 vs. 1/2).

Sampling Fractions in Zero Blocks. The "zero blocks" had no occupied dwelling units on them at the time of the last United States Census. Since, to the best of our knowledge, there are no occupied dwelling units on these blocks, it is impossible to develop a within-block sampling fraction. A practical alternative is to include every dwelling unit which now exists on each zero block which gets into the block sample under the basic block fraction. If this procedure is followed, we tend to oversample heavily in particular zero blocks. However, since no new buildings have been built on many of the zero blocks since the census, the net addition to total interviews and therefore the effect on the total survey is minimal. Other, more complex methods, beyond the scope of this Appendix, should be followed if the net addition to the population of the city has exceeded 5 per cent since the census used as a base for sampling computations.

The sampling fraction in the zero blocks under this plan will be:

Block fraction		Within-block fraction		Basic fraction
$\dfrac{1}{21}$	$\times$	$\dfrac{1}{1}$	$=$	$\dfrac{1}{21}$

Note that, for all strata, the basic sampling fraction will be the same. We know that, in 1950, of the 72,350 dwelling units in Omaha, 67,575 (93.4%) are to be found in the small blocks and 4,775 (6.6%) are to be found in the large blocks. Therefore, of the 3,600 dwelling units used in the sample, 3,362 (93.4%) should be in the small blocks and 238 (6.6%) should be in the large blocks.

If these proportions are maintained, then:

Small blocks	=	Large blocks	=	All blocks	=	Basic sampling fraction
$\dfrac{3,362}{67,575}$	$=$	$\dfrac{238}{4,775}$	$=$	$\dfrac{3,600}{72,350}$	$=$	$\dfrac{1}{21}$

Therefore, if the block and within-block fractions for the small blocks are equated to the basic sampling fraction, the proper proportion of interviews will automatically be drawn from the small blocks. Likewise, as is shown below, if the block and within-block fractions for the large blocks are equated to the basic sampling fraction of 1/21, the proper proportion of interviews will automatically be drawn from the large blocks.

We now have all the working tools necessary for drawing our sample:

Small block fraction is 1/10, which means that we must draw 1/10 of the small blocks (Stratum II).

Large block fraction is 1/3, which means that we must draw 1/3 of the large blocks (Stratum III).

Zero block fraction is 1/21, the basic sampling fraction (Stratum I).

The within-block fraction for *small* blocks is 1/2, which means that we include 1/2 of all the occupied dwellings in every small block included in the sample.

The within-block fraction for *large* blocks is 1/7, which means that we must include 1/7 of all the occupied dwellings in every large block included in the sample.

We include all occupied dwellings in zero blocks included in the sample.

Step 6. Selecting the Sample Blocks

It is now necessary to apply the sampling fractions to the work tables which were developed above in Step 4 in order to select the specific blocks in which field work will be undertaken. The cumulative block totals which have been computed for each tract (Table B) serve as a basis for this selection. This is done as follows:

a) For each stratum a random starting point for the selection of blocks from the census tables is determined. This starting point is selected with reference to the block sampling fraction in each stratum. In Stratum II, for example, the block fraction is 1/10. The starting point in this stratum was selected between 1 and 10 from a table of random numbers. The starting point selected was 9, or the ninth block in Stratum II, which occurs in Tract 2.

b) Starting with the ninth block in Stratum II, every 10.5th block thereafter falls into the block sample. In practice, this interval of 10.5 is accomplished by skipping first to block 10, then to block 11, then to block 10, and so on.

The starting point was entered into a tape adding machine. The interval was added to this starting point successively until the total number of blocks within the stratum was cumulated. Therefore, 9 is entered into the adding machine and 10, then 11, then 10, etc., are successively added. The tape totals are as follows:

Starting point and intervals:
9 + 10 + 11 + 10 + 11 + 10 + 11 + 10 + 11 + 10 + 11 + 10 + 11 +
10 + 11 + 10, etc.

Accumulated totals:
9, 19, 30, 40, 51, 61, 72, 82, 93, 103, 114, 124, 135, 145, 156, 166, etc.

Comparison of the cumulative block totals and the adding machine tape totals indicates:

1. No sample blocks are found in Tract 1.
2. The first eight blocks are to be found in Tract 2, starting with the ninth Stratum II block in Tract 2.
3. The next four blocks are to be found in Tract 3, starting with the first Stratum II block in Tract 3.
4. The next five blocks are to be found in Tract 4, starting with the sixth Stratum II block in Tract 4, etc.

The use of this method is most helpful when the block interval is great because it permits rapid location of tracts containing sample blocks without onerous and time-consuming counting off of the intervening nonsample blocks.

We are now ready to pick the actual blocks to be sampled in Stratum II. This is done by counting down the column "Total Occupied Dwelling Units." For Stratum II only blocks which have from

1 to 99 occupied dwellings are counted, since zero blocks (no dwellings) are Stratum I and all blocks having 100 or more occupied dwellings are Stratum III. Thus, to locate the ninth block in this stratum, block No. 1 in Tract 1 is skipped, and in Tract 2, blocks Nos. 3, 4, 5, 6, 7, and 8 are counted, block No. 11 is skipped and blocks Nos. 2, 12, 13, and 14 are counted (see Table A). Since we have now reached a total of nine counted blocks, we locate our starting point (the first block in the sample) at block 14. We now continue to count down the column until we reach the point at which we have counted 10 more blocks that have from 1 to 99 dwelling units (to reach our second accumulative total of 19). This brings us to block No. 24, which becomes the second one selected for the sample. This process is continued according to the pattern established above until all blocks are selected for Stratum II. The same procedure is followed to select a group of blocks for Stratum I (counting only those with no occupied dwellings on the tract maps) and a group for Stratum III (counting only blocks with 100 or more occupied dwelling units).

The blocks actually selected are now colored on street maps. Three colors were used in Omaha: red for Stratum I, blue for Stratum II, and green for Stratum III.

Step 7. Selecting Households Within Blocks

When the interviewer goes to a block to select the homes to be taken in the sample, two factors must be controlled. The first of these factors is the identification of the dwelling to be used as a starting point. The second is the counting of dwellings to identify the ones which are to be skipped and those to be taken in the sample.

The starting point in the Omaha research was the first dwelling facing north in the northwest corner of the block. The interviewer then proceeded around the block in clockwise fashion, selecting dwellings according to the following instructions:

Each interviewer will receive a street map of Omaha. On this map, the blocks in which you will interview have been marked in colored pencil. As you can see, three colors have been used in marking these assigned blocks (red, blue, and green).

Red blocks: In any block marked in red, you will contact every home.
Blue blocks: In any block marked in blue, you will contact every second home.
Green blocks: In any block marked in green, you will contact every seventh home.

Multiple Dwelling Units

As you work around the assigned blocks, you may encounter multiple dwelling units buildings—apartments, flats, or duplexes. Each family unit is treated as a separate dwelling.

In apartment buildings, you should continue using the assigned interval for the block (i.e., one in two, one in seven, or every dwelling). You should cover *all* floors in the apartment building, working from top to bottom of the building.

Duplexes (two homes in the same building, side by side) should be treated as separate houses.

Flats should be worked from top to bottom.

This example shows a complete sampling operation for one market. Additional examples on a national scale may be found in cases in the Selected Readings for Chapter 12.

INDEX OF NAMES

INDEX OF SUBJECTS